P9-CCE-747

Class Declaration

```java
public class CashRegister
{
    private int itemCount;          ⎤ Instance variables
    private double totalPrice;      ⎦

    public void addItem(double price)   ⎤
    {                                   ⎟
        itemCount++;                    ⎬ Method
        totalPrice = totalPrice + price;⎟
    }                                   ⎦
    . . .
}
```

Selected Operators and Their Precedence

(See Appendix B for the complete list.)

[]	Array element access
++ -- !	Increment, decrement, Boolean *not*
* / %	Multiplication, division, remainder
+ -	Addition, subtraction
< <= > >=	Comparisons
== !=	Equal, not equal
&&	Boolean *and*
||	Boolean *or*
=	Assignment

Conditional Statement

```java
          Condition
            ╱
if (floor >= 13)
{
    actualFloor = floor - 1;    ⎤ Executed when condition is true
}
else if (floor >= 0)     Second condition (optional)
{
    actualFloor = floor;
}
else
{
    System.out.println("Floor negative");  ⎤ Executed when
}                                           ⎦ all conditions are
                                              false (optional)
```

Loop Statements

```java
          Condition
            ╱
while (balance < TARGET)
{
    year++;                                   ⎤ Executed while
    balance = balance * (1 + rate / 100);     ⎦ condition is true
}
```

```java
   Initialization  Condition  Update
        ╱            ╱         ╱
for (int i = 0; i < 10; i++)
{
    System.out.println(i);
}
```

Variable and Constant Declarations

```java
  Type    Name    Initial value
   ╱       ╱         ╱
int cansPerPack = 6;

final double CAN_VOLUME = 0.335;
```

Method Declaration

```java
                                        Parameter
  Modifiers      Return type            type and name
   ╱    ╲           ╱                    ╱        ╱
public static double cubeVolume(double sideLength)
{
    double volume = sideLength * sideLength * sideLength;
    return volume;
}               Exits method and
                returns result.
```

Mathematical Operations

Math.pow(x, y)	Raising to a power x^y
Math.sqrt(x)	Square root $\sqrt{x}$
Math.log10(x)	Decimal log $\log_{10}(x)$
Math.abs(x)	Absolute value $\lvert x \rvert$
Math.sin(x)	⎤
Math.cos(x)	⎬ Sine, cosine, tangent of x (x in radians)
Math.tan(x)	⎦

String Operations

```java
String s = "Hello";
int n = s.length(); // 5
char ch = s.charAt(1); // 'e'
String t = s.substring(1, 4); // "ell"
String u = s.toUpperCase(); // "HELLO"
if (u.equals("HELLO")) ... // Use equals, not ==
for (int i = 0; i < s.length(); i++)
{
    char ch = s.charAt(i);
    Process ch
}
```

```java
do                    Loop body executed
{                       at least once
    System.out.print("Enter a positive integer: ");
    input = in.nextInt();
}
while (input <= 0);
```

```java
                 Set to a new element in each iteration        An array or collection
                                                                ╱
for (double value : values)
{
    sum = sum + value;    ⎤ Executed for each element
}
```

JAVA CONCEPTS

Early Objects

Seventh Edition

JAVA CONCEPTS
Early Objects

Seventh Edition

CAY HORSTMANN

San Jose State University

WILEY

PUBLISHER	Don Fowley
EXECUTIVE EDITOR	Beth Lang Golub
CONTENT MANAGER	Kevin Holm
EDITORIAL PROGRAM ASSISTANT	Katherine Willis
EXECUTIVE MARKETING MANAGER	Christopher Ruel
CREATIVE DIRECTOR	Harry Nolan
SENIOR DESIGNER	Madelyn Lesure
SENIOR PHOTO EDITOR	Lisa Gee
SENIOR CONTENT EDITOR	Wendy Ashenberg
SENIOR PRODUCT DESIGNER	Jenny Welter
EDITORIAL OPERATIONS MANAGER	Melissa Edwards
PRODUCTION EDITOR	Tim Lindner
PRODUCTION MANAGEMENT SERVICES	Cindy Johnson, Publishing Services
COVER PHOTOS	(bird) © FLPA/John Holmes/Age Fotostock America, Inc.; (monkey) © S Sailer/A Sailer/Age Fotostock America, Inc.; (tiger) © Frans Lemmens/SuperStock
INTERIOR DESIGN	Maureen Eide

This book was set in Stempel Garamond by Publishing Services, and printed and bound by Quad/Graphics Versailles.

This book is printed on acid-free paper. ∞

Founded in 1807, John Wiley & Sons, Inc. has been a valued source of knowledge and understanding for more than 200 years, helping people around the world meet their needs and fulfill their aspirations. Our company is built on a foundation of principles that include responsibility to the communities we serve and where we live and work. In 2008, we launched a Corporate Citizenship Initiative, a global effort to address the environmental, social, economic, and ethical challenges we face in our business. Among the issues we are addressing are carbon impact, paper specifications and procurement, ethical conduct within our business and among our vendors, and community and charitable support. For more information, please visit our website: www.wiley.com/go/citizenship.

Copyright © 2014 John Wiley & Sons, Inc. All rights reserved. No part of this publication may be reproduced, stored in a retrieval system, or transmitted in any form or by any means, electronic, mechanical, photocopying, recording, scanning or otherwise, except as permitted under Sections 107 or 108 of the 1976 United States Copyright Act, without either the prior written permission of the Publisher, or authorization through payment of the appropriate per-copy fee to the Copyright Clearance Center, Inc., 222 Rosewood Drive, Danvers, MA 01923 (Web site: www.copyright.com). Requests to the Publisher for permission should be addressed to the Permissions Department, John Wiley & Sons, Inc., 111 River Street, Hoboken, NJ 07030-5774, (201) 748-6011, fax (201) 748-6008, or online at: www.wiley.com/go/permissions.

Evaluation copies are provided to qualified academics and professionals for review purposes only, for use in their courses during the next academic year. These copies are licensed and may not be sold or transferred to a third party. Upon completion of the review period, please return the evaluation copy to Wiley. Return instructions and a free of charge return shipping label are available at: www.wiley.com/go/returnlabel. If you have chosen to adopt this textbook for use in your course, please accept this book as your complimentary desk copy. Outside of the United States, please contact your local sales representative.

ISBN 978-1-118-43112-2 (Main Book)
ISBN 978-1-118-42301-1 (Binder-Ready Version)

Printed in the United States of America

10 9 8 7 6 5 4

PREFACE

This book is an introduction to Java and computer programming that focuses on the essentials—and on effective learning. The book is designed to serve a wide range of student interests and abilities and is suitable for a first course in programming for computer scientists, engineers, and students in other disciplines. No prior programming experience is required, and only a modest amount of high school algebra is needed. Here are the key features of this book:

Start objects early, teach object orientation gradually.

In Chapter 2, students learn how to use objects and classes from the standard library. Chapter 3 shows the mechanics of implementing classes from a given specification. Students then use simple objects as they master branches, loops, and arrays. Object-oriented design starts in Chapter 8. This gradual approach allows students to use objects throughout their study of the core algorithmic topics, without teaching bad habits that must be un-learned later.

Guidance and worked examples help students succeed.

Beginning programmers often ask "How do I start? Now what do I do?" Of course, an activity as complex as programming cannot be reduced to cookbook-style instructions. However, step-by-step guidance is immensely helpful for building confidence and providing an outline for the task at hand. "Problem Solving" sections stress the importance of design and planning. "How To" guides help students with common programming tasks. Additional Worked Examples are available online.

Practice makes perfect.

Of course, programming students need to be able to implement nontrivial programs, but they first need to have the confidence that they can succeed. This book contains a substantial number of self-check questions at the end of each section. "Practice It" pointers suggest exercises to try after each section. And additional practice opportunities, including lab exercises and skill-oriented multiple-choice questions are available online.

A visual approach motivates the reader and eases navigation.

Photographs present visual analogies that explain the nature and behavior of computer concepts. Step-by-step figures illustrate complex program operations. Syntax boxes and example tables present a variety of typical and special cases in a compact format. It is easy to get the "lay of the land" by browsing the visuals, before focusing on the textual material.

Visual features help the reader with navigation.

Focus on the essentials while being technically accurate.

An encyclopedic coverage is not helpful for a beginning programmer, but neither is the opposite—reducing the material to a list of simplistic bullet points. In this book, the essentials are presented in digestible chunks, with separate notes that go deeper into good practices or language features when the reader is ready for the additional information. You will not find artificial over-simplifications that give an illusion of knowledge.

Reinforce sound engineering practices.

A multitude of useful tips on software quality and common errors encourage the development of good programming habits. The optional testing track focuses on test-driven development, encouraging students to test their programs systematically.

Provide an optional graphics track.

Graphical shapes are splendid examples of objects. Many students enjoy writing programs that create drawings or use graphical user interfaces. If desired, these topics can be integrated into the course by using the materials at the end of Chapters 2, 3, and 10.

New to This Edition

Problem Solving Strategies

This edition adds practical, step-by-step illustrations of techniques that can help students devise and evaluate solutions to programming problems. Introduced where they are most relevant, these strategies address barriers to success for many students. Strategies included are:

- Algorithm Design (with pseudocode)
- Tracing Objects
- First Do It By Hand (doing sample calculations by hand)
- Flowcharts
- Selecting Test Cases
- Hand-Tracing
- Storyboards
- Adapting Algorithms
- Discovering Algorithms by Manipulating Physical Objects
- Patterns for Object Data
- Thinking Recursively
- Estimating the Running Time of an Algorithm

Optional Science and Business Exercises

End-of-chapter exercises have been enhanced with problems from scientific and business domains. Designed to engage students, the exercises illustrate the value of programming in applied fields.

New and Reorganized Topics

All chapters were revised and enhanced to respond to user feedback and improve the flow of topics. Loop algorithms are now introduced explicitly in Chapter 6. Additional array algorithms are presented in Chapter 7 and incorporated into the problem-solving sections. Chapter 8 is more clearly focused on the design of a single class, whereas Chapter 12 deals with relationships between classes. Chapter 15 shows how to use the basic data structures from the standard library. New example tables, photographs, and exercises appear throughout the book.

A Tour of the Book

The book can be naturally grouped into three parts, as illustrated by Figure 1. The organization of chapters offers the same flexibility as the previous edition; dependencies among the chapters are also shown in the figure.

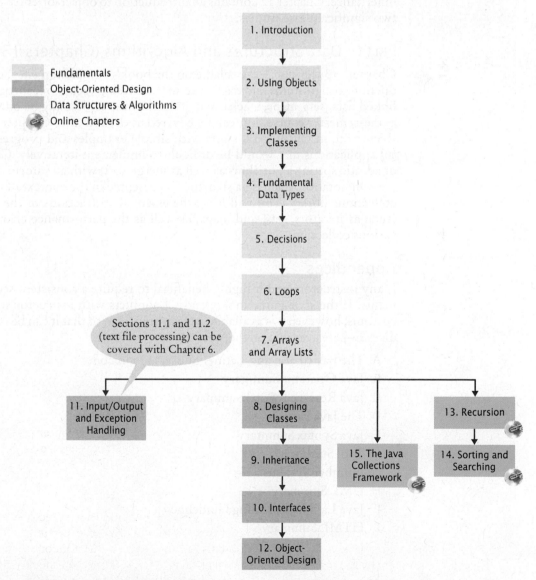

Figure 1   Chapter Dependencies

Part A: Fundamentals (Chapters 1–7)

Chapter 1 contains a brief introduction to computer science and Java programming. Chapter 2 shows how to manipulate objects of predefined classes. In Chapter 3, you will build your own simple classes from given specifications. Fundamental data types, branches, loops, and arrays are covered in Chapters 4–7.

Part B: Object-Oriented Design (Chapters 8–12)

Chapter 8 takes up the subject of class design in a systematic fashion, and it introduces a very simple subset of the UML notation. The discussion of polymorphism and inheritance is split into two chapters. Chapter 9 covers inheritance and polymorphism, whereas Chapter 10 covers interfaces. Exception handling and basic file input/output are covered in Chapter 11. The exception hierarchy gives a useful example for inheritance. Chapter 12 contains an introduction to object-oriented design, including two significant case studies.

Part C: Data Structures and Algorithms (Chapters 13–15)

Chapters 13 through 15 (available on the book's companion sites) contain an introduction to algorithms and data structures, covering recursion, sorting and searching, linked lists, sets, maps, stacks, and queues. These topics may be outside the scope of a one-semester course, but can be covered as desired after Chapter 7 (see Figure 1). Recursion, in Chapter 13, starts with simple examples and progresses to meaningful applications that would be difficult to implement iteratively. Chapter 14 covers quadratic sorting algorithms as well as merge sort, with an informal introduction to big-Oh notation. Each data structure is presented in the context of the standard Java collections library. You will learn the essential abstractions of the standard library (such as iterators, sets, and maps) as well as the performance characteristics of the various collections.

Appendices

Many instructors find it highly beneficial to require a consistent style for all assignments. If the style guide in Appendix I conflicts with instructor sentiment or local customs, however, it is available in electronic form so that it can be modified. Appendices E–J are available on the Web.

- A. The Basic Latin and Latin-1 Subsets of Unicode
- B. Java Operator Summary
- C. Java Reserved Word Summary
- D. The Java Library
- E. Java Syntax Summary
- F. Tool Summary
- G. Number Systems
- H. UML Summary
- I. Java Language Coding Guidelines
- J. HTML Summary

Custom Book and eBook Options

Java Concepts may be ordered as a custom print or eBook that includes your choice of chapters—including those from other Horstmann titles. Visit customselect.wiley.com to create your custom book order.

To order the Wiley Select Edition of *Java Concepts* with all 15 chapters in the printed book, specify ISBN 978-1-119-93669-5 when you order books.

Java Concepts is available in a variety of eBook formats at prices that are significantly lower than the printed book. Please contact your Wiley sales rep for more information or check www.wiley.com/college/horstmann for available versions.

Web Resources

This book is complemented by a complete suite of online resources. Go to www.wiley.com/college/horstmann to visit the online companion sites, which include

- "CodeCheck," a new online service currently in development by Cay Horstmann that students can use to check their homework assignments and to work on additional practice problems. Visit http://horstmann.com/codecheck to learn more and to try it out.
- Source code for all example programs in the book and in online examples.
- Worked Examples that apply the problem-solving steps in the book to other realistic examples.
- Animations of key concepts.
- Lab exercises that apply chapter concepts (with solutions for instructors only).
- Lecture presentation slides (for instructors only).
- Solutions to all review and programming exercises (for instructors only).
- A test bank that focuses on skills, not just terminology (for instructors only). This extensive set of multiple-choice questions can be used with a word processor or imported into a course management system.

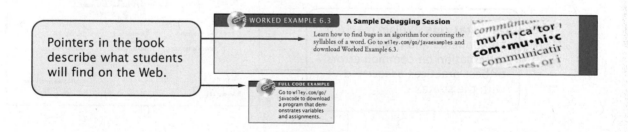

Pointers in the book describe what students will find on the Web.

WORKED EXAMPLE 6.3   **A Sample Debugging Session**

Learn how to find bugs in an algorithm for counting the syllables of a word. Go to wiley.com/go/javaexamples and download Worked Example 6.3.

FULL CODE EXAMPLE

Go to wiley.con/go/javacode to download a program that demonstrates variables and assignments.

A Walkthrough of the Learning Aids

The pedagogical elements in this book work together to focus on and reinforce key concepts and fundamental principles of programming, with additional tips and detail organized to support and deepen these fundamentals. In addition to traditional features, such as chapter objectives and a wealth of exercises, each chapter contains elements geared to today's visual learner.

Throughout each chapter, **margin notes** show where new concepts are introduced and provide an outline of key ideas.

Additional **full code examples** provides complete programs for students to run and modify.

Annotated **syntax boxes** provide a quick, visual overview of new language constructs.

Annotations explain required components and point to more information on common errors or best practices associated with the syntax.

Analogies to everyday objects are used to explain the nature and behavior of concepts such as variables, data types, loops, and more.

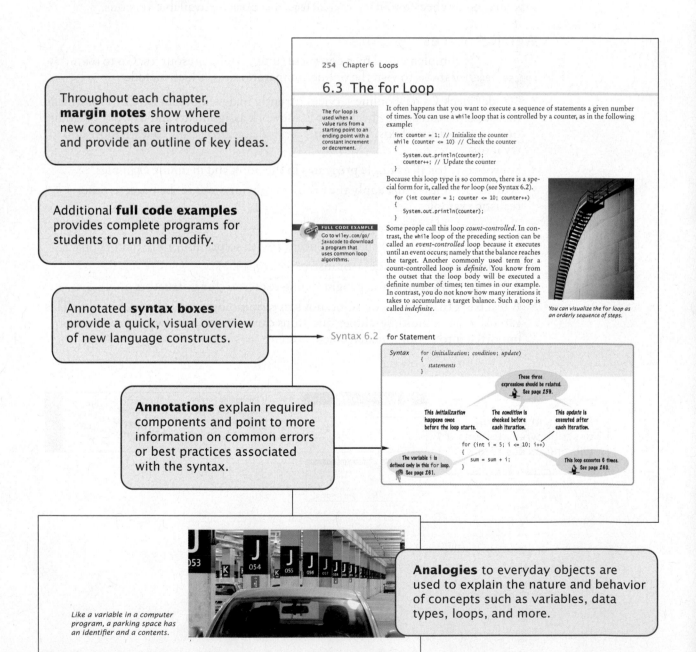

254   Chapter 6   Loops

6.3 The for Loop

The for loop is used when a value runs from a starting point to an ending point with a constant increment or decrement.

It often happens that you want to execute a sequence of statements a given number of times. You can use a while loop that is controlled by a counter, as in the following example:

```
int counter = 1; // Initialize the counter
while (counter <= 10) // Check the counter
{
    System.out.println(counter);
    counter++; // Update the counter
}
```

Because this loop type is so common, there is a special form for it, called the for loop (see Syntax 6.2).

```
for (int counter = 1; counter <= 10; counter++)
{
    System.out.println(counter);
}
```

Some people call this loop *count-controlled*. In contrast, the while loop of the preceding section can be called an *event-controlled* loop because it executes until an event occurs; namely that the balance reaches the target. Another commonly used term for a count-controlled loop is *definite*. You know from the outset that the loop body will be executed a definite number of times; ten times in our example. In contrast, you do not know how many iterations it takes to accumulate a target balance. Such a loop is called *indefinite*.

FULL CODE EXAMPLE

Go to wiley.com/go/ javacode to download a program that uses common loop algorithms.

You can visualize the for loop as an orderly sequence of steps.

Syntax 6.2   for Statement

```
Syntax    for (initialization; condition; update)
          {
              statements
          }
```

These three expressions should be related. See page 259.

This *initialization* happens once before the loop starts.

The *condition* is checked before each iteration.

This *update* is executed after each iteration.

```
for (int i = 5; i <= 10; i++)
{
    sum = sum + i;
}
```

The variable i is defined only in this for loop. See page 261.

This loop executes 6 times. See page 260.

Like a variable in a computer program, a parking space has an identifier and a contents.

Memorable photos reinforce analogies and help students remember the concepts.

In the same way that there can be a street named "Main Street" in different cities, a Java program can have multiple variables with the same name.

Problem Solving sections teach techniques for generating ideas and evaluating proposed solutions, often using pencil and paper or other artifacts. These sections emphasize that most of the planning and problem solving that makes students successful happens away from the computer.

7.5   Problem Solving: Discovering Algorithms by Manipulating Physical Objects   339

Now how does that help us with our problem, switching the first and the second half of the array?

Let's put the first coin into place, by swapping it with the fifth coin. However, as Java programmers, we will say that we swap the coins in positions 0 and 4:

Next, we swap the coins in positions 1 and 5:

HOW TO 6.1   **Writing a Loop**

This How To walks you through the process of implementing a loop statement. We will illustrate the steps with the following example problem.

Problem Statement   Read twelve temperature values (one for each month) and display the number of the month with the highest temperature. For example, according to worldclimate.com, the average maximum temperatures for Death Valley are (in order by month, in degrees Celsius):

18.2 22.6 26.4 31.1 36.6 42.2 **45.7** 44.5 40.2 33.1 24.2 17.6

In this case, the month with the highest temperature (45.7 degrees Celsius) is July, and the program should display 7.

Step 1   Decide what work must be done *inside* the loop.

Every loop needs to do some kind of repetitive work, such as

* Reading another item.
* Updating a value (such as a bank balance or total).
* Incrementing a counter.

If you can't figure out what needs to go inside the loop, start by writing down the steps that

How To guides give step-by-step guidance for common programming tasks, emphasizing planning and testing. They answer the beginner's question, "Now what do I do?" and integrate key concepts into a problem-solving sequence.

 WORKED EXAMPLE 6.1   **Credit Card Processing**

Learn how to use a loop to remove spaces from a credit card number. Go to wiley.com/go/javaexamples and download Worked Example 6.1.

Worked Examples apply the steps in the How To to a different example, showing how they can be used to plan, implement, and test a solution to another programming problem.

Table 1 Variable Declarations in Java

Variable Name	Comment
int width = 20;	Declares an integer variable and initializes it with 20.
int perimeter = 4 * width;	The initial value need not be a fixed value. (Of course, width must have been previously declared.)
String greeting = "Hi!";	This variable has the type String and is initialized with the string "Hi".
⊘ height = 30;	**Error:** The type is missing. This statement is not a declaration but an assignment of a new value to an existing variable—see Section 2.2.5
⊘ int width = "20";	**Error:** You cannot initialize a number with the string "20". (Note the quotation marks.)
int width;	Declares an integer variable without initializing it. This can be a cause for errors—see Common Error 2.1 on page 42.
int width, height;	Declares two integer variables in a single statement. In this book, we will declare each variable in a separate statement.

Example tables support beginners with multiple, concrete examples. These tables point out common errors and present another quick reference to the section's topic.

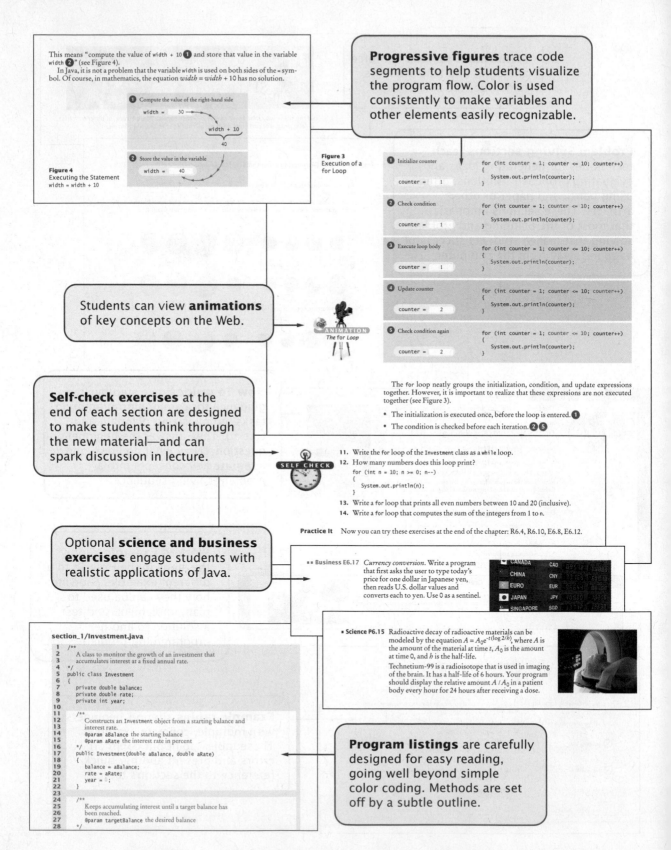

This means "compute the value of width + 10 ❶ and store that value in the variable width ❷" (see Figure 4).

In Java, it is not a problem that the variable width is used on both sides of the = symbol. Of course, in mathematics, the equation *width* = *width* + 10 has no solution.

❶ Compute the value of the right-hand side

    width =   30

            width + 10
                 40

Figure 4
Executing the Statement
width = width + 10

❷ Store the value in the variable

    width =   40

Progressive figures trace code segments to help students visualize the program flow. Color is used consistently to make variables and other elements easily recognizable.

Figure 3
Execution of a for Loop

❶ Initialize counter
```
for (int counter = 1; counter <= 10; counter++)
{
    System.out.println(counter);
}
```
    counter =   1

❷ Check condition
```
for (int counter = 1; counter <= 10; counter++)
{
    System.out.println(counter);
}
```
    counter =   1

❸ Execute loop body
```
for (int counter = 1; counter <= 10; counter++)
{
    System.out.println(counter);
}
```
    counter =   1

❹ Update counter
```
for (int counter = 1; counter <= 10; counter++)
{
    System.out.println(counter);
}
```
    counter =   2

❺ Check condition again
```
for (int counter = 1; counter <= 10; counter++)
{
    System.out.println(counter);
}
```
    counter =   2

Students can view **animations** of key concepts on the Web.

ANIMATION
The for Loop

The for loop neatly groups the initialization, condition, and update expressions together. However, it is important to realize that these expressions are not executed together (see Figure 3).

• The initialization is executed once, before the loop is entered. ❶
• The condition is checked before each iteration. ❷ ❺

Self-check exercises at the end of each section are designed to make students think through the new material—and can spark discussion in lecture.

SELF CHECK

11. Write the for loop of the Investment class as a while loop.
12. How many numbers does this loop print?
```
for (int n = 10; n >= 0; n--)
{
    System.out.println(n);
}
```
13. Write a for loop that prints all even numbers between 10 and 20 (inclusive).
14. Write a for loop that computes the sum of the integers from 1 to n.

Practice It   Now you can try these exercises at the end of the chapter: R6.4, R6.10, E6.8, E6.12.

Optional **science and business exercises** engage students with realistic applications of Java.

•• Business E6.17 *Currency conversion.* Write a program that first asks the user to type today's price for one dollar in Japanese yen, then reads U.S. dollar values and converts each to yen. Use 0 as a sentinel.

CANADA	CAD
CHINA	CNY
EURO	EUR
JAPAN	JPY
SINGAPORE	SGD

• Science P6.15 Radioactive decay of radioactive materials can be modeled by the equation $A = A_0 e^{-t (\log 2/h)}$, where A is the amount of the material at time t, A_0 is the amount at time 0, and h is the half-life.

Technetium-99 is a radioisotope that is used in imaging of the brain. It has a half-life of 6 hours. Your program should display the relative amount A / A_0 in a patient body every hour for 24 hours after receiving a dose.

section_1/Investment.java
```
1   /**
2       A class to monitor the growth of an investment that
3       accumulates interest at a fixed annual rate.
4   */
5   public class Investment
6   {
7       private double balance;
8       private double rate;
9       private int year;
10
11      /**
12          Constructs an Investment object from a starting balance and
13          interest rate.
14          @param aBalance the starting balance
15          @param aRate the interest rate in percent
16      */
17      public Investment(double aBalance, double aRate)
18      {
19          balance = aBalance;
20          rate = aRate;
21          year = 0;
22      }
23
24      /**
25          Keeps accumulating interest until a target balance has
26          been reached.
27          @param targetBalance the desired balance
28      */
```

Program listings are carefully designed for easy reading, going well beyond simple color coding. Methods are set off by a subtle outline.

Common Errors describe the kinds of errors that students often make, with an explanation of why the errors occur, and what to do about them.

Common Error 7.4

Length and Size

Unfortunately, the Java syntax for determining the number of elements in an array, an array list, and a string is not at all consistent. It is a common error to confuse these. You just have to remember the correct syntax for every data type.

Data Type	Number of Elements
Array	a.length
Array list	a.size()
String	a.length()

Programming Tips explain good programming practices, and encourage students to be more productive with tips and techniques such as hand-tracing.

Programming Tip 5.5

Hand-Tracing

A very useful technique for understanding whether a program works correctly is called *hand-tracing*. You simulate the program's activity on a sheet of paper. You can use this method with pseudocode or Java code.

Get an index card, a cocktail napkin, or whatever sheet of paper is within reach. Make a column for each variable. Have the program code ready. Use a marker, such as a paper clip, to mark the current statement. In your mind, execute statements one at a time. Every time the value of a variable changes, cross out the old value and write the new value below the old one.

For example, let's trace the getTax method with the data from the program run above.

Hand-tracing helps you understand whether a program works correctly.

When the TaxReturn object is constructed, the income instance variable is set to 80,000 and status is set to MARRIED. Then the getTax method is called. In lines 31 and 32 of TaxReturn.java, tax1 and tax2 are initialized to 0.

```
29  public double getTax()
30  {
31      double tax1 = 0;
32      double tax2 = 0;
33
```

income	status	tax1	tax2
80000	MARRIED	0	0

Because status is not SINGLE, we move to the else branch of the outer if statement (line 46).

```
34      if (status == SINGLE)
35      {
36          if (income <= RATE1_SINGLE_LIMIT)
37          {
38              tax1 = RATE1 * income;
39          }
40          else
41          {
42              tax1 = RATE1 * RATE1_SINGLE_LIMIT;
43              tax2 = RATE2 * (income - RATE1_SINGLE_LIMIT);
```

Special Topics present optional topics and provide additional explanation of others. New features of Java 7 are also covered in these notes.

Special Topic 11.2

File Dialog Boxes

In a program with a graphical user interface, you will want to use a file dialog box (such as the one shown in the figure below) whenever the users of your program need to pick a file. The JFileChooser class implements a file dialog box for the Swing user-interface toolkit.

The JFileChooser class has many options to fine-tune the display of the dialog box, but in its most basic form it is quite simple: Construct a file chooser object; then call the showOpenDialog or showSaveDialog method. Both methods show the same dialog box, but the button for selecting a file is labeled "Open" or "Save", depending on which method you call.

For better placement of the dialog box on the screen, you can specify the user-interface component over which to pop up the dialog box. If you don't care where the dialog box pops up, you can simply pass null. The showOpenDialog and showSaveDialog methods return either JFileChooser.APPROVE_OPTION, if the user has chosen a file, or JFileChooser.CANCEL_OPTION, if the user canceled the selection. If a file was chosen, then you call the getSelectedFile method to obtain a File object that describes the file. Here is a complete example:

FULL CODE EXAMPLE
Go to wiley.com/go/javacode to download a program that demonstrates how to use a file chooser.

```
JFileChooser chooser = new JFileChooser();
Scanner in = null;
if (chooser.showOpenDialog(null) == JFileChooser.APPROVE_OPTION)
{
    File selectedFile = chooser.getSelectedFile();
    in = new Scanner(selectedFile);
    . . .
}
```

Call with showOpenDialog method

Computing & Society presents social and historical topics on computing—for interest and to fulfill the "historical and social context" requirements of the ACM/IEEE curriculum guidelines.

Computing & Society 1.1 Computers Are Everywhere

When computers were first invented in the 1940s, a computer filled an entire room. The photo below shows the ENIAC (electronic numerical integrator and computer), completed in 1946 at the University of Pennsylvania. The ENIAC was used by the military to compute the trajectories of projectiles. Nowadays, computing facilities of search engines, Internet shops, and social networks fill huge buildings called data centers. At the other end of the spectrum, computers are all around us. Your cell phone has a computer inside, as do many credit cards and fare cards for public transit. A modern car has several computers—to control the engine, brakes, lights, and the radio.

The advent of ubiquitous computing changed many aspects of our lives. Factories used to employ people to do repetitive assembly tasks that are today carried out by computer-controlled robots, operated by a few people who know how to work with those computers. Books, music, and movies are nowadays often consumed on computers, and computers are almost always involved in their production. The book that you are reading right now

This transit card contains a computer.

could not have been written without computers.

Web Resources

CodeCheck "CodeCheck" is a new online service currently in development by Cay Horstmann that students can use to check their homework and to work on additional practice problems. Visit http://horstmann.com/codecheck to learn more and to try it out.

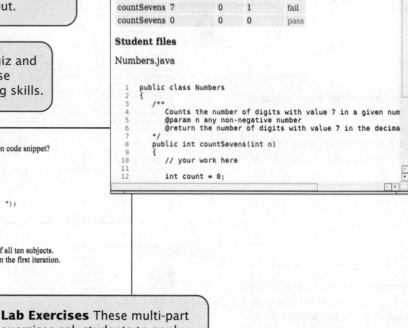

```
bj4cc:ch06/c06_exp_6_105:check                              _ □ ×
Web
◄ ➡    http://horstmann.com/codecheck/                    C  ▣
```

Calling method

Method	Arguments	Actual	Expected	
countSevens	1797	1	2	fail
countSevens	7777777	6	7	fail
countSevens	1985	0	0	pass
countSevens	7	0	1	fail
countSevens	0	0	0	pass

Student files

Numbers.java

```
 1   public class Numbers
 2   {
 3      /**
 4         Counts the number of digits with value 7 in a given num
 5         @param n any non-negative number
 6         @return the number of digits with value 7 in the decima
 7      */
 8      public int countSevens(int n)
 9      {
10         // your work here
11
12         int count = 0;
```

Test Bank Instructors can use quiz and test questions designed to exercise students' code reading and writing skills.

10) What is displayed after executing the given code snippet?

```
int[] mymarks = new int[10];
int total = 0;
Scanner in = new Scanner(System.in);
for (int cnt = 1; cnt <= 10; cnt++)
{
   System.out.print("Enter the marks: ");
   mymarks[cnt] = in.nextInt();
   total = total + mymarks[cnt];
}
System.out.println(total);
```

a) The code snippet displays the total marks of all ten subjects.
b) The for loop causes a run-time time error on the first iteration.
c) The code snippet causes a bounds error.
d) The code snippet displays zero.

Lab Exercises These multi-part exercises ask students to apply chapter concepts. They can serve as "warm-ups" in the lab or to provide additional practice.

1.1) Consider the following Card class.

```
public class Card
{
   private String name;

   public Card()
   {
      name = "";
   }

   public Card(String n)
   {
      name = n;
   }

   public String getName()
   {
      return name;
   }

   public boolean isExpired()
   {
      return false;
   }

   public String format()
   {
      return "Card holder: " + name;
   }
}
```

Use this class as a superclass to implement a hierarchy of related classes:

Class	Data
IDCard	ID number
CallingCard	Card number, PIN
DriverLicense	Expiration year

Write declarations for each of the subclasses. For each subclass, supply private instance variables. Leave the bodies of the constructors and the format methods blank for now.

Animations Students can play and replay dynamic explanations of concepts and program flow.

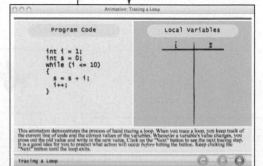

```
○○○                     Animation: Tracing a Loop

        Program Code              Local Variables
                                    i         s
        int i = 1;
        int s = 0;
        while (i <= 10)
        {
           s = s + i;
           i++;
        }

This animation demonstrates the process of hand tracing a loop. When you trace a loop, you keep track of
the current line of code and the current values of the variables. Whenever a variable's value changes, you
cross out the old value and write in the new value. Click on the "Next" button to see the next tracing step.
It is a good idea for you to predict what action will occur before hitting the button. Keep clicking the
"Next" button until the loop exits.

Tracing a Loop                              ○  ○  ○
```

Acknowledgments

Many thanks to Beth Lang Golub, Don Fowley, Elizabeth Mills, Katherine Willis, Jenny Welter, Wendy Ashenberg, Lisa Gee, Kevin Holm, and Tim Lindner at John Wiley & Sons, and Vickie Piercey at Publishing Services for their help with this project. An especially deep acknowledgment and thanks goes to Cindy Johnson for her hard work, sound judgment, and amazing attention to detail.

I am grateful to Jose Cordova, *University of Louisiana*, James Johnson, Norm Krumpe, *Miami University Ohio*, Kathy Liszka, *University of Akron*, Donald Smith, *Columbia College*, Brent Wilson, *George Fox University*, and David Woolbright, *Columbus State University*, for their excellent contributions to the supplementary materials.

Many thanks to the individuals who reviewed the manuscript for this edition, made valuable suggestions, and brought an embarrassingly large number of errors and omissions to my attention. They include:

Eric Aaron, *Wesleyan University*

James Agnew, *Anne Arundel Community College*

Greg Ballinger, *Miami Dade College*

Jon Beck, *Truman State University*

Matt Boutell, *Rose-Hulman Institute of Technology*

John Bundy, *DeVry University Chicago*

Michael Carney, *Finger Lakes Community College*

Christopher Cassa, *Massachusetts Institute of Technology*

Dr. Suchindran S. Chatterjee, *Arizona State University*

Tina Comston, *Franklin University*

Lennie Cooper, *Miami Dade College*

Sherif Elfayoumy, *University of North Florida*

Henry A Etlinger, *Rochester Institute of Technology*

Guy Helmer, *Iowa State University*

Ed Holden, *Rochester Institute of Technology*

Steven Janke, *Colorado College*

Mark Jones, *Lock Haven University of Pennsylvania*

Dr. Mustafa Kamal, *University of Central Missouri*

Gary J. Koehler, *University of Florida*

Ronald Krawitz, *DeVry University*

Norm Krumpe, *Miami University Ohio*

Jim Leone, *Rochester Institute of Technology*

Kevin Lillis, *St. Ambrose University*

Darren Lim, *Siena College*

Hong Lin, *DeVry University*

Kuber Maharjan, *Purdue University College of Technology at Columbus*

Patricia McDermott-Wells, *Florida International University*

Bill Mongan, *Drexel University*

George Novacky, *University of Pittsburgh*

Mimi Opkins, *California State University Long Beach*

Derek Pao, *City University of Hong Kong*

Katherine Salch, *Illinois Central College*

Javad Shakib, *DeVry University*

Charlie Shu, *Franklin University*

Joslyn A. Smith, *Florida International University*

Robert Strader, *Stephen F. Austin State University*

Jonathan S. Weissman, *Finger Lakes Community College*

Katherine H. Winters, *University of Tennessee Chattanooga*

Tom Wulf, *University of Cincinnati*

Qi Yu, *Rochester Institute of Technology*

Every new edition builds on the suggestions and experiences of prior reviewers and users. I am grateful for the invaluable contributions these individuals have made:

Tim Andersen, *Boise State University*

Ivan Bajic, *San Diego State University*

Ted Bangay, *Sheridan Institute of Technology*

Ian Barland, *Radford University*

George Basham, *Franklin University*

Sambit Bhattacharya, *Fayetteville State University*

Rick Birney, *Arizona State University*

Paul Bladek, *Edmonds Community College*

Joseph Bowbeer, *Vizrea Corporation*

Timothy A. Budd, *Oregon State University*

Robert P. Burton, *Brigham Young University*

Frank Butt, *IBM*

Jerry Cain, *Stanford University*

Adam Cannon, *Columbia University*

Nancy Chase, *Gonzaga University*

Archana Chidanandan, *Rose-Hulman Institute of Technology*

Vincent Cicirello, *The Richard Stockton College of New Jersey*

Teresa Cole, *Boise State University*

Deborah Coleman, *Rochester Institute of Technology*

Jose Cordova, *University of Louisiana, Monroe*

Valentino Crespi, *California State University, Los Angeles*

Jim Cross, *Auburn University*

Russell Deaton, *University of Arkansas*

Geoffrey Decker, *Northern Illinois University*

H. E. Dunsmore, *Purdue University*

Robert Duvall, *Duke University*

Eman El-Sheikh, *University of West Florida*

John Fendrich, *Bradley University*

David Freer, *Miami Dade College*

John Fulton, *Franklin University*

David Geary, *Sabreware, Inc.*

Margaret Geroch, *Wheeling Jesuit University*

Ahmad Ghafarian, *North Georgia College & State University*

Rick Giles, *Acadia University*

Stacey Grasso, *College of San Mateo*

Jianchao Han, *California State University, Dominguez Hills*

Lisa Hansen, *Western New England College*

Elliotte Harold

Eileen Head, *Binghamton University*

Cecily Heiner, *University of Utah*

Brian Howard, *Depauw University*

Lubomir Ivanov, *Iona College*

Norman Jacobson, *University of California, Irvine*

Curt Jones, *Bloomsburg University*

Aaron Keen, *California Polytechnic State University, San Luis Obispo*

Mugdha Khaladkar, *New Jersey Institute of Technology*

Elliot Koffman, *Temple University*

Kathy Liszka, *University of Akron*

Hunter Lloyd, *Montana State University*

Youmin Lu, *Bloomsburg University*

John S. Mallozzi, *Iona College*

John Martin, *North Dakota State University*

Jeanna Matthews, *Clarkson University*

Scott McElfresh, *Carnegie Mellon University*

Joan McGrory, *Christian Brothers University*

Carolyn Miller, *North Carolina State University*

Sandeep R. Mitra, *State University of New York, Brockport*

Teng Moh, *San Jose State University*

John Moore, *The Citadel*

Jose-Arturo Mora-Soto, Jesica Rivero-Espinosa, and Julio-Angel Cano-Romero, *University of Madrid*

Faye Navabi, *Arizona State University*

Parviz Partow-Navid, *California State University, Los Angeles*

Kevin O'Gorman, *California Polytechnic State University, San Luis Obispo*

Michael Olan, *Richard Stockton College*

Kevin Parker, *Idaho State University*

Jim Perry, *Ulster County Community College*

Cornel Pokorny, *California Polytechnic State University, San Luis Obispo*

Roger Priebe, *University of Texas, Austin*

C. Robert Putnam, *California State University, Northridge*

Kai Qian, *Southern Polytechnic State University*

Cyndi Rader, *Colorado School of Mines*

Neil Rankin, *Worcester Polytechnic Institute*

Brad Rippe, *Fullerton College*

Pedro I. Rivera Vega, *University of Puerto Rico, Mayaguez*

Daniel Rogers, *SUNY Brockport*

Chaman Lal Sabharwal, *Missouri University of Science and Technology*

John Santore, *Bridgewater State College*

Carolyn Schauble, *Colorado State University*

Brent Seales, *University of Kentucky*

Christian Shin, *SUNY Geneseo*

Jeffrey Six, *University of Delaware*

Don Slater, *Carnegie Mellon University*

Ken Slonneger, *University of Iowa*

Donald Smith, *Columbia College*

Stephanie Smullen, *University of Tennessee, Chattanooga*

Monica Sweat, *Georgia Institute of Technology*

Peter Stanchev, *Kettering University*

Shannon Tauro, *University of California, Irvine*

Ron Taylor, *Wright State University*

Russell Tessier, *University of Massachusetts, Amherst*

Jonathan L. Tolstedt, *North Dakota State University*

David Vineyard, *Kettering University*

Joseph Vybihal, *McGill University*

Xiaoming Wei, *Iona College*

Todd Whittaker, *Franklin University*

Robert Willhoft, *Roberts Wesleyan College*

Lea Wittie, *Bucknell University*

David Womack, *University of Texas at San Antonio*

David Woolbright, *Columbus State University*

Catherine Wyman, *DeVry University*

Arthur Yanushka, *Christian Brothers University*

Salih Yurttas, *Texas A&M University*

CONTENTS

ALPHABETICAL LIST OF SYNTAX BOXES

CHAPTER	Common Errors	How Tos and Worked Examples
1 Introduction	Omitting Semicolons 14 Misspelling Words 16	Describing an Algorithm with Pseudocode 20 Writing an Algorithm for Tiling a Floor 22
2 Using Objects	Using Undeclared or Uninitialized Variables 42 Confusing Variable Declarations and Assignment Statements 42 Trying to Invoke a Constructor Like a Method 50	How Many Days Have You Been Alive? Working with Pictures
3 Implementing Classes	Declaring a Constructor as void 92 Ignoring Parameter Variables 98 Duplicating Instance Variables in Local Variables 108 Providing Unnecessary Instance Variables 108 Forgetting to Initialize Object References in a Constructor 109	Implementing a Class 98 Making a Simple Menu Drawing Graphical Shapes 116
4 Fundamental Data Types	Unintended Integer Division 144 Unbalanced Parentheses 144	Carrying out Computations 151 Computing the Volume and Surface Area of a Pyramid Computing Travel Time

Available online at www.wiley.com/college/horstmann.

Programming Tips

 Special Topics

 Computing & Society

CHAPTER	Common Errors	How Tos and Worked Examples
5 Decisions	A Semicolon After the if Condition 184 Using == to Compare Strings 192 The Dangling else Problem 204 Combining Multiple Relational Operators 216 Confusing && and || Conditions 216	Implementing an if Statement 193 Extracting the Middle 🍜
6 Loops	Don't Think "Are We There Yet?" 247 Infinite Loops 248 Off-by-One Errors 248	Writing a Loop 276 Credit Card Processing 🍜 Manipulating the Pixels in an Image 🍜 Debugging 289 A Sample Debugging Session 🍜
7 Arrays and Array Lists	Bounds Errors 318 Uninitialized and Unfilled Arrays 318 Underestimating the Size of a Data Set 331 Length and Size 356	Working with Arrays 334 Rolling the Dice 🍜 A World Population Table 🍜
8 Designing Classes	Trying to Access Instance Variables in Static Methods 398 Confusing Dots 403	Programming with Packages 404

🍜 Available online at www.wiley.com/college/horstmann.

Programming Tips

 Special Topics

 Computing & Society

CHAPTER	Common Errors	How Tos and Worked Examples

Programming Tips

 Special Topics

 Computing & Society

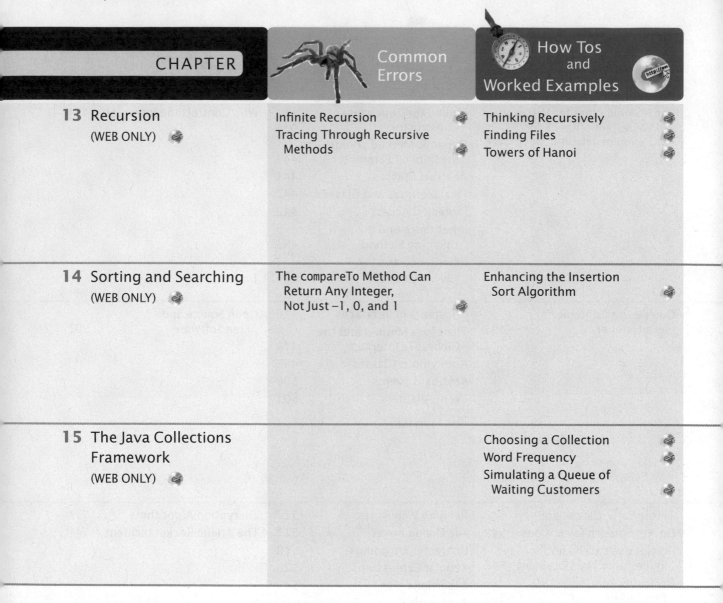

CHAPTER	Common Errors	How Tos and Worked Examples
13 Recursion (WEB ONLY)	Infinite Recursion Tracing Through Recursive Methods	Thinking Recursively Finding Files Towers of Hanoi
14 Sorting and Searching (WEB ONLY)	The compareTo Method Can Return Any Integer, Not Just –1, 0, and 1	Enhancing the Insertion Sort Algorithm
15 The Java Collections Framework (WEB ONLY)		Choosing a Collection Word Frequency Simulating a Queue of Waiting Customers

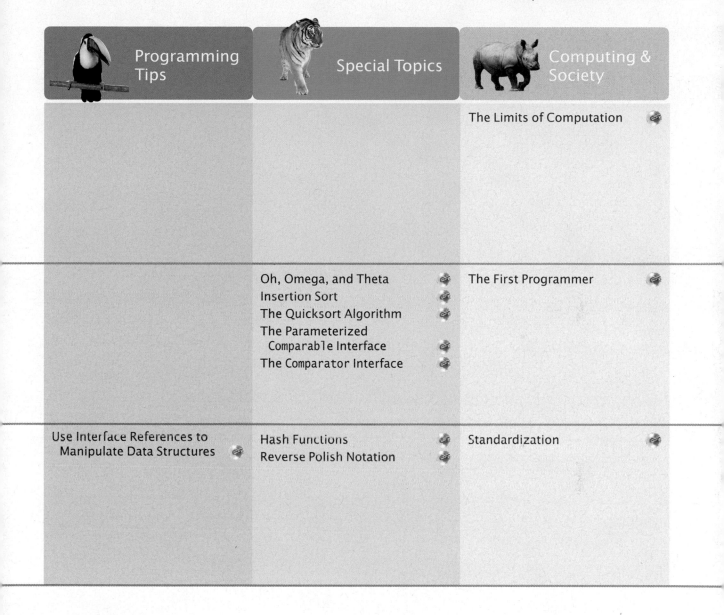

Programming Tips	Special Topics	Computing & Society
		The Limits of Computation
	Oh, Omega, and Theta Insertion Sort The Quicksort Algorithm The Parameterized Comparable Interface The Comparator Interface	The First Programmer
Use Interface References to Manipulate Data Structures	Hash Functions Reverse Polish Notation	Standardization

INTRODUCTION

CHAPTER GOALS

To learn about computers
and programming

To compile and run your first Java program

To recognize compile-time and run-time errors

To describe an algorithm with pseudocode

CHAPTER CONTENTS

Just as you gather tools, study a project, and make a plan for tackling it, in this chapter you will gather up the basics you need to start learning to program. After a brief introduction to computer hardware, software, and programming in general, you will learn how to write and run your first Java program. You will also learn how to diagnose and fix programming errors, and how to use pseudocode to describe an algorithm—a step-by-step description of how to solve a problem—as you plan your computer programs.

1.1 Computer Programs

Computers execute very basic instructions in rapid succession.

You have probably used a computer for work or fun. Many people use computers for everyday tasks such as electronic banking or writing a term paper. Computers are good for such tasks. They can handle repetitive chores, such as totaling up numbers or placing words on a page, without getting bored or exhausted.

The flexibility of a computer is quite an amazing phenomenon. The same machine can balance your checkbook, lay out your term paper, and play a game. In contrast, other machines carry out a much narrower range of tasks; a car drives and a toaster toasts. Computers can carry out a wide range of tasks because they execute different programs, each of which directs the computer to work on a specific task.

A computer program is a sequence of instructions and decisions.

The computer itself is a machine that stores data (numbers, words, pictures), interacts with devices (the monitor, the sound system, the printer), and executes programs. A **computer program** tells a computer, in minute detail, the sequence of steps that are needed to fulfill a task. The physical computer and peripheral devices are collectively called the **hardware**. The programs the computer executes are called the **software**.

Today's computer programs are so sophisticated that it is hard to believe that they are composed of extremely primitive instructions. A typical instruction may be one of the following:

- Put a red dot at a given screen position.
- Add up two numbers.
- If this value is negative, continue the program at a certain instruction.

The computer user has the illusion of smooth interaction because a program contains a huge number of such instructions, and because the computer can execute them at great speed.

Programming is the act of designing and implementing computer programs.

The act of designing and implementing computer programs is called **programming**. In this book, you will learn how to program a computer—that is, how to direct the computer to execute tasks.

To write a computer game with motion and sound effects or a word processor that supports fancy fonts and pictures is a complex task that requires a team of many highly-skilled programmers. Your first programming efforts will be more mundane. The concepts and skills you learn in this book form an important foundation, and you should not be disappointed if your first programs do not rival the sophisticated software that is familiar to you. Actually, you will find that there is an immense thrill even in simple programming tasks. It is an amazing experience to see the computer precisely and quickly carry out a task that would take you hours of drudgery, to make small changes in a program that lead to immediate improvements, and to see the computer become an extension of your mental powers.

SELF CHECK

1. What is required to play music on a computer?
2. Why is a CD player less flexible than a computer?
3. What does a computer user need to know about programming in order to play a video game?

1.2 The Anatomy of a Computer

To understand the programming process, you need to have a rudimentary understanding of the building blocks that make up a computer. We will look at a personal computer. Larger computers have faster, larger, or more powerful components, but they have fundamentally the same design.

At the heart of the computer lies the **central processing unit (CPU)** (see Figure 3). The inside wiring of the CPU is enormously complicated. For example, the Intel Core processor (a popular CPU for personal computers at the time of this writing) is composed of several hundred million structural elements, called *transistors*.

> The central processing unit (CPU) performs program control and data processing.

The CPU performs program control and data processing. That is, the CPU locates and executes the program instructions; it carries out arithmetic operations such as addition, subtraction, multiplication, and division; it fetches data from external memory or devices and places processed data into storage.

Figure 1   Central Processing Unit

> Storage devices include memory and secondary storage.

There are two kinds of storage. Primary storage or memory is made from electronic circuits that can store data, provided they are supplied with electric power. **Secondary storage**, usually a **hard disk** (see Figure 2)

Figure 2   A Hard Disk

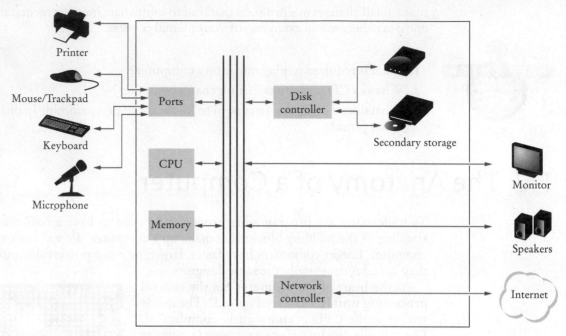

Figure 3   Schematic Design of a Personal Computer

or a solid-state drive, provides slower and less expensive storage that persists without electricity. A hard disk consists of rotating platters, which are coated with a magnetic material. A solid-state drive uses electronic components that can retain information without power, and without moving parts.

To interact with a human user, a computer requires peripheral devices. The computer transmits information (called *output*) to the user through a display screen, speakers, and printers. The user can enter information (called *input*) for the computer by using a keyboard or a pointing device such as a mouse.

Some computers are self-contained units, whereas others are interconnected through **networks**. Through the network cabling, the computer can read data and programs from central storage locations or send data to other computers. To the user of a networked computer, it may not even be obvious which data reside on the computer itself and which are transmitted through the network.

Figure 3 gives a schematic overview of the architecture of a personal computer. Program instructions and data (such as text, numbers, audio, or video) reside in secondary storage or elsewhere on the network. When a program is started, its instructions are brought into memory, where the CPU can read them. The CPU reads and executes one instruction at a time. As directed by these instructions, the CPU reads data, modifies it, and writes it back to memory or secondary storage. Some program instructions will cause the CPU to place dots on the display screen or printer or to vibrate the speaker. As these actions happen many times over and at great speed, the human user will perceive images and sound. Some program instructions read user input from the keyboard, mouse, touch sensor, or microphone. The program analyzes the nature of these inputs and then executes the next appropriate instruction.

4. Where is a program stored when it is not currently running?

5. Which part of the computer carries out arithmetic operations, such as addition and multiplication?

6. A modern smartphone is a computer, comparable to a desktop computer. Which components of a smartphone correspond to those shown in Figure 3?

Practice It   Now you can try these exercises at the end of the chapter: R1.2, R1.3.

Computing & Society 1.1 Computers Are Everywhere

When computers were first invented in the 1940s, a computer filled an entire room. The photo below shows the ENIAC (*electronic numerical integrator and computer*), completed in 1946 at the University of Pennsylvania. The ENIAC was used by the military to compute the trajectories of projectiles. Nowadays, computing facilities of search engines, Internet shops, and social networks fill huge buildings called data centers. At the other end of the spectrum, computers are all around us. Your cell phone has a computer inside, as do many credit cards and fare cards for public transit. A modern car has several computers—to control the engine, brakes, lights, and the radio.

The advent of ubiquitous computing changed many aspects of our lives. Factories used to employ people to do repetitive assembly tasks that are today carried out by computer-controlled robots, operated by a few people who know how to work with those computers. Books, music, and movies nowadays are often consumed on computers, and computers are almost always involved in their production. The book that you are reading right now

This transit card contains a computer.

could not have been written without computers.

Knowing about computers and how to program them has become an essential skill in many careers. Engineers design computer-controlled cars and medical equipment that preserve lives. Computer scientists develop programs that help people come together to support social causes. For example, activists used social networks to share videos showing abuse by repressive regimes, and this information was instrumental in changing public opinion.

As computers, large and small, become ever more embedded in our everyday lives, it is increasingly important for everyone to understand how they work, and how to work with them. As you use this book to learn how to program a computer, you will develop a good understanding of computing fundamentals that will make you a more informed citizen and, perhaps, a computing professional.

The ENIAC

1.3 The Java Programming Language

In order to write a computer program, you need to provide a sequence of instructions that the CPU can execute. A computer program consists of a large number of simple CPU instructions, and it is tedious and error-prone to specify them one by one. For that reason, **high-level programming languages** have been created. In a high-level language, you specify the actions that your program should carry out. A **compiler** translates the high-level instructions into the more detailed instructions (called **machine code**) required by the CPU. Many different programming languages have been designed for different purposes.

James Gosling

In 1991, a group led by James Gosling and Patrick Naughton at Sun Microsystems designed a programming language, code-named "Green", for use in consumer devices, such as intelligent television "set-top" boxes. The language was designed to be simple, secure, and usable for many different processor types. No customer was ever found for this technology.

> Java was originally designed for programming consumer devices, but it was first successfully used to write Internet applets.

Gosling recounts that in 1994 the team realized, "We could write a really cool browser. It was one of the few things in the client/server mainstream that needed some of the weird things we'd done: architecture neutral, real-time, reliable, secure." Java was introduced to an enthusiastic crowd at the SunWorld exhibition in 1995, together with a browser that ran **applets**—Java code that can be located anywhere on the Internet. Figure 4 shows a typical example of an applet.

Figure 4 An Applet for Visualizing Molecules Running in a Browser Window (http://jmol.sourceforge.net/)

Table 1	Java Versions	
Version	Year	Important New Features
1.0	1996	
1.1	1997	Inner classes
1.2	1998	Swing, Collections framework
1.3	2000	Performance enhancements
1.4	2002	Assertions, XML support
5	2004	Generic classes, enhanced for loop, auto-boxing, enumerations, annotations
6	2006	Library improvements
7	2011	Small language changes and library improvements

Since then, Java has grown at a phenomenal rate. Programmers have embraced the language because it is easier to use than its closest rival, C++. In addition, Java has a rich **library** that makes it possible to write portable programs that can bypass proprietary operating systems—a feature that was eagerly sought by those who wanted to be independent of those proprietary systems and was bitterly fought by their vendors. A "micro edition" and an "enterprise edition" of the Java library allow Java programmers to target hardware ranging from smart cards and cell phones to the largest Internet servers.

Because Java was designed for the Internet, it has two attributes that make it very suitable for beginners: safety and portability.

You can run a Java program in your browser without fear. The safety features of the Java language ensure that a program is terminated if it tries to do something unsafe. Having a safe environment is also helpful for anyone learning Java. When you make an error that results in unsafe behavior, your program is terminated and you receive an accurate error report.

The other benefit of Java is portability. The same Java program will run, without change, on Windows, UNIX, Linux, or Macintosh. In order to achieve portability, the Java compiler does not translate Java programs directly into CPU instructions. Instead, compiled Java programs contain instructions for the Java **virtual machine**, a program that simulates a real CPU. Portability is another benefit for the beginning student. You do not have to learn how to write programs for different platforms.

At this time, Java is firmly established as one of the most important languages for general-purpose programming as well as for computer science instruction. However, although Java is a good language for beginners, it is not perfect, for three reasons.

Because Java was not specifically designed for students, no thought was given to making it really simple to write basic programs. A certain amount of technical machinery is necessary to write even the simplest programs. This is not a problem for professional programmers, but it can be a nuisance for beginning students. As you learn how to program in Java, there will be times when you will be asked to be satisfied with a preliminary explanation and wait for more complete detail in a later chapter.

Java has been extended many times during its life—see Table 1. In this book, we assume that you have Java version 5 or later.

Java was designed to be safe and portable, benefiting both Internet users and students.

Java programs are distributed as instructions for a virtual machine, making them platform-independent.

Java has a very large library. Focus on learning those parts of the library that you need for your programming projects.

Finally, you cannot hope to learn all of Java in one course. The Java language itself is relatively simple, but Java contains a vast set of *library packages* that are required to write useful programs. There are packages for graphics, user-interface design, cryptography, networking, sound, database storage, and many other purposes. Even expert Java programmers cannot hope to know the contents of all of the packages — they just use those that they need for particular projects.

Using this book, you should expect to learn a good deal about the Java language and about the most important packages. Keep in mind that the central goal of this book is not to make you memorize Java minutiae, but to teach you how to think about programming.

SELF CHECK

7. What are the two most important benefits of the Java language?

8. How long does it take to learn the entire Java library?

Practice It   Now you can try this exercise at the end of the chapter: R1.5.

1.4 Becoming Familiar with Your Programming Environment

Set aside some time to become familiar with the programming environment that you will use for your class work.

Many students find that the tools they need as programmers are very different from the software with which they are familiar. You should spend some time making yourself familiar with your programming environment. Because computer systems vary widely, this book can only give an outline of the steps you need to follow. It is a good idea to participate in a hands-on lab, or to ask a knowledgeable friend to give you a tour.

Step 1   Start the Java development environment.

An editor is a program for entering and modifying text, such as a Java program.

Computer systems differ greatly in this regard. On many computers there is an **integrated development environment** in which you can write and test your programs. On other computers you first launch an **editor**, a program that functions like a word processor, in which you can enter your Java instructions; you then open a *console window* and type commands to execute your program. You need to find out how to get started with your environment.

Step 2   Write a simple program.

The traditional choice for the very first program in a new programming language is a program that displays a simple greeting: "Hello, World!". Let us follow that tradition. Here is the "Hello, World!" program in Java:

```java
public class HelloPrinter
{
    public static void main(String[] args)
    {
        System.out.println("Hello, World!");
    }
}
```

We will examine this program in the next section.

Figure 5
Running the
HelloPrinter
Program in an
Integrated
Development
Environment

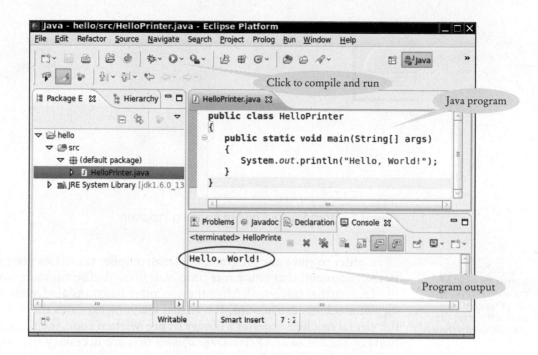

No matter which programming environment you use, you begin your activity by typing the program statements into an editor window.

Create a new file and call it HelloPrinter.java, using the steps that are appropriate for your environment. (If your environment requires that you supply a project name in addition to the file name, use the name hello for the project.) Enter the program instructions *exactly* as they are given above. Alternatively, locate the electronic copy in this book's companion code and paste it into your editor.

Java is case sensitive. You must be careful about distinguishing between upper- and lowercase letters.

As you write this program, pay careful attention to the various symbols, and keep in mind that Java is **case sensitive**. You must enter upper- and lowercase letters exactly as they appear in the program listing. You cannot type MAIN or PrintLn. If you are not careful, you will run into problems—see Common Error 1.2 on page 16.

Step 3   Run the program.

The process for running a program depends greatly on your programming environment. You may have to click a button or enter some commands. When you run the test program, the message

    Hello, World!

will appear somewhere on the screen (see Figures 5 and 6).

Figure 6
Running the HelloPrinter
Program in a Console Window

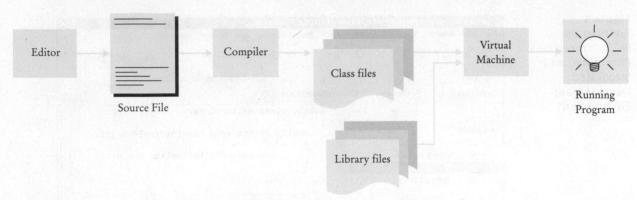

Figure 7   From Source Code to Running Program

The Java compiler translates source code into class files that contain instructions for the Java virtual machine.

In order to run your program, the Java compiler translates your **source files** (that is, the statements that you wrote) into *class files*. (A class file contains instructions for the Java virtual machine.) After the compiler has translated your **source code** into virtual machine instructions, the virtual machine executes them. During execution, the virtual machine accesses a library of pre-written code, including the implementations of the System and PrintStream classes that are necessary for displaying the program's output. Figure 7 summarizes the process of creating and running a Java program. In some programming environments, the compiler and virtual machine are essentially invisible to the programmer—they are automatically executed whenever you ask to run a Java program. In other environments, you need to launch the compiler and virtual machine explicitly.

Step 4   Organize your work.

ANIMATION
Compilation Process

As a programmer, you write programs, try them out, and improve them. You store your programs in **files**. Files are stored in **folders** or **directories**. A folder can contain files as well as other folders, which themselves can contain more files and folders (see Figure 8). This hierarchy can be quite large, and you need not be concerned with all of its branches. However, you should create folders for organizing your work. It is a good idea to make a separate folder for your programming class. Inside that folder, make a separate folder for each program.

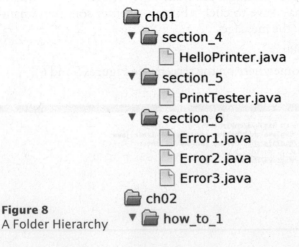

Figure 8
A Folder Hierarchy

Some programming environments place your programs into a default location if you don't specify a folder yourself. In that case, you need to find out where those files are located.

Be sure that you understand where your files are located in the folder hierarchy. This information is essential when you submit files for grading, and for making backup copies (see Programming Tip 1.1).

SELF CHECK

9. Where is the `HelloPrinter.java` file stored on your computer?

10. What do you do to protect yourself from data loss when you work on programming projects?

Practice It   Now you can try this exercise at the end of the chapter: R1.6.

Programming Tip 1.1

Backup Copies

You will spend many hours creating and improving Java programs. It is easy to delete a file by accident, and occasionally files are lost because of a computer malfunction. Retyping the contents of lost files is frustrating and time-consuming. It is therefore crucially important that you learn how to safeguard files and get in the habit of doing so *before* disaster strikes. Backing up files on a memory stick is an easy and convenient storage method for many people. Another increasingly popular form of backup is Internet file storage. Here are a few pointers to keep in mind:

- *Back up often.* Backing up a file takes only a few seconds, and you will hate yourself if you have to spend many hours recreating work that you could have saved easily. I recommend that you back up your work once every thirty minutes.

- *Rotate backups.* Use more than one directory for backups, and rotate them. That is, first back up onto the first directory. Then back up onto the second directory. Then use the third, and then go back to the first. That way you always have three recent backups. If your recent changes made matters worse, you can then go back to the older version.

> Develop a strategy for keeping backup copies of your work before disaster strikes.

- *Pay attention to the backup direction.* Backing up involves copying files from one place to another. It is important that you do this right—that is, copy from your work location to the backup location. If you do it the wrong way, you will overwrite a newer file with an older version.

- *Check your backups once in a while.* Double-check that your backups are where you think they are. There is nothing more frustrating than to find out that the backups are not there when you need them.

- *Relax, then restore.* When you lose a file and need to restore it from a backup, you are likely to be in an unhappy, nervous state. Take a deep breath and think through the recovery process before you start. It is not uncommon for an agitated computer user to wipe out the last backup when trying to restore a damaged file.

1.5 Analyzing Your First Program

In this section, we will analyze the first Java program in detail. Here again is the source code:

section_5/HelloPrinter.java

```
1  public class HelloPrinter
2  {
3     public static void main(String[] args)
4     {
5        // Display a greeting in the console window
6
7        System.out.println("Hello, World!");
8     }
9  }
```

The line

```
public class HelloPrinter
```

indicates the declaration of a **class** called HelloPrinter.

> Classes are the fundamental building blocks of Java programs.

Every Java program consists of one or more classes. We will discuss classes in more detail in Chapters 2 and 3.

The word public denotes that the class is usable by the "public". You will later encounter private features.

In Java, every source file can contain at most one public class, and the name of the public class must match the name of the file containing the class. For example, the class HelloPrinter must be contained in a file named HelloPrinter.java.

The construction

```
public static void main(String[] args)
{
   . . .
}
```

> Every Java application contains a class with a main method. When the application starts, the instructions in the main method are executed.

declares a **method** called main. A method contains a collection of programming instructions that describe how to carry out a particular task. Every Java application must have a **main method**. Most Java programs contain other methods besides main, and you will see in Chapter 3 how to write other methods.

The term static is explained in more detail in Chapter 8, and the meaning of String[] args is covered in Chapter 11. At this time, simply consider

> Each class contains declarations of methods. Each method contains a sequence of instructions.

```
public class ClassName
{
   public static void main(String[] args)
   {
      . . .
   }
}
```

as a part of the "plumbing" that is required to create a Java program. Our first program has all instructions inside the main method of the class.

The main method contains one or more instructions called **statements**. Each statement ends in a semicolon (;). When a program runs, the statements in the main method are executed one by one.

Syntax 1.1   Java Program

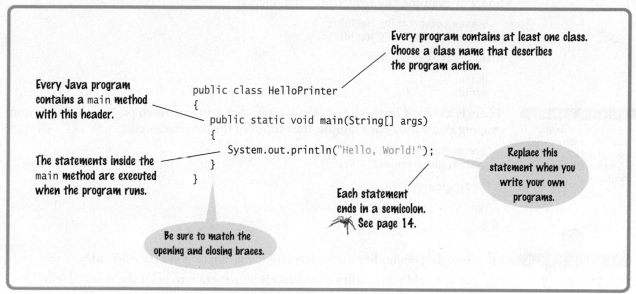

Every program contains at least one class.
Choose a class name that describes
the program action.

Every Java program
contains a `main` **method**
with this header.

```java
public class HelloPrinter
{
   public static void main(String[] args)
   {
      System.out.println("Hello, World!");
   }
}
```

The statements inside the
`main` **method** are executed
when the program runs.

Replace this
statement when you
write your own
programs.

Each statement
ends in a semicolon.
See page 14.

Be sure to match the
opening and closing braces.

In our example program, the `main` method has a single statement:

```java
System.out.println("Hello, World!");
```

This statement prints a line of text, namely "Hello, World!". In this statement, we *call* a method which, for reasons that we will not explain here, is specified by the rather long name `System.out.println`.

We do not have to implement this method—the programmers who wrote the Java library already did that for us. We simply want the method to perform its intended task, namely to print a value.

Whenever you call a method in Java, you need to specify

1. The method you want to use (in this case, `System.out.println`).
2. Any values the method needs to carry out its task (in this case, `"Hello, World!"`). The technical term for such a value is an **argument**. Arguments are enclosed in parentheses. Multiple arguments are separated by commas.

A method is called
by specifying the
method and
its arguments.

A sequence of characters enclosed in quotation marks

```java
"Hello, World!"
```

A string is a sequence
of characters
enclosed in
quotation marks.

is called a **string**. You must enclose the contents of the string inside quotation marks so that the compiler knows you literally mean `"Hello, World!"`. There is a reason for this requirement. Suppose you need to print the word *main*. By enclosing it in quotation marks, `"main"`, the compiler knows you mean the sequence of characters m a i n, not the method named `main`. The rule is simply that you must enclose all text strings in quotation marks, so that the compiler considers them plain text and does not try to interpret them as program instructions.

You can also print numerical values. For example, the statement

```java
System.out.println(3 + 4);
```

evaluates the expression 3 + 4 and displays the number 7.

The `System.out.println` method prints a string or a number and then starts a new line. For example, the sequence of statements

```
System.out.println("Hello");
System.out.println("World!");
```

prints two lines of text:

```
Hello
World!
```

FULL CODE EXAMPLE

Go to wiley.com/go/javacode to download a program to demonstrate print commands.

There is a second method, `System.out.print`, that you can use to print an item without starting a new line. For example, the output of the two statements

```
System.out.print("00");
System.out.println(3 + 4);
```

is the single line

```
007
```

SELF CHECK

11. How do you modify the `HelloPrinter` program to greet you instead?

12. How would you modify the `HelloPrinter` program to print the word "Hello" vertically?

13. Would the program continue to work if you replaced line 7 with this statement?

    ```
    System.out.println(Hello);
    ```

14. What does the following set of statements print?

    ```
    System.out.print("My lucky number is");
    System.out.println(3 + 4 + 5);
    ```

15. What do the following statements print?

    ```
    System.out.println("Hello");
    System.out.println("");
    System.out.println("World");
    ```

Practice It   Now you can try these exercises at the end of the chapter: R1.7, R1.8, E1.5, E1.7.

Common Error 1.1

Omitting Semicolons

In Java every statement must end in a semicolon. Forgetting to type a semicolon is a common error. It confuses the compiler, because the compiler uses the semicolon to find where one statement ends and the next one starts. The compiler does not use line breaks or closing braces to recognize the end of statements. For example, the compiler considers

```
System.out.println("Hello")
System.out.println("World!");
```

a single statement, as if you had written

```
System.out.println("Hello") System.out.println("World!");
```

Then it doesn't understand that statement, because it does not expect the word `System` following the closing parenthesis after `"Hello"`.

The remedy is simple. Scan every statement for a terminating semicolon, just as you would check that every English sentence ends in a period. However, do not add a semicolon at the end of `public class Hello` or `public static void main`. These lines are not statements.

1.6 Errors

Experiment a little with the `HelloPrinter` program. What happens if you make a typing error such as

```
System.ou.println("Hello, World!");
System.out.println("Hello, Word!");
```

Programmers spend a fair amount of time fixing compile-time and run-time errors.

> A compile-time error is a violation of the programming language rules that is detected by the compiler.

In the first case, the compiler will complain. It will say that it has no clue what you mean by `ou`. The exact wording of the error message is dependent on your development environment, but it might be something like "Cannot find symbol ou". This is a **compile-time error**. Something is wrong according to the rules of the language and the compiler finds it. For this reason, compile-time errors are often called **syntax errors**. When the compiler finds one or more errors, it refuses to translate the program into Java virtual machine instructions, and as a consequence you have no program that you can run. You must fix the error and compile again. In fact, the compiler is quite picky, and it is common to go through several rounds of fixing compile-time errors before compilation succeeds for the first time.

If the compiler finds an error, it will not simply stop and give up. It will try to report as many errors as it can find, so you can fix them all at once.

Sometimes, an error throws the compiler off track. Suppose, for example, you forget the quotation marks around a string: `System.out.println(Hello, World!)`. The compiler will not complain about the missing quotation marks. Instead, it will report "Cannot find symbol Hello". Unfortunately, the compiler is not very smart and it does not realize that you meant to use a string. It is up to you to realize that you need to enclose strings in quotation marks.

The error in the second line above is of a different kind. The program will compile and run, but its output will be wrong. It will print

```
Hello, Word!
```

> A run-time error causes a program to take an action that the programmer did not intend.

This is a **run-time error**. The program is syntactically correct and does something, but it doesn't do what it is supposed to do. Because run-time errors are caused by logical flaws in the program, they are often called **logic errors**.

This particular run-time error did not include an error message. It simply produced the wrong output. Some kinds of run-time errors are so severe that they generate an **exception**: an error message from the Java virtual machine. For example, if your program includes the statement

```
System.out.println(1 / 0);
```

you will get a run-time error message "Division by zero".

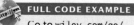

FULL CODE EXAMPLE

Go to wiley.com/go/javacode to download three programs to illustrate errors.

During program development, errors are unavoidable. Once a program is longer than a few lines, it would require superhuman concentration to enter it correctly without slipping up once. You will find yourself omitting semicolons or quotation marks more often than you would like, but the compiler will track down these problems for you.

Run-time errors are more troublesome. The compiler will not find them—in fact, the compiler will cheerfully translate any program as long as its syntax is correct—

but the resulting program will do something wrong. It is the responsibility of the program author to test the program and find any run-time errors.

SELF CHECK

16. Suppose you omit the "" characters around `Hello, World!` from the `HelloPrinter.java` program. Is this a compile-time error or a run-time error?

17. Suppose you change `println` to `printline` in the `HelloPrinter.java` program. Is this a compile-time error or a run-time error?

18. Suppose you change `main` to `hello` in the `HelloPrinter.java` program. Is this a compile-time error or a run-time error?

19. When you used your computer, you may have experienced a program that "crashed" (quit spontaneously) or "hung" (failed to respond to your input). Is that behavior a compile-time error or a run-time error?

20. Why can't you test a program for run-time errors when it has compiler errors?

Practice It   Now you can try these exercises at the end of the chapter: R1.9, R1.10, R1.11.

Common Error 1.2

Misspelling Words

If you accidentally misspell a word, then strange things may happen, and it may not always be completely obvious from the error messages what went wrong. Here is a good example of how simple spelling errors can cause trouble:

```
public class HelloPrinter
{
    public static void Main(String[] args)
    {
        System.out.println("Hello, World!");
    }
}
```

This class declares a method called `Main`. The compiler will not consider this to be the same as the `main` method, because `Main` starts with an uppercase letter and the Java language is case sensitive. Upper- and lowercase letters are considered to be completely different from each other, and to the compiler `Main` is no better match for `main` than `rain`. The compiler will cheerfully compile your `Main` method, but when the Java virtual machine reads the compiled file, it will complain about the missing `main` method and refuse to run the program. Of course, the message "missing main method" should give you a clue where to look for the error.

If you get an error message that seems to indicate that the compiler or virtual machine is on the wrong track, check for spelling and capitalization. If you misspell the name of a symbol (for example, `ou` instead of `out`), the compiler will produce a message such as "cannot find symbol ou". That error message is usually a good clue that you made a spelling error.

1.7 Problem Solving: Algorithm Design

You will soon learn how to program calculations and decision making in Java. But before we look at the mechanics of implementing computations in the next chapter, let's consider how you can describe the steps that are necessary for finding the solution to a problem.

1.7.1 The Algorithm Concept

You may have run across advertisements that encourage you to pay for a computerized service that matches you up with a love partner. Think how this might work. You fill out a form and send it in. Others do the same. The data are processed by a computer program. Is it reasonable to assume that the computer can perform the task of finding the best match for you? Suppose your younger brother, not the computer, had all the forms on his desk. What instructions could you give him? You can't say, "Find the best-looking person who likes inline skating and browsing the Internet". There is no objective standard for good looks, and your brother's opinion (or that of a computer program analyzing the photos of prospective partners) will likely be different from yours. If you can't give written instructions for someone to solve the problem, there is no way the computer can magically find the right solution. The computer can only do what you tell it to do. It just does it faster, without getting bored or exhausted.

Finding the perfect partner is not a problem that a computer can solve.

For that reason, a computerized match-making service cannot guarantee to find the optimal match for you. Instead, you may be presented with a set of potential partners who share common interests with you. That is a task that a computer program can solve.

In order for a computer program to provide an answer to a problem that computes an answer, it must follow a sequence of steps that is

- Unambiguous
- Executable
- Terminating

An algorithm for solving a problem is a sequence of steps that is unambiguous, executable, and terminating.

The step sequence is *unambiguous* when there are precise instructions for what to do at each step and where to go next. There is no room for guesswork or personal opinion. A step is *executable* when it can be carried out in practice. For example, a computer can list all people that share your hobbies, but it can't predict who will be your life-long partner. Finally, a sequence of steps is *terminating* if it will eventually come to an end. A program that keeps working without delivering an answer is clearly not useful.

A sequence of steps that is unambiguous, executable, and terminating is called an **algorithm**. Although there is no algorithm for finding a partner, many problems do have algorithms for solving them. The next section gives an example.

An algorithm is a recipe for finding a solution.

1.7.2 An Algorithm for Solving an Investment Problem

Consider the following investment problem:

You put $10,000 into a bank account that earns 5 percent interest per year. How many years does it take for the account balance to be double the original?

Could you solve this problem by hand? Sure, you could. You figure out the balance as follows:

year	interest	balance
0		10000
1	10000.00 x 0.05 = 500.00	10000.00 + 500.00 = 10500.00
2	10500.00 x 0.05 = 525.00	10500.00 + 525.00 = 11025.00
3	11025.00 x 0.05 = 551.25	11025.00 + 551.25 = 11576.25
4	11576.25 x 0.05 = 578.81	11576.25 + 578.81 = 12155.06

You keep going until the balance is at least $20,000. Then the last number in the year column is the answer.

Of course, carrying out this computation is intensely boring to you or your younger brother. But computers are very good at carrying out repetitive calculations quickly and flawlessly. What is important to the computer is a description of the steps for finding the solution. Each step must be clear and unambiguous, requiring no guesswork. Here is such a description:

Start with a year value of 0, a column for the interest, and a balance of $10,000.

year	interest	balance
0		10000

Repeat the following steps while the balance is less than $20,000
    Add 1 to the year value.
    Compute the interest as balance x 0.05 (i.e., 5 percent interest).
    Add the interest to the balance.

year	interest	balance
0		10000
1	500.00	10500.00
14	942.82	19799.32
(15)	989.96	20789.28

Report the final year value as the answer.

These steps are not yet in a language that a computer can understand, but you will soon learn how to formulate them in Java. This informal description is called **pseudocode**. We examine the rules for writing pseudocode in the next section.

1.7.3 Pseudocode

Pseudocode is an informal description of a sequence of steps for solving a problem.

There are no strict requirements for pseudocode because it is read by human readers, not a computer program. Here are the kinds of pseudocode statements and how we will use them in this book:

- Use statements such as the following to describe how a value is set or changed:

  total cost = purchase price + operating cost
  Multiply the balance value by 1.05.
  Remove the first and last character from the word.

- Describe decisions and repetitions as follows:

  If total cost 1 < total cost 2
  While the balance is less than $20,000
  For each picture in the sequence

  Use indentation to indicate which statements should be selected or repeated:

  For each car
      operating cost = 10 x annual fuel cost
      total cost = purchase price + operating cost

  Here, the indentation indicates that both statements should be executed for each car.

- Indicate results with statements such as:

  Choose car 1.
  Report the final year value as the answer.

1.7.4 From Algorithms to Programs

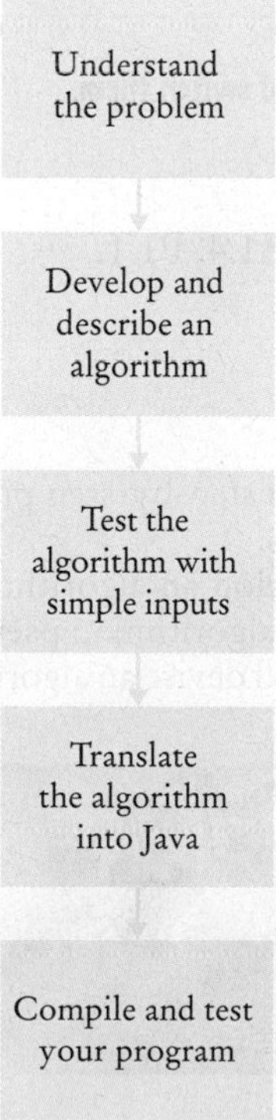

Understand the problem

↓

Develop and describe an algorithm

↓

Test the algorithm with simple inputs

↓

Translate the algorithm into Java

↓

Compile and test your program

In Section 1.7.2, we developed pseudocode for finding how long it takes to double an investment. Let's double-check that the pseudocode represents an algorithm; that is, that it is unambiguous, executable, and terminating.

Our pseudocode is unambiguous. It simply tells how to update values in each step. The pseudocode is executable because we use a fixed interest rate. Had we said to use the actual interest rate that will be charged in years to come, and not a fixed rate of 5 percent per year, the instructions would not have been executable. There is no way for anyone to know what the interest rate will be in the future. It requires a bit of thought to see that the steps are terminating: With every step, the balance goes up by at least $500, so eventually it must reach $20,000.

Therefore, we have found an algorithm to solve our investment problem, and we know we can find the solution by programming a computer. The existence of an algorithm is an essential prerequisite for programming a task. You need to first discover and describe an algorithm for the task before you start programming (see Figure 9). In the chapters that follow, you will learn how to express algorithms in the Java language.

Figure 9   The Software Development Process

SELF CHECK

21. Suppose the interest rate was 20 percent. How long would it take for the investment to double?

22. Suppose your cell phone carrier charges you $29.95 for up to 300 minutes of calls, and $0.45 for each additional minute, plus 12.5 percent taxes and fees. Give an algorithm to compute the monthly charge from a given number of minutes.

23. Consider the following pseudocode for finding the most attractive photo from a sequence of photos:

Pick the first photo and call it "the best so far".
For each photo in the sequence
    If it is more attractive than the "best so far"
        Discard "the best so far".
        Call this photo "the best so far".
The photo called "the best so far" is the most attractive photo in the sequence.

Is this an algorithm that will find the most attractive photo?

24. Suppose each photo in Self Check 23 had a price tag. Give an algorithm for finding the most expensive photo.

25. Suppose you have a random sequence of black and white marbles and want to rearrange it so that the black and white marbles are grouped together. Consider this algorithm:

Repeat until sorted
    Locate the first black marble that is preceded by a white marble, and switch them.

What does the algorithm do with the sequence ○●○●●? Spell out the steps until the algorithm stops.

26. Suppose you have a random sequence of colored marbles. Consider this pseudocode:

Repeat until sorted
    Locate the first marble that is preceded by a marble of a different color, and switch them.

Why is this not an algorithm?

Practice It   Now you can try these exercises at the end of the chapter: R1.15, E1.4, P1.1.

HOW TO 1.1

Describing an Algorithm with Pseudocode

This is the first of many "How To" sections in this book that give you step-by-step procedures for carrying out important tasks in developing computer programs.

Before you are ready to write a program in Java, you need to develop an algorithm—a method for arriving at a solution for a particular problem. Describe the algorithm in pseudocode: a sequence of precise steps formulated in English. To illustrate, we'll devise an algorithm for this problem:

Problem Statement   You have the choice of buying two cars. One is more fuel efficient than the other, but also more expensive. You know the price and fuel efficiency (in miles per gallon, mpg) of both cars. You plan to keep the car for ten years. Assume a price of $4 per gallon of gas and usage of 15,000 miles per year. You will pay cash for the car and not worry about financing costs. Which car is the better deal?

Step 1   Determine the inputs and outputs.

In our sample problem, we have these inputs:
- **purchase price1** and **fuel efficiency1**, the price and fuel efficiency (in mpg) of the first car
- **purchase price2** and **fuel efficiency2**, the price and fuel efficiency of the second car

We simply want to know which car is the better buy. That is the desired output.

Step 2   Break down the problem into smaller tasks.

For each car, we need to know the total cost of driving it. Let's do this computation separately for each car. Once we have the total cost for each car, we can decide which car is the better deal.

The total cost for each car is **purchase price + operating cost.**

We assume a constant usage and gas price for ten years, so the operating cost depends on the cost of driving the car for one year.

The operating cost is **10 x annual fuel cost.**

The annual fuel cost is **price per gallon x annual fuel consumed.**

The annual fuel consumed is **annual miles driven / fuel efficiency.** For example, if you drive the car for 15,000 miles and the fuel efficiency is 15 miles/gallon, the car consumes 1,000 gallons.

Step 3   Describe each subtask in pseudocode.

In your description, arrange the steps so that any intermediate values are computed before they are needed in other computations. For example, list the step

    total cost = purchase price + operating cost

after you have computed **operating cost.**

Here is the algorithm for deciding which car to buy:

    For each car, compute the total cost as follows:
        annual fuel consumed = annual miles driven / fuel efficiency
        annual fuel cost = price per gallon x annual fuel consumed
        operating cost = 10 x annual fuel cost
        total cost = purchase price + operating cost
    If total cost1 < total cost2
        Choose car1.
    Else
        Choose car2.

Step 4   Test your pseudocode by working a problem.

We will use these sample values:

    Car 1: $25,000, 50 miles/gallon
    Car 2: $20,000, 30 miles/gallon

Here is the calculation for the cost of the first car:

    annual fuel consumed = annual miles driven / fuel efficiency = 15000 / 50 = 300
    annual fuel cost = price per gallon x annual fuel consumed = 4 x 300 = 1200
    operating cost = 10 x annual fuel cost = 10 x 1200 = 12000
    total cost = purchase price + operating cost = 25000 + 12000 = 37000

Similarly, the total cost for the second car is $40,000. Therefore, the output of the algorithm is to choose car 1.

The following Worked Example demonstrates how to use the concepts in this chapter and the steps in the How To feature to solve another problem. In this case, you will see how to develop an algorithm for laying tile in an alternating pattern of colors. You should read the Worked Example to review what you have learned, or for help in tackling another problem.

In future chapters, Worked Examples are provided for you on the book's companion Web site. A brief description of the problem tackled in the example will appear with the reminder to download it from www.wiley.com/go/javaexamples. You will find any code related to the Worked Example included with the companion code for the chapter. When you see the Worked Example description, download the example and the code to learn how the problem was solved.

WORKED EXAMPLE 1.1   Writing an Algorithm for Tiling a Floor

Problem Statement   Write an algorithm for tiling a rectangular bathroom floor with alternating black and white tiles measuring 4 × 4 inches. The floor dimensions, measured in inches, are multiples of 4.

Step 1   Determine the inputs and outputs.

The inputs are the floor dimensions (length × width), measured in inches. The output is a tiled floor.

Step 2   Break down the problem into smaller tasks.

A natural subtask is to lay one row of tiles. If you can solve that task, then you can solve the problem by laying one row next to the other, starting from a wall, until you reach the opposite wall.

How do you lay a row? Start with a tile at one wall. If it is white, put a black one next to it. If it is black, put a white one next to it. Keep going until you reach the opposite wall. The row will contain **width / 4** tiles.

Step 3   Describe each subtask in pseudocode.

In the pseudocode, you want to be more precise about exactly where the tiles are placed.

> Place a black tile in the northwest corner.
> While the floor is not yet filled, repeat the following steps:
>   Repeat this step width / 4 – 1 times:
>   Place a tile east of the previously placed tile. If the previously placed tile was white, pick a black one;
>   otherwise, a white one.
>   Locate the tile at the beginning of the row that you just placed. If there is space to the south, place a tile of
>   the opposite color below it.

Step 4   Test your pseudocode by working a problem.

Suppose you want to tile an area measuring 20 × 12 inches.

The first step is to place a black tile in the northwest corner.

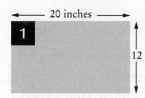

Next, alternate four tiles until reaching the east wall. (**width / 4 − 1 = 20 / 4 − 1 = 4**)

There is room to the south. Locate the tile at the beginning of the completed row. It is black. Place a white tile south of it.

Complete the row.

There is still room to the south. Locate the tile at the beginning of the completed row. It is white. Place a black tile south of it.

Complete the row.

Now the entire floor is filled, and you are done.

CHAPTER SUMMARY

Define "computer program" and programming.

- Computers execute very basic instructions in rapid succession.
- A computer program is a sequence of instructions and decisions.
- Programming is the act of designing and implementing computer programs.

Describe the components of a computer.

- The central processing unit (CPU) performs program control and data processing.
- Storage devices include memory and secondary storage.

Describe the process of translating high-level languages to machine code.

- Java was originally designed for programming consumer devices, but it was first successfully used to write Internet applets.
- Java was designed to be safe and portable, benefiting both Internet users and students.
- Java programs are distributed as instructions for a virtual machine, making them platform-independent.
- Java has a very large library. Focus on learning those parts of the library that you need for your programming projects.

Become familiar with your Java programming environment.

- Set aside some time to become familiar with the programming environment that you will use for your class work.
- An editor is a program for entering and modifying text, such as a Java program.
- Java is case sensitive. You must be careful about distinguishing between upper- and lowercase letters.
- The Java compiler translates source code into class files that contain instructions for the Java virtual machine.
- Develop a strategy for keeping backup copies of your work before disaster strikes.

Describe the building blocks of a simple program.

- Classes are the fundamental building blocks of Java programs.
- Every Java application contains a class with a main method. When the application starts, the instructions in the main method are executed.
- Each class contains declarations of methods. Each method contains a sequence of instructions.
- A method is called by specifying the method and its arguments.
- A string is a sequence of characters enclosed in quotation marks.

Classify program errors as compile-time and run-time errors.

- A compile-time error is a violation of the programming language rules that is detected by the compiler.
- A run-time error causes a program to take an action that the programmer did not intend.

Write pseudocode for simple algorithms.

- An algorithm for solving a problem is a sequence of steps that is unambiguous, executable, and terminating.
- Pseudocode is an informal description of a sequence of steps for solving a problem.

STANDARD LIBRARY ITEMS INTRODUCED IN THIS CHAPTER

```
java.io.PrintStream
print
println
```

```
java.lang.System
out
```

REVIEW QUESTIONS

- **R1.1** Explain the difference between using a computer program and programming a computer.

- **R1.2** Which parts of a computer can store program code? Which can store user data?

- **R1.3** Which parts of a computer serve to give information to the user? Which parts take user input?

- **R1.4** A toaster is a single-function device, but a computer can be programmed to carry out different tasks. Is your cell phone a single-function device, or is it a programmable computer? (Your answer will depend on your cell phone model.)

- **R1.5** Explain two benefits of using Java over machine code.

- **R1.6** On your own computer or on a lab computer, find the exact location (folder or directory name) of
    - **a.** The sample file `HelloPrinter.java`, which you wrote with the editor
    - **b.** The Java program launcher `java.exe` or `java`
    - **c.** The library file `rt.jar` that contains the run-time library

- **R1.7** What does this program print?
```
public class Test
{
    public static void main(String[] args)
    {
        System.out.println("39 + 3");
        System.out.println(39 + 3);
    }
}
```

■■ **R1.8** What does this program print? Pay close attention to spaces.

```java
public class Test
{
    public static void main(String[] args)
    {
        System.out.print("Hello");
        System.out.println("World");
    }
}
```

■■ **R1.9** What is the compile-time error in this program?

```java
public class Test
{
    public static void main(String[] args)
    {
        System.out.println("Hello", "World!");
    }
}
```

■■ **R1.10** Write three versions of the HelloPrinter.java program that have different compile-time errors. Write a version that has a run-time error.

■ **R1.11** How do you discover syntax errors? How do you discover logic errors?

■■ **R1.12** Write an algorithm to settle the following question: A bank account starts out with $10,000. Interest is compounded monthly at 6 percent per year (0.5 percent per month). Every month, $500 is withdrawn to meet college expenses. After how many years is the account depleted?

■■■ **R1.13** Consider the question in Exercise R1.12. Suppose the numbers ($10,000, 6 percent, $500) were user selectable. Are there values for which the algorithm you developed would not terminate? If so, change the algorithm to make sure it always terminates.

■■■ **R1.14** In order to estimate the cost of painting a house, a painter needs to know the surface area of the exterior. Develop an algorithm for computing that value. Your inputs are the width, length, and height of the house, the number of windows and doors, and their dimensions. (Assume the windows and doors have a uniform size.)

■■ **R1.15** In How To 1.1, you made assumptions about the price of gas and annual usage to compare cars. Ideally, you would like to know which car is the better deal without making these assumptions. Why can't a computer program solve that problem?

■■ **R1.16** Suppose you put your younger brother in charge of backing up your work. Write a set of detailed instructions for carrying out his task. Explain how often he should do it, and what files he needs to copy from which folder to which location. Explain how he should verify that the backup was carried out correctly.

■ **R1.17** Write pseudocode for an algorithm that describes how to prepare Sunday breakfast in your household.

■■ **R1.18** The ancient Babylonians had an algorithm for determining the square root of a number a. Start with an initial guess of $a / 2$. Then find the average of your guess g and a / g. That's your next guess. Repeat until two consecutive guesses are close enough. Write pseudocode for this algorithm.

PRACTICE EXERCISES

■ E1.1 Write a program that prints a greeting of your choice, perhaps in a language other than English.

■■ E1.2 Write a program that prints the sum of the first ten positive integers, $1 + 2 + \ldots + 10$.

■■ E1.3 Write a program that prints the product of the first ten positive integers, $1 \times 2 \times \ldots \times 10$. (Use * to indicate multiplication in Java.)

■■ E1.4 Write a program that prints the balance of an account after the first, second, and third year. The account has an initial balance of $1,000 and earns 5 percent interest per year.

■ E1.5 Write a program that displays your name inside a box on the screen, like this:

```
Dave
```

Do your best to approximate lines with characters such as | - +.

■■■ E1.6 Write a program that prints your name in large letters, such as

```
*     *    **    ****    ****    *   *
*     *   *  *   *   *   *   *   *   *
*****   *    *   ****    ****     * *
*     * ******  *   *   *   *      *
*     * *    *  *   *   *   *      *
```

■■ E1.7 Write a program that prints a face similar to (but different from) the following:

```
   /////
  +"""""+
  (| o o |)
  |   ^   |
  |  '-'  |
  +-----+
```

■■ E1.8 Write a program that prints an imitation of a Pict Mondrian painting. (Search the Internet if you are not familiar with his paintings.) Use character sequences such as @@@ or ::: to indicate different colors, and use - and | to form lines.

■■ E1.9 Write a program that prints a house that looks exactly like the following:

```
      +
     + +
    +   +
  +-----+
  | .-. |
  | | | |
  +-+-+-+
```

■■■ E1.10 Write a program that prints an animal speaking a greeting, similar to (but different from) the following:

```
  /\_/\     -----
 ( ' ' )  / Hello \'
 (  -  ) < Junior |
  | | |   \ Coder!/
 (_|_)     -----
```

- **E1.11** Write a program that prints three items, such as the names of your three best friends or favorite movies, on three separate lines.

- **E1.12** Write a program that prints a poem of your choice. If you don't have a favorite poem, search the Internet for "Emily Dickinson" or "e e cummings".

- - **E1.13** Write a program that prints the United States flag, using * and = characters.

- - **E1.14** Type in and run the following program:

```java
import javax.swing.JOptionPane;

public class DialogViewer
{
    public static void main(String[] args)
    {
        JOptionPane.showMessageDialog(null, "Hello, World!");
    }
}
```

Then modify the program to show the message "Hello, *your name*!".

- - **E1.15** Type in and run the following program:

```java
import javax.swing.JOptionPane;

public class DialogViewer
{
    public static void main(String[] args)
    {
        String name = JOptionPane.showInputDialog("What is your name?");
        System.out.println(name);
    }
}
```

Then modify the program to print "Hello, *name*!", displaying the name that the user typed in.

- - - **E1.16** Modify the program from Exercise E1.15 so that the dialog continues with the message "My name is Hal! What would you like me to do?" Discard the user's input and display a message such as

```
I'm sorry, Dave. I'm afraid I can't do that.
```

Replace Dave with the name that was provided by the user.

- - **E1.17** Type in and run the following program:

```java
import java.net.URL;
import javax.swing.ImageIcon;
import javax.swing.JOptionPane;

public class Test
{
    public static void main(String[] args) throws Exception
    {
        URL imageLocation = new URL(
                "http://horstmann.com/java4everyone/duke.gif");
        JOptionPane.showMessageDialog(null, "Hello", "Title",
                JOptionPane.PLAIN_MESSAGE, new ImageIcon(imageLocation));
    }
}
```

Then modify it to show a different greeting and image.

■ **Business E1.18** Write a program that prints a two-column list of your friends' birthdays. In the first column, print the names of your best friends; in the second column, print their birthdays.

■ **Business E1.19** In the United States there is no federal sales tax, so every state may impose its own sales taxes. Look on the Internet for the sales tax charged in five U.S. states, then write a program that prints the tax rate for five states of your choice.

```
Sales Tax Rates
---------------
Alaska:    0%
Hawaii:    4%
. . .
```

■ **Business E1.20** To speak more than one language is a valuable skill in the labor market today. One of the basic skills is learning to greet people. Write a program that prints a two-column list with the greeting phrases shown in the following table; in the first column, print the phrase in English, in the second column, print the phrase in a language of your choice. If you don't speak any language other than English, use an online translator or ask a friend.

List of Phrases to Translate
Good morning.
It is a pleasure to meet you.
Please call me tomorrow.
Have a nice day!

PROGRAMMING PROJECTS

■■ **P1.1** You want to decide whether you should drive your car to work or take the train. You know the one-way distance from your home to your place of work, and the fuel efficiency of your car (in miles per gallon). You also know the one-way price of a train ticket. You assume the cost of gas at $4 per gallon, and car maintenance at 5 cents per mile. Write an algorithm to decide which commute is cheaper.

■■ **P1.2** You want to find out which fraction of your car's use is for commuting to work, and which is for personal use. You know the one-way distance from your home to work. For a particular period, you recorded the beginning and ending mileage on the odometer and the number of work days. Write an algorithm to settle this question.

■■■ **P1.3** The value of π can be computed according to the following formula:

$$\frac{\pi}{4} = 1 - \frac{1}{3} + \frac{1}{5} - \frac{1}{7} + \frac{1}{9} - \cdots$$

Write an algorithm to compute π. Because the formula is an infinite series and an algorithm must stop after a finite number of steps, you should stop when you have the result determined to six significant digits.

■ **Business P1.4** Imagine that you and a number of friends go to a luxury restaurant, and when you ask for the bill you want to split the amount and the tip (15 percent) between all. Write pseudocode for calculating the amount of money that everyone has to pay. Your program should print the amount of the bill, the tip, the total cost, and the amount each person has to pay. It should also print how much of what each person pays is for the bill and for the tip.

■■ **P1.5** Write an algorithm to create a tile pattern composed of black and white tiles, with a fringe of black tiles all around and two or three black tiles in the center, equally spaced from the boundary. The inputs to your algorithm are the total number of rows and columns in the pattern.

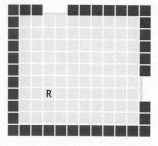

■■■ **P1.6** Suppose you received a loyalty promotion that lets you purchase one item, valued up to $100, from an online catalog. You want to make the best of the offer. You have a list of all items for sale, some of which are less than $100, some more. Write an algorithm to produce the item that is closest to $100. If there is more than one such item, list them all. Remember that a computer will inspect one item at a time—it can't just glance at a list and find the best one.

■■■ **P1.7** Consider a robot that is placed in a room. The robot can do the following:

- Move forward by one unit
- Turn left or right
- Sense what is in front of it: a wall, a window, or neither

Write an algorithm that enables the robot, placed anywhere in the room, to count the number of windows. For example, in the room at right, the robot (marked as R) should find that it has two windows.

■■■ **P1.8** Consider a robot that has been placed in a maze. The right-hand rule tells you how to escape from a maze: Always have the right hand next to a wall, and eventually you will find an exit.

The robot can do the following:

- Move forward by one unit
- Turn left or right
- Sense what is in front of it: a wall, an exit, or neither

Write an algorithm that lets the robot escape the maze. You may assume that there is an exit that is reachable by the right-hand rule. Your challenge is to deal with situations in which the path turns. The robot can't see turns. It can only see what is directly in front of it.

■■ Science P1.9 A television manufacturer advertises that a television set has a certain size, measured diagonally. You wonder how the set will fit into your living room. Write an algorithm that yields the horizontal and vertical size of the television. Your inputs are the diagonal size and the aspect ratio (the ratio of width to height, usually 16 : 9 for television sets).

■■■ Science P1.10 Cameras today can correct "red eye" problems caused when the photo flash makes eyes look red. Write pseudocode for an algorithm that can detect red eyes. Your input is a pattern of colors, such as

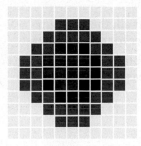

You are given the number of rows and columns. For any row or column number, you can query the color, which will be red, black, or something else. If you find that the center of the black pixels coincides with the center of the red pixels, you have found a red eye, and your output should be "yes". Otherwise, your output is "no".

ANSWERS TO SELF-CHECK QUESTIONS

1. A program that reads the data on the CD and sends output to the speakers and the screen.

2. A CD player can do one thing—play music CDs. It cannot execute programs.

3. Nothing.

4. In secondary storage, typically a hard disk.

5. The central processing unit.

6. A smartphone has a CPU and memory, like any computer. A few smartphones have keyboards. Generally, the touchpad is used instead of a mouse. Secondary storage is in the form of a solid state drive. Of course, smartphones have a display, speaker, and microphone. The network connection uses the wireless radio to connect to a cell tower.

7. Safety and portability.

8. No one person can learn the entire library—it is too large.

9. The answer varies among systems. A typical answer might be `/home/dave/cs1/hello/Hello-`

`Printer.java` or `c:\Users\Dave\Workspace\hello\HelloPrinter.java`

10. You back up your files and folders.

11. Change `World` to your name (here, `Dave`):

    `System.out.println("Hello, Dave!");`

12. `System.out.println("H");`
    `System.out.println("e");`
    `System.out.println("l");`
    `System.out.println("l");`
    `System.out.println("o");`

13. No. The compiler would look for an item whose name is `Hello`. You need to enclose `Hello` in quotation marks:

    `System.out.println("Hello");`

14. The printout is `My lucky number is12`. It would be a good idea to add a space after the `is`.

15. `Hello`
    a blank line
    `World`

16. This is a compile-time error. The compiler will complain that it does not know the meanings of the words `Hello` and `World`.

17. This is a compile-time error. The compiler will complain that `System.out` does not have a method called `printline`.

18. This is a run-time error. It is perfectly legal to give the name `hello` to a method, so the compiler won't complain. But when the program is run, the virtual machine will look for a `main` method and won't find one.

19. It is a run-time error. After all, the program had been compiled in order for you to run it.

20. When a program has compiler errors, no class file is produced, and there is nothing to run.

21. 4 years:

```
0  10,000
1  12,000
2  14,400
3  17,280
4  20,736
```

22. Is the number of minutes at most 300?

   a. If so, the answer is $29.95 \times 1.125 = \$33.70$.

   b. If not,

   1. Compute the difference: (number of minutes) – 300.

   2. Multiply that difference by 0.45.

   3. Add $29.95.

   4. Multiply the total by 1.125. That is the answer.

23. No. The step **If it is more attractive than the "best so far"** is not executable because there is no objective way of deciding which of two photos is more attractive.

24. **Pick the first photo and call it "the most expensive so far".**
For each photo in the sequence
   If it is more expensive than "the most expensive so far"
      Discard "the most expensive so far".
      Call this photo "the most expensive so far".
The photo called "the most expensive so far" is the most expensive photo in the sequence.

25. The first black marble that is preceded by a white one is marked in blue:

○●○●●

Switching the two yields

●○○●●

The next black marble to be switched is

●○○●●

yielding

●○○○●

The next steps are

●●○○●

●●○●○

●●●○○

Now the sequence is sorted.

26. The sequence doesn't terminate. Consider the input ○●○●○. The first two marbles keep getting switched.

CHAPTER 2

USING OBJECTS

CHAPTER GOALS

To learn about variables

To understand the concepts of classes and objects

To be able to call methods

To learn about arguments and return values

To be able to browse the API documentation

To implement test programs

To understand the difference between objects and object references

To write programs that display simple shapes

CHAPTER CONTENTS

Most useful programs don't just manipulate numbers and strings. Instead, they deal with data items that are more complex and that more closely represent entities in the real world. Examples of these data items include bank accounts, employee records, and graphical shapes.

The Java language is ideally suited for designing and manipulating such data items, or *objects*. In Java, you implement *classes* that describe the behavior of these objects. In this chapter, you will learn how to manipulate objects that belong to classes that have already been implemented. This will prepare you for the next chapter, in which you will learn how to implement your own classes.

2.1 Objects and Classes

When you write a computer program, you put it together from certain "building blocks". In Java, you build programs from *objects*. Each object has a particular behavior, and you can manipulate it to achieve certain effects.

As an analogy, think of a home builder who constructs a house from certain parts: doors, windows, walls, pipes, a furnace, a water heater, and so on. Each of these elements has a particular function, and they work together to fulfill a common purpose. Note that the home builder is not concerned with how to build a window or a water heater. These elements are readily available, and the builder's job is to integrate them into the house.

Of course, computer programs are more abstract than houses, and the objects that make up a computer program aren't as tangible as a window or a water heater. But the analogy holds well: A programmer produces a working

Each part that a home builder uses, such as a furnace or a water heater, fulfills a particular function. Similarly, you build programs from objects, each of which has a particular behavior.

program from elements with the desired functionality—the objects. In this chapter, you will learn the basics about using objects written by other programmers.

2.1.1 Using Objects

Objects are entities in your program that you manipulate by calling methods.

An **object** is an entity that you can manipulate by calling one or more of its **methods**. A method consists of a sequence of instructions that can access the internal data of an object. When you call the method, you do not know exactly what those instructions are, or even how the object is organized internally. However, the behavior of the method is well defined, and that is what matters to us when we use it.

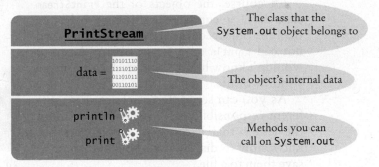

Figure 1 Representation of the `System.out` Object

A method is a sequence of instructions that accesses the data of an object.

For example, you saw in Chapter 1 that `System.out` refers to an object. You manipulate it by calling the `println` method. When the `println` method is called, some activities occur inside the object, and the ultimate effect is that text appears in the console window. You don't know how that happens, and that's OK. What matters is that the method carries out the work that you requested.

Figure 1 shows a representation of the `System.out` object. The internal data is symbolized by a sequence of zeroes and ones. Think of each method (symbolized by the gears) as a piece of machinery that carries out its assigned task.

In general, think of an object as an entity that can do work for you when you call its methods. How the work is done is not important to the programmer using the object.

In the remainder of this chapter, you will see other objects and the methods that they can carry out.

You can think of a water heater as an object that can carry out the "get hot water" method. When you call that method to enjoy a hot shower, you don't care whether the water heater uses gas or solar power.

2.1.2 Classes

In Chapter 1, you encountered two objects:

- `System.out`
- `"Hello, World!"`

A class describes a set of objects with the same behavior.

Each of these objects belongs to a different **class**. The `System.out` object belongs to the `PrintStream` class. The `"Hello, World!"` object belongs to the `String` class. Of course, there are many more `String` objects, such as `"Goodbye"` or `"Mississippi"`. They all have something in common—you can invoke the same methods on all strings. You will see some of these methods in Section 2.3.

As you will see in Chapter 11, you can construct objects of the `PrintStream` class other than `System.out`. Those objects write data to files or other destinations instead of the console. Still, all `PrintStream` objects share common behavior. You can invoke the `println` and `print` methods on any `PrintStream` object, and the printed values are sent to their destination.

Of course, the objects of the `PrintStream` class have a completely different behavior than the objects of the `String` class. You could not call `println` on a `String` object. A string wouldn't know how to send itself to a console window or file.

As you can see, different classes have different responsibilities. A string knows about the letters that it contains, but it does not know how to display them to a human or to save them to a file.

All objects of a `Window` class share the same behavior.

SELF CHECK

1. In Java, objects are grouped into classes according to their behavior. Would a window object and a water heater object belong to the same class or to different classes? Why?
2. Some light bulbs use a glowing filament, others use a fluorescent gas. If you consider a light bulb a Java object with an "illuminate" method, would you need to know which kind of bulb it is?

Practice It   Now you can try these exercises at the end of the chapter: R2.1, R2.2.

2.2 Variables

Before we continue with the main topic of this chapter—the behavior of objects—we need to go over some basic programming terminology. In the following sections, you will learn about the concepts of variables, types, and assignment.

2.2.1 Variable Declarations

When your program manipulates objects, you will want to store the objects and the values that their methods return, so that you can use them later. In a Java program, you use variables to store values. The following statement declares a variable named `width`:

```
int width = 20;
```

Like a variable in a computer program, a parking space has an identifier and a contents.

Syntax 2.1 Variable Declaration

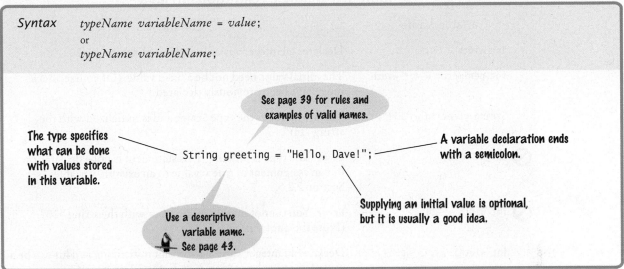

Syntax

    typeName variableName = value;
    or
    typeName variableName;

See page 39 for rules and examples of valid names.

The type specifies what can be done with values stored in this variable.

```
String greeting = "Hello, Dave!";
```

A variable declaration ends with a semicolon.

Use a descriptive variable name. See page 43.

Supplying an initial value is optional, but it is usually a good idea.

A variable is a storage location with a name.

A **variable** is a storage location in a computer program. Each variable has a name and holds a value.

A variable is similar to a parking space in a parking garage. The parking space has an identifier (such as "J 053"), and it can hold a vehicle. A variable has a name (such as width), and it can hold a value (such as 20). When declaring a variable, you usually want to **initialize** it. That is, you specify the value that should be stored in the variable. Consider again this variable declaration:

When declaring a variable, you usually specify an initial value.

```
int width = 20;
```

The variable width is initialized with the value 20.

Like a parking space that is restricted to a certain type of vehicle (such as a compact car, motorcycle, or electric vehicle), a variable in Java stores data of a specific type. Java supports quite a few data types: numbers, text strings, files, dates, and many others. You must specify the type whenever you declare a variable (see Syntax 2.1).

When declaring a variable, you also specify the type of its values.

The width variable is an **integer**, a whole number without a fractional part. In Java, this type is called int.

Note that the type comes before the variable name:

```
int width = 20;
```

After you have declared and initialized a variable, you can use it. For example,

```
int width = 20;
System.out.println(width);
int area = width * width;
```

Table 1 shows several examples of variable declarations.

Each parking space is suitable for a particular type of vehicle, just as each variable holds a value of a particular type.

Table 1 Variable Declarations in Java

Variable Name	Comment
`int width = 20;`	Declares an integer variable and initializes it with 20.
`int perimeter = 4 * width;`	The initial value need not be a fixed value. (Of course, `width` must have been previously declared.)
`String greeting = "Hi!";`	This variable has the type `String` and is initialized with the string "Hi".
🚫 `height = 30;`	**Error:** The type is missing. This statement is not a declaration but an assignment of a new value to an existing variable—see Section 2.2.5.
🚫 `int width = "20";`	**Error:** You cannot initialize a number with the string "20". (Note the quotation marks.)
`int width;`	Declares an integer variable without initializing it. This can be a cause for errors—see Common Error 2.1 on page 42.
`int width, height;`	Declares two integer variables in a single statement. In this book, we will declare each variable in a separate statement.

2.2.2 Types

Use the int type for numbers that cannot have a fractional part.

In Java, there are several different types of numbers. You use the `int` type to denote a whole number without a fractional part. For example, suppose you count the number of cars in a parking lot. The counter must be an integer number—you cannot have a fraction of a car.

When a fractional part is required (such as in the number 22.5), we use **floating-point numbers**. The most commonly used type for floating-point numbers in Java is called `double`. Here is the declaration of a floating-point variable:

```
double milesPerGallon = 22.5;
```

Use the double type for floating-point numbers.

You can combine numbers with the + and - operators, as in `width + 10` or `width - 1`. To multiply two numbers, use the * operator. For example, $2 \times width$ is written as `2 * width`. Use the / operator for division, such as `width / 2`.

Numbers can be combined by arithmetic operators such as +, -, and *.

As in mathematics, the * and / operator bind more strongly than the + and - operators. That is, `width + height * 2` means the sum of `width` and the product `height * 2`. If you want to multiply the sum by 2, use parentheses: `(width + height) * 2`.

Not all types are number types. For example, the value `"Hello"` has the type `String`. You need to specify that type when you define a variable that holds a string:

```
String greeting = "Hello";
```

A type specifies the operations that can be carried out with its values.

Types are important because they indicate what you can do with a variable. For example, consider the variable `width`. It's type is `int`. Therefore, you can multiply the value that it holds with another number. But the type of `greeting` is `String`. You can't multiply a string with another number. (You will see in Section 2.3.1 what you can do with strings.)

2.2.3 Names

When you declare a variable, you should pick a name that explains its purpose. For example, it is better to use a descriptive name, such as milesPerGallon, than a terse name, such as mpg.

In Java, there are a few simple rules for the names of variables, methods, and classes:

1. Names must start with a letter or the underscore (_) character, and the remaining characters must be letters, numbers, or underscores. (Technically, the $ symbol is allowed as well, but you should not use it—it is intended for names that are automatically generated by tools.)

2. You cannot use other symbols such as ? or %. Spaces are not permitted inside names either. You can use uppercase letters to denote word boundaries, as in milesPerGallon. This naming convention is called *camel case* because the uppercase letters in the middle of the name look like the humps of a camel.)

3. Names are **case sensitive**, that is, milesPerGallon and milespergallon are different names.

4. You cannot use **reserved words** such as double or class as names; these words are reserved exclusively for their special Java meanings. (See Appendix C for a listing of all reserved words in Java.)

> By convention, variable names should start with a lowercase letter.

It is a convention among Java programmers that names of variables and methods start with a lowercase letter (such as milesPerGallon). Class names should start with an uppercase letter (such as HelloPrinter). That way, it is easy to tell them apart.

Table 2 shows examples of legal and illegal variable names in Java.

Table 2 Variable Names in Java	
Variable Name	**Comment**
distance_1	Names consist of letters, numbers, and the underscore character.
x	In mathematics, you use short variable names such as x or y. This is legal in Java, but not very common, because it can make programs harder to understand (see Programming Tip 2.1 on page 43).
⚠ CanVolume	**Caution:** Names are case sensitive. This variable name is different from canVolume, and it violates the convention that variable names should start with a lowercase letter.
🚫 6pack	**Error:** Names cannot start with a number.
🚫 can volume	**Error:** Names cannot contain spaces.
🚫 double	**Error:** You cannot use a reserved word as a name.
🚫 miles/gal	**Error:** You cannot use symbols such as / in names.

2.2.4 Comments

As your programs get more complex, you should add **comments**, explanations for human readers of your code. For example, here is a comment that explains the value used to initialize a variable:

```
double milesPerGallon = 33.8; // The average fuel efficiency of new U.S. cars in 2011
```

This comment explains the significance of the value 33.8 to a human reader. The compiler does not process comments at all. It ignores everything from a // delimiter to the end of the line.

> Use comments to add explanations for humans who read your code. The compiler ignores comments.

It is a good practice to provide comments. This helps programmers who read your code understand your intent. In addition, you will find comments helpful when you review your own programs.

You use the // delimiter for short comments. If you have a longer comment, enclose it between /* and */ delimiters. The compiler ignores these delimiters and everything in between. For example,

```
/*
    In most countries, fuel efficiency is measured in liters per hundred
    kilometer. Perhaps that is more useful—it tells you how much gas you need
    to purchase to drive a given distance. Here is the conversion formula.
*/
double fuelEfficiency = 235.214583 / milesPerGallon;
```

2.2.5 Assignment

> Use the assignment operator (=) to change the value of a variable.

You can change the value of a variable with the assignment operator (=). For example, consider the variable declaration

```
int width = 10; ❶
```

If you want to change the value of the variable, simply assign the new value:

```
width = 20; ❷
```

The assignment replaces the original value of the variable (see Figure 2).

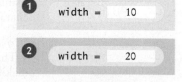

Figure 2
Assigning a New Value to a Variable

ANIMATION
Variable Initialization and Assignment

It is an error to use a variable that has never had a value assigned to it. For example, the following assignment statement has an error:

```
int height;
int width = height;   // ERROR—uninitialized variable height
```

The compiler will complain about an **"uninitialized variable"** when you use a variable that has never been assigned a value. (See Figure 3.)

Figure 3
An Uninitialized Variable

 height = [   ] No value has been assigned.

Syntax 2.2 Assignment

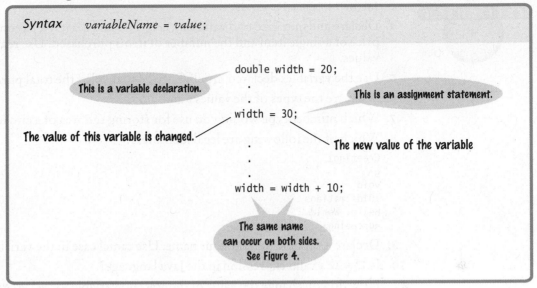

Syntax *variableName = value;*

This is a variable declaration.

    double width = 20;

This is an assignment statement.

The value of this variable is changed.

    width = 30;

The new value of the variable

    width = width + 10;

The same name can occur on both sides. See Figure 4.

All variables must be initialized before you access them.

The remedy is to assign a value to the variable before you use it:

    int height = 20;
    int width = height; // OK

The right-hand side of the = symbol can be a mathematical expression. For example,

    width = height + 10;

This means "compute the value of height + 10 and store that value in the variable width".

The assignment operator = does *not* denote mathematical equality.

In the Java programming language, the = operator denotes an *action*, namely to replace the value of a variable. This usage differs from the mathematical usage of the = symbol as a statement about equality. For example, in Java, the following statement is entirely legal:

    width = width + 10;

This means "compute the value of width + 10 ❶ and store that value in the variable width ❷" (see Figure 4).

In Java, it is not a problem that the variable width is used on both sides of the = symbol. Of course, in mathematics, the equation *width = width + 10* has no solution.

FULL CODE EXAMPLE

Go to wiley.com/go/javacode to download a program that demonstrates variables and assignments.

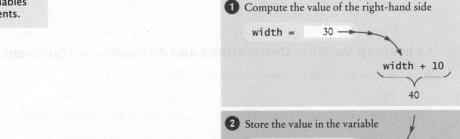

❶ Compute the value of the right-hand side

    width =   30

    width + 10

    40

❷ Store the value in the variable

    width =   40

Figure 4
Executing the Statement
width = width + 10

SELF CHECK

3. What is wrong with the following variable declaration?

```
int miles per gallon = 39.4
```

4. Declare and initialize two variables, `unitPrice` and `quantity`, to contain the unit price of a single item and the number of items purchased. Use reasonable initial values.

5. Use the variables declared in Self Check 4 to display the total purchase price.

6. What are the types of the values 0 and "0"?

7. Which number type would you use for storing the area of a circle?

8. Which of the following are legal identifiers?

```
Greeting1
g
void
101dalmatians
Hello, World
<greeting>
```

9. Declare a variable to hold your name. Use camel case in the variable name.

10. Is 12 = 12 a valid expression in the Java language?

11. How do you change the value of the `greeting` variable to "Hello, Nina!"?

12. How would you explain assignment using the parking space analogy?

Practice It Now you can try these exercises at the end of the chapter: R2.3, R2.4, R2.6.

Common Error 2.1

Using Undeclared or Uninitialized Variables

You must declare a variable before you use it for the first time. For example, the following sequence of statements would not be legal:

```
int perimeter = 4 * width; // ERROR: width not yet declared
int width = 20;
```

In your program, the statements are compiled in order. When the compiler reaches the first statement, it does not know that `width` will be declared in the next line, and it reports an error. The remedy is to reorder the declarations so that each variable is declared before it is used.

A related error is to leave a variable uninitialized:

```
int width;
int perimeter = 4 * width; // ERROR: width not yet initialized
```

The Java compiler will complain that you are using a variable that has not yet been given a value. The remedy is to assign a value to the variable before it is used.

Common Error 2.2

Confusing Variable Declarations and Assignment Statements

Suppose your program declares a variable as follows:

```
int width = 20;
```

If you want to change the value of the variable, you use an assignment statement:

```
width = 30;
```

It is a common error to accidentally use another variable declaration:

```
int width = 30; // ERROR—starts with int and is therefore a declaration
```

But there is already a variable named `width`. The compiler will complain that you are trying to declare another variable with the same name.

Programming Tip 2.1

Choose Descriptive Variable Names

In algebra, variable names are usually just one letter long, such as p or A, maybe with a subscript such as p_1. You might be tempted to save yourself a lot of typing by using short variable names in your Java programs:

```
int a = w * h;
```

Compare that statement with the following one:

```
int area = width * height;
```

The advantage is obvious. Reading `width` is much easier than reading `w` and then figuring out that it must mean "width".

In practical programming, descriptive variable names are particularly important when programs are written by more than one person. It may be obvious to you that `w` stands for width, but is it obvious to the person who needs to update your code years later? For that matter, will you yourself remember what `w` means when you look at the code a month from now?

2.3 Calling Methods

A program performs useful work by calling methods on its objects. In this section, we examine how to supply values in a method, and how to obtain the result of the method.

2.3.1 The Public Interface of a Class

You use an object by calling its methods. All objects of a given class share a common set of methods. For example, the `PrintStream` class provides methods for its objects (such as `println` and `print`). Similarly, the `String` class provides methods that you can apply to `String` objects. One of them is the `length` method. The `length` method counts the number of characters in a string. You can apply that method to any object of type `String`. For example, the sequence of statements:

```
String greeting = "Hello, World!";
int numberOfCharacters = greeting.length();
```

sets `numberOfCharacters` to the length of the `String` object "`Hello, World!`". After the instructions in the `length` method are executed, `numberOfCharacters` is set to 13. (The quotation marks are not part of the string, and the `length` method does not count them.)

When calling the `length` method, you do not supply any values inside the parentheses. Also note that the `length` method does not produce any visible output. It returns a value that is subsequently used in the program.

Let's look at another method of the `String` class. When you apply the `toUpperCase` method to a `String` object, the method creates another `String` object that contains the characters of the original string, with lowercase letters converted to uppercase. For example, the sequence of statements

```
String river = "Mississippi";
String bigRiver = river.toUpperCase();
```

sets `bigRiver` to the `String` object "`MISSISSIPPI`".

The public interface of a class specifies what you can do with its objects. The hidden implementation describes how these actions are carried out.

The String class declares many other methods besides the length and toUpper-Case methods—you will learn about many of them in Chapter 4. Collectively, the methods form the **public interface** of the class, telling you what you can do with the objects of the class. A class also declares a *private implementation*, describing the data inside its objects and the instructions for its methods. Those details are hidden from the programmers who use objects and call methods.

The controls of a car form its public interface. The private implementation is under the hood.

Figure 5 shows two objects of the String class. Each object stores its own data (drawn as boxes that contain characters). Both objects support the same set of methods—the public interface that is specified by the String class.

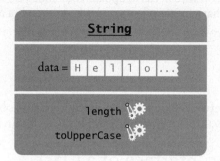 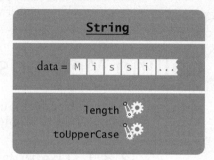

Figure 5 A Representation of Two String Objects

2.3.2 Method Arguments

An argument is a value that is supplied in a method call.

Most methods require values that give details about the work that the method needs to do. For example, when you call the println method, you must supply the string that should be printed. Computer scientists use the technical term **argument** for method inputs. We say that the string greeting is an argument of the method call

```
System.out.println(greeting);
```

Figure 6 illustrates passing the argument to the method.

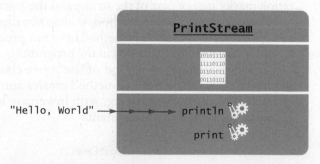

Figure 6 Passing an Argument to the println Method

At this tailor shop, the customer's measurements and the fabric are the arguments of the sew *method. The return value is the finished garment.*

Some methods require multiple arguments; others don't require any arguments at all. An example of the latter is the `length` method of the `String` class (see Figure 7). All the information that the `length` method requires to do its job—namely, the character sequence of the string—is stored in the object that carries out the method.

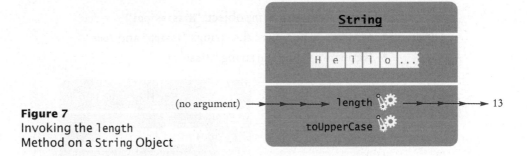

Figure 7
Invoking the `length`
Method on a `String` Object

2.3.3 Return Values

The return value of a method is a result that the method has computed.

Some methods, such as the `println` method, carry out an action for you. Other methods compute and return a value. For example, the `length` method returns a value, namely the number of characters in the string. You can store the return value in a variable:

```
int numberOfCharacters = greeting.length();
```

You can also use the return value of one method as an argument of another method:

```
System.out.println(greeting.length());
```

The method call `greeting.length()` returns a value—the integer 13. The return value becomes an argument of the `println` method. Figure 8 shows the process.

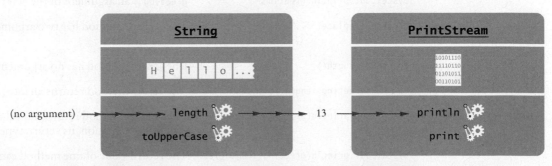

Figure 8 Passing the Result of a Method Call to Another Method

ANIMATION
Parameter Passing

Not all methods return values. One example is the `println` method. The `println` method interacts with the operating system, causing characters to appear in a window. But it does not return a value to the code that calls it.

Let us analyze a more complex method call. Here, we will call the `replace` method of the `String` class. The `replace` method carries out a search-and-replace operation, similar to that of a word processor. For example, the call

```
river.replace("issipp", "our")
```

constructs a new string that is obtained by replacing all occurrences of `"issipp"` in `"Mississippi"` with `"our"`. (In this situation, there was only one replacement.) The method returns the `String` object `"Missouri"`. You can save that string in a variable:

```
river = river.replace("issipp", "our");
```

Or you can pass it to another method:

```
System.out.println(river.replace("issipp", "our"));
```

As Figure 9 shows, this method call

- Is invoked on a `String` object: `"Mississippi"`
- Has two arguments: the strings `"issipp"` and `"our"`
- Returns a value: the string `"Missouri"`

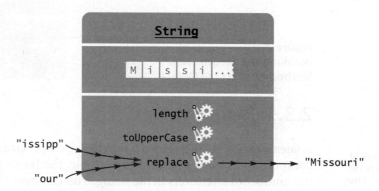

Figure 9 Calling the `replace` Method

Table 3 Method Arguments and Return Values

Example	Comments
`System.out.println(greeting)`	`greeting` is an argument of the `println` method.
`greeting.replace("e","3")`	The `replace` method has two arguments, in this case `"e"` and `"3"`.
`greeting.length()`	The `length` method has no arguments.
`int n = greeting.length();`	The `length` method returns an integer value.
`System.out.println(n);`	The `println` method returns no value. In the API documentation, its return type is `void`.
`System.out.println(greeting.length());`	The return value of one method can become the argument of another.

2.3.4 Method Declarations

When a method is declared in a class, the declaration specifies the types of the arguments and the return value. For example, the String class declares the length method as

```
public int length()
```

That is, there are no arguments, and the return value has the type int. (For now, all the methods that we consider will be "public" methods—see Chapter 9 for more restricted methods.)

The replace method is declared as

```
public String replace(String target, String replacement)
```

To call the replace method, you supply two arguments, target and replacement, which both have type String. The returned value is another string.

When a method returns no value, the return type is declared with the reserved word **void**. For example, the PrintStream class declares the println method as

```
public void println(String output)
```

Occasionally, a class declares two methods with the same name and different argument types. For example, the PrintStream class declares a second method, also called println, as

```
public void println(int output)
```

That method is used to print an integer value. We say that the println name is **overloaded** because it refers to more than one method.

FULL CODE EXAMPLE

Go to wiley.com/go/javacode to download a program that demonstrates method calls.

SELF CHECK

13. How can you compute the length of the string "Mississippi"?
14. How can you print out the uppercase version of "Hello, World!"?
15. Is it legal to call river.println()? Why or why not?
16. What are the arguments in the method call river.replace("p", "s")?
17. What is the result of the call river.replace("p", "s")?
18. What is the result of the call greeting.replace("World", "Dave").length()?
19. How is the toUpperCase method declared in the String class?

Practice It Now you can try these exercises at the end of the chapter: R2.7, R2.8, R2.9.

Programming Tip 2.2

Learn By Trying

When you learn about a new method, write a small program to try it out. For example, you can go right now to your Java development environment and run this program:

```java
public class ReplaceDemo
{
   public static void main(String[] args)
   {
      String river = "Mississippi";
      System.out.println(river.replace("issipp", "our"));
   }
}
```

Then you can see with your own eyes what the replace method does. Also, you can run experiments. Does replace change every match, or only the first one? Try it out:

```
System.out.println(river.replace("i", "x"));
```

Set up your work environment to make this kind of experimentation easy and natural. Keep a file with the blank outline of a Java program around, so you can copy and paste it when needed. Alternatively, some development environments will automatically type the class and main method. Find out if yours does. Some environments even let you type commands into a window and show you the result right away, without having to make a main method to call System. out.println (see Figure 10).

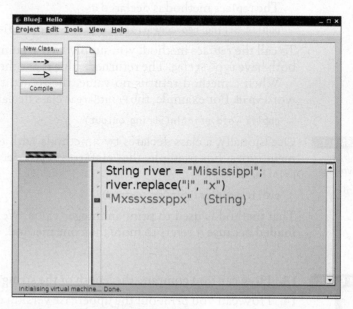

Figure 10 The Code Pad in BlueJ

2.4 Constructing Objects

Generally, when you want to use objects in your program, you need to specify their initial properties by *constructing* them.

To learn about object construction, we need to go beyond String objects and the System.out object. Let us turn to another class in the Java library: the Rectangle class. Objects of type Rectangle describe rectangular shapes. These objects are useful for a variety of purposes. You can assemble rectangles into bar charts, and you can program simple games by moving rectangles inside a window.

Note that a Rectangle object isn't a rectangular shape—it's an object that contains a set of numbers. The numbers *describe* the rectangle (see Figure 11). Each rectangle is described by the x- and y-coordinates of its top-left corner, its width, and its height.

Objects of the Rectangle *class describe rectangular shapes.*

Rectangle		Rectangle		Rectangle	
x =	5	x =	35	x =	45
y =	10	y =	30	y =	0
width =	20	width =	20	width =	30
height =	30	height =	20	height =	20

Figure 11   Rectangle Objects

It is very important that you understand this distinction. In the computer, a Rectangle object is a block of memory that holds four numbers, for example $x = 5$, $y = 10$, *width* = 20, *height* = 30. In the imagination of the programmer who uses a Rectangle object, the object describes a geometric figure.

To make a new rectangle, you need to specify the *x*, *y*, *width*, and *height* values. Then *invoke the new operator*, specifying the name of the class and the argument(s) required for constructing a new object. For example, you can make a new rectangle with its top-left corner at (5, 10), width 20, and height 30 as follows:

> **Use the new operator, followed by a class name and arguments, to construct new objects.**

```
new Rectangle(5, 10, 20, 30)
```

Here is what happens in detail:

1. The new operator makes a Rectangle object.
2. It uses the arguments (in this case, 5, 10, 20, and 30) to initialize the object's data.
3. It returns the object.

The process of creating a new object is called **construction**. The four values 5, 10, 20, and 30 are called the *construction arguments*.

The new expression yields an object, and you need to store the object if you want to use it later. Usually you assign the output of the new operator to a variable. For example,

```
Rectangle box = new Rectangle(5, 10, 20, 30);
```

Syntax 2.3   Object Construction

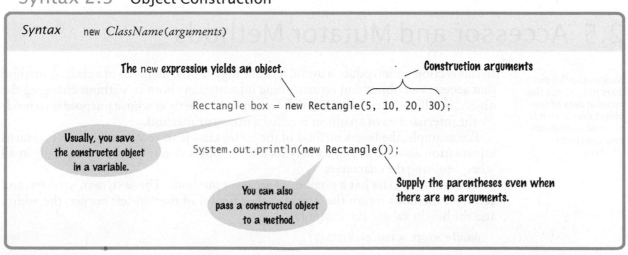

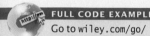

FULL CODE EXAMPLE

Go to wiley.com/go/javacode to download a program that demonstrates constructors.

Some classes let you construct objects in multiple ways. For example, you can also obtain a Rectangle object by supplying no construction arguments at all (but you must still supply the parentheses):

```
new Rectangle()
```

This expression constructs a (rather useless) rectangle with its top-left corner at the origin (0, 0), width 0, and height 0.

SELF CHECK

20. How do you construct a square with center (100, 100) and side length 20?

21. Initialize the variables box and box2 with two rectangles that touch each other.

22. The getWidth method returns the width of a Rectangle object. What does the following statement print?

```
System.out.println(new Rectangle().getWidth());
```

23. The PrintStream class has a constructor whose argument is the name of a file. How do you construct a PrintStream object with the construction argument "output.txt"?

24. Write a statement to save the object that you constructed in Self Check 23 in a variable.

Practice It Now you can try these exercises at the end of the chapter: R2.11, R2.14, R2.16.

Common Error 2.3

Trying to Invoke a Constructor Like a Method

Constructors are not methods. You can only use a constructor with the new operator, not to reinitialize an existing object:

```
box.Rectangle(20, 35, 20, 30); // Error—can't reinitialize object
```

The remedy is simple: Make a new object and overwrite the current one stored by box.

```
box = new Rectangle(20, 35, 20, 30); // OK
```

2.5 Accessor and Mutator Methods

An accessor method does not change the internal data of the object on which it is invoked. A mutator method changes the data.

In this section we introduce a useful terminology for the methods of a class. A method that accesses an object and returns some information about it, without changing the object, is called an **accessor method**. In contrast, a method whose purpose is to modify the internal data of an object is called a **mutator method**.

For example, the length method of the String class is an accessor method. It returns information about a string, namely its length. But it doesn't modify the string at all when counting the characters.

The Rectangle class has a number of accessor methods. The getX, getY, getWidth, and getHeight methods return the x- and y-coordinates of the top-left corner, the width, and the height values. For example,

```
double width = box.getWidth();
```

Now let us consider a mutator method. Programs that manipulate rectangles frequently need to move them around, for example, to display animations. The `Rectangle` class has a method for that purpose, called `translate`. (Mathematicians use the term "translation" for a rigid motion of the plane.) This method moves a rectangle by a certain distance in the *x*- and *y*-directions. The method call,

```
box.translate(15, 25);
```

FULL CODE EXAMPLE

Go to wiley.com/go/
javacode to download a program that demonstrates accessors and mutators.

moves the rectangle by 15 units in the *x*-direction and 25 units in the *y*-direction (see Figure 12). Moving a rectangle doesn't change its width or height, but it changes the top-left corner. Afterward, the rectangle that had its top-left corner at (5, 10) now has it at (20, 35).

This method is a mutator because it modifies the object on which the method is invoked.

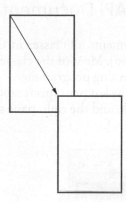

Figure 12   Using the `translate` Method to Move a Rectangle

SELF CHECK

25. What does this sequence of statements print?

```
Rectangle box = new Rectangle(5, 10, 20, 30);
System.out.println("Before: " + box.getX());
box.translate(25, 40);
System.out.println("After: " + box.getX());
```

26. What does this sequence of statements print?

```
Rectangle box = new Rectangle(5, 10, 20, 30);
System.out.println("Before: " + box.getWidth());
box.translate(25, 40);
System.out.println("After: " + box.getWidth());
```

27. What does this sequence of statements print?

```
String greeting = "Hello";
System.out.println(greeting.toUpperCase());
System.out.println(greeting);
```

28. Is the `toUpperCase` method of the `String` class an accessor or a mutator?

29. Which call to `translate` is needed to move the rectangle declared by `Rectangle box = new Rectangle(5, 10, 20, 30)` so that its top-left corner is the origin (0, 0)?

Practice It   Now you can try these exercises at the end of the chapter: R2.17, E2.6, E2.8.

2.6 The API Documentation

The API (Application Programming Interface) documentation lists the classes and methods of the Java library.

The classes and methods of the Java library are listed in the **API documentation**. The API is the "application programming interface". A programmer who uses the Java classes to put together a computer program (or *application*) is an *application programmer*. That's you. In contrast, the programmers who designed and implemented the library classes such as PrintStream and Rectangle are *system programmers*.

You can find the API documentation on the Web. Point your web browser to http://docs.oracle.com/javase/7/docs/api/index.html. An abbreviated version of the API documentation is provided in Appendix D that may be easier to use at first, but you should eventually move on to the real thing.

2.6.1 Browsing the API Documentation

The API documentation documents all classes in the Java library—there are thousands of them (see Figure 13, top). Most of the classes are rather specialized, and only a few are of interest to the beginning programmer.

Locate the Rectangle link in the left pane, preferably by using the search function of your browser. Click on the link, and the right pane shows all the features of the Rectangle class (see Figure 13, bottom).

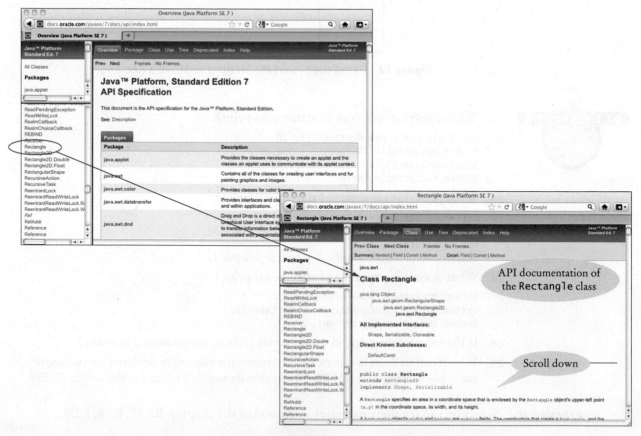

Figure 13 The API Documentation of the Standard Java Library

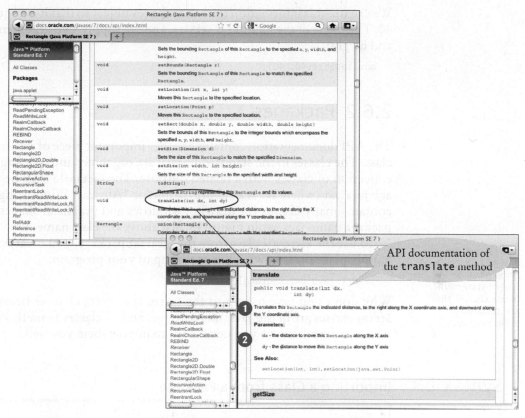

Figure 14 The Method Summary for the Rectangle Class

The API documentation for each class starts out with a section that describes the purpose of the class. Then come summary tables for the constructors and methods (see Figure 14, top). Click on a method's link to get a detailed description (see Figure 14, bottom).

The detailed description of a method shows

- The action that the method carries out. ❶
- The types and names of the parameter variables that receive the arguments when the method is called. ❷
- The value that it returns (or the reserved word void if the method doesn't return any value).

As you can see, the Rectangle class has quite a few methods. While occasionally intimidating for the beginning programmer, this is a strength of the standard library. If you ever need to do a computation involving rectangles, chances are that there is a method that does all the work for you.

For example, suppose you want to change the width or height of a rectangle. If you browse through the API documentation, you will find a setSize method with the description "Sets the size of this Rectangle to the specified width and height." The method has two arguments, described as

- width - the new width for this Rectangle
- height - the new height for this Rectangle

We can use this information to change the box object so that it is a square of side length 40. The name of the method is setSize, and we supply two arguments: the new width and height:

```
box.setSize(40, 40);
```

2.6.2 Packages

The API documentation contains another important piece of information about each class. The classes in the standard library are organized into **packages**. A package is a collection of classes with a related purpose. The Rectangle class belongs to the package java.awt (where awt is an abbreviation for "Abstract Windowing Toolkit"), which contains many classes for drawing windows and graphical shapes. You can see the package name java.awt in Figure 13, just above the class name.

To use the Rectangle class from the java.awt package, you must *import* the package. Simply place the following line at the top of your program:

> Java classes are grouped into packages. Use the import statement to use classes that are declared in other packages.

```
import java.awt.Rectangle;
```

Why don't you have to import the System and String classes? Because the System and String classes are in the java.lang package, and all classes from this package are automatically imported, so you never need to import them yourself.

Syntax 2.4   Importing a Class from a Package

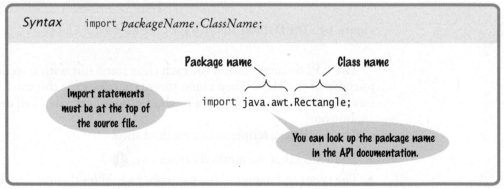

SELF CHECK

30. Look at the API documentation of the String class. Which method would you use to obtain the string "hello, world!" from the string "Hello, World!"?

31. In the API documentation of the String class, look at the description of the trim method. What is the result of applying trim to the string " Hello, Space ! "? (Note the spaces in the string.)

32. Look into the API documentation of the Rectangle class. What is the difference between the methods void translate(int x, int y) and void setLocation(int x, int y)?

33. The Random class is declared in the java.util package. What do you need to do in order to use that class in your program?

34. In which package is the BigInteger class located? Look it up in the API documentation.

Practice It   Now you can try these exercises at the end of the chapter: R2.18, E2.4, E2.11.

Programming Tip 2.3

Don't Memorize—Use Online Help

The Java library has thousands of classes and methods. It is neither necessary nor useful trying to memorize them. Instead, you should become familiar with using the API documentation. Because you will need to use the API documentation all the time, it is best to download and install it onto your computer, particularly if your computer is not always connected to the Internet. You can download the documentation from http://www.oracle.com/technetwork/java/javase/downloads/index.html.

2.7 Implementing a Test Program

A test program
verifies that methods
behave as expected.

In this section, we discuss the steps that are necessary to implement a test program. The purpose of a test program is to verify that one or more methods have been implemented correctly. A test program calls methods and checks that they return the expected results. Writing test programs is a very important skill.

In this section, we will develop a simple program that tests a method in the Rectangle class using these steps:

1. Provide a tester class.
2. Supply a main method.
3. Inside the main method, construct one or more objects.
4. Apply methods to the objects.
5. Display the results of the method calls.
6. Display the values that you expect to get.

Our sample test program tests the behavior of the translate method. Here are the key steps (which have been placed inside the main method of the MoveTester class).

```
Rectangle box = new Rectangle(5, 10, 20, 30);

// Move the rectangle
box.translate(15, 25);

// Print information about the moved rectangle
System.out.print("x: ");
System.out.println(box.getX());
System.out.println("Expected: 20");
```

We print the value that is returned by the getX method, and then we print a message that describes the value we expect to see.

Determining the
expected result
in advance is an
important part
of testing.

This is a very important step. You want to spend some time thinking about the expected result before you run a test program. This thought process will help you understand how your program should behave, and it can help you track down errors at an early stage. Finding and fixing errors early is a very effective strategy that can save you a great deal of time.

In our case, the rectangle has been constructed with the top-left corner at (5, 10). The *x*-direction is moved by 15, so we expect an *x*-value of 5 + 15 = 20 after the move. Here is the program that tests the moving of a rectangle:

section_7/MoveTester.java

```
1   import java.awt.Rectangle;
2
3   public class MoveTester
4   {
5      public static void main(String[] args)
6      {
7         Rectangle box = new Rectangle(5, 10, 20, 30);
8
9         // Move the rectangle
10        box.translate(15, 25);
11
12        // Print information about the moved rectangle
13        System.out.print("x: ");
14        System.out.println(box.getX());
15        System.out.println("Expected: 20");
16
17        System.out.print("y: ");
18        System.out.println(box.getY());
19        System.out.println("Expected: 35");
20     }
21  }
```

Program Run

```
x: 20
Expected: 20
y: 35
Expected: 35
```

SELF CHECK

35. Suppose we had called `box.translate(25, 15)` instead of `box.translate(15, 25)`. What are the expected outputs?

36. Why doesn't the `MoveTester` program need to print the width and height of the rectangle?

Practice It Now you can try these exercises at the end of the chapter: E2.1, E2.7, E2.13.

Special Topic 2.1

Testing Classes in an Interactive Environment

Some development environments are specifically designed to help students explore objects without having to provide tester classes. These environments can be very helpful for gaining insight into the behavior of objects, and for promoting object-oriented thinking. The BlueJ environment (shown in the figure) displays objects as blobs on a workbench.

You can construct new objects, put them on the workbench, invoke methods, and see the return values, all without writing a line of code. You can download BlueJ at no charge from www.bluej.org. Another excellent environment for interactively exploring objects is Dr. Java at drjava.sourceforge.net.

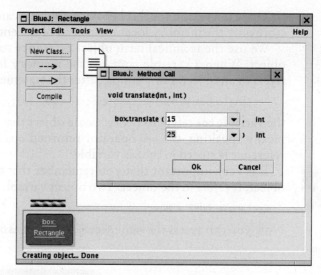

Testing a Method Call in BlueJ

![netpli] **WORKED EXAMPLE 2.1** **How Many Days Have You Been Alive?**

Explore the API of a class Day that represents a calendar day. Using that class, learn to write a program that computes how many days have elapsed since the day you were born. Go to wiley.com/go/javaexamples and download Worked Example 2.1.

![netpli] **WORKED EXAMPLE 2.2** **Working with Pictures**

Learn how to use the API of a Picture class to edit photos. Go to wiley.com/go/javaexamples and download Worked Example 2.2.

2.8 Object References

In Java, an object variable (that is, a variable whose type is a class) does not actually hold an object. It merely holds the *memory location* of an object. The object itself is stored elsewhere—see Figure 15.

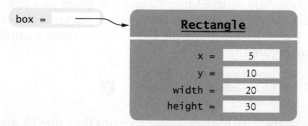

Figure 15 An Object Variable Containing an Object Reference

There is a reason for this behavior. Objects can be very large. It is more efficient to store only the memory location instead of the entire object.

An object reference describes the location of an object.

We use the technical term **object reference** to denote the memory location of an object. When a variable contains the memory location of an object, we say that it *refers* to an object. For example, after the statement

```
Rectangle box = new Rectangle(5, 10, 20, 30);
```

the variable box refers to the Rectangle object that the new operator constructed. Technically speaking, the new operator returned a reference to the new object, and that reference is stored in the box variable.

It is very important that you remember that the box variable *does not contain* the object. It *refers* to the object. Two object variables can refer to the same object:

```
Rectangle box2 = box;
```

Multiple object variables can contain references to the same object.

Now you can access the same Rectangle object as box and as box2, as shown in Figure 16.

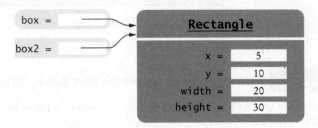

Figure 16 Two Object Variables Referring to the Same Object

In Java, numbers are not objects. Number variables actually store numbers. When you declare

```
int luckyNumber = 13;
```

then the luckyNumber variable holds the number 13, not a reference to the number (see Figure 17). The reason is again efficiency. Because numbers require little storage, it is more efficient to store them directly in a variable.

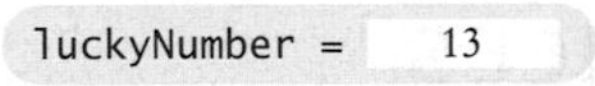

luckyNumber =   13

Figure 17 A Number Variable Stores a Number

Number variables store numbers. Object variables store references.

You can see the difference between number variables and object variables when you make a copy of a variable. When you copy a number, the original and the copy of the number are independent values. But when you copy an object reference, both the original and the copy are references to the same object.

Consider the following code, which copies a number and then changes the copy (see Figure 18):

```
int luckyNumber = 13;      1
int luckyNumber2 = luckyNumber;   2
luckyNumber2 = 12;    3
```

Now the variable luckyNumber contains the value 13, and luckyNumber2 contains 12.

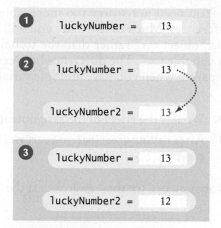

Figure 18 Copying Numbers

FULL CODE EXAMPLE

Go to wiley.com/go/
javacode to down-
load a program that
demonstrates the
difference between
copying numbers and
object references.

Now consider the seemingly analogous code with Rectangle objects (see Figure 19).

```
Rectangle box = new Rectangle(5, 10, 20, 30); ①
Rectangle box2 = box; ②
box2.translate(15, 25); ③
```

Because box and box2 refer to the same rectangle after step ②, both variables refer to the moved rectangle after the call to the translate method.

ANIMATION
Object References

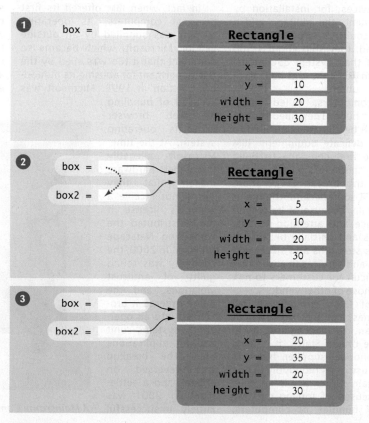

Figure 19 Copying Object References

You need not worry too much about the difference between objects and object references. Much of the time, you will have the correct intuition when you think of the "object box" rather than the technically more accurate "object reference stored in variable box". The difference between objects and object references only becomes apparent when you have multiple variables that refer to the same object.

SELF CHECK

37. What is the effect of the assignment `String greeting2 = greeting`?

38. After calling `greeting2.toUpperCase()`, what are the contents of `greeting` and `greeting2`?

Practice It   Now you can try these exercises at the end of the chapter: R2.15, R2.19.

Computing & Society 2.1 Computer Monopoly

When International Business Machines Corporation (IBM), a successful manufacturer of punched-card equipment for tabulating data, first turned its attention to designing computers in the early 1950s, its planners assumed that there was a market for perhaps 50 such devices, for installation by the government, the military, and a few of the country's largest corporations. Instead, they sold about 1,500 machines of their System 650 model and went on to build and sell more powerful computers.

These computers, called mainframes, were huge. They filled rooms, which had to be climate-controlled to protect the delicate equipment. IBM was not the first company to build mainframe computers; that honor belongs to the Univac Corporation. However, IBM soon became the major player, partially because of its technical excellence and attention to customer needs and partially because it exploited its strengths and structured its products and services in a way that made it difficult for customers to mix them with those of other vendors.

As all of IBM's competitors fell on hard times, the U.S. government brought an antitrust suit against IBM in 1969. In the United States, it is legal to be a monopoly supplier, but it is not legal to use one's monopoly in one market to gain supremacy in another. IBM was accused of forcing customers to buy bundles of computers, software, and peripherals, making it impossible for other vendors of software and peripherals to compete.

The suit went to trial in 1975 and dragged on until 1982, when it was abandoned, largely because new waves of smaller computers had made it irrelevant.

In fact, when IBM offered its first personal computers, its operating system was supplied by an outside vendor, Microsoft, which became so dominant that it too was sued by the U.S. goverment for abusing its monopoly position in 1998. Microsoft was accused of bundling its web browser with its operating system. At the time, Microsoft allegedly threatened hardware makers that they would not receive a Windows license if they distributed the competing Netscape browser. In 2000, the company was found guilty of antitrust violations, and the judge ordered it broken up into an operating systems unit and an applications unit. The breakup was reversed on appeal, and a settlement in 2001 was largely unsuccessful in establishing alternatives for desktop software.

Now the computing landscape is shifting once again, toward mobile devices and cloud computing. As you observe that change, you may well see new monopolies in the making. When a software vendor needs the permission of a hardware vendor in order to place a product into an "app store", or when a maker of a digital book reader tries to coerce publishers into a particular pricing structure, the question arises whether such conduct is illegal exploitation of a monopoly position.

A Mainframe Computer

2.9 Graphical Applications

The following optional sections teach you how to write *graphical applications:* applications that display drawings inside a window. The drawings are made up of shape objects: rectangles, ellipses, and lines. The shape objects provide another source of examples, and many students enjoy the visual feedback.

2.9.1 Frame Windows

> To show a frame, construct a JFrame object, set its size, and make it visible.

A graphical application shows information inside a **frame**: a window with a title bar, as shown in Figure 20. In this section, you will learn how to display a frame. In Section 2.9.2, you will learn how to create a drawing inside the frame.

A graphical application shows information inside a frame.

To show a frame, carry out the following steps:

1. Construct an object of the JFrame class:

   ```
   JFrame frame = new JFrame();
   ```

2. Set the size of the frame:

   ```
   frame.setSize(300, 400);
   ```

   This frame will be 300 pixels wide and 400 pixels tall. If you omit this step the frame will be 0 by 0 pixels, and you won't be able to see it. (Pixels are the tiny dots from which digital images are composed.)

3. If you'd like, set the title of the frame:

   ```
   frame.setTitle("An empty frame");
   ```

   If you omit this step, the title bar is simply left blank.

4. Set the "default close operation":

   ```
   frame.setDefaultCloseOperation(JFrame.EXIT_ON_CLOSE);
   ```

   When the user closes the frame, the program automatically exits. Don't omit this step. If you do, the program keeps running even after the frame is closed.

5. Make the frame visible:

   ```
   frame.setVisible(true);
   ```

The simple program below shows all of these steps. It produces the empty frame shown in Figure 20.

The JFrame class is a part of the javax.swing package. Swing is the nickname for the graphical user interface library in Java. The "x" in javax denotes the fact that Swing started out as a Java *extension* before it was added to the standard library.

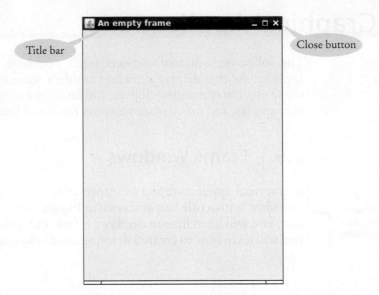

Title bar

Close button

Figure 20 A Frame Window

We will go into much greater detail about Swing programming in Chapters 3, 10, and 19. For now, consider this program to be the essential plumbing that is required to show a frame.

section_9_1/EmptyFrameViewer.java

```
1   import javax.swing.JFrame;
2
3   public class EmptyFrameViewer
4   {
5      public static void main(String[] args)
6      {
7         JFrame frame = new JFrame();
8         frame.setSize(300, 400);
9         frame.setTitle("An empty frame");
10        frame.setDefaultCloseOperation(JFrame.EXIT_ON_CLOSE);
11        frame.setVisible(true);
12     }
13  }
```

2.9.2 Drawing on a Component

In this section, you will learn how to make shapes appear inside a frame window. The first drawing will be exceedingly modest: just two rectangles (see Figure 21). You'll soon see how to produce more interesting drawings. The purpose of this example is to show you the basic outline of a program that creates a drawing.

You cannot draw directly onto a frame. Instead, drawing happens in a **component** object. In the Swing toolkit, the JComponent class represents a blank component.

Because we don't want to add a blank component, we have to modify the JComponent class and specify how the component should be painted. The solution is to declare a new class that extends the JComponent class. You will learn about the process of extending classes in Chapter 9.

In order to display a drawing in a frame, declare a class that extends the JComponent class.

Figure 21
Drawing Rectangles

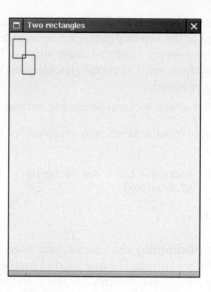

For now, simply use the following code as a template:

```
public class RectangleComponent extends JComponent
{
    public void paintComponent(Graphics g)
    {
        Drawing instructions
    }
}
```

> Place drawing instructions inside the paintComponent method. That method is called whenever the component needs to be repainted.

The extends reserved word indicates that our component class, RectangleComponent, can be used like a JComponent. However, the RectangleComponent class will be different from the plain JComponent class in one respect: Its paintComponent method will contain instructions to draw the rectangles.

When the component is shown for the first time, the paintComponent method is called automatically. The method is also called when the window is resized, or when it is shown again after it was hidden.

The paintComponent method receives an object of type Graphics as its argument. The Graphics object stores the graphics state—the current color, font, and so on—that are used for drawing operations. However, the Graphics class is not very useful. When programmers clamored for a more object-oriented approach to drawing graphics, the designers of Java created the Graphics2D class, which extends the Graphics class. Whenever the Swing toolkit calls the paintComponent method, it actually passes an object of type Graphics2D as the argument. Because we want to use the more sophisticated methods to draw two-dimensional graphics objects, we need to use the Graphics2D class. This is accomplished by using a **cast**:

> Use a cast to recover the Graphics2D object from the Graphics argument of the paintComponent method.

```
public class RectangleComponent extends JComponent
{
    public void paintComponent(Graphics g)
    {
        // Recover Graphics2D
        Graphics2D g2 = (Graphics2D) g;
        . . .
    }
}
```

Chapter 9 has more information about casting. For now, you should simply include the cast at the top of your paintComponent methods.

Now you are ready to draw shapes. The draw method of the Graphics2D class can draw shapes, such as rectangles, ellipses, line segments, polygons, and arcs. Here we draw a rectangle:

```java
public class RectangleComponent extends JComponent
{
    public void paintComponent(Graphics g)
    {
        . . .
        Rectangle box = new Rectangle(5, 10, 20, 30);
        g2.draw(box);
        . . .
    }
}
```

When positioning the shapes, you need to pay attention to the coordinate system. It is different from the one used in mathematics. The origin (0, 0) is at the upper-left corner of the component, and the y-coordinate grows downward.

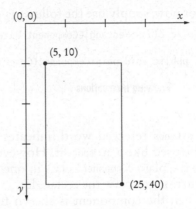

Following is the source code for the RectangleComponent class. Note that the paintComponent method of the RectangleComponent class draws two rectangles. As you can see from the import statements, the Graphics and Graphics2D classes are part of the java.awt package.

section_9_2/RectangleComponent.java

```java
1   import java.awt.Graphics;
2   import java.awt.Graphics2D;
3   import java.awt.Rectangle;
4   import javax.swing.JComponent;
5
6   /**
7       A component that draws two rectangles.
8   */
9   public class RectangleComponent extends JComponent
10  {
11      public void paintComponent(Graphics g)
12      {
13          // Recover Graphics2D
14          Graphics2D g2 = (Graphics2D) g;
15
```

```
16        // Construct a rectangle and draw it
17        Rectangle box = new Rectangle(5, 10, 20, 30);
18        g2.draw(box);
19
20        // Move rectangle 15 units to the right and 25 units down
21        box.translate(15, 25);
22
23        // Draw moved rectangle
24        g2.draw(box);
25    }
26 }
```

2.9.3 Displaying a Component in a Frame

In a graphical application, you need a frame to show the application, and you need a component for the drawing. In this section, you will see how to combine the two. Follow these steps:

1. Construct a frame object and configure it.
2. Construct an object of your component class:

   ```
   RectangleComponent component = new RectangleComponent();
   ```

3. Add the component to the frame:

   ```
   frame.add(component);
   ```

4. Make the frame visible.

The following listing shows the complete process.

section_9_3/RectangleViewer.java

```
1   import javax.swing.JFrame;
2
3   public class RectangleViewer
4   {
5      public static void main(String[] args)
6      {
7         JFrame frame = new JFrame();
8
9         frame.setSize(300, 400);
10        frame.setTitle("Two rectangles");
11        frame.setDefaultCloseOperation(JFrame.EXIT_ON_CLOSE);
12
13        RectangleComponent component = new RectangleComponent();
14        frame.add(component);
15
16        frame.setVisible(true);
17     }
18  }
```

Note that the rectangle drawing program consists of two classes:

- The RectangleComponent class, whose paintComponent method produces the drawing.
- The RectangleViewer class, whose main method constructs a frame and a Rectangle-Component, adds the component to the frame, and makes the frame visible.

39. How do you display a square frame with a title bar that reads "Hello, World!"?
40. How can a program display two frames at once?
41. How do you modify the program to draw two squares?
42. How do you modify the program to draw one rectangle and one square?
43. What happens if you call g.draw(box) instead of g2.draw(box)?

Practice It   Now you can try these exercises at the end of the chapter: R2.20, R2.24, E2.17.

2.10 Ellipses, Lines, Text, and Color

In Section 2.9 you learned how to write a program that draws rectangles. In the following sections, you will learn how to draw other shapes: ellipses and lines. With these graphical elements, you can draw quite a few interesting pictures.

2.10.1 Ellipses and Circles

To draw an ellipse, you specify its bounding box (see Figure 22) in the same way that you would specify a rectangle, namely by the x- and y-coordinates of the top-left corner and the width and height of the box.

You can make simple drawings out of lines, rectangles, and circles.

> The Ellipse2D.Double and Line2D.Double classes describe graphical shapes.

However, there is no simple Ellipse class that you can use. Instead, you must use one of the two classes Ellipse2D.Float and Ellipse2D.Double, depending on whether you want to store the ellipse coordinates as single- or double-precision floating-point values. Because the latter are more convenient to use in Java, we will always use the Ellipse2D.Double class.

Here is how you construct an ellipse:

```
Ellipse2D.Double ellipse = new Ellipse2D.Double(x, y, width, height);
```

The class name Ellipse2D.Double looks different from the class names that you have encountered up to now. It consists of two class names Ellipse2D and Double separated

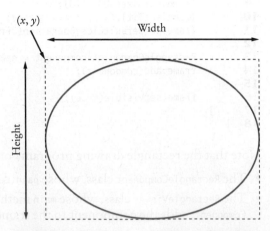

Figure 22   An Ellipse and Its Bounding Box

by a period (.). This indicates that Ellipse2D.Double is a so-called **inner class** inside Ellipse2D. When constructing and using ellipses, you don't actually need to worry about the fact that Ellipse2D.Double is an inner class—just think of it as a class with a long name. However, in the import statement at the top of your program, you must be careful that you import only the outer class:

```
import java.awt.geom.Ellipse2D;
```

Drawing an ellipse is easy: Use exactly the same draw method of the Graphics2D class that you used for drawing rectangles.

```
g2.draw(ellipse);
```

To draw a circle, simply set the width and height to the same values:

```
Ellipse2D.Double circle = new Ellipse2D.Double(x, y, diameter, diameter);
g2.draw(circle);
```

Notice that (x, y) is the top-left corner of the bounding box, not the center of the circle.

2.10.2 Lines

To draw a line, use an object of the Line2D.Double class. A line is constructed by specifying its two end points. You can do this in two ways. Give the *x*- and *y*-coordinates of both end points:

```
Line2D.Double segment = new Line2D.Double(x1, y1, x2, y2);
```

Or specify each end point as an object of the Point2D.Double class:

```
Point2D.Double from = new Point2D.Double(x1, y1);
Point2D.Double to = new Point2D.Double(x2, y2);

Line2D.Double segment = new Line2D.Double(from, to);
```

The second option is more object-oriented and is often more useful, particularly if the point objects can be reused elsewhere in the same drawing.

2.10.3 Drawing Text

The drawString method draws a string, starting at its basepoint.

You often want to put text inside a drawing, for example, to label some of the parts. Use the drawString method of the Graphics2D class to draw a string anywhere in a window. You must specify the string and the *x*- and *y*-coordinates of the basepoint of the first character in the string (see Figure 23). For example,

```
g2.drawString("Message", 50, 100);
```

Figure 23 Basepoint and Baseline

2.10.4 Colors

When you first start drawing, all shapes and strings are drawn with a black pen. To change the color, you need to supply an object of type Color. Java uses the RGB color model. That is, you specify a color by the amounts of the primary colors—red, green, and blue—that make up the color. The amounts are given as integers between 0 (primary color not present) and 255 (maximum amount present). For example,

```
Color magenta = new Color(255, 0, 255);
```

constructs a Color object with maximum red, no green, and maximum blue, yielding a bright purple color called magenta.

For your convenience, a variety of colors have been declared in the Color class. Table 4 shows those colors and their RGB values. For example, Color.PINK has been declared to be the same color as new Color(255, 175, 175).

To draw a shape in a different color, first set the color of the Graphics2D object, then call the draw method:

```
g2.setColor(Color.RED);
g2.draw(circle); // Draws the shape in red
```

> When you set a new color in the graphics context, it is used for subsequent drawing operations.

If you want to color the inside of the shape, use the fill method instead of the draw method. For example,

```
g2.fill(circle);
```

fills the inside of the circle with the current color.

Table 4 Predefined Colors

Color		RGB Values
Color.BLACK		0, 0, 0
Color.BLUE		0, 0, 255
Color.CYAN		0, 255, 255
Color.GRAY		128, 128, 128
Color.DARK_GRAY		64, 64, 64
Color.LIGHT_GRAY		192, 192, 192
Color.GREEN		0, 255, 0
Color.MAGENTA		255, 0, 255
Color.ORANGE		255, 200, 0
Color.PINK		255, 175, 175
Color.RED		255, 0, 0
Color.WHITE		255, 255, 255
Color.YELLOW		255, 255, 0

Figure 24 An Alien Face

The following program puts all these shapes to work, creating a simple drawing (see Figure 24).

section_10/FaceComponent.java

```java
1   import java.awt.Color;
2   import java.awt.Graphics;
3   import java.awt.Graphics2D;
4   import java.awt.Rectangle;
5   import java.awt.geom.Ellipse2D;
6   import java.awt.geom.Line2D;
7   import javax.swing.JComponent;
8
9   /**
10     A component that draws an alien face.
11  */
12  public class FaceComponent extends JComponent
13  {
14     public void paintComponent(Graphics g)
15     {
16        // Recover Graphics2D
17        Graphics2D g2 = (Graphics2D) g;
18
19        // Draw the head
20        Ellipse2D.Double head = new Ellipse2D.Double(5, 10, 100, 150);
21        g2.draw(head);
22
23        // Draw the eyes
24        g2.setColor(Color.GREEN);
25        Rectangle eye = new Rectangle(25, 70, 15, 15);
26        g2.fill(eye);
27        eye.translate(50, 0);
28        g2.fill(eye);
29
30        // Draw the mouth
31        Line2D.Double mouth = new Line2D.Double(30, 110, 80, 110);
32        g2.setColor(Color.RED);
33        g2.draw(mouth);
34
35        // Draw the greeting
36        g2.setColor(Color.BLUE);
37        g2.drawString("Hello, World!", 5, 175);
38     }
39  }
```

section_10/FaceViewer.java

```java
1    import javax.swing.JFrame;
2
3    public class FaceViewer
4    {
5       public static void main(String[] args)
6       {
7          JFrame frame = new JFrame();
8          frame.setSize(150, 250);
9          frame.setTitle("An Alien Face");
10         frame.setDefaultCloseOperation(JFrame.EXIT_ON_CLOSE);
11
12         FaceComponent component = new FaceComponent();
13         frame.add(component);
14
15         frame.setVisible(true);
16      }
17   }
```

SELF CHECK

44. Give instructions to draw a circle with center (100, 100) and radius 25.

45. Give instructions to draw a letter "V" by drawing two line segments.

46. Give instructions to draw a string consisting of the letter "V".

47. What are the RGB color values of Color.BLUE?

48. How do you draw a yellow square on a red background?

Practice It   Now you can try these exercises at the end of the chapter: R2.25, E2.18, E2.19.

CHAPTER SUMMARY

Identify objects, methods, and classes.

- Objects are entities in your program that you manipulate by calling methods.
- A method is a sequence of instructions that accesses the data of an object.
- A class describes a set of objects with the same behavior.

Write variable declarations and assignments.

- A variable is a storage location with a name.
- When declaring a variable, you usually specify an initial value.
- When declaring a variable, you also specify the type of its values.
- Use the int type for numbers that cannot have a fractional part.
- Use the double type for floating-point numbers.
- Numbers can be combined by arithmetic operators such as +, -, and *.
- By convention, variable names should start with a lowercase letter.
- Use comments to add explanations for humans who read your code. The compiler ignores comments.

- Use the assignment operator (=) to change the value of a variable.
- All variables must be initialized before you access them.
- The assignment operator = does *not* denote mathematical equality.

Recognize arguments and return values of methods.

- The public interface of a class specifies what you can do with its objects. The hidden implementation describes how these actions are carried out.
- An argument is a value that is supplied in a method call.
- The return value of a method is a result that the method has computed.

Use constructors to construct new objects.

- Use the new operator, followed by a class name and arguments, to construct new objects.

Classify methods as accessor and mutator methods.

- An accessor method does not change the internal data of the object on which it is invoked. A mutator method changes the data.

Use the API documentation for finding method descriptions and packages.

- The API (Application Programming Interface) documentation lists the classes and methods of the Java library.
- Java classes are grouped into packages. Use the import statement to use classes that are declared in other packages.

Write programs that test the behavior of methods.

- A test program verifies that methods behave as expected.
- Determining the expected result in advance is an important part of testing.

Describe how multiple object references can refer to the same object.

- An object reference describes the location of an object.
- Multiple object variables can contain references to the same object.
- Number variables store numbers. Object variables store references.

Write programs that display frame windows.

- To show a frame, construct a JFrame object, set its size, and make it visible.
- In order to display a drawing in a frame, declare a class that extends the JComponent class.

- Place drawing instructions inside the paintComponent method. That method is called whenever the component needs to be repainted.
- Use a cast to recover the Graphics2D object from the Graphics argument of the paint-Component method.

Use the Java API for drawing simple figures.

- The Ellipse2D.Double and Line2D.Double classes describe graphical shapes.
- The drawString method draws a string, starting at its basepoint.
- When you set a new color in the graphics context, it is used for subsequent drawing operations.

STANDARD LIBRARY ITEMS INTRODUCED IN THIS CHAPTER

```
java.awt.Color                    java.awt.Rectangle
java.awt.Component                   getX
   getHeight                         getY
   getWidth                          getHeight
   setSize                           getWidth
   setVisible                        setSize
java.awt.Frame                       translate
   setTitle                       java.lang.String
java.awt.geom.Ellipse2D.Double       length
java.awt.geom.Line2D.Double          replace
java.awt.geom.Point2D.Double         toLowerCase
java.awt.Graphics                    toUpperCase
   setColor                       javax.swing.JComponent
java.awt.Graphics2D                  paintComponent
   draw                           javax.swing.JFrame
   drawString                        setDefaultCloseOperation
   fill
```

REVIEW QUESTIONS

- **R2.1** Explain the difference between an object and a class.

- **R2.2** What is the *public interface* of a class? How does it differ from the *implementation* of a class?

- **R2.3** Declare and initialize variables for holding the price and the description of an article that is available for sale.

- **R2.4** What is the value of mystery after this sequence of statements?

```
int mystery = 1;
mystery = 1 - 2 * mystery;
mystery = mystery + 1;
```

- **R2.5** What is wrong with the following sequence of statements?

```
int mystery = 1;
mystery = mystery + 1;
int mystery = 1 - 2 * mystery;
```

■■ R2.6 Explain the difference between the = symbol in Java and in mathematics.

■■ R2.7 Give an example of a method that has an argument of type int. Give an example of a method that has a return value of type int. Repeat for the type String.

■■ R2.8 Write Java statements that initialize a string message with "Hello" and then change it to "HELLO". Use the toUpperCase method.

■■ R2.9 Write Java statements that initialize a string message with "Hello" and then change it to "hello". Use the replace method.

■ R2.10 Explain the difference between an object and an object variable.

■■ R2.11 Give the Java code for constructing an *object* of class Rectangle, and for declaring an *object variable* of class Rectangle.

■■ R2.12 Give Java code for objects with the following descriptions:

    a. A rectangle with center (100, 100) and all side lengths equal to 50

    b. A string with the contents "Hello, Dave"

Create objects, not object variables.

■■ R2.13 Repeat Exercise R2.12, but now declare object variables that are initialized with the required objects.

■■ R2.14 Write a Java statement to initialize a variable square with a rectangle object whose top left corner is (10, 20) and whose sides all have length 40. Then write a statement that replaces square with a rectangle of the same size and top left corner (20, 20).

■■ R2.15 Write Java statements that initialize two variables square1 and square2 to refer to the same square with center (20, 20) and side length 40.

■■ R2.16 Find the errors in the following statements:

    a. `Rectangle r = (5, 10, 15, 20);`

    b. `double width = Rectangle(5, 10, 15, 20).getWidth();`

    c. `Rectangle r;`
        `r.translate(15, 25);`

    d. `r = new Rectangle();`
        `r.translate("far, far away!");`

■ R2.17 Name two accessor methods and two mutator methods of the Rectangle class.

■■ R2.18 Consult the API documentation to find methods for

    • Concatenating two strings, that is, making a string consisting of the first string, followed by the second string.

    • Removing leading and trailing white space of a string.

    • Converting a rectangle to a string.

    • Computing the smallest rectangle that contains two given rectangles.

    • Returning a random floating-point number.

For each method, list the class in which it is defined, the return type, the method name, and the types of the arguments.

■ R2.19 Explain the difference between an object and an object reference.

■ Graphics R2.20 What is the difference between a console application and a graphical application?

■■ Graphics R2.21 Who calls the paintComponent method of a component? When does the call to the paintComponent method occur?

■■ Graphics R2.22 Why does the argument of the paintComponent method have type Graphics and not Graphics2D?

■■ Graphics R2.23 What is the purpose of a graphics context?

■■ Graphics R2.24 Why are separate viewer and component classes used for graphical programs?

■ Graphics R2.25 How do you specify a text color?

PRACTICE EXERCISES

■ Testing E2.1 Write an AreaTester program that constructs a Rectangle object and then computes and prints its area. Use the getWidth and getHeight methods. Also print the expected answer.

■ Testing E2.2 Write a PerimeterTester program that constructs a Rectangle object and then computes and prints its perimeter. Use the getWidth and getHeight methods. Also print the expected answer.

E2.3 Write a program that constructs a rectangle with area 42 and a rectangle with perimeter 42. Print the widths and heights of both rectangles.

■■ Testing E2.4 Look into the API documentation of the Rectangle class and locate the method

```
void add(int newx, int newy)
```

Read through the method documentation. Then determine the result of the following statements:

```
Rectangle box = new Rectangle(5, 10, 20, 30);
box.add(0, 0);
```

Write a program AddTester that prints the expected and actual location, width, and height of box after the call to add.

■■ Testing E2.5 Write a program ReplaceTester that encodes a string by replacing all letters "i" with "!" and all letters "s" with "$". Use the replace method. Demonstrate that you can correctly encode the string "Mississippi". Print both the actual and expected result.

■■■ E2.6 Write a program HollePrinter that switches the letters "e" and "o" in a string. Use the replace method repeatedly. Demonstrate that the string "Hello, World!" turns into "Holle, Werld!"

■ Testing E2.7 The StringBuilder class has a method for reversing a string. In a ReverseTester class, construct a StringBuilder from a given string (such as "desserts"), call the reverse method followed by the toString method, and print the result. Also print the expected value.

■■ E2.8 In the Java library, a color is specified by its red, green, and blue components between 0 and 255 (see Table 4 on page 68). Write a program BrighterDemo that constructs a Color object with red, green, and blue values of 50, 100, and 150. Then apply the brighter method of the Color class and print the red, green, and blue values of the resulting color. (You won't actually see the color—see Exercise E2.9 on how to display the color.)

·· Graphics E2.9 Repeat Exercise E2.8, but place your code into the following class. Then the color will be displayed.

```java
import java.awt.Color;
import javax.swing.JFrame;

public class BrighterDemo
{
    public static void main(String[] args)
    {
        JFrame frame = new JFrame();
        frame.setSize(200, 200);
        Color myColor = ...;
        frame.getContentPane().setBackground(myColor);
        frame.setDefaultCloseOperation(JFrame.EXIT_ON_CLOSE);
        frame.setVisible(true);
    }
}
```

·· E2.10 Repeat Exercise E2.8, but apply the darker method of the Color class twice to the object Color.RED. Call your class DarkerDemo.

·· E2.11 The Random class implements a *random number generator*, which produces sequences of numbers that appear to be random. To generate random integers, you construct an object of the Random class, and then apply the nextInt method. For example, the call generator.nextInt(6) gives you a random number between 0 and 5.

Write a program DieSimulator that uses the Random class to simulate the cast of a die, printing a random number between 1 and 6 every time that the program is run.

·· E2.12 Write a program RandomPrice that prints a random price between $10.00 and $19.95 every time the program is run.

·· Testing E2.13 Look at the API of the Point class and find out how to construct a Point object. In a PointTester program, construct two points with coordinates (3, 4) and (–3, –4). Find the distance between them, using the distance method. Print the distance, as well as the expected value. (Draw a sketch on graph paper to find the value you will expect.)

· E2.14 Using the Day class of Worked Example 2.1, write a DayTester program that constructs a Day object representing today, adds ten days to it, and then computes the difference between that day and today. Print the difference and the expected value.

·· E2.15 Using the Picture class of Worked Example 2.2, write a HalfSizePicture program that loads a picture and shows it at half the original size, centered in the window.

·· E2.16 Using the Picture class of Worked Example 2.2, write a DoubleSizePicture program that loads a picture, doubles its size, and shows the center of the picture in the window.

·· Graphics E2.17 Write a graphics program that draws two squares, both with the same center. Provide a class TwoSquareViewer and a class TwoSquareComponent.

·· Graphics E2.18 Write a program that draws two solid squares: one in pink and one in purple. Use a standard color for one of them and a custom color for the other. Provide a class TwoSquareViewer and a class TwoSquareComponent.

·· Graphics E2.19 Write a graphics program that draws your name in red, contained inside a blue rectangle. Provide a class NameViewer and a class NameComponent.

PROGRAMMING PROJECTS

•• P2.1 Write a program called `FourRectanglePrinter` that constructs a `Rectangle` object, prints its location by calling `System.out.println(box)`, and then translates and prints it three more times, so that, if the rectangles were drawn, they would form one large rectangle, as shown at right.

Your program will not produce a drawing. It will simply print the locations of the four rectangles.

•• P2.2 Write a `GrowSquarePrinter` program that constructs a `Rectangle` object square representing a square with top-left corner (100, 100) and side length 50, prints its location by calling `System.out.println(square)`, applies the `translate` and `grow` methods, and calls `System.out.println(square)` again. The calls to `translate` and `grow` should modify the square so that it has twice the size and the same top-left corner as the original. If the squares were drawn, they would look like the figure at right.

Your program will not produce a drawing. It will simply print the locations of square before and after calling the mutator methods.

Look up the description of the `grow` method in the API documentation.

••• P2.3 The `intersection` method computes the *intersection* of two rectangles — that is, the rectangle that would be formed by two overlapping rectangles if they were drawn, as shown at right.

You call this method as follows:

```
Rectangle r3 = r1.intersection(r2);
```

Write a program `IntersectionPrinter` that constructs two rectangle objects, prints them as described in Exercise P2.1, and then prints the rectangle object that describes the intersection. Then the program should print the result of the `intersection` method when the rectangles do not overlap. Add a comment to your program that explains how you can tell whether the resulting rectangle is empty.

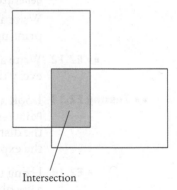

Intersection

••• Graphics P2.4 In this exercise, you will explore a simple way of visualizing a `Rectangle` object. The `setBounds` method of the `JFrame` class moves a frame window to a given rectangle. Complete the following program to visually show the `translate` method of the `Rectangle` class:

```java
import java.awt.Rectangle;
import javax.swing.JFrame;
import javax.swing.JOptionPane;

public class TranslateDemo
{
    public static void main(String[] args)
    {
        // Construct a frame and show it
        JFrame frame = new JFrame();
        frame.setDefaultCloseOperation(JFrame.EXIT_ON_CLOSE);
```

```
                frame.setVisible(true);

                // Your work goes here:
                // Construct a rectangle and set the frame bounds

                JOptionPane.showMessageDialog(frame, "Click OK to continue");

                // Your work goes here:
                // Move the rectangle and set the frame bounds again
        }
}
```

■■■ P2.5 Write a program LotteryPrinter that picks a combination in a lottery. In this lottery, players can choose 6 numbers (possibly repeated) between 1 and 49. Construct an object of the Random class and invoke an appropriate method to generate each number. (In a real lottery, repetitions aren't allowed, but we haven't yet discussed the programming constructs that would be required to deal with that problem.) Your program should print out a sentence such as "Play this combination—it'll make you rich!", followed by a lottery combination.

■■ P2.6 Using the Day class of Worked Example 1, write a program that generates a Day object representing February 28 of this year, and three more such objects that represent February 28 of the next three years. Advance each object by one day, and print each object. Also print the expected values:

```
2012-02-29
Expected: 2012-02-29
2013-03-01
Expected: 2013-03-01
. . .
```

■■■ P2.7 The GregorianCalendar class describes a point in time, as measured by the Gregorian calendar, the standard calendar that is commonly used throughout the world today. You construct a GregorianCalendar object from a year, month, and day of the month, like this:

```
GregorianCalendar cal = new GregorianCalendar(); // Today's date
GregorianCalendar eckertsBirthday = new GregorianCalendar(1919,
        Calendar.APRIL, 9);
```

Use the values Calendar.JANUARY . . . Calendar.DECEMBER to specify the month.

The add method can be used to add a number of days to a GregorianCalendar object:

```
cal.add(Calendar.DAY_OF_MONTH, 10); // Now cal is ten days from today
```

This is a mutator method—it changes the cal object.

The get method can be used to query a given GregorianCalendar object:

```
int dayOfMonth = cal.get(Calendar.DAY_OF_MONTH);
int month = cal.get(Calendar.MONTH);
int year = cal.get(Calendar.YEAR);
int weekday = cal.get(Calendar.DAY_OF_WEEK);
    // 1 is Sunday, 2 is Monday, . . . , 7 is Saturday
```

Your task is to write a program that prints:
- The date and weekday that is 100 days from today.
- The weekday of your birthday.
- The date that is 10,000 days from your birthday.

Use the birthday of a computer scientist if you don't want to reveal your own birthday.

Hint: The GregorianCalendar class is complex, and it is a really good idea to write a few test programs to explore the API before tackling the whole problem. Start with a program that constructs today's date, adds ten days, and prints out the day of the month and the weekday.

■■■ Testing P2.8 Write a program LineDistanceTester that constructs a line joining the points (100, 100) and (200, 200), then constructs points (100, 200), (150, 150), and (250, 50). Print the distance from the line to each of the three points, using the ptSegDist method of the Line2D class. Also print the expected values. (Draw a sketch on graph paper to find what values you expect.)

■■ Graphics P2.9 Repeat Exercise P2.8, but now write a graphical application that shows the line and the points. Draw each point as a tiny circle. Use the drawString method to draw each distance next to the point, using calls

```
g2.drawString("Distance: " + distance, p.getX(), p.getY());
```

■■ Graphics P2.10 Write a graphics program that draws 12 strings, one each for the 12 standard colors (except Color.WHITE), each in its own color. Provide a class ColorNameViewer and a class ColorNameComponent.

■■ Graphics P2.11 Write a program to plot the face at right. Provide a class FaceViewer and a class FaceComponent.

■■ Graphics P2.12 Write a graphical program that draws a traffic light.

■■ Graphics P2.13 Run the following program:

```java
import java.awt.Color;
import javax.swing.JFrame;
import javax.swing.JLabel;

public class FrameViewer
{
    public static void main(String[] args)
    {
        JFrame frame = new JFrame();
        frame.setSize(200, 200);
        JLabel label = new JLabel("Hello, World!");
        label.setOpaque(true);
        label.setBackground(Color.PINK);
        frame.add(label);
        frame.setDefaultCloseOperation(JFrame.EXIT_ON_CLOSE);
        frame.setVisible(true);
    }
}
```

Modify the program as follows:
- Double the frame size.
- Change the greeting to "Hello, *your name*!".
- Change the background color to pale green (see Exercise E2.9).
- For extra credit, add an image of yourself. (*Hint:* Construct an `ImageIcon`.)

ANSWERS TO SELF-CHECK QUESTIONS

1. Objects with the same behavior belong to the same class. A window lets in light while protecting a room from the outside wind and heat or cold. A water heater has completely different behavior. It heats water. They belong to different classes.

2. When one calls a method, one is not concerned with how it does its job. As long as a light bulb illuminates a room, it doesn't matter to the occupant how the photons are produced.

3. There are three errors:
   - You cannot have spaces in variable names.
   - The variable type should be `double` because it holds a fractional value.
   - There is a semicolon missing at the end of the statement.

4. ```
   double unitPrice = 1.95;
   int quantity = 2;
   ```

5. ```
   System.out.print("Total price: ");
   System.out.println(unitPrice * quantity);
   ```

6. `int` and `String`

7. `double`

8. Only the first two are legal identifiers.

9. `String myName = "John Q. Public";`

10. No, the left-hand side of the = operator must be a variable.

11. `greeting = "Hello, Nina!";`

    Note that

    `String greeting = "Hello, Nina!";`

    is not the right answer—that statement declares a new variable.

12. Assignment would occur when one car is replaced by another in the parking space.

13. `river.length()` or `"Mississippi".length()`

14. `System.out.println(greeting.toUpperCase());`

    or

    ```
    System.out.println(
        "Hello, World!".toUpperCase());
    ```

15. It is not legal. The variable `river` has type `String`. The `println` method is not a method of the `String` class.

16. The arguments are the strings "p" and "s".

17. `"Missississi"`

18. 12

19. As `public String toUpperCase()`, with no argument and return type `String`.

20. `new Rectangle(90, 90, 20, 20)`

21. ```
    Rectangle box = new Rectangle(5, 10, 20, 30);
    Rectangle box2 = new Rectangle(25, 10, 20, 30);
    ```

22. 0

23. `new PrintStream("output.txt");`

24. `PrintStream out = new PrintStream("output.txt");`

25. ```
    Before: 5
    After: 30
    ```

26. ```
    Before: 20
    After: 20
    ```

    Moving the rectangle does not affect its width or height. You can change the width and height with the `setSize` method.

27. ```
    HELLO
    hello
    ```

    Note that calling `toUpperCase` doesn't modify the string.

28. An accessor—it doesn't modify the original string but returns a new string with uppercase letters.

29. `box.translate(-5, -10)`, provided the method is called immediately after storing the new rectangle into `box`.

30. `toLowerCase`

31. `"Hello, Space !"` — only the leading and trailing spaces are trimmed.

32. The arguments of the `translate` method tell how far to move the rectangle in the *x*- and *y*-directions. The arguments of the `setLocation` method indicate the new *x*- and *y*-values for the top-left corner.

For example, `box.move(1, 1)` moves the box one pixel down and to the right. `box.setLocation(1, 1)` moves box to the top-left corner of the screen.

33. Add the statement `import java.util.Random;` at the top of your program.

34. In the `java.math` package.

35. x: 30, y: 25

36. Because the `translate` method doesn't modify the shape of the rectangle.

37. Now `greeting` and `greeting2` both refer to the same `String` object.

38. Both variables still refer to the same string, and the string has not been modified. Recall that the `toUpperCase` method constructs a new string that contains uppercase characters, leaving the original string unchanged.

39. Modify the `EmptyFrameViewer` program as follows:

```
frame.setSize(300, 300);
frame.setTitle("Hello, World!");
```

40. Construct two `JFrame` objects, set each of their sizes, and call `setVisible(true)` on each of them.

41. Change line 17 of `RectangleComponent` to

```
Rectangle box = new Rectangle(5, 10, 20, 20);
```

42. Replace the call to `box.translate(15, 25)` with

```
box = new Rectangle(20, 35, 20, 20);
```

43. The compiler complains that `g` doesn't have a draw method.

44. `g2.draw(new Ellipse2D.Double(75, 75, 50, 50));`

45.
```
Line2D.Double segment1
   = new Line2D.Double(0, 0, 10, 30);
g2.draw(segment1);
Line2D.Double segment2
   = new Line2D.Double(10, 30, 20, 0);
g2.draw(segment2);
```

46. `g2.drawString("V", 0, 30);`

47. 0, 0, 255

48. First fill a big red square, then fill a small yellow square inside:

```
g2.setColor(Color.RED);
g2.fill(new Rectangle(0, 0, 200, 200));
g2.setColor(Color.YELLOW);
g2.fill(new Rectangle(50, 50, 100, 100));
```

CHAPTER **3**

IMPLEMENTING CLASSES

CHAPTER GOALS

To become familiar with the process of
implementing classes

To be able to implement and test
simple methods

To understand the purpose and use of constructors

To understand how to access instance variables and
local variables

To be able to write javadoc comments

To implement classes for drawing graphical shapes

CHAPTER CONTENTS

In this chapter, you will learn how to implement your own classes. You will start with a given design that specifies the public interface of the class—that is, the methods through which programmers can manipulate the objects of the class. Then you will learn the steps to completing the class—creating the internal "workings" like the inside of an air conditioner shown here. You need to implement the methods, which entails finding a data representation for the objects and supplying the instructions for each method. You need to document your efforts so that other programmers can understand and use your creation. And you need to provide a tester to validate that your class works correctly.

3.1 Instance Variables and Encapsulation

In Chapter 2, you learned how to use objects from existing classes. In this chapter, you will start implementing your own classes. We begin with a very simple example that shows you how objects store their data, and how methods access the data of an object. Our first example is a class that models a *tally counter*, a mechanical device that is used to count people—for example, to find out how many people attend a concert or board a bus (see Figure 1).

Figure 1 A Tally Counter

3.1.1 Instance Variables

Whenever the operator clicks the button of a tally counter, the counter value advances by one. We model this operation with a click method of a Counter class. A physical counter has a display to show the current value. In our simulation, we use a getValue method to get the current value. For example,

```
Counter tally = new Counter();
tally.click();
tally.click();
int result = tally.getValue(); // Sets result to 2
```

When implementing the Counter class, you need to determine the data that each counter object contains. In this simple example, that is very straightforward. Each counter needs a variable that keeps track of the number of simulated button clicks.

An object stores its data in **instance variables**. An *instance* of a class is an object of the class. Thus, an instance variable is a storage location that is present in each object of the class.

> An object's instance variables store the data required for executing its methods.

You specify instance variables in the class declaration:

```
public class Counter
{
    private int value;
    . . .
}
```

Syntax 3.1   Instance Variable Declaration

Syntax   ```
public class ClassName
{
    private typeName variableName;
    . . .
}
```

```
public class Counter
{
    private int value;
    . . .
}
```

Instance variables should always be private.

Each object of this class has a separate copy of this instance variable.

Type of the variable

An instance variable declaration consists of the following parts:

- An **access specifier** (private)
- The **type** of the instance variable (such as int)
- The name of the instance variable (such as value)

Each object of a class has its own set of instance variables.

Each object of a class has its own set of instance variables. For example, if concert-Counter and boardingCounter are two objects of the Counter class, then each object has its own value variable (see Figure 2). As you will see in Section 3.3, the instance variable value is set to 0 when a Counter object is constructed.

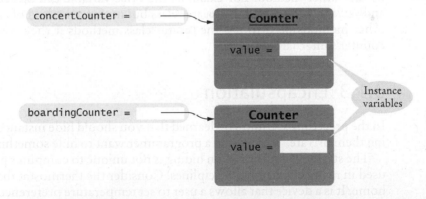

concertCounter =

Counter

value =

boardingCounter =

Counter

value =

Instance variables

Figure 2
Instance Variables

These clocks have common behavior, but each of them has a different state. Similarly, objects of a class can have their instance variables set to different values.
```

3.1.2 The Methods of the Counter Class

In this section, we will look at the implementation of the methods of the Counter class.

The click method advances the counter value by 1. You have seen the method header syntax in Chapter 2. Now, focus on the body of the method inside the braces.

```
public void click()
{
    value = value + 1;
}
```

Note how the click method accesses the instance variable value. *Which* instance variable? The one belonging to the object on which the method is invoked. For example, consider the call

```
concertCounter.click();
```

This call advances the value variable of the concertCounter object.

The getValue method returns the current value:

```
public int getValue()
{
    return value;
}
```

The return statement is a special statement that terminates the method call and returns a result (the **return value**) to the method's caller.

> Private instance variables can only be accessed by methods of the same class.

Instance variables are generally declared with the access specifier private. That specifier means that they can be accessed only by the methods of the *same class*, not by any other method. For example, the value variable can be accessed by the click and getValue methods of the Counter class but not by a method of another class. Those other methods need to use the Counter class methods if they want to manipulate a counter's internal data.

3.1.3 Encapsulation

In the preceding section, you learned that you should hide instance variables by making them private. Why would a programmer want to hide something?

The strategy of information hiding is not unique to computer programming—it is used in many engineering disciplines. Consider the thermostat that you find in your home. It is a device that allows a user to set temperature preferences and that controls the furnace and the air conditioner. If you ask your contractor what is inside the thermostat, you will likely get a shrug.

The thermostat is a *black box*, something that magically does its thing. A contractor would never open the control module—it contains electronic parts that can only be serviced at the factory. In general, engineers use the term "black box" to describe any device whose inner workings are hidden. Note that a black box is not totally mysterious. Its interface with the outside world is well-defined. For example, the contractor understands how the thermostat must be connected with the furnace and air conditioner.

> Encapsulation is the process of hiding implementation details and providing methods for data access.

The process of hiding implementation details while publishing an interface is called **encapsulation**. In Java, the class construct provides encapsulation. The public methods of a class are the interface through which the private implementation is manipulated.

Why do contractors use prefabricated components such as thermostats and furnaces? These "black boxes" greatly simplify the work of the contractor. In ancient times, builders had to know how to construct furnaces from brick and mortar, and how to produce some rudimentary temperature controls. Nowadays, a contractor just makes a trip to the hardware store, without needing to know what goes on inside the components.

A thermostat functions as a "black box" whose inner workings are hidden.

Similarly, a programmer using a class is not burdened by unnecessary detail, as you know from your own experience. In Chapter 2, you used classes for strings, streams, and windows without worrying how these classes are implemented.

Encapsulation also helps with diagnosing errors. A large program may consist of hundreds of classes and thousands of methods, but if there is an error with the internal data of an object, you only need to look at the methods of one class. Finally, encapsulation makes it possible to change the implementation of a class without having to tell the programmers who use the class.

In Chapter 2, you learned to be an object user. You saw how to obtain objects, how to manipulate them, and how to assemble them into a program. In that chapter, you treated objects as black boxes. Your role was roughly analogous to the contractor who installs a new thermostat.

In this chapter, you will move on to implementing classes. In these sections, your role is analogous to the hardware manufacturer who puts together a thermostat from buttons, sensors, and other electronic parts. You will learn the necessary Java programming techniques that enable your objects to carry out the desired behavior.

> **Encapsulation allows a programmer to use a class without having to know its implementation.**

> **Information hiding makes it simpler for the implementor of a class to locate errors and change implementations.**

> **FULL CODE EXAMPLE**
> Go to wiley.com/go/javacode to download a demonstration of the Counter class.

section_1/Counter.java

```java
1  /**
2     This class models a tally counter.
3  */
4  public class Counter
5  {
6     private int value;
7
8     /**
9        Gets the current value of this counter.
10       @return the current value
11    */
12    public int getValue()
13    {
14       return value;
15    }
16
17    /**
18       Advances the value of this counter by 1.
19    */
20    public void click()
21    {
22       value = value + 1;
23    }
24
```

```
25      /**
26          Resets the value of this counter to 0.
27      */
28      public void reset()
29      {
30          value = 0;
31      }
32  }
```

SELF CHECK

1. Supply the body of a method `public void unclick()` that undoes an unwanted button click.
2. Suppose you use a class `Clock` with private instance variables `hours` and `minutes`. How can you access these variables in your program?
3. Consider the `Counter` class. A counter's value starts at 0 and is advanced by the `click` method, so it should never be negative. Suppose you found a negative value variable during testing. Where would you look for the error?
4. In Chapters 1 and 2, you used `System.out` as a black box to cause output to appear on the screen. Who designed and implemented `System.out`?
5. Suppose you are working in a company that produces personal finance software. You are asked to design and implement a class for representing bank accounts. Who will be the users of your class?

Practice It   Now you can try these exercises at the end of the chapter: R3.1, R3.3, E3.1.

3.2 Specifying the Public Interface of a Class

In the following sections, we will discuss the process of specifying the public interface of a class. Imagine that you are a member of a team that works on banking software. A fundamental concept in banking is a *bank account*. Your task is to design a `BankAccount` class that can be used by other programmers to manipulate bank accounts. What methods should you provide? What information should you give the programmers who use this class? You will want to settle these questions before you implement the class.

3.2.1 Specifying Methods

In order to implement a class, you first need to know which methods are required.

You need to know exactly what operations of a bank account need to be implemented. Some operations are essential (such as taking deposits), whereas others are not important (such as giving a gift to a customer who opens a bank account). Deciding which operations are essential is not always an easy task. We will revisit that issue in Chapters 8 and 12. For now, we will assume that a competent designer has decided that the following are considered the essential operations of a bank account:

- Deposit money
- Withdraw money
- Get the current balance

In Java, you call a method when you want to apply an operation to an object. To figure out the exact specification of the method calls, imagine how a programmer would carry out the bank account operations. We'll assume that the variable harrysChecking contains a reference to an object of type BankAccount. We want to support method calls such as the following:

```
harrysChecking.deposit(2240.59);
harrysChecking.withdraw(500);
double currentBalance = harrysChecking.getBalance();
```

The first two methods are mutators. They modify the balance of the bank account and don't return a value. The third method is an accessor. It returns a value that you store in a variable or pass to a method.

From the sample calls, we decide the BankAccount class should declare three methods:

- public void deposit(double amount)
- public void withdraw(double amount)
- public double getBalance()

Recall from Chapter 2 that double denotes the double-precision floating-point type, and void indicates that a method does not return a value.

Here we only give the method *headers*. When you declare a method, you also need to provide the method **body**, which consists of statements that are executed when the method is called.

```
public void deposit(double amount)
{
    method body—implementation filled in later
}
```

We will supply the method bodies in Section 3.3.

Note that the methods have been declared as public, indicating that all other methods in a program can call them. Occasionally, it can be useful to have private methods. They can only be called from other methods of the same class.

Some people like to fill in the bodies so that they compile, like this:

```
public double getBalance()
{
    // TODO: fill in implementation
    return 0;
}
```

That is a good idea if you compose your specification in your development environment—you won't get warnings about incorrect code.

3.2.2 Specifying Constructors

Constructors set the initial data for objects.

As you know from Chapter 2, constructors are used to initialize objects. In Java, a **constructor** is very similar to a method, with two important differences:

- The name of the constructor is always the same as the name of the class (e.g., BankAccount).
- Constructors have no return type (not even void).

We want to be able to construct bank accounts that initially have a zero balance, as well as accounts that have a given initial balance.

For this purpose, we specify two constructors:

- `public BankAccount()`
- `public BankAccount(double initialBalance)`

They are used as follows:

```
BankAccount harrysChecking = new BankAccount();
BankAccount momsSavings = new BankAccount(5000);
```

Don't worry about the fact that there are two constructors with the same name—*all* constructors of a class have the same name, that is, the name of the class. The compiler can tell them apart because they take different arguments. The first constructor takes no arguments at all. Such a constructor is called a **no-argument constructor**. The second constructor takes an argument of type `double`.

> The constructor name is always the same as the class name.

Just like a method, a constructor also has a body—a sequence of statements that is executed when a new object is constructed.

```
public BankAccount()
{
    constructor body—implementation filled in later
}
```

The statements in the constructor body will set the instance variables of the object that is being constructed—see Section 3.3.

When declaring a class, you place all constructor and method declarations inside, like this:

```
public class BankAccount
{
    private instance variables—filled in later

    // Constructors
    public BankAccount()
    {
        implementation—filled in later
    }

    public BankAccount(double initialBalance)
    {
        implementation—filled in later
    }

    // Methods
    public void deposit(double amount)
    {
        implementation—filled in later
    }

    public void withdraw(double amount)
    {
        implementation—filled in later
    }

    public double getBalance()
    {
        implementation—filled in later
    }
}
```

Syntax 3.2   Class Declaration

Syntax   *accessSpecifier* class *ClassName*
{
    instance variables
    constructors
    methods
}

```
public class Counter
{
    private int value;

    public Counter(int initialValue) { value = initialValue; }

    public void click() { value = value + 1; }
    public int getValue() { return value; }
}
```

Public interface

Private implementation

The public constructors and methods of a class form the **public interface** of the class. These are the operations that any programmer can use to create and manipulate BankAccount objects.

3.2.3 Using the Public Interface

Our BankAccount class is simple, but it allows programmers to carry out all of the important operations that commonly occur with bank accounts. For example, consider this program segment, authored by a programmer who uses the BankAccount class. These statements transfer an amount of money from one bank account to another:

```
// Transfer from one account to another
double transferAmount = 500;
momsSavings.withdraw(transferAmount);
harrysChecking.deposit(transferAmount);
```

And here is a program segment that adds interest to a savings account:

```
double interestRate = 5; // 5 percent interest
double interestAmount = momsSavings.getBalance() * interestRate / 100;
momsSavings.deposit(interestAmount);
```

As you can see, programmers can use objects of the BankAccount class to carry out meaningful tasks, without knowing how the BankAccount objects store their data or how the BankAccount methods do their work.

Of course, as implementors of the BankAccount class, we will need to supply the private implementation. We will do so in Section 3.3. First, however, an important step remains: *documenting* the public interface. That is the topic of the next section.

3.2.4 Commenting the Public Interface

When you implement classes and methods, you should get into the habit of thoroughly *commenting* their behaviors. In Java there is a very useful standard form for

documentation comments. If you use this form in your classes, a program called **javadoc** can automatically generate a neat set of HTML pages that describe them. (See Programming Tip 3.1 on page 92 for a description of this utility.)

> Use documentation comments to describe the classes and public methods of your programs.

A documentation comment is placed before the class or method declaration that is being documented. It starts with a /**, a special comment delimiter used by the java-doc utility. Then you describe the method's *purpose*. Then, for each argument, you supply a line that starts with @param, followed by the name of the variable that holds the argument (which is called a **parameter variable**). Supply a short explanation for each argument after the variable name. Finally, you supply a line that starts with @return, describing the return value. You omit the @param tag for methods that have no arguments, and you omit the @return tag for methods whose return type is void.

The javadoc utility copies the *first* sentence of each comment to a summary table in the HTML documentation. Therefore, it is best to write that first sentence with some care. It should start with an uppercase letter and end with a period. It does not have to be a grammatically complete sentence, but it should be meaningful when it is pulled out of the comment and displayed in a summary.

Here are two typical examples:

```
/**
    Withdraws money from the bank account.
    @param amount the amount to withdraw
*/
public void withdraw(double amount)
{
    implementation—filled in later
}
```

```
/**
    Gets the current balance of the bank account.
    @return the current balance
*/
public double getBalance()
{
    implementation—filled in later
}
```

The comments you have just seen explain individual *methods*. Supply a brief comment for each *class*, too, explaining its purpose. Place the documentation comment above the class declaration:

```
/**
    A bank account has a balance that can be changed by
    deposits and withdrawals.
*/
public class BankAccount
{
    . . .
}
```

Your first reaction may well be "Whoa! Am I supposed to write all this stuff?" Sometimes, documentation comments seem pretty repetitive, but in most cases, they are informative. Even with seemingly repetitive comments, you should take the time to write them.

It is always a good idea to write the method comment *first*, before writing the code in the method body. This is an excellent test to see that you firmly understand what you need to program. If you can't explain what a class or method does, you aren't ready to implement it.

What about very simple methods? You can easily spend more time pondering whether a comment is too trivial to write than it takes to write it. In practical programming, very simple methods are rare. It is harmless to have a trivial method overcommented, whereas a complicated method without any comment can cause real grief to future maintenance programmers. According to the standard Java documentation style, *every* class, *every* method, *every* parameter variable, and *every* return value should have a comment.

> Provide documentation comments for every class, every method, every parameter variable, and every return value.

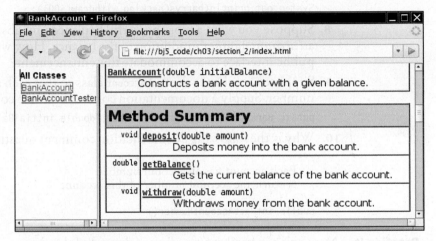

Figure 3   A Method Summary Generated by `javadoc`

> **FULL CODE EXAMPLE**
>
> Go to wiley.com/go/javacode to download the BankAccount class with documentation but without implementation.

The `javadoc` utility formats your comments into a neat set of documents that you can view in a web browser. It makes good use of the seemingly repetitive phrases. The first sentence of the comment is used for a *summary table* of all methods of your class (see Figure 3). The `@param` and `@return` comments are neatly formatted in the detail description of each method (see Figure 4). If you omit any of the comments, then javadoc generates documents that look strangely empty.

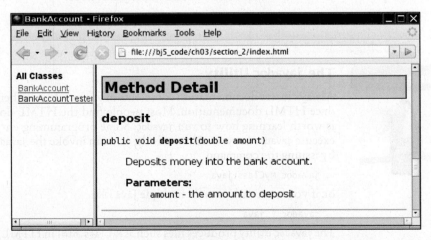

Figure 4   Method Detail Generated by `javadoc`

This documentation format should look familiar. The programmers who implement the Java library use javadoc themselves. They too document every class, every method, every parameter variable, and every return value, and then use javadoc to extract the documentation in HTML format.

SELF CHECK

6. How can you use the methods of the public interface to *empty* the harrysChecking bank account?

7. What is wrong with this sequence of statements?

```
BankAccount harrysChecking = new BankAccount(10000);
System.out.println(harrysChecking.withdraw(500));
```

8. Suppose you want a more powerful bank account abstraction that keeps track of an *account number* in addition to the balance. How would you change the public interface to accommodate this enhancement?

9. Suppose we enhance the BankAccount class so that each account has an account number. Supply a documentation comment for the constructor

```
public BankAccount(int accountNumber, double initialBalance)
```

10. Why is the following documentation comment questionable?

```
/**
    Each account has an account number.
    @return the account number of this account
*/
public int getAccountNumber()
```

Practice It   Now you can try these exercises at the end of the chapter: R3.7, R3.8, R3.9.

Common Error 3.1

Declaring a Constructor as void

Do not use the void reserved word when you declare a constructor:

```
public void BankAccount()   // Error—don't use void!
```

This would declare a method with return type void and *not* a constructor. Unfortunately, the Java compiler does not consider this a syntax error.

Programming Tip 3.1

The javadoc Utility

Always insert documentation comments in your code, whether or not you use javadoc to produce HTML documentation. Most people find the HTML documentation convenient, so it is worth learning how to run javadoc. Some programming environments (such as BlueJ) can execute javadoc for you. Alternatively, you can invoke the javadoc utility from a shell window, by issuing the command

```
javadoc MyClass.java
```

or, if you want to document multiple Java files,

```
javadoc *.java
```

The javadoc utility produces files such as MyClass.html in HTML format, which you can inspect in a browser. If you know HTML (see Appendix H), you can embed HTML tags into the comments to specify fonts or add images. Perhaps most importantly, javadoc automatically provides *hyperlinks* to other classes and methods.

You can run javadoc before implementing any methods. Just leave all the method bodies empty. Don't run the compiler—it would complain about missing return values. Simply run javadoc on your file to generate the documentation for the public interface that you are about to implement.

The javadoc tool is wonderful because it does one thing right: It allows you to put the documentation *together with your code*. That way, when you update your programs, you can see right away which documentation needs to be updated. Hopefully, you will update it right then and there. Afterward, run javadoc again and get updated information that is timely and nicely formatted.

3.3 Providing the Class Implementation

Now that you understand the specification of the public interface of the BankAccount class, let's provide the implementation.

3.3.1 Providing Instance Variables

The private implementation of a class consists of instance variables, and the bodies of constructors and methods.

First, we need to determine the data that each bank account object contains. In the case of our simple bank account class, each object needs to store a single value, the current balance. (A more complex bank account class might store additional data—perhaps an account number, the interest rate paid, the date for mailing out the next statement, and so on.)

```
public class BankAccount
{
    private double balance;
    // Methods and constructors below
    . . .
}
```

In general, it can be challenging to find a good set of instance variables. Ask yourself what an object needs to remember so that it can carry out any of its methods.

Like a wilderness explorer who needs to carry all items that may be needed, an object needs to store the data required for its method calls.

3.3.2 Providing Constructors

A **constructor** has a simple job: to initialize the instance variables of an object.

Recall that we designed the BankAccount class to have two constructors. The first constructor simply sets the balance to zero:

```
public BankAccount()
{
    balance = 0;
}
```

The second constructor sets the balance to the value supplied as the construction argument:

```
public BankAccount(double initialBalance)
{
    balance = initialBalance;
}
```

To see how these constructors work, let us trace the statement

```
BankAccount harrysChecking = new BankAccount(1000);
```

one step at a time.

Here are the steps that are carried out when the statement executes (see Figure 5):

- Create a new object of type BankAccount. **1**
- Call the second constructor (because an argument is supplied in the constructor call).
- Set the parameter variable initialBalance to 1000. **2**
- Set the balance instance variable of the newly created object to initialBalance. **3**
- Return an object reference, that is, the memory location of the object, as the value of the new expression.
- Store that object reference in the harrysChecking variable. **4**

In general, when you implement constructors, be sure that each constructor initializes all instance variables, and that you make use of all parameter variables (see Common Error 3.2 on page 98).

A constructor is like a set of assembly instructions for an object.

Figure 5
How a Constructor Works

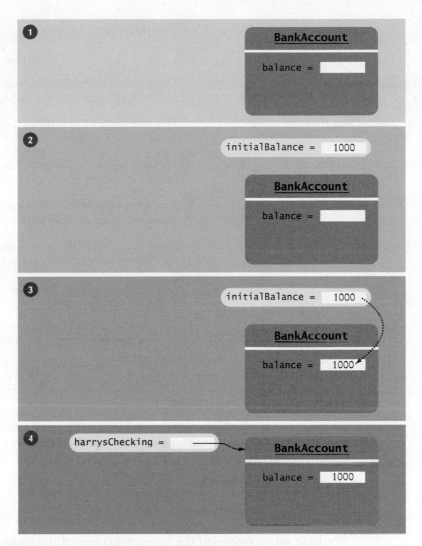

3.3.3 Providing Methods

In this section, we finish implementing the methods of the BankAccount class.

When you implement a method, ask yourself whether it is an accessor or mutator method. A mutator method needs to update the instance variables in some way. An accessor method retrieves or computes a result.

Here is the deposit method. It is a mutator method, updating the balance:

```java
public void deposit(double amount)
{
    balance = balance + amount;
}
```

The withdraw method is very similar to the deposit method:

```java
public void withdraw(double amount)
{
    balance = balance - amount;
}
```

Table 1   Implementing Classes

Example	Comments
`public class BankAccount { . . . }`	This is the start of a class declaration. Instance variables, methods, and constructors are placed inside the braces.
`private double balance;`	This is an instance variable of type `double`. Instance variables should be declared as `private`.
`public double getBalance() { . . . }`	This is a method declaration. The body of the method must be placed inside the braces.
`. . . { return balance; }`	This is the body of the `getBalance` method. The `return` statement returns a value to the caller of the method.
`public void deposit(double amount) { . . . }`	This is a method with a parameter variable (`amount`). Because the method is declared as `void`, it has no return value.
`. . . { balance = balance + amount; }`	This is the body of the `deposit` method. It does not have a `return` statement.
`public BankAccount() { . . . }`	This is a constructor declaration. A constructor has the same name as the class and no return type.
`. . . { balance = 0; }`	This is the body of the constructor. A constructor should initialize the instance variables.

There is one method left, `getBalance`. Unlike the `deposit` and `withdraw` methods, which modify the instance variable of the object on which they are invoked, the `getBalance` method returns a value:

```java
public double getBalance()
{
    return balance;
}
```

We have now completed the implementation of the `BankAccount` class—see the code listing below. There is only one step remaining: testing that the class works correctly. That is the topic of the next section.

section_3/BankAccount.java

```java
1  /**
2      A bank account has a balance that can be changed by
3      deposits and withdrawals.
4  */
5  public class BankAccount
6  {
7      private double balance;
8
9      /**
10         Constructs a bank account with a zero balance.
11     */
12     public BankAccount()
13     {
14         balance = 0;
15     }
```

```
16
17      /**
18         Constructs a bank account with a given balance.
19         @param initialBalance the initial balance
20      */
21      public BankAccount(double initialBalance)
22      {
23         balance = initialBalance;
24      }
25
26      /**
27         Deposits money into the bank account.
28         @param amount the amount to deposit
29      */
30      public void deposit(double amount)
31      {
32         balance = balance + amount;
33      }
34
35      /**
36         Withdraws money from the bank account.
37         @param amount the amount to withdraw
38      */
39      public void withdraw(double amount)
40      {
41         balance = balance - amount;
42      }
43
44      /**
45         Gets the current balance of the bank account.
46         @return the current balance
47      */
48      public double getBalance()
49      {
50         return balance;
51      }
52   }
```

SELF CHECK

11. Suppose we modify the BankAccount class so that each bank account has an account number. How does this change affect the instance variables?

12. Why does the following code not succeed in robbing mom's bank account?

```
public class BankRobber
{
    public static void main(String[] args)
    {
        BankAccount momsSavings = new BankAccount(1000);
        momsSavings.balance = 0;
    }
}
```

13. The Rectangle class has four instance variables: x, y, width, and height. Give a possible implementation of the getWidth method.

14. Give a possible implementation of the translate method of the Rectangle class.

Practice It   Now you can try these exercises at the end of the chapter: R3.4, R3.10, E3.4.

Common Error 3.2

Ignoring Parameter Variables

A surprisingly common beginner's error is to ignore parameter variables of methods or constructors. This usually happens when an assignment gives an example with specific values. For example, suppose you are asked to provide a class Letter with a recipient and a sender, and you are given a sample letter like this:

```
Dear John:

I am sorry we must part.
I wish you all the best.

Sincerely,

Mary
```

Now look at this incorrect attempt:

```
public class Letter
{
   private String recipient;
   private String sender;

   public Letter(String aRecipient, String aSender)
   {
      recipient = "John"; // Error—should use parameter variable
      sender = "Mary"; // Same error
   }
   . . .
}
```

The constructor ignores the names of the recipient and sender arguments that were provided to the constructor. If a user constructs a

```
new Letter("John", "Yoko")
```

the sender is still set to "Mary", which is bound to be embarrassing.

The constructor should use the parameter variables, like this:

```
public Letter(String aRecipient, String aSender)
{
   recipient = aRecipient;
   sender = aSender;
}
```

HOW TO 3.1

Implementing a Class

This "How To" section tells you how you implement a class from a given specification.

Problem Statement   Implement a class that models a self-service cash register. The customer scans the price tags and deposits money in the machine. The machine dispenses the change.

Step 1   Find out which methods you are asked to supply.

In a simulation, you won't have to provide every feature that occurs in the real world—there are too many. In the cash register example, we don't deal with sales tax or credit card payments. The assignment tells you *which aspects* of the self-service cash register your class should simulate. Make a list of them:

- Process the price of each purchased item.
- Receive payment.
- Calculate the amount of change due to the customer.

Step 2   Specify the public interface.

Turn the list in Step 1 into a set of methods, with specific types for the parameter variables and the return values. Many programmers find this step simpler if they write out method calls that are applied to a sample object, like this:

```
CashRegister register = new CashRegister();
register.recordPurchase(29.95);
register.recordPurchase(9.95);
register.receivePayment(50);
double change = register.giveChange();
```

Now we have a specific list of methods:

- `public void recordPurchase(double amount)`
- `public void receivePayment(double amount)`
- `public double giveChange()`

To complete the public interface, you need to specify the constructors. Ask yourself what information you need in order to construct an object of your class. Sometimes you will want two constructors: one that sets all instance variables to a default and one that sets them to user-supplied values.

In the case of the cash register example, we can get by with a single constructor that creates an empty register. A more realistic cash register might start out with some coins and bills so that we can give exact change, but that is well beyond the scope of our assignment.

Thus, we add a single constructor:

- `public CashRegister()`

Step 3   Document the public interface.

Here is the documentation, with comments, that describes the class and its methods:

```java
/**
    A cash register totals up sales and computes change due.
*/
public class CashRegister
{
    /**
        Constructs a cash register with no money in it.
    */
    public CashRegister()
    {
    }

    /**
        Records the sale of an item.
        @param amount the price of the item
    */
    public void recordPurchase(double amount)
    {
```

```
    }

    /**
        Processes a payment received from the customer.
        @param amount the amount of the payment
    */
    public void receivePayment(double amount)
    {
    }

    /**
        Computes the change due and resets the machine for the next customer.
        @return the change due to the customer
    */
    public double giveChange()
    {
    }
}
```

Step 4   Determine instance variables.

Ask yourself what information an object needs to store to do its job. Remember, the methods can be called in any order. The object needs to have enough internal memory to be able to process every method using just its instance variables and the parameter variables. Go through each method, perhaps starting with a simple one or an interesting one, and ask yourself what you need to carry out the method's task. Make instance variables to store the information that the method needs.

Just as importantly, don't introduce unnecessary instance variables (see Common Error 3.3). If a value can be computed from other instance variables, it is generally better to compute it on demand than to store it.

In the cash register example, you need to keep track of the total purchase amount and the payment. You can compute the change due from these two amounts.

```
public class CashRegister
{
    private double purchase;
    private double payment;
    . . .
}
```

Step 5   Implement constructors and methods.

Implement the constructors and methods in your class, one at a time, starting with the easiest ones. Here is the implementation of the recordPurchase method:

```
public void recordPurchase(double amount)
{
    purchase = purchase + amount;
}
```

The receivePayment method looks almost the same,

```
public void receivePayment(double amount)
{
    payment = payment + amount;
}
```

but why does the method add the amount, instead of simply setting payment = amount? A customer might provide two separate payments, such as two $10 bills, and the machine must process them both. Remember, methods can be called more than once, and they can be called in any order.

Finally, here is the giveChange method. This method is a bit more sophisticated—it computes the change due, and it also resets the cash register for the next sale.

```java
public double giveChange()
{
    double change = payment - purchase;
    purchase = 0;
    payment = 0;
    return change;
}
```

If you find that you have trouble with the implementation, you may need to rethink your choice of instance variables. It is common for a beginner to start out with a set of instance variables that cannot accurately reflect the state of an object. Don't hesitate to go back and add or modify instance variables.

You can find the complete implementation in the how_to_1 directory of the book's companion code.

Step 6 Test your class.

Write a short tester program and execute it. The tester program should carry out the method calls that you found in Step 2.

```java
public class CashRegisterTester
{
    public static void main(String[] args)
    {
        CashRegister register = new CashRegister();

        register.recordPurchase(29.50);
        register.recordPurchase(9.25);
        register.receivePayment(50);

        double change = register.giveChange();

        System.out.println(change);
        System.out.println("Expected: 11.25");
    }
}
```

The output of this test program is:

```
11.25
Expected: 11.25
```

WORKED EXAMPLE 3.1   **Making a Simple Menu**

Learn how to implement a class that constructs simple text-based menus. Go to wiley.com/go/javaexamples and download Worked Example 3.1.

3.4 Unit Testing

In the preceding section, we completed the implementation of the BankAccount class. What can you do with it? Of course, you can compile the file BankAccount.java. However, you can't *execute* the resulting BankAccount.class file. It doesn't contain a main method. That is normal—most classes don't contain a main method.

> A unit test verifies that a class works correctly in isolation, outside a complete program.

In the long run, your class may become a part of a larger program that interacts with users, stores data in files, and so on. However, before integrating a class into a program, it is always a good idea to test it in isolation. Testing in isolation, outside a complete program, is called **unit testing**.

An engineer tests a part in isolation. This is an example of unit testing.

To test your class, you have two choices. Some interactive development environments have commands for constructing objects and invoking methods (see Special Topic 2.1). Then you can test a class simply by constructing an object, calling methods, and verifying that you get the expected return values. Figure 6 shows the result of calling the get-Balance method on a BankAccount object in BlueJ.

> To test a class, use an environment for interactive testing, or write a tester class to execute test instructions.

Alternatively, you can write a *tester class*. A tester class is a class with a main method that contains statements to run methods of another class. As discussed in Section 2.7, a tester class typically carries out the following steps:

1. Construct one or more objects of the class that is being tested.
2. Invoke one or more methods.
3. Print out one or more results.
4. Print the expected results.

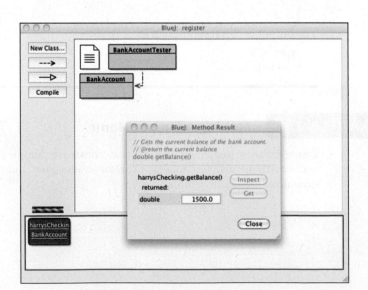

Figure 6 The Return Value of the getBalance Method in BlueJ

The MoveTester class in Section 2.7 is a good example of a tester class. That class runs methods of the Rectangle class—a class in the Java library.

Following is a class to run methods of the BankAccount class. The main method constructs an object of type BankAccount, invokes the deposit and withdraw methods, and then displays the remaining balance on the console.

We also print the value that we expect to see. In our sample program, we deposit $2,000 and withdraw $500. We therefore expect a balance of $1,500.

section_4/BankAccountTester.java

```
1   /**
2         A class to test the BankAccount class.
3   */
4   public class BankAccountTester
5   {
6      /**
7            Tests the methods of the BankAccount class.
8            @param args not used
9      */
10     public static void main(String[] args)
11     {
12        BankAccount harrysChecking = new BankAccount();
13        harrysChecking.deposit(2000);
14        harrysChecking.withdraw(500);
15        System.out.println(harrysChecking.getBalance());
16        System.out.println("Expected: 1500");
17     }
18  }
```

Program Run

```
1500
Expected: 1500
```

To produce a program, you need to combine the BankAccount and the BankAccountTester classes. The details for building the program depend on your compiler and development environment. In most environments, you need to carry out these steps:

1. Make a new subfolder for your program.
2. Make two files, one for each class.
3. Compile both files.
4. Run the test program.

Many students are surprised that such a simple program contains two classes. However, this is normal. The two classes have entirely different purposes. The BankAccount class describes objects that compute bank balances. The BankAccountTester class runs a test that puts a BankAccount object through its paces.

SELF CHECK

15. When you run the BankAccountTester program, how many objects of class Bank-Account are constructed? How many objects of type BankAccountTester?

16. Why is the BankAccountTester class unnecessary in development environments that allow interactive testing, such as BlueJ?

Practice It   Now you can try these exercises at the end of the chapter: E3.3, E3.10.

Computing & Society 3.1 Electronic Voting Machines

In the 2000 presidential elections in the United States, votes were tallied by a variety of machines. Some machines processed cardboard ballots into which voters punched holes to indicate their choices (see below). When voters were not careful, remains of paper—the now infamous "chads"—were partially stuck in the punch cards, causing votes to be miscounted. A manual recount was necessary, but it was not carried out everywhere due to time constraints and procedural wrangling. The election was very close, and there remain doubts in the minds of many people whether the election outcome would have been different if the voting machines had accurately counted the intent of the voters.

Punch Card Ballot

Subsequently, voting machine manufacturers have argued that electronic voting machines would avoid the problems caused by punch cards or optically scanned forms. In an electronic voting machine, voters indicate their preferences by pressing buttons or touching icons on a computer screen. Typically, each voter is presented with a summary screen for review before casting the ballot. The process is very similar to using a bank's automated teller machine.

It seems plausible that these machines make it more likely that a vote is counted in the same way that the voter intends. However, there has been significant controversy surrounding some types of electronic voting machines. If a machine simply records the votes and prints out the totals after the election has been completed, then how do you know that the machine worked correctly? Inside the machine is a computer that executes a program, and, as you may know from your own experience, programs can have bugs.

In fact, some electronic voting machines do have bugs. There have been isolated cases where machines reported tallies that were impossible. When a machine reports far more or far fewer votes than voters, then it is clear that it malfunctioned. Unfortunately, it is then impossible to find out the actual votes. Over time, one would expect these bugs to be fixed in the software. More insidiously, if the results are plausible, nobody may ever investigate.

Many computer scientists have spoken out on this issue and confirmed that it is impossible, with today's technology, to tell that software is error free and has not been tampered with. Many of them recommend that electronic voting machines should employ a *voter verifiable audit trail*. (A good source of information is http://verifiedvoting.org.) Typically, a voter-verifiable machine prints out a ballot. Each voter has a chance to review the printout, and then deposits it in an old-fashioned ballot box. If there is a problem with the electronic equipment, the printouts can be scanned or counted by hand.

As this book is written, this concept is strongly resisted both by manufacturers of electronic voting machines and by their customers, the cities and counties that run elections. Manufacturers are reluctant to increase the cost of the machines because they may not be able to pass the cost increase on to their customers, who tend to have tight budgets. Election officials fear problems with malfunctioning printers, and some of them have publicly stated that they actually prefer equipment that eliminates bothersome recounts.

What do you think? You probably use an automated bank teller machine to get cash from your bank account. Do you review the paper record that the machine issues? Do you check your bank statement? Even if you don't, do you put your faith in other people who double-check their balances, so that the bank won't get away with widespread cheating?

Is the integrity of banking equipment more important or less important than that of voting machines? Won't every voting process have some room for error and fraud anyway? Is the added cost for equipment, paper, and staff time reasonable to combat a potentially slight risk of malfunction and fraud? Computer scientists cannot answer these questions—an informed society must make these tradeoffs. But, like all professionals, they have an obligation to speak out and give accurate testimony about the capabilities and limitations of computing equipment.

Touch Screen Voting Machine

3.5 Problem Solving: Tracing Objects

Researchers have studied why some students have an easier time learning how to program than others. One important skill of successful programmers is the ability to simulate the actions of a program with pencil and paper. In this section, you will see how to develop this skill by tracing method calls on objects.

Write the methods on the front of a card and the instance variables on the back.

Use an index card or a sticky note for each object. On the front, write the methods that the object can execute. On the back, make a table for the values of the instance variables.

Here is a card for a CashRegister object:

```
CashRegister reg1

recordPurchase
receivePayment
giveChange
```
front

reg1.purchase	reg1.payment

back

In a small way, this gives you a feel for encapsulation. An object is manipulated through its public interface (on the front of the card), and the instance variables are hidden in the back.

When an object is constructed, fill in the initial values of the instance variables:

reg1.purchase	reg1.payment
0	0

Update the values of the instance variables when a mutator method is called.

Whenever a mutator method is executed, cross out the old values and write the new ones below. Here is what happens after a call to the recordPurchase method:

reg1.purchase	reg1.payment
~~0~~ 19.95	0

If you have more than one object in your program, you will have multiple cards, one for each object:

reg1.purchase	reg1.payment
~~0~~ 19.95	~~0~~ 19.95

reg2.purchase	reg2.payment
~~0~~ ~~20.50~~ 9.25	~~0~~ 50.00

These diagrams are also useful when you design a class. Suppose you are asked to enhance the CashRegister class to compute the sales tax. Add methods recordTaxablePurchase and getSalesTax to the front of the card. Now turn the card over, look over the instance variables, and ask yourself whether the object has sufficient information to compute the answer. Remember that each object is an autonomous unit. Any value that can be used in a computation must be

- An instance variable.
- A method argument.
- A static variable (uncommon; see Section 8.4).

To compute the sales tax, we need to know the tax rate and the total of the taxable items. (Food items are usually not subject to sales tax.) We don't have that information available. Let us introduce additional instance variables for the tax rate and the taxable total. The tax rate can be set in the constructor (assuming it stays fixed for the lifetime of the object). When adding an item, we need to be told whether the item is taxable. If so, we add its price to the taxable total.

For example, consider the following statements.

```
CashRegister reg3(7.5); // 7.5 percent sales tax
reg3.recordPurchase(3.95); // Not taxable
reg3.recordTaxablePurchase(19.95); // Taxable
```

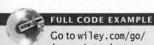

FULL CODE EXAMPLE

Go to wiley.com/go/javacode to download an enhanced CashRegister class that computes the sales tax.

When you record the effect on a card, it looks like this:

reg3.purchase	reg3.taxablePurchase	reg3.payment	reg3.taxRate
~~0~~ 3.95	~~0~~ 19.95	0	7.5

With this information, we can compute the tax. It is **taxablePurchase x taxRate / 100**. Tracing the object helped us understand the need for additional instance variables.

SELF CHECK

17. Consider a Car class that simulates fuel consumption in a car. We will assume a fixed efficiency (in miles per gallon) that is supplied in the constructor. There are methods for adding gas, driving a given distance, and checking the amount of gas left in the tank. Make a card for a Car object, choosing suitable instance variables and showing their values after the object was constructed.

18. Trace the following method calls:

```
Car myCar(25);
myCar.addGas(20);
myCar.drive(100);
myCar.drive(200);
myCar.addGas(5);
```

19. Suppose you are asked to simulate the odometer of the car, by adding a method getMilesDriven. Add an instance variable to the object's card that is suitable for computing this method's result.

20. Trace the methods of Self Check 18, updating the instance variable that you added in Self Check 19.

Practice It Now you can try these exercises at the end of the chapter: R3.18, R3.19, R3.20.

3.6 Local Variables

In this section, we discuss the behavior of *local* variables. A **local variable** is a variable that is declared in the body of a method. For example, the giveChange method in How To 3.1 declares a local variable change:

> Local variables are declared in the body of a method.

```
public double giveChange()
{
    double change = payment - purchase;
    purchase = 0;
    payment = 0;
    return change;
}
```

ANIMATION
Lifetime of Variables

Parameter variables are similar to local variables, but they are declared in method headers. For example, the following method declares a parameter variable amount:

```
public void receivePayment(double amount)
```

> When a method exits, its local variables are removed.

Local and parameter variables belong to methods. When a method runs, its local and parameter variables come to life. When the method exits, they are removed immediately. For example, if you call register.giveChange(), then a variable change is created. When the method exits, that variable is removed.

In contrast, instance variables belong to objects, not methods. When an object is constructed, its instance variables are created. The instance variables stay alive until no method uses the object any longer. (The Java virtual machine contains an agent called a **garbage collector** that periodically reclaims objects when they are no longer used.)

> Instance variables are initialized to a default value, but you must initialize local variables.

An important difference between instance variables and local variables is initialization. You must **initialize** all local variables. If you don't initialize a local variable, the compiler complains when you try to use it. (Note that parameter variables are initialized when the method is called.)

FULL CODE EXAMPLE

Go to wiley.com/go/javacode to download a demonstration of local variables.

Instance variables are initialized with a default value before a constructor is invoked. Instance variables that are numbers are initialized to 0. Object references are set to a special value called null. If an object reference is null, then it refers to no object at all. We will discuss the null value in greater detail in Section 5.2.5.

21. What do local variables and parameter variables have in common? In which essential aspect do they differ?

22. Why was it necessary to introduce the local variable change in the giveChange method? That is, why didn't the method simply end with the statement

```
return payment - purchase;
```

23. Consider a CashRegister object reg1 whose payment instance variable has the value 20 and whose purchase instance variable has the value 19.5. Trace the call reg1.giveChange(). Include the local variable change. Draw an X in its column when the variable ceases to exist.

Practice It Now you can try these exercises at the end of the chapter: R3.14, R3.15.

Common Error 3.3

Duplicating Instance Variables in Local Variables

Beginning programmers commonly add types to assignment statements, thereby changing them into local variable declarations. For example,

```
public double giveChange()
{
    double change = payment - purchase;
    double purchase = 0; // ERROR! This declares a local variable.
    double payment = 0;  // ERROR! The instance variable is not updated.
    return change;
}
```

Another common error is to declare a parameter variable with the same name as an instance variable. For example, consider this BankAccount constructor:

```
public BankAccount(double balance)
{
    balance = balance; // ERROR! Does not set the instance variable
}
```

This constructor simply sets the parameter variable to itself, leaving it unchanged. A simple remedy is to come up with a different name for the parameter variable:

```
public BankAccount(double initialBalance)
{
    balance = initialBalance; // OK
}
```

Common Error 3.4

Providing Unnecessary Instance Variables

A common beginner's mistake is to use instance variables when local variables would be more appropriate. For example, consider the change variable of the giveChange method. It is not needed anywhere else—that's why it is local to the method. But what if it had been declared as an instance variable?

```
public class CashRegister
{
    private double purchase;
    private double payment;
    private double change; // Not appropriate
```

```
public double giveChange()
{
    change = payment - purchase;
    purchase = 0;
    payment = 0;
    return change;
}
. . .
}
```

This class will work, but there is a hidden danger. Other methods can read and write to the change instance variable, which can be a source of confusion.

Use instance variables for values that an object needs to remember between method calls. Use local variables for values that don't need to be retained when a method has completed.

Common Error 3.5

Forgetting to Initialize Object References in a Constructor

Just as it is a common error to forget to initialize a local variable, it is easy to forget about instance variables. Every constructor needs to ensure that all instance variables are set to appropriate values.

If you do not initialize an instance variable, the Java compiler will initialize it for you. Numbers are initialized with 0, but object references—such as string variables—are set to the null reference.

Of course, 0 is often a convenient default for numbers. However, null is hardly ever a convenient default for objects. Consider this "lazy" constructor for a modified version of the BankAccount class:

```
public class BankAccount
{
    private double balance;
    private String owner;
    . . .
    public BankAccount(double initialBalance)
    {
        balance = initialBalance;
    }
}
```

Then balance is initialized, but the owner variable is set to a null reference. This can be a problem—it is illegal to call methods on the null reference.

To avoid this problem, it is a good idea to initialize every instance variable:

```
public BankAccount(double initialBalance)
{
    balance = initialBalance;
    owner = "None";
}
```

3.7 The this Reference

When you call a method, you pass two kinds of inputs to the method:

• The object on which you invoke the method
• The method arguments

For example, when you call

```
momsSavings.deposit(500);
```

the deposit method needs to know the account object (momsSavings) as well as the amount that is being deposited (500).

When you implement the method, you provide a parameter variable for each argument. But you don't need to provide a parameter variable for the object on which the method is being invoked. That object is called the **implicit parameter**. All other parameter variables (such as the amount to be deposited in our example) are called **explicit parameters**.

Look again at the code of the deposit method:

```
public void deposit(double amount)
{
    balance = balance + amount;
}
```

Here, amount is an explicit parameter. You don't see the implicit parameter—that is why it is called "implicit". But consider what balance means exactly. After all, our program may have multiple BankAccount objects, and *each of them* has its own balance.

Because we are depositing the money into momsSavings, balance must mean momsSavings.balance. In general, when you refer to an instance variable inside a method, it means the instance variable of the implicit parameter.

In any method, you can access the implicit parameter—the object on which the method is called—with the reserved word this. For example, in the preceding method invocation, this refers to the same object as momsSavings (see Figure 7).

The statement

```
balance = balance + amount;
```

actually means

```
this.balance = this.balance + amount;
```

When you refer to an instance variable in a method, the compiler automatically applies it to the this reference. Some programmers actually prefer to manually insert the this reference before every instance variable because they find it makes the code clearer. Here is an example:

```
public BankAccount(double initialBalance)
{
    this.balance = initialBalance;
}
```

You may want to try it out and see if you like that style.

> Use of an instance variable name in a method denotes the instance variable of the implicit parameter.

> The this reference denotes the implicit parameter.

Figure 7　The Implicit Parameter of a Method Call

The this reference can also be used to distinguish between instance variables and local or parameter variables. Consider the constructor

```java
public BankAccount(double balance)
{
    this.balance = balance;
}
```

The expression this.balance clearly refers to the balance instance variable. However, the expression balance by itself seems ambiguous. It could denote either the parameter variable or the instance variable. The Java language specifies that in this situation the local variable wins out. It "shadows" the instance variable. Therefore,

```java
this.balance = balance;
```

means: "Set the instance variable balance to the parameter variable balance".

There is another situation in which it is important to understand implicit parameters. Consider the following modification to the BankAccount class. We add a method to apply the monthly account fee:

```java
public class BankAccount
{
    . . .
    public void monthlyFee()
    {
        withdraw(10); // Withdraw $10 from this account
    }
}
```

> A local variable shadows an instance variable with the same name. You can access the instance variable name through the this reference.

That means to withdraw from the *same* bank account object that is carrying out the monthlyFee operation. In other words, the implicit parameter of the withdraw method is the (invisible) implicit parameter of the monthlyFee method.

If you find it confusing to have an invisible parameter, you can use the this reference to make the method easier to read:

```java
public class BankAccount
{
    . . .
    public void monthlyFee()
    {
        this.withdraw(10); // Withdraw $10 from this account
    }
}
```

> A method call without an implicit parameter is applied to the same object.

You have now seen how to use objects and implement classes, and you have learned some important technical details about variables and method parameters. The remainder of this chapter continues the optional graphics track. In the next chapter, you will learn more about the most fundamental data types of the Java language.

FULL CODE EXAMPLE
Go to wiley.com/go/javacode to download a program that demonstrates the this reference.

SELF CHECK

24. How many implicit and explicit parameters does the withdraw method of the BankAccount class have, and what are their names and types?
25. In the deposit method, what is the meaning of this.amount? Or, if the expression has no meaning, why not?
26. How many implicit and explicit parameters does the main method of the BankAccountTester class have, and what are they called?

Practice It   Now you can try these exercises at the end of the chapter: R3.11, R3.12.

Special Topic 3.1

Calling One Constructor from Another

Consider the BankAccount class. It has two constructors: a no-argument constructor to initialize the balance with zero, and another constructor to supply an initial balance. Rather than explicitly setting the balance to zero, one constructor can call another constructor of the same class instead. There is a shorthand notation to achieve this result:

```
public class BankAccount
{
   public BankAccount(double initialBalance)
   {
      balance = initialBalance;
   }

   public BankAccount()
   {
      this(0);
   }
   . . .
}
```

The command this(0); means "Call another constructor of this class and supply the value 0". Such a call to another constructor can occur only as the *first line in a constructor*.

This syntax is a minor convenience. We will not use it in this book. Actually, the use of the reserved word this is a little confusing. Normally, this denotes a reference to the implicit parameter, but if this is followed by parentheses, it denotes a call to another constructor of the same class.

3.8 Shape Classes

In this section, we continue the optional graphics track by discussing how to organize complex drawings in a more object-oriented fashion.

When you produce a drawing that has multiple shapes, or parts made of multiple shapes, such as the car in Figure 8, it is a good idea to make a separate class for each part. The class should have a draw method that draws the shape, and a constructor to set the position of the shape. For example, here is the outline of the Car class:

> It is a good idea to make a class for any part of a drawing that can occur more than once.

```
public class Car
{
   public Car(int x, int y)
   {
      // Remember position
      . . .
   }

   public void draw(Graphics2D g2)
   {
      // Drawing instructions
      . . .
   }
}
```

You will find the complete class declaration at the end of this section. The draw method contains a rather long sequence of instructions for drawing the body, roof, and tires.

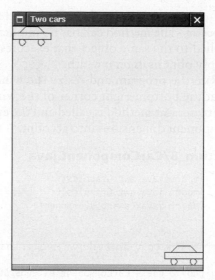

Figure 8   The Car Component Draws Two Car Shapes

The coordinates of the car parts seem a bit arbitrary. To come up with suitable values, draw the image on graph paper and read off the coordinates (Figure 9).

> To figure out how to draw a complex shape, make a sketch on graph paper.

The program that produces Figure 8 is composed of three classes.

- The Car class is responsible for drawing a single car. Two objects of this class are constructed, one for each car.
- The CarComponent class displays the drawing.
- The CarViewer class shows a frame that contains a CarComponent.

Let us look more closely at the CarComponent class. The paintComponent method draws two cars. We place one car in the top-left corner of the window, and the other car in the bottom-right corner. To compute the bottom-right position, we call the getWidth and getHeight methods of the JComponent class. These methods return the dimensions of the component. We subtract the dimensions of the car to determine the position of car2:

```
Car car1 = new Car(0, 0);
int x = getWidth() - 60;
int y = getHeight() - 30;
Car car2 = new Car(x, y);
```

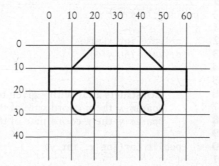

Figure 9
Using Graph Paper to
Find Shape Coordinates

Pay close attention to the call to getWidth inside the paintComponent method of Car-Component. The method call has no implicit parameter, which means that the method is applied to the same object that executes the paintComponent method. The component simply obtains *its own* width.

Run the program and resize the window. Note that the second car always ends up at the bottom-right corner of the window. Whenever the window is resized, the paintComponent method is called and the car position is recomputed, taking the current component dimensions into account.

section_8/CarComponent.java

```
1   import java.awt.Graphics;
2   import java.awt.Graphics2D;
3   import javax.swing.JComponent;
4
5   /**
6      This component draws two car shapes.
7   */
8   public class CarComponent extends JComponent
9   {
10     public void paintComponent(Graphics g)
11     {
12        Graphics2D g2 = (Graphics2D) g;
13
14        Car car1 = new Car(0, 0);
15
16        int x = getWidth() - 60;
17        int y = getHeight() - 30;
18
19        Car car2 = new Car(x, y);
20
21        car1.draw(g2);
22        car2.draw(g2);
23     }
24  }
```

section_8/Car.java

```
1   import java.awt.Graphics2D;
2   import java.awt.Rectangle;
3   import java.awt.geom.Ellipse2D;
4   import java.awt.geom.Line2D;
5   import java.awt.geom.Point2D;
6
7   /**
8      A car shape that can be positioned anywhere on the screen.
9   */
10  public class Car
11  {
12     private int xLeft;
13     private int yTop;
14
15     /**
16        Constructs a car with a given top left corner.
17        @param x the x-coordinate of the top-left corner
18        @param y the y-coordinate of the top-left corner
19     */
20     public Car(int x, int y)
21     {
```

```
22          xLeft = x;
23          yTop = y;
24       }
25
26       /**
27          Draws the car.
28          @param g2  the graphics context
29       */
30       public void draw(Graphics2D g2)
31       {
32          Rectangle body = new Rectangle(xLeft, yTop + 10, 60, 10);
33          Ellipse2D.Double frontTire
34                = new Ellipse2D.Double(xLeft + 10, yTop + 20, 10, 10);
35          Ellipse2D.Double rearTire
36                = new Ellipse2D.Double(xLeft + 40, yTop + 20, 10, 10);
37
38          // The bottom of the front windshield
39          Point2D.Double r1 = new Point2D.Double(xLeft + 10, yTop + 10);
40          // The front of the roof
41          Point2D.Double r2 = new Point2D.Double(xLeft + 20, yTop);
42          // The rear of the roof
43          Point2D.Double r3 = new Point2D.Double(xLeft + 40, yTop);
44          // The bottom of the rear windshield
45          Point2D.Double r4 = new Point2D.Double(xLeft + 50, yTop + 10);
46
47          Line2D.Double frontWindshield = new Line2D.Double(r1, r2);
48          Line2D.Double roofTop = new Line2D.Double(r2, r3);
49          Line2D.Double rearWindshield = new Line2D.Double(r3, r4);
50
51          g2.draw(body);
52          g2.draw(frontTire);
53          g2.draw(rearTire);
54          g2.draw(frontWindshield);
55          g2.draw(roofTop);
56          g2.draw(rearWindshield);
57       }
58    }
```

section_8/CarViewer.java

```
1     import javax.swing.JFrame;
2
3     public class CarViewer
4     {
5        public static void main(String[] args)
6        {
7           JFrame frame = new JFrame();
8
9           frame.setSize(300, 400);
10          frame.setTitle("Two cars");
11          frame.setDefaultCloseOperation(JFrame.EXIT_ON_CLOSE);
12
13          CarComponent component = new CarComponent();
14          frame.add(component);
15
16          frame.setVisible(true);
17       }
18    }
```

SELF CHECK

27. Which class needs to be modified to have the two cars positioned next to each other?

28. Which class needs to be modified to have the car tires painted in black, and what modification do you need to make?

29. How do you make the cars twice as big?

Practice It   Now you can try these exercises at the end of the chapter: E3.16, E3.21.

HOW TO 3.2   Drawing Graphical Shapes

Suppose you want to write a program that displays graphical shapes such as cars, aliens, charts, or any other images that can be obtained from rectangles, lines, and ellipses. These instructions give you a step-by-step procedure for decomposing a drawing into parts and implementing a program that produces the drawing.

Problem Statement   Create a program that draws a national flag.

Step 1   Determine the shapes that you need for the drawing.

You can use the following shapes:
- Squares and rectangles
- Circles and ellipses
- Lines

The outlines of these shapes can be drawn in any color, and you can fill the insides of these shapes with any color. You can also use text to label parts of your drawing.

Some national flags consist of three equally wide sections of different colors, side by side.

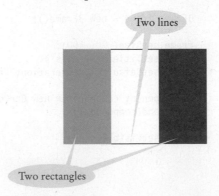

You could draw such a flag using three rectangles. But if the middle rectangle is white, as it is, for example, in the flag of Italy (green, white, red), it is easier and looks better to draw a line on the top and bottom of the middle portion:

Two lines

Two rectangles

Step 2   Find the coordinates for the shapes.

You now need to find the exact positions for the geometric shapes.

- For rectangles, you need the x- and y-position of the top-left corner, the width, and the height.
- For ellipses, you need the top-left corner, width, and height of the bounding rectangle.
- For lines, you need the x- and y-positions of the start and end points.
- For text, you need the x- and y-position of the basepoint.

A commonly-used size for a window is 300 by 300 pixels. You may not want the flag crammed all the way to the top, so perhaps the upper-left corner of the flag should be at point (100, 100).

Many flags, such as the flag of Italy, have a width : height ratio of 3 : 2. (You can often find exact proportions for a particular flag by doing a bit of Internet research on one of several Flags of the World sites.) For example, if you make the flag 90 pixels wide, then it should be 60 pixels tall. (Why not make it 100 pixels wide? Then the height would be $100 \cdot 2 / 3 \approx 67$, which seems more awkward.)

Now you can compute the coordinates of all the important points of the shape:

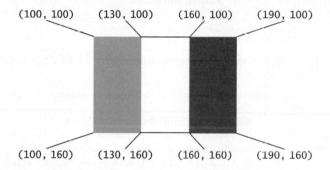

Step 3   Write Java statements to draw the shapes.

In our example, there are two rectangles and two lines:

```
Rectangle leftRectangle = new Rectangle(100, 100, 30, 60);
Rectangle rightRectangle = new Rectangle(160, 100, 30, 60);
Line2D.Double topLine = new Line2D.Double(130, 100, 160, 100);
Line2D.Double bottomLine = new Line2D.Double(130, 160, 160, 160);
```

If you are more ambitious, then you can express the coordinates in terms of a few variables. In the case of the flag, we have arbitrarily chosen the top-left corner and the width. All other coordinates follow from those choices. If you decide to follow the ambitious approach, then the rectangles and lines are determined as follows:

```
Rectangle leftRectangle = new Rectangle(
    xLeft, yTop,
    width / 3, width * 2 / 3);
Rectangle rightRectangle = new Rectangle(
    xLeft + 2 * width / 3, yTop,
    width / 3, width * 2 / 3);
Line2D.Double topLine = new Line2D.Double(
    xLeft + width / 3, yTop,
    xLeft + width * 2 / 3, yTop);
Line2D.Double bottomLine = new Line2D.Double(
    xLeft + width / 3, yTop + width * 2 / 3,
    xLeft + width * 2 / 3, yTop + width * 2 / 3);
```

Now you need to fill the rectangles and draw the lines. For the flag of Italy, the left rectangle is green and the right rectangle is red. Remember to switch colors before the filling and drawing operations:

```
g2.setColor(Color.GREEN);
g2.fill(leftRectangle);
g2.setColor(Color.RED);
g2.fill(rightRectangle);
g2.setColor(Color.BLACK);
g2.draw(topLine);
g2.draw(bottomLine);
```

Step 4   Combine the drawing statements with the component "plumbing".

```
public class MyComponent extends JComponent
{
    public void paintComponent(Graphics g)
    {
        Graphics2D g2 = (Graphics2D) g;
        // Drawing instructions
        . . .
    }
}
```

In our simple example, you could add all shapes and drawing instructions inside the paint-Component method:

```
public class ItalianFlagComponent extends JComponent
{
    public void paintComponent(Graphics g)
    {
        Graphics2D g2 = (Graphics2D) g;
        Rectangle leftRectangle = new Rectangle(100, 100, 30, 60);
        . . .
        g2.setColor(Color.GREEN);
        g2.fill(leftRectangle);
        . . .
    }
}
```

That approach is acceptable for simple drawings, but it is not very object-oriented. After all, a flag is an object. It is better to make a separate class for the flag. Then you can draw different flags at different positions. Specify the sizes in a constructor and supply a draw method:

```
public class ItalianFlag
{
    private int xLeft;
    private int yTop;
    private int width;

    public ItalianFlag(int x, int y, int aWidth)
    {
        xLeft = x;
        yTop = y;
        width = aWidth;
    }

    public void draw(Graphics2D g2)
    {
        Rectangle leftRectangle = new Rectangle(
            xLeft, yTop,
            width / 3, width * 2 / 3);
```

```
              . . .
        g2.setColor(Color.GREEN);
        g2.fill(leftRectangle);
              . . .
    }
}
```

You still need a separate class for the component, but it is very simple:

```
public class ItalianFlagComponent extends JComponent
{
    public void paintComponent(Graphics g)
    {
        Graphics2D g2 = (Graphics2D) g;
        ItalianFlag flag = new ItalianFlag(100, 100, 90);
        flag.draw(g2);
    }
}
```

Step 5   Write the viewer class.

Provide a viewer class, with a main method in which you construct a frame, add your component, and make your frame visible. The viewer class is completely routine; you only need to change a single line to show a different component.

```
public class ItalianFlagViewer
{
    public static void main(String[] args)
    {
        JFrame frame = new JFrame();

        frame.setSize(300, 400);
        frame.setDefaultCloseOperation(JFrame.EXIT_ON_CLOSE);

        ItalianFlagComponent component = new ItalianFlagComponent();
        frame.add(component);

        frame.setVisible(true);
    }
}
```

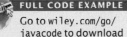

FULL CODE EXAMPLE
Go to wiley.com/go/
javacode to download
the complete flag
drawing program.

CHAPTER SUMMARY

Understand instance variables and the methods that access them.

- An object's instance variables store the data required for executing its methods.
- Each object of a class has its own set of instance variables.
- Private instance variables can only be accessed by methods of the same class.
- Encapsulation is the process of hiding implementation details and providing methods for data access.
- Encapsulation allows a programmer to use a class without having to know its implementation.
- Information hiding makes it simpler for the implementor of a class to locate errors and change implementations.

Write method and constructor headers that describe the public interface of a class.

- In order to implement a class, you first need to know which methods are required.
- Constructors set the initial data for objects.
- The constructor name is always the same as the class name.
- Use documentation comments to describe the classes and public methods of your programs.
- Provide documentation comments for every class, every method, every parameter variable, and every return value.

Implement a class.

- The private implementation of a class consists of instance variables, and the bodies of constructors and methods.

Write tests that verify that a class works correctly.

- A unit test verifies that a class works correctly in isolation, outside a complete program.
- To test a class, use an environment for interactive testing, or write a tester class to execute test instructions.

Use the technique of object tracing for visualizing object behavior.

- Write the methods on the front of a card and the instance variables on the back.
- Update the values of the instance variables when a mutator method is called.

Compare initialization and lifetime of instance, local, and parameter variables.

- Local variables are declared in the body of a method.
- When a method exits, its local variables are removed.
- Instance variables are initialized to a default value, but you must initialize local variables.

Recognize the use of the implicit parameter in method declarations.

- Use of an instance variable name in a method denotes the instance variable of the implicit parameter.
- The this reference denotes the implicit parameter.
- A local variable shadows an instance variable with the same name. You can access the instance variable name through the this reference.
- A method call without an implicit parameter is applied to the same object.

Implement classes that draw graphical shapes.

- It is a good idea to make a class for any part of a drawing that can occur more than once.
- To figure out how to draw a complex shape, make a sketch on graph paper.

- **R3.1** What is the public interface of the Counter class in Section 3.1? How does it differ from the implementation of the class?

- **R3.2** What is encapsulation? Why is it useful?

- **R3.3** Instance variables are a part of the hidden implementation of a class, but they aren't actually hidden from programmers who have the source code of the class. Explain to what extent the private reserved word provides information hiding.

- **R3.4** Consider a class Grade that represents a letter grade, such as A+ or B. Give two choices of instance variables that can be used for implementing the Grade class.

- **R3.5** Consider a class Time that represents a point in time, such as 9 A.M. or 3:30 P.M. Give two different sets of instance variables that can be used for implementing the Time class.

- **R3.6** Suppose the implementor of the Time class of Exercise R3.5 changes from one implementation strategy to another, keeping the public interface unchanged. What do the programmers who use the Time class need to do?

- **R3.7** You can read the value instance variable of the Counter class with the getValue accessor method. Should there be a setValue mutator method to change it? Explain why or why not.

- **R3.8** **a.** Show that the BankAccount(double initialBalance) constructor is not strictly necessary. That is, if we removed that constructor from the public interface, how could a programmer still obtain BankAccount objects with an arbitrary balance?
  b. Conversely, could we keep only the BankAccount(double initialBalance) constructor and remove the BankAccount() constructor?

- **R3.9** Why does the BankAccount class not have a reset method?

- **R3.10** What happens in our implementation of the BankAccount class when more money is withdrawn from the account than the current balance?

- **R3.11** What is the this reference? Why would you use it?

- **R3.12** What does the following method do? Give an example of how you can call the method.
  ```
  public class BankAccount
  {
      public void mystery(BankAccount that, double amount)
      {
          this.balance = this.balance - amount;
          that.balance = that.balance + amount;
      }
      . . . // Other bank account methods
  }
  ```

- **R3.13** Suppose you want to implement a class TimeDepositAccount. A time deposit account has a fixed interest rate that should be set in the constructor, together with the initial balance. Provide a method to get the current balance. Provide a method to add the earned interest to the account. This method should have no arguments because the interest rate is already known. It should have no return value because you already provided a method for obtaining the current balance. It is not possible to deposit additional funds into this account. Provide a `withdraw` method that removes the entire balance. Partial withdrawals are not allowed.

■ R3.14 Consider the following implementation of a class `Square`:

```
public class Square
{
    private int sideLength;
    private int area; // Not a good idea

    public Square(int length)
    {
        sideLength = length;
    }

    public int getArea()
    {
        area = sideLength * sideLength;
        return area;
    }
}
```

Why is it not a good idea to introduce an instance variable for the area? Rewrite the class so that area is a local variable.

■■ R3.15 Consider the following implementation of a class `Square`:

```
public class Square
{
    private int sideLength;
    private int area;

    public Square(int initialLength)
    {
        sideLength = initialLength;
        area = sideLength * sideLength;
    }

    public int getArea() { return area; }
    public void grow() { sideLength = 2 * sideLength; }
}
```

What error does this class have? How would you fix it?

■■ Testing R3.16 Provide a unit test class for the `Counter` class in Section 3.1.

■■ Testing R3.17 Read Exercise E3.9, but do not implement the `Car` class yet. Write a tester class that tests a scenario in which gas is added to the car, the car is driven, more gas is added, and the car is driven again. Print the actual and expected amount of gas in the tank.

■ R3.18 Using the object tracing technique described in Section 3.5, trace the program at the end of Section 3.4.

■■ R3.19 Using the object tracing technique described in Section 3.5, trace the program in How To 3.1.

■■ R3.20 Using the object tracing technique described in Section 3.5, trace the program in Worked Example 3.1.

■■■ **R3.21** Design a modification of the BankAccount class in which the first five transactions per month are free and a $1 fee is charged for every additional transaction. Provide a method that deducts the fee at the end of a month. What additional instance variables do you need? Using the object tracing technique described in Section 3.5, trace a scenario that shows how the fees are computed over two months.

■■ **Graphics R3.22** Suppose you want to extend the car viewer program in Section 3.8 to show a suburban scene, with several cars and houses. Which classes do you need?

■■■ **Graphics R3.23** Explain why the calls to the getWidth and getHeight methods in the CarComponent class have no explicit parameter.

■■ **Graphics R3.24** How would you modify the Car class in order to show cars of varying sizes?

PRACTICE EXERCISES

■ **E3.1** We want to add a button to the tally counter in Section 3.1 that allows an operator to undo an accidental button click. Provide a method

```
public void undo()
```

that simulates such a button. As an added precaution, make sure that clicking the undo button more often than the click button has no effect. (*Hint:* The call Math.max(n, 0) returns n if n is greater than zero, zero otherwise.)

■ **E3.2** Simulate a tally counter that can be used to admit a limited number of people. First, the limit is set with a call

```
public void setLimit(int maximum)
```

If the click button is clicked more often than the limit, it has no effect. (*Hint:* The call Math.min(n, limit) returns n if n is less than limit, and limit otherwise.).

■ **Testing E3.3** Write a BankAccountTester class whose main method constructs a bank account, deposits $1,000, withdraws $500, withdraws another $400, and then prints the remaining balance. Also print the expected result.

■ **E3.4** Add a method

```
public void addInterest(double rate)
```

to the BankAccount class that adds interest at the given rate. For example, after the statements

```
BankAccount momsSavings = new BankAccount(1000);
momsSavings.addInterest(10); // 10 percent interest
```

the balance in momsSavings is $1,100. Also supply a BankAccountTester class that prints the actual and expected balance.

■ **E3.5** Write a class SavingsAccount that is similar to the BankAccount class, except that it has an added instance variable interest. Supply a constructor that sets both the initial balance and the interest rate. Supply a method addInterest (with no explicit parameter) that adds interest to the account. Write a SavingsAccountTester class that constructs a savings account with an initial balance of $1,000 and an interest rate of 10 percent. Then apply the addInterest method and print the resulting balance. Also compute the expected result by hand and print it.

■■■ **E3.6** Add a method printReceipt to the CashRegister class. The method should print the prices of all purchased items and the total amount due. *Hint:* You will need to form a string of all prices. Use the concat method of the String class to add additional items to that string. To turn a price into a string, use the call String.valueOf(price).

■ **E3.7** After closing time, the store manager would like to know how much business was transacted during the day. Modify the CashRegister class to enable this functionality. Supply methods getSalesTotal and getSalesCount to get the total amount of all sales and the number of sales. Supply a method reset that resets any counters and totals so that the next day's sales start from zero.

■■ **E3.8** Implement a class Employee. An employee has a name (a string) and a salary (a double). Provide a constructor with two arguments

```
public Employee(String employeeName, double currentSalary)
```

and methods

```
public String getName()
public double getSalary()
public void raiseSalary(double byPercent)
```

These methods return the name and salary, and raise the employee's salary by a certain percentage. Sample usage:

```
Employee harry = new Employee("Hacker, Harry", 50000);
harry.raiseSalary(10); // Harry gets a 10 percent raise
```

Supply an EmployeeTester class that tests all methods.

■■ **E3.9** Implement a class Car with the following properties. A car has a certain fuel efficiency (measured in miles/gallon or liters/km — pick one) and a certain amount of fuel in the gas tank. The efficiency is specified in the constructor, and the initial fuel level is 0. Supply a method drive that simulates driving the car for a certain distance, reducing the amount of gasoline in the fuel tank. Also supply methods getGasInTank, returning the current amount of gasoline in the fuel tank, and addGas, to add gasoline to the fuel tank. Sample usage:

```
Car myHybrid = new Car(50); // 50 miles per gallon
myHybrid.addGas(20); // Tank 20 gallons
myHybrid.drive(100); // Drive 100 miles
double gasLeft = myHybrid.getGasInTank(); // Get gas remaining in tank
```

You may assume that the drive method is never called with a distance that consumes more than the available gas. Supply a CarTester class that tests all methods.

■ **E3.10** Implement a class Product. A product has a name and a price, for example new Product("Toaster", 29.95). Supply methods getName, getPrice, and reducePrice. Supply a program ProductPrinter that makes two products, prints the name and price, reduces their prices by $5.00, and then prints the prices again.

■■ **E3.11** Provide a class for authoring a simple letter. In the constructor, supply the names of the sender and the recipient:

```
public Letter(String from, String to)
```

Supply a method

```
public void addLine(String line)
```

to add a line of text to the body of the letter.

Supply a method

```
public String getText()
```

that returns the entire text of the letter. The text has the form:

Dear *recipient name*:
blank line
first line of the body
second line of the body
. . .
last line of the body
blank line
Sincerely,
blank line
sender name

Also supply a class `LetterPrinter` that prints this letter.

Dear John:

I am sorry we must part.
I wish you all the best.

Sincerely,

Mary

Construct an object of the `Letter` class and call `addLine` twice.

Hints: (1) Use the concat method to form a longer string from two shorter strings.
(2) The special string "\n" represents a new line. For example, the statement

```
body = body.concat("Sincerely,").concat("\n");
```

adds a line containing the string "Sincerely," to the body.

■■ **E3.12** Write a class `Bug` that models a bug moving along a horizontal line. The bug moves either to the right or left. Initially, the bug moves to the right, but it can turn to change its direction. In each move, its position changes by one unit in the current direction. Provide a constructor

```
public Bug(int initialPosition)
```

and methods

```
public void turn()
public void move()
public int getPosition()
```

Sample usage:

```
Bug bugsy = new Bug(10);
bugsy.move(); // Now the position is 11
bugsy.turn();
bugsy.move(); // Now the position is 10
```

Your `BugTester` should construct a bug, make it move and turn a few times, and print the actual and expected position.

■■ **E3.13** Implement a class `Moth` that models a moth flying along a straight line. The moth has a position, which is the distance from a fixed origin. When the moth moves toward a point of light, its new position is halfway between its old position and the position of the light source. Supply a constructor

```
public Moth(double initialPosition)
```

and methods

```
public void moveToLight(double lightPosition)
public double getPosition()
```

Your MothTester should construct a moth, move it toward a couple of light sources, and check that the moth's position is as expected.

■■■ **Graphics E3.14** Write a program that fills the window with a large ellipse, with a black outline and filled with your favorite color. The ellipse should touch the window boundaries, even if the window is resized. Call the getWidth and getHeight methods of the JComponent class in the paintComponent method.

■■ **Graphics E3.15** Draw a shooting target—a set of concentric rings in alternating black and white colors. *Hint:* Fill a black circle, then fill a smaller white circle on top, and so on. Your program should be composed of classes Target, TargetComponent, and TargetViewer.

■■ **Graphics E3.16** Write a program that draws a picture of a house. It could be as simple as the accompanying figure, or if you like, make it more elaborate (3-D, skyscraper, marble columns in the entryway, whatever). Implement a class House and supply a method draw(Graphics2D g2) that draws the house.

■■ **Graphics E3.17** Extend Exercise E3.16 by supplying a House constructor for specifying the position and size. Then populate your screen with a few houses of different sizes.

■■ **Graphics E3.18** Change the car viewer program in Section 3.8 to make the cars appear in different colors. Each Car object should store its own color. Supply modified Car and CarComponent classes.

■■ **Graphics E3.19** Change the Car class so that the size of a car can be specified in the constructor. Change the CarComponent class to make one of the cars appear twice the size of the original example.

■■ **Graphics E3.20** Write a program to plot the string "HELLO", using only lines and circles. Do not call drawString, and do not use System.out. Make classes LetterH, LetterE, LetterL, and LetterO.

■■ **Graphics E3.21** Write a program that displays the Olympic rings. Color the rings in the Olympic colors. Provide classes OlympicRing, OlympicRingViewer and OlympicRingComponent.

■■ **Graphics E3.22** Make a bar chart to plot the following data set. Label each bar. Make the bars horizontal for easier labeling. Provide a class BarChartViewer and a class BarChartComponent.

Bridge Name	Longest Span (ft)
Golden Gate	4,200
Brooklyn	1,595
Delaware Memorial	2,150
Mackinac	3,800

PROGRAMMING PROJECTS

■ P3.1 Enhance the CashRegister class so that it counts the purchased items. Provide a get-ItemCount method that returns the count.

■■■ P3.2 Support computing sales tax in the CashRegister class. The tax rate should be supplied when constructing a CashRegister object. Add recordTaxablePurchase and getTotal-Tax methods. (Amounts added with recordPurchase are not taxable.) The giveChange method should correctly reflect the sales tax that is charged on taxable items.

■■ P3.3 Implement a class Balloon. A balloon starts out with radius 0. Supply a method

```
public void inflate(double amount)
```

that increases the radius by the given amount. Supply a method

```
public double getVolume()
```

that returns the current volume of the balloon. Use Math.PI for the value of π. To compute the cube of a value r, just use r * r * r.

■■■ P3.4 Implement a class Student. For the purpose of this exercise, a student has a name and a total quiz score. Supply an appropriate constructor and methods getName(), addQuiz(int score), getTotalScore(), and getAverageScore(). To compute the average, you also need to store the *number of quizzes* that the student took.

Supply a StudentTester class that tests all methods.

■ P3.5 Write a class Battery that models a rechargeable battery. A battery has a constructor

```
public Battery(double capacity)
```

where capacity is a value measured in milliampere hours. A typical AA battery has a capacity of 2000 to 3000 mAh. The method

```
public void drain(double amount)
```

drains the capacity of the battery by the given amount. The method

```
public void charge()
```

charges the battery to its original capacity.

The method

```
public double getRemainingCapacity()
```

gets the remaining capacity of the battery.

■■ Graphics P3.6 Write a program that draws three stars. Use classes Star, StarComponent, and StarViewer. Each star should look like this:

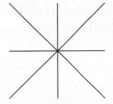

■■ P3.7 Implement a class RoachPopulation that simulates the growth of a roach population. The constructor takes the size of the initial roach population. The breed method simulates a period in which the roaches breed, which doubles their population. The spray(double percent) method simulates spraying with insecticide, which reduces the population by the given percentage. The getRoaches method returns the current number of roaches. A program called RoachSimulation simulates a population that starts out with 10 roaches. Breed, spray to reduce the population by 10 percent, and print the roach count. Repeat three more times.

■■ **P3.8** Implement a VotingMachine class that can be used for a simple election. Have methods to clear the machine state, to vote for a Democrat, to vote for a Republican, and to get the tallies for both parties.

■■■ **P3.9** In this project, you will enhance the BankAccount class and see how abstraction and encapsulation enable evolutionary changes to software.

Begin with a simple enhancement: charging a fee for every deposit and withdrawal. Supply a mechanism for setting the fee and modify the deposit and withdraw methods so that the fee is levied. Test your resulting class and check that the fee is computed correctly.

Now make a more complex change. The bank will allow a fixed number of free transactions (deposits or withdrawals) every month, and charge for transactions exceeding the free allotment. The charge is not levied immediately but at the end of the month.

Supply a new method deductMonthlyCharge to the BankAccount class that deducts the monthly charge and resets the transaction count. (*Hint:* Use Math.max(actual transaction count, free transaction count) in your computation.)

Produce a test program that verifies that the fees are calculated correctly over several months.

■■■ **P3.10** In this project, you will explore an object-oriented alternative to the "Hello, World" program in Chapter 1.

Begin with a simple Greeter class that has a single method, sayHello. That method should *return* a string, not print it. Create two objects of this class and invoke their sayHello methods. Of course, both objects return the same answer.

Enhance the Greeter class so that each object produces a customized greeting. For example, the object constructed as new Greeter("Dave") should say "Hello, Dave". (Use the concat method to combine strings to form a longer string, or peek ahead at Section 4.5 to see how you can use the + operator for the same purpose.)

Add a method sayGoodbye to the Greeter class.

Finally, add a method refuseHelp to the Greeter class. It should return a string such as "I am sorry, Dave. I am afraid I can't do that."

If you use BlueJ, place two Greeter objects on the workbench (one that greets the world and one that greets Dave) and invoke methods on them. Otherwise, write a tester program that constructs these objects, invokes methods, and prints the results.

ANSWERS TO SELF-CHECK QUESTIONS

1.
```
public void unclick()
{
    value = value - 1;
}
```

2. You can only access them by invoking the methods of the Clock class.

3. In one of the methods of the Counter class.

4. The programmers who designed and implemented the Java library.

5. Other programmers who work on the personal finance application.

6.
```
harrysChecking.withdraw(
    harrysChecking.getBalance())
```

7. The withdraw method has return type void. It doesn't return a value. Use the getBalance method to obtain the balance after the withdrawal.

8. Add an accountNumber parameter variable to the constructors, and add a getAccountNumber method. There is no need for a setAccountNumber method—the account number never changes after construction.

9.
```
/**
    Constructs a new bank account with a given
    initial balance.
    @param accountNumber the account number for
    this account
    @param initialBalance the initial balance for
    this account
*/
```

10. The first sentence of the method description should describe the method—it is displayed in isolation in the summary table.

11. An instance variable needs to be added to the class:

```
private int accountNumber;
```

12. Because the balance instance variable is accessed from the main method of BankRobber. The compiler will report an error because main is not a method of the BankAccount class and has no access to BankAccount instance variables.

13.
```
public int getWidth()
{
    return width;
}
```

14. There is more than one correct answer. One possible implementation is as follows:

```
public void translate(int dx, int dy)
{
    int newx = x + dx;
    x = newx;
    int newy = y + dy;
    y = newy;
}
```

15. One BankAccount object, no BankAccountTester object. The purpose of the BankAccountTester class is merely to hold the main method.

16. In those environments, you can issue interactive commands to construct BankAccount objects, invoke methods, and display their return values.

17.

Car myCar
Car(mpg)
addGas(amount)
drive(distance)
getGasLeft

front

gasLeft	milesPerGallon
0	25

back

18.

gasLeft	milesPerGallon
~~0~~	25
~~20~~	
~~16~~	
~~8~~	
13	

19.

gasLeft	milesPerGallon	totalMiles
0	25	0

20.

gasLeft	milesPerGallon	totalMiles
~~0~~ ~~20~~ ~~16~~ ~~8~~ 13	25	0 100 300

21. Variables of both categories belong to methods—they come alive when the method is called, and they die when the method exits. They differ in their initialization. Parameter variables are initialized with the values supplied as arguments in the call; local variables must be explicitly initialized.

22. After computing the change due, payment and purchase were set to zero. If the method returned payment - purchase, it would always return zero.

23.

reg1.purchase	reg1.payment	change
~~19.5~~ 0	~~20~~ 0	0.5 X

24. One implicit parameter, called this, of type BankAccount, and one explicit parameter, called amount, of type double.

25. It is not a legal expression. this is of type BankAccount and the BankAccount class has no instance variable named amount.

26. No implicit parameter—the main method is not invoked on any object—and one explicit parameter, called args.

27. CarComponent

28. In the draw method of the Car class, call

```
g2.fill(frontTire);
g2.fill(rearTire);
```

29. Double all measurements in the draw method of the Car class.

CHAPTER 4

FUNDAMENTAL DATA TYPES

CHAPTER GOALS

To understand integer and floating-point numbers

To recognize the limitations of the numeric types

To become aware of causes for overflow and roundoff errors

To understand the proper use of constants

To write arithmetic expressions in Java

To use the String type to manipulate character strings

To write programs that read input and produce formatted output

CHAPTER CONTENTS

Numbers and character strings (such as the ones on this display board) are important data types in any Java program. In this chapter, you will learn how to work with numbers and text, and how to write simple programs that perform useful tasks with them. We also cover the important topic of input and output, which enables you to implement interactive programs.

4.1 Numbers

We start this chapter with information about numbers. The following sections tell you how to choose the most appropriate number types for your numeric values, and how to work with constants—numeric values that do not change.

4.1.1 Number Types

Java has eight primitive types, including four integer types and two floating-point types.

In Java, every value is either a reference to an object, or it belongs to one of the eight **primitive types** shown in Table 1.

Six of the primitive types are number types; four of them for integers and two for floating-point numbers.

Each of the number types has a different range. Appendix G explains why the range limits are related to powers of two. The largest number that can be represented in an int is denoted by Integer.MAX_VALUE. Its value is about 2.14 billion. Similarly, the smallest integer is Integer.MIN_VALUE, about −2.14 billion.

Table 1 Primitive Types		
Type	Description	Size
int	The integer type, with range −2,147,483,648 (Integer.MIN_VALUE) . . . 2,147,483,647 (Integer.MAX_VALUE, about 2.14 billion)	4 bytes
byte	The type describing a single byte, with range −128 . . . 127	1 byte
short	The short integer type, with range −32,768 . . . 32,767	2 bytes
long	The long integer type, with range −9,223,372,036,854,775,808 . . . 9,223,372,036,854,775,807	8 bytes
double	The double-precision floating-point type, with a range of about $\pm 10^{308}$ and about 15 significant decimal digits	8 bytes
float	The single-precision floating-point type, with a range of about $\pm 10^{38}$ and about 7 significant decimal digits	4 bytes
char	The character type, representing code units in the Unicode encoding scheme (see Computing & Society 4.2 on page 163)	2 bytes
boolean	The type with the two truth values false and true (see Chapter 5)	1 bit

	Table 2 Number Literals in Java		
Number	Type	Comment	
6	int	An integer has no fractional part.	
-6	int	Integers can be negative.	
0	int	Zero is an integer.	
0.5	double	A number with a fractional part has type double.	
1.0	double	An integer with a fractional part .0 has type double.	
1E6	double	A number in exponential notation: 1×10^6 or 1000000. Numbers in exponential notation always have type double.	
2.96E-2	double	Negative exponent: $2.96 \times 10^{-2} = 2.96 / 100 = 0.0296$	
🚫 100,000		**Error:** Do not use a comma as a decimal separator.	
🚫 3 1/2		**Error:** Do not use fractions; use decimal notation: 3.5	

When a value such as 6 or 0.335 occurs in a Java program, it is called a **number literal**. If a number literal has a decimal point, it is a floating-point number; otherwise, it is an integer. Table 2 shows how to write integer and floating-point literals in Java.

Generally, you will use the int type for integer quantities. Occasionally, however, calculations involving integers can *overflow*. This happens if the result of a computation exceeds the range for the number type. For example,

> **A numeric computation overflows if the result falls outside the range for the number type.**

```java
int n = 1000000;
System.out.println(n * n);   // Prints –727379968, which is clearly wrong
```

The product n * n is 10^{12}, which is larger than the largest integer (about $2 \cdot 10^9$). The result is truncated to fit into an int, yielding a value that is completely wrong. Unfortunately, there is no warning when an integer overflow occurs.

If you run into this problem, the simplest remedy is to use the long type. Special Topic 4.1 on page 138 shows you how to use the BigInteger type in the unlikely event that even the long type overflows.

Overflow is not usually a problem for double-precision floating-point numbers. The double type has a range of about $\pm 10^{308}$. Floating-point numbers have a different problem—limited precision. The double type has about 15 significant digits, and there are many numbers that cannot be accurately represented as double values.

> **Rounding errors occur when an exact representation of a floating-point number is not possible.**

When a value cannot be represented exactly, it is rounded to the nearest match. Consider this example:

```java
double f = 4.35;
System.out.println(100 * f); // Prints 434.99999999999994
```

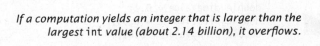

If a computation yields an integer that is larger than the largest int *value (about 2.14 billion), it overflows.*

Floating-point numbers have limited precision. Not every value can be represented precisely, and roundoff errors can occur.

The problem arises because computers represent numbers in the binary number system. In the binary number system, there is no exact representation of the fraction 1/10, just as there is no exact representation of the fraction 1/3 = 0.33333 in the decimal number system. (See Appendix G for more information.)

For this reason, the `double` type is not appropriate for financial calculations. In this book, we will continue to use `double` values for bank balances and other financial quantities so that we keep our programs as simple as possible. However, professional programs need to use the `BigDecimal` type for this purpose — see Special Topic 4.1.

In Java, it is legal to assign an integer value to a floating-point variable:

```
int dollars = 100;
double balance = dollars; // OK
```

But the opposite assignment is an error: You cannot assign a floating-point expression to an integer variable.

```
double balance = 13.75;
int dollars = balance; // Error
```

You will see in Section 4.2.5 how to convert a value of type `double` into an integer.

In this book, we do not use the `float` type. It has less than 7 significant digits, which greatly increases the risk of **roundoff errors**. Some programmers use `float` to save on memory if they need to store a huge set of numbers that do not require much precision.

4.1.2 Constants

In many programs, you need to use numerical **constants**—values that do not change and that have a special significance for a computation.

A typical example for the use of constants is a computation that involves coin values, such as the following:

```
payment = dollars + quarters * 0.25 + dimes * 0.1
        + nickels * 0.05 + pennies * 0.01;
```

Most of the code is self-documenting. However, the four numeric quantities, 0.25, 0.1, 0.05, and 0.01 are included in the arithmetic expression without any explanation. Of course, in this case, you know that the value of a nickel is five cents, which explains the 0.05, and so on. However, the next person who needs to maintain this code may live in another country and may not know that a nickel is worth five cents.

Thus, it is a good idea to use symbolic names for all values, even those that appear obvious. Here is a clearer version of the computation of the total:

```
double quarterValue = 0.25;
double dimeValue = 0.1;
double nickelValue = 0.05;
double pennyValue = 0.01;
```

```
payment = dollars + quarters * quarterValue + dimes * dimeValue
    + nickels * nickelValue + pennies * pennyValue;
```

There is another improvement we can make. There is a difference between the nickels and nickelValue variables. The nickels variable can truly vary over the life of the program, as we calculate different payments. But nickelValue is always 0.05.

A final variable is a constant. Once its value has been set, it cannot be changed.

In Java, constants are identified with the reserved word final. A variable tagged as final can never change after it has been set. If you try to change the value of a final variable, the compiler will report an error and your program will not compile.

Many programmers use all-uppercase names for constants (final variables), such as NICKEL_VALUE. That way, it is easy to distinguish between variables (with mostly lowercase letters) and constants. We will follow this convention in this book. However, this rule is a matter of good style, not a requirement of the Java language. The compiler will not complain if you give a final variable a name with lowercase letters.

Use named constants to make your programs easier to read and maintain.

Here is an improved version of the code that computes the value of a payment.

```
final double QUARTER_VALUE = 0.25;
final double DIME_VALUE = 0.1;
final double NICKEL_VALUE = 0.05;
final double PENNY_VALUE = 0.01;
payment = dollars + quarters * QUARTER_VALUE + dimes * DIME_VALUE
    + nickels * NICKEL_VALUE + pennies * PENNY_VALUE;
```

Frequently, constant values are needed in several methods. Then you should declare them together with the instance variables of a class and tag them as static and final. As before, final indicates that the value is a constant. The static reserved word means that the constant belongs to the class—this is explained in greater detail in Chapter 8.)

```
public class CashRegister
{
    // Constants
    public static final double QUARTER_VALUE = 0.25;
    public static final double DIME_VALUE = 0.1;
    public static final double NICKEL_VALUE = 0.05;
    public static final double PENNY_VALUE = 0.01;

    // Instance variables
    private double purchase;
    private double payment;

    // Methods
    . . .
}
```

We declared the constants as public. There is no danger in doing this because constants cannot be modified. Methods of other classes can access a public constant by first specifying the name of the class in which it is declared, then a period, then the name of the constant, such as CashRegister.NICKEL_VALUE.

The Math class from the standard library declares a couple of useful constants:

```
public class Math
{
    . . .
    public static final double E = 2.7182818284590452354;
    public static final double PI = 3.14159265358979323846;
}
```

You can refer to these constants as Math.PI and Math.E in any method. For example,

```
double circumference = Math.PI * diameter;
```

Syntax 4.1 Constant Declaration

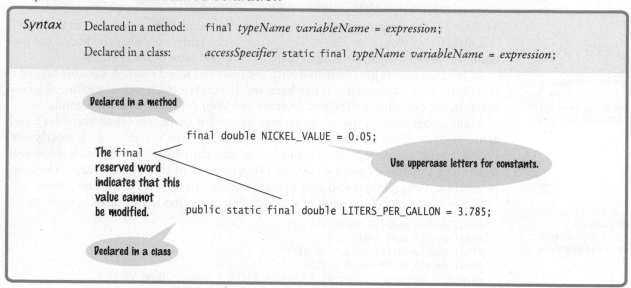

Syntax   Declared in a method: `final typeName variableName = expression;`

Declared in a class: *accessSpecifier* `static final typeName variableName = expression;`

Declared in a method

`final double NICKEL_VALUE = 0.05;`

The `final` reserved word indicates that this value cannot be modified.

Use uppercase letters for constants.

`public static final double LITERS_PER_GALLON = 3.785;`

Declared in a class

The sample program below puts constants to work. The program shows a refinement of the CashRegister class of How To 3.1. The public interface of that class has been modified in order to solve a common business problem.

Busy cashiers sometimes make mistakes totaling up coin values. Our CashRegister class features a method whose inputs are the *coin counts.* For example, the call

```
register.receivePayment(1, 2, 1, 1, 4);
```

processes a payment consisting of one dollar, two quarters, one dime, one nickel, and four pennies. The receivePayment method figures out the total value of the payment, $1.69. As you can see from the code listing, the method uses named constants for the coin values.

section_1/CashRegister.java

```java
1   /**
2       A cash register totals up sales and computes change due.
3   */
4   public class CashRegister
5   {
6       public static final double QUARTER_VALUE = 0.25;
7       public static final double DIME_VALUE = 0.1;
8       public static final double NICKEL_VALUE = 0.05;
9       public static final double PENNY_VALUE = 0.01;
10
11      private double purchase;
12      private double payment;
13
14      /**
15          Constructs a cash register with no money in it.
16      */
17      public CashRegister()
18      {
19          purchase = 0;
20          payment = 0;
```

```
21        }
22
23        /**
24            Records the purchase price of an item.
25            @param amount the price of the purchased item
26        */
27        public void recordPurchase(double amount)
28        {
29            purchase = purchase + amount;
30        }
31
32        /**
33            Processes the payment received from the customer.
34            @param dollars the number of dollars in the payment
35            @param quarters the number of quarters in the payment
36            @param dimes the number of dimes in the payment
37            @param nickels the number of nickels in the payment
38            @param pennies the number of pennies in the payment
39        */
40        public void receivePayment(int dollars, int quarters,
41                int dimes, int nickels, int pennies)
42        {
43            payment = dollars + quarters * QUARTER_VALUE + dimes * DIME_VALUE
44                + nickels * NICKEL_VALUE + pennies * PENNY_VALUE;
45        }
46
47        /**
48            Computes the change due and resets the machine for the next customer.
49            @return the change due to the customer
50        */
51        public double giveChange()
52        {
53            double change = payment - purchase;
54            purchase = 0;
55            payment = 0;
56            return change;
57        }
58    }
```

section_1/CashRegisterTester.java

```
1     /**
2         This class tests the CashRegister class.
3     */
4     public class CashRegisterTester
5     {
6         public static void main(String[] args)
7         {
8             CashRegister register = new CashRegister();
9
10            register.recordPurchase(0.75);
11            register.recordPurchase(1.50);
12            register.receivePayment(2, 0, 5, 0, 0);
13            System.out.print("Change: ");
14            System.out.println(register.giveChange());
15            System.out.println("Expected: 0.25");
16
17            register.recordPurchase(2.25);
18            register.recordPurchase(19.25);
19            register.receivePayment(23, 2, 0, 0, 0);
```

```
20          System.out.print("Change: ");
21          System.out.println(register.giveChange());
22          System.out.println("Expected: 2.0");
23      }
24  }
```

Program Run

```
Change: 0.25
Expected: 0.25
Change: 2.0
Expected: 2.0
```

SELF CHECK

1. Which are the most commonly used number types in Java?

2. Suppose you want to write a program that works with population data from various countries. Which Java data type should you use?

3. Which of the following initializations are incorrect, and why?

   a. int dollars = 100.0;

   b. double balance = 100;

4. What is the difference between the following two statements?

   final double CM_PER_INCH = 2.54;

   and

   public static final double CM_PER_INCH = 2.54;

5. What is wrong with the following statement sequence?

   double diameter = . . .;
   double circumference = 3.14 * diameter;

Practice It   Now you can try these exercises at the end of the chapter: R4.1, R4.21, E4.20.

Special Topic 4.1

Big Numbers

If you want to compute with really large numbers, you can use big number objects. Big number objects are objects of the BigInteger and BigDecimal classes in the java.math package. Unlike the number types such as int or double, big number objects have essentially no limits on their size and precision. However, computations with big number objects are much slower than those that involve number types. Perhaps more importantly, you can't use the familiar arithmetic operators such as (+ - *) with them. Instead, you have to use methods called add, subtract, and multiply. Here is an example of how to create a BigInteger object and how to call the multiply method:

```
BigInteger n = new BigInteger("1000000");
BigInteger r = n.multiply(n);
System.out.println(r); // Prints 1000000000000
```

The BigDecimal type carries out floating-point computations without roundoff errors. For example,

```
BigDecimal d = new BigDecimal("4.35");
BigDecimal e = new BigDecimal("100");
BigDecimal f = d.multiply(e);
System.out.println(f); // Prints 435.00
```

Programming Tip 4.1

Do Not Use Magic Numbers

A **magic number** is a numeric constant that appears in your code without explanation. For example, consider the following scary example that actually occurs in the Java library source:

```
h = 31 * h + ch;
```

Why 31? The number of days in January? One less than the number of bits in an integer? Actually, this code computes a "hash code" from a string—a number that is derived from the characters in such a way that different strings are likely to yield different hash codes. The value 31 turns out to scramble the character values nicely.

A better solution is to use a named constant:

```
final int HASH_MULTIPLIER = 31;
h = HASH_MULTIPLIER * h + ch;
```

You should never use magic numbers in your code. Any number that is not completely self-explanatory should be declared as a named constant. Even the most reasonable cosmic constant is going to change one day. You think there are 365 days in a year? Your customers on Mars are going to be pretty unhappy about your silly prejudice. Make a constant

We prefer programs that are easy to understand over those that appear to work by magic.

```
final int DAYS_PER_YEAR = 365;
```

4.2 Arithmetic

In this section, you will learn how to carry out arithmetic calculations in Java.

4.2.1 Arithmetic Operators

Java supports the same four basic arithmetic operations as a calculator—addition, subtraction, multiplication, and division—but it uses different symbols for the multiplication and division **operators**.

You must write a * b to denote multiplication. Unlike in mathematics, you cannot write a b, a · b, or a × b. Similarly, division is always indicated with the / operator, never a ÷ or a fraction bar. For example, $\frac{a+b}{2}$ becomes (a + b) / 2.

The combination of variables, literals, operators, and/or method calls is called an **expression**. For example, (a + b) / 2 is an expression.

Parentheses are used just as in algebra: to indicate in which order the parts of the expression should be computed. For example, in the expression (a + b) / 2, the sum a + b is computed first, and then the sum is divided by 2. In contrast, in the expression

```
a + b / 2
```

only b is divided by 2, and then the sum of a and b / 2 is formed. As in regular algebraic notation, multiplication and division have a *higher precedence* than addition and subtraction. For example, in the expression a + b / 2, the / is carried out first, even though the + operation occurs further to the left (see Appendix B).

Mixing integers and floating-point values in an arithmetic expression yields a floating-point value.

If you mix integer and floating-point values in an arithmetic expression, the result is a floating-point value. For example, 7 + 4.0 is the floating-point value 11.0.

4.2.2 Increment and Decrement

The ++ operator adds 1 to a variable; the -- operator subtracts 1.

Changing a variable by adding or subtracting 1 is so common that there is a special shorthand for it. The ++ operator increments a variable (see Figure 1):

```
counter++; // Adds 1 to the variable counter
```

Similarly, the -- operator decrements a variable:

```
counter--; // Subtracts 1 from counter
```

Figure 1   Incrementing a Variable

4.2.3 Integer Division and Remainder

If both arguments of / are integers, the remainder is discarded.

Division works as you would expect, as long as at least one of the numbers involved is a floating-point number. That is,

```
7.0 / 4.0
7 / 4.0
7.0 / 4
```

all yield 1.75. However, if *both* numbers are integers, then the result of the **integer division** is always an integer, with the remainder discarded. That is,

```
7 / 4
```

evaluates to 1 because 7 divided by 4 is 1 with a remainder of 3 (which is discarded). This can be a source of subtle programming errors—see Common Error 4.1.

The % operator computes the remainder of an integer division.

If you are interested in the remainder only, use the % operator:

```
7 % 4
```

Integer division and the % operator yield the dollar and cent values of a piggybank full of pennies.

is 3, the remainder of the integer division of 7 by 4. The % symbol has no analog in algebra. It was chosen because it looks similar to /, and the remainder operation is related to division. The operator is called **modulus**. (Some people call it *modulo* or *mod*.) It has no relationship with the percent operation that you find on some calculators.

Here is a typical use for the integer / and % operations. Suppose you have an amount of pennies in a piggybank:

```
int pennies = 1729;
```

You want to determine the value in dollars and cents. You obtain the dollars through an integer division by 100:

```
int dollars = pennies / 100;   // Sets dollars to 17
```

Table 3 Integer Division and Remainder

Expression (where n = 1729)	Value	Comment
n % 10	9	n % 10 is always the last digit of n.
n / 10	172	This is always n without the last digit.
n % 100	29	The last two digits of n.
n / 10.0	172.9	Because 10.0 is a floating-point number, the fractional part is not discarded.
-n % 10	-9	Because the first argument is negative, the remainder is also negative.
n % 2	1	n % 2 is 0 if n is even, 1 or -1 if n is odd.

The integer division discards the remainder. To obtain the remainder, use the % operator:

```
int cents = pennies % 100;   // Sets cents to 29
```

See Table 3 for additional examples.

4.2.4 Powers and Roots

In Java, there are no symbols for powers and roots. To compute them, you must call methods. To take the square root of a number, you use the `Math.sqrt` method. For example, $\sqrt{x}$ is written as `Math.sqrt(x)`. To compute x^n, you write `Math.pow(x, n)`.

In algebra, you use fractions, exponents, and roots to arrange expressions in a compact two-dimensional form. In Java, you have to write all expressions in a linear arrangement. For example, the mathematical expression

$$b \times \left(1 + \frac{r}{100}\right)^n$$

becomes

```
b * Math.pow(1 + r / 100, n)
```

Figure 2 shows how to analyze such an expression. Table 4 shows additional mathematical methods.

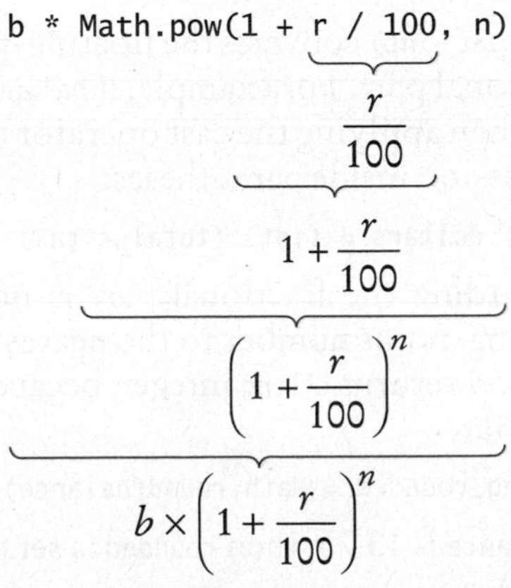

The Java library declares many mathematical functions, such as Math.sqrt (square root) and Math.pow (raising to a power).

$$b * \text{Math.pow}(1 + \underbrace{r / 100}_{\frac{r}{100}}, n)$$

$$\underbrace{1 + \frac{r}{100}}$$

$$\underbrace{\left(1 + \frac{r}{100}\right)^n}$$

$$\underbrace{b \times \left(1 + \frac{r}{100}\right)^n}$$

Figure 2
Analyzing an Expression

Table 4 Mathematical Methods

Method	Returns	Method	Returns
Math.sqrt(x)	Square root of x (≥ 0)	Math.abs(x)	Absolute value $\|x\|$
Math.pow(x, y)	x^y ($x > 0$, or $x = 0$ and $y > 0$, or $x < 0$ and y is an integer)	Math.max(x, y)	The larger of x and y
Math.sin(x)	Sine of x (x in radians)	Math.min(x, y)	The smaller of x and y
Math.cos(x)	Cosine of x	Math.exp(x)	e^x
Math.tan(x)	Tangent of x	Math.log(x)	Natural log ($\ln(x)$, $x > 0$)
Math.round(x)	Closest integer to x (as a long)	Math.log10(x)	Decimal log ($\log_{10}(x)$, $x > 0$)
Math.ceil(x)	Smallest integer $\geq x$ (as a double)	Math.floor(x)	Largest integer $\leq x$ (as a double)
Math.toRadians(x)	Convert x degrees to radians (i.e., returns $x \cdot \pi/180$)	Math.toDegrees(x)	Convert x radians to degrees (i.e., returns $x \cdot 180/\pi$)

4.2.5 Converting Floating-Point Numbers to Integers

Occasionally, you have a value of type double that you need to convert to the type int. It is an error to assign a floating-point value to an integer:

```
double balance = total + tax;
int dollars = balance; // Error: Cannot assign double to int
```

The compiler disallows this assignment because it is potentially dangerous:

- The fractional part is lost.
- The magnitude may be too large. (The largest integer is about 2 billion, but a floating-point number can be much larger.)

> You use a cast (*typeName*) to convert a value to a different type.

You must use the **cast** operator (int) to convert a convert floating-point value to an integer. Write the cast operator before the expression that you want to convert:

```
double balance = total + tax;
int dollars = (int) balance;
```

The cast (int) converts the floating-point value balance to an integer by discarding the fractional part. For example, if balance is 13.75, then dollars is set to 13.

When applying the cast operator to an arithmetic expression, you need to place the expression inside parentheses:

```
int dollars = (int) (total + tax);
```

Discarding the fractional part is not always appropriate. If you want to round a floating-point number to the nearest whole number, use the Math.round method. This method returns a long integer, because large floating-point numbers cannot be stored in an int.

```
long rounded = Math.round(balance);
```

If balance is 13.75, then rounded is set to 14.

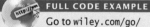

FULL CODE EXAMPLE

Go to wiley.com/go/javacode to download a program that demonstrates casts, rounding, and the % operator.

Syntax 4.2 Cast

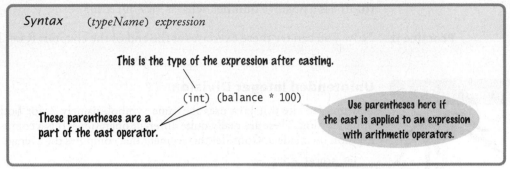

Syntax   *(typeName) expression*

This is the type of the expression after casting.

(int) (balance * 100)

These parentheses are a part of the cast operator.

Use parentheses here if the cast is applied to an expression with arithmetic operators.

If you know that the result can be stored in an `int` and does not require a `long`, you can use a cast:

```
int rounded = (int) Math.round(balance);
```

Table 5 Arithmetic Expressions

Mathematical Expression	Java Expression	Comments
$\dfrac{x + y}{2}$	`(x + y) / 2`	The parentheses are required; `x + y / 2` computes $x + \frac{y}{2}$.
$\dfrac{xy}{2}$	`x * y / 2`	Parentheses are not required; operators with the same precedence are evaluated left to right.
$\left(1 + \dfrac{r}{100}\right)^{n}$	`Math.pow(1 + r / 100, n)`	Use `Math.pow(x, n)` to compute x^{n}.
$\sqrt{a^2 + b^2}$	`Math.sqrt(a * a + b * b)`	`a * a` is simpler than `Math.pow(a, 2)`.
$\dfrac{i + j + k}{3}$	`(i + j + k) / 3.0`	If i, j, and k are integers, using a denominator of 3.0 forces floating-point division.
π	`Math.PI`	`Math.PI` is a constant declared in the `Math` class.

SELF CHECK

6. A bank account earns interest once per year. In Java, how do you compute the interest earned in the first year? Assume variables `percent` and `balance` of type `double` have already been declared.

7. In Java, how do you compute the side length of a square whose area is stored in the variable `area`?

8. The volume of a sphere is given by

$$V = \frac{4}{3}\pi r^{3}$$

If the radius is given by a variable `radius` of type `double`, write a Java expression for the volume.

9. What is the value of 1729 / 100 and 1729 % 100?

10. If *n* is a positive number, what is (n / 10) % 10?

Practice It   Now you can try these exercises at the end of the chapter: R4.4, R4.6, E4.4, E4.23.

Common Error 4.1

Unintended Integer Division

It is unfortunate that Java uses the same symbol, namely /, for both integer and floating-point division. These are really quite different operations. It is a common error to use **integer division** by accident. Consider this segment that computes the average of three integers:

```
int score1 = 10;
int score2 = 4;
int score3 = 9;

double average = (score1 + score2 + score3) / 3; // Error
System.out.println("Average score: " + average); // Prints 7.0, not 7.666666666666667
```

What could be wrong with that? Of course, the average of score1, score2, and score3 is

$$\frac{score1 + score2 + score3}{3}$$

Here, however, the / does not mean division in the mathematical sense. It denotes integer division because both 3 and the sum of score1 + score2 + score3 are integers. Because the scores add up to 23, the average is computed to be 7, the result of the integer division of 23 by 3. That integer 7 is then moved into the floating-point variable average. The remedy is to make the numerator or denominator into a floating-point number:

```
double total = score1 + score2 + score3;
double average = total / 3;
```

or

```
double average = (score1 + score2 + score3) / 3.0;
```

Common Error 4.2

Unbalanced Parentheses

Consider the expression

```
((a + b) * t / 2 * (1 - t)
```

What is wrong with it? Count the parentheses. There are three (and two). The parentheses are *unbalanced*. This kind of typing error is very common with complicated expressions. Now consider this expression.

```
(a + b) * t) / (2 * (1 - t)
```

This expression has three (and three), but it still is not correct. In the middle of the expression,

```
(a + b) * t) / (2 * (1 - t)
          ↑
```

there is only one (but two), which is an error. In the middle of an expression, the count of (must be greater than or equal to the count of), and at the end of the expression the two counts must be the same.

Here is a simple trick to make the counting easier without using pencil and paper. It is difficult for the brain to keep two counts simultaneously. Keep only one count when scanning the expression. Start with 1 at the first opening parenthesis, add 1 whenever you see an opening parenthesis, and subtract one whenever you see a closing parenthesis. Say the numbers aloud as you scan the expression. If the count ever drops below zero, or is not zero at the end, the parentheses are unbalanced. For example, when scanning the previous expression, you would mutter

```
(a + b) * t) / (2 * (1 - t)
1       0  -1
```

and you would find the error.

Programming Tip 4.2

Spaces in Expressions

It is easier to read

```
x1 = (-b + Math.sqrt(b * b - 4 * a * c)) / (2 * a);
```

than

```
x1=(-b+Math.sqrt(b*b-4*a*c))/(2*a);
```

Simply put spaces around all operators + - * / % =. However, don't put a space after a *unary* minus: a – used to negate a single quantity, such as -b. That way, it can be easily distinguished from a *binary* minus, as in a - b.

It is customary not to put a space after a method name. That is, write Math.sqrt(x) and not Math.sqrt (x).

Special Topic 4.2

Combining Assignment and Arithmetic

In Java, you can combine arithmetic and assignment. For example, the instruction

```
balance += amount;
```

is a shortcut for

```
balance = balance + amount;
```

Similarly,

```
total *= 2;
```

is another way of writing

```
total = total * 2;
```

Many programmers find this a convenient shortcut. If you like it, go ahead and use it in your own code. For simplicity, we won't use it in this book, though.

Special Topic 4.3

Instance Methods and Static Methods

In the preceding section, you encountered the Math class, which contains a collection of helpful methods for carrying out mathematical computations. These methods do not operate on an object. That is, you don't call

```
double root = 2.sqrt(); // Error
```

In Java, numbers are not objects, so you can never invoke a method on a number. Instead, you pass a number as an argument (explicit parameter) to a method, enclosing the number in parentheses after the method name:

```
double root = Math.sqrt(2);
```

Such methods are called **static methods**. (The term "static" is a historical holdover from the C and C++ programming languages. It has nothing to do with the usual meaning of the word.)

Static methods do not operate on objects, but they are still declared inside classes. When calling the method, you specify the class to which the sqrt method belongs:

The name of the class   The name of the static method

`Math.sqrt(2)`

In contrast, a method that is invoked on an object is called an **instance method**. As a rule of thumb, you use static methods when you manipulate numbers. You will learn more about the distinction between static and instance methods in Chapter 8.

Computing & Society 4.1 The Pentium Floating-Point Bug

In 1994, Intel Corporation released what was then its most powerful processor, the Pentium. Unlike previous generations of its processors, it had a very fast floating-point unit. Intel's goal was to compete aggressively with the makers of higher-end processors for engineering workstations. The Pentium was a huge success immediately.

In the summer of 1994, Dr. Thomas Nicely of Lynchburg College in Virginia ran an extensive set of computations to analyze the sums of reciprocals of certain sequences of prime numbers. The results were not always what his theory predicted, even after he took into account the inevitable roundoff errors. Then Dr. Nicely noted that the same program did produce the correct results when running on the slower 486 processor that preceded the Pentium in Intel's lineup. This should not have happened. The optimal round-off behavior of floating-point calculations has been standardized by the Institute for Electrical and Electronic Engineers (IEEE) and Intel claimed to adhere to the IEEE standard in both the 486 and the Pentium processors. Upon further checking, Dr. Nicely discovered that indeed there was a very small set of numbers for which the product of two numbers was computed differently on the two processors. For example,

$$4{,}195{,}835 - \left((4{,}195{,}835/3{,}145{,}727) \times 3{,}145{,}727\right)$$

is mathematically equal to 0, and it did compute as 0 on a 486 processor. On his Pentium processor the result was 256.

As it turned out, Intel had independently discovered the bug in its testing and had started to produce chips that fixed it. The bug was caused by an error in a table that was used to speed up the floating-point multiplication algorithm of the processor. Intel determined that the problem was exceedingly rare. They claimed that under normal use, a typical consumer would only notice the problem once every 27,000 years. Unfortunately for Intel, Dr. Nicely had not been a normal user.

Now Intel had a real problem on its hands. It figured that the cost of replacing all Pentium processors that it had sold so far would cost a great deal of money. Intel already had more orders for the chip than it could produce, and it would be particularly galling to have to give out the scarce chips as free replacements instead of selling them. Intel's management decided to punt on the issue and initially offered to replace the processors only for those customers who could prove that their work required absolute precision in mathematical calculations. Naturally, that did not go over well with the hundreds of thousands of customers who had paid retail prices of $700 and more for a Pentium chip and did not want to live with the nagging feeling that perhaps, one day, their income tax program would produce a faulty return.

Ultimately, Intel caved in to public demand and replaced all defective chips, at a cost of about 475 million dollars.

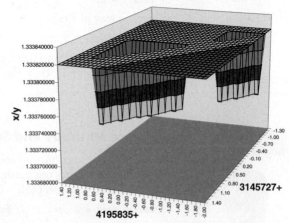

This graph shows a set of numbers for which the original Pentium processor obtained the wrong quotient.

4.3 Input and Output

In the following sections, you will see how to read user input and how to control the appearance of the output that your programs produce.

4.3.1 Reading Input

You can make your programs more flexible if you ask the program user for inputs rather than using fixed values. Consider, for example, a program that processes prices and quantities of soda containers. Prices and quantities are likely to fluctuate. The program user should provide them as inputs.

When a program asks for user input, it should first print a message that tells the user which input is expected. Such a message is called a **prompt**.

```
System.out.print("Please enter the number of bottles: "); // Display prompt
```

Use the print method, not println, to display the prompt. You want the input to appear after the colon, not on the following line. Also remember to leave a space after the colon.

Because output is sent to System.out, you might think that you use System.in for input. Unfortunately, it isn't quite that simple. When Java was first designed, not much attention was given to reading keyboard input. It was assumed that all programmers would produce graphical user interfaces with text fields and menus. System.in was given a minimal set of features and must be combined with other classes to be useful.

To read keyboard input, you use a class called Scanner. You obtain a Scanner object by using the following statement:

```
Scanner in = new Scanner(System.in);
```

A supermarket scanner reads bar codes. The Java Scanner *reads numbers and text.*

Once you have a scanner, you use its nextInt method to read an integer value:

```
System.out.print("Please enter the number of bottles: ");
int bottles = in.nextInt();
```

Use the Scanner class to read keyboard input in a console window.

Syntax 4.3   Input Statement

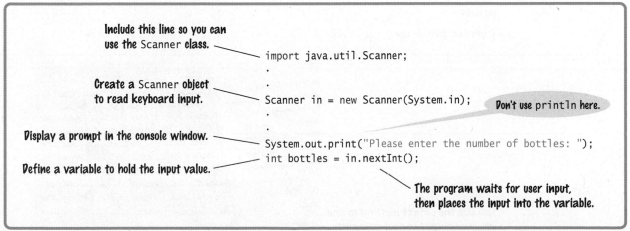

Include this line so you can use the Scanner class.
```
import java.util.Scanner;
```

Create a Scanner object to read keyboard input.
```
Scanner in = new Scanner(System.in);
```
Don't use println here.

Display a prompt in the console window.
```
System.out.print("Please enter the number of bottles: ");
```
Define a variable to hold the input value.
```
int bottles = in.nextInt();
```
The program waits for user input, then places the input into the variable.

When the `nextInt` method is called, the program waits until the user types a number and presses the Enter key. After the user supplies the input, the number is placed into the `bottles` variable, and the program continues.

To read a floating-point number, use the `nextDouble` method instead:

```
System.out.print("Enter price: ");
double price = in.nextDouble();
```

The `Scanner` class belongs to the package `java.util`. When using the `Scanner` class, import it by placing the following declaration at the top of your program file:

```
import java.util.Scanner;
```

4.3.2 Formatted Output

When you print the result of a computation, you often want to control its appearance. For example, when you print an amount in dollars and cents, you usually want it to be rounded to two significant digits. That is, you want the output to look like

```
Price per liter: 1.22
```

instead of

```
Price per liter: 1.215962441314554
```

> Use the `printf` method to specify how values should be formatted.

The following command displays the price with two digits after the decimal point:

```
System.out.printf("%.2f", price);
```

You can also specify a *field width*:

```
System.out.printf("%10.2f", price);
```

The price is printed using ten characters: six spaces followed by the four characters 1.22.

```
      1 . 2 2
```

The construct `%10.2f` is called a *format specifier:* it describes how a value should be formatted. The letter `f` at the end of the format specifier indicates that we are displaying a floating-point number. Use `d` for an integer and `s` for a string; see Table 6 for examples. A format string contains format specifiers and literal characters. Any characters that are not format specifiers are printed verbatim. For example, the command

```
System.out.printf("Price per liter:%10.2f", price);
```

prints

```
Price per liter:      1.22
```

You use the `printf` *method to line up your output in neat columns.*

Table 6 Format Specifier Examples

Format String	Sample Output	Comments
"%d"	24	Use d with an integer.
"%5d"	24	Spaces are added so that the field width is 5.
"Quantity:%5d"	Quantity: 24	Characters inside a format string but outside a format specifier appear in the output.
"%f"	1.21997	Use f with a floating-point number.
"%.2f"	1.22	Prints two digits after the decimal point.
"%7.2f"	1.22	Spaces are added so that the field width is 7.
"%s"	Hello	Use s with a string.
"%d %.2f"	24 1.22	You can format multiple values at once.

You can print multiple values with a single call to the printf method. Here is a typical example:

```
System.out.printf("Quantity: %d Total: %10.2f", quantity, total);
```

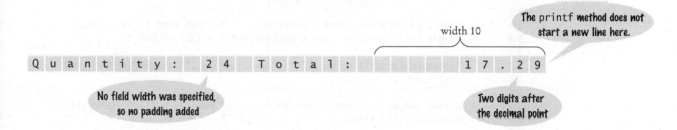

width 10

The printf method does not start a new line here.

Quantity: 24 Total: 17.29

No field width was specified, so no padding added

Two digits after the decimal point

The printf method, like the print method, does not start a new line after the output. If you want the next output to be on a separate line, you can call System.out.println(). Alternatively, Section 4.5.4 shows you how to add a newline character to the format string.

Our next example program will prompt for the price of a six-pack of soda and a two-liter bottle, and then print out the price per liter for both. The program puts to work what you just learned about reading input and formatting output.

What is the better deal? A six-pack of 12-ounce cans or a two-liter bottle?

section_3/Volume.java

```java
1   import java.util.Scanner;
2
3   /**
4      This program prints the price per liter for a six-pack of cans and
5      a two-liter bottle.
6   */
7   public class Volume
8   {
9      public static void main(String[] args)
10     {
11        // Read price per pack
12
13        Scanner in = new Scanner(System.in);
14
15        System.out.print("Please enter the price for a six-pack: ");
16        double packPrice = in.nextDouble();
17
18        // Read price per bottle
19
20        System.out.print("Please enter the price for a two-liter bottle: ");
21        double bottlePrice = in.nextDouble();
22
23        final double CANS_PER_PACK = 6;
24        final double CAN_VOLUME = 0.355; // 12 oz. = 0.355 l
25        final double BOTTLE_VOLUME = 2;
26
27        // Compute and print price per liter
28
29        double packPricePerLiter = packPrice / (CANS_PER_PACK * CAN_VOLUME);
30        double bottlePricePerLiter = bottlePrice / BOTTLE_VOLUME;
31
32        System.out.printf("Pack price per liter:   %8.2f", packPricePerLiter);
33        System.out.println();
34
35        System.out.printf("Bottle price per liter: %8.2f", bottlePricePerLiter);
36        System.out.println();
37     }
38  }
```

Program Run

```
Please enter the price for a six-pack: 2.95
Please enter the price for a two-liter bottle: 2.85
Pack price per liter:      1.38
Bottle price per liter:    1.43
```

SELF CHECK

11. Write statements to prompt for and read the user's age using a Scanner variable named in.

12. What is wrong with the following statement sequence?

```java
System.out.print("Please enter the unit price: ");
double unitPrice = in.nextDouble();
int quantity = in.nextInt();
```

13. What is problematic about the following statement sequence?

```
System.out.print("Please enter the unit price: ");
double unitPrice = in.nextInt();
```

14. What is problematic about the following statement sequence?

```
System.out.print("Please enter the number of cans");
int cans = in.nextInt();
```

15. What is the output of the following statement sequence?

```
int volume = 10;
System.out.printf("The volume is %5d", volume);
```

16. Using the `printf` method, print the values of the integer variables `bottles` and `cans` so that the output looks like this:

```
Bottles:       8
Cans:         24
```

The numbers to the right should line up. (You may assume that the numbers have at most 8 digits.)

Practice It   Now you can try these exercises at the end of the chapter: R4.11, E4.6, E4.7.

HOW TO 4.1   Carrying Out Computations

Many programming problems require arithmetic computations. This How To shows you how to turn a problem statement into pseudocode and, ultimately, a Java program.

Problem Statement   Suppose you are asked to write a program that simulates a vending machine. A customer selects an item for purchase and inserts a bill into the vending machine. The vending machine dispenses the purchased item and gives change. We will assume that all item prices are multiples of 25 cents, and the machine gives all change in dollar coins and quarters. Your task is to compute how many coins of each type to return.

Step 1   Understand the problem: What are the inputs? What are the desired outputs?

In this problem, there are two inputs:

- The denomination of the bill that the customer inserts
- The price of the purchased item

There are two desired outputs:

- The number of dollar coins that the machine returns
- The number of quarters that the machine returns

Step 2   Work out examples by hand.

This is a very important step. If you can't compute a couple of solutions by hand, it's unlikely that you'll be able to write a program that automates the computation.

Let's assume that a customer purchased an item that cost $2.25 and inserted a $5 bill. The customer is due $2.75, or two dollar coins and three quarters, in change.

That is easy for you to see, but how can a Java program come to the same conclusion? The key is to work in pennies, not dollars. The change due the customer is 275 pennies. Dividing by 100 yields 2, the number of dollars. Dividing the remainder (75) by 25 yields 3, the number of quarters.

Step 3   Write pseudocode for computing the answers.

In the previous step, you worked out a specific instance of the problem. You now need to come up with a method that works in general.

Given an arbitrary item price and payment, how can you compute the coins due? First, compute the change due in pennies:

> change due = 100 x bill value - item price in pennies

To get the dollars, divide by 100 and discard the remainder:

> dollar coins = change due / 100 (without remainder)

The remaining change due can be computed in two ways. If you are familiar with the modulus operator, you can simply compute

> change due = change due % 100

Alternatively, subtract the penny value of the dollar coins from the change due:

> change due = change due - 100 x dollar coins

To get the quarters due, divide by 25:

> quarters = change due / 25

Step 4   Declare the variables and constants that you need, and specify their types.

Here, we have five variables:

- billValue
- itemPrice
- changeDue
- dollarCoins
- quarters

Should we introduce constants to explain 100 and 25 as PENNIES_PER_DOLLAR and PENNIES_PER_QUARTER? Doing so will make it easier to convert the program to international markets, so we will take this step.

It is very important that changeDue and PENNIES_PER_DOLLAR are of type int because the computation of dollarCoins uses integer division. Similarly, the other variables are integers.

Step 5   Turn the pseudocode into Java statements.

If you did a thorough job with the pseudocode, this step should be easy. Of course, you have to know how to express mathematical operations (such as powers or integer division) in Java.

```
changeDue = PENNIES_PER_DOLLAR * billValue - itemPrice;
dollarCoins = changeDue / PENNIES_PER_DOLLAR;
changeDue = changeDue % PENNIES_PER_DOLLAR;
quarters = changeDue / PENNIES_PER_QUARTER;
```

Step 6   Provide input and output.

Before starting the computation, we prompt the user for the bill value and item price:

```
System.out.print("Enter bill value (1 = $1 bill, 5 = $5 bill, etc.): ");
billValue = in.nextInt();
System.out.print("Enter item price in pennies: ");
itemPrice = in.nextInt();
```

When the computation is finished, we display the result. For extra credit, we use the printf method to make sure that the output lines up neatly.

```
System.out.printf("Dollar coins: %6d", dollarCoins);
System.out.printf("Quarters:     %6d", quarters);
```

A vending machine takes bills and gives change in coins.

Step 7   Provide a class with a main method.

Your computation needs to be placed into a class. Find an appropriate name for the class that describes the purpose of the computation. In our example, we will choose the name Vending-Machine.

Inside the class, supply a main method.

In the main method, you need to declare constants and variables (Step 4), carry out computations (Step 5), and provide input and output (Step 6). Clearly, you will want to first get the input, then do the computations, and finally show the output. Declare the constants at the beginning of the method, and declare each variable just before it is needed.

Here is the complete program, how_to_1/VendingMachine.java:

```java
import java.util.Scanner;

/**
    This program simulates a vending machine that gives change.
*/
public class VendingMachine
{
    public static void main(String[] args)
    {
        Scanner in = new Scanner(System.in);

        final int PENNIES_PER_DOLLAR = 100;
        final int PENNIES_PER_QUARTER = 25;

        System.out.print("Enter bill value (1 = $1 bill, 5 = $5 bill, etc.): ");
        int billValue = in.nextInt();
        System.out.print("Enter item price in pennies: ");
        int itemPrice = in.nextInt();

        // Compute change due

        int changeDue = PENNIES_PER_DOLLAR * billValue - itemPrice;
        int dollarCoins = changeDue / PENNIES_PER_DOLLAR;
        changeDue = changeDue % PENNIES_PER_DOLLAR;
        int quarters = changeDue / PENNIES_PER_QUARTER;

        // Print change due

        System.out.printf("Dollar coins: %6d", dollarCoins);
        System.out.println();
```

```
                        System.out.printf("Quarters:      %6d", quarters);
                        System.out.println();
                }
        }
```

Program Run

```
Enter bill value (1 = $1 bill, 5 = $5 bill, etc.): 5
Enter item price in pennies: 225
Dollar coins:    2
Quarters:        3
```

WORKED EXAMPLE 4.1   **Computing the Volume and Surface Area of a Pyramid**

Learn how to design a class for computing the volume and surface area of a pyramid. Go to wiley.com/go/javaexamples and download Worked Example 4.1.

4.4 Problem Solving: First Do It By Hand

A very important step for developing an algorithm is to first carry out the computations *by hand*. If you can't compute a solution yourself, it's unlikely that you'll be able to write a program that automates the computation.

To illustrate the use of hand calculations, consider the following problem.

A row of black and white tiles needs to be placed along a wall. For aesthetic reasons, the architect has specified that the first and last tile shall be black.

Your task is to compute the number of tiles needed and the gap at each end, given the space available and the width of each tile.

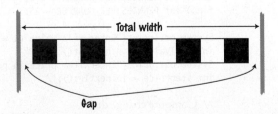

Pick concrete values for a typical situation to use in a hand calculation.

To make the problem more concrete, let's assume the following dimensions:

- Total width: 100 inches
- Tile width: 5 inches

The obvious solution would be to fill the space with 20 tiles, but that would not work—the last tile would be white.

Instead, look at the problem this way: The first tile must always be black, and then we add some number of white/black pairs:

The first tile takes up 5 inches, leaving 95 inches to be covered by pairs. Each pair is 10 inches wide. Therefore the number of pairs is 95 / 10 = 9.5. However, we need to discard the fractional part since we can't have fractions of tile pairs.

Therefore, we will use 9 tile pairs or 18 tiles, plus the initial black tile. Altogether, we require 19 tiles.

The tiles span $19 \times 5 = 95$ inches, leaving a total gap of $100 - 19 \times 5 = 5$ inches.

The gap should be evenly distributed at both ends. At each end, the gap is $(100 - 19 \times 5) / 2 = 2.5$ inches.

This computation gives us enough information to devise an algorithm with arbitrary values for the total width and tile width.

FULL CODE EXAMPLE
Go to wiley.com/go/javacode to download a program that implements this algorithm.

> number of pairs = integer part of (total width – tile width) / (2 × tile width)
> number of tiles = 1 + 2 × number of pairs
> gap at each end = (total width – number of tiles × tile width) / 2

As you can see, doing a hand calculation gives enough insight into the problem that it becomes easy to develop an algorithm.

SELF CHECK

17. Translate the pseudocode for computing the number of tiles and the gap width into Java.

18. Suppose the architect specifies a pattern with black, gray, and white tiles, like this:

Again, the first and last tile should be black. How do you need to modify the algorithm?

19. A robot needs to tile a floor with alternating black and white tiles. Develop an algorithm that yields the color (0 for black, 1 for white), given the row and column number. Start with specific values for the row and column, and then generalize.

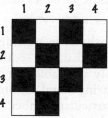

20. For a particular car, repair and maintenance costs in year 1 are estimated at $100; in year 10, at $1,500. Assuming that the repair cost increases by the same amount every year, develop pseudocode to compute the repair cost in year 3 and then generalize to year **n**.

21. The shape of a bottle is approximated by two cylinders of radius r_1 and r_2 and heights h_1 and h_2, joined by a cone section of height h_3.

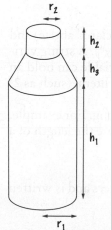

Using the formulas for the volume of a cylinder, $V = \pi r^2 h$, and a cone section,

$$V = \pi \frac{\left(r_1^2 + r_1 r_2 + r_2^2\right)h}{3},$$

develop pseudocode to compute the volume of the bottle. Using an actual bottle with known volume as a sample, make a hand calculation of your pseudocode.

Practice It   Now you can try these exercises at the end of the chapter: R4.16, R4.18, R4.19.

WORKED EXAMPLE 4.2   **Computing Travel Time**

Learn how to develop a hand calculation to compute the time that a robot requires to retrieve an item from rocky terrain. Go to wiley.com/go/javaexamples and download Worked Example 4.2.

4.5 Strings

Strings are sequences of characters.

Many programs process text, not numbers. Text consists of **characters**: letters, numbers, punctuation, spaces, and so on. A **string** is a sequence of characters. For example, the string "Harry" is a sequence of five characters.

4.5.1 The String Type

You can declare variables that hold strings.

```
String name = "Harry";
```

We distinguish between string variables (such as the variable name declared above) and string **literals** (character sequences enclosed in quotes, such as "Harry"). A string variable is simply a variable that can hold a string, just as an integer variable can hold an integer. A string literal denotes a particular string, just as a number literal (such as 2) denotes a particular number.

The length method yields the number of characters in a string.

The number of characters in a string is called the *length* of the string. For example, the length of "Harry" is 5. As you saw in Section 2.3, you can compute the length of a string with the length method.

```
int n = name.length();
```

A string of length 0 is called the *empty string*. It contains no characters and is written as " ".

4.5.2 Concatenation

Use the + operator to *concatenate* strings; that is, to put them together to yield a longer string.

Given two strings, such as "Harry" and "Morgan", you can **concatenate** them to one long string. The result consists of all characters in the first string, followed by all characters in the second string. In Java, you use the + operator to concatenate two strings.

For example,

```
String fName = "Harry";
String lName = "Morgan";
String name = fName + lName;
```

results in the string

```
"HarryMorgan"
```

What if you'd like the first and last name separated by a space? No problem:

```
String name = fName + " " + lName;
```

This statement concatenates three strings: fName, the string literal " ", and lName. The result is

```
"Harry Morgan"
```

When the expression to the left or the right of a + operator is a string, the other one is automatically forced to become a string as well, and both strings are concatenated.

For example, consider this code:

```
String jobTitle = "Agent";
int employeeId = 7;
String bond = jobTitle + employeeId;
```

Whenever one of the arguments of the + operator is a string, the other argument is converted to a string.

Because jobTitle is a string, employeeId is converted from the integer 7 to the string "7". Then the two strings "Agent" and "7" are concatenated to form the string "Agent7".

This concatenation is very useful for reducing the number of System.out.print instructions. For example, you can combine

```
System.out.print("The total is ");
System.out.println(total);
```

to the single call

```
System.out.println("The total is " + total);
```

The concatenation "The total is " + total computes a single string that consists of the string "The total is ", followed by the string equivalent of the number total.

4.5.3 String Input

Use the next method of the Scanner class to read a string containing a single word.

You can read a string from the console:

```
System.out.print("Please enter your name: ");
String name = in.next();
```

When a string is read with the next method, only one word is read. For example, suppose the user types

```
Harry Morgan
```

as the response to the prompt. This input consists of two words. The call in.next() yields the string "Harry". You can use another call to in.next() to read the second word.

4.5.4 Escape Sequences

To include a quotation mark in a literal string, precede it with a backslash (\), like this:

```
"He said \"Hello\""
```

The backslash is not included in the string. It indicates that the quotation mark that follows should be a part of the string and not mark the end of the string. The sequence \" is called an **escape sequence**.

To include a backslash in a string, use the escape sequence \\, like this:

```
"C:\\Temp\\Secret.txt"
```

Another common escape sequence is \n, which denotes a **newline** character. Printing a newline character causes the start of a new line on the display. For example, the statement

```
System.out.print("*\n**\n***\n");
```

prints the characters

```
*
**
***
```

on three separate lines.

You often want to add a newline character to the end of the format string when you use System.out.printf:

```
System.out.printf("Price: %10.2f\n", price);
```

4.5.5 Strings and Characters

Strings are sequences of **Unicode** characters (see Computing & Society 4.2). In Java, a **character** is a value of the type char. Characters have numeric values. You can find the values of the characters that are used in Western European languages in Appendix A. For example, if you look up the value for the character 'H', you can see that it is actually encoded as the number 72.

A string is a sequence of characters.

Character literals are delimited by single quotes, and you should not confuse them with strings.

- 'H' is a character, a value of type char.
- "H" is a string containing a single character, a value of type String.

The charAt method returns a char value from a string. The first string position is labeled 0, the second one 1, and so on.

> *String positions are counted starting with 0.*

```
H a r r y
0 1 2 3 4
```

The position number of the last character (4 for the string "Harry") is always one less than the length of the string.

For example, the statement

```
String name = "Harry";
char start = name.charAt(0);
char last = name.charAt(4);
```

sets start to the value 'H' and last to the value 'y'.

4.5.6 Substrings

Use the substring method to extract a part of a string.

Once you have a string, you can extract substrings by using the substring method. The method call

```
str.substring(start, pastEnd)
```

returns a string that is made up of the characters in the string str, starting at position start, and containing all characters up to, but not including, the position pastEnd. Here is an example:

```
String greeting = "Hello, World!";
String sub = greeting.substring(0, 5); // sub is "Hello"
```

Here the substring operation makes a string that consists of the first five characters taken from the string greeting.

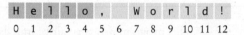

Let's figure out how to extract the substring "World". Count characters starting at 0, not 1. You find that W has position number 7. The first character that you don't want, !, is the character at position 12. Therefore, the appropriate substring command is

```
String sub2 = greeting.substring(7, 12);
```

It is curious that you must specify the position of the first character that you do want and then the first character that you don't want. There is one advantage to this setup. You can easily compute the length of the substring: It is pastEnd - start. For example, the string "World" has length 12 − 7 = 5.

If you omit the end position when calling the substring method, then all characters from the starting position to the end of the string are copied. For example,

```
String tail = greeting.substring(7); // Copies all characters from position 7 on
```

sets tail to the string "World!".

Following is a simple program that puts these concepts to work. The program asks for your name and that of your significant other. It then prints out your initials.

The operation `first.substring(0, 1)` makes a string consisting of one character, taken from the start of `first`. The program does the same for the second. Then it concatenates the resulting one-character strings with the string literal `"&"` to get a string of length 3, the `initials` string. (See Figure 3.)

Initials are formed from the first letter of each name.

```
first =  R  o  d  o  l  f  o
         0  1  2  3  4  5  6

second = S  a  l  l  y
         0  1  2  3  4

initials = R  &  S
           0  1  2
```

Figure 3 Building the initials String

section_5/Initials.java

```java
1   import java.util.Scanner;
2
3   /**
4      This program prints a pair of initials.
5   */
6   public class Initials
7   {
8      public static void main(String[] args)
9      {
10        Scanner in = new Scanner(System.in);
11
12        // Get the names of the couple
13
14        System.out.print("Enter your first name: ");
15        String first = in.next();
16        System.out.print("Enter your significant other's first name: ");
17        String second = in.next();
18
19        // Compute and display the inscription
20
21        String initials = first.substring(0, 1)
22           + "&" + second.substring(0, 1);
23        System.out.println(initials);
24     }
25  }
```

Program Run

```
Enter your first name: Rodolfo
Enter your significant other's first name: Sally
R&S
```

Table 7 String Operations

Statement	Result	Comment
`string str = "Ja";` `str = str + "va";`	str is set to "Java"	When applied to strings, + denotes concatenation.
`System.out.println("Please"` `   + " enter your name: ");`	Prints Please enter your name:	Use concatenation to break up strings that don't fit into one line.
`team = 49 + "ers"`	team is set to "49ers"	Because "ers" is a string, 49 is converted to a string.

`String first = in.next();`
`String last = in.next();`
`(User input: Harry Morgan)`
	first contains "Harry"
	last contains "Morgan"
		The next method places the next word into the string variable.

`String greeting = "H & S";` `int n = greeting.length();`	n is set to 5	Each space counts as one character.
`String str = "Sally";` `char ch = str.charAt(1);`	ch is set to 'a'	This is a char value, not a String. Note that the initial position is 0.
`String str = "Sally";` `String str2 = str.substring(1, 4);`	str2 is set to "all"	Extracts the substring starting at position 1 and ending before position 4.
`String str = "Sally";` `String str2 = str.substring(1);`	str2 is set to "ally"	If you omit the end position, all characters from the position until the end of the string are included.
`String str = "Sally";` `String str2 = str.substring(1, 2);`	str2 is set to "a"	Extracts a String of length 1; contrast with str.charAt(1).
`String last = str.substring(` `   str.length() - 1);`	last is set to the string containing the last character in str	The last character has position str.length() - 1.

SELF CHECK

22. What is the length of the string `"Java Program"`?

23. Consider this string variable.

    String str = "Java Program";

Give a call to the `substring` method that returns the substring `"gram"`.

24. Use string concatenation to turn the string variable str from Self Check 23 into `"Java Programming"`.

25. What does the following statement sequence print?

    String str = "Harry";
    int n = str.length();
    String mystery = str.substring(0, 1) + str.substring(n - 1, n);
    System.out.println(mystery);

26. Give an input statement to read a name of the form "John Q. Public".

Practice It   Now you can try these exercises at the end of the chapter: R4.8, R4.12, E4.14, P4.6.

Programming Tip 4.3

Reading Exception Reports

You will often have programs that terminate and display an error message, such as

```
Exception in thread "main" java.lang.StringIndexOutOfBoundsException:
    String index out of range: -4
  at java.lang.String.substring(String.java:1444)
  at Homework1.main(Homework1.java:16)
```

If this happens to you, don't say "it didn't work," or "my program died." Instead, read the error message. Admittedly, the format of the exception report is not very friendly. But it is actually easy to decipher it.

When you have a close look at the error message, you will notice two pieces of useful information:

1. The name of the exception, such as StringIndexOutOfBoundsException
2. The line number of the code that contained the statement that caused the exception, such as Homework1.java:16

The name of the exception is always in the first line of the report, and it ends in Exception. If you get a StringIndexOutOfBoundsException, then there was a problem with accessing an invalid position in a string. That is useful information.

The line number of the offending code is a little harder to determine. The exception report contains the entire **stack trace**—that is, the names of all methods that were pending when the exception hit. The first line of the stack trace is the method that actually generated the exception. The last line of the stack trace is a line in main. Often, the exception was thrown by a method that is in the standard library. Look for the first line in your code that appears in the exception report. For example, skip the line that refers to

```
java.lang.String.substring(String.java:1444)
```

The next line in our example mentions a line number in your code, Homework1.java. Once you have the line number in your code, open up the file, go to that line, and look at it! Also look at the name of the exception. In most cases, these two pieces of information will make it completely obvious what went wrong, and you can easily fix your error.

Special Topic 4.4

Using Dialog Boxes for Input and Output

Most program users find the console window rather old-fashioned. The easiest alternative is to create a separate pop-up window for each input.

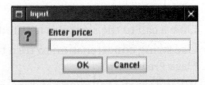

An Input Dialog Box

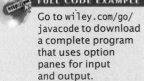

FULL CODE EXAMPLE

Go to wiley.com/go/ javacode to download a complete program that uses option panes for input and output.

Call the static showInputDialog method of the JOptionPane class, and supply the string that prompts the input from the user. For example,

```
String input = JOptionPane.showInputDialog("Enter price:");
```

That method returns a String object. Of course, often you need the input as a number. Use the Integer.parseInt and Double.parseDouble methods to convert the string to a number:

```
double price = Double.parseDouble(input);
```

You can also display output in a dialog box:

```
JOptionPane.showMessageDialog(null, "Price: " + price);
```

Computing & Society 4.2 International Alphabets and Unicode

The English alphabet is pretty simple: upper- and lowercase *a* to *z*. Other European languages have accent marks and special characters. For example, German has three so-called *umlaut* characters, ä, ö, ü, and a *double-s* character ß. These are not optional frills; you couldn't write a page of German text without using these characters a few times. German keyboards have keys for these characters.

Hebrew, Arabic, and English

Many countries don't use the Roman script at all. Russian, Greek, Hebrew, Arabic, and Thai letters, to name just a few, have completely different shapes. To complicate matters, Hebrew and Arabic are typed from right to left. Each of these alphabets has about as many characters as the English alphabet.

The Chinese languages as well as Japanese and Korean use Chinese characters. Each character represents an idea or thing. Words are made up of one or more of these ideographic characters. Over 70,000 ideographs are known.

Starting in 1987, a consortium of hardware and software manufacturers developed a uniform encoding scheme called Unicode that is capable of encoding text in essentially all written languages of the world. An early version of Unicode used 16 bits for each character. The Java char type corresponds to that encoding.

Today Unicode has grown to a 21-bit code, with definitions for over 100,000 characters (www.unicode.org). There are even plans to add codes for extinct languages, such as Egyptian hieroglyphics. Unfortunately, that means that a Java char value does not always correspond to a Unicode character. Some characters in languages such as Chinese or ancient Egyptian occupy two char values.

The German Keyboard Layout

The Chinese Script

<hr/>

CHAPTER SUMMARY

Choose appropriate types for representing numeric data.

- Java has eight primitive types, including four integer types and two floating-point types.
- A numeric computation overflows if the result falls outside the range for the number type.
- Rounding errors occur when an exact conversion between numbers is not possible.
- A final variable is a constant. Once its value has been set, it cannot be changed.
- Use named constants to make your programs easier to read and maintain.

Write arithmetic expressions in Java.

- Mixing integers and floating-point values in an arithmetic expression yields a floating-point value.
- The ++ operator adds 1 to a variable; the -- operator subtracts 1.
- If both arguments of / are integers, the remainder is discarded.
- The % operator computes the remainder of an integer division.
- The Java library declares many mathematical functions, such as Math.sqrt (square root) and Math.pow (raising to a power).
- You use a cast (*typeName*) to convert a value to a different type.

Write programs that read user input and print formatted output.

- Use the Scanner class to read keyboard input in a console window.
- Use the printf method to specify how values should be formatted.

Carry out hand calculations when developing an algorithm.

- Pick concrete values for a typical situation to use in a hand calculation.

Write programs that process strings.

- Strings are sequences of characters.
- The length method yields the number of characters in a string.
- Use the + operator to *concatenate* strings; that is, to put them together to yield a longer string.
- Whenever one of the arguments of the + operator is a string, the other argument is converted to a string.
- Use the next method of the Scanner class to read a string containing a single word.
- String positions are counted starting with 0.
- Use the substring method to extract a part of a string.

STANDARD LIBRARY ITEMS INTRODUCED IN THIS CHAPTER

java.io.PrintStream	exp	java.lang.String	java.math.BigInteger
printf	log	charAt	add
java.lang.Double	log10	length	multiply
parseDouble	max	substring	subtract
java.lang.Integer	min	java.lang.System	java.util.Scanner
MAX_VALUE	pow	in	next
MIN_VALUE	round	java.math.BigDecimal	nextDouble
parseInt	sin	add	nextInt
java.lang.Math	sqrt	multiply	javax.swing.JOptionPane
PI	tan	subtract	showInputDialog
abs	toDegrees		showMessageDialog
cos	toRadians		

REVIEW QUESTIONS

▪ R4.1 Write declarations for storing the following quantities. Choose between integers and floating-point numbers. Declare constants when appropriate.

a. The number of days per week

b. The number of days until the end of the semester

c. The number of centimeters in an inch

d. The height of the tallest person in your class, in centimeters

▪ R4.2 What is the value of mystery after this sequence of statements?

```
int mystery = 1;
mystery = 1 - 2 * mystery;
mystery = mystery + 1;
```

▪ R4.3 What is wrong with the following sequence of statements?

```
int mystery = 1;
mystery = mystery + 1;
int mystery = 1 - 2 * mystery;
```

▪▪ R4.4 Write the following Java expressions in mathematical notation.

a. `dm = m * (Math.sqrt(1 + v / c) / Math.sqrt(1 - v / c) - 1);`

b. `volume = Math.PI * r * r * h;`

c. `volume = 4 * Math.PI * Math.pow(r, 3) / 3;`

d. `z = Math.sqrt(x ^ x + y ^ y);`

▪▪ R4.5 Write the following mathematical expressions in Java.

$$s = s_0 + v_0 t + \frac{1}{2} g t^2$$

$$G = 4\pi^2 \frac{a^3}{p^2(m_1 + m_2)}$$

$$FV = PV \cdot \left(1 + \frac{INT}{100}\right)^{YRS}$$

$$c = \sqrt{a^2 + b^2 - 2ab\cos\gamma}$$

▪▪ R4.6 What are the values of the following expressions? In each line, assume that

```
double x = 2.5;
double y = -1.5;
int m = 18;
int n = 4;
```

a. `x + n * y - (x + n) * y`

b. `m / n + m % n`

c. `5 * x - n / 5`

d. `1 - (1 - (1 - (1 - (1 - n))))`

e. `Math.sqrt(Math.sqrt(n))`

- **R4.7** What are the values of the following expressions, assuming that n is 17 and m is 18?

    a. n / 10 + n % 10
    b. n % 2 + m % 2
    c. (m + n) / 2
    d. (m + n) / 2.0
    e. (int) (0.5 * (m + n))
    f. (int) Math.round(0.5 * (m + n))

- **R4.8** What are the values of the following expressions? In each line, assume that

    ```
    String s = "Hello";
    String t = "World";
    ```

    a. s.length() + t.length()
    b. s.substring(1, 2)
    c. s.substring(s.length() / 2, s.length())
    d. s + t
    e. t + s

- **R4.9** Find at least five *compile-time* errors in the following program.

    ```
    public class HasErrors
    {
        public static void main();
        {
            System.out.print(Please enter two numbers:)
            x = in.readDouble;
            y = in.readDouble;
            System.out.printline("The sum is " + x + y);
        }
    }
    ```

- **R4.10** Find three *run-time* errors in the following program.

    ```
    public class HasErrors
    {
        public static void main(String[] args)
        {
            int x = 0;
            int y = 0;
            Scanner in = new Scanner("System.in");
            System.out.print("Please enter an integer:");
            x = in.readInt();
            System.out.print("Please enter another integer: ");
            x = in.readInt();
            System.out.println("The sum is " + x + y);
        }
    }
    ```

- **R4.11** Consider the following code:

    ```
    CashRegister register = new CashRegister();
    register.recordPurchase(19.93);
    register.receivePayment(20, 0, 0, 0, 0);
    System.out.print("Change: ");
    System.out.println(register.giveChange());
    ```

    The code segment prints the total as 0.07000000000000028. Explain why. Give a recommendation to improve the code so that users will not be confused.

- **R4.12** Explain the differences between 2, 2.0, '2', "2", and "2.0".

- **R4.13** Explain what each of the following program segments computes.

    a. x = 2;
        y = x + x;
    b. s = "2";
        t = s + s;

- ■ **R4.14** Write pseudocode for a program that reads a word and then prints the first character, the last character, and the characters in the middle. For example, if the input is Harry, the program prints H y arr.

- ■ **R4.15** Write pseudocode for a program that reads a name (such as Harold James Morgan) and then prints a monogram consisting of the initial letters of the first, middle, and last name (such as HJM).

- ■■ **R4.16** Write pseudocode for a program that computes the first and last digit of a number. For example, if the input is 23456, the program should print 2 and 6. *Hint:* %, Math.log10.

- ■ **R4.17** Modify the pseudocode for the program in How To 4.1 so that the program gives change in quarters, dimes, and nickels. You can assume that the price is a multiple of 5 cents. To develop your pseudocode, first work with a couple of specific values.

- ■ **R4.18** A cocktail shaker is composed of three cone sections.

    Using realistic values for the radii and heights, compute the total volume, using the formula given in Self Check 21 for a cone section. Then develop an algorithm that works for arbitrary dimensions.

- ■■ **R4.19** You are cutting off a piece of pie like this, where c is the length of the straight part (called the chord length) and h is the height of the piece.

    There is an approximate formula for the area:

    $$A \approx \frac{2}{3}ch + \frac{h^3}{2c}$$

    However, h is not so easy to measure, whereas the diameter d of a pie is usually well-known. Calculate the area where the diameter of the pie is 12 inches and the chord length of the segment is 10 inches. Generalize to an algorithm that yields the area for any diameter and chord length.

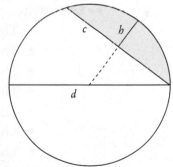

- ■■ **R4.20** The following pseudocode describes how to obtain the name of a day, given the day number (0 = Sunday, 1 = Monday, and so on.)

    > Declare a string called names containing "SunMonTueWedThuFriSat".
    > Compute the starting position as 3 x the day number.
    > Extract the substring of names at the starting position with length 3.

    Check this pseudocode, using the day number 4. Draw a diagram of the string that is being computed, similar to Figure 3.

- ■■ **R4.21** The following pseudocode describes how to swap two letters in a word.

    > We are given a string str and two positions i and j. (i comes before j)
    > Set first to the substring from the start of the string to the last position before i.

Set middle to the substring from positions i + 1 to j - 1.
Set last to the substring from position j + 1 to the end of the string.
Concatenate the following five strings: first, the string containing just the character at position j, middle, the string containing just the character at position i, and last.

Check this pseudocode, using the string "Gateway" and positions 2 and 4. Draw a diagram of the string that is being computed, similar to Figure 3.

•• R4.22 How do you get the first character of a string? The last character? How do you remove the first character? The last character?

••• R4.23 Write a program that prints the values

```
3 * 1000 * 1000 * 1000
3.0 * 1000 * 1000 * 1000
```

Explain the results.

PRACTICE EXERCISES

• E4.1 Write a program that displays the dimensions of a letter-size (8.5 × 11 inches) sheet of paper in millimeters. There are 25.4 millimeters per inch. Use constants and comments in your program.

• E4.2 Write a program that computes and displays the perimeter of a letter-size (8.5 × 11 inches) sheet of paper and the length of its diagonal.

• E4.3 Write a program that reads a number and displays the square, cube, and fourth power. Use the Math.pow method only for the fourth power.

•• E4.4 Write a program that prompts the user for two integers and then prints
  • The sum
  • The difference
  • The product
  • The average
  • The distance (absolute value of the difference)
  • The maximum (the larger of the two)
  • The minimum (the smaller of the two)
  Hint: The max and min functions are declared in the Math class.

•• E4.5 Enhance the output of Exercise E4.4 so that the numbers are properly aligned:

```
Sum:            45
Difference:     -5
Product:        500
Average:        22.50
Distance:       5
Maximum:        25
Minimum:        20
```

•• E4.6 Write a program that prompts the user for a measurement in meters and then converts it to miles, feet, and inches.

• E4.7 Write a program that prompts the user for a radius and then prints
- The area and circumference of a circle with that radius
- The volume and surface area of a sphere with that radius

•• E4.8 Write a program that asks the user for the lengths of a rectangle's sides. Then print
- The area and perimeter of the rectangle
- The length of the diagonal (use the Pythagorean theorem)

• E4.9 Improve the program discussed in How To 4.1 to allow input of quarters in addition to bills.

•• E4.10 Write a program that asks the user to input
- The number of gallons of gas in the tank
- The fuel efficiency in miles per gallon
- The price of gas per gallon

Then print the cost per 100 miles and how far the car can go with the gas in the tank.

• E4.11 *File names and extensions.* Write a program that prompts the user for the drive letter (C), the path (\Windows\System), the file name (Readme), and the extension (txt). Then print the complete file name C:\Windows\System\Readme.txt. (If you use UNIX or a Macintosh, skip the drive name and use / instead of \ to separate directories.)

••• E4.12 Write a program that reads a number between 1,000 and 999,999 from the user, where the user enters a comma in the input. Then print the number without a comma.

Here is a sample dialog; the user input is in color:

```
Please enter an integer between 1,000 and 999,999: 23,456
23456
```

Hint: Read the input as a string. Measure the length of the string. Suppose it contains *n* characters. Then extract substrings consisting of the first $n - 4$ characters and the last three characters.

•• E4.13 Write a program that reads a number between 1,000 and 999,999 from the user and prints it with a comma separating the thousands. Here is a sample dialog; the user input is in color:

```
Please enter an integer between 1000 and 999999: 23456
23,456
```

• E4.14 *Printing a grid.* Write a program that prints the following grid to play tic-tac-toe.

```
+--+--+--+
|  |  |  |
+--+--+--+
|  |  |  |
+--+--+--+
|  |  |  |
+--+--+--+
```

Of course, you could simply write seven statements of the form

```
System.out.println("+--+--+--+");
```

You should do it the smart way, though. Declare string variables to hold two kinds of patterns: a comb-shaped pattern and the bottom line. Print the comb three times and the bottom line once.

•• **E4.15** Write a program that reads in an integer and breaks it into a sequence of individual digits. For example, the input 16384 is displayed as

```
1 6 3 8 4
```

You may assume that the input has no more than five digits and is not negative.

•• **E4.16** Write a program that reads two times in military format (0900, 1730) and prints the number of hours and minutes between the two times. Here is a sample run. User input is in color.

```
Please enter the first time: 0900
Please enter the second time: 1730
8 hours 30 minutes
```

Extra credit if you can deal with the case where the first time is later than the second:

```
Please enter the first time: 1730
Please enter the second time: 0900
15 hours 30 minutes
```

••• **E4.17** *Writing large letters.* A large letter H can be produced like this:

```
*   *
*   *
*****
*   *
*   *
```

It can be declared as a string literal like this:

```
final string LETTER_H = "*   *\n*   *\n*****\n*   *\n*   *\n";
```

(The \n escape sequence denotes a "newline" character that causes subsequent characters to be printed on a new line.) Do the same for the letters E, L, and O. Then write the message

```
H
E
L
L
O
```

in large letters.

•• **E4.18** Write a program that transforms numbers 1, 2, 3, ..., 12 into the corresponding month names January, February, March, ..., December. *Hint:* Make a very long string "January February March ...", in which you add spaces such that each month name has *the same length*. Then use substring to extract the month you want.

•• **E4.19** Write a program that prints a Christmas tree:

```
    /\
   /  \
  /    \
 /      \
 --------
   "  "
   "  "
   "  "
```

Remember to use escape sequences.

E4.20 Enhance the `CashRegister` class by adding separate methods `enterDollars`, `enterQuarters`, `enterDimes`, `enterNickels`, and `enterPennies`.

Use this tester class:

```
public class CashRegisterTester
{
    public static void main (String[] args)
    {
        CashRegister register = new CashRegister();
        register.recordPurchase(20.37);
        register.enterDollars(20);
        register.enterQuarters(2);
        System.out.println("Change: " + register.giveChange());
        System.out.println("Expected: 0.13");
    }
}
```

■■ E4.21 Implement a class `IceCreamCone` with methods `getSurfaceArea()` and `getVolume()`. In the constructor, supply the height and radius of the cone. Be careful when looking up the formula for the surface area—you should only include the outside area along the side of the cone since the cone has an opening on the top to hold the ice cream.

■■ E4.22 Implement a class `SodaCan` whose constructor receives the height and diameter of the soda can. Supply methods `getVolume` and `getSurfaceArea`. Supply a `SodaCanTester` class that tests your class.

■■■ E4.23 Implement a class `Balloon` that models a spherical balloon that is being filled with air. The constructor constructs an empty balloon. Supply these methods:

- `void addAir(double amount)` adds the given amount of air
- `double getVolume()` gets the current volume
- `double getSurfaceArea()` gets the current surface area
- `double getRadius()` gets the current radius

Supply a `BalloonTester` class that constructs a balloon, adds 100 cm^3 of air, tests the three accessor methods, adds another 100 cm^3 of air, and tests the accessor methods again.

PROGRAMMING PROJECTS

■■■ P4.1 Write a program that helps a person decide whether to buy a hybrid car. Your program's inputs should be:

- The cost of a new car
- The estimated miles driven per year
- The estimated gas price
- The efficiency in miles per gallon
- The estimated resale value after 5 years

Compute the total cost of owning the car for five years. (For simplicity, we will not take the cost of financing into account.)

Obtain realistic prices for a new and used hybrid and a comparable car from the Web. Run your program twice, using today's gas price and 15,000 miles per year. Include pseudocode and the program runs with your assignment.

■■ P4.2 Easter Sunday is the first Sunday after the first full moon of spring. To compute the date, you can use this algorithm, invented by the mathematician Carl Friedrich Gauss in 1800:

1. Let y be the year (such as 1800 or 2001).
2. Divide y by 19 and call the remainder a. Ignore the quotient.
3. Divide y by 100 to get a quotient b and a remainder c.
4. Divide b by 4 to get a quotient d and a remainder e.
5. Divide 8 * b + 13 by 25 to get a quotient g. Ignore the remainder.
6. Divide 19 * a + b - d - g + 15 by 30 to get a remainder h. Ignore the quotient.
7. Divide c by 4 to get a quotient j and a remainder k.
8. Divide a + 11 * h by 319 to get a quotient m. Ignore the remainder.
9. Divide 2 * e + 2 * j - k - h + m + 32 by 7 to get a remainder r. Ignore the quotient.
10. Divide h - m + r + 90 by 25 to get a quotient n. Ignore the remainder.
11. Divide h - m + r + n + 19 by 32 to get a remainder p. Ignore the quotient.

Then Easter falls on day p of month n. For example, if y is 2001:

```
a = 6              h = 18           n = 4
b = 20, c = 1      j = 0, k = 1     p = 15
d = 5, e = 0       m = 0
g = 6              r = 6
```

Therefore, in 2001, Easter Sunday fell on April 15. Write a program that prompts the user for a year and prints out the month and day of Easter Sunday.

■■■ P4.3 In this project, you will perform calculations with triangles. A triangle is defined by the *x*- and *y*-coordinates of its three corner points.

Your job is to compute the following properties of a given triangle:

- the lengths of all sides
- the angles at all corners
- the perimeter
- the area

Implement a `Triangle` class with appropriate methods. Supply a program that prompts a user for the corner point coordinates and produces a nicely formatted table of the triangle properties.

■■■ P4.4 The `CashRegister` class has an unfortunate limitation: It is closely tied to the coin system in the United States and Canada. Research the system used in most of Europe. Your goal is to produce a cash register that works with euros and cents. Rather than designing another limited `CashRegister` implementation for the European market, you should design a separate `Coin` class and a cash register that can work with coins of all types.

■■ Business P4.5 The following pseudocode describes how a bookstore computes the price of an order from the total price and the number of the books that were ordered.

Read the total book price and the number of books.
Compute the tax (7.5 percent of the total book price).
Compute the shipping charge ($2 per book).
The price of the order is the sum of the total book price, the tax, and the shipping charge.
Print the price of the order.

Translate this pseudocode into a Java program.

■■ Business P4.6 The following pseudocode describes how to turn a string containing a ten-digit phone number (such as "4155551212") into a more readable string with parentheses and dashes, like this: "(415) 555-1212".

Take the substring consisting of the first three characters and surround it with "(" and ") ". This is the area code.
Concatenate the area code, the substring consisting of the next three characters, a hyphen, and the substring consisting of the last four characters. This is the formatted number.

Translate this pseudocode into a Java program that reads a telephone number into a string variable, computes the formatted number, and prints it.

■■ Business P4.7 The following pseudocode describes how to extract the dollars and cents from a price given as a floating-point value. For example, a price 2.95 yields values 2 and 95 for the dollars and cents.

Assign the price to an integer variable dollars.
Multiply the difference price - dollars by 100 and add 0.5.
Assign the result to an integer variable cents.

Translate this pseudocode into a Java program. Read a price and print the dollars and cents. Test your program with inputs 2.95 and 4.35.

■■ Business P4.8 *Giving change.* Implement a program that directs a cashier how to give change. The program has two inputs: the amount due and the amount received from the customer. Display the dollars, quarters, dimes, nickels, and pennies that the customer should receive in return. In order to avoid roundoff errors, the program user should supply both amounts in pennies, for example 274 instead of 2.74.

■ Business P4.9 An online bank wants you to create a program that shows prospective customers how their deposits will grow. Your program should read the initial balance and the annual interest rate. Interest is compounded monthly. Print out the balances after the first three months. Here is a sample run:

```
Initial balance: 1000
Annual interest rate in percent: 6.0
After first month:    1005.00
After second month:   1010.03
After third month:    1015.08
```

■■ Business P4.10 A video club wants to reward its best members with a discount based on the member's number of movie rentals and the number of new members referred by the member. The discount is in percent and is equal to the sum of the rentals and the referrals, but it cannot exceed 75 percent. (*Hint:* Math.min.) Write a program Discount-Calculator to calculate the value of the discount.

Here is a sample run:

```
Enter the number of movie rentals: 56
Enter the number of members referred to the video club: 3
The discount is equal to:     59.00 percent.
```

· Science P4.11 Consider the following circuit.

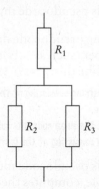

Write a program that reads the resistances of the three resistors and computes the total resistance, using Ohm's law.

·· Science P4.12 The dew point temperature T_d can be calculated (approximately) from the relative humidity RH and the actual temperature T by

$$T_d = \frac{b \cdot f(T, RH)}{a - f(T, RH)}$$

$$f(T, RH) = \frac{a \cdot T}{b + T} + \ln(RH)$$

where $a = 17.27$ and $b = 237.7°$ C.

Write a program that reads the relative humidity (between 0 and 1) and the temperature (in degrees C) and prints the dew point value. Use the Java function log to compute the natural logarithm.

··· Science P4.13 The pipe clip temperature sensors shown here are robust sensors that can be clipped directly onto copper pipes to measure the temperature of the liquids in the pipes.

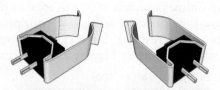

Each sensor contains a device called a *thermistor*. Thermistors are semiconductor devices that exhibit a temperature-dependent resistance described by:

$$R = R_0\, e^{\beta\left(\frac{1}{T} - \frac{1}{T_0}\right)}$$

where R is the resistance (in Ω) at the temperature T (in $°$K), and R_0 is the resistance (in Ω) at the temperature T_0 (in $°$K). β is a constant that depends on the material used to make the thermistor. Thermistors are specified by providing values for R_0, T_0, and β.

The thermistors used to make the pipe clip temperature sensors have $R_0 = 1075\ \Omega$ at $T_0 = 85\ °C$, and $\beta = 3969\ °K$. (Notice that β has units of $°K$. Recall that the temperature in $°K$ is obtained by adding 273 to the temperature in $°C$.) The liquid temperature, in $°C$, is determined from the resistance R, in Ω, using

$$T = \frac{\beta T_0}{T_0 \ln\left(\dfrac{R}{R_0}\right) + \beta} - 273$$

Write a Java program that prompts the user for the thermistor resistance R and prints a message giving the liquid temperature in $°C$.

••• Science P4.24 The circuit shown below illustrates some important aspects of the connection between a power company and one of its customers. The customer is represented by three parameters, V_t, P, and pf. V_t is the voltage accessed by plugging into a wall outlet. Customers depend on having a dependable value of V_t in order for their appliances to work properly. Accordingly, the power company regulates the value of V_t carefully.

P describes the amount of power used by the customer and is the primary factor in determining the customer's electric bill. The power factor, pf, is less familiar. (The power factor is calculated as the cosine of an angle so that its value will always be between zero and one.) In this problem you will be asked to write a Java program to investigate the significance of the power factor.

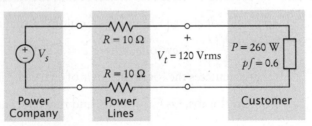

In the figure, the power lines are represented, somewhat simplistically, as resistances in Ohms. The power company is represented as an AC voltage source. The source voltage, V_s, required to provide the customer with power P at voltage V_t can be determined using the formula

$$V_s = \sqrt{\left(V_t + \frac{2RP}{V_t}\right)^2 + \left(\frac{2RP}{pf V_t}\right)^2 \left(1 - pf^2\right)}$$

(V_s has units of Vrms.) This formula indicates that the value of V_s depends on the value of pf. Write a Java program that prompts the user for a power factor value and then prints a message giving the corresponding value of V_s, using the values for P, R, and V_t shown in the figure above.

••• Science P4.25 Consider the following tuning circuit connected to an antenna, where C is a variable capacitor whose capacitance ranges from C_{min} to C_{max}.

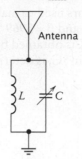

Antenna

L C

The tuning circuit selects the frequency $f = \dfrac{2\pi}{\sqrt{LC}}$. To design this circuit for a given frequency, take $C = \sqrt{C_{min}C_{max}}$ and calculate the required inductance L from f and C. Now the circuit can be tuned to any frequency in the range $f_{min} = \dfrac{2\pi}{\sqrt{LC_{max}}}$ to $f_{max} = \dfrac{2\pi}{\sqrt{LC_{min}}}$.

Write a Java program to design a tuning circuit for a given frequency, using a variable capacitor with given values for C_{min} and C_{max}. (A typical input is $f = 16.7$ MHz, $C_{min} = 14$ pF, and $C_{max} = 365$ pF.) The program should read in f (in Hz), C_{min} and C_{max} (in F), and print the required inductance value and the range of frequencies to which the circuit can be tuned by varying the capacitance.

• Science P4.26 According to the Coulomb force law, the electric force between two charged particles of charge Q_1 and Q_2 Coulombs, that are a distance r meters apart, is

$F = \dfrac{Q_1 Q_2}{4\pi\varepsilon r^2}$ Newtons, where $\varepsilon = 8.854 \times 10^{-12}$ Farads/meter. Write a program that calculates the force on a pair of charged particles, based on the user input of Q_1 Coulombs, Q_2 Coulombs, and r meters, and then computes and displays the electric force.

ANSWERS TO SELF-CHECK QUESTIONS

1. `int` and `double`.

2. The world's most populous country, China, has about 1.2×10^9 inhabitants. Therefore, individual population counts could be held in an `int`. However, the world population is over 6×10^9. If you compute totals or averages of multiple countries, you can exceed the largest `int` value. Therefore, `double` is a better choice. You could also use `long`, but there is no benefit because the exact population of a country is not known at any point in time.

3. The first initialization is incorrect. The right hand side is a value of type `double`, and it is not legal to initialize an `int` variable with a `double` value. The second initialization is correct—an `int` value can always be converted to a `double`.

4. The first declaration is used inside a method, the second inside a class.

5. Two things: You should use a named constant, not the "magic number" 3.14, and 3.14 is not an accurate representation of π.

6. `double interest = balance * percent / 100;`

7. `double sideLength = Math.sqrt(area);`

8. `4 * PI * Math.pow(radius, 3) / 3`
   or `(4.0 / 3) * PI * Math.pow(radius, 3)`,
   but not `(4 / 3) * PI * Math.pow(radius, 3)`

9. 17 and 29

10. It is the second-to-last digit of n. For example, if n is 1729, then n / 10 is 172, and (n / 10) % 10 is 2.

11. `System.out.print("How old are you? ");`
    `int age = in.nextInt();`

12. There is no prompt that alerts the program user to enter the quantity.

13. The second statement calls `nextInt`, not `nextDouble`. If the user were to enter a price such as 1.95, the program would be terminated with an "input mismatch exception".

14. There is no colon and space at the end of the prompt. A dialog would look like this:
    `Please enter the number of cans6`

15. `The total volume is    10`

    There are four spaces between is and 10. One space originates from the format string (the

space between s and %), and three spaces are added before 10 to achieve a field width of 5.

16. Here is a simple solution:
    ```
    System.out.printf("Bottles: %8d\n", bottles);
    System.out.printf("Cans:    %8d\n", cans);
    ```
    Note the spaces after `Cans:`. Alternatively, you can use format specifiers for the strings. You can even combine all output into a single statement:
    ```
    System.out.printf("%-9s%8d\n%-9s%8d\n",
    "Bottles: ", bottles, "Cans:", cans);
    ```

17. ```
    int pairs = (totalWidth - tileWidth)
        / (2 * tileWidth);
    int tiles = 1 + 2 * pairs;
    double gap = (totalWidth -
        tiles * tileWidth) / 2.0;
    ```
    Be sure that `pairs` is declared as an `int`.

18. Now there are groups of four tiles (gray/white/gray/black) following the initial black tile. Therefore, the algorithm is now

    number of groups = integer part of (total width – tile width) / (4 x tile width)
    number of tiles = 1 + 4 x number of groups

    The formula for the gap is not changed.

19. The answer depends only on whether the row and column numbers are even or odd, so let's first take the remainder after dividing by 2. Then we can enumerate all expected answers:

Row % 2	Column % 2	Color
0	0	0
0	1	1
1	0	1
1	1	0

    In the first three entries of the table, the color is simply the sum of the remainders. In the fourth entry, the sum would be 2, but we want a zero. We can achieve that by taking another remainder operation:

    color = ((row % 2) + (column % 2)) % 2

20. In nine years, the repair costs increased by $1,400. Therefore, the increase per year is $1,400 / 9 \approx $156. The repair cost in year 3 would be $100 + 2 \times $156 = $412. The repair cost in year n is $100 + n \times $156. To avoid accumulation of roundoff errors, it is actually
    ```

a good idea to use the original expression that yielded $156, that is,

Repair cost in year n = 100 + n x 1400 / 9

21. The pseudocode follows from the equations:

bottom volume = π x r_1^2 x h_1
top volume = π x r_2^2 x h_2
middle volume = π x (r_1^2 + r_1 x r_2 + r_2^2) x h_3 / 3
total volume = bottom volume + top volume + middle volume

Measuring a typical wine bottle yields $r_1 = 3.6, r_2 = 1.2, h_1 = 15, h_2 = 7, h_3 = 6$ (all in centimeters). Therefore,

bottom volume = 610.73

top volume = 31.67

middle volume = 135.72

total volume = 778.12

The actual volume is 750 ml, which is close enough to our computation to give confidence that it is correct.

22. The length is 12. The space counts as a character.

23. `str.substring(8, 12)` or `str.substring(8)`

24. `str = str + "ming";`

25. `Hy`

26. ```
String first = in.next();
String middle = in.next();
String last = in.next();
```
```

DECISIONS

One of the essential features of computer programs is their ability to make decisions. Like a train that changes tracks depending on how the switches are set, a program can take different actions depending on inputs and other circumstances.

In this chapter, you will learn how to program simple and complex decisions. You will apply what you learn to the task of checking user input.

5.1 The if Statement

The if statement allows a program to carry out different actions depending on the nature of the data to be processed.

The if statement is used to implement a decision (see Syntax 5.1). When a condition is fulfilled, one set of statements is executed. Otherwise, another set of statements is executed.

Here is an example using the if statement: In many countries, the number 13 is considered unlucky. Rather than offending superstitious tenants, building owners sometimes skip the thirteenth floor; floor 12 is immediately followed by floor 14. Of course, floor 13 is not usually left empty or, as some conspiracy theorists believe, filled with secret offices and research labs. It is simply called floor 14. The computer that controls the building elevators needs to compensate for this foible and adjust all floor numbers above 13.

Let's simulate this process in Java. We will ask the user to type in the desired floor number and then compute the actual floor. When the input is above 13, then we need to decrement the input to obtain the actual floor. For example, if the user provides an input of 20, the program determines the actual floor to be 19. Otherwise, it simply uses the supplied floor number.

This elevator panel "skips" the thirteenth floor. The floor is not actually missing—the computer that controls the elevator adjusts the floor numbers above 13.

```java
int actualFloor;

if (floor > 13)
{
   actualFloor = floor - 1;
}
else
{
   actualFloor = floor;
}
```

The flowchart in Figure 1 shows the branching behavior.

In our example, each branch of the if statement contains a single statement. You can include as many statements in each branch as you like. Sometimes, it happens that

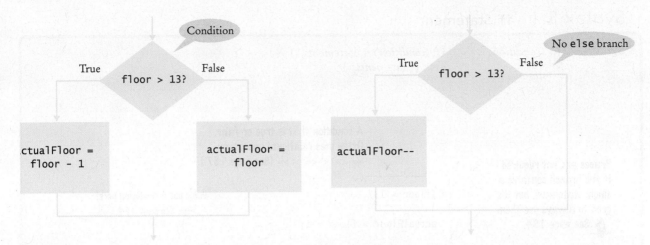

Figure 1
Flowchart for if Statement

Figure 2
Flowchart for if Statement with No else Branch

there is nothing to do in the else branch of the statement. In that case, you can omit it entirely, such as in this example:

```
int actualFloor = floor;

if (floor > 13)
{
   actualFloor--;
} // No else needed
```

See Figure 2 for the flowchart.

An if statement is like a fork in the road. Depending upon a decision, different parts of the program are executed.

Syntax 5.1 if Statement

Syntax
```
if (condition)              if (condition) { statements₁ }
{                           else { statements₂ }
    statements
}
```

A condition that is true or false.
Often uses relational operators:
== != < <= > >= (See page 187.)

Braces are not required
if the branch contains a
single statement, but it's
good to always use them.
See page 184.

```
if (floor > 13)
{
    actualFloor = floor - 1;
}
else
{
    actualFloor = floor;
}
```

Don't put a semicolon here!
See page 184.

If the condition is true, the statement(s)
in this branch are executed in sequence;
if the condition is false, they are skipped.

Omit the else branch
if there is nothing to do.

If the condition is false, the statement(s)
in this branch are executed in sequence;
if the condition is true, they are skipped.

Lining up braces
is a good idea.
See page 184.

The following program puts the if statement to work. This program asks for the desired floor and then prints out the actual floor.

section_1/ElevatorSimulation.java

```java
1   import java.util.Scanner;
2
3   /**
4       This program simulates an elevator panel that skips the 13th floor.
5   */
6   public class ElevatorSimulation
7   {
8       public static void main(String[] args)
9       {
10          Scanner in = new Scanner(System.in);
11          System.out.print("Floor: ");
12          int floor = in.nextInt();
13
14          // Adjust floor if necessary
15
16          int actualFloor;
17          if (floor > 13)
18          {
19              actualFloor = floor - 1;
20          }
21          else
22          {
```

```
23          actualFloor = floor;
24       }
25
26       System.out.println("The elevator will travel to the actual floor "
27          + actualFloor);
28    }
29 }
```

Program Run

```
Floor: 20
The elevator will travel to the actual floor 19
```

SELF CHECK

1. In some Asian countries, the number 14 is considered unlucky. Some building owners play it safe and skip *both* the thirteenth and the fourteenth floor. How would you modify the sample program to handle such a building?

2. Consider the following if statement to compute a discounted price:

```
if (originalPrice > 100)
{
    discountedPrice = originalPrice - 20;
}
else
{
    discountedPrice = originalPrice - 10;
}
```

What is the discounted price if the original price is 95? 100? 105?

3. Compare this if statement with the one in Self Check 2:

```
if (originalPrice < 100)
{
    discountedPrice = originalPrice - 10;
}
else
{
    discountedPrice = originalPrice - 20;
}
```

Do the two statements always compute the same value? If not, when do the values differ?

4. Consider the following statements to compute a discounted price:

```
discountedPrice = originalPrice;
if (originalPrice > 100)
{
    discountedPrice = originalPrice - 10;
}
```

What is the discounted price if the original price is 95? 100? 105?

5. The variables fuelAmount and fuelCapacity hold the actual amount of fuel and the size of the fuel tank of a vehicle. If less than 10 percent is remaining in the tank, a status light should show a red color; otherwise it shows a green color. Simulate this process by printing out either "red" or "green".

Practice It   Now you can try these exercises at the end of the chapter: R5.5, R5.6, E5.9.

Programming Tip 5.1

Brace Layout

The compiler doesn't care where you place braces. In this book, we follow the simple rule of making { and } line up.

```
if (floor > 13)
{
    floor--;
}
```

This style makes it easy to spot matching braces. Some programmers put the opening brace on the same line as the if:

```
if (floor > 13) {
    floor--;
}
```

Properly lining up your code makes your programs easier to read.

This style makes it harder to match the braces, but it saves a line of code, allowing you to view more code on the screen without scrolling. There are passionate advocates of both styles.

It is important that you pick a layout style and stick with it consistently within a given programming project. Which style you choose may depend on your personal preference or a coding style guide that you need to follow.

Programming Tip 5.2

Always Use Braces

When the body of an if statement consists of a single statement, you need not use braces. For example, the following is legal:

```
if (floor > 13)
    floor--;
```

However, it is a good idea to always include the braces:

```
if (floor > 13)
{
    floor--;
}
```

The braces make your code easier to read. They also make it easier for you to maintain the code because you won't have to worry about adding braces when you add statements inside an if statement.

Common Error 5.1

A Semicolon After the if Condition

The following code fragment has an unfortunate error:

```
if (floor > 13) ; // ERROR
{
    floor--;
}
```

There should be no semicolon after the if condition. The compiler interprets this statement as follows: If floor is greater than 13, execute the statement that is denoted by a single semicolon, that is, the do-nothing statement. The statement enclosed in braces is no longer a part of the if statement. It is always executed. In other words, even if the value of floor is not above 13, it is decremented.

Programming Tip 5.3

Tabs

Block-structured code has the property that nested statements are indented by one or more levels:

```
public class ElevatorSimulation
{
|   public static void main(String[] args)
|   {
|   |   int floor;
|   |   . . .
|   |   if (floor > 13)
|   |   {
|   |   |   floor--;
|   |   }
|   |   . . .
|   }
|   |   |   |
0   1   2   3     Indentation level
```

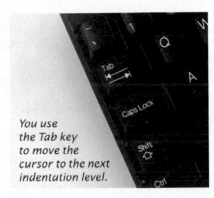

You use the Tab key to move the cursor to the next indentation level.

How do you move the cursor from the leftmost column to the appropriate indentation level? A perfectly reasonable strategy is to hit the space bar a sufficient number of times. With most editors, you can use the Tab key instead. A tab moves the cursor to the next indentation level. Some editors even have an option to fill in the tabs automatically.

While the Tab *key* is nice, some editors use *tab characters* for alignment, which is not so nice. Tab characters can lead to problems when you send your file to another person or a printer. There is no universal agreement on the width of a tab character, and some software will ignore tab characters altogether. It is therefore best to save your files with spaces instead of tabs. Most editors have a setting to automatically convert all tabs to spaces. Look at the documentation of your development environment to find out how to activate this useful setting.

Special Topic 5.1

The Conditional Operator

Java has a *conditional operator* of the form

   condition ? *value₁* : *value₂*

The value of that expression is either *value₁* if the test passes or *value₂* if it fails. For example, we can compute the actual floor number as

```
actualFloor = floor > 13 ? floor - 1 : floor;
```

which is equivalent to

```
if (floor > 13) { actualFloor = floor - 1; } else { actualFloor = floor; }
```

You can use the conditional operator anywhere that a value is expected, for example:

```
System.out.println("Actual floor: " + (floor > 13 ? floor - 1 : floor));
```

We don't use the conditional operator in this book, but it is a convenient construct that you will find in many Java programs.

Avoid Duplication in Branches

Look to see whether you *duplicate code* in each branch. If so, move it out of the `if` statement. Here is an example of such duplication:

```
if (floor > 13)
{
   actualFloor = floor - 1;
   System.out.println("Actual floor: " + actualFloor);
}
else
{
   actualFloor = floor;
   System.out.println("Actual floor: " + actualFloor);
}
```

The output statement is exactly the same in both branches. This is not an error—the program will run correctly. However, you can simplify the program by moving the duplicated statement, like this:

```
if (floor > 13)
{
   actualFloor = floor - 1;
}
else
{
   actualFloor = floor;
}
System.out.println("Actual floor: " + actualFloor);
```

Removing duplication is particularly important when programs are maintained for a long time. When there are two sets of statements with the same effect, it can easily happen that a programmer modifies one set but not the other.

5.2 Comparing Values

Use relational
operators
(< <= > >= == !=)
to compare numbers.

Every `if` statement contains a condition. In many cases, the condition involves comparing two values. In the following sections, you will learn how to implement comparisons in Java.

5.2.1 Relational Operators

Relational operators
compare values. The
== operator tests for
equality.

A **relational operator** tests the relationship between two values. An example is the > operator that we used in the test `floor > 13`. Java has six relational operators (see Table 1).

In Java, you use a relational operator to check whether one value is greater than another.

Table 1 Relational Operators		
Java	Math Notation	Description
>	>	Greater than
>=	≥	Greater than or equal
<	<	Less than
<=	≤	Less than or equal
==	=	Equal
!=	≠	Not equal

As you can see, only two Java relational operators (> and <) look as you would expect from the mathematical notation. Computer keyboards do not have keys for ≥, ≤, or ≠, but the >=, <=, and != operators are easy to remember because they look similar. The == operator is initially confusing to most newcomers to Java.

In Java, = already has a meaning, namely assignment. The == operator denotes equality testing:

```
floor = 13; // Assign 13 to floor
```

```
if (floor == 13)   // Test whether floor equals 13
```

You must remember to use == inside tests and to use = outside tests.

Syntax 5.2   Comparisons

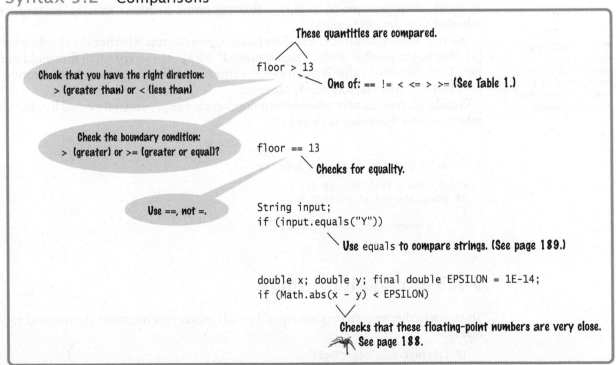

These quantities are compared.

```
floor > 13
```

Check that you have the right direction:
> (greater than) or < (less than)

One of: == != < <= > >= (See Table 1.)

Check the boundary condition:
> (greater) or >= (greater or equal)?

```
floor == 13
```

Checks for equality.

Use ==, not =.

```
String input;
if (input.equals("Y"))
```

Use equals to compare strings. (See page 189.)

```
double x; double y; final double EPSILON = 1E-14;
if (Math.abs(x - y) < EPSILON)
```

Checks that these floating-point numbers are very close.
See page 188.

The relational operators in Table 1 have a lower precedence than the arithmetic operators. That means you can write arithmetic expressions on either side of the relational operator without using parentheses. For example, in the expression

```
floor - 1 < 13
```

both sides (`floor - 1` and `13`) of the `<` operator are evaluated, and the results are compared. Appendix B shows a table of the Java operators and their precedence.

5.2.2 Comparing Floating-Point Numbers

You have to be careful when comparing floating-point numbers in order to cope with roundoff errors. For example, the following code multiplies the square root of 2 by itself and then subtracts 2.

```java
double r = Math.sqrt(2);
double d = r * r - 2;
if (d == 0)
{
    System.out.println("sqrt(2) squared minus 2 is 0");
}
else
{
    System.out.println("sqrt(2) squared minus 2 is not 0 but " + d);
}
```

Even though the laws of mathematics tell us that $\left(\sqrt{2}\right)^2 - 2$ equals 0, this program fragment prints

```
sqrt(2) squared minus 2 is not 0 but 4.440892098500626E-16
```

Unfortunately, such roundoff errors are unavoidable. It plainly does not make sense in most circumstances to compare floating-point numbers exactly. Instead, test whether they are *close enough*.

To test whether a number x is close to zero, you can test whether the absolute value $|x|$ (that is, the number with its sign removed) is less than a very small threshold number. That threshold value is often called ε (the Greek letter epsilon). It is common to set ε to 10^{-14} when testing `double` numbers.

Similarly, you can test whether two numbers are approximately equal by checking whether their difference is close to 0.

> When comparing floating-point numbers, don't test for equality. Instead, check whether they are close enough.

$$|x - y| \le \varepsilon$$

In Java, we program the test as follows:

```java
final double EPSILON = 1E-14;
if (Math.abs(x - y) <= EPSILON)
{
    // x is approximately equal to y
}
```

5.2.3 Comparing Strings

To test whether two strings are equal to each other, you must use the method called `equals`:

```java
if (string1.equals(string2)) . . .
```

Do not use the == operator to compare strings. The comparison

```
if (string1 == string2) // Not useful
```

has an unrelated meaning. It tests whether the two strings are stored in the same memory location. You can have strings with identical contents stored in different locations, so this test never makes sense in actual programming; see Common Error 5.2 on page 192.

If two strings are not identical, you still may want to know the relationship between them. The compareTo method compares strings in **lexicographic order**. This ordering is very similar to the way in which words are sorted in a dictionary. If

```
string1.compareTo(string2) < 0
```

then the string string1 comes before the string string2 in the dictionary. For example, this is the case if string1 is "Harry", and string2 is "Hello".

Conversely, if

```
string1.compareTo(string2) > 0
```

then string1 comes after string2 in dictionary order.

Finally, if

```
string1.compareTo(string2) == 0
```

then string1 and string2 are equal.

There are a few technical differences between the ordering in a dictionary and the lexicographic ordering in Java. In Java:

- All uppercase letters come before the lowercase letters. For example, "Z" comes before "a".
- The space character comes before all printable characters.
- Numbers come before letters.
- For the ordering of punctuation marks, see Appendix A.

When comparing two strings, you compare the first letters of each word, then the second letters, and so on, until one of the strings ends or you find the first letter pair that doesn't match.

If one of the strings ends, the longer string is considered the "larger" one. For example, compare "car" with "cart". The first three letters match, and we reach the end of the first string. Therefore "car" comes before "cart" in lexicographic ordering.

When you reach a mismatch, the string containing the "larger" character is considered "larger". For example, compare "cat" with "cart". The first two letters match. Because t comes after r, the string "cat" comes after "cart" in the lexicographic ordering.

Margin notes:

Do not use the == operator to compare strings. Use the equals method instead.

The compareTo method compares strings in lexicographic order.

| c | a | r |

| c | a | r | t |

| c | a | t |

Letters   r comes
match   before t

Lexicographic Ordering

To see which of two terms comes first in the dictionary, consider the first letter in which they differ.

5.2.4 Comparing Objects

If you compare two object references with the == operator, you test whether the references refer to the same object. Here is an example:

```
Rectangle box1 = new Rectangle(5, 10, 20, 30);
Rectangle box2 = box1;
Rectangle box3 = new Rectangle(5, 10, 20, 30);
```

The comparison

```
box1 == box2
```

is true. Both object variables refer to the same object. But the comparison

```
box1 == box3
```

> The == operator tests whether two object references are identical. To compare the contents of objects, you need to use the equals method.

is false. The two object variables refer to different objects (see Figure 3). It does not matter that the objects have identical contents.

You can use the equals method to test whether two rectangles have the same contents, that is, whether they have the same upper-left corner and the same width and height. For example, the test

```
box1.equals(box3)
```

is true.

However, you must be careful when using the equals method. It works correctly only if the implementors of the class have supplied it. The Rectangle class has an equals method that is suitable for comparing rectangles.

For your own classes, you need to supply an appropriate equals method. You will learn how to do that in Chapter 9. Until that point, you should not use the equals method to compare objects of your own classes.

Figure 3
Comparing Object References

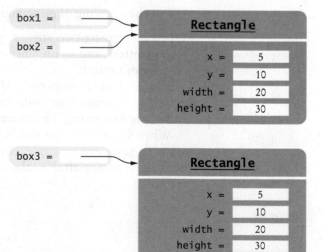

5.2.5 Testing for null

> The null reference refers to no object.

An object reference can have the special value null if it refers to no object at all. It is common to use the null value to indicate that a value has never been set. For example,

```
String middleInitial = null; // Not set
if ( . . . )
{
    middleInitial = middleName.substring(0, 1);
}
```

You use the == operator (and not equals) to test whether an object reference is a null reference:

```
if (middleInitial == null)
{
    System.out.println(firstName + " " + lastName);
}
else
{
    System.out.println(firstName + " " + middleInitial + ". " + lastName);
}
```

FULL CODE EXAMPLE

Go to wiley.com/
go/javacode to
download a program
that demonstrates
comparisons of
numbers and strings

Note that the **null reference** is not the same as the empty string "". The empty string is a valid string of length 0, whereas a null indicates that a string variable refers to no string at all.

Table 2 summarizes how to compare values in Java.

Table 2 Relational Operator Examples

Expression	Value	Comment
3 <= 4	true	3 is less than 4; <= tests for "less than or equal".
🚫 3 =< 4	**Error**	The "less than or equal" operator is <=, not =<. The "less than" symbol comes first.
3 > 4	false	> is the opposite of <=.
4 < 4	false	The left-hand side must be strictly smaller than the right-hand side.
4 <= 4	true	Both sides are equal; <= tests for "less than or equal".
3 == 5 - 2	true	== tests for equality.
3 != 5 - 1	true	!= tests for inequality. It is true that 3 is not 5 − 1.
🚫 3 = 6 / 2	**Error**	Use == to test for equality.
1.0 / 3.0 == 0.333333333	false	Although the values are very close to one another, they are not exactly equal. See Section 5.2.2.
🚫 "10" > 5	**Error**	You cannot compare a string to a number.
"Tomato".substring(0, 3).equals("Tom")	true	Always use the equals method to check whether two strings have the same contents.
"Tomato".substring(0, 3) == ("Tom")	false	Never use == to compare strings; it only checks whether the strings are stored in the same location. See Common Error 5.2 on page 192.

6. Which of the following conditions are true, provided a is 3 and b is 4?

a. `a + 1 <= b`

b. `a + 1 >= b`

c. `a + 1 != b`

7. Give the opposite of the condition

`floor > 13`

8. What is the error in this statement?

```
if (scoreA = scoreB)
{
    System.out.println("Tie");
}
```

9. Supply a condition in this `if` statement to test whether the user entered a Y:

```
System.out.println("Enter Y to quit.");
String input = in.next();
if (. . .)
{
    System.out.println("Goodbye.");
}
```

10. Give two ways of testing that a string `str` is the empty string.

11. What is the value of `s.length()` if s is

a. the empty string `""`?

b. the string `" "` containing a space?

c. `null`?

12. Which of the following comparisons are syntactically incorrect? Which of them are syntactically correct, but logically questionable?

```
String a = "1";
String b = "one";
double x = 1;
double y = 3 * (1.0 / 3);
```

a. `a == "1"`

b. `a == null`

c. `a.equals("")`

d. `a == b`

e. `a == x`

f. `x == y`

g. `x - y == null`

h. `x.equals(y)`

Practice It   Now you can try these exercises at the end of the chapter: R5.4, R5.7, E5.13.

Common Error 5.2

Using == to Compare Strings

If you write

```
if (nickname == "Rob")
```

then the test succeeds only if the variable `nickname` refers to the exact same location as the string literal "Rob".

The test will pass if a string variable was initialized with the same string literal:

```
String nickname = "Rob";
. . .
if (nickname == "Rob") // Test is true
```

However, if the string with the letters R o b has been assembled in some other way, then the test will fail:

```
String name = "Robert";
String nickname = name.substring(0, 3);
. . .
if (nickname == "Rob") // Test is false
```

In this case, the substring method produces a string in a different memory location. Even though both strings have the same contents, the comparison fails.

You must remember never to use == to compare strings. Always use equals to check whether two strings have the same contents.

HOW TO 5.1   **Implementing an if Statement**

This How To walks you through the process of implementing an if statement. We will illustrate the steps with the following example problem.

Problem Statement   The university bookstore has a Kilobyte Day sale every October 24, giving an 8 percent discount on all computer accessory purchases if the price is less than $128, and a 16 percent discount if the price is at least $128. Write a program that asks the cashier for the original price and then prints the discounted price.

Step 1   Decide upon the branching condition.

In our sample problem, the obvious choice for the condition is:

original price < 128?

That is just fine, and we will use that condition in our solution.

But you could equally well come up with a correct solution if you choose the opposite condition: Is the original price at least $128? You might choose this condition if you put yourself into the position of a shopper who wants to know when the bigger discount applies.

Sales discounts are often higher for expensive products. Use the if statement to implement such a decision.

Step 2   Give pseudocode for the work that needs to be done when the condition is true.

In this step, you list the action or actions that are taken in the "positive" branch. The details depend on your problem. You may want to print a message, compute values, or even exit the program.

In our example, we need to apply an 8 percent discount:

discounted price = 0.92 x original price

Step 3   Give pseudocode for the work (if any) that needs to be done when the condition is *not* true.

What do you want to do in the case that the condition of Step 1 is not satisfied? Sometimes, you want to do nothing at all. In that case, use an `if` statement without an `else` branch.

In our example, the condition tested whether the price was less than $128. If that condition is *not* true, the price is at least $128, so the higher discount of 16 percent applies to the sale:

> discounted price = 0.84 x original price

Step 4   Double-check relational operators.

First, be sure that the test goes in the right *direction*. It is a common error to confuse > and <. Next, consider whether you should use the < operator or its close cousin, the <= operator.

What should happen if the original price is exactly $128? Reading the problem carefully, we find that the lower discount applies if the original price is *less than* $128, and the higher discount applies when it is *at least* $128. A price of $128 should therefore *not* fulfill our condition, and we must use <, not <=.

Step 5   Remove duplication.

Check which actions are common to both branches, and move them outside. (See Programming Tip 5.4 on page 186.)

In our example, we have two statements of the form

> discounted price = ___ x original price

They only differ in the discount rate. It is best to just set the rate in the branches, and to do the computation afterwards:

> If original price < 128
>   discount rate = 0.92
> Else
>   discount rate = 0.84
> discounted price = discount rate x original price

Step 6   Test both branches.

Formulate two test cases, one that fulfills the condition of the `if` statement, and one that does not. Ask yourself what should happen in each case. Then follow the pseudocode and act each of them out.

In our example, let us consider two scenarios for the original price: $100 and $200. We expect that the first price is discounted by $8, the second by $32.

When the original price is 100, then the condition 100 < 128 is true, and we get

> discount rate = 0.92
> discounted price = 0.92 x 100 = 92

When the original price is 200, then the condition 200 < 128 is false, and

> discount rate = 0.84
> discounted price = 0.84 x 200 = 168

In both cases, we get the expected answer.

Step 7   Assemble the `if` statement in Java.

Type the skeleton

```
if ()
{
}
else
{
```

```
}
```
and fill it in, as shown in Syntax 5.1 on page 182. Omit the else branch if it is not needed. In our example, the completed statement is

```
if (originalPrice < 128)
{
    discountRate = 0.92;
}
else
{
    discountRate = 0.84;
}
discountedPrice = discountRate * originalPrice;
```

FULL CODE EXAMPLE

Go to wiley.com/go/javacode to download the complete program for calculating a discounted price.

WORKED EXAMPLE 5.1   **Extracting the Middle**

Learn how to extract the middle character from a string, or the two middle characters if the length of the string is even. Go to www.wiley.com/go/javaexamples and download Worked Example 5.1.

c	r	a	t	e
0	1	2	3	4

Computing & Society 5.1 Denver's Luggage Handling System

Making decisions is an essential part of any computer program. Nowhere is this more obvious than in a computer system that helps sort luggage at an airport. After scanning the luggage identification codes, the system sorts the items and routes them to different conveyor belts. Human operators then place the items onto trucks. When the city of Denver built a huge airport to replace an outdated and congested facility, the luggage system contractor went a step further. The new system was designed to replace the human operators with robotic carts. Unfortunately, the system plainly did not work. It was plagued by mechanical problems, such as luggage falling onto the tracks and jamming carts. Equally frustrating were the software glitches. Carts would uselessly accumulate at some locations when they were needed elsewhere.

The airport had been scheduled to open in 1993, but without a functioning luggage system, the opening was delayed for over a year while the contractor tried to fix the problems. The contractor never succeeded, and ultimately a manual system was installed. The delay cost the city and airlines close to a billion dollars, and the contractor, once the leading luggage systems vendor in the United States, went bankrupt.

Clearly, it is very risky to build a large system based on a technology that has never been tried on a smaller scale. As robots and the software that controls them get better over time, they will take on a larger share of luggage handling in the future. But it is likely that this will happen in an incremental fashion.

The Denver airport originally had a fully automatic system for moving luggage, replacing human operators with robotic carts. Unfortunately, the system never worked and was dismantled before the airport was opened.

5.3 Multiple Alternatives

Multiple if statements can be combined to evaluate complex decisions.

In Section 5.1, you saw how to program a two-way branch with an if statement. In many situations, there are more than two cases. In this section, you will see how to implement a decision with multiple alternatives.

For example, consider a program that displays the effect of an earthquake, as measured by the Richter scale (see Table 3).

The 1989 Loma Prieta earthquake that damaged the Bay Bridge in San Francisco and destroyed many buildings measured 7.1 on the Richter scale.

Table 3 Richter Scale	
Value	Effect
8	Most structures fall
7	Many buildings destroyed
6	Many buildings considerably damaged, some collapse
4.5	Damage to poorly constructed buildings

The Richter scale is a measurement of the strength of an earthquake. Every step in the scale, for example from 6.0 to 7.0, signifies a tenfold increase in the strength of the quake.

In this case, there are five branches: one each for the four descriptions of damage, and one for no destruction. Figure 4 shows the flowchart for this multiple-branch statement.

You use multiple if statements to implement multiple alternatives, like this:

ANIMATION
Multiple Alternatives

```
if (richter >= 8.0)
{
    description = "Most structures fall";
}
else if (richter >= 7.0)
{
    description = "Many buildings destroyed";
}
else if (richter >= 6.0)
{
    description = "Many buildings considerably damaged, some collapse";
}
else if (richter >= 4.5)
{
    description = "Damage to poorly constructed buildings";
}
else
{
    description = "No destruction of buildings";
}
```

As soon as one of the four tests succeeds, the effect is displayed, and no further tests are attempted. If none of the four cases applies, the final else clause applies, and a default message is printed.

Figure 4
Multiple Alternatives

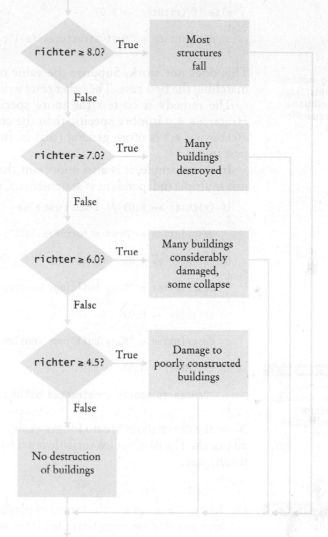

Here you must sort the conditions and test against the largest cutoff first.
Suppose we reverse the order of tests:

```
if (richter >= 4.5) // Tests in wrong order
{
   description = "Damage to poorly constructed buildings";
}
else if (richter >= 6.0)
{
   description = "Many buildings considerably damaged, some collapse";
}
else if (richter >= 7.0)
{
   description = "Many buildings destroyed";
```

```
    }
    else if (richter >= 8.0)
    {
        description = "Most structures fall";
    }
```

When using multiple
if statements, test
general conditions
after more specific
conditions.

This does not work. Suppose the value of `richter` is 7.1. That value is at least 4.5, matching the first case. The other tests will never be attempted.

The remedy is to test the more specific conditions first. Here, the condition `richter >= 8.0` is more specific than the condition `richter >= 7.0`, and the condition `richter >= 4.5` is more general (that is, fulfilled by more values) than either of the first two.

In this example, it is also important that we use an `if/else if/else` sequence, not just multiple independent `if` statements. Consider this sequence of independent tests.

```
    if (richter >= 8.0) // Didn't use else
    {
        description = "Most structures fall";
    }
    if (richter >= 7.0)
    {
        description = "Many buildings destroyed";
    }
    if (richter >= 6.0)
    {
        description = "Many buildings considerably damaged, some collapse";
    }
    if (richter >= 4.5)
    {
        "Damage to poorly constructed buildings";
    }
```

FULL CODE EXAMPLE

Go to `wiley.com/go/javacode` to download the program for printing earthquake descriptions.

Now the alternatives are no longer exclusive. If `richter` is 7.1, then the last *three* tests all match. The `description` variable is set to three different strings, ending up with the wrong one.

SELF CHECK

13. In a game program, the scores of players A and B are stored in variables `scoreA` and `scoreB`. Assuming that the player with the larger score wins, write an `if/else if/else` sequence that prints out `"A won"`, `"B won"`, or `"Game tied"`.

14. Write a conditional statement with three branches that sets s to 1 if x is positive, to −1 if x is negative, and to 0 if x is zero.

15. How could you achieve the task of Self Check 14 with only two branches?

16. Beginners sometimes write statements such as the following:

```
    if (price > 100)
    {
        discountedPrice = price - 20;
    }
    else if (price <= 100)
    {
        discountedPrice = price - 10;
    }
```

Explain how this code can be improved.

17. Suppose the user enters -1 into the earthquake program. What is printed?

18. Suppose we want to have the earthquake program check whether the user entered a negative number. What branch would you add to the if statement, and where?

Practice It Now you can try these exercises at the end of the chapter: R5.22, E5.10, E5.24.

Special Topic 5.2

The switch Statement

An if/else if/else sequence that compares a *value* against several alternatives can be implemented as a switch statement. For example,

```
int digit = . . .;
switch (digit)
{
   case 1: digitName = "one"; break;
   case 2: digitName = "two"; break;
   case 3: digitName = "three"; break;
   case 4: digitName = "four"; break;
   case 5: digitName = "five"; break;
   case 6: digitName = "six"; break;
   case 7: digitName = "seven"; break;
   case 8: digitName = "eight"; break;
   case 9: digitName = "nine"; break;
   default: digitName = ""; break;
}
```

The switch statement lets you choose from a fixed set of alternatives.

This is a shortcut for

```
int digit = . . .;
if (digit == 1) { digitName = "one"; }
else if (digit == 2) { digitName = "two"; }
else if (digit == 3) { digitName = "three"; }
else if (digit == 4) { digitName = "four"; }
else if (digit == 5) { digitName = "five"; }
else if (digit == 6) { digitName = "six"; }
else if (digit == 7) { digitName = "seven"; }
else if (digit == 8) { digitName = "eight"; }
else if (digit == 9) { digitName = "nine"; }
else { digitName = ""; }
```

It isn't much of a shortcut, but it has one advantage—it is obvious that all branches test the *same* value, namely digit.

The switch statement can be applied only in narrow circumstances. The values in the case clauses must be constants. They can be integers or characters. As of Java 7, strings are permitted as well. You cannot use a switch statement to branch on floating-point values.

Every branch of the switch should be terminated by a break instruction. If the break is missing, execution *falls through* to the next branch, and so on, until a break or the end of the switch is reached. In practice, this fall-through behavior is rarely useful, but it is a common cause of errors. If you accidentally forget a break statement, your program compiles but executes unwanted code. Many programmers consider the switch statement somewhat dangerous and prefer the if statement.

We leave it to you to use the switch statement for your own code or not. At any rate, you need to have a reading knowledge of switch in case you find it in other programmers' code.

5.4 Nested Branches

When a decision statement is contained inside the branch of another decision statement, the statements are *nested*.

It is often necessary to include an if statement inside another. Such an arrangement is called a *nested* set of statements.

Here is a typical example: In the United States, different tax rates are used depending on the taxpayer's marital status. There are different tax schedules for single and for married taxpayers. Married taxpayers add their income together and pay taxes on the total. Table 4 gives the tax rate computations, using a simplification of the schedules that were in effect for the 2008 tax year. A different tax rate applies to each "bracket". In this schedule, the income in the first bracket is taxed at 10 percent, and the income in the second bracket is taxed at 25 percent. The income limits for each bracket depend on the marital status.

Table 4 Federal Tax Rate Schedule

If your status is Single and if the taxable income is	the tax is	of the amount over
at most $32,000	10%	$0
over $32,000	$3,200 + 25%	$32,000

If your status is Married and if the taxable income is	the tax is	of the amount over
at most $64,000	10%	$0
over $64,000	$6,400 + 25%	$64,000

Nested decisions are required for problems that have two levels of decision making.

Now compute the taxes due, given a marital status and an income figure. The key point is that there are two *levels* of decision making. First, you must branch on the marital status. Then, for each marital status, you must have another branch on income level.

The two-level decision process is reflected in two levels of if statements in the program at the end of this section. (See Figure 5 for a flowchart.) In theory, nesting can go deeper than two levels. A three-level decision process (first by state, then by marital status, then by income level) requires three nesting levels.

ANIMATION
Nested Branches

Computing income taxes requires multiple levels of decisions.

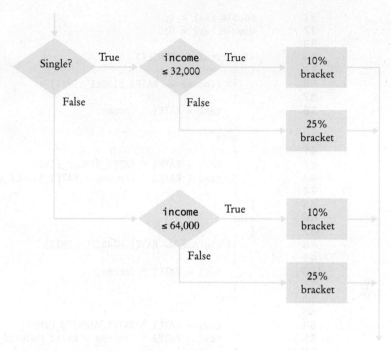

Figure 5   Income Tax Computation

section_4/TaxReturn.java

```java
1    /**
2       A tax return of a taxpayer in 2008.
3    */
4    public class TaxReturn
5    {
6       public static final int SINGLE = 1;
7       public static final int MARRIED = 2;
8
9       private static final double RATE1 = 0.10;
10      private static final double RATE2 = 0.25;
11      private static final double RATE1_SINGLE_LIMIT = 32000;
12      private static final double RATE1_MARRIED_LIMIT = 64000;
13
14      private double income;
15      private int status;
16
17      /**
18         Constructs a TaxReturn object for a given income and
19         marital status.
20         @param anIncome the taxpayer income
21         @param aStatus either SINGLE or MARRIED
22      */
23      public TaxReturn(double anIncome, int aStatus)
24      {
25         income = anIncome;
26         status = aStatus;
27      }
28
29      public double getTax()
30      {
```

```
31       double tax1 = 0;
32       double tax2 = 0;
33
34       if (status == SINGLE)
35       {
36          if (income <= RATE1_SINGLE_LIMIT)
37          {
38             tax1 = RATE1 * income;
39          }
40          else
41          {
42             tax1 = RATE1 * RATE1_SINGLE_LIMIT;
43             tax2 = RATE2 * (income - RATE1_SINGLE_LIMIT);
44          }
45       }
46       else
47       {
48          if (income <= RATE1_MARRIED_LIMIT)
49          {
50             tax1 = RATE1 * income;
51          }
52          else
53          {
54             tax1 = RATE1 * RATE1_MARRIED_LIMIT;
55             tax2 = RATE2 * (income - RATE1_MARRIED_LIMIT);
56          }
57       }
58
59       return tax1 + tax2;
60    }
61 }
```

section_4/TaxCalculator.java

```
 1   import java.util.Scanner;
 2
 3   /**
 4      This program calculates a simple tax return.
 5   */
 6   public class TaxCalculator
 7   {
 8      public static void main(String[] args)
 9      {
10         Scanner in = new Scanner(System.in);
11
12         System.out.print("Please enter your income: ");
13         double income = in.nextDouble();
14
15         System.out.print("Are you married? (Y/N) ");
16         String input = in.next();
17         int status;
18         if (input.equals("Y"))
19         {
20            status = TaxReturn.MARRIED;
21         }
22         else
23         {
24            status = TaxReturn.SINGLE;
25         }
26         TaxReturn aTaxReturn = new TaxReturn(income, status);
```

```
27        System.out.println("Tax: "
28                + aTaxReturn.getTax());
29     }
30 }
```

Program Run

```
Please enter your income: 80000
Are you married? (Y/N) Y
Tax: 10400.0
```

SELF CHECK

19. What is the amount of tax that a single taxpayer pays on an income of $32,000?

20. Would that amount change if the first nested if statement changed from

    ```
    if (income <= RATE1_SINGLE_LIMIT)
    ```

    to

    ```
    if (income < RATE1_SINGLE_LIMIT)
    ```

21. Suppose Harry and Sally each make $40,000 per year. Would they save taxes if they married?

22. How would you modify the TaxCalculator.java program in order to check that the user entered a correct value for the marital status (i.e., Y or N)?

23. Some people object to higher tax rates for higher incomes, claiming that you might end up with less money after taxes when you get a raise for working hard. What is the flaw in this argument?

Practice It Now you can try these exercises at the end of the chapter: R5.9, R5.21, E5.14, E5.17.

Programming Tip 5.5

Hand-Tracing

A very useful technique for understanding whether a program works correctly is called *hand-tracing*. You simulate the program's activity on a sheet of paper. You can use this method with pseudocode or Java code.

Get an index card, a cocktail napkin, or whatever sheet of paper is within reach. Make a column for each variable. Have the program code ready. Use a marker, such as a paper clip, to mark the current statement. In your mind, execute statements one at a time. Every time the value of a variable changes, cross out the old value and write the new value below the old one.

For example, let's trace the getTax method with the data from the program run above.

When the TaxReturn object is constructed, the income instance variable is set to 80,000 and status is set to MARRIED. Then the getTax method is called. In lines 31 and 32 of TaxReturn.java, tax1 and tax2 are initialized to 0.

Hand-tracing helps you understand whether a program works correctly.

```
29 public double getTax()
30 {
31     double tax1 = 0;
32     double tax2 = 0;
33
```

income	status	tax1	tax2
80000	MARRIED	0	0

Because status is not SINGLE, we move to the else branch of the outer if statement (line 46).

```
34    if (status == SINGLE)
35    {
36       if (income <= RATE1_SINGLE_LIMIT)
37       {
38          tax1 = RATE1 * income;
39       }
40       else
41       {
42          tax1 = RATE1 * RATE1_SINGLE_LIMIT;
43          tax2 = RATE2 * (income - RATE1_SINGLE_LIMIT);
44       }
45    }
46    else
47    {
```

Because income is not <= 64000, we move to the else branch of the inner if statement (line 52).

```
48       if (income <= RATE1_MARRIED_LIMIT)
49       {
50          tax1 = RATE1 * income;
51       }
52       else
53       {
54          tax1 = RATE1 * RATE1_MARRIED_LIMIT;
55          tax2 = RATE2 * (income - RATE1_MARRIED_LIMIT);
56       }
```

The values of tax1 and tax2 are updated.

```
53       {
54          tax1 = RATE1 * RATE1_MARRIED_LIMIT;
55          tax2 = RATE2 * (income - RATE1_MARRIED_LIMIT);
56       }
57    }
```

income	status	tax1	tax2
80000	MARRIED	~~0~~	~~0~~
		6400	4000

Their sum is returned and the method ends.

```
58
59    return tax1 + tax2;
60 }
```

Because the program trace shows the expected return value ($10,400), it successfully demonstrates that this test case works correctly.

income	status	tax1	tax2	return value
80000	MARRIED	~~0~~	~~0~~	
		6400	4000	10400

Common Error 5.3

The Dangling else Problem

When an if statement is nested inside another if statement, the following error may occur.

```
double shippingCharge = 5.00; // $5 inside continental U.S.
if (country.equals("USA"))
    if (state.equals("HI"))
        shippingCharge = 10.00; // Hawaii is more expensive
else // Pitfall!
    shippingCharge = 20.00; // As are foreign shipments
```

The indentation level seems to suggest that the else is grouped with the test country.equals("USA"). Unfortunately, that is not the case. The compiler ignores all indentation and matches the else with the preceding if. That is, the code is actually

```
double shippingCharge = 5.00; // $5 inside continental U.S.
if (country.equals("USA"))
    if (state.equals("HI"))
        shippingCharge = 10.00; // Hawaii is more expensive
    else // Pitfall!
        shippingCharge = 20.00; // As are foreign shipments
```

That isn't what you want. You want to group the `else` with the first `if`.

The ambiguous `else` is called a *dangling else*. You can avoid this pitfall if you always use braces, as recommended in Programming Tip 5.2 on page 184:

```java
double shippingCharge = 5.00; // $5 inside continental U.S.
if (country.equals("USA"))
{
   if (state.equals("HI"))
   {
      shippingCharge = 10.00; // Hawaii is more expensive
   }
}
else
{
   shippingCharge = 20.00; // As are foreign shipments
}
```

Special Topic 5.3

Block Scope

A *block* is a sequence of statements that is enclosed in braces. For example, consider this statement:

```java
if (status == TAXABLE)
{
   double tax = price * TAX_RATE;
   price = price + tax;
}
```

The highlighted part is a block. You can declare a variable in a block, such as the tax variable in this example. Such a variable is only visible inside the block.

```java
{
   double tax = price * TAX_RATE; // Variable declared inside a block
   price = price + tax;
}
// You can no longer access the tax variable here
```

In fact, the variable is only created after the program enters the block, and it is removed as soon as the program exits the block. Such a variable is said to have *block scope*. In general, the **scope** of a variable is the part of the program in which the variable can be accessed. A variable with block scope is visible only inside a block.

It is considered good design to minimize the scope of a variable. This reduces the possibility of accidental modification and name conflicts. For example, as long as the tax variable is not

In the same way that there can be a street named "Main Street" in different cities, a Java program can have multiple variables with the same name.

needed outside the block, it is a good idea to declare it inside the block. However, if you need the variable outside the block, you must define it outside. For example,

```
double tax = 0;
if (status == TAXABLE)
{
    tax = price * TAX_RATE;
}
price = price + tax;
```

Here, the tax variable is used outside the block of the if statement, and you must declare it outside.

In Java, the scope of a local variable can never contain the declaration of another local variable with the same name. For example, the following is an error:

```
double tax = 0;
if (status == TAXABLE)
{
    double tax = price * TAX_RATE;
    // Error: Cannot declare another variable with the same name
    price = price + tax;
}
```

However, you can have local variables with identical names if their scopes do not overlap, such as

```
if (Math.random() > 0.5)
{
    Rectangle r = new Rectangle(5, 10, 20, 30);
    . . .
} // Scope of r ends here
else
{
    int r = 5;
    // OK—it is legal to declare another r here
    . . .
}
```

These variables are independent from each other. You can have local variables with the same name, as long as their scopes don't overlap.

Enumeration Types

In many programs, you use variables that can hold one of a finite number of values. For example, in the tax return class, the status instance variable holds one of the values SINGLE or MARRIED. We arbitrarily declared SINGLE as the number 1 and MARRIED as 2. If, due to some programming error, the status variable is set to another integer value (such as -1, 0, or 3), then the programming logic may produce invalid results.

In a simple program, this is not really a problem. But as programs grow over time, and more cases are added (such as the "married filing separately" status), errors can slip in. Java version 5.0 introduces a remedy: **enumeration types**. An enumeration type has a finite set of values, for example

```
public enum FilingStatus { SINGLE, MARRIED, MARRIED_FILING_SEPARATELY }
```

You can have any number of values, but you must include them all in the enum declaration.

You can declare variables of the enumeration type:

```
FilingStatus status = FilingStatus.SINGLE;
```

If you try to assign a value that isn't a `FilingStatus`, such as 2 or "S", then the compiler reports an error.

Use the == operator to compare enumeration values, for example:

```
if (status == FilingStatus.SINGLE) . . .
```

Place the `enum` declaration inside the class that implements your program, such as

```
public class TaxReturn
{
    public enum FilingStatus { SINGLE, MARRIED, MARRIED_FILING_SEPARATELY }
    . . .
}
```

5.5 Problem Solving: Flowcharts

Flow charts are made up of elements for tasks, input/output, and decisions.

You have seen examples of flowcharts earlier in this chapter. A flowchart shows the structure of decisions and tasks that are required to solve a problem. When you have to solve a complex problem, it can help to draw a flowchart to visualize the flow of control.

The basic flowchart elements are shown in Figure 6.

Figure 6
Flowchart Elements

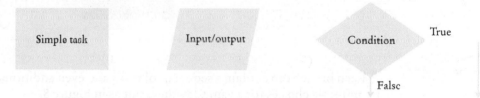

Each branch of a decision can contain tasks and further decisions.

The basic idea is simple enough. Link tasks and input/output boxes in the sequence in which they should be executed. Whenever you need to make a decision, draw a diamond with two outcomes (see Figure 7).

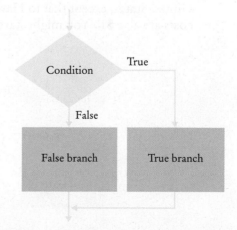

Figure 7
Flowchart with Two Outcomes

Figure 8
Flowchart with Multiple Choices

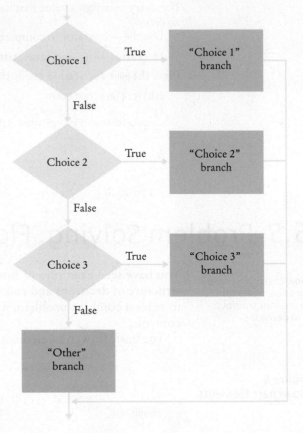

Each branch can contain a sequence of tasks and even additional decisions. If there are multiple choices for a value, lay them out as in Figure 8.

There is one issue that you need to be aware of when drawing flowcharts. Unconstrained branching and merging can lead to "spaghetti code", a messy network of possible pathways through a program.

There is a simple rule for avoiding spaghetti code: Never point an arrow *inside another branch*.

> Never point an arrow inside another branch.

To understand the rule, consider this example: Shipping costs are $5 inside the United States, except that to Hawaii and Alaska they are $10. International shipping costs are also $10. You might start out with a flowchart like the following:

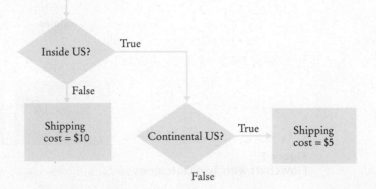

Now you may be tempted to reuse the "shipping cost = $10" task:

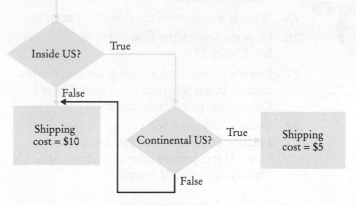

Don't do that! The red arrow points inside a different branch. Instead, add another task that sets the shipping cost to $10, like this:

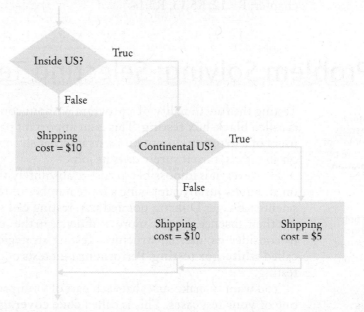

FULL CODE EXAMPLE

Go to wiley.com/go/
javacode to
download a program
that computes
shipping costs.

Not only do you avoid spaghetti code, but it is also a better design. In the future it may well happen that the cost for international shipments is different from that to Alaska and Hawaii.

Flowcharts can be very useful for getting an intuitive understanding of the flow of an algorithm. However, they get large rather quickly when you add more details. At that point, it makes sense to switch from flowcharts to pseudocode.

*Spaghetti code has so many pathways that
it becomes impossible to understand.*

SELF CHECK

24. Draw a flowchart for a program that reads a value temp and prints "Frozen" if it is less than zero.
25. What is wrong with the flowchart at right?
26. How do you fix the flowchart of Self Check 25?
27. Draw a flowchart for a program that reads a value x. If it is less than zero, print "Error". Otherwise, print its square root.
28. Draw a flowchart for a program that reads a value temp. If it is less than zero, print "Ice". If it is greater than 100, print "Steam". Otherwise, print "Liquid".

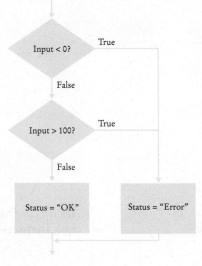

Practice It Now you can try these exercises at the end of the chapter: R5.12, R5.13, R5.14.

5.6 Problem Solving: Selecting Test Cases

> Black-box testing describes a testing method that does not take the structure of the implementation into account.

> White-box testing uses information about the structure of a program.

> Code coverage is a measure of how many parts of a program have been tested.

Testing the functionality of a program without consideration of its internal structure is called **black-box testing**. This is an important part of testing, because, after all, the users of a program do not know its internal structure. If a program works perfectly on all inputs, then it surely does its job.

However, it is impossible to ensure absolutely that a program will work correctly on all inputs just by supplying a finite number of test cases. As the famous computer scientist Edsger Dijkstra pointed out, testing can show only the presence of bugs—not their absence. To gain more confidence in the correctness of a program, it is useful to consider its internal structure. Testing strategies that look inside a program are called **white-box testing**. Performing unit tests of each method is a part of white-box testing.

You want to make sure that each part of your program is exercised at least once by one of your test cases. This is called **code coverage**. If some code is never executed by any of your test cases, you have no way of knowing whether that code would perform correctly if it ever were executed by user input. That means that you need to look at every if/else branch to see that each of them is reached by some test case. Many conditional branches are in the code only to take care of strange and abnormal inputs, but they still do something. It is a common phenomenon that they end up doing something incorrectly, but those faults are never discovered during testing, because nobody supplied the strange and abnormal inputs. The remedy is to ensure that each part of the code is covered by some test case.

For example, in testing the getTax method of the TaxReturn class, you want to make sure that every if statement is entered for at least one test case. You should test both single and married taxpayers, with incomes in each of the three tax brackets.

When you select test cases, you should make it a habit to include **boundary test cases**: legal values that lie at the boundary of the set of acceptable inputs.

Boundary test cases are test cases that are at the boundary of acceptable inputs.

Here is a plan for obtaining a comprehensive set of test cases for the tax program:

- There are two possibilities for the marital status and two tax brackets for each status, yielding four test cases.
- Test a handful of *boundary* conditions, such as an income that is at the boundary between two brackets, and a zero income.
- If you are responsible for error checking (which is discussed in Section 5.8), also test an invalid input, such as a negative income.

Make a list of the test cases and the expected outputs:

Test Case	Married	Expected Output	Comment
30,000	N	3,000	10% bracket
72,000	N	13,200	3,200 + 25% of 40,000
50,000	Y	5,000	10% bracket
104,000	Y	16,400	6,400 + 25% of 40,000
32,000	N	3,200	boundary case
0		0	boundary case

It is a good idea to design test cases before implementing a program.

When you develop a set of test cases, it is helpful to have a flowchart of your program (see Section 5.5). Check off each branch that has a test case. Include test cases for the boundary cases of each decision. For example, if a decision checks whether an input is less than 100, test with an input of 100.

It is always a good idea to design test cases *before* starting to code. Working through the test cases gives you a better understanding of the algorithm that you are about to implement.

SELF CHECK

29. Using Figure 1 on page 181 as a guide, follow the process described in this section to design a set of test cases for the ElevatorSimulation.java program in Section 5.1.

30. What is a boundary test case for the algorithm in How To 5.1 on page 193? What is the expected output?

31. Using Figure 4 on page 197 as a guide, follow the process described in Section 5.6 to design a set of test cases for the Earthquake.java program in Section 5.3.

32. Suppose you are designing a part of a program for a medical robot that has a sensor returning an x- and y-location (measured in cm). You need to check whether the sensor location is inside the circle, outside the circle, or on the boundary (specifically, having a distance of less than 1 mm from the boundary). Assume the circle has center (0, 0) and a radius of 2 cm. Give a set of test cases.

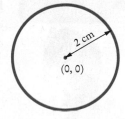

Practice It   Now you can try these exercises at the end of the chapter: R5.15, R5.16.

Programming Tip 5.6

Make a Schedule and Make Time for Unexpected Problems

Commercial software is notorious for being delivered later than promised. For example, Microsoft originally promised that its Windows Vista operating system would be available late in 2003, then in 2005, then in March 2006; it finally was released in January 2007. Some of the early promises might not have been realistic. It was in Microsoft's interest to let prospective customers expect the imminent availability of the product. Had customers known the actual delivery date, they might have switched to a different product in the meantime. Undeniably, though, Microsoft had not anticipated the full complexity of the tasks it had set itself to solve.

Microsoft can delay the delivery of its product, but it is likely that you cannot. As a student or a programmer, you are expected to manage your time wisely and to finish your assignments on time. You can probably do simple programming exercises the night before the due date, but an assignment that looks twice as hard may well take four times as long, because more things can go wrong. You should therefore make a schedule whenever you start a programming project.

First, estimate realistically how much time it will take you to:

- Design the program logic.
- Develop test cases.
- Type the program in and fix syntax errors.
- Test and debug the program.

For example, for the income tax program I might estimate an hour for the design; 30 minutes for developing test cases; an hour for data entry and fixing syntax errors; and an hour for testing and debugging. That is a total of 3.5 hours. If I work two hours a day on this project, it will take me almost two days.

Make a schedule for your programming work and build in time for problems.

Then think of things that can go wrong. Your computer might break down. You might be stumped by a problem with the computer system. (That is a particularly important concern for beginners. It is *very* common to lose a day over a trivial problem just because it takes time to track down a person who knows the magic command to overcome it.) As a rule of thumb, *double* the time of your estimate. That is, you should start four days, not two days, before the due date. If nothing went wrong, great; you have the program done two days early. When the inevitable problem occurs, you have a cushion of time that protects you from embarrassment and failure.

Special Topic 5.5

Logging

Sometimes you run a program and you are not sure where it spends its time. To get a printout of the program flow, you can insert **trace messages** into the program, such as this one:

```
if (status == SINGLE)
{
    System.out.println("status is SINGLE");
    . . .
}
```

However, there is a problem with using `System.out.println` for trace messages. When you are done testing the program, you need to remove all print statements that produce trace messages. If you find another error, however, you need to stick the print statements back in.

To overcome this problem, you should use the Logger class, which allows you to turn off the trace messages without removing them from the program.

Instead of printing directly to System.out, use the global logger object that is returned by the call Logger.getGlobal(). (Prior to Java 7, you obtained the global logger as Logger.getLogger("global").) Then call the info method:

```
Logger.getGlobal().info("status is SINGLE");
```

By default, the message is printed. But if you call

```
Logger.getGlobal().setLevel(Level.OFF);
```

> Logging messages can be deactivated when testing is complete.

at the beginning of the main method of your program, all log message printing is suppressed. Set the level to Level.INFO to turn logging of info messages on again. Thus, you can turn off the log messages when your program works fine, and you can turn them back on if you find another error. In other words, using Logger.getGlobal().info is just like System.out.println, except that you can easily activate and deactivate the logging.

The Logger class has many other options for industrial-strength logging. Check out the API documentation if you want to have more control over logging.

5.7 Boolean Variables and Operators

> The Boolean type boolean has two values, false and true.

A Boolean variable is also called a flag because it can be either up (true) or down (false).

Sometimes, you need to evaluate a logical condition in one part of a program and use it elsewhere. To store a condition that can be true or false, you use a *Boolean variable*. Boolean variables are named after the mathematician George Boole (1815–1864), a pioneer in the study of logic.

In Java, the boolean data type has exactly two values, denoted false and true. These values are not strings or integers; they are special values, just for Boolean variables. Here is a declaration of a Boolean variable:

```
boolean failed = true;
```

You can use the value later in your program to make a decision:

```
if (failed) // Only executed if failed has been set to true
{
   . . .
}
```

When you make complex decisions, you often need to combine Boolean values. An operator that combines Boolean conditions is called a **Boolean operator**. In Java, the && operator (called *and*) yields true only when both conditions are true. The || operator (called *or*) yields the result true if at least one of the conditions is true.

A	B	A && B	A	B	A || B	A	!A
true	true	true	true	true	true	true	false
true	false	false	true	false	true	false	true
false	true	false	false	true	true		
false	false	false	false	false	false		

Figure 9 Boolean Truth Tables

At this geyser in Iceland, you can see ice, liquid water, and steam.

Suppose you write a program that processes temperature values, and you want to test whether a given temperature corresponds to liquid water. (At sea level, water freezes at 0 degrees Celsius and boils at 100 degrees.) Water is liquid if the temperature is greater than zero *and* less than 100:

> Java has two Boolean operators that combine conditions: && (*and*) and || (*or*).

```
if (temp > 0 && temp < 100) { System.out.println("Liquid"); }
```

The condition of the test has two parts, joined by the && operator. Each part is a Boolean value that can be true or false. The combined expression is true if both individual expressions are true. If either one of the expressions is false, then the result is also false (see Figure 9).

The Boolean operators && and || have a lower precedence than the relational operators. For that reason, you can write relational expressions on either side of the Boolean operators without using parentheses. For example, in the expression

FULL CODE EXAMPLE

Go to wiley.com/go/javacode to download a program comparing numbers using Boolean expressions.

```
temp > 0 && temp < 100
```

the expressions temp > 0 and temp < 100 are evaluated first. Then the && operator combines the results. Appendix B shows a table of the Java operators and their precedence.

Conversely, let's test whether water is *not* liquid at a given temperature. That is the case when the temperature is at most 0 *or* at least 100.

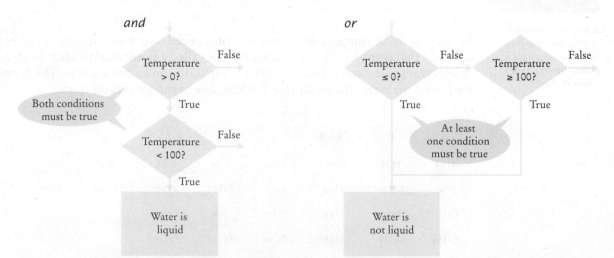

Figure 10   Flowcharts for *and* and *or* Combinations

Table 5 Boolean Operator Examples

Expression	Value	Comment
`0 < 200 && 200 < 100`	`false`	Only the first condition is true.
`0 < 200 || 200 < 100`	`true`	The first condition is true.
`0 < 200 || 100 < 200`	`true`	The || is not a test for "either-or". If both conditions are true, the result is true.
`0 < x && x < 100 || x == -1`	`(0 < x && x < 100)` `|| x == -1`	The && operator has a higher precedence than the || operator (see Appendix B).
🚫 `0 < x < 100`	**Error**	**Error:** This expression does not test whether x is between 0 and 100. The expression 0 < x is a Boolean value. You cannot compare a Boolean value with the integer 100.
🚫 `x && y > 0`	**Error**	**Error:** This expression does not test whether x and y are positive. The left-hand side of && is an integer, x, and the right-hand side, y > 0, is a Boolean value. You cannot use && with an integer argument.
`!(0 < 200)`	`false`	0 < 200 is true, therefore its negation is false.
`frozen == true`	`frozen`	There is no need to compare a Boolean variable with true.
`frozen == false`	`!frozen`	It is clearer to use ! than to compare with false.

Use the || (*or*) operator to combine the expressions:

```
if (temp <= 0 || temp >= 100) { System.out.println("Not liquid"); }
```

Figure 10 shows flowcharts for these examples.

Sometimes you need to *invert* a condition with the *not* Boolean operator. The ! operator takes a single condition and evaluates to true if that condition is false and to false if the condition is true. In this example, output occurs if the value of the Boolean variable frozen is false: .

> To invert a condition, use the ! (*not*) operator.

```
if (!frozen) { System.out.println("Not frozen"); }
```

Table 5 illustrates additional examples of evaluating Boolean operators.

SELF CHECK

33. Suppose x and y are two integers. How do you test whether both of them are zero?

34. How do you test whether at least one of them is zero?

35. How do you test whether *exactly one of them* is zero?

36. What is the value of !!frozen?

37. What is the advantage of using the type boolean rather than strings "false"/"true" or integers 0/1?

Practice It   Now you can try these exercises at the end of the chapter: R5.29, E5.22, E5.23.

Common Error 5.4

Combining Multiple Relational Operators

Consider the expression

```
if (0 <= temp <= 100) // Error
```

This looks just like the mathematical test $0 \le \text{temp} \le 100$. But in Java, it is a compile-time error.

Let us dissect the condition. The first half, `0 <= temp`, is a test with an outcome `true` or `false`. The outcome of that test (`true` or `false`) is then compared against 100. This seems to make no sense. Is `true` larger than 100 or not? Can one compare truth values and numbers? In Java, you cannot. The Java compiler rejects this statement.

Instead, use `&&` to combine two separate tests:

```
if (0 <= temp && temp <= 100) . . .
```

Another common error, along the same lines, is to write

```
if (input == 1 || 2) . . . // Error
```

to test whether `input` is 1 or 2. Again, the Java compiler flags this construct as an error. You cannot apply the `||` operator to numbers. You need to write two Boolean expressions and join them with the `||` operator:

```
if (input == 1 || input == 2) . . .
```

Common Error 5.5

Confusing && and || Conditions

It is a surprisingly common error to confuse *and* and *or* conditions. A value lies between 0 and 100 if it is at least 0 *and* at most 100. It lies outside that range if it is less than 0 *or* greater than 100. There is no golden rule; you just have to think carefully.

Often the *and* or *or* is clearly stated, and then it isn't too hard to implement it. But sometimes the wording isn't as explicit. It is quite common that the individual conditions are nicely set apart in a bulleted list, but with little indication of how they should be combined.

Consider these instructions for filing a tax return. You can claim single filing status if any one of the following is true:

- You were never married.

- You were legally separated or divorced on the last day of the tax year.

- You were widowed, and did not remarry.

Because the test passes if *any one* of the conditions is true, you must combine the conditions with *or*.

Elsewhere, the same instructions state that you may use the more advantageous status of married filing jointly if all five of the following conditions are true:

- Your spouse died less than two years ago and you did not remarry.

- You have a child whom you can claim as dependent.

- That child lived in your home for all of the tax year.

- You paid over half the cost of keeping up your home for this child.

- You filed a joint return with your spouse the year he or she died.

Because *all* of the conditions must be true for the test to pass, you must combine them with an *and*.

Special Topic 5.6

Short-Circuit Evaluation of Boolean Operators

The && and || operators are computed using short-circuit evaluation. In other words, logical expressions are evaluated from left to right, and evaluation stops as soon as the truth value is determined. When an && is evaluated and the first condition is false, the second condition is not evaluated, because it does not matter what the outcome of the second test is.

For example, consider the expression

```
quantity > 0 && price / quantity < 10
```

> The && and || operators are computed using *short-circuit evaluation:* As soon as the truth value is determined, no further conditions are evaluated.

Suppose the value of quantity is zero. Then the test quantity > 0 fails, and the second test is not attempted. That is just as well, because it is illegal to divide by zero.

Similarly, when the first condition of an || expression is true, then the remainder is not evaluated because the result must be true.

This process is called **short-circuit evaluation**.

In a short circuit, electricity travels along the path of least resistance. Similarly, short-circuit evaluation takes the fastest path for computing the result of a Boolean expression.

Special Topic 5.7

De Morgan's Law

Humans generally have a hard time comprehending logical conditions with *not* operators applied to *and/or* expressions. **De Morgan's Law**, named after the logician Augustus De Morgan (1806–1871), can be used to simplify these Boolean expressions.

Suppose we want to charge a higher shipping rate if we don't ship within the continental United States:

```
if (!(country.equals("USA") && !state.equals("AK") && !state.equals("HI")))
{
    shippingCharge = 20.00;
}
```

This test is a little bit complicated, and you have to think carefully through the logic. When it is *not* true that the country is USA *and* the state is not Alaska *and* the state is not Hawaii, then charge $20.00. Huh? It is not true that some people won't be confused by this code.

The computer doesn't care, but it takes human programmers to write and maintain the code. Therefore, it is useful to know how to simplify such a condition.

De Morgan's Law has two forms: one for the negation of an *and* expression and one for the negation of an *or* expression:

> De Morgan's Law tells you how to negate && and || conditions.

!(A && B) is the same as !A || !B
!(A || B) is the same as !A && !B

Pay particular attention to the fact that the *and* and *or* operators are *reversed* by moving the *not* inward. For example, the negation of "the state is Alaska *or* it is Hawaii",

```
!(state.equals("AK") || state.equals("HI"))
```

is "the state is not Alaska *and* it is not Hawaii":

```
!state.equals("AK") && !state.equals("HI")
```

Now apply the law to our shipping charge computation:

```
!(country.equals("USA")
    && !state.equals("AK")
    && !state.equals("HI"))
```

is equivalent to

```
!country.equals("USA")
    || !!state.equals("AK")
    || !!state.equals("HI"))
```

Because two ! cancel each other out, the result is the simpler test

```
!country.equals("USA")
    || state.equals("AK")
    || state.equals("HI"))
```

In other words, higher shipping charges apply when the destination is outside the United States or to Alaska or Hawaii.

To simplify conditions with negations of *and* or *or* expressions, it is usually a good idea to apply De Morgan's Law to move the negations to the innermost level.

5.8 Application: Input Validation

Like a quality control worker, you want to make sure that user input is correct before processing it.

An important application for the `if` statement is *input validation*. Whenever your program accepts user input, you need to make sure that the user-supplied values are valid before you use them in your computations.

Consider our elevator simulation program. Assume that the elevator panel has buttons labeled 1 through 20 (but not 13). The following are illegal inputs:

- The number 13
- Zero or a negative number
- A number larger than 20
- An input that is not a sequence of digits, such as `five`

In each of these cases, we want to give an error message and exit the program. It is simple to guard against an input of 13:

```
if (floor == 13)
{
    System.out.println("Error: There is no thirteenth floor.");
}
```

Here is how you ensure that the user doesn't enter a number outside the valid range:

```
if (floor <= 0 || floor > 20)
{
    System.out.println("Error: The floor must be between 1 and 20.");
}
```

However, dealing with an input that is not a valid integer is a more serious problem. When the statement

```
floor = in.nextInt();
```

is executed, and the user types in an input that is not an integer (such as `five`), then the integer variable `floor` is not set. Instead, a run-time exception occurs and the program is terminated. To avoid this problem, you should first call the `hasNextInt` method

Call the hasNextInt
or hasNextDouble
method to ensure
that the next input is
a number.

which checks whether the next input is an integer. If that method returns true, you can safely call nextInt. Otherwise, print an error message and exit the program:

```java
if (in.hasNextInt())
{
    int floor = in.nextInt();
    Process the input value.
}
else
{
    System.out.println("Error: Not an integer.");
}
```

Here is the complete elevator simulation program with input validation:

section_8/ElevatorSimulation2.java

```java
1   import java.util.Scanner;
2
3   /**
4       This program simulates an elevator panel that skips the 13th floor, checking for
5       input errors.
6   */
7   public class ElevatorSimulation2
8   {
9       public static void main(String[] args)
10      {
11          Scanner in = new Scanner(System.in);
12          System.out.print("Floor: ");
13          if (in.hasNextInt())
14          {
15              // Now we know that the user entered an integer
16
17              int floor = in.nextInt();
18
19              if (floor == 13)
20              {
21                  System.out.println("Error: There is no thirteenth floor.");
22              }
23              else if (floor <= 0 || floor > 20)
24              {
25                  System.out.println("Error: The floor must be between 1 and 20.");
26              }
27              else
28              {
29                  // Now we know that the input is valid
30
31                  int actualFloor = floor;
32                  if (floor > 13)
33                  {
34                      actualFloor = floor - 1;
35                  }
36
37                  System.out.println("The elevator will travel to the actual floor "
38                      + actualFloor);
39              }
40          }
41          else
42          {
43              System.out.println("Error: Not an integer.");
```

```
44          }
45        }
46  }
```

Program Run

```
Floor: 13
Error: There is no thirteenth floor.
```

SELF CHECK

38. In the `ElevatorSimulation2` program, what is the output when the input is

    a. 100?

    b. −1?

    c. 20?

    d. thirteen?

39. Your task is to rewrite lines 19–26 of the `ElevatorSimulation2` program so that there is a single `if` statement with a complex condition. What is the condition?

```
if (. . .)
{
    System.out.println("Error: Invalid floor number");
}
```

40. In the Sherlock Holmes story "The Adventure of the Sussex Vampire", the inimitable detective uttered these words: "Matilda Briggs was not the name of a young woman, Watson, … It was a ship which is associated with the giant rat of Sumatra, a story for which the world is not yet prepared." Over a hundred years later, researchers found giant rats in Western New Guinea, another part of Indonesia.

Suppose you are charged with writing a program that processes rat weights. It contains the statements

```
System.out.print("Enter weight in kg: ");
double weight = in.nextDouble();
```

What input checks should you supply?

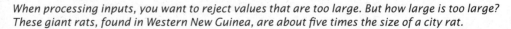

When processing inputs, you want to reject values that are too large. But how large is too large? These giant rats, found in Western New Guinea, are about five times the size of a city rat.

41. Run the following test program and supply inputs 2 and `three` at the prompts. What happens? Why?

```
import java.util.Scanner

public class Test
{
    public static void main(String[] args)
    {
        Scanner in = new Scanner(System.in);
        System.out.print("Enter an integer: ");
        int m = in.nextInt();
        System.out.print("Enter another integer: ");
        int n = in.nextInt();
        System.out.println(m + " " + n);
    }
}
```

Practice It   Now you can try these exercises at the end of the chapter: R5.3, R5.32, E5.12.

Computing & Society 5.2 Artificial Intelligence

When one uses a sophisticated computer program such as a tax preparation package, one is bound to attribute some intelligence to the computer. The computer asks sensible questions and makes computations that we find a mental challenge. After all, if doing one's taxes were easy, we wouldn't need a computer to do it for us.

As programmers, however, we know that all this apparent intelligence is an illusion. Human programmers have carefully "coached" the software in all possible scenarios, and it simply replays the actions and decisions that were programmed into it.

Would it be possible to write computer programs that are genuinely intelligent in some sense? From the earliest days of computing, there was a sense that the human brain might be nothing but an immense computer, and that it might well be feasible to program computers to imitate some processes of human thought. Serious research into *artificial intelligence* began in the mid-1950s, and the first twenty years brought some impressive successes. Programs that play chess—surely an activity that appears to require remarkable intellectual powers—have become so good that they now routinely beat all but the best human players. As far back as 1975, an *expert-system* program called Mycin gained fame for being better in diagnosing meningitis in patients than the average physician.

However, there were serious setbacks as well. From 1982 to 1992, the Japanese government embarked on a massive research project, funded at over 40 billion Japanese yen. It was known as the *Fifth-Generation Project*. Its goal was to develop new hardware and software to greatly improve the performance of expert system software. At its outset, the project created fear in other countries that the Japanese computer industry was about to become the undisputed leader in the field. However, the end results were disappointing and did little to bring

artificial intelligence applications to market.

From the very outset, one of the stated goals of the AI community was to produce software that could translate text from one language to another, for example from English to Russian. That undertaking proved to be enormously complicated. Human language appears to be much more subtle and interwoven with the human experience than had originally been thought. Even the grammar-checking tools that come with word-processing programs today are more of a gimmick than a useful tool, and analyzing grammar is just the first step in translating sentences.

The CYC (from en*cyc*lopedia) project, started by Douglas Lenat in 1984, tries to codify the implicit assumptions that underlie human speech and writing. The team members started out analyzing news articles and asked themselves what unmentioned facts are necessary to actually understand the sentences. For example, consider the sentence, "Last fall she enrolled in Michigan State". The reader automatically realizes that "fall" is not related to falling down in this context, but refers to the season. While there is a state of Michigan, here Michigan State denotes the university. A priori, a computer program has none of this

knowledge. The goal of the CYC project is to extract and store the requisite facts—that is, (1) people enroll in universities; (2) Michigan is a state; (3) many states have universities named X State University, often abbreviated as X State; (4) most people enroll in a university in the fall. By 1995, the project had codified about 100,000 common-sense concepts and about a million facts of knowledge relating them. Even this massive amount of data has not proven sufficient for useful applications.

In recent years, artificial intelligence technology has seen substantial advances. One of the most astounding examples is the outcome of a series of "grand challenges" for autonomous vehicles posed by the Defense Advanced Research Projects Agency (DARPA). Competitors were invited to submit a computer-controlled vehicle that had to complete an obstacle course without a human driver or remote control. The first event, in 2004, was a disappointment, with none of the entrants finishing the route. In 2005, five vehicles completed a grueling 212 km course in the Mojave desert. Stanford's Stanley came in first, with an average speed of 30 km/h. In 2007, DARPA moved the competition to an "urban" environment, an abandoned air force base. Vehicles had to be able to interact with each other, following California traffic laws. As Stanford's Sebastian Thrun explained: "In the last Grand Challenge, it didn't really matter whether an obstacle was a rock or a bush, because either way you'd just drive around it. The current challenge is to move from just sensing the environment to understanding it."

Winner of the 2007 DARPA Urban Challenge

CHAPTER SUMMARY

Use the `if` statement to implement a decision.

- The `if` statement allows a program to carry out different actions depending on the nature of the data to be processed.

Implement comparisons of numbers and objects.

- Use relational operators (`< <= > >= == !=`) to compare numbers.
- Relational operators compare values. The `==` operator tests for equality.
- When comparing floating-point numbers, don't test for equality. Instead, check whether they are close enough.
- Do not use the `==` operator to compare strings. Use the `equals` method instead.
- The `compareTo` method compares strings in lexicographic order.
- The `==` operator tests whether two object references are identical. To compare the contents of objects, you need to use the `equals` method.
- The `null` reference refers to no object.

Implement complex decisions that require multiple `if` statements.

- Multiple `if` statements can be combined to evaluate complex decisions.
- When using multiple `if` statements, test general conditions after more specific conditions.

Implement decisions whose branches require further decisions.

- When a decision statement is contained inside the branch of another decision statement, the statements are *nested*.
- Nested decisions are required for problems that have two levels of decision making.

Draw flowcharts for visualizing the control flow of a program.

- Flow charts are made up of elements for tasks, input/output, and decisions.
- Each branch of a decision can contain tasks and further decisions.
- Never point an arrow inside another branch.

Design test cases for your programs.

- Black-box testing describes a testing method that does not take the structure of the implementation into account.
- White-box testing uses information about the structure of a program.
- Code coverage is a measure of how many parts of a program have been tested.
- Boundary test cases are test cases that are at the boundary of acceptable inputs.
- It is a good idea to design test cases before implementing a program.
- Logging messages can be deactivated when testing is complete.

Use the Boolean data type to store and combine conditions that can be true or false.

- The Boolean type `boolean` has two values, `false` and `true`.
- Java has two Boolean operators that combine conditions: `&&` (*and*) and `||` (*or*).
- To invert a condition, use the `!` (*not*) operator.
- The `&&` and `||` operators are computed using **short-circuit evaluation**: As soon as the truth value is determined, no further conditions are evaluated.
- De Morgan's Law tells you how to negate `&&` and `||` conditions.

Apply `if` statements to detect whether user input is valid.

- Call the `hasNextInt` or `hasNextDouble` method to ensure that the next input is a number.

STANDARD LIBRARY ITEMS INTRODUCED IN THIS CHAPTER

```
java.awt.Rectangle                java.util.logging.Level
   equals                            INFO
java.lang.String                     OFF
   equals                         java.util.logging.Logger
   compareTo                         getGlobal
java.util.Scanner                    info
   hasNextDouble                     setLevel
   hasNextInt
```

REVIEW QUESTIONS

- **R5.1** What is the value of each variable after the `if` statement?

  a. `int n = 1; int k = 2; int r = n;`
  `if (k < n) { r = k; }`

  b. `int n = 1; int k = 2; int r;`
  `if (n < k) { r = k; }`
  `else { r = k + n; }`

  c. `int n = 1; int k = 2; int r = k;`
  `if (r < k) { n = r; }`
  `else { k = n; }`

  d. `int n = 1; int k = 2; int r = 3;`
  `if (r < n + k) { r = 2 * n; }`
  `else { k = 2 * r; }`

R5.2 Explain the difference between

```
s = 0;
if (x > 0) { s++; }
if (y > 0) { s++; }
```

and

```
s = 0;
if (x > 0) { s++; }
else if (y > 0) { s++; }
```

R5.3 Find the errors in the following if statements.

a. if x > 0 then System.out.print(x);

b. if (1 + x > Math.pow(x, Math.sqrt(2))) { y = y + x; }

c. if (x = 1) { y++; }

d.
```
x = in.nextInt();
if (in.hasNextInt())
{
    sum = sum + x;
}
else
{
    System.out.println("Bad input for x");
}
```

e.
```
String letterGrade = "F";
if (grade >= 90) { letterGrade = "A"; }
if (grade >= 80) { letterGrade = "B"; }
if (grade >= 70) { letterGrade = "C"; }
if (grade >= 60) { letterGrade = "D"; }
```

R5.4 What do these code fragments print?

a.
```
int n = 1;
int m = -1;
if (n < -m) { System.out.print(n); }
else { System.out.print(m); }
```

b.
```
int n = 1;
int m = -1;
if (-n >= m) { System.out.print(n); }
else { System.out.print(m); }
```

c.
```
double x = 0;
double y = 1;
if (Math.abs(x - y) < 1) { System.out.print(x); }
else { System.out.print(y); }
```

d.
```
double x = Math.sqrt(2);
double y = 2;
if (x * x == y) { System.out.print(x); }
else { System.out.print(y); }
```

R5.5 Suppose x and y are variables of type double. Write a code fragment that sets y to x if x is positive and to 0 otherwise.

R5.6 Suppose x and y are variables of type double. Write a code fragment that sets y to the absolute value of x without calling the Math.abs function. Use an if statement.

R5.7 Explain why it is more difficult to compare floating-point numbers than integers. Write Java code to test whether an integer n equals 10 and whether a floating-point number x is approximately equal to 10.

■ R5.8 It is easy to confuse the = and == operators. Write a test program containing the statement

```
if (floor = 13)
```

What error message do you get? Write another test program with the statement

```
count == 0;
```

What does your compiler do when you compile the program?

■■ R5.9 Each square on a chess board can be described by a letter and number, such as g5 in the example at right.

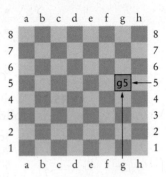

The following pseudocode describes an algorithm that determines whether a square with a given letter and number is dark (black) or light (white).

> If the letter is an a, c, e, or g
>   If the number is odd
>   color = "black"
>   Else
>   color = "white"
> Else
>   If the number is even
>   color = "black"
>   Else
>   color = "white"

Using the procedure in Programming Tip 5.5, trace this pseudocode with input g5.

■■ Testing R5.10 Give a set of four test cases for the algorithm of Exercise R5.9 that covers all branches.

■■ R5.11 In a scheduling program, we want to check whether two appointments overlap. For simplicity, appointments start at a full hour, and we use military time (with hours 0–24). The following pseudocode describes an algorithm that determines whether the appointment with start time **start1** and end time **end1** overlaps with the appointment with start time **start2** and end time **end2**.

> If start1 > start2
>   s = start1
> Else
>   s = start2
> If end1 < end2
>   e = end1
> Else
>   e = end2
> If s < e
>   The appointments overlap.
> Else
>   The appointments don't overlap.

Trace this algorithm with an appointment from 10–12 and one from 11–13, then with an appointment from 10–11 and one from 12–13.

■ R5.12 Draw a flow chart for the algorithm in Exercise R5.11.

■ R5.13 Draw a flow chart for the algorithm in Exercise E5.13.

- **R5.14** Draw a flow chart for the algorithm in Exercise E5.14.

■■ **Testing R5.15** Develop a set of test cases for the algorithm in Exercise R5.11.

■■ **Testing R5.16** Develop a set of test cases for the algorithm in Exercise E5.14.

■■ **R5.17** Write pseudocode for a program that prompts the user for a month and day and prints out whether it is one of the following four holidays:
- New Year's Day (January 1)
- Independence Day (July 4)
- Veterans Day (November 11)
- Christmas Day (December 25)

■■ **R5.18** Write pseudocode for a program that assigns letter grades for a quiz, according to the following table:

Score	Grade
90-100	A
80-89	B
70-79	C
60-69	D
< 60	F

■■ **R5.19** Explain how the lexicographic ordering of strings in Java differs from the ordering of words in a dictionary or telephone book. *Hint:* Consider strings such as IBM, wiley.com, Century 21, and While-U-Wait.

■■ **R5.20** Of the following pairs of strings, which comes first in lexicographic order?
- **a.** "Tom", "Jerry"
- **b.** "Tom", "Tomato"
- **c.** "church", "Churchill"
- **d.** "car manufacturer", "carburetor"
- **e.** "Harry", "hairy"
- **f.** "Java", " Car"
- **g.** "Tom", "Tom"
- **h.** "Car", "Carl"
- **i.** "car", "bar"

- **R5.21** Explain the difference between an if/else if/else sequence and nested if statements. Give an example of each.

■■ **R5.22** Give an example of an if/else if/else sequence where the order of the tests does not matter. Give an example where the order of the tests matters.

- **R5.23** Rewrite the condition in Section 5.3 to use < operators instead of >= operators. What is the impact on the order of the comparisons?

■■ **Testing R5.24** Give a set of test cases for the tax program in Exercise P5.2. Manually compute the expected results.

- **R5.25** Make up a Java code example that shows the dangling else problem using the following statement: A student with a GPA of at least 1.5, but less than 2, is on probation. With less than 1.5, the student is failing.

■■■ **R5.26** Complete the following truth table by finding the truth values of the Boolean expressions for all combinations of the Boolean inputs p, q, and r.

p	q	r	(p && q) || !r	!(p && (q || !r))
false	false	false		
false	false	true		
false	true	false		
...				
5 more combinations				
...				

■■■ **R5.27** True or false? *A* && *B* is the same as *B* && *A* for any Boolean conditions *A* and *B*.

■ **R5.28** The "advanced search" feature of many search engines allows you to use Boolean operators for complex queries, such as "(cats OR dogs) AND NOT pets". Contrast these search operators with the Boolean operators in Java.

■■ **R5.29** Suppose the value of b is false and the value of x is 0. What is the value of each of the following expressions?

a. b && x == 0

b. b || x == 0

c. !b && x == 0

d. !b || x == 0

e. b && x != 0

f. b || x != 0

g. !b && x != 0

h. !b || x != 0

■■ **R5.30** Simplify the following expressions. Here, b is a variable of type boolean.

a. b == true

b. b == false

c. b != true

d. b != false

■■■ **R5.31** Simplify the following statements. Here, b is a variable of type boolean and n is a variable of type int.

a. if (n == 0) { b = true; } else { b = false; }

   (*Hint:* What is the value of n == 0?)

b. if (n == 0) { b = false; } else { b = true; }

c. b = false; if (n > 1) { if (n < 2) { b = true; } }

d. if (n < 1) { b = true; } else { b = n > 2; }

■ **R5.32** What is wrong with the following program?

```
System.out.print("Enter the number of quarters: ");
int quarters = in.nextInt();
if (in.hasNextInt())
{
    total = total + quarters * 0.25;
    System.out.println("Total: " + total);
```

```
    }
    else
    {
        System.out.println("Input error.");
    }
```

PRACTICE EXERCISES

■ **E5.1** Write a program that reads an integer and prints whether it is negative, zero, or positive.

■■ **E5.2** Write a program that reads a floating-point number and prints "zero" if the number is zero. Otherwise, print "positive" or "negative". Add "small" if the absolute value of the number is less than 1, or "large" if it exceeds 1,000,000.

■■ **E5.3** Write a program that reads an integer and prints how many digits the number has, by checking whether the number is ≥ 10, ≥ 100, and so on. (Assume that all integers are less than ten billion.) If the number is negative, first multiply it with –1.

■■ **E5.4** Write a program that reads three numbers and prints "all the same" if they are all the same, "all different" if they are all different, and "neither" otherwise.

■■ **E5.5** Write a program that reads three numbers and prints "increasing" if they are in increasing order, "decreasing" if they are in decreasing order, and "neither" otherwise. Here, "increasing" means "strictly increasing", with each value larger than its predecessor. The sequence 3 4 4 would not be considered increasing.

■■ **E5.6** Repeat Exercise E5.5, but before reading the numbers, ask the user whether increasing/decreasing should be "strict" or "lenient". In lenient mode, the sequence 3 4 4 is increasing and the sequence 4 4 4 is both increasing and decreasing.

■■ **E5.7** Write a program that reads in three integers and prints "in order" if they are sorted in ascending *or* descending order, or "not in order" otherwise. For example,

```
1 2 5    in order
1 5 2    not in order
5 2 1    in order
1 2 2    in order
```

■■ **E5.8** Write a program that reads four integers and prints "two pairs" if the input consists of two matching pairs (in some order) and "not two pairs" otherwise. For example,

```
1 2 2 1    two pairs
1 2 2 3    not two pairs
2 2 2 2    two pairs
```

■■ **Business E5.9** Write a program that reads in the name and salary of an employee. Here the salary will denote an *hourly* wage, such as $9.25. Then ask how many hours the employee worked in the past week. Be sure to accept fractional hours. Compute the pay. Any overtime work (over 40 hours per week) is paid at 150 percent of the regular wage. Print a paycheck for the employee. In your solution, implement a class Paycheck.

■ **E5.10** Write a program that reads a temperature value and the letter C for Celsius or F for Fahrenheit. Print whether water is liquid, solid, or gaseous at the given temperature at sea level.

E5.11 The boiling point of water drops by about one degree centigrade for every 300 meters (or 1,000 feet) of altitude. Improve the program of Exercise E5.10 to allow the user to supply the altitude in meters or feet.

E5.12 Add error handling to Exercise E5.11. If the user does not enter a number when expected, or provides an invalid unit for the altitude, print an error message and end the program.

E5.13 When two points in time are compared, each given as hours (in military time, ranging from 0 and 23) and minutes, the following pseudocode determines which comes first.

> If hour1 < hour2
>   time1 comes first.
> Else if hour1 and hour2 are the same
>   If minute1 < minute2
>   time1 comes first.
>   Else if minute1 and minute2 are the same
>   time1 and time2 are the same.
>   Else
>   time2 comes first.
> Else
>   time2 comes first.

Write a program that prompts the user for two points in time and prints the time that comes first, then the other time. In your program, supply a class Time and a method

```
public int compareTo(Time other)
```

that returns −1 if the time comes before the other, 0 if both are the same, and 1 otherwise.

E5.14 The following algorithm yields the season (Spring, Summer, Fall, or Winter) for a given month and day.

> If month is 1, 2, or 3, season = "Winter"
> Else If month is 4, 5, or 6, season = "Spring"
> Else if month is 7, 8, or 9, season = "Summer"
> Else if month is 10, 11, or 12, season = "Fall"
> If month is divisible by 3 and day >= 21
>   If season is "Winter", season = "Spring"
>   Else if season is "Spring", season = "Summer"
>   Else if season is "Summer", season = "Fall"
>   Else season = "Winter"

Write a program that prompts the user for a month and day and then prints the season, as determined by this algorithm. Use a class Date with a method getSeason.

E5.15 Write a program that translates a letter grade into a number grade. Letter grades are A, B, C, D, and F, possibly followed by + or −. Their numeric values are 4, 3, 2, 1, and 0. There is no F+ or F−. A + increases the numeric value by 0.3, a − decreases it by 0.3. However, an A+ has value 4.0.

```
Enter a letter grade: B-
The numeric value is 2.7.
```

Use a class Grade with a method getNumericGrade.

■■ E5.16 Write a program that translates a number between 0 and 4 into the closest letter grade. For example, the number 2.8 (which might have been the average of several grades) would be converted to B–. Break ties in favor of the better grade; for example 2.85 should be a B.

Use a class `Grade` with a method `getNumericGrade`.

■■ E5.17 The original U.S. income tax of 1913 was quite simple. The tax was

- 1 percent on the first $50,000.
- 2 percent on the amount over $50,000 up to $75,000.
- 3 percent on the amount over $75,000 up to $100,000.
- 4 percent on the amount over $100,000 up to $250,000.
- 5 percent on the amount over $250,000 up to $500,000.
- 6 percent on the amount over $500,000.

There was no separate schedule for single or married taxpayers. Write a program that computes the income tax according to this schedule.

■■ E5.18 Write a program that takes user input describing a playing card in the following shorthand notation:

A	Ace
2 ... 10	Card values
J	Jack
Q	Queen
K	King
D	Diamonds
H	Hearts
S	Spades
C	Clubs

Your program should print the full description of the card. For example,

```
Enter the card notation: QS
Queen of Spades
```

Implement a class `Card` whose constructor takes the card notation string and whose `getDescription` method returns a description of the card. If the notation string is not in the correct format, the `getDescription` method should return the string `"Unknown"`.

■■ E5.19 Write a program that reads in three floating-point numbers and prints the largest of the three inputs. For example:

```
Please enter three numbers: 4 9 2.5
The largest number is 9.
```

■■ E5.20 Write a program that reads in three strings and sorts them lexicographically.

```
Enter three strings: Charlie Able Baker
Able
Baker
Charlie
```

•• E5.21 Write a program that reads in two floating-point numbers and tests whether they are the same up to two decimal places. Here are two sample runs.

```
Enter two floating-point numbers: 2.0 1.99998
They are the same up to two decimal places.
Enter two floating-point numbers: 2.0 1.98999
They are different.
```

• E5.22 Write a program that prompts the user to provide a single character from the alphabet. Print Vowel or Consonant, depending on the user input. If the user input is not a letter (between a and z or A and Z), or is a string of length > 1, print an error message.

•• E5.23 Write a program that asks the user to enter a month (1 for January, 2 for February, etc.) and then prints the number of days in the month. For February, print "28 days".

```
Enter a month: 5
30 days
```

Use a class Month with a method

```
public int getLength()
```

Do not use a separate if/else branch for each month. Use Boolean operators.

• Business E5.24 A supermarket awards coupons depending on how much a customer spends on groceries. For example, if you spend $50, you will get a coupon worth eight percent of that amount. The following table shows the percent used to calculate the coupon awarded for different amounts spent. Write a program that calculates and prints the value of the coupon a person can receive based on groceries purchased.

Here is a sample run:

```
Please enter the cost of your groceries: 14
You win a discount coupon of $ 1.12. (8% of your purchase)
```

Money Spent	Coupon Percentage
Less than $10	No coupon
From $10 to $60	8%
More than $60 to $150	10%
More than $150 to $210	12%
More than $210	14%

PROGRAMMING PROJECTS

•• P5.1 Write a program that prompts for the day and month of the user's birthday and then prints a horoscope. Make up fortunes for programmers, like this:

```
Please enter your birthday (month and day): 6 16
Gemini are experts at figuring out the behavior of complicated programs.
You feel where bugs are coming from and then stay one step ahead. Tonight,
your style wins approval from a tough critic.
```

Each fortune should contain the name of the astrological sign. (You will find the names and date ranges of the signs at a distressingly large number of sites on the Internet.) Use a class Date with a method getFortune.

• • P5.2   Write a program that computes taxes for the following schedule.

If your status is Single and if the taxable income is over	but not over	the tax is	of the amount over
$0	$8,000	10%	$0
$8,000	$32,000	$800 + 15%	$8,000
$32,000		$4,400 + 25%	$32,000
If your status is Married and if the taxable income is over	**but not over**	**the tax is**	**of the amount over**
$0	$16,000	10%	$0
$16,000	$64,000	$1,600 + 15%	$16,000
$64,000		$8,800 + 25%	$64,000

• • • P5.3   The TaxReturn.java program uses a simplified version of the 2008 U.S. income tax schedule. Look up the tax brackets and rates for the current year, for both single and married filers, and implement a program that computes the actual income tax.

• • • P5.4   *Unit conversion.* Write a unit conversion program that asks the users from which unit they want to convert (fl. oz, gal, oz, lb, in, ft, mi) and to which unit they want to convert (ml, l, g, kg, mm, cm, m, km). Reject incompatible conversions (such as gal → km). Ask for the value to be converted, then display the result:

```
Convert from? gal
Convert to? ml
Value? 2.5
2.5 gal = 9462.5 ml
```

• • • P5.5   A year with 366 days is called a leap year. Leap years are necessary to keep the calendar synchronized with the sun because the earth revolves around the sun once every 365.25 days. Actually, that figure is not entirely precise, and for all dates after 1582 the *Gregorian correction* applies. Usually years that are divisible by 4 are leap years, for example 1996. However, years that are divisible by 100 (for example, 1900) are not leap years, but years that are divisible by 400 are leap years (for example, 2000). Write a program that asks the user for a year and computes whether that year is a leap year. Provide a class Year with a method isLeapYear. Use a single if statement and Boolean operators.

• • • P5.6   *Roman numbers.* Write a program that converts a positive integer into the Roman number system. The Roman number system has digits

I	1
V	5
X	10
L	50
C	100
D	500
M	1,000

Numbers are formed according to the following rules:

a. Only numbers up to 3,999 are represented.

b. As in the decimal system, the thousands, hundreds, tens, and ones are expressed separately.

c. The numbers 1 to 9 are expressed as

I	1	VI	6
II	2	VII	7
III	3	VIII	8
IV	4	IX	9
V	5		

As you can see, an I preceding a V or X is subtracted from the value, and you can never have more than three I's in a row.

d. Tens and hundreds are done the same way, except that the letters X, L, C and C, D, M are used instead of I, V, X, respectively.

Your program should take an input, such as 1978, and convert it to Roman numerals, MCMLXXVIII.

■■■ **P5.7** French country names are feminine when they end with the letter e, masculine otherwise, except for the following which are masculine even though they end with e:

- le Belize
- le Cambodge
- le Mexique
- le Mozambique
- le Zaïre
- le Zimbabwe

Write a program that reads the French name of a country and adds the article: le for masculine or la for feminine, such as le Canada or la Belgique.

However, if the country name starts with a vowel, use l'; for example, l'Afghanistan.

For the following plural country names, use les:

- les Etats-Unis
- les Pays-Bas

■■■ **Business P5.8** Write a program to simulate a bank transaction. There are two bank accounts: checking and savings. First, ask for the initial balances of the bank accounts; reject negative balances. Then ask for the transactions; options are deposit, withdrawal, and transfer. Then ask for the account; options are checking and savings. Reject transactions that overdraw an account. At the end, print the balances of both accounts.

■■ **Business P5.9** When you use an automated teller machine (ATM) with your bank card, you need to use a personal identification number (PIN) to access your account. If a user fails more than three times when entering the PIN, the machine will block the card. Assume that the user's PIN is "1234" and write a program that asks the user for the PIN no more than three times, and does the following:

• If the user enters the right number, print a message saying, "Your PIN is correct", and end the program.

• If the user enters a wrong number, print a message saying, "Your PIN is incorrect" and, if you have asked for the PIN less than three times, ask for it again.

• If the user enters a wrong number three times, print a message saying "Your bank card is blocked" and end the program.

• Business P5.10 Calculating the tip when you go to a restaurant is not difficult, but your restaurant wants to suggest a tip according to the service diners receive. Write a program that calculates a tip according to the diner's satisfaction as follows:

• Ask for the diners' satisfaction level using these ratings: 1 = Totally satisfied, 2 = Satisfied, 3 = Dissatisfied.

• If the diner is totally satisfied, calculate a 20 percent tip.

• If the diner is satisfied, calculate a 15 percent tip.

• If the diner is dissatisfied, calculate a 10 percent tip.

• Report the satisfaction level and tip in dollars and cents.

• Science P5.11 Write a program that prompts the user for a wavelength value and prints a description of the corresponding part of the electromagnetic spectrum, as given in the following table.

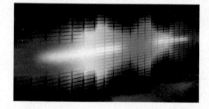

Electromagnetic Spectrum		
Type	Wavelength (m)	Frequency (Hz)
Radio Waves	$> 10^{-1}$	$< 3 \times 10^9$
Microwaves	10^{-3} to 10^{-1}	3×10^9 to 3×10^{11}
Infrared	7×10^{-7} to 10^{-3}	3×10^{11} to 4×10^{14}
Visible light	4×10^{-7} to 7×10^{-7}	4×10^{14} to 7.5×10^{14}
Ultraviolet	10^{-8} to 4×10^{-7}	7.5×10^{14} to 3×10^{16}
X-rays	10^{-11} to 10^{-8}	3×10^{16} to 3×10^{19}
Gamma rays	$< 10^{-11}$	$> 3 \times 10^{19}$

• Science P5.12 Repeat Exercise P5.11, modifying the program so that it prompts for the frequency instead.

•• Science P5.13 Repeat Exercise P5.11, modifying the program so that it first asks the user whether the input will be a wavelength or a frequency.

••• Science P5.14 A minivan has two sliding doors. Each door can be opened by either a dashboard switch, its inside handle, or its outside handle. However, the inside handles do not work if a child lock switch is activated. In order for the sliding doors to open, the gear shift must be in park, *and* the master unlock switch must be activated. (This book's author is the long-suffering owner of just such a vehicle.)

Your task is to simulate a portion of the control software for the vehicle. The input is a sequence of values for the switches and the gear shift, in the following order:

- Dashboard switches for left and right sliding door, child lock, and master unlock (0 for off or 1 for activated)
- Inside and outside handles on the left and right sliding doors (0 or 1)
- The gear shift setting (one of P N D 1 2 3 R).

A typical input would be 0 0 0 1 0 1 0 0 P.

Print "left door opens" and/or "right door opens" as appropriate. If neither door opens, print "both doors stay closed".

Science P5.15 Sound level L in units of decibel (dB) is determined by

$$L = 20 \log_{10}(p/p_0)$$

where p is the sound pressure of the sound (in Pascals, abbreviated Pa), and p_0 is a reference sound pressure equal to 20×10^{-6} Pa (where L is 0 dB). The following table gives descriptions for certain sound levels.

Threshold of pain	130 dB
Possible hearing damage	120 dB
Jack hammer at 1 m	100 dB
Traffic on a busy roadway at 10 m	90 dB
Normal conversation	60 dB
Calm library	30 dB
Light leaf rustling	0 dB

Write a program that reads a value and a unit, either dB or Pa, and then prints the closest description from the list above.

Science P5.16 The electric circuit shown below is designed to measure the temperature of the gas in a chamber.

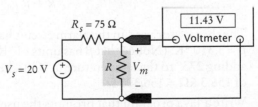

The resistor R represents a temperature sensor enclosed in the chamber. The resistance R, in Ω, is related to the temperature T, in °C, by the equation

$$R = R_0 + kT$$

In this device, assume $R_0 = 100\ \Omega$ and $k = 0.5$. The voltmeter displays the value of the voltage, V_m, across the sensor. This voltage V_m indicates the temperature, T, of the gas according to the equation

$$T = \frac{R}{k} - \frac{R_0}{k} = \frac{R_s}{k} \frac{V_m}{V_s - V_m} - \frac{R_0}{k}$$

Suppose the voltmeter voltage is constrained to the range $V_{min} = 12$ volts $\leq V_m \leq V_{max} = 18$ volts. Write a program that accepts a value of V_m and checks that it's between 12 and 18. The program should return the gas temperature in degrees Celsius when V_m is between 12 and 18 and an error message when it isn't.

■■■ **Science P5.17** Crop damage due to frost is one of the many risks confronting farmers. The figure below shows a simple alarm circuit designed to warn of frost. The alarm circuit uses a device called a thermistor to sound a buzzer when the temperature drops below freezing. Thermistors are semiconductor devices that exhibit a temperature dependent resistance described by the equation

$$R = R_0 e^{\beta\left(\frac{1}{T} - \frac{1}{T_0}\right)}$$

where R is the resistance, in Ω, at the temperature T, in °K, and R_0 is the resistance, in Ω, at the temperature T_0, in°K. β is a constant that depends on the material used to make the thermistor.

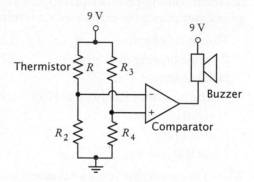

The circuit is designed so that the alarm will sound when

$$\frac{R_2}{R + R_2} < \frac{R_4}{R_3 + R_4}$$

The thermistor used in the alarm circuit has $R_0 = 33,192\ \Omega$ at $T_0 = 40$ °C, and $\beta = 3,310$ °K. (Notice that β has units of °K. The temperature in °K is obtained by adding 273° to the temperature in °C.) The resistors R_2, R_3, and R_4 have a resistance of 156.3 kΩ = 156,300 Ω.

Write a Java program that prompts the user for a temperature in °F and prints a message indicating whether or not the alarm will sound at that temperature.

■ **Science P5.18** A mass $m = 2$ kilograms is attached to the end of a rope of length $r = 3$ meters. The mass is whirled around at high speed. The rope can withstand a maximum tension of $T = 60$ Newtons. Write a program that accepts a rotation speed v and determines whether such a speed will cause the rope to break. *Hint:* $T = mv^2/r$.

■ **Science P5.19** A mass m is attached to the end of a rope of length $r = 3$ meters. The rope can only be whirled around at speeds of 1, 10, 20, or 40 meters per second. The rope can withstand a maximum tension of $T = 60$ Newtons. Write a program where the user enters the value of the mass m, and the program determines the greatest speed at which it can be whirled without breaking the rope. *Hint:* $T = mv^2/r$.

■■ **Science P5.20** The average person can jump off the ground with a velocity of 7 mph without fear of leaving the planet. However, if an astronaut jumps with this velocity while standing on Halley's Comet, will the astronaut ever come back down? Create a program that allows the user to input a launch velocity (in mph) from the surface of Halley's Comet and determine whether a jumper will return to the surface. If not, the program should calculate how much more massive the comet must be in order to return the jumper to the surface.

Hint: Escape velocity is $v_{escape} = \sqrt{2\dfrac{G\,M}{R}}$, where $G = 6.67 \times 10^{-11}\,N\,m^2 / kg^2$ is the gravitational constant, $M = 1.3 \times 10^{22}\,kg$ is the mass of Halley's comet, and $R = 1.153 \times 10^6\,m$ is its radius.

ANSWERS TO SELF-CHECK QUESTIONS

1. Change the `if` statement to
```
if (floor > 14)
{
    actualFloor = floor - 2;
}
```

2. 85, 90, 85.

3. The only difference is if `originalPrice` is 100. The statement in Self Check 2 sets `discountedPrice` to 90; this one sets it to 80.

4. 95, 100, 95.

5.
```
if (fuelAmount < 0.10 * fuelCapacity)
{
    System.out.println("red");
}
else
{
    System.out.println("green");
}
```

6. (a) and (b) are both true, (c) is false.

7. `floor <= 13`

8. The values should be compared with ==, not =.

9. `input.equals("Y")`

10. `str.equals("")` or `str.length() == 0`

11. (a) 0; (b) 1; (c) An exception occurs.

12. Syntactically incorrect: e, g, h. Logically questionable: a, d, f.

13.
```
if (scoreA > scoreB)
{
    System.out.println("A won");
}
else if (scoreA < scoreB)
{
    System.out.println("B won");
}
else
{
    System.out.println("Game tied");
}
```

14.
```
if (x > 0) { s = 1; }
else if (x < 0) { s = -1; }
else { s = 0; }
```

15. You could first set s to one of the three values:
```
s = 0;
if (x > 0) { s = 1; }
else if (x < 0) { s = -1; }
```

16. The `if (price <= 100)` can be omitted (leaving just `else`), making it clear that the `else` branch is the sole alternative.

17. No destruction of buildings.

18. Add a branch before the final `else`:
```
else if (richter < 0)
{
    System.out.println("Error: Negative input");
}
```

19. 3200.

20. No. Then the computation is $0.10 \times 32000 + 0.25 \times (32000 - 32000)$.

21. No. Their individual tax is $5,200 each, and if they married, they would pay $10,400. Actually, taxpayers in higher tax brackets (which our program does not model) may pay higher taxes when they marry, a phenomenon known as the *marriage penalty*.

22. Change `else` in line 22 to

```
else if (maritalStatus.equals("N"))
```

and add another branch after line 25:

```
else
{
   System.out.println(
   "Error: Please answer Y or N.");
}
```

23. The higher tax rate is only applied on the income in the higher bracket. Suppose you are single and make $31,900. Should you try to get a $200 raise? Absolutely: you get to keep 90 percent of the first $100 and 75 percent of the next $100.

24.

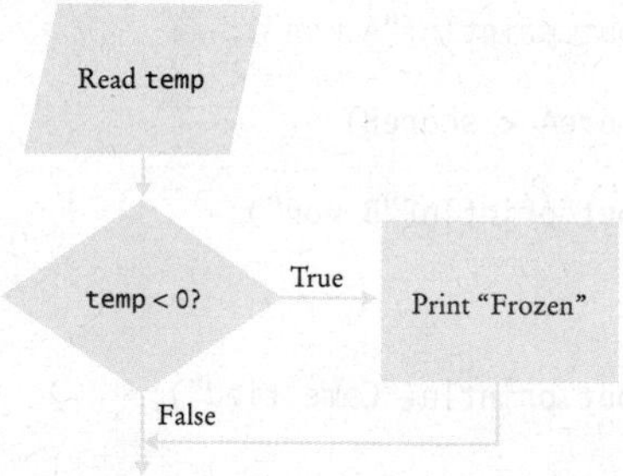

25. The "True" arrow from the first decision points into the "True" branch of the second decision, creating spaghetti code.

26. Here is one solution. In Section 5.7, you will see how you can combine the conditions for a more elegant solution.

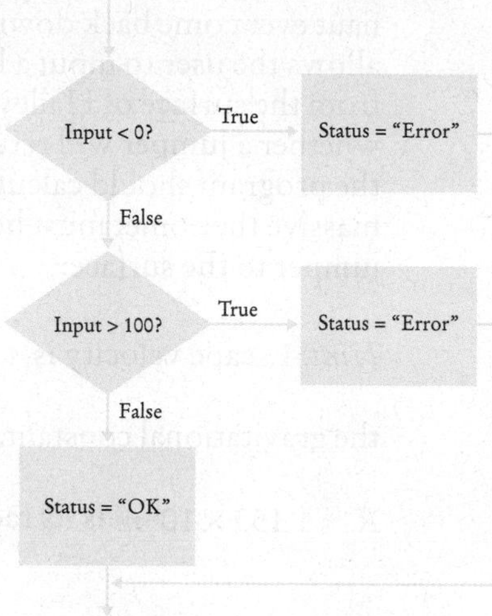

27.

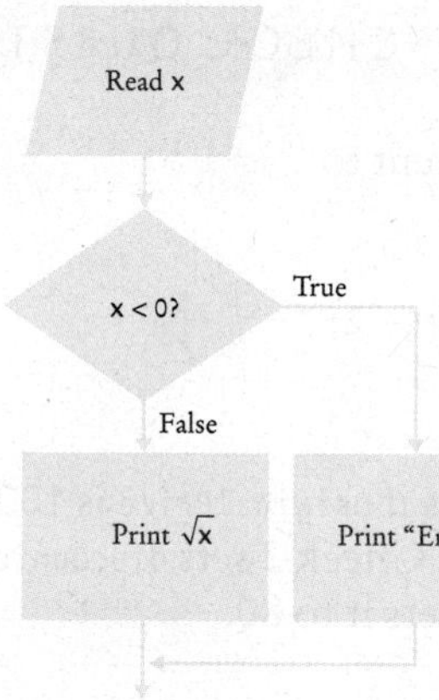

28.

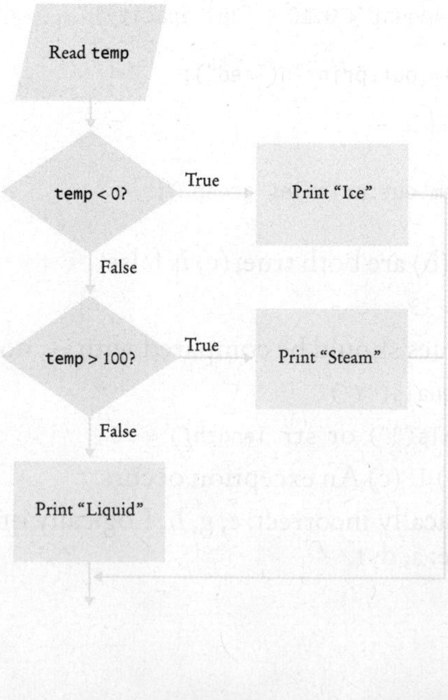

29.

Test Case	Expected Output	Comment
12	12	Below 13th floor
14	13	Above 13th floor
13	?	The specification is not clear— See Section 5.8 for a version of this program with error handling

30. A boundary test case is a price of $128. A 16 percent discount should apply because the problem statement states that the larger discount applies if the price is *at least* $128. Thus, the expected output is $107.52.

31.

Test Case	Expected Output	Comment
9	Most structures fall	
7.5	Many buildings destroyed	
6.5	Many buildings ...	
5	Damage to poorly...	
3	No destruction...	
8.0	Most structures fall	Boundary case. In this program, boundary cases are not as significant because the behavior of an earthquake changes gradually.
-1		The specification is not clear—see Self Check 18 for a version of this program with error handling.

32.

Test Case	Expected Output	Comment
(0.5, 0.5)	inside	
(4, 2)	outside	
(0, 2)	on the boundary	Exactly on the boundary
(1.414, 1.414)	on the boundary	Close to the boundary
(0, 1.9)	inside	Not less than 1 mm from the boundary
(0, 2.1)	outside	Not less than 1 mm from the boundary

33. x == 0 && y == 0

34. x == 0 || y == 0

35. (x == 0 && y != 0) || (y == 0 && x != 0)

36. The same as the value of frozen.

37. You are guaranteed that there are no other values. With strings or integers, you would need to check that no values such as "maybe" or –1 enter your calculations.

38. (a) Error: The floor must be between 1 and 20.
(b) Error: The floor must be between 1 and 20.
(c) 19 (d) Error: Not an integer.

39. floor == 13 || floor <= 0 || floor > 20

40. Check for in.hasNextDouble(), to make sure a researcher didn't supply an input such as oh my. Check for weight <= 0, because any rat must surely have a positive weight. We don't know how giant a rat could be, but the New Guinea rats weighed no more than 2 kg. A regular house rat (*rattus rattus*) weighs up to 0.2 kg, so we'll say that any weight > 10 kg was surely an input error, perhaps confusing grams and kilograms. Thus, the checks are

```java
if (in.hasNextDouble())
{
    double weight = in.nextDouble();
    if (weight < 0)
    {
        System.out.println(
            "Error: Weight cannot be negative.");
    }
    else if (weight > 10)
    {
        System.out.println(
            "Error: Weight > 10 kg.");
    }
    else
    {
        Process valid weight.
    }
}
else
{
    System.out.print("Error: Not a number");
}
```

41. The second input fails, and the program terminates without printing anything.

LOOPS

CHAPTER GOALS

To implement while, for, and do loops

To hand-trace the execution of a program

To learn to use common loop algorithms

To understand nested loops

To implement programs that read and process data sets

To use a computer for simulations

To learn about the debugger

CHAPTER CONTENTS

In a loop, a part of a program is repeated over and over, until a specific goal is reached. Loops are important for calculations that require repeated steps and for processing input consisting of many data items. In this chapter, you will learn about loop statements in Java, as well as techniques for writing programs that process input and simulate activities in the real world.

6.1 The while Loop

In this section, you will learn about *loop statements* that repeatedly execute instructions until a goal has been reached.

Recall the investment problem from Chapter 1. You put $10,000 into a bank account that earns 5 percent interest per year. How many years does it take for the account balance to be double the original investment?

In Chapter 1 we developed the following algorithm for this problem:

Because the interest earned also earns interest, a bank balance grows exponentially.

Start with a year value of 0, a column for the interest, and a balance of $10,000.

year	interest	balance
0		$10,000

Repeat the following steps while the balance is less than $20,000.
  Add 1 to the year value.
  Compute the interest as balance x 0.05 (i.e., 5 percent interest).
  Add the interest to the balance.
Report the final year value as the answer.

You now know how to declare and update the variables in Java. What you don't yet know is how to carry out "Repeat steps while the balance is less than $20,000".

In a particle accelerator, subatomic particles traverse a loop-shaped tunnel multiple times, gaining the speed required for physical experiments. Similarly, in computer science, statements in a loop are executed while a condition is true.

Figure 1 Flowchart of a while Loop

A loop executes
instructions
repeatedly while a
condition is true.

In Java, the while statement implements such a repetition (see Syntax 6.1). It has the form

```
while (condition)
{
    statements
}
```

As long as the condition remains true, the statements inside the while statement are executed. These statements are called the **body** of the while statement.

In our case, we want to increment the year counter and add interest while the balance is less than the target balance of $20,000:

```
while (balance < targetBalance)
{
    year++;
    double interest = balance * RATE / 100;
    balance = balance + interest;
}
```

A while statement is an example of a **loop**. If you draw a flowchart, the flow of execution loops again to the point where the condition is tested (see Figure 1).

Syntax 6.1   while Statement

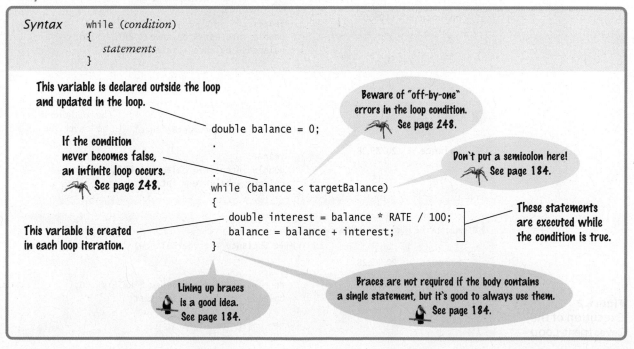

Syntax
```
while (condition)
{
    statements
}
```

This variable is declared outside the loop and updated in the loop.

Beware of "off-by-one" errors in the loop condition. See page 248.

If the condition never becomes false, an infinite loop occurs. See page 248.

```
double balance = 0;
.
.
.
while (balance < targetBalance)
{
    double interest = balance * RATE / 100;
    balance = balance + interest;
}
```

Don't put a semicolon here! See page 184.

These statements are executed while the condition is true.

This variable is created in each loop iteration.

Lining up braces is a good idea. See page 184.

Braces are not required if the body contains a single statement, but it's good to always use them. See page 184.

When you declare a variable *inside* the loop body, the variable is created for each iteration of the loop and removed after the end of each iteration. For example, consider the `interest` variable in this loop:

```
while (balance < targetBalance)
{
    year++;
    double interest = balance * RATE / 100;
    balance = balance + interest;
}
// interest no longer declared here
```

A new `interest` variable is created in each iteration.

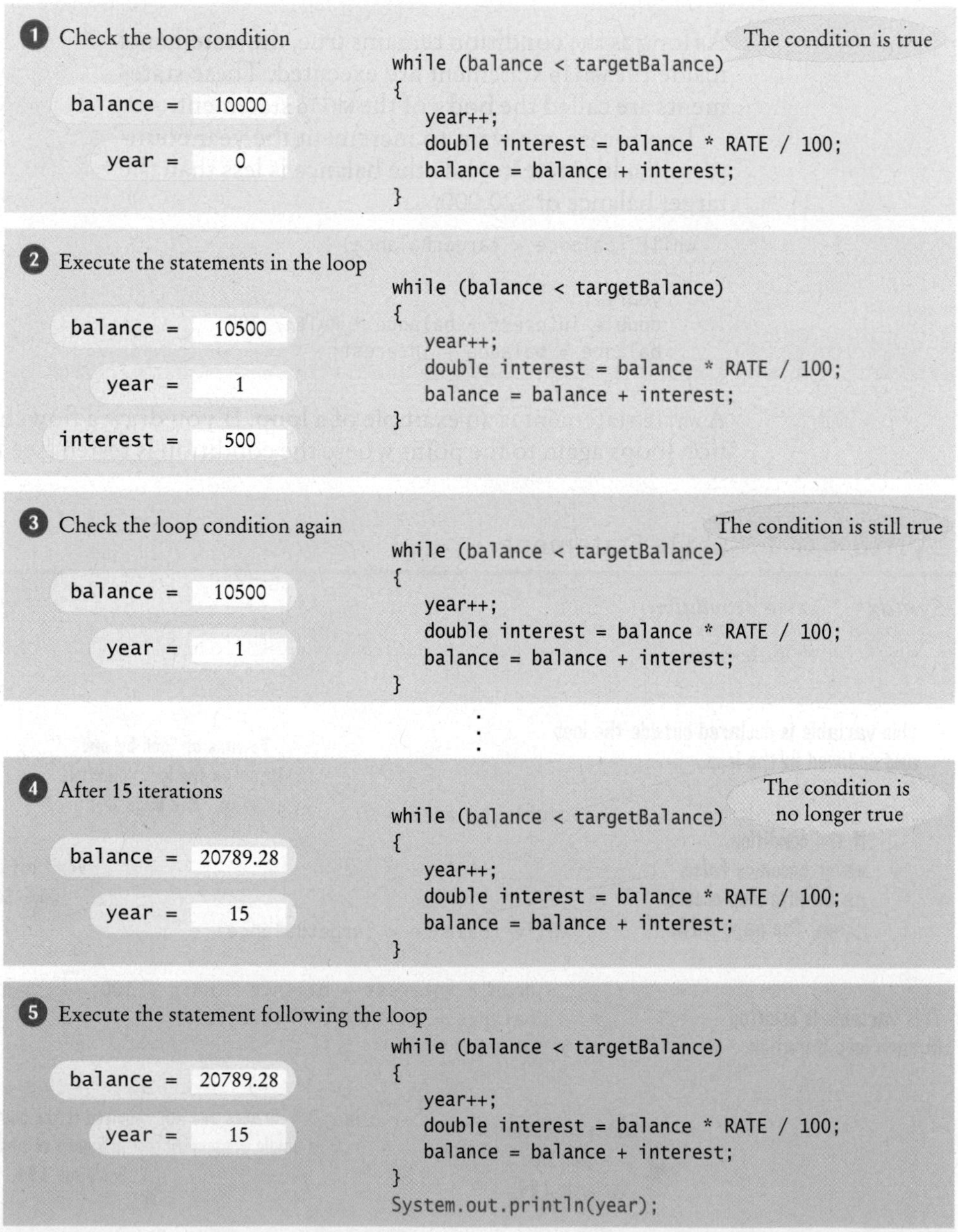

1 Check the loop condition

balance = 10000

year = 0

The condition is true

```
while (balance < targetBalance)
{
    year++;
    double interest = balance * RATE / 100;
    balance = balance + interest;
}
```

2 Execute the statements in the loop

balance = 10500

year = 1

interest = 500

```
while (balance < targetBalance)
{
    year++;
    double interest = balance * RATE / 100;
    balance = balance + interest;
}
```

3 Check the loop condition again

balance = 10500

year = 1

The condition is still true

```
while (balance < targetBalance)
{
    year++;
    double interest = balance * RATE / 100;
    balance = balance + interest;
}
```

⋮

4 After 15 iterations

balance = 20789.28

year = 15

The condition is no longer true

```
while (balance < targetBalance)
{
    year++;
    double interest = balance * RATE / 100;
    balance = balance + interest;
}
```

5 Execute the statement following the loop

balance = 20789.28

year = 15

```
while (balance < targetBalance)
{
    year++;
    double interest = balance * RATE / 100;
    balance = balance + interest;
}
System.out.println(year);
```

Figure 2
Execution of the
Investment Loop

In contrast, the balance and year variables were declared outside the loop body. That way, the same variable is used for all iterations of the loop.

Here is the program that solves the investment problem. Figure 2 illustrates the program's execution.

section_1/Investment.java

```java
1   /**
2       A class to monitor the growth of an investment that
3       accumulates interest at a fixed annual rate.
4   */
5   public class Investment
6   {
7       private double balance;
8       private double rate;
9       private int year;
10
11      /**
12          Constructs an Investment object from a starting balance and
13          interest rate.
14          @param aBalance the starting balance
15          @param aRate the interest rate in percent
16      */
17      public Investment(double aBalance, double aRate)
18      {
19          balance = aBalance;
20          rate = aRate;
21          year = 0;
22      }
23
24      /**
25          Keeps accumulating interest until a target balance has
26          been reached.
27          @param targetBalance the desired balance
28      */
29      public void waitForBalance(double targetBalance)
30      {
31          while (balance < targetBalance)
32          {
33              year++;
34              double interest = balance * rate / 100;
35              balance = balance + interest;
36          }
37      }
38
39      /**
40          Gets the current investment balance.
41          @return the current balance
42      */
43      public double getBalance()
44      {
45          return balance;
46      }
47
48      /**
49          Gets the number of years this investment has accumulated
50          interest.
51          @return the number of years since the start of the investment
```

```
52      */
53      public int getYears()
54      {
55         return year;
56      }
57   }
```

section_1/InvestmentRunner.java

```
1    /**
2        This program computes how long it takes for an investment
3        to double.
4    */
5    public class InvestmentRunner
6    {
7       public static void main(String[] args)
8       {
9          final double INITIAL_BALANCE = 10000;
10         final double RATE = 5;
11         Investment invest = new Investment(INITIAL_BALANCE, RATE);
12         invest.waitForBalance(2 * INITIAL_BALANCE);
13         int years = invest.getYears();
14         System.out.println("The investment doubled after "
15            + years + " years");
16      }
17   }
```

Program Run

```
The investment doubled after 15 years.
```

SELF CHECK

1. How many years does it take for the investment to triple? Modify the program and run it.
2. If the interest rate is 10 percent per year, how many years does it take for the investment to double? Modify the program and run it.
3. Modify the program so that the balance after each year is printed. How did you do that?
4. Suppose we change the program so that the condition of the `while` loop is

   ```
   while (balance <= targetBalance)
   ```

   What is the effect on the program? Why?
5. What does the following loop print?

   ```
   int n = 1;
   while (n < 100)
   {
      n = 2 * n;
      System.out.print(n + " ");
   }
   ```

Practice It   Now you can try these exercises at the end of the chapter: R6.1, R6.5, E6.13.

Table 1 while Loop Examples

Loop	Output	Explanation
| ```
i = 0; sum = 0;
while (sum < 10)
{
    i++; sum = sum + i;
    Print i and sum;
}
``` | 1 1<br>2 3<br>3 6<br>4 10 | When sum is 10, the loop condition is false, and the loop ends. |
| ```
i = 0; sum = 0;
while (sum < 10)
{
    i++; sum = sum - i;
    Print i and sum;
}
``` | 1 -1<br>2 -3<br>3 -6<br>4 -10<br>. . . | Because sum never reaches 10, this is an "infinite loop" (see Common Error 6.2 on page 248). |
| ```
i = 0; sum = 0;
while (sum < 0)
{
    i++; sum = sum - i;
    Print i and sum;
}
``` | (No output) | The statement sum < 0 is false when the condition is first checked, and the loop is never executed. |
| ```
i = 0; sum = 0;
while (sum >= 10)
{
    i++; sum = sum + i;
    Print i and sum;
}
``` | (No output) | The programmer probably thought, "Stop when the sum is at least 10." However, the loop condition controls when the loop is executed, not when it ends (see Common Error 6.1 on page 247). |
| ```
i = 0; sum = 0;
while (sum < 10) ;
{
    i++; sum = sum + i;
    Print i and sum;
}
``` | (No output, program does not terminate) | Note the semicolon before the {. This loop has an empty body. It runs forever, checking whether sum < 10 and doing nothing in the body. |

Common Error 6.1

Don't Think "Are We There Yet?"

When doing something repetitive, most of us want to know when we are done. For example, you may think, "I want to get at least $20,000," and set the loop condition to

```
balance >= targetBalance
```

But the while loop thinks the opposite: How long am I allowed to keep going? The correct loop condition is

```
while (balance < targetBalance)
```

In other words: "Keep at it while the balance is less than the target."

When writing a loop condition, don't ask, "Are we there yet?" The condition determines how long the loop will keep going.
```

Infinite Loops

A very annoying loop error is an *infinite loop:* a loop that runs forever and can be stopped only by killing the program or restarting the computer. If there are output statements in the program, then reams and reams of output flash by on the screen. Otherwise, the program just sits there and *hangs,* seeming to do nothing. On some systems, you can kill a hanging program by hitting Ctrl + C. On others, you can close the window in which the program runs.

A common reason for infinite loops is forgetting to update the variable that controls the loop:

```java
int year = 1;
while (year <= 20)
{
    double interest = balance * RATE / 100;
    balance = balance + interest;
}
```

Like this hamster who can't stop running in the treadmill, an infinite loop never ends.

Here the programmer forgot to add a year++ command in the loop. As a result, the year always stays at 1, and the loop never comes to an end.

Another common reason for an infinite loop is accidentally incrementing a counter that should be decremented (or vice versa). Consider this example:

```java
int year = 20;
while (year > 0)
{
    double interest = balance * RATE / 100;
    balance = balance + interest;
    year++;
}
```

The year variable really should have been decremented, not incremented. This is a common error because incrementing counters is so much more common than decrementing that your fingers may type the ++ on autopilot. As a consequence, year is always larger than 0, and the loop never ends. (Actually, year may eventually exceed the largest representable positive integer and *wrap around* to a negative number. Then the loop ends—of course, with a completely wrong result.)

Off-by-One Errors

Consider our computation of the number of years that are required to double an investment:

```java
int year = 0;
while (balance < targetBalance)
{
    year++;
    balance = balance * (1 + RATE / 100);
}
System.out.println("The investment doubled after "
    + year + " years.");
```

Should year start at 0 or at 1? Should you test for balance < targetBalance or for balance <= targetBalance? It is easy to be *off by one* in these expressions.

Some people try to solve **off-by-one errors** by randomly inserting +1 or -1 until the program seems to work—a terrible strategy. It can take a long time to compile and test all the various possibilities. Expending a small amount of mental effort is a real time saver.

Fortunately, off-by-one errors are easy to avoid, simply by thinking through a couple of test cases and using the information from the test cases to come up with a rationale for your decisions.

Should year start at 0 or at 1? Look at a scenario with simple values: an initial balance of $100 and an interest rate of 50 percent. After year 1, the balance is $150, and after year 2 it is $225, or over $200. So the investment doubled after 2 years. The loop executed two times, incrementing year each time. Hence year must start at 0, not at 1.

> An off-by-one error is a common error when programming loops. Think through simple test cases to avoid this type of error.

year	balance
0	$100
1	$150
2	$225

In other words, the balance variable denotes the balance after the end of the year. At the outset, the balance variable contains the balance after year 0 and not after year 1.

Next, should you use a < or <= comparison in the test? This is harder to figure out, because it is rare for the balance to be exactly twice the initial balance. There is one case when this happens, namely when the interest is 100 percent. The loop executes once. Now year is 1, and balance is exactly equal to 2 * INITIAL_BALANCE. Has the investment doubled after one year? It has. Therefore, the loop should not execute again. If the test condition is balance < targetBalance, the loop stops, as it should. If the test condition had been balance <= targetBalance, the loop would have executed once more.

In other words, you keep adding interest while the balance *has not yet doubled*.

6.2 Problem Solving: Hand-Tracing

> Hand-tracing is a simulation of code execution in which you step through instructions and track the values of the variables.

In Programming Tip 5.5, you learned about the method of hand-tracing. When you hand-trace code or pseudocode, you write the names of the variables on a sheet of paper, mentally execute each step of the code, and update the variables.

It is best to have the code written or printed on a sheet of paper. Use a marker, such as a paper clip, to mark the current line. Whenever a variable changes, cross out the old value and write the new value below. When a program produces output, also write down the output in another column.

Consider this example. What value is displayed?

```java
int n = 1729;
int sum = 0;
while (n > 0)
{
   int digit = n % 10;
   sum = sum + digit;
   n = n / 10;
}
System.out.println(sum);
```

There are three variables: n, sum, and digit.

n	sum	digit

The first two variables are initialized with 1729 and 0 before the loop is entered.

```
int n = 1729;
int sum = 0;
while (n > 0)
{
    int digit = n % 10;
    sum = sum + digit;
    n = n / 10;
}
System.out.println(sum);
```

n	sum	digit
1729	0	

Because n is greater than zero, enter the loop. The variable digit is set to 9 (the remainder of dividing 1729 by 10). The variable sum is set to 0 + 9 = 9.

```
int n = 1729;
int sum = 0;
while (n > 0)
{
    int digit = n % 10;
    sum = sum + digit;
    n = n / 10;
}
System.out.println(sum);
```

n	sum	digit
1729	0̸	
	9	9

Finally in this iteration, n becomes 172. (Recall that the remainder in the division 1729 / 10 is discarded because both arguments are integers.)

Cross out the old values and write the new ones under the old ones.

```
int n = 1729;
int sum = 0;
while (n > 0)
{
    int digit = n % 10;
    sum = sum + digit;
    n = n / 10;
}
System.out.println(sum);
```

n	sum	digit
1̶7̶2̶9̶	0̸	
172	9	9

Now check the loop condition again.

```
int n = 1729;
int sum = 0;
while (n > 0)
{
    int digit = n % 10;
    sum = sum + digit;
    n = n / 10;
}
System.out.println(sum);
```

Because n is still greater than zero, repeat the loop. Now digit becomes 2, sum is set to $9 + 2 = 11$, and n is set to 17.

n	sum	digit
~~1729~~	~~0~~	
~~171~~	~~9~~	~~9~~
17	11	2

Repeat the loop once again, setting digit to 7, sum to $11 + 7 = 18$, and n to 1.

n	sum	digit
~~1729~~	~~0~~	
~~171~~	~~9~~	~~9~~
~~17~~	~~11~~	~~2~~
1	18	7

Enter the loop for one last time. Now digit is set to 1, sum to 19, and n becomes zero.

n	sum	digit
~~1729~~	~~0~~	
~~171~~	~~9~~	~~9~~
~~17~~	~~11~~	~~2~~
~~1~~	~~18~~	~~7~~
0	19	1

```java
int n = 1729;
int sum = 0;
while (n > 0)
{
   int digit = n % 10;
   sum = sum + digit;
   n = n / 10;
}
System.out.println(sum);
```

> Because n equals zero, this condition is not true.

The condition n > 0 is now false. Continue with the statement after the loop.

```java
int n = 1729;
int sum = 0;
while (n > 0)
{
   int digit = n % 10;
   sum = sum + digit;
   n = n / 10;
}
System.out.println(sum);
```

n	sum	digit	output
~~1729~~	~~0~~		
~~171~~	~~9~~	~~9~~	
~~17~~	~~11~~	~~2~~	
~~1~~	~~18~~	~~7~~	
0	19	1	19

ANIMATION
Tracing a Loop

This statement is an output statement. The value that is output is the value of sum, which is 19.

Of course, you can get the same answer by just running the code. However, hand-tracing can give you an *insight* that you would not get if you simply ran the code. Consider again what happens in each iteration:

- We extract the last digit of n.
- We add that digit to sum.
- We strip the digit off n.

In other words, the loop forms the sum of the digits in n. You now know what the loop does for any value of n, not just the one in the example. (Why would anyone want to form the sum of the digits? Operations of this kind are useful for checking the validity of credit card numbers and other forms of ID numbers.)

Hand-tracing does not just help you understand code that works correctly. It is a powerful technique for finding errors in your code. When a program behaves in a way that you don't expect, get out a sheet of paper and track the values of the variables as you mentally step through the code.

You don't need a working program to do hand-tracing. You can hand-trace pseudocode. In fact, it is an excellent idea to hand-trace your pseudocode before you go to the trouble of translating it into actual code, to confirm that it works correctly.

> Hand-tracing can help you understand how an unfamiliar algorithm works.

> Hand-tracing can show errors in code or pseudocode.

SELF CHECK

6. Hand-trace the following code, showing the value of n and the output.

```java
int n = 5;
while (n >= 0)
{
   n--;
   System.out.print(n);
}
```

7. Hand-trace the following code, showing the value of n and the output. What potential error do you notice?

```java
int n = 1;
while (n <= 3)
{
   System.out.print(n + ", ");
   n++;
}
```

8. Hand-trace the following code, assuming that a is 2 and n is 4. Then explain what the code does for arbitrary values of a and n.

```java
int r = 1;
int i = 1;
while (i <= n)
{
   r = r * a;
   i++;
}
```

9. Trace the following code. What error do you observe?

```java
int n = 1;
while (n != 50)
{
   System.out.println(n);
   n = n + 10;
}
```

10. The following pseudocode is intended to count the number of digits in the number n:

```
count = 1
temp = n
while (temp > 10)
    Increment count.
    Divide temp by 10.0.
```

Trace the pseudocode for n = 123 and n = 100. What error do you find?

Practice It   Now you can try these exercises at the end of the chapter: R6.3, R6.6.

Computing & Society 6.1   Software Piracy

As you read this, you will have written a few computer programs and experienced firsthand how much effort it takes to write even the humblest of programs. Writing a real software product, such as a financial application or a computer game, takes a lot of time and money. Few people, and fewer companies, are going to spend that kind of time and money if they don't have a reasonable chance to make more money from their effort. (Actually, some companies give away their software in the hope that users will upgrade to more elaborate paid versions. Other companies give away the software that enables users to read and use files but sell the software needed to create those files. Finally, there are individuals who donate their time, out of enthusiasm, and produce programs that you can copy freely.)

When selling software, a company must rely on the honesty of its customers. It is an easy matter for an unscrupulous person to make copies of computer programs without paying for them. In most countries that is illegal. Most governments provide legal protection, such as copyright laws and patents, to encourage the development of new products. Countries that tolerate widespread piracy have found that they have an ample cheap supply of foreign software, but no local manufacturers willing to design good software for their own citizens, such as word processors in the local script or financial programs adapted to the local tax laws.

When a mass market for software first appeared, vendors were enraged by the money they lost through piracy. They tried to fight back by various schemes to ensure that only the legitimate owner could use the software, such as *dongles*—devices that must be attached to a printer port before the software will run. Legitimate users hated these measures. They paid for the software, but they had to suffer through inconveniences, such as having multiple dongles stick out from their computer. In the United States, market pressures forced most vendors to give up on these copy protection schemes, but they are still commonplace in other parts of the world.

Because it is so easy and inexpensive to pirate software, and the chance of being found out is minimal, you have to make a moral choice for yourself. If a package that you would really like to have is too expensive for your budget, do you steal it, or do you stay honest and get by with a more affordable product?

Of course, piracy is not limited to software. The same issues arise for other digital products as well. You may have had the opportunity to obtain copies of songs or movies without payment. Or you may have been frustrated by a copy protection device on your music player that made it difficult for you to listen to songs that you paid for. Admittedly, it can be difficult to have a lot of sympathy for a musical ensemble whose publisher charges a lot of money for what seems to have been very little effort on their part, at least when compared to the effort that goes into designing and implementing a software package. Nevertheless, it seems only fair that artists and authors receive some compensation for their efforts. How to pay artists, authors, and programmers fairly, without burdening honest customers, is an unsolved problem at the time of this writing, and many computer scientists are engaged in research in this area.

6.3 The for Loop

The for loop is used when a value runs from a starting point to an ending point with a constant increment or decrement.

It often happens that you want to execute a sequence of statements a given number of times. You can use a while loop that is controlled by a counter, as in the following example:

```java
int counter = 1; // Initialize the counter
while (counter <= 10) // Check the counter
{
    System.out.println(counter);
    counter++; // Update the counter
}
```

Because this loop type is so common, there is a special form for it, called the for loop (see Syntax 6.2).

```java
for (int counter = 1; counter <= 10; counter++)
{
    System.out.println(counter);
}
```

Some people call this loop *count-controlled*. In contrast, the while loop of the preceding section can be called an *event-controlled* loop because it executes until an event occurs; namely that the balance reaches the target. Another commonly used term for a count-controlled loop is *definite*. You know from the outset that the loop body will be executed a definite number of times; ten times in our example. In contrast, you do not know how many iterations it takes to accumulate a target balance. Such a loop is called *indefinite*.

You can visualize the for *loop as an orderly sequence of steps.*

Syntax 6.2   for Statement

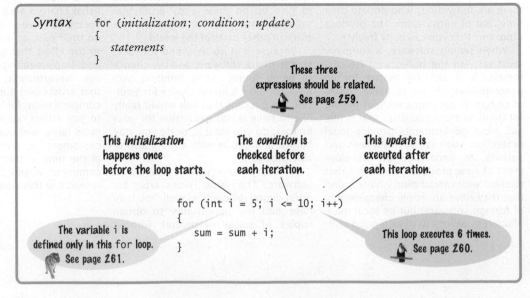

Syntax
```java
for (initialization; condition; update)
{
    statements
}
```

These three expressions should be related.
See page 259.

This *initialization* happens once before the loop starts.

The *condition* is checked before each iteration.

This *update* is executed after each iteration.

```java
for (int i = 5; i <= 10; i++)
{
    sum = sum + i;
}
```

The variable i is defined only in this for loop.
See page 261.

This loop executes 6 times.
See page 260.

The for loop neatly groups the initialization, condition, and update expressions together. However, it is important to realize that these expressions are not executed together (see Figure 3).

ANIMATION
The for Loop

- The initialization is executed once, before the loop is entered. ❶
- The condition is checked before each iteration. ❷ ❺
- The update is executed after each iteration. ❹

❶ Initialize counter

```
for (int counter = 1; counter <= 10; counter++)
{
    System.out.println(counter);
}
```

counter = 1

❷ Check condition

```
for (int counter = 1; counter <= 10; counter++)
{
    System.out.println(counter);
}
```

counter = 1

❸ Execute loop body

```
for (int counter = 1; counter <= 10; counter++)
{
    System.out.println(counter);
}
```

counter = 1

❹ Update counter

```
for (int counter = 1; counter <= 10; counter++)
{
    System.out.println(counter);
}
```

counter = 2

❺ Check condition again

```
for (int counter = 1; counter <= 10; counter++)
{
    System.out.println(counter);
}
```

counter = 2

Figure 3
Execution of a
for Loop

A for loop can count down instead of up:

```
for (int counter = 10; counter >= 0; counter--) . . .
```

The increment or decrement need not be in steps of 1:

```
for (int counter = 0; counter <= 10; counter = counter + 2) . . .
```

See Table 2 on page 258 for additional variations.

So far, we have always declared the counter variable in the loop initialization:

```
for (int counter = 1; counter <= 10; counter++)
{
    . . .
}
// counter  no longer declared here
```

Such a variable is declared for all iterations of the loop, but you cannot use it after the loop. If you declare the counter variable before the loop, you can continue to use it after the loop:

```
int counter;
for (counter = 1; counter <= 10; counter++)
{
   . . .
}
// counter still declared here
```

A common use of the for loop is to traverse all characters of a string:

```
for (int i = 0; i < str.length(); i++)
{
    char ch = str.charAt(i);
    Process ch.
}
```

Note that the counter variable i starts at 0, and the loop is terminated when i reaches the length of the string. For example, if str has length 5, i takes on the values 0, 1, 2, 3, and 4. These are the valid positions in the string.

Here is another typical use of the for loop. We want to compute the growth of our savings account over a period of years, as shown in this table:

Year	Balance
1	10500.00
2	11025.00
3	11576.25
4	12155.06
5	12762.82

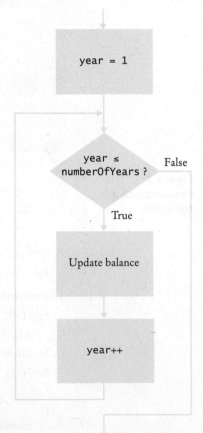

The for loop pattern applies because the variable year starts at 1 and then moves in constant increments until it reaches the target:

```
for (int year = 1; year <= numberOfYears; year++)
{
    Update balance.
}
```

Following is the complete program. Figure 4 shows the corresponding flowchart.

Figure 4   Flowchart of a for Loop

section_3/Investment.java

```java
1   /**
2       A class to monitor the growth of an investment that
3       accumulates interest at a fixed annual rate.
4   */
5   public class Investment
6   {
7       private double balance;
8       private double rate;
9       private int year;
10
11      /**
12          Constructs an Investment object from a starting balance and
13          interest rate.
14          @param aBalance the starting balance
15          @param aRate the interest rate in percent
16      */
17      public Investment(double aBalance, double aRate)
18      {
19          balance = aBalance;
20          rate = aRate;
21          year = 0;
22      }
23
24      /**
25          Keeps accumulating interest until a target balance has
26          been reached.
27          @param targetBalance the desired balance
28      */
29      public void waitForBalance(double targetBalance)
30      {
31          while (balance < targetBalance)
32          {
33              year++;
34              double interest = balance * rate / 100;
35              balance = balance + interest;
36          }
37      }
38
39      /**
40          Keeps accumulating interest for a given number of years.
41          @param numberOfYears the number of years to wait
42      */
43      public void waitYears(int numberOfYears)
44      {
45          for (int i = 1; i <= numberOfYears; i++)
46          {
47              double interest = balance * rate / 100;
48              balance = balance + interest;
49          }
50          year = year + n;
51      }
52
53      /**
54          Gets the current investment balance.
55          @return the current balance
56      */
57      public double getBalance()
58      {
```

```
59          return balance;
60       }
61
62       /**
63          Gets the number of years this investment has accumulated
64          interest.
65          @return the number of years since the start of the investment
66       */
67       public int getYears()
68       {
69          return year;
70       }
71    }
```

section_3/InvestmentRunner.java

```
1    /**
2       This program computes how much an investment grows in
3       a given number of years.
4    */
5    public class InvestmentRunner
6    {
7       public static void main(String[] args)
8       {
9          final double INITIAL_BALANCE = 10000;
10         final double RATE = 5;
11         final int YEARS = 20;
12         Investment invest = new Investment(INITIAL_BALANCE, RATE);
13         invest.waitYears(YEARS);
14         double balance = invest.getBalance();
15         System.out.printf("The balance after %d years is %.2f\n",
16             YEARS, balance);
17      }
18   }
```

Program Run

```
The balance after 20 years is 26532.98
```

Table 2 for Loop Examples

Loop	Values of i	Comment
for (i = 0; i <= 5; i++)	0 1 2 3 4 5	Note that the loop is executed 6 times. (See Programming Tip 6.3 on page 260.)
for (i = 5; i >= 0; i--)	5 4 3 2 1 0	Use i-- for decreasing values.
for (i = 0; i < 9; i = i + 2)	0 2 4 6 8	Use i = i + 2 for a step size of 2.
for (i = 0; i != 9; i = i + 2)	0 2 4 6 8 10 12 14 ... (infinite loop)	You can use < or <= instead of != to avoid this problem.
for (i = 1; i <= 20; i = i * 2)	1 2 4 8 16	You can specify any rule for modifying i, such as doubling it in every step.
for (i = 0; i < str.length(); i++)	0 1 2 ... until the last valid index of the string str	In the loop body, use the expression str.charAt(i) to get the ith character.

SELF CHECK

11. Write the for loop of the Investment class as a while loop.

12. How many numbers does this loop print?

```
for (int n = 10; n >= 0; n--)
{
    System.out.println(n);
}
```

13. Write a for loop that prints all even numbers between 10 and 20 (inclusive).

14. Write a for loop that computes the sum of the integers from 1 to n.

15. How would you modify the InvestmentRunner.java program to print the balances after 20, 40, ..., 100 years?

Practice It Now you can try these exercises at the end of the chapter: R6.4, R6.10, E6.8, E6.12.

Programming Tip 6.1

Use for Loops for Their Intended Purpose Only

A for loop is an *idiom* for a loop of a particular form. A value runs from the start to the end, with a constant increment or decrement.

The compiler won't check whether the initialization, condition, and update expressions are related. For example, the following loop is legal:

```
// Confusing—unrelated expressions
for (System.out.print("Inputs: "); in.hasNextDouble(); sum = sum + x)
{
    x = in.nextDouble();
}
```

However, programmers reading such a for loop will be confused because it does not match their expectations. Use a while loop for iterations that do not follow the for idiom.

You should also be careful not to update the loop counter in the body of a for loop. Consider the following example:

```
for (int counter = 1; counter <= 100; counter++)
{
    if (counter % 10 == 0) // Skip values that are divisible by 10
    {
        counter++; // Bad style—you should not update the counter in a for loop
    }
    System.out.println(counter);
}
```

Updating the counter inside a for loop is confusing because the counter is updated *again* at the end of the loop iteration. In some loop iterations, counter is incremented once, in others twice. This goes against the intuition of a programmer who sees a for loop.

If you find yourself in this situation, you can either change from a for loop to a while loop, or implement the "skipping" behavior in another way. For example:

```
for (int counter = 1; counter <= 100; counter++)
{
    if (counter % 10 != 0) // Skip values that are divisible by 10
    {
        System.out.println(counter);
    }
}
```

Programming Tip 6.2

Choose Loop Bounds That Match Your Task

Suppose you want to print line numbers that go from 1 to 10. Of course, you will use a loop:

```
for (int i = 1; i <= 10; i++)
```

The values for i are bounded by the relation $1 \leq i \leq 10$. Because there are $\leq$ on both bounds, the bounds are called **symmetric bounds**.

When traversing the characters in a string, it is more natural to use the bounds

```
for (int i = 0; i < str.length(); i++)
```

In this loop, i traverses all valid positions in the string. You can access the ith character as str.charAt(i). The values for i are bounded by $0 \leq i < str.length()$, with a $\leq$ to the left and a $<$ to the right. That is appropriate, because str.length() is not a valid position. Such bounds are called **asymmetric bounds**.

In this case, it is not a good idea to use symmetric bounds:

```
for (int i = 0; i <= str.length() - 1; i++) // Use < instead
```

The asymmetric form is easier to understand.

Programming Tip 6.3

Count Iterations

Finding the correct lower and upper bounds for an iteration can be confusing. Should you start at 0 or at 1? Should you use <= b or < b as a termination condition?

Counting the number of iterations is a very useful device for better understanding a loop. Counting is easier for loops with asymmetric bounds. The loop

```
for (int i = a; i < b; i++)
```

is executed b - a times. For example, the loop traversing the characters in a string,

```
for (int i = 0; i < str.length(); i++)
```

runs str.length() times. That makes perfect sense, because there are str.length() characters in a string.

The loop with symmetric bounds,

```
for (int i = a; i <= b; i++)
```

is executed b - a + 1 times. That "+1" is the source of many programming errors.

For example,

```
for (int i = 0; i <= 10; i++)
```

runs 11 times. Maybe that is what you want; if not, start at 1 or use < 10.

One way to visualize this "+1" error is by looking at a fence. Each section has one fence post to the left, and there is a final post on the right of the last section. Forgetting to count the last value is often called a "fence post error".

How many posts do you need for a fence with four sections? It is easy to be "off by one" with problems such as this one.

Special Topic 6.1

Variables Declared in a for Loop Header

As mentioned, it is legal in Java to declare a variable in the header of a for loop. Here is the most common form of this syntax:

```
for (int i = 1; i <= n; i++)
{
    . . .
}
```

```
// i no longer defined here
```

The scope of the variable extends to the end of the for loop. Therefore, i is no longer defined after the loop ends. If you need to use the value of the variable beyond the end of the loop, then you need to declare it outside the loop. In this loop, you don't need the value of i—you know it is n + 1 when the loop is finished. (Actually, that is not quite true—it is possible to break out of a loop before its end; see Special Topic 6.4 on page 267). When you have two or more exit conditions, though, you may still need the variable. For example, consider the loop

```
for (i = 1; balance < targetBalance && i <= n; i++)
{
    . . .
}
```

You want the balance to reach the target but you are willing to wait only a certain number of years. If the balance doubles sooner, you may want to know the value of i. Therefore, in this case, it is not appropriate to declare the variable in the loop header.

Note that the variables named i in the following pair of for loops are independent:

```
for (int i = 1; i <= 10; i++)
{
    System.out.println(i * i);
}
for (int i = 1; i <= 10; i++) // Declares a new variable i
{
    System.out.println(i * i * i);
}
```

In the loop header, you can declare multiple variables, as long as they are of the same type, and you can include multiple update expressions, separated by commas:

```
for (int i = 0, j = 10; i <= 10; i++, j--)
{
    . . .
}
```

However, many people find it confusing if a for loop controls more than one variable. I recommend that you not use this form of the for statement (see Programming Tip 6.2 on page 260). Instead, make the for loop control a single counter, and update the other variable explicitly:

```
int j = 10;
for (int i = 0; i <= 10; i++)
{
    . . .
    j--;
}
```

6.4 The do Loop

The do loop is appropriate when the loop body must be executed at least once.

Sometimes you want to execute the body of a loop at least once and perform the loop test after the body is executed. The do loop serves that purpose:

```
do
{
    statements
}
while (condition);
```

The body of the do loop is executed first, then the condition is tested.

Some people call such a loop a *post-test loop* because the condition is tested after completing the loop body. In contrast, while and for loops are *pre-test loops*. In those loop types, the condition is tested before entering the loop body.

A typical example for a do loop is input validation. Suppose you ask a user to enter a value < 100. If the user doesn't pay attention and enters a larger value, you ask again, until the value is correct. Of course, you cannot test the value until the user has entered it. This is a perfect fit for the do loop (see Figure 5):

FULL CODE EXAMPLE

Go to wiley.com/go/javacode to download a program that illustrates the use of the do loop for input validation.

```
int value;
do
{
    System.out.print("Enter an integer < 100: ");
    value = in.nextInt();
}
while (value >= 100);
```

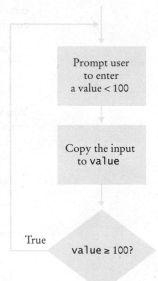

Prompt user
to enter
a value < 100

Copy the input
to value

True

value ≥ 100?

False

Figure 5   Flowchart of a do Loop

SELF CHECK

16. Suppose that we want to check for inputs that are at least 0 and at most 100. Modify the do loop for this check.

17. Rewrite the input check do loop using a while loop. What is the disadvantage of your solution?

18. Suppose Java didn't have a do loop. Could you rewrite any do loop as a while loop?

19. Write a do loop that reads integers and computes their sum. Stop when reading the value 0.

20. Write a do loop that reads integers and computes their sum. Stop when reading a zero or the same value twice in a row. For example, if the input is 1 2 3 4 4, then the sum is 14 and the loop stops.

Practice It   Now you can try these exercises at the end of the chapter: R6.9, R6.16, R6.17.

Programming Tip 6.4

Flowcharts for Loops

In Section 5.5, you learned how to use flowcharts to visualize the flow of control in a program. There are two types of loops that you can include in a flowchart; they correspond to a `while` loop and a `do` loop in Java. They differ in the placement of the condition—either before or after the loop body.

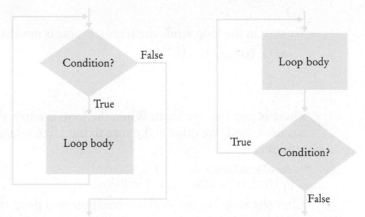

As described in Section 5.5, you want to avoid "spaghetti code" in your flowcharts. For loops, that means that you never want to have an arrow that points inside a loop body.

6.5 Application: Processing Sentinel Values

In this section, you will learn how to write loops that read and process a sequence of input values.

A sentinel value denotes the end of a data set, but it is not part of the data.

Whenever you read a sequence of inputs, you need to have some method of indicating the end of the sequence. Sometimes you are lucky and no input value can be zero. Then you can prompt the user to keep entering numbers, or 0 to finish the sequence. If zero is allowed but negative numbers are not, you can use –1 to indicate termination.

Such a value, which is not an actual input, but serves as a signal for termination, is called a **sentinel**.

Let's put this technique to work in a program that computes the average of a set of salary values. In our sample program, we will use –1 as a sentinel. An employee would surely not work for a negative salary, but there may be volunteers who work for free.

In the military, a sentinel guards a border or passage. In computer science, a sentinel value denotes the end of an input sequence or the border between input sequences.

Inside the loop, we read an input. If the input is not –1, we process it. In order to compute the average, we need the total sum of all salaries, and the number of inputs.

```
salary = in.nextDouble();
if (salary != -1)
{
    sum = sum + salary;
    count++;
}
```

We stay in the loop while the sentinel value is not detected.

```
while (salary != -1)
{
    . . .
}
```

There is just one problem: When the loop is entered for the first time, no data value has been read. We must make sure to initialize salary with some value other than the sentinel:

```
double salary = 0;
// Any value other than –1 will do
```

After the loop has finished, we compute and print the average. Here is the complete program:

section_5/SentinelDemo.java

```
 1  import java.util.Scanner;
 2
 3  /**
 4     This program prints the average of salary values that are terminated with a sentinel.
 5  */
 6  public class SentinelDemo
 7  {
 8     public static void main(String[] args)
 9     {
10        double sum = 0;
11        int count = 0;
12        double salary = 0;
13        System.out.print("Enter salaries, -1 to finish: ");
14        Scanner in = new Scanner(System.in);
15
16        // Process data until the sentinel is entered
17
18        while (salary != -1)
19        {
20           salary = in.nextDouble();
21           if (salary != -1)
22           {
23              sum = sum + salary;
24              count++;
25           }
26        }
27
28        // Compute and print the average
29
30        if (count > 0)
31        {
32           double average = sum / count;
```

```
33          System.out.println("Average salary: " + average);
34       }
35       else
36       {
37          System.out.println("No data");
38       }
39    }
40 }
```

Program Run

```
Enter salaries, -1 to finish: 10 10 40 -1
Average salary: 20
```

> You can use a Boolean variable to control a loop. Set the variable before entering the loop, then set it to the opposite to leave the loop.

Some programmers don't like the "trick" of initializing the input variable with a value other than the sentinel. Another approach is to use a Boolean variable:

```
System.out.print("Enter salaries, -1 to finish: ");
boolean done = false;
while (!done)
{
   value = in.nextDouble();
   if (value == -1)
   {
      done = true;
   }
   else
   {
      Process value.
   }
}
```

Special Topic 6.4 on page 267 shows an alternative mechanism for leaving such a loop.

Now consider the case in which any number (positive, negative, or zero) can be an acceptable input. In such a situation, you must use a sentinel that is not a number (such as the letter Q). As you have seen in Section 5.8, the condition

```
in.hasNextDouble()
```

is false if the next input is not a floating-point number. Therefore, you can read and process a set of inputs with the following loop:

```
System.out.print("Enter values, Q to quit: ");
while (in.hasNextDouble())
{
   value = in.nextDouble();
   Process value.
}
```

SELF CHECK

21. What does the SentinelDemo.java program print when the user immediately types −1 when prompted for a value?

22. Why does the SentinelDemo.java program have *two* checks of the form
```
salary != -1
```

23. What would happen if the declaration of the salary variable in SentinelDemo.java was changed to
```
double salary = -1;
```

24. In the last example of this section, we prompt the user "Enter values, Q to quit: " What happens when the user enters a different letter?

25. What is wrong with the following loop for reading a sequence of values?

```java
System.out.print("Enter values, Q to quit: ");
do
{
    double value = in.nextDouble();
    sum = sum + value;
    count++;
}
while (in.hasNextDouble());
```

Practice It   Now you can try these exercises at the end of the chapter: R6.13, E6.17, E6.18.

Special Topic 6.2

Redirection of Input and Output

Consider the `SentinelDemo` program that computes the average value of an input sequence. If you use such a program, then it is quite likely that you already have the values in a file, and it seems a shame that you have to type them all in again. The command line interface of your operating system provides a way to link a file to the input of a program, as if all the characters in the file had actually been typed by a user. If you type

> Use input redirection to read input from a file. Use output redirection to capture program output in a file.

```
java SentinelDemo < numbers.txt
```

the program is executed, but it no longer expects input from the keyboard. All input commands get their input from the file numbers.txt. This process is called input **redirection**.

Input redirection is an excellent tool for testing programs. When you develop a program and fix its bugs, it is boring to keep entering the same input every time you run the program. Spend a few minutes putting the inputs into a file, and use redirection.

You can also redirect output. In this program, that is not terribly useful. If you run

```
java SentinelDemo < numbers.txt > output.txt
```

the file output.txt contains the input prompts and the output, such as

```
Enter salaries, -1 to finish: Enter salaries, -1 to finish:
Enter salaries, -1 to finish: Enter salaries, -1 to finish:
Average salary: 15
```

However, redirecting output is obviously useful for programs that produce lots of output. You can format or print the file containing the output.

Special Topic 6.3

The "Loop and a Half" Problem

Reading input data sometimes requires a loop such as the following, which is somewhat unsightly:

```java
boolean done = false;
while (!done)
{
    String input = in.next();
    if (input.equals("Q"))
    {
        done = true;
```

```
   }
   else
   {
       Process data.
   }
}
```

The true test for loop termination is in the middle of the loop, not at the top. This is called a "loop and a half", because one must go halfway into the loop before knowing whether one needs to terminate.

Some programmers dislike the introduction of an additional Boolean variable for loop control. Two Java language features can be used to alleviate the "loop and a half" problem. I don't think either is a superior solution, but both approaches are fairly common, so it is worth knowing about them when reading other people's code.

You can combine an assignment and a test in the loop condition:

```
while (!(input = in.next()).equals("Q"))
{
    Process data.
}
```

The expression

```
(input = in.next()).equals("Q")
```

means, "First call in.next(), then assign the result to input, then test whether it equals "Q"". This is an expression with a side effect. The primary purpose of the expression is to serve as a test for the while loop, but it also does some work—namely, reading the input and storing it in the variable input. In general, it is a bad idea to use side effects, because they make a program hard to read and maintain. In this case, however, that practice is somewhat seductive, because it eliminates the control variable done, which also makes the code hard to read and maintain.

The other solution is to exit the loop from the middle, either by a return statement or by a break statement (see Special Topic 6.4 on page 267).

```
public void processInput(Scanner in)
{
    while (true)
    {
        String input = in.next();
        if (input.equals("Q"))
        {
            return;
        }
        Process data.
    }
}
```

Special Topic 6.4

The break **and** continue **Statements**

You already encountered the break statement in Special Topic 5.2, where it was used to exit a switch statement. In addition to breaking out of a switch statement, a break statement can also be used to exit a while, for, or do loop.

For example, the break statement in the following loop terminates the loop when the end of input is reached.

```
while (true)
{
```

```
        String input = in.next();
        if (input.equals("Q"))
        {
            break;
        }
        double x = Double.parseDouble(input);
        data.add(x);
    }
```

A loop with break statements can be difficult to understand because you have to look closely to find out how to exit the loop. However, when faced with the bother of introducing a separate loop control variable, some programmers find that break statements are beneficial in the "loop and a half" case. This issue is often the topic of heated (and quite unproductive) debate. In this book, we won't use the break statement, and we leave it to you to decide whether you like to use it in your own programs.

In Java, there is a second form of the break statement that is used to break out of a nested statement. The statement break *label*; immediately jumps to the *end* of the statement that is tagged with a label. Any statement (including if and block statements) can be tagged with a label—the syntax is

label: *statement*

The labeled break statement was invented to break out of a set of nested loops.

```
outerloop:
while (outer loop condition)
{ . . .
    while (inner loop condition)
    { . . .
        if (something really bad happened)
        {
            break outerloop;
        }
    }
}
Jumps here if something really bad happened.
```

Naturally, this situation is quite rare. We recommend that you try to introduce additional methods instead of using complicated nested loops.

Finally, there is the continue statement, which jumps to the end of the *current iteration* of the loop. Here is a possible use for this statement:

```
while (!done)
{
    String input = in.next();
    if (input.equals("Q"))
    {
        done = true;
        continue; // Jump to the end of the loop body
    }
    double x = Double.parseDouble(input);
    data.add(x);
    // continue statement jumps here
}
```

By using the continue statement, you don't need to place the remainder of the loop code inside an else clause. This is a minor benefit. Few programmers use this statement.

6.6 Problem Solving: Storyboards

When you design a program that interacts with a user, you need to make a plan for that interaction. What information does the user provide, and in which order? What information will your program display, and in which format? What should happen when there is an error? When does the program quit?

> A storyboard consists of annotated sketches for each step in an action sequence.

This planning is similar to the development of a movie or a computer game, where *storyboards* are used to plan action sequences. A storyboard is made up of panels that show a sketch of each step. Annotations explain what is happening and note any special situations. Storyboards are also used to develop software—see Figure 6.

Making a storyboard is very helpful when you begin designing a program. You need to ask yourself which information you need in order to compute the answers that the program user wants. You need to decide how to present those answers. These are important considerations that you want to settle before you design an algorithm for computing the answers.

> Developing a storyboard helps you understand the inputs and outputs that are required for a program.

Let's look at a simple example. We want to write a program that helps users with questions such as "How many tablespoons are in a pint?" or "How many inches are 30 centimeters?"

What information does the user provide?

- The quantity and unit to convert from
- The unit to convert to

What if there is more than one quantity? A user may have a whole table of centimeter values that should be converted into inches.

What if the user enters units that our program doesn't know how to handle, such as ångström?

What if the user asks for impossible conversions, such as inches to gallons?

Figure 6
Storyboard for the Design of a Web Application

Let's get started with a storyboard panel. It is a good idea to write the user inputs in a different color. (Underline them if you don't have a color pen handy.)

Converting a Sequence of Values

What unit do you want to convert from? cm
What unit do you want to convert to? in
Enter values, terminated by zero ——————— Allows conversion of multiple values
30
30 cm = 11.81 in ——————
100   Format makes clear what got converted
100 cm = 39.37 in
0
What unit do you want to convert from?

The storyboard shows how we deal with a potential confusion. A user who wants to know how many inches are 30 centimeters may not read the first prompt carefully and specify inches. But then the output is "30 in = 76.2 cm", alerting the user to the problem.

The storyboard also raises an issue. How is the user supposed to know that "cm" and "in" are valid units? Would "centimeter" and "inches" also work? What happens when the user enters a wrong unit? Let's make another storyboard to demonstrate error handling.

Handling Unknown Units (needs improvement)

What unit do you want to convert from? cm
What unit do you want to convert to? inches
Sorry, unknown unit.
What unit do you want to convert to? inch
Sorry, unknown unit.
What unit do you want to convert to? grrr

To eliminate frustration, it is better to list the units that the user can supply.

From unit (in, ft, mi, mm, cm, m, km, oz, lb, g, kg, tsp, tbsp, pint, gal): cm
To unit: in ——————
            —————— No need to list the units again

We switched to a shorter prompt to make room for all the unit names. Exercise R6.22 explores a different alternative.

There is another issue that we haven't addressed yet. How does the user quit the program? The first storyboard suggests that the program will go on forever.

We can ask the user after seeing the sentinel that terminates an input sequence.

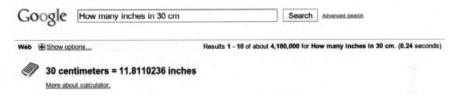

> **Exiting the Program**
>
> From unit (in, ft, mi, mm, cm, m, km, oz, lb, g, kg, tsp, tbsp, pint, gal): cm
> To unit: in
> Enter values, terminated by zero
> 30
> 30 cm = 11.81 in
> 0
> More conversions (y, n)? n ——— Sentinel triggers the prompt to exit
> (Program exits)

As you can see from this case study, a storyboard is essential for developing a working program. You need to know the flow of the user interaction in order to structure your program.

SELF CHECK

26. Provide a storyboard panel for a program that reads a number of test scores and prints the average score. The program only needs to process one set of scores. Don't worry about error handling.

27. Google has a simple interface for converting units. You just type the question, and you get the answer.

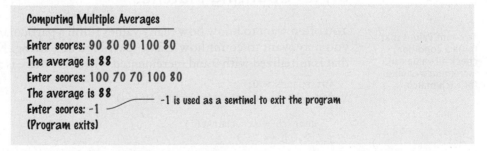

Make storyboards for an equivalent interface in a Java program. Show a scenario in which all goes well, and show the handling of two kinds of errors.

28. Consider a modification of the program in Self Check 26. Suppose we want to drop the lowest score before computing the average. Provide a storyboard for the situation in which a user only provides one score.

29. What is the problem with implementing the following storyboard in Java?

> **Computing Multiple Averages**
>
> Enter scores: 90 80 90 100 80
> The average is 88
> Enter scores: 100 70 70 100 80
> The average is 88 ——— -1 is used as a sentinel to exit the program
> Enter scores: -1
> (Program exits)

30. Produce a storyboard for a program that compares the growth of a $10,000 investment for a given number of years under two interest rates.

Practice It   Now you can try these exercises at the end of the chapter: R6.21, R6.22, R6.23.

6.7 Common Loop Algorithms

In the following sections, we discuss some of the most common algorithms that are implemented as loops. You can use them as starting points for your loop designs.

6.7.1 Sum and Average Value

Computing the sum of a number of inputs is a very common task. Keep a *running total*, a variable to which you add each input value. Of course, the total should be initialized with 0.

```
double total = 0;
while (in.hasNextDouble())
{
    double input = in.nextDouble();
    total = total + input;
}
```

Note that the total variable is declared outside the loop. We want the loop to update a single variable. The input variable is declared inside the loop. A separate variable is created for each input and removed at the end of each loop iteration.

To compute an average, keep a total and a count of all values.

To compute an average, count how many values you have, and divide by the count. Be sure to check that the count is not zero.

```
double total = 0;
int count = 0;
while (in.hasNextDouble())
{
    double input = in.nextDouble();
    total = total + input;
    count++;
}
double average = 0;
if (count > 0)
{
    average = total / count;
}
```

6.7.2 Counting Matches

To count values that fulfill a condition, check all values and increment a counter for each match.

You often want to know how many values fulfill a particular condition. For example, you may want to count how many spaces are in a string. Keep a *counter*, a variable that is initialized with 0 and incremented whenever there is a match.

```
int spaces = 0;
for (int i = 0; i < str.length(); i++)
{
    char ch = str.charAt(i);
    if (ch == ' ')
    {
        spaces++;
    }
}
```

For example, if str is "My Fair Lady", spaces is incremented twice (when i is 2 and 7).

Note that the spaces variable is declared outside the loop. We want the loop to update a single variable. The ch variable is declared inside the loop. A separate variable is created for each iteration and removed at the end of each loop iteration.

This loop can also be used for scanning inputs. The following loop reads text a word at a time and counts the number of words with at most three letters:

```java
int shortWords = 0;
while (in.hasNext())
{
    String input = in.next();
    if (input.length() <= 3)
    {
        shortWords++;
    }
}
```

In a loop that counts matches, a counter is incremented whenever a match is found.

6.7.3 Finding the First Match

If your goal is to find a match, exit the loop when the match is found.

When you count the values that fulfill a condition, you need to look at all values. However, if your task is to find a match, then you can stop as soon as the condition is fulfilled.

Here is a loop that finds the first space in a string. Because we do not visit all elements in the string, a while loop is a better choice than a for loop:

```java
boolean found = false;
char ch = '?';
int position = 0;
while (!found && position < str.length())
{
    ch = str.charAt(position);
    if (ch == ' ') { found = true; }
    else { position++; }
}
```

If a match was found, then found is true, ch is the first matching character, and position is the index of the first match. If the loop did not find a match, then found remains false after the end of the loop.

Note that the variable ch is declared *outside* the while loop because you may want to use the input after the loop has finished. If it had been declared inside the loop body, you would not be able to use it outside the loop.

When searching, you look at items until a match is found.

6.7.4 Prompting Until a Match is Found

In the preceding example, we searched a string for a character that matches a condition. You can apply the same process to user input. Suppose you are asking a user to enter a positive value < 100. Keep asking until the user provides a correct input:

```java
boolean valid = false;
double input = 0;
while (!valid)
{
    System.out.print("Please enter a positive value < 100: ");
    input = in.nextDouble();
    if (0 < input && input < 100) { valid = true; }
    else { System.out.println("Invalid input."); }
}
```

Note that the variable input is declared *outside* the while loop because you will want to use the input after the loop has finished.

6.7.5 Maximum and Minimum

To find the largest value, update the largest value seen so far whenever you see a larger one.

To compute the largest value in a sequence, keep a variable that stores the largest element that you have encountered, and update it when you find a larger one.

```java
double largest = in.nextDouble();
while (in.hasNextDouble())
{
    double input = in.nextDouble();
    if (input > largest)
    {
        largest = input;
    }
}
```

This algorithm requires that there is at least one input.

To compute the smallest value, simply reverse the comparison:

```java
double smallest = in.nextDouble();
while (in.hasNextDouble())
{
    double input = in.nextDouble();
    if (input < smallest)
    {
        smallest = input;
    }
}
```

To find the height of the tallest bus rider, remember the largest value so far, and update it whenever you see a taller one.

6.7.6 Comparing Adjacent Values

To compare adjacent inputs, store the preceding input in a variable.

When processing a sequence of values in a loop, you sometimes need to compare a value with the value that just preceded it. For example, suppose you want to check whether a sequence of inputs, such as 1 7 2 9 9 4 9, contains adjacent duplicates.

Now you face a challenge. Consider the typical loop for reading a value:

```java
double input;
while (in.hasNextDouble())
{
    input = in.nextDouble();
    . . .
}
```

How can you compare the current input with the preceding one? At any time, input contains the current input, overwriting the previous one.

The answer is to store the previous input, like this:

```java
double input = 0;
while (in.hasNextDouble())
{
    double previous = input;
    input = in.nextDouble();
    if (input == previous)
    {
        System.out.println("Duplicate input");
    }
}
```

When comparing adjacent values, store the previous value in a variable.

One problem remains. When the loop is entered for the first time, input has not yet been read. You can solve this problem with an initial input operation outside the loop:

```java
double input = in.nextDouble();
while (in.hasNextDouble())
{
    double previous = input;
    input = in.nextDouble();
    if (input == previous)
    {
        System.out.println("Duplicate input");
    }
}
```

FULL CODE EXAMPLE

Go to wiley.com/go/javacode to download a program that uses common loop algorithms.

SELF CHECK

31. What total is computed when no user input is provided in the algorithm in Section 6.7.1?

32. How do you compute the total of all positive inputs?

33. What are the values of position and ch when no match is found in the algorithm in Section 6.7.3?

34. What is wrong with the following loop for finding the position of the first space in a string?

```java
boolean found = false;
for (int position = 0; !found && position < str.length(); position++)
{
```

```
            char ch = str.charAt(position);
            if (ch == ' ') { found = true; }
        }
```

35. How do you find the position of the *last* space in a string?

36. What happens with the algorithm in Section 6.7.6 when no input is provided at all? How can you overcome that problem?

Practice It   Now you can try these exercises at the end of the chapter: E6.5, E6.9, E6.10.

HOW TO 6.1   Writing a Loop

This How To walks you through the process of implementing a loop statement. We will illustrate the steps with the following example problem.

Problem Statement   Read twelve temperature values (one for each month) and display the number of the month with the highest temperature. For example, according to worldclimate.com, the average maximum temperatures for Death Valley are (in order by month, in degrees Celsius):

    18.2 22.6 26.4 31.1 36.6 42.2 45.7 44.5 40.2 33.1 24.2 17.6

In this case, the month with the highest temperature (45.7 degrees Celsius) is July, and the program should display 7.

Step 1   Decide what work must be done *inside* the loop.

Every loop needs to do some kind of repetitive work, such as

• Reading another item.

• Updating a value (such as a bank balance or total).

• Incrementing a counter.

If you can't figure out what needs to go inside the loop, start by writing down the steps that you would take if you solved the problem by hand. For example, with the temperature reading problem, you might write

Read first value.
Read second value.
If second value is higher than the first, set highest temperature to that value, highest month to 2.
Read next value.
If value is higher than the first and second, set highest temperature to that value, highest month to 3.
Read next value.
If value is higher than the highest temperature seen so far, set highest temperature to that value,
    highest month to 4.
. . .

Now look at these steps and reduce them to a set of *uniform* actions that can be placed into the loop body. The first action is easy:

Read next value.

The next action is trickier. In our description, we used tests "higher than the first", "higher than the first and second", "higher than the highest temperature seen so far". We need to settle on one test that works for all iterations. The last formulation is the most general.

Similarly, we must find a general way of setting the highest month. We need a variable that stores the current month, running from 1 to 12. Then we can formulate the second loop action:

If value is higher than the highest temperature, set highest temperature to that value, highest month to current month.

Altogether our loop is

Repeat
    Read next value.
    If value is higher than the highest temperature,
        set highest temperature to that value,
        set highest month to current month.
    Increment current month.

Step 2   Specify the loop condition.

What goal do you want to reach in your loop? Typical examples are

- Has a counter reached its final value?
- Have you read the last input value?
- Has a value reached a given threshold?

In our example, we simply want the current month to reach 12.

Step 3   Determine the loop type.

We distinguish between two major loop types. A *count-controlled* loop is executed a definite number of times. In an *event-controlled* loop, the number of iterations is not known in advance—the loop is executed until some event happens.

Count-controlled loops can be implemented as `for` statements. For other loops, consider the loop condition. Do you need to complete one iteration of the loop body before you can tell when to terminate the loop? In that case, choose a `do` loop. Otherwise, use a `while` loop.

Sometimes, the condition for terminating a loop changes in the middle of the loop body. In that case, you can use a Boolean variable that specifies when you are ready to leave the loop. Follow this pattern:

```
boolean done = false;
while (!done)
{
    Do some work.
    If all work has been completed
    {
        done = true;
    }
    else
    {
        Do more work.
    }
}
```

Such a variable is called a **flag**.

In summary,

- If you know in advance how many times a loop is repeated, use a `for` loop.
- If the loop body must be executed at least once, use a `do` loop.
- Otherwise, use a `while` loop.

In our example, we read 12 temperature values. Therefore, we choose a `for` loop.

Step 4   Set up variables for entering the loop for the first time.

List all variables that are used and updated in the loop, and determine how to initialize them. Commonly, counters are initialized with 0 or 1, totals with 0.

In our example, the variables are

```
current month
highest value
highest month
```

We need to be careful how we set up the highest temperature value. We can't simply set it to 0. After all, our program needs to work with temperature values from Antarctica, all of which may be negative.

A good option is to set the highest temperature value to the first input value. Of course, then we need to remember to read in only 11 more values, with the current month starting at 2.

We also need to initialize the highest month with 1. After all, in an Australian city, we may never find a month that is warmer than January.

Step 5   Process the result after the loop has finished.

In many cases, the desired result is simply a variable that was updated in the loop body. For example, in our temperature program, the result is the highest month. Sometimes, the loop computes values that contribute to the final result. For example, suppose you are asked to average the temperatures. Then the loop should compute the sum, not the average. After the loop has completed, you are ready to compute the average: divide the sum by the number of inputs.

Here is our complete loop.

```
Read first value; store as highest value.
highest month = 1
For current month from 2 to 12
    Read next value.
    If value is higher than the highest value
        Set highest value to that value.
        Set highest month to current month.
```

Step 6   Trace the loop with typical examples.

Hand trace your loop code, as described in Section 6.2. Choose example values that are not too complex—executing the loop 3–5 times is enough to check for the most common errors. Pay special attention when entering the loop for the first and last time.

Sometimes, you want to make a slight modification to make tracing feasible. For example, when hand-tracing the investment doubling problem, use an interest rate of 20 percent rather than 5 percent. When hand-tracing the temperature loop, use 4 data values, not 12.

Let's say the data are 22.6 36.6 44.5 24.2. Here is the walkthrough:

current month	current value	highest month	highest value
		~~1~~	~~22.6~~
~~2~~	36.6	~~2~~	~~36.6~~
~~3~~	44.5	3	44.5
4	24.2		

The trace demonstrates that **highest month** and **highest value** are properly set.

Step 7   Implement the loop in Java.

Here's the loop for our example. Exercise E6.4 asks you to complete the program.

```java
double highestValue;
highestValue = in.nextDouble();
int highestMonth = 1;
```

```
for (int currentMonth = 2; currentMonth <= 12; currentMonth++)
{
   double nextValue = in.nextDouble();
   if (nextValue > highestValue)
   {
      highestValue = nextValue;
      highestMonth = currentMonth;
   }
}
System.out.println(highestMonth);
```

WORKED EXAMPLE 6.1   **Credit Card Processing**

Learn how to use a loop to remove spaces from a credit card number. Go to wiley.com/go/javaexamples and download Worked Example 6.1.

6.8 Nested Loops

When the body of a loop contains another loop, the loops are nested. A typical use of nested loops is printing a table with rows and columns.

In Section 5.4, you saw how to nest two if statements. Similarly, complex iterations sometimes require a **nested loop**: a loop inside another loop statement. When processing tables, nested loops occur naturally. An outer loop iterates over all rows of the table. An inner loop deals with the columns in the current row.

In this section you will see how to print a table. For simplicity, we will simply print the powers of x, x^n, as in the table at right.

Here is the pseudocode for printing the table:

Print table header.
For x from 1 to 10
    Print table row.
    Print new line.

How do you print a table row? You need to print a value for each exponent. This requires a second loop.

For n from 1 to 4
    Print x^n.

x^1	x^2	x^3	x^4
1	1	1	1
2	4	8	16
3	9	27	81
...	...	...	...
10	100	1000	10000

This loop must be placed inside the preceding loop. We say that the inner loop is *nested* inside the outer loop.

The hour and minute displays in a digital clock are an example of nested loops. The hours loop 12 times, and for each hour, the minutes loop 60 times.

Figure 7
Flowchart of a Nested Loop

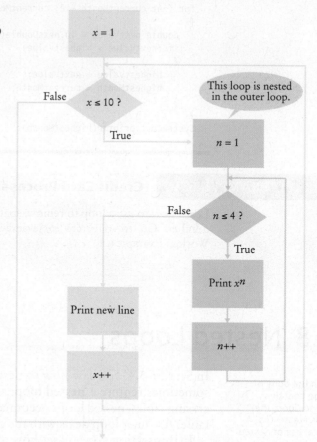

There are 10 rows in the outer loop. For each x, the program prints four columns in the inner loop (see Figure 7). Thus, a total of $10 \times 4 = 40$ values are printed.

Following is the complete program. Note that we also use two loops to print the table header. However, those loops are not nested.

section_8/PowerTable.java

```
1   /**
2       This program prints a table of powers of x.
3   */
4   public class PowerTable
5   {
6       public static void main(String[] args)
7       {
8           final int NMAX = 4;
9           final double XMAX = 10;
10
11          // Print table header
12
13          for (int n = 1; n <= NMAX; n++)
14          {
15              System.out.printf("%10d", n);
16          }
17          System.out.println();
```

```
18        for (int n = 1; n <= NMAX; n++)
19        {
20           System.out.printf("%10s", "x ");
21        }
22        System.out.println();
23
24        // Print table body
25
26        for (double x = 1; x <= XMAX; x++)
27        {
28           // Print table row
29
30           for (int n = 1; n <= NMAX; n++)
31           {
32              System.out.printf("%10.0f", Math.pow(x, n));
33           }
34           System.out.println();
35        }
36     }
37  }
```

Program Run

1	2	3	4
x	x	x	x
1	1	1	1
2	4	8	16
3	9	27	81
4	16	64	256
5	25	125	625
6	36	216	1296
7	49	343	2401
8	64	512	4096
9	81	729	6561
10	100	1000	10000

SELF CHECK

37. Why is there a statement System.out.println(); in the outer loop but not in the inner loop?

38. How would you change the program to display all powers from x^0 to x^5?

39. If you make the change in Self Check 38, how many values are displayed?

40. What do the following nested loops display?

```
for (int i = 0; i < 3; i++)
{
   for (int j = 0; j < 4; j++)
   {
      System.out.print(i + j);
   }
   System.out.println();
}
```

41. Write nested loops that make the following pattern of brackets:

```
[][][][]
[][][][]
[][][][]
```

Practice It   Now you can try these exercises at the end of the chapter: R6.27, E6.14, E6.16.

Table 3 Nested Loop Examples

Nested Loops	Output	Explanation

```for (i = 1; i <= 3; i++)```
```{```
```   for (j = 1; j <= 4; j++) { Print "*" }```
```   System.out.println();```
```}```
	```****```
	```****```
	```****```
		Prints 3 rows of 4 asterisks each.

```for (i = 1; i <= 4; i++)```
```{```
```   for (j = 1; j <= 3; j++) { Print "*" }```
```   System.out.println();```
```}```
	```***```
	```***```
	```***```
	```***```
		Prints 4 rows of 3 asterisks each.

```for (i = 1; i <= 4; i++)```
```{```
```   for (j = 1; j <= i; j++) { Print "*" }```
```   System.out.println();```
```}```
	```*```
	```**```
	```***```
	```****```
		Prints 4 rows of lengths 1, 2, 3, and 4.

```for (i = 1; i <= 3; i++)```
```{```
```   for (j = 1; j <= 5; j++)```
```   {```
```   if (j % 2 == 0) { Print "*" }```
```   else { Print "-" }```
```   }```
```   System.out.println();```
```}```
	```-*-*-```
	```-*-*-```
	```-*-*-```
		Prints asterisks in even columns, dashes in odd columns.

```for (i = 1; i <= 3; i++)```
```{```
```   for (j = 1; j <= 5; j++)```
```   {```
```   if (i % 2 == j % 2) { Print "*" }```
```   else { Print " " }```
```   }```
```   System.out.println();```
```}```
	```* * *```
	``` * * ```
	```* * *```
		Prints a checkerboard pattern.

WORKED EXAMPLE 6.2   Manipulating the Pixels in an Image

Learn how to use nested loops for manipulating the pixels in an image. The outer loop traverses the rows of the image, and the inner loop accesses each pixel of a row. Go to wiley.com/go/javaexamples and download Worked Example 6.2.

6.9 Application: Random Numbers and Simulations

In a simulation, you use the computer to simulate an activity.

A *simulation program* uses the computer to simulate an activity in the real world (or an imaginary one). Simulations are commonly used for predicting climate change, analyzing traffic, picking stocks, and many other applications in science and business. In many simulations, one or more loops are used to modify the state of a system and observe the changes. You will see examples in the following sections.

6.9.1 Generating Random Numbers

Many events in the real world are difficult to predict with absolute precision, yet we can sometimes know the average behavior quite well. For example, a store may know from experience that a customer arrives every five minutes. Of course, that is an average—customers don't arrive in five minute intervals. To accurately model customer traffic, you want to take that random fluctuation into account. Now, how can you run such a simulation in the computer?

You can introduce randomness by calling the random number generator.

The Random class of the Java library implements a *random number generator* that produces numbers that appear to be completely random. To generate random numbers, you construct an object of the Random class, and then apply one of the following methods:

Method	Returns
nextInt(n)	A random integer between the integers 0 (inclusive) and n (exclusive)
nextDouble()	A random floating-point number between 0 (inclusive) and 1 (exclusive)

For example, you can simulate the cast of a die as follows:

```
Random generator = new Random();
int d = 1 + generator.nextInt(6);
```

The call generator.nextInt(6) gives you a random number between 0 and 5 (inclusive). Add 1 to obtain a number between 1 and 6.

To give you a feeling for the random numbers, run the following program a few times.

section_9_1/Die.java

```
1   import java.util.Random;
2
3   /**
4      This class models a die that, when cast, lands on a
5      random face.
6   */
7   public class Die
8   {
9      private Random generator;
10     private int sides;
```

```
11
12    /**
13        Constructs a die with a given number of sides.
14        @param s the number of sides, e.g., 6 for a normal die
15    */
16    public Die(int s)
17    {
18        sides = s;
19        generator = new Random();
20    }
21
22    /**
23        Simulates a throw of the die.
24        @return the face of the die
25    */
26    public int cast()
27    {
28        return 1 + generator.nextInt(sides);
29    }
30 }
```

section_9_1/DieSimulator.java

```
1  /**
2      This program simulates casting a die ten times.
3  */
4  public class DieSimulator
5  {
6      public static void main(String[] args)
7      {
8          Die d = new Die(6);
9          final int TRIES = 10;
10         for (int i = 1; i <= TRIES; i++)
11         {
12             int n = d.cast();
13             System.out.print(n + " ");
14         }
15         System.out.println();
16     }
17 }
```

Typical Program Run

```
6 5 6 3 2 6 3 4 4 1
```

Typical Program Run (Second Run)

```
3 2 2 1 6 5 3 4 1 2
```

As you can see, this program produces a different stream of simulated die casts every time it is run.

Actually, the numbers are not completely random. They are drawn from very long sequences of numbers that don't repeat for a long time. These sequences are computed from fairly simple formulas; they just behave like random numbers. For that reason, they are often called **pseudorandom numbers**. Generating good sequences of numbers that behave like truly random sequences is an important and well-studied problem in computer science. We won't investigate this issue further, though; we'll just use the random numbers produced by the Random class.

6.9.2 The Monte Carlo Method

The Monte Carlo method is an ingenious method for finding approximate solutions to problems that cannot be precisely solved. (The method is named after the famous casino in Monte Carlo.) Here is a typical example. It is difficult to compute the number π, but you can approximate it quite well with the following simulation.

Simulate shooting a dart into a square surrounding a circle of radius 1. That is easy: generate random x- and y- coordinates between -1 and 1.

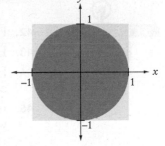

If the generated point lies inside the circle, we count it as a *hit*. That is the case when $x^2 + y^2 \leq 1$. Because our shots are entirely random, we expect that the ratio of *hits / tries* is approximately equal to the ratio of the areas of the circle and the square, that is, $\pi / 4$. Therefore, our estimate for π is $4 \times$ *hits / tries*. This method yields an estimate for π, using nothing but simple arithmetic.

To generate a random floating-point value between -1 and 1, you compute:

```
double r = generator.nextDouble(); // 0 ≤ r < 1
double x = -1 + 2 * r; // −1 ≤ x < 1
```

As r ranges from 0 (inclusive) to 1 (exclusive), x ranges from $-1 + 2 \times 0 = -1$ (inclusive) to $-1 + 2 \times 1 = 1$ (exclusive). In our application, it does not matter that x never reaches 1. The points that fulfill the equation $x = 1$ lie on a line with area 0.

Here is the program that carries out the simulation:

section_9_2/MonteCarlo.java

```
1   import java.util.Random;
2
3   /**
4      This program computes an estimate of pi by simulating dart throws onto a square.
5   */
6   public class MonteCarlo
7   {
8      public static void main(String[] args)
9      {
10         final int TRIES = 10000;
11         Random generator = new Random();
12
13         int hits = 0;
14         for (int i = 1; i <= TRIES; i++)
15         {
16            // Generate two random numbers between −1 and 1
17
18            double r = generator.nextDouble();
19            double x = -1 + 2 * r; // Between −1 and 1
20            r = generator.nextDouble();
21            double y = -1 + 2 * r;
22
```

```
23              // Check whether the point lies in the unit circle
24
25              if (x * x + y * y <= 1) { hits++; }
26          }
27
28          /*
29              The ratio hits / tries is approximately the same as the ratio
30              circle area / square area = pi / 4
31          */
32
33          double piEstimate = 4.0 * hits / TRIES;
34          System.out.println("Estimate for pi: " + piEstimate);
35      }
36  }
```

Program Run

```
Estimate for pi: 3.1504
```

SELF CHECK

42. How do you simulate a coin toss with the Random class?

43. How do you simulate the picking of a random playing card?

44. How would you modify the DieSimulator program to simulate tossing a pair of dice?

45. In many games, you throw a pair of dice to get a value between 2 and 12. What is wrong with this simulated throw of a pair of dice?

```
int sum = 2 + generator.nextInt(11);
```

46. How do you generate a random floating-point number ≥ 0 and < 100?

Practice It   Now you can try these exercises at the end of the chapter: R6.28, E6.7, E6.19.

6.10 Using a Debugger

A debugger is a program that you can use to execute another program and analyze its run-time behavior.

As you have undoubtedly realized by now, computer programs rarely run perfectly the first time. At times, it can be quite frustrating to find the bugs. Of course, you can insert print commands, run the program, and try to analyze the printout. If the printout does not clearly point to the problem, you may need to add and remove print commands and run the program again. That can be a time-consuming process.

Modern development environments contain special programs, called **debuggers**, that help you locate bugs by letting you follow the execution of a program. You can stop and restart your program and see the contents of variables whenever your program is temporarily stopped. At each stop, you have the choice of what variables to inspect and how many program steps to run until the next stop.

Some people feel that debuggers are just a tool to make programmers lazy. Admittedly some people write sloppy programs and then fix them up with a debugger, but the majority of programmers make an honest effort to write the best program they can before trying to run it through a debugger. These programmers realize that a debugger, while more convenient than print commands, is not cost-free. It does take time to set up and carry out an effective debugging session.

In actual practice, you cannot avoid using a debugger. The larger your programs get, the harder it is to debug them simply by inserting print commands. The time invested in learning about a debugger will be amply repaid in your programming career.

Like compilers, debuggers vary widely from one system to another. Some are quite primitive and require you to memorize a small set of arcane commands; others have an intuitive window interface. Figure 8 shows the debugger in the Eclipse development environment, downloadable for free from the Eclipse Foundation (eclipse.org). Other integrated environments, such as BlueJ, also include debuggers. A free standalone debugger called JSwat is available from code.google.com/p/jswat.

You will have to find out how to prepare a program for debugging and how to start a debugger on your system. If you use an integrated development environment (with an editor, compiler, and debugger), this step is usually easy. You build the program in the usual way and pick a command to start debugging. On some systems, you must manually build a debug version of your program and invoke the debugger.

Once you have started the debugger, you can go a long way with just three debugging commands: "set breakpoint", "single step", and "inspect variable". The names and keystrokes or mouse clicks for these commands differ widely, but all debuggers support these basic commands. You can find out how, either from the documentation or a lab manual, or by asking someone who has used the debugger before.

When you start the debugger, it runs at full speed until it reaches a **breakpoint**. Then execution stops, and the breakpoint that causes the stop is displayed (Figure 8). You can now inspect variables and step through the program one line at a time, or continue running the program at full speed until it reaches the next breakpoint. When the program terminates, the debugger stops as well.

> You can make effective use of a debugger by mastering just three concepts: breakpoints, single-stepping, and inspecting variables.

> When a debugger executes a program, the execution is suspended whenever a breakpoint is reached.

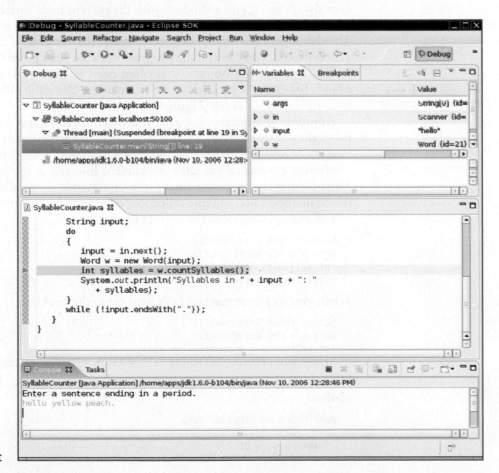

Figure 8
Stopping at a Breakpoint

Figure 9   Inspecting Variables

Breakpoints stay active until you remove them, so you should periodically clear the breakpoints that you no longer need.

Once the program has stopped, you can look at the current values of variables. Again, the method for selecting the variables differs among debuggers. Some debuggers always show you a window with the current local variables. On other debuggers you issue a command such as "inspect variable" and type in or click on the variable. The debugger then displays the contents of the variable. If all variables contain what you expected, you can run the program until the next point where you want to stop.

When inspecting objects, you often need to give a command to "open up" the object, for example by clicking on a tree node. Once the object is opened up, you see its instance variables (see Figure 9).

Running to a breakpoint gets you there speedily, but you don't know how the program got there. You can also step through the program one line at a time. Then you know how the program flows, but it can take a long time to step through it. The *single-step command* executes the current line and stops at the next program line. Most debuggers have two single-step commands, one called *step into*, which steps inside method calls, and one called *step over*, which skips over method calls.

For example, suppose the current line is

> The single-step command executes the program one line at a time.

```
String input = in.next();
Word w = new Word(input);
int syllables = w.countSyllables();
System.out.println("Syllables in " + input + ": " + syllables);
```

When you step over method calls, you get to the next line:

```
String input = in.next();
Word w = new Word(input);
int syllables = w.countSyllables();
System.out.println("Syllables in " + input + ": " + syllables);
```

However, if you step into method calls, you enter the first line of the countSyllables method.

```
public int countSyllables()
{
    int count = 0;
```

```
int end = text.length() - 1;
    . . .
}
```

You should step *into* a method to check whether it carries out its job correctly. You should step *over* a method if you know it works correctly.

Finally, when the program has finished running, the debug session is also finished. To debug the program again, you must restart it in the debugger.

A debugger can be an effective tool for finding and removing bugs in your program. However, it is no substitute for good design and careful programming. If the debugger does not find any errors, it does not mean that your program is bug-free. Testing and debugging can only show the presence of bugs, not their absence.

SELF CHECK

47. In the debugger, you are reaching a call to System.out.println. Should you step into the method or step over it?

48. In the debugger, you are reaching the beginning of a method with a couple of loops inside. You want to find out the return value that is computed at the end of the method. Should you set a breakpoint, or should you step through the method?

49. When using the debugger, you find that a variable has an unexpected value. How can you go backwards to see when the variable changed?

50. When using a debugger, should you insert statements to print the values of variables?

51. Instead of using a debugger, could you simply trace a program by hand?

Practice It Now you can try these exercises at the end of the chapter: R6.30, R6.31, R6.32.

HOW TO 6.2 **Debugging**

Knowing all about the mechanics of debugging may still leave you helpless when you fire up a debugger to look at a sick program. This How To presents a number of strategies that you can use to recognize bugs and their causes.

Step 1 Reproduce the error.

As you test your program, you notice that it sometimes does something wrong. It gives the wrong output, it seems to print something random, it goes in an infinite loop, or it crashes. Find out exactly how to reproduce that behavior. What numbers did you enter? Where did you click with the mouse?

Run the program again; type in exactly the same numbers, and click with the mouse on the same spots (or as close as you can get). Does the program exhibit the same behavior? If so, then it makes sense to fire up a debugger to study this particular problem. Debuggers are good for analyzing particular failures. They aren't terribly useful for studying a program in general.

Step 2 Simplify the error.

Before you start up a debugger, it makes sense to spend a few minutes trying to come up with a simpler input that also produces an error. Can you use shorter words or simpler numbers and still have the program misbehave? If so, use those values during your debugging session.

Step 3   Divide and conquer.

> Use the divide-and-conquer technique to locate the point of failure of a program.

Now that you have a particular failure, you want to get as close to the failure as possible. The key point of debugging is to locate the code that produces the failure. Just as with real insect pests, finding the bug can be hard, but once you find it, squashing it is usually the easy part. Suppose your program dies with a division by 0. Because there are many division operations in a typical program, it is often not feasible to set breakpoints to all of them. Instead, use a technique of *divide and conquer*. Step over the methods in main, but don't step inside them. Eventually, the failure will happen again. Now you know which method contains the bug: It is the last method that was called from main before the program died. Restart the debugger and go back to that line in main, then step inside that method. Repeat the process.

Eventually, you will have pinpointed the line that contains the bad division. Maybe it is obvious from the code why the denominator is not correct. If not, you need to find the location where it is computed. Unfortunately, you can't go back in the debugger. You need to restart the program and move to the point where the denominator computation happens.

Step 4   Know what your program should do.

> During debugging, compare the actual contents of variables against the values you know they should have.

A debugger shows you what the program does. You must know what the program *should* do, or you will not be able to find bugs. Before you trace through a loop, ask yourself how many iterations you expect the program to make. Before you inspect a variable, ask yourself what you expect to see. If you have no clue, set aside some time and think first. Have a calculator handy to make independent computations. When you know what the value should be, inspect the variable. If the value is what you expected, you must look further for the bug. If the value is different, you may be on to something. Double-check your computation. If you are sure your value is correct, find out why your program comes up with a different value.

In many cases, program bugs are the result of simple errors such as loop termination conditions that are off by one. Quite often, however, programs make computational errors. Maybe they are supposed to add two numbers, but by accident the code was written to subtract them. Programs don't make a special effort to ensure that everything is a simple integer (and neither do real-world problems). You will need to make some calculations with large integers or nasty floating-point numbers. Sometimes these calculations can be avoided if you just ask yourself, "Should this quantity be positive? Should it be larger than that value?" Then inspect variables to verify those theories.

Step 5   Look at all details.

When you debug a program, you often have a theory about what the problem is. Nevertheless, keep an open mind and look at all details. What strange messages are displayed? Why does the program take another unexpected action? These details count. When you run a debugging session, you really are a detective who needs to look at every clue available.

If you notice another failure on the way to the problem that you are about to pin down, don't just say, "I'll come back to it later". That very failure may be the original cause for your current problem. It is better to make a note of the current problem, fix what you just found, and then return to the original mission.

Step 6   Make sure you understand each bug before you fix it.

Once you find that a loop makes too many iterations, it is very tempting to apply a "Band-Aid" solution and subtract 1 from a variable so that the particular problem doesn't appear again. Such a quick fix has an overwhelming probability of creating trouble elsewhere. You really need to have a thorough understanding of how the program should be written before you apply a fix.

It does occasionally happen that you find bug after bug and apply fix after fix, and the problem just moves around. That usually is a symptom of a larger problem with the program logic. There is little you can do with the debugger. You must rethink the program design and reorganize it.

WORKED EXAMPLE 6.3   **A Sample Debugging Session**

Learn how to find bugs in an algorithm for counting the syllables of a word. Go to wiley.com/go/javaexamples and download Worked Example 6.3.

Computing & Society 6.2 The First Bug

According to legend, the first bug was found in the Mark II, a huge electromechanical computer at Harvard University. It really was caused by a bug—a moth was trapped in a relay switch.

Actually, from the note that the operator left in the log book next to the moth (see the photo), it appears as if the term "bug" had already been in active use at the time.

The pioneering computer scientist Maurice Wilkes wrote, "Somehow, at the Moore School and afterwards, one had always assumed there would be no particular difficulty in getting programs right. I can remember the exact instant in time at which it dawned on me that a great part of my future life would be spent finding mistakes in my own programs."

The First Bug

CHAPTER SUMMARY

Explain the flow of execution in a loop.

- A loop executes instructions repeatedly while a condition is true.
- An off-by-one error is a common error when programming loops. Think through simple test cases to avoid this type of error.

Use the technique of hand-tracing to analyze the behavior of a program.

- Hand-tracing is a simulation of code execution in which you step through instructions and track the values of the variables.
- Hand-tracing can help you understand how an unfamiliar algorithm works.
- Hand-tracing can show errors in code or pseudocode.

Use for loops for implementing count-controlled loops.

- The for loop is used when a value runs from a starting point to an ending point with a constant increment or decrement.

Choose between the while loop and the do loop.

- The do loop is appropriate when the loop body must be executed at least once.

Implement loops that read sequences of input data.

- A sentinel value denotes the end of a data set, but it is not part of the data.
- You can use a Boolean variable to control a loop. Set the variable to true before entering the loop, then set it to false to leave the loop.
- Use input redirection to read input from a file. Use output redirection to capture program output in a file.

Use the technique of storyboarding for planning user interactions.

- A storyboard consists of annotated sketches for each step in an action sequence.
- Developing a storyboard helps you understand the inputs and outputs that are required for a program.

Know the most common loop algorithms.

- To compute an average, keep a total and a count of all values.
- To count values that fulfill a condition, check all values and increment a counter for each match.
- If your goal is to find a match, exit the loop when the match is found.
- To find the largest value, update the largest value seen so far whenever you see a larger one.
- To compare adjacent inputs, store the preceding input in a variable.

Use nested loops to implement multiple levels of iteration.

- When the body of a loop contains another loop, the loops are nested. A typical use of nested loops is printing a table with rows and columns.

Apply loops to the implementation of simulations.

- In a simulation, you use the computer to simulate an activity.
- You can introduce randomness by calling the random number generator.

Use a debugger to analyze your programs.

- A debugger is a program that you can use to execute another program and analyze its run-time behavior.
- You can make effective use of a debugger by mastering just three concepts: break-points, single-stepping, and inspecting variables.
- When a debugger executes a program, the execution is suspended whenever a breakpoint is reached.
- The single-step command executes the program one line at a time.
- Use the divide-and-conquer technique to locate the point of failure of a program.
- During debugging, compare the actual contents of variables against the values you know they should have.

STANDARD LIBRARY ITEMS INTRODUCED IN THIS CHAPTER

```
java.util.Random
    nextDouble
    nextInt
```

REVIEW QUESTIONS

- **R6.1** Write a while loop that prints
  - **a.** All squares less than n. For example, if n is 100, print 0 1 4 9 16 25 36 49 64 81.
  - **b.** All positive numbers that are divisible by 10 and less than n. For example, if n is 100, print 10 20 30 40 50 60 70 80 90
  - **c.** All powers of two less than n. For example, if n is 100, print 1 2 4 8 16 32 64.

- **R6.2** Write a loop that computes
  - **a.** The sum of all even numbers between 2 and 100 (inclusive).
  - **b.** The sum of all squares between 1 and 100 (inclusive).
  - **c.** The sum of all odd numbers between a and b (inclusive).
  - **d.** The sum of all odd digits of n. (For example, if n is 32677, the sum would be 3 + 7 + 7 = 17.)

- **R6.3** Provide trace tables for these loops.
  - **a.** `int i = 0; int j = 10; int n = 0;`
    `while (i < j) { i++; j--; n++; }`
  - **b.** `int i = 0; int j = 0; int n = 0;`
    `while (i < 10) { i++; n = n + i + j; j++; }`
  - **c.** `int i = 10; int j = 0; int n = 0;`
    `while (i > 0) { i--; j++; n = n + i - j; }`
  - **d.** `int i = 0; int j = 10; int n = 0;`
    `while (i != j) { i = i + 2; j = j - 2; n++; }`

- **R6.4** What do these loops print?

    a. for (int i = 1; i < 10; i++) { System.out.print(i + " "); }
    b. for (int i = 1; i < 10; i += 2) { System.out.print(i + " "); }
    c. for (int i = 10; i > 1; i--) { System.out.print(i + " "); }
    d. for (int i = 0; i < 10; i++) { System.out.print(i + " "); }
    e. for (int i = 1; i < 10; i = i * 2) { System.out.print(i + " "); }
    f. for (int i = 1; i < 10; i++) { if (i % 2 == 0) { System.out.print(i + " "); } }

- **R6.5** What is an infinite loop? On your computer, how can you terminate a program that executes an infinite loop?

- **R6.6** Write a program trace for the pseudocode in Exercise E6.6, assuming the input values are 4 7 –2 –5 0.

- ■ **R6.7** What is an "off-by-one" error? Give an example from your own programming experience.

- **R6.8** What is a sentinel value? Give a simple rule when it is appropriate to use a numeric sentinel value.

- **R6.9** Which loop statements does Java support? Give simple rules for when to use each loop type.

- **R6.10** How many iterations do the following loops carry out? Assume that i is not changed in the loop body.

    a. for (int i = 1; i <= 10; i++) . . .
    b. for (int i = 0; i < 10; i++) . . .
    c. for (int i = 10; i > 0; i--) . . .
    d. for (int i = -10; i <= 10; i++) . . .
    e. for (int i = 10; i >= 0; i++) . . .
    f. for (int i = -10; i <= 10; i = i + 2) . . .
    g. for (int i = -10; i <= 10; i = i + 3) . . .

- ■ **R6.11** Write pseudocode for a program that prints a calendar such as the following.

    ```
    Su  M  T  W Th  F Sa
                 1  2  3  4
     5  6  7  8  9 10 11
    12 13 14 15 16 17 18
    19 20 21 22 23 24 25
    26 27 28 29 30 31
    ```

- **R6.12** Write pseudocode for a program that prints a Celsius/Fahrenheit conversion table such as the following.

    ```
    Celsius | Fahrenheit
    --------+-----------
          0 |         32
         10 |         50
         20 |         68
      . . .        . . .
        100 |        212
    ```

- **R6.13** Write pseudocode for a program that reads a student record, consisting of the student's first and last name, followed by a sequence of test scores and a sentinel of –1.

The program should print the student's average score. Then provide a trace table for this sample input:

```
Harry Morgan 94 71 86 95 -1
```

■■ R6.14 Write pseudocode for a program that reads a sequence of student records and prints the total score for each student. Each record has the student's first and last name, followed by a sequence of test scores and a sentinel of –1. The sequence is terminated by the word END. Here is a sample sequence:

```
Harry Morgan 94 71 86 95 -1
Sally Lin 99 98 100 95 90 -1
END
```

Provide a trace table for this sample input.

■ R6.15 Rewrite the following for loop into a while loop.

```
int s = 0;
for (int i = 1; i <= 10; i++)
{
    s = s + i;
}
```

■ R6.16 Rewrite the following do loop into a while loop.

```
int n = in.nextInt();
double x = 0;
double s;
do
{
    s = 1.0 / (1 + n * n);
    n++;
    x = x + s;
}
while (s > 0.01);
```

■ R6.17 Provide trace tables of the following loops.

```
a. int s = 1;
   int n - 1;
   while (s < 10) { s = s + n; }
   n++;
b. int s = 1;
   for (int n = 1; n < 5; n++) { s = s + n; }
c. int s = 1;
   int n = 1;
   do
   {
       s = s + n;
       n++;
   }
   while (s < 10 * n);
```

■ R6.18 What do the following loops print? Work out the answer by tracing the code, not by using the computer.

```
a. int s = 1;
   for (int n = 1; n <= 5; n++)
   {
       s = s + n;
       System.out.print(s + " ");
   }
```

b.
```
int s = 1;
for (int n = 1; s <= 10; System.out.print(s + " "))
{
    n = n + 2;
    s = s + n;
}
```

c.
```
int s = 1;
int n;
for (n = 1; n <= 5; n++)
{
    s = s + n;
    n++;
}
System.out.print(s + " " + n);
```

- **R6.19** What do the following program segments print? Find the answers by tracing the code, not by using the computer.

    a.
    ```
    int n = 1;
    for (int i = 2; i < 5; i++) { n = n + i; }
    System.out.print(n);
    ```

    b.
    ```
    int i;
    double n = 1 / 2;
    for (i = 2; i <= 5; i++) { n = n + 1.0 / i; }
    System.out.print(i);
    ```

    c.
    ```
    double x = 1;
    double y = 1;
    int i = 0;
    do
    {
        y = y / 2;
        x = x + y;
        i++;
    }
    while (x < 1.8);
    System.out.print(i);
    ```

    d.
    ```
    double x = 1;
    double y = 1;
    int i = 0;
    while (y >= 1.5)
    {
        x = x / 2;
        y = x + y;
        i++;
    }
    System.out.print(i);
    ```

- **R6.20** Give an example of a for loop where symmetric bounds are more natural. Give an example of a for loop where asymmetric bounds are more natural.

- **R6.21** Add a storyboard panel for the conversion program in Section 6.6 on page 269 that shows a scenario where a user enters incompatible units.

- **R6.22** In Section 6.6, we decided to show users a list of all valid units in the prompt. If the program supports many more units, this approach is unworkable. Give a storyboard panel that illustrates an alternate approach: If the user enters an unknown unit, a list of all known units is shown.

- **R6.23** Change the storyboards in Section 6.6 to support a menu that asks users whether they want to convert units, see program help, or quit the program. The menu should be displayed at the beginning of the program, when a sequence of values has been converted, and when an error is displayed.

- **R6.24** Draw a flow chart for a program that carries out unit conversions as described in Section 6.6.

- **R6.25** In Section 6.7.5, the code for finding the largest and smallest input initializes the largest and smallest variables with an input value. Why can't you initialize them with zero?

- **R6.26** What are nested loops? Give an example where a nested loop is typically used.

- **R6.27** The nested loops

  ```
  for (int i = 1; i <= height; i++)
  {
     for (int j = 1; j <= width; j++) { System.out.print("*"); }
     System.out.println();
  }
  ```

  display a rectangle of a given width and height, such as

  ```
  ****
  ****
  ****
  ```

  Write a *single* for loop that displays the same rectangle.

- **R6.28** Suppose you design an educational game to teach children how to read a clock. How do you generate random values for the hours and minutes?

- **R6.29** In a travel simulation, Harry will visit one of his friends that are located in three states. He has ten friends in California, three in Nevada, and two in Utah. How do you produce a random number between 1 and 3, denoting the destination state, with a probability that is proportional to the number of friends in each state?

- **Testing R6.30** Explain the differences between these debugger operations:
  - Stepping into a method
  - Stepping over a method

- **Testing R6.31** Explain in detail how to inspect the string stored in a String object in your debugger.

- **Testing R6.32** Explain in detail how to inspect the information stored in a Rectangle object in your debugger.

- **Testing R6.33** Explain in detail how to use your debugger to inspect the balance stored in a Bank-Account object.

- **Testing R6.34** Explain the divide-and-conquer strategy to get close to a bug in a debugger.

PRACTICE EXERCISES

- **E6.1** Write programs with loops that compute
  - **a.** The sum of all even numbers between 2 and 100 (inclusive).
  - **b.** The sum of all squares between 1 and 100 (inclusive).

    c. All powers of 2 from 2^0 up to 2^{20}.

    d. The sum of all odd numbers between a and b (inclusive), where a and b are inputs.

    e. The sum of all odd digits of an input. (For example, if the input is 32677, the sum would be $3 + 7 + 7 = 17$.)

■■ E6.2 Write programs that read a sequence of integer inputs and print

    a. The smallest and largest of the inputs.

    b. The number of even and odd inputs.

    c. Cumulative totals. For example, if the input is 1 7 2 9, the program should print 1 8 10 19.

    d. All adjacent duplicates. For example, if the input is 1 3 3 4 5 5 6 6 6 2, the program should print 3 5 6.

■■ E6.3 Write programs that read a line of input as a string and print

    a. Only the uppercase letters in the string.

    b. Every second letter of the string.

    c. The string, with all vowels replaced by an underscore.

    d. The number of vowels in the string.

    e. The positions of all vowels in the string.

■■ E6.4 Complete the program in How To 6.1 on page 276. Your program should read twelve temperature values and print the month with the highest temperature.

■■ E6.5 Write a program that reads a set of floating-point values. Ask the user to enter the values (prompting only a single time for the values), then print

    • the average of the values.

    • the smallest of the values.

    • the largest of the values.

    • the range, that is the difference between the smallest and largest.

    Your program should use a class `DataSet`. That class should have a method

```
public void add(double value)
```

    and methods `getAverage`, `getSmallest`, `getLargest`, and `getRange`.

■ E6.6 Translate the following pseudocode for finding the minimum value from a set of inputs into a Java program.

> Set a Boolean variable "first" to true.
> While another value has been read successfully
>   If first is true
>   Set the minimum to the value.
>   Set first to false.
>   Else if the value is less than the minimum
>   Set the minimum to the value.
> Print the minimum.

■■■ E6.7 Translate the following pseudocode for randomly permuting the characters in a string into a Java program.

> Read a word.
> Repeat word.length() times
>   Pick a random position i in the word, but not the last position.
>   Pick a random position j > i in the word.
>   Swap the letters at positions j and i.
> Print the word.

To swap the letters, construct substrings as follows:

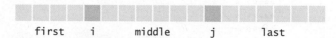

Then replace the string with

    first + word.charAt(j) + middle + word.charAt(i) + last

■ E6.8 Write a program that reads a word and prints each character of the word on a separate line. For example, if the user provides the input "Harry", the program prints

    H
    a
    r
    r
    y

■■ E6.9 Write a program that reads a word and prints the word in reverse. For example, if the user provides the input "Harry", the program prints

    yrraH

■ E6.10 Write a program that reads a word and prints the number of vowels in the word. For this exercise, assume that a e i o u y are vowels. For example, if the user provides the input "Harry", the program prints 2 vowels.

■■■ E6.11 Write a program that reads a word and prints all substrings, sorted by length. For example, if the user provides the input "rum", the program prints

    r
    u
    m
    ru
    um
    rum

■ E6.12 Write a program that prints all powers of 2 from 2^0 up to 2^{20}.

■■ E6.13 Write a program that reads a number and prints all of its *binary digits:* Print the remainder number % 2, then replace the number with number / 2. Keep going until the number is 0. For example, if the user provides the input 13, the output should be

    1
    0
    1
    1

■ **E6.14** Write a program that prints a multiplication table, like this:

```
1    2    3    4    5    6    7    8    9   10
2    4    6    8   10   12   14   16   18   20
3    6    9   12   15   18   21   24   27   30
.    .    .
10   20   30   40   50   60   70   80   90  100
```

■■ **E6.15** Write a program that reads an integer and displays, using asterisks, a filled and hollow square, placed next to each other. For example if the side length is 5, the program should display

```
***** *****
***** *   *
***** *   *
***** *   *
***** *****
```

■■ **E6.16** Write a program that reads an integer and displays, using asterisks, a filled diamond of the given side length. For example, if the side length is 4, the program should display

```
   *
  ***
 *****
*******
 *****
  ***
   *
```

■■ **Business E6.17** *Currency conversion*. Write a program that first asks the user to type today's price for one dollar in Japanese yen, then reads U.S. dollar values and converts each to yen. Use 0 as a sentinel.

■■ **Business E6.18** Write a program that first asks the user to type in today's price of one dollar in Japanese yen, then reads U.S. dollar values and converts each to Japanese yen. Use 0 as the sentinel value to denote the end of dollar inputs. Then the program reads a sequence of yen amounts and converts them to dollars. The second sequence is terminated by another zero value.

■■ **E6.19** *The Monty Hall Paradox*. Marilyn vos Savant described the following problem (loosely based on a game show hosted by Monty Hall) in a popular magazine: "Suppose you're on a game show, and you're given the choice of three doors: Behind one door is a car; behind the others, goats. You pick a door, say No. 1, and the host, who knows what's behind the doors, opens another door, say No. 3, which has a goat. He then says to you, "Do you want to pick door No. 2?" Is it to your advantage to switch your choice?"

Ms. vos Savant proved that it is to your advantage, but many of her readers, including some mathematics professors, disagreed, arguing that the probability would not change because another door was opened.

Your task is to simulate this game show. In each iteration, randomly pick a door number between 1 and 3 for placing the car. Randomly have the player pick a door.

Randomly have the game show host pick a door having a goat (but not the door that the player picked). Increment a counter for strategy 1 if the player wins by switching to the host's choice, and increment a counter for strategy 2 if the player wins by sticking with the original choice. Run 1,000 iterations and print both counters.

PROGRAMMING PROJECTS

■■ P6.1 *Mean and standard deviation.* Write a program that reads a set of floating-point data values. Choose an appropriate mechanism for prompting for the end of the data set.

When all values have been read, print out the count of the values, the average, and the standard deviation. The average of a data set $\{x_1, \ldots, x_n\}$ is $\bar{x} = \sum x_i / n$, where $\sum x_i = x_1 + \ldots + x_n$ is the sum of the input values. The standard deviation is

$$s = \sqrt{\frac{\sum \left(x_i - \bar{x}\right)^2}{n-1}}$$

However, this formula is not suitable for the task. By the time the program has computed $\bar{x}$, the individual x_i are long gone. Until you know how to save these values, use the numerically less stable formula

$$s = \sqrt{\frac{\sum x_i^2 - \frac{1}{n}\left(\sum x_i\right)^2}{n-1}}$$

You can compute this quantity by keeping track of the count, the sum, and the sum of squares as you process the input values.

Your program should use a class `DataSet`. That class should have a method

```
public void add(double value)
```

and methods `getAverage` and `getStandardDeviation`.

■■ P6.2 The *Fibonacci numbers* are defined by the sequence

$$f_1 = 1$$
$$f_2 = 1$$
$$f_n = f_{n-1} + f_{n-2}$$

Reformulate that as

```
fold1 = 1;
fold2 = 1;
fnew = fold1 + fold2;
```

Fibonacci numbers describe the growth of a rabbit population.

After that, discard `fold2`, which is no longer needed, and set `fold2` to `fold1` and `fold1` to `fnew`. Repeat an appropriate number of times.

Implement a program that prompts the user for an integer n and prints the nth Fibonacci number, using the above algorithm.

■■■ **P6.3** *Factoring of integers.* Write a program that asks the user for an integer and then prints out all its factors. For example, when the user enters 150, the program should print

```
2
3
5
5
```

Use a class `FactorGenerator` with a constructor `FactorGenerator(int numberToFactor)` and methods `nextFactor` and `hasMoreFactors`. Supply a class `FactorPrinter` whose `main` method reads a user input, constructs a `FactorGenerator` object, and prints the factors.

■■■ **P6.4** *Prime numbers.* Write a program that prompts the user for an integer and then prints out all prime numbers up to that integer. For example, when the user enters 20, the program should print

```
2
3
5
7
11
13
17
19
```

Recall that a number is a prime number if it is not divisible by any number except 1 and itself.

Use a class `PrimeGenerator` with methods `nextPrime` and `isPrime`. Supply a class `PrimePrinter` whose `main` method reads a user input, constructs a `PrimeGenerator` object, and prints the primes.

■■■ **P6.5** *The game of Nim.* This is a well-known game with a number of variants. The following variant has an interesting winning strategy. Two players alternately take marbles from a pile. In each move, a player chooses how many marbles to take. The player must take at least one but at most half of the marbles. Then the other player takes a turn. The player who takes the last marble loses.

Write a program in which the computer plays against a human opponent. Generate a random integer between 10 and 100 to denote the initial size of the pile. Generate a random integer between 0 and 1 to decide whether the computer or the human takes the first turn. Generate a random integer between 0 and 1 to decide whether the computer plays *smart* or *stupid*. In stupid mode the computer simply takes a random legal value (between 1 and *n*/2) from the pile whenever it has a turn. In smart mode the computer takes off enough marbles to make the size of the pile a power of two minus 1—that is, 3, 7, 15, 31, or 63. That is always a legal move, except when the size of the pile is currently one less than a power of two. In that case, the computer makes a random legal move.

You will note that the computer cannot be beaten in smart mode when it has the first move, unless the pile size happens to be 15, 31, or 63. Of course, a human player who has the first turn and knows the winning strategy can win against the computer.

■■ **P6.6** *The Drunkard's Walk.* A drunkard in a grid of streets randomly picks one of four directions and stumbles to the next intersection, then again randomly picks one of four directions, and so on. You might think that on average the drunkard doesn't move very far because the choices cancel each other out, but that is not the case.

Represent locations as integer pairs (x, y). Implement the drunkard's walk over 100 intersections, starting at $(0, 0)$, and print the ending location.

■ **P6.7** A simple random generator is obtained by the formula

$$r_{new} = (a \cdot r_{old} + b) \% m$$

and then setting r_{old} to r_{new}. If m is chosen as 2^{32}, then you can compute

$$r_{new} = a \cdot r_{old} + b$$

because the truncation of an overflowing result to the int type is equivalent to computing the remainder.

Write a program that asks the user to enter a value for r_{old}. (Such a value is often called a *seed*). Then print the first 100 random integers generated by this formula, using $a = 32310901$ and $b = 1729$.

■■ **P6.8** *The Buffon Needle Experiment.* The following experiment was devised by Comte Georges-Louis Leclerc de Buffon (1707–1788), a French naturalist. A needle of length 1 inch is dropped onto paper that is ruled with lines 2 inches apart. If the needle drops onto a line, we count it as a *hit*. (See Figure 10.) Buffon discovered that the quotient *tries/hits* approximates π.

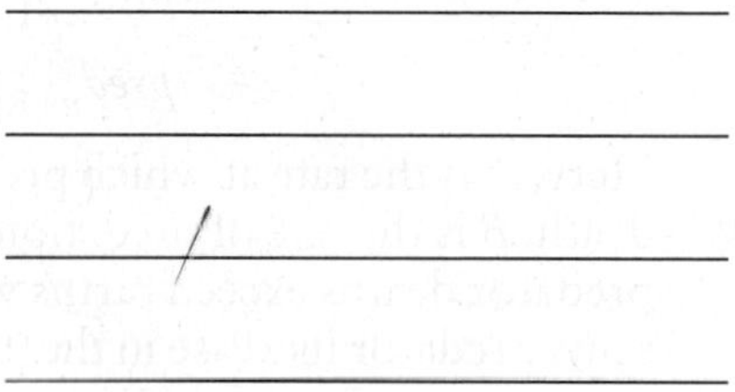

Figure 10
The Buffon Needle Experiment

For the Buffon needle experiment, you must generate two random numbers: one to describe the starting position and one to describe the angle of the needle with the x-axis. Then you need to test whether the needle touches a grid line.

Generate the *lower* point of the needle. Its x-coordinate is irrelevant, and you may assume its y-coordinate y_{low} to be any random number between 0 and 2. The angle α between the needle and the x-axis can be any value between 0 degrees and 180 degrees (π radians). The upper end of the needle has y-coordinate

$$y_{high} = y_{low} + \sin \alpha$$

The needle is a hit if y_{high} is at least 2, as shown in Figure 11. Stop after 10,000 tries and print the quotient *tries/hits*. (This program is not suitable for computing the value of π. You need π in the computation of the angle.)

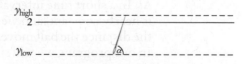

Figure 11
A Hit in the Buffon Needle Experiment

■■ Business P6.9 Your company has shares of stock it would like to sell when their value exceeds a certain target price. Write a program that reads the target price and then reads the current stock price until it is at least the target price. Your program should use a Scanner to read a sequence of double values from standard input. Once the minimum is reached, the program should report that the stock price exceeds the target price.

■■ Business P6.10 Write an application to pre-sell a limited number of cinema tickets. Each buyer can buy as many as 4 tickets. No more than 100 tickets can be sold. Implement a program called TicketSeller that prompts the user for the desired number of tickets and then displays the number of remaining tickets. Repeat until all tickets have been sold, and then display the total number of buyers.

■■ Business P6.11 You need to control the number of people who can be in an oyster bar at the same time. Groups of people can always leave the bar, but a group cannot enter the bar if they would make the number of people in the bar exceed the maximum of 100 occupants. Write a program that reads the sizes of the groups that arrive or depart. Use negative numbers for departures. After each input, display the current number of occupants. As soon as the bar holds the maximum number of people, report that the bar is full and exit the program.

■■ Science P6.12 In a predator-prey simulation, you compute the populations of predators and prey, using the following equations:

$$prey_{n+1} = prey_n \times \left(1 + A - B \times pred_n\right)$$
$$pred_{n+1} = pred_n \times \left(1 - C + D \times prey_n\right)$$

Here, A is the rate at which prey birth exceeds natural death, B is the rate of predation, C is the rate at which predator deaths exceed births without food, and D represents predator increase in the presence of food.

Write a program that prompts users for these rates, the initial population sizes, and the number of periods. Then print the populations for the given number of periods. As inputs, try $A = 0.1$, $B = C = 0.01$, and $D = 0.00002$ with initial prey and predator populations of 1,000 and 20.

■■ Science P6.13 *Projectile flight.* Suppose a cannonball is propelled straight into the air with a starting velocity v_0. Any calculus book will state that the position of the ball after t seconds is $s(t) = -\frac{1}{2}gt^2 + v_0 t$, where $g = 9.81 \text{ m/s}^2$ is the gravitational force of the earth. No calculus textbook ever mentions why someone would want to carry out such an obviously dangerous experiment, so we will do it in the safety of the computer.

In fact, we will confirm the theorem from calculus by a simulation. In our simulation, we will consider how the ball moves in very short time intervals Δt. In a short time interval the velocity v is nearly constant, and we can compute the distance the ball moves as $\Delta s = v \Delta t$. In our program, we will simply set

```
const double DELTA_T = 0.01;
```

and update the position by

```
s = s + v * DELTA_T;
```

The velocity changes constantly—in fact, it is reduced by the gravitational force of the earth. In a short time interval, $\Delta v = -g\Delta t$, we must keep the velocity updated as

```
v = v - g * DELTA_T;
```

In the next iteration the new velocity is used to update the distance.

Now run the simulation until the cannonball falls back to the earth. Get the initial velocity as an input (100 m/s is a good value). Update the position and velocity 100 times per second, but print out the position only every full second. Also printout the values from the exact formula $s(t) = -\frac{1}{2}gt^2 + v_0t$ for comparison.

Note: You may wonder whether there is a benefit to this simulation when an exact formula is available. Well, the formula from the calculus book is *not* exact. Actually, the gravitational force diminishes the farther the cannonball is away from the surface of the earth. This complicates the algebra sufficiently that it is not possible to give an exact formula for the actual motion, but the computer simulation can simply be extended to apply a variable gravitational force. For cannonballs, the calculus-book formula is actually good enough, but computers are necessary to compute accurate trajectories for higher-flying objects such as ballistic missiles.

■■■ Science P6.14   A simple model for the hull of a ship is given by

$$|y| = \frac{B}{2}\left[1 - \left(\frac{2x}{L}\right)^2\right]\left[1 - \left(\frac{z}{T}\right)^2\right]$$

where B is the beam, L is the length, and T is the draft. (*Note:* There are two values of y for each x and z because the hull is symmetric from starboard to port.)

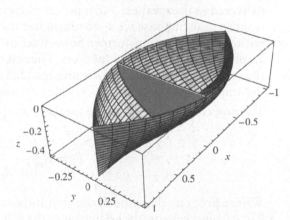

The cross-sectional area at a point x is called the "section" in nautical parlance. To compute it, let z go from 0 to $-T$ in n increments, each of size T/n. For each value of z, compute the value for y. Then sum the areas of trapezoidal strips. At right are the strips where $n = 4$.

Write a program that reads in values for B, L, T, x, and n and then prints out the cross-sectional area at x.

■ Science P6.15 Radioactive decay of radioactive materials can be modeled by the equation $A = A_0 e^{-t(\log 2/h)}$, where A is the amount of the material at time t, A_0 is the amount at time 0, and h is the half-life.

Technetium-99 is a radioisotope that is used in imaging of the brain. It has a half-life of 6 hours. Your program should display the relative amount A/A_0 in a patient body every hour for 24 hours after receiving a dose.

■ ■ ■ Science P6.16 The photo at left shows an electric device called a "transformer". Transformers are often constructed by wrapping coils of wire around a ferrite core. The figure below illustrates a situation that occurs in various audio devices such as cell phones and music players. In this circuit, a transformer is used to connect a speaker to the output of an audio amplifier.

tockphoto

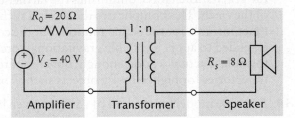

The symbol used to represent the transformer is intended to suggest two coils of wire. The parameter n of the transformer is called the "turns ratio" of the transformer. (The number of times that a wire is wrapped around the core to form a coil is called the number of turns in the coil. The turns ratio is literally the ratio of the number of turns in the two coils of wire.)

When designing the circuit, we are concerned primarily with the value of the power delivered to the speakers—that power causes the speakers to produce the sounds we want to hear. Suppose we were to connect the speakers directly to the amplifier without using the transformer. Some fraction of the power available from the amplifier would get to the speakers. The rest of the available power would be lost in the amplifier itself. The transformer is added to the circuit to increase the fraction of the amplifier power that is delivered to the speakers.

The power, P_s, delivered to the speakers is calculated using the formula

$$P_s = R_s \left(\frac{n V_s}{n^2 R_0 + R_s} \right)^2$$

Write a program that models the circuit shown and varies the turns ratio from 0.01 to 2 in 0.01 increments, then determines the value of the turns ratio that maximizes the power delivered to the speakers.

■ Graphics P6.17 Write a graphical application that displays a checkerboard with 64 squares, alternating white and black.

■ ■ ■ Graphics P6.18 Write a graphical application that draws a spiral, such as this one:

•• Graphics P6.19 It is easy and fun to draw graphs of curves with the Java graphics library. Simply draw 100 line segments joining the points $(x, f(x))$ and $(x + d, f(x + d))$, where x ranges from x_{min} to x_{max} and $d = (x_{max} - x_{min})/100$.

Draw the curve $f(x) = 0.00005x^3 - 0.03x^2 + 4x + 200$, where x ranges from 0 to 400 in this fashion.

••• Graphics P6.20 Draw a picture of the "four-leaved rose" whose equation in polar coordinates is $r = \cos(2\theta)$. Let θ go from 0 to 2π in 100 steps. Each time, compute r and then compute the (x, y) coordinates from the polar coordinates by using the formula

$$x = r \cdot \cos(\theta), \quad y = r \cdot \sin(\theta)$$

ANSWERS TO SELF-CHECK QUESTIONS

1. 23 years.

2. 8 years.

3. Add a statement

```
System.out.println(balance);
```

as the last statement in the while loop.

4. The program prints the same output. This is because the balance after 14 years is slightly below $20,000, and after 15 years, it is slightly above $20,000.

5. 2 4 8 16 32 64 128

Note that the value 128 is printed even though it is larger than 100.

6.
n	output
5	
4	4
3	3
2	2
1	1
0	0
-1	-1

7.
n	output
1	1,
2	1, 2,
3	1, 2, 3,
4	

There is a comma after the last value. Usually, commas are between values only.

8.
a	n	r	i
2	4	1	1
		2	2
		4	3
		8	4
		16	5

The code computes a^n.

9.
n	output
1	1
11	11
21	21
31	31
41	41
51	51
61	61
...	

This is an infinite loop. n is never equal to 50.

10.
count	temp
1	123
2	12.3
3	1.23

This yields the correct answer. The number 123 has 3 digits.

count	temp
1	100
2	10.0

This yields the wrong answer. The number 100 also has 3 digits. The loop condition should have been **while (temp >= 10)**.

11.
```
int year = 1;
while (year <= numberOfYears)
{
    double interest = balance * RATE / 100;
    balance = balance + interest;
    year++;
}
```

12. 11 numbers: 10 9 8 7 6 5 4 3 2 1 0

13.
```
for (int i = 10; i <= 20; i = i + 2)
{
    System.out.println(i);
}
```

14.
```
int sum = 0;
for (int i = 1; i <= n; i++)
{
    sum = sum + i;
}
```

15.
```
final int PERIODS = 5;
for (int i = 1; i <= PERIODS; i++)
{
    invest.waitYears(YEARS);
    System.out.printf(
        "The balance after %d years is %.2f\n",
        invest.getYears(), invest.getBalance());
}
```

16.
```
do
{
    System.out.print(
        "Enter a value between 0 and 100: ");
    value = in.nextInt();
}
while (value < 0 || value > 100);
```

17.
```
int value = 100;
while (value >= 100)
{
    System.out.print("Enter a value < 100: ");
    value = in.nextInt();
}
```

Here, the variable value had to be initialized with an artificial value to ensure that the loop is entered at least once.

18. Yes. The do loop

do { *body* } while (*condition*);

is equivalent to this while loop:

```
boolean first = true;
while (first || condition)
{
    body;
    first = false;
}
```

19.
```
int x;
int sum = 0;
do
{
    x = in.nextInt();
    sum = sum + x;
}
while (x != 0);
```

20.
```
int x = 0;
int previous;
do
{
    previous = x;
    x = in.nextInt();
    sum = sum + x;
}
while (x != 0 && previous != x);
```

21. No data

22. The first check ends the loop after the sentinel has been read. The second check ensures that the sentinel is not processed as an input value.

23. The while loop would never be entered. The user would never be prompted for input. Because count stays 0, the program would then print "No data".

24. The nextDouble method also returns false. A more accurate prompt would have been: "Enter values, a key other than a digit to quit:" But that might be more confusing to the program user who would need to ponder which key to choose.

25. If the user doesn't provide any numeric input, the first call to in.nextDouble() will fail.

26. *Computing the average*

```
Enter scores, Q to quit: 90 80 90 100 80 Q
The average is 88
(Program exits)
```

27. *Simple conversion*

```
                                          Only one value can be converted
Your conversion question: How many in are 30 cm
30 cm = 11.81 in
(Program exits)          Run program again for another question
```

Unknown unit

```
Your conversion question: How many inches are 30 cm?
Unknown unit: inches
Known units are in, ft, mi, mm, cm, m, km, oz, lb, g, kg, tsp, tbsp, pint, gal
(Program exits)
```

Program doesn't understand question syntax

```
Your conversion question: What is an ångström?
Please formulate your question as "How many (unit) are (value) (unit)?"
(Program exits)
```

28. *One score is not enough*

```
Enter scores, Q to quit: 90 Q
Error: At least two scores are required.
(Program exits)
```

29. It would not be possible to implement this interface using the Java features we have covered up to this point. There is no way for the program to know when the first set of inputs ends. (When you read numbers with value = in.nextDouble(), it is your choice

whether to put them on a single line or multiple lines.)

30. *Comparing two interest rates*

First interest rate in percent: *5*
Second interest rate in percent: *10*
Years: *5*

Year	5%	10%
0	10000.00	10000.00
1	10500.00	11000.00
2	11025.00	12100.00
3	11576.25	13310.00
4	12155.06	14641.00
5	12762.82	16105.10

This row clarifies that 1 means the end of the first year

31. The total is zero.

32.
```
double total = 0;
while (in.hasNextDouble())
{
    double input = in.nextDouble();
    if (input > 0) { total = total + input; }
}
```

33. position is str.length() and ch is unchanged from its initial value, '?'. Note that ch must be initialized with some value—otherwise the compiler will complain about a possibly uninitialized variable.

34. The loop will stop when a match is found, but you cannot access the match because neither position nor ch are defined outside the loop.

35. Start the loop at the end of string:
```
boolean found = false;
int i = str.length() - 1;
while (!found && i >= 0)
{
    char ch = str.charAt(i);
    if (ch == ' ') { found = true; }
    else { i--; }
}
```

36. The initial call to in.nextDouble() fails, terminating the program. One solution is to do all input in the loop and introduce a Boolean variable that checks whether the loop is entered for the first time.
```
double input = 0;
boolean first = true;
while (in.hasNextDouble())
{
    double previous = input;
    input = in.nextDouble();
    if (first) { first = false; }
    else if (input == previous)
    {
```
```
        System.out.println("Duplicate input");
    }
}
```

37. All values in the inner loop should be displayed on the same line.

38. Change lines 13, 18, and 30 to for (int n = 0; n <= NMAX; n++). Change NMAX to 5.

39. 60: The outer loop is executed 10 times, and the inner loop 6 times.

40. 0123
1234
2345

41.
```
for (int i = 1; i <= 3; i++)
{
    for (int j = 1; j <= 4; j++)
    {
        System.out.print("[]");
    }
    System.out.println();
}
```

42. Compute generator.nextInt(2), and use 0 for heads, 1 for tails, or the other way around.

43. Compute generator.nextInt(4) and associate the numbers 0 . . . 3 with the four suits. Then compute generator.nextInt(13) and associate the numbers 0 . . . 12 with Jack, Ace, 2 . . . 10, Queen, and King.

44. Construct two Die objects:
```
Die d1 = new Die(6);
Die d2 = new Die(6);
```
Then cast and print both of them:
```
System.out.println(
    d1.cast() + " " + d2.cast());
```

45. The call will produce a value between 2 and 12, but all values have the same probability. When throwing a pair of dice, the number 7 is six times as likely as the number 2. The correct formula is
```
int sum = generator.nextInt(6)
    + generator.nextInt(6) + 2;
```

46. generator.nextDouble() * 100.0

47. You should step over it because you are not interested in debugging the internals of the println method.

48. You should set a breakpoint. Stepping through loops can be tedious.

49. Unfortunately, most debuggers do not support going backwards. Instead, you must restart the program. Try setting breakpoints at the lines in which the variable is changed.

50. No, there is no need. You can just inspect the variables in the debugger.

51. For short programs, you certainly could. But when programs get longer, it would be very time-consuming to trace them manually.

CHAPTER 7

ARRAYS AND ARRAY LISTS

To collect elements using arrays and array lists

To use the enhanced for loop for traversing arrays and array lists

To learn common algorithms for processing arrays and array lists

To work with two-dimensional arrays

To understand the concept of regression testing

In many programs, you need to collect large numbers of values. In Java, you use the array and array list constructs for this purpose. Arrays have a more concise syntax, whereas array lists can automatically grow to any desired size. In this chapter, you will learn about arrays, array lists, and common algorithms for processing them.

7.1 Arrays

We start this chapter by introducing the array data type. Arrays are the fundamental mechanism in Java for collecting multiple values. In the following sections, you will learn how to declare arrays and how to access array elements.

7.1.1 Declaring and Using Arrays

Suppose you write a program that reads a sequence of values and prints out the sequence, marking the largest value, like this:

```
32
54
67.5
29
35
80
115 <= largest value
44.5
100
65
```

You do not know which value to mark as the largest one until you have seen them all. After all, the last value might be the largest one. Therefore, the program must first store all values before it can print them.

Could you simply store each value in a separate variable? If you know that there are ten values, then you could store the values in ten variables value1, value2, value3, ..., value10. However, such a sequence of variables is not very practical to use. You would have to write quite a bit of code ten times, once for each of the variables. In Java, an **array** is a much better choice for storing a sequence of values of the same type.

> An array collects a sequence of values of the same type.

Here we create an array that can hold ten values of type double:

```
new double[10]
```

The number of elements (here, 10) is called the *length* of the array.

The new operator constructs the array. You will want to store the array in a variable so that you can access it later.

The type of an array variable is the type of the element to be stored, followed by []. In this example, the type is double[], because the element type is double.

Here is the declaration of an array variable of type double[] (see Figure 1):

```
double[] values; ❶
```

When you declare an array variable, it is not yet initialized. You need to initialize the variable with the array:

```
double[] values = new double[10]; ❷
```

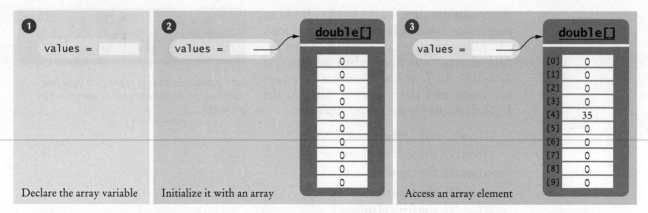

Figure 1 An Array of Size 10

Now `values` is initialized with an array of 10 numbers. By default, each number in the array is 0.

When you declare an array, you can specify the initial values. For example,

```
double[] moreValues = { 32, 54, 67.5, 29, 35, 80, 115, 44.5, 100, 65 };
```

When you supply initial values, you don't use the `new` operator. The compiler determines the length of the array by counting the initial values.

To access a value in an array, you specify which "slot" you want to use. That is done with the `[]` operator:

> Individual elements in an array are accessed by an integer index i, using the notation *array*[i].

```
values[4] = 35; ❸
```

Now the number 4 slot of `values` is filled with 35 (see Figure 1). This "slot number" is called an *index*. Each slot in an array contains an *element*.

Because `values` is an array of `double` values, each element `values[i]` can be used like any variable of type `double`. For example, you can display the element with index 4 with the following command:

> An array element can be used like any variable.

```
System.out.println(values[4]);
```

Syntax 7.1 Arrays

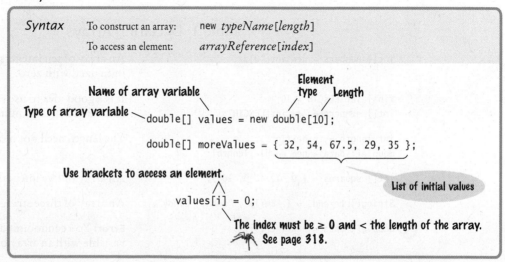

Before continuing, we must take care of an important detail of Java arrays. If you look carefully at Figure 1, you will find that the *fifth* element was filled when we changed values[4]. In Java, the elements of arrays are numbered *starting at 0*. That is, the legal elements for the values array are

Like a mailbox that is identified by a box number, an array element is identified by an index.

values[0], the first element

values[1], the second element

values[2], the third element

values[3], the fourth element

values[4], the fifth element

...

values[9], the tenth element

In other words, the declaration

```
double[] values = new double[10];
```

creates an array with ten elements. In this array, an index can be any integer ranging from 0 to 9.

> An array index must be at least zero and less than the size of the array.

You have to be careful that the index stays within the valid range. Trying to access an element that does not exist in the array is a serious error. For example, if values has ten elements, you are not allowed to access values[20]. Attempting to access an element whose index is not within the valid index range is called a **bounds error**. The compiler does not catch this type of error. When a bounds error occurs at run time, it causes a run-time exception.

Here is a very common bounds error:

> A bounds error, which occurs if you supply an invalid array index, can cause your program to terminate.

```
double[] values = new double[10];
values[10] = value;
```

There is no values[10] in an array with ten elements — the index can range from 0 to 9.

To avoid bounds errors, you will want to know how many elements are in an array. The expression values.length yields the length of the values array. Note that there are no parentheses following length.

Table 1 Declaring Arrays

`int[] numbers = new int[10];`	An array of ten integers. All elements are initialized with zero.
`final int LENGTH = 10;` `int[] numbers = new int[LENGTH];`	It is a good idea to use a named constant instead of a "magic number".
`int length = in.nextInt();` `double[] data = new double[length];`	The length need not be a constant.
`int[] squares = { 0, 1, 4, 9, 16 };`	An array of five integers, with initial values.
`String[] friends = { "Emily", "Bob", "Cindy" };`	An array of three strings.
🚫 `double[] data = new int[10];`	**Error:** You cannot initialize a double[] variable with an array of type int[].

The following code ensures that you only access the array when the index variable i is within the legal bounds:

Use the expression array.length to find the number of elements in an array.

```
if (0 <= i && i < values.length) { values[i] = value; }
```

Arrays suffer from a significant limitation: *their length is fixed.* If you start out with an array of 10 elements and later decide that you need to add additional elements, then you need to make a new array and copy all elements of the existing array into the new array. We will discuss this process in detail in Section 7.3.9.

To visit all elements of an array, use a variable for the index. Suppose values has ten elements and the integer variable i is set to 0, 1, 2, and so on, up to 9. Then the expression values[i] yields each element in turn. For example, this loop displays all elements in the values array:

```
for (int i = 0; i < 10; i++)
{
    System.out.println(values[i]);
}
```

Note that in the loop condition the index is *less than* 10 because there is no element corresponding to values[10].

7.1.2 Array References

If you look closely at Figure 1, you will note that the variable values does not store any numbers. Instead, the array is stored elsewhere and the values variable holds a **reference** to the array. (The reference denotes the location of the array in memory.) You have already seen this behavior with objects in Section 2.8. When you access an object or array, you need not be concerned about the fact that Java uses references. This only becomes important when you copy a reference.

An array reference specifies the location of an array. Copying the reference yields a second reference to the same array.

When you copy an array variable into another, both variables refer to the same array (see Figure 2).

```
int[] scores = { 10, 9, 7, 4, 5 };
int[] values = scores; // Copying array reference
```

You can modify the array through either of the variables:

```
scores[3] = 10;
System.out.println(values[3]); // Prints 10
```

Section 7.3.9 shows how you can make a copy of the *contents* of the array.

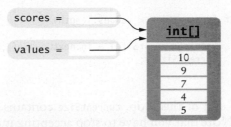

Figure 2
Two Array Variables Referencing the Same Array

7.1.3 Using Arrays with Methods

Arrays can be method arguments and return values, just like any other values.

> Arrays can occur as method arguments and return values.

When you define a method with an array argument, you provide a parameter variable for the array. For example, the following method adds scores to a student object:

```java
public void addScores(int[] values)
{
    for (int i = 0; i < values.length; i++)
    {
        totalScore = totalScore + values[i];
    }
}
```

To call this method, you have to provide an array:

```java
int[] scores = { 10, 9, 7, 10 };
fred.addScores(scores);
```

Conversely, a method can return an array. For example, a Student class can have a method

```java
public int[] getScores()
```

that returns an array with all of the student's scores.

7.1.4 Partially Filled Arrays

With a partially filled array, you need to remember how many elements are filled.

An array cannot change size at run time. This is a problem when you don't know in advance how many elements you need. In that situation, you must come up with a good guess on the maximum number of elements that you need to store. For example, we may decide that we sometimes want to store more than ten elements, but never more than 100:

```java
final int LENGTH = 100;
double[] values = new double[LENGTH];
```

In a typical program run, only a part of the array will be occupied by actual elements. We call such an array a **partially filled array**. You must keep a *companion variable* that counts how many elements are actually used. In Figure 3 we call the companion variable currentSize.

The following loop collects inputs and fills up the values array:

```java
int currentSize = 0;
Scanner in = new Scanner(System.in);
while (in.hasNextDouble())
{
    if (currentSize < values.length)
    {
        values[currentSize] = in.nextDouble();
        currentSize++;
    }
}
```

> With a partially filled array, keep a companion variable for the current size.

At the end of this loop, currentSize contains the actual number of elements in the array. Note that you have to stop accepting inputs if the currentSize companion variable reaches the array length.

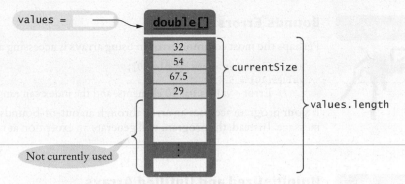

Figure 3 A Partially Filled Array

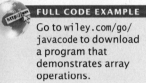
FULL CODE EXAMPLE
Go to wiley.com/go/
javacode to download
a program that
demonstrates array
operations.

To process the gathered array elements, you again use the companion variable, not the array length. This loop prints the partially filled array:

```
for (int i = 0; i < currentSize; i++)
{
    System.out.println(values[i]);
}
```

SELF CHECK

1. Declare an array of integers containing the first five prime numbers.

2. Assume the array primes has been initialized as described in Self Check 1. What does it contain after executing the following loop?

```
for (int i = 0; i < 2; i++)
{
    primes[4 - 1] = primes[1];
}
```

3. Assume the array primes has been initialized as described in Self Check 1. What does it contain after executing the following loop?

```
for (int i = 0; i < 5; i++)
{
    primes[i]++;
}
```

4. Given the declaration

```
int[] values = new int[10];
```

write statements to put the integer 10 into the elements of the array values with the lowest and the highest valid index.

5. Declare an array called words that can hold ten elements of type String.

6. Declare an array containing two strings, "Yes", and "No".

7. Can you produce the output on page 312 without storing the inputs in an array, by using an algorithm similar to the algorithm for finding the maximum in Section 6.7.5?

8. Declare a method of a class Lottery that returns a combination of n numbers. You don't need to implement the method.

Practice It Now you can try these exercises at the end of the chapter: R7.1, R7.2, R7.6, E7.1.

Common Error 7.1

Bounds Errors

Perhaps the most common error in using arrays is accessing a nonexistent element.

```
double[] values = new double[10];
values[10] = 5.4;
    // Error—values has 10 elements, and the index can range from 0 to 9
```

If your program accesses an array through an out-of-bounds index, there is no compiler error message. Instead, the program will generate an exception at run time.

Common Error 7.2

Uninitialized and Unfilled Arrays

A common error is to allocate an array variable, but not an actual array.

```
double[] values;
values[0] = 29.95; // Error—values not initialized
```

Array variables work exactly like object variables—they are only references to the actual array. To construct the actual array, you must use the new operator:

```
double[] values = new double[10];
```

Another common error is to allocate an array of objects and expect it to be filled with objects.

```
BankAccount[] accounts = new BankAccount[10]; // Contains ten null references
```

This array contains null references, not default bank accounts. You need to remember to fill the array, for example:

```
for (int i = 0; i < 10; i++)
{
    accounts[i] = new BankAccount();
}
```

Programming Tip 7.1

Use Arrays for Sequences of Related Items

Arrays are intended for storing sequences of values with the same meaning. For example, an array of test scores makes perfect sense:

```
int[] scores = new int[NUMBER_OF_SCORES];
```

But an array

```
int[] personalData = new int[3];
```

that holds a person's age, bank balance, and shoe size in positions 0, 1, and 2 is bad design. It would be tedious for the programmer to remember which of these data values is stored in which array location. In this situation, it is far better to use three separate variables.

Programming Tip 7.2

Make Parallel Arrays into Arrays of Objects

Programmers who are familiar with arrays, but unfamiliar with object-oriented programming, sometimes distribute information across separate arrays. Here is a typical example: A program needs to manage bank data, consisting of account numbers and balances. Don't store the account numbers and balances in separate arrays.

```
// Don't do this
int[] accountNumbers;
double[] balances;
```

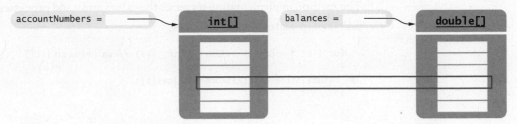

Figure 4 Avoid Parallel Arrays

Arrays such as these are called **parallel arrays** (see Figure 4). The ith slice (accountNumbers[i] and balances[i]) contains data that need to be processed together.

If you find yourself using two arrays that have the same length, ask yourself whether you couldn't replace them with a single array of a class type. Look at a slice and find the concept that it represents. Then make the concept into a class. In our example each slice contains an account number and a balance, describing a bank account. Therefore, it is an easy matter to use a single array of objects

> Avoid parallel arrays by changing them into arrays of objects.

```
BankAccount[] accounts;
```

(See Figure 5.)

Why is this beneficial? Think ahead. Maybe your program will change and you will need to store the owner of the bank account as well. It is a simple matter to update the BankAccount class. It may well be quite complicated to add a new array and make sure that all methods that accessed the original two arrays now also correctly access the third one.

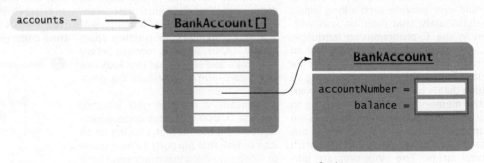

Figure 5 Reorganizing Parallel Arrays into an Array of Objects

Special Topic 7.1

Methods with a Variable Number of Arguments

It is possible to declare methods that receive a variable number of arguments. For example, we can write a method that can add an arbitrary number of scores to a student:

```
fred.addScores(10, 7); // This method call has two arguments
fred.addScores(1, 7, 2, 9); // Another call to the same method, now with four arguments
```

The method must be declared as

```
public void addScores(int... values)
```

The int... type indicates that the method can receive any number of int arguments. The values parameter variable is actually an int[] array that contains all arguments that were passed to the method.

The method implementation traverses the values array and processes the elements:

```
public void addScores(int... values)
{
   for (int i = 0; i < values.length; i++) // values is an int[]
   {
      totalScore = totalScore + values[i];
   }
}
```

Computing & Society 7.1 Computer Viruses

In November 1988, Robert Morris, a student at Cornell University, launched a so-called virus program that infected a significant fraction of computers connected to the Internet (which was much smaller then than it is now).

In order to attack a computer, a virus has to find a way to get its instructions executed. This particular program carried out a "buffer overrun" attack, providing an unexpectedly large input to a program on another machine. That program allocated an array of 512 characters, under the assumption that nobody would ever provide such a long input. Unfortunately, that program was written in the C programming language. C, unlike Java, does not check that an array index is less than the length of the array. If you write into an array using an index that is too large, you simply overwrite memory locations that belong to some other objects. C programmers are supposed to provide safety checks, but that had not happened in the program under attack. The virus program purposefully filled the 512-character array with 536 bytes. The excess 24 bytes overwrote a return address, which the attacker knew was stored just after the array. When the method that read the input was finished, it didn't return to its caller but to code supplied by the virus (see the figure). The virus was thus able to execute its code on a remote machine and infect it.

In Java, as in C, all programmers must be very careful not to overrun array boundaries. However, in Java, this error causes a run-time exception, and it never corrupts memory outside the array. This is one of the safety features of Java. One may well speculate what would possess the virus author to spend weeks designing a program that disabled thousands of computers. It appears that the break-in was fully intended by the author, but the disabling of the computers was a bug caused by continuous reinfection. Morris was sentenced to 3 years probation, 400 hours of community service, and a $10,000 fine.

In recent years, computer attacks have intensified and the motives have become more sinister. Instead of disabling computers, viruses often take permanent residence in the attacked computers. Criminal enterprises rent out the processing power of millions of hijacked computers for sending spam e-mail. Other viruses monitor every keystroke and send those that look like credit card numbers or banking passwords to their master.

Typically, a machine gets infected because a user executes code downloaded from the Internet, clicking on an icon or link that purports to be a game or video clip. Antivirus programs check all downloaded programs against an ever-growing list of known viruses.

When you use a computer for managing your finances, you need to be aware of the risk of infection. If a virus reads your banking password and empties your account, you will have a hard time convincing your financial institution that it wasn't your act, and you will most likely lose your money. Keep your operating system and antivirus program up to date, and don't click on suspicious links on a web page or your e-mail inbox. Use banks that require "two-factor authentication" for major transactions, such as a callback on your cell phone.

Viruses are even used for military purposes. In 2010, a virus, dubbed Stuxnet, spread through Microsoft Windows and infected USB sticks. The virus looked for Siemens industrial computers and reprogrammed them in subtle ways. It appears that the virus was designed to damage the centrifuges of the Iranian nuclear enrichment operation. The computers controlling the centrifuges were not connected to the Internet, but they were configured with USB sticks, some of which were infected. It is rumored that the virus was developed by U.S. and Israeli intelligence agencies, and that it was successful in slowing down the Iranian nuclear program.

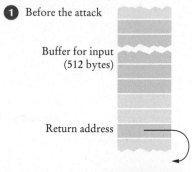

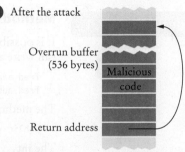

A "Buffer Overrun" Attack

7.2 The Enhanced for Loop

Often, you need to visit all elements of an array. The *enhanced* for *loop* makes this process particularly easy to program.

You can use the enhanced for loop to visit all elements of an array.

Here is how you use the enhanced for loop to total up all elements in an array named values:

```java
double[] values = . . .;
double total = 0;
for (double element : values)
{
    total = total + element;
}
```

The loop body is executed for each element in the array values. At the beginning of each loop iteration, the next element is assigned to the variable element. Then the loop body is executed. You should read this loop as "for each element in values".

This loop is equivalent to the following for loop and an explicit index variable:

```java
for (int i = 0; i < values.length; i++)
{
    double element = values[i];
    total = total + element;
}
```

Note an important difference between the enhanced for loop and the basic for loop. In the enhanced for loop, the *element variable* is assigned values[0], values[1], and so on. In the basic for loop, the *index variable* i is assigned 0, 1, and so on.

Use the enhanced for loop if you do not need the index values in the loop body.

Keep in mind that the enhanced for loop has a very specific purpose: getting the elements of a collection, from the beginning to the end. It is not suitable for all array algorithms. In particular, the enhanced for loop does not allow you to modify the contents of an array. The following loop does not fill an array with zeroes:

```java
for (double element : values)
{
    element = 0; // ERROR: this assignment does not modify array elements
}
```

When the loop is executed, the variable element is set to values[0]. Then element is set to 0, then to values[1], then to 0, and so on. The values array is not modified. The remedy is simple: Use a basic for loop:

```java
for (int i = 0; i < values.length; i++)
{
    values[i] = 0; // OK
}
```

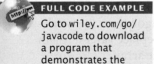

FULL CODE EXAMPLE

Go to wiley.com/go/javacode to download a program that demonstrates the enhanced for loop.

The enhanced for *loop is a convenient mechanism for traversing all elements in a collection.*

Syntax 7.2 The Enhanced for Loop

```
Syntax        for (typeName variable : collection)
              {
                  statements
              }
```

This variable is set in each loop iteration.
It is only defined inside the loop.

An array

```
for (double element : values)
{
    sum = sum + element;
}
```

These statements are executed for each element.

The variable contains an element, not an index.

SELF CHECK

9. What does this enhanced for loop do?

```
int counter = 0;
for (double element : values)
{
    if (element == 0) { counter++; }
}
```

10. Write an enhanced for loop that prints all elements in the array values.

11. Write an enhanced for loop that multiplies all elements in a double[] array named factors, accumulating the result in a variable named product.

12. Why is the enhanced for loop not an appropriate shortcut for the following basic for loop?

```
for (int i = 0; i < values.length; i++) { values[i] = i * i; }
```

Practice It   Now you can try these exercises at the end of the chapter: R7.7, R7.8, R7.9.

7.3 Common Array Algorithms

In the following sections, we discuss some of the most common algorithms for working with arrays. If you use a partially filled array, remember to replace values.length with the companion variable that represents the current size of the array.

7.3.1 Filling

This loop fills an array with squares (0, 1, 4, 9, 16, ...). Note that the element with index 0 contains 0^2, the element with index 1 contains 1^2, and so on.

```
for (int i = 0; i < values.length; i++)
{
    values[i] = i * i;
}
```

7.3.2 Sum and Average Value

You have already encountered this algorithm in Section 6.7.1. When the values are located in an array, the code looks much simpler:

```
double total = 0;
for (double element : values)
{
    total = total + element;
}
double average = 0;
if (values.length > 0) { average = total / values.length; }
```

7.3.3 Maximum and Minimum

Use the algorithm from Section 6.7.5 that keeps a variable for the largest element already encountered. Here is the implementation of that algorithm for an array:

```
double largest = values[0];
for (int i = 1; i < values.length; i++)
{
    if (values[i] > largest)
    {
        largest = values[i];
    }
}
```

Note that the loop starts at 1 because we initialize largest with values[0].

To compute the smallest element, reverse the comparison.

These algorithms require that the array contain at least one element.

7.3.4 Element Separators

When separating elements, don't place a separator before the first element.

When you display the elements of an array, you usually want to separate them, often with commas or vertical lines, like this:

```
32 | 54 | 67.5 | 29 | 35
```

Note that there is one fewer separator than there are numbers. Print the separator before each element in the sequence *except the initial one* (with index 0) like this:

```
for (int i = 0; i < values.length; i++)
{
    if (i > 0)
    {
        System.out.print(" | ");
    }
    System.out.print(values[i]);
}
```

To print five elements, you need four separators.

If you want comma separators, you can use the Arrays.toString method. (You'll need to import java.util.Arrays.) The expression

```
Arrays.toString(values)
```

returns a string describing the contents of the array values in the form

```
[32, 54, 67.5, 29, 35]
```

The elements are surrounded by a pair of brackets and separated by commas. This method can be convenient for debugging:

```java
System.out.println("values=" + Arrays.toString(values));
```

7.3.5 Linear Search

To search for a specific element, visit the elements and stop when you encounter the match.

You often need to search for the position of a specific element in an array so that you can replace or remove it. Visit all elements until you have found a match or you have come to the end of the array. Here we search for the position of the first element in an array that is equal to 100:

```java
int searchedValue = 100;
int pos = 0;
boolean found = false;
while (pos < values.length && !found)
{
    if (values[pos] == searchedValue)
    {
        found = true;
    }
    else
    {
        pos++;
    }
}
if (found) { System.out.println("Found at position: " + pos); }
else { System.out.println("Not found"); }
```

A linear search inspects elements in sequence until a match is found.

This algorithm is called **linear search** or *sequential search* because you inspect the elements in sequence. If the array is sorted, you can use the more efficient **binary search** algorithm. We discuss binary search in Chapter 14.

7.3.6 Removing an Element

Suppose you want to remove the element with index pos from the array values. As explained in Section 7.1.4, you need a companion variable for tracking the number of elements in the array. In this example, we use a companion variable called currentSize.

If the elements in the array are not in any particular order, simply overwrite the element to be removed with the *last* element of the array, then decrement the currentSize variable. (See Figure 6.)

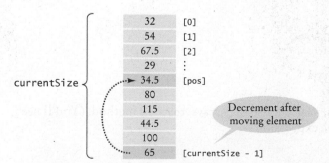

Figure 6
Removing an Element in an Unordered Array

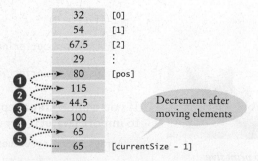

Figure 7
Removing an Element in an Ordered Array

```
values[pos] = values[currentSize - 1];
currentSize--;
```

ANIMATION
*Removing from
an Array*

The situation is more complex if the order of the elements matters. Then you must move all elements following the element to be removed to a lower index, and then decrement the variable holding the size of the array. (See Figure 7.)

```
for (int i = pos + 1; i < currentSize; i++)
{
    values[i - 1] = values[i];
}
currentSize--;
```

7.3.7 Inserting an Element

ANIMATION
*Inserting into
an Array*

In this section, you will see how to insert an element into an array. Note that you need a companion variable for tracking the array size, as explained in Section 7.1.4.

If the order of the elements does not matter, you can simply insert new elements at the end, incrementing the variable tracking the size.

```
if (currentSize < values.length)
{
    currentSize++;
    values[currentSize - 1] = newElement;
}
```

It is more work to insert an element at a particular position in the middle of an array. First, move all elements after the insertion location to a higher index. Then insert the new element (see Figure 9).

Note the order of the movement: When you remove an element, you first move the next element to a lower index, then the one after that, until you finally get to the end of the array. When you insert an element, you start at the end of the array, move that element to a higher index, then move the one before that, and so on until you finally get to the insertion location.

Before inserting an element, move elements to the end of the array *starting with the last one.*

```
if (currentSize < values.length)
{
    currentSize++;
    for (int i = currentSize - 1; i > pos; i--)
    {
        values[i] = values[i - 1];
    }
    values[pos] = newElement;
}
```

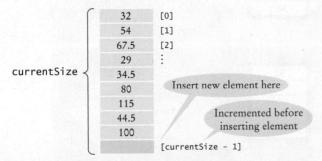

Figure 8
Inserting an Element in an Unordered Array

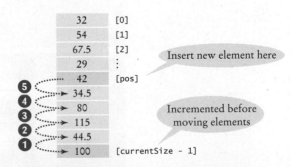

Figure 9
Inserting an Element in an Ordered Array

7.3.8 Swapping Elements

You often need to swap elements of an array. For example, you can sort an array by repeatedly swapping elements that are not in order.

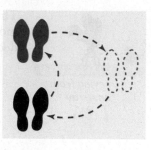

Consider the task of swapping the elements at positions i and j of an array values. We'd like to set values[i] to values[j]. But that overwrites the value that is currently stored in values[i], so we want to save that first:

```
double temp = values[i];
values[i] = values[j];
```

Now we can set values[j] to the saved value.

```
values[j] = temp;
```

Figure 10 shows the process.

Use a temporary variable when swapping two elements.

To swap two elements, you need a temporary variable.

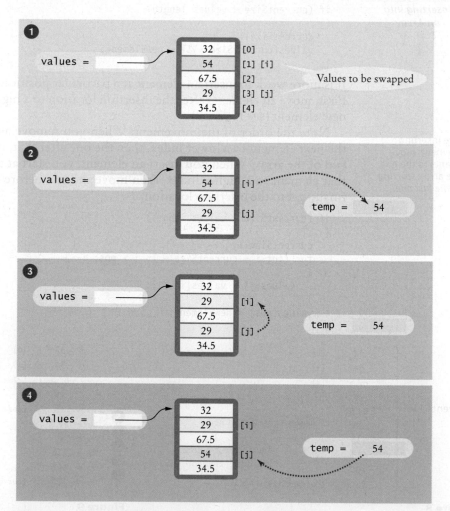

Figure 10 Swapping Array Elements

7.3.9 Copying Arrays

Array variables do not themselves hold array elements. They hold a reference to the actual array. If you copy the reference, you get another reference to the same array (see Figure 11):

```
double[] values = new double[6];
. . . // Fill array
double[] prices = values;  ❶
```

If you want to make a true copy of an array, call the Arrays.copyOf method (as shown in Figure 11).

Use the Arrays.
copyOf method to
copy the elements of
an array into a
new array.

```
double[] prices = Arrays.copyOf(values, values.length);  ❷
```

The call Arrays.copyOf(values, n) allocates an array of length n, copies the first n elements of values (or the entire values array if n > values.length) into it, and returns the new array.

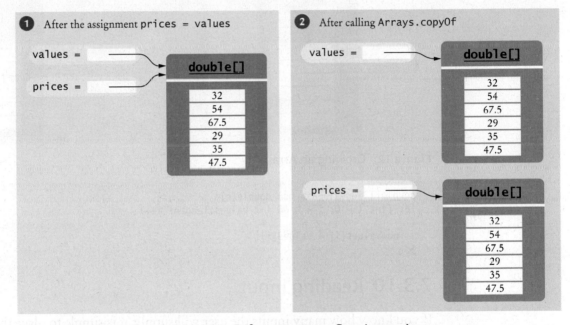

Figure 11 Copying an Array Reference versus Copying an Array

In order to use the Arrays class, you need to add the following statement to the top of your program:

```
import java.util.Arrays;
```

Another use for Arrays.copyOf is to grow an array that has run out of space. The following statements have the effect of doubling the length of an array (see Figure 12):

```
double[] newValues = Arrays.copyOf(values, 2 * values.length);  ❶
values = newValues;  ❷
```

The copyOf method was added in Java 6. If you use Java 5, replace

```
double[] newValues = Arrays.copyOf(values, n)
```

with

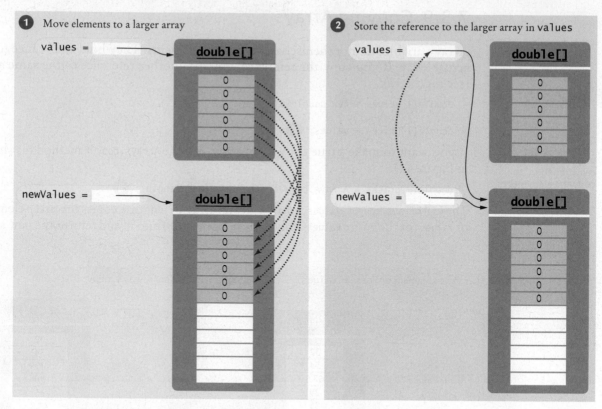

Figure 12   Growing an Array

```
double[] newValues = new double[n];
for (int i = 0; i < n && i < values.length; i++)
{
    newValues[i] = values[i];
}
```

7.3.10 Reading Input

If you know how many inputs the user will supply, it is simple to place them into an array:

```
double[] inputs = new double[NUMBER_OF_INPUTS];
for (i = 0; i < inputs.length; i++)
{
    inputs[i] = in.nextDouble();
}
```

However, this technique does not work if you need to read a sequence of arbitrary length. In that case, add the inputs to an array until the end of the input has been reached.

```
int currentSize = 0;
while (in.hasNextDouble() && currentSize < inputs.length)
{
    inputs[currentSize] = in.nextDouble();
    currentSize++;
}
```

Now `inputs` is a partially filled array, and the companion variable `currentSize` is set to the number of inputs.

However, this loop silently throws away inputs that don't fit into the array. A better approach is to grow the array to hold all inputs.

```
double[] inputs = new double[INITIAL_SIZE];
int currentSize = 0;
while (in.hasNextDouble())
{
    // Grow the array if it has been completely filled
    if (currentSize >= inputs.length)
    {
        inputs = Arrays.copyOf(inputs, 2 * inputs.length); // Grow the inputs array
    }

    inputs[currentSize] = in.nextDouble();
    currentSize++;
}
```

When you are done, you can discard any excess (unfilled) elements:

```
inputs = Arrays.copyOf(inputs, currentSize);
```

The following program puts these algorithms to work, solving the task that we set ourselves at the beginning of this chapter: to mark the largest value in an input sequence.

section_3/LargestInArray.java

```
1   import java.util.Scanner;
2
3   /**
4       This program reads a sequence of values and prints them, marking the largest value.
5   */
6   public class LargestInArray
7   {
8       public static void main(String[] args)
9       {
10          final int LENGTH = 100;
11          double[] values = new double[LENGTH];
12          int currentSize = 0;
13
14          // Read inputs
15
16          System.out.println("Please enter values, Q to quit:");
17          Scanner in = new Scanner(System.in);
18          while (in.hasNextDouble() && currentSize < values.length)
19          {
20              values[currentSize] = in.nextDouble();
21              currentSize++;
22          }
23
24          // Find the largest value
25
26          double largest = values[0];
27          for (int i = 1; i < currentSize; i++)
28          {
29              if (values[i] > largest)
30              {
31                  largest = values[i];
32              }
33          }
```

```
34
35        // Print all values, marking the largest
36
37        for (int i = 0; i < currentSize; i++)
38        {
39            System.out.print(values[i]);
40            if (values[i] == largest)
41            {
42                System.out.print(" <== largest value");
43            }
44            System.out.println();
45        }
46    }
47 }
```

Program Run

```
Please enter values, Q to quit:
34.5 80 115 44.5 Q
34.5
80
115 <== largest value
44.5
```

SELF CHECK

13. Given these inputs, what is the output of the LargestInArray program?

    ```
    20 10 20 Q
    ```

14. Write a loop that counts how many elements in an array are equal to zero.

15. Consider the algorithm to find the largest element in an array. Why don't we initialize largest and i with zero, like this?

    ```
    double largest = 0;
    for (int i = 0; i < values.length; i++)
    {
        if (values[i] > largest)
        {
            largest = values[i];
        }
    }
    ```

16. When printing separators, we skipped the separator before the initial element. Rewrite the loop so that the separator is printed *after* each element, except for the last element.

17. What is wrong with these statements for printing an array with separators?

    ```
    System.out.print(values[0]);
    for (int i = 1; i < values.length; i++)
    {
        System.out.print(", " + values[i]);
    }
    ```

18. When finding the position of a match, we used a while loop, not a for loop. What is wrong with using this loop instead?

    ```
    for (pos = 0; pos < values.length && !found; pos++)
    {
        if (values[pos] > 100)
        {
            found = true;
        }
    ```

}

19. When inserting an element into an array, we moved the elements with larger index values, starting at the end of the array. Why is it wrong to start at the insertion location, like this?

```
for (int i = pos; i < currentSize - 1; i++)
{
    values[i + 1] = values[i];
}
```

Practice It   Now you can try these exercises at the end of the chapter: R7.15, R7.18, E7.8.

Common Error 7.3

Underestimating the Size of a Data Set

Programmers commonly underestimate the amount of input data that a user will pour into an unsuspecting program. Suppose you write a program to search for text in a file. You store each line in a string, and keep an array of strings. How big do you make the array? Surely nobody is going to challenge your program with an input that is more than 100 lines. Really? It is very easy to feed in the entire text of *Alice in Wonderland* or *War and Peace* (which are available on the Internet). All of a sudden, your program has to deal with tens or hundreds of thousands of lines. You either need to allow for large inputs or politely reject the excess input.

Special Topic 7.2

Sorting with the Java Library

Sorting an array efficiently is not an easy task. You will learn in Chapter 14 how to implement efficient sorting algorithms. Fortunately, the Java library provides an efficient sort method.

To sort an array values, call

```
Arrays.sort(values);
```

If the array is partially filled, call

```
Arrays.sort(values, 0, currentSize);
```

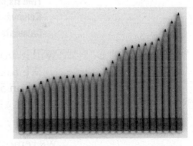

7.4 Problem Solving: Adapting Algorithms

By combining fundamental algorithms, you can solve complex programming tasks.

In Section 7.3, you were introduced to a number of fundamental array algorithms. These algorithms form the building blocks for many programs that process arrays. In general, it is a good problem-solving strategy to have a repertoire of fundamental algorithms that you can combine and adapt.

Consider this example problem: You are given the quiz scores of a student. You are to compute the final quiz score, which is the sum of all scores after dropping the lowest one. For example, if the scores are

8   7   8.5   9.5   7   4   10

then the final score is 50.

We do not have a ready-made algorithm for this situation. Instead, consider which algorithms may be related. These include:

- Calculating the sum (Section 7.3.2)
- Finding the minimum value (Section 7.3.3)
- Removing an element (Section 7.3.6)

We can formulate a plan of attack that combines these algorithms:

Find the minimum.
Remove it from the array.
Calculate the sum.

Let's try it out with our example. The minimum of

	[0]	[1]	[2]	[3]	[4]	[5]	[6]
	8	7	8.5	9.5	7	4	10

is 4. How do we remove it?

Now we have a problem. The removal algorithm in Section 7.3.6 locates the element to be removed by using the *position* of the element, not the value.

But we have another algorithm for that:

- Linear search (Section 7.3.5)

We need to fix our plan of attack:

Find the minimum value.
Find its position.
Remove that position from the array.
Calculate the sum.

Will it work? Let's continue with our example.

We found a minimum value of 4. Linear search tells us that the value 4 occurs at position 5.

	[0]	[1]	[2]	[3]	[4]	[5]	[6]
	8	7	8.5	9.5	7	4	10

We remove it:

	[0]	[1]	[2]	[3]	[4]	[5]
	8	7	8.5	9.5	7	10

Finally, we compute the sum: 8 + 7 + 8.5 + 9.5 + 7 + 10 = 50.

This walkthrough demonstrates that our strategy works.

Can we do better? It seems a bit inefficient to find the minimum and then make another pass through the array to obtain its position.

We can adapt the algorithm for finding the minimum to yield the position of the minimum. Here is the original algorithm:

> You should be familiar with the implementation of fundamental algorithms so that you can adapt them.

```
double smallest = values[0];
for (int i = 1; i < values.length; i++)
{
    if (values[i] < smallest)
    {
        smallest = values[i];
    }
}
```

}

When we find the smallest value, we also want to update the position:

```
if (values[i] < smallest)
{
   smallest = values[i];
   smallestPosition = i;
}
```

In fact, then there is no reason to keep track of the smallest value any longer. It is simply `values[smallestPosition]`. With this insight, we can adapt the algorithm as follows:

```
int smallestPosition = 0;
for (int i = 1; i < values.length; i++)
{
   if (values[i] < values[smallestPosition])
   {
      smallestPosition = i;
   }
}
```

FULL CODE EXAMPLE

Go to wiley.com/go/javacode to download a program that computes the score using the adapted algorithm for finding the minimum.

With this adaptation, our problem is solved with the following strategy:

Find the position of the minimum.
Remove it from the array.
Calculate the sum.

The next section shows you a technique for discovering a new algorithm when none of the fundamental algorithms can be adapted to a task.

SELF CHECK

20. Section 7.3.6 has two algorithms for removing an element. Which of the two should be used to solve the task described in this section?

21. It isn't actually necessary to *remove* the minimum in order to compute the total score. Describe an alternative.

22. How can you print the number of positive and negative values in a given array, using one or more of the algorithms in Section 6.7?

23. How can you print all positive values in an array, separated by commas?

24. Consider the following algorithm for collecting all matches in an array:

```
int matchesSize = 0;
for (int i = 0; i < values.length; i++)
{
   if (values[i] fulfills the condition)
   {
      matches[matchesSize] = values[i];
      matchesSize++;
   }
}
```

How can this algorithm help you with Self Check 23?

Practice It   Now you can try these exercises at the end of the chapter: R7.24, R7.25.

HOW TO 7.1   **Working with Arrays**

In many data processing situations, you need to process a sequence of values. This How To walks you through the steps for storing input values in an array and carrying out computations with the array elements.

Problem Statement Consider again the problem from Section 7.4: A final quiz score is computed by adding all the scores, except for the lowest one. For example, if the scores are

8 7 8.5 9.5 7 5 10

then the final score is 50.

Step 1 Decompose your task into steps.

You will usually want to break down your task into multiple steps, such as

• Reading the data into an array.
• Processing the data in one or more steps.
• Displaying the results.

When deciding how to process the data, you should be familiar with the array algorithms in Section 7.3. Most processing tasks can be solved by using one or more of these algorithms.

In our sample problem, we will want to read the data. Then we will remove the minimum and compute the total. For example, if the input is 8 7 8.5 9.5 7 5 10, we will remove the minimum of 5, yielding 8 7 8.5 9.5 7 10. The sum of those values is the final score of 50.

Thus, we have identified three steps:

Read inputs.
Remove the minimum.
Calculate the sum.

Step 2 Determine which algorithm(s) you need.

Sometimes, a step corresponds to exactly one of the basic array algorithms in Section 7.3. That is the case with calculating the sum (Section 7.3.2) and reading the inputs (Section 7.3.10). At other times, you need to combine several algorithms. To remove the minimum value, you can find the minimum value (Section 7.3.3), find its position (Section 7.3.5), and remove the element at that position (Section 7.3.6).

We have now refined our plan as follows:

Read inputs.
Find the minimum.
Find its position.
Remove the minimum.
Calculate the sum.

This plan will work—see Section 7.4. But here is an alternate approach. It is easy to compute the sum and subtract the minimum. Then we don't have to find its position. The revised plan is

Read inputs.
Find the minimum.
Calculate the sum.
Subtract the minimum.

Step 3   Use classes and methods to structure the program.

Even though it may be possible to put all steps into the main method, this is rarely a good idea. It is better to carry out each processing step in a separate method. It is also a good idea to come up with a class that is responsible for collecting and processing the data.

In our example, let's provide a class Student. A student has an array of scores.

```java
public class Student
{
    private double[] scores;
    private double scoresSize;
    . . .
    public Student(int capacity) { . . . }
    public boolean addScore(double score) { . . . }
    public double finalScore() { . . . }
}
```

A second class, ScoreAnalyzer, is responsible for reading the user input and displaying the result. Its main method simply calls the Student methods:

```java
Student fred = new Student(100);
System.out.println("Please enter values, Q to quit:");
while (in.hasNextDouble())
{
    if (!fred.addScore(in.nextDouble()))
    {
        System.out.println("Too many scores.");
        return;
    }
}
System.out.println("Final score: " + fred.finalScore());
```

Now the finalScore method must do the heavy lifting. It too should not have to do all the work. Instead, we will supply helper methods

```java
public double sum()
public double minimum()
```

These methods simply implement the algorithms in Sections 7.3.2 and 7.3.3.

Then the finalScore method becomes

```java
public double finalScore()
{
    if (scoresSize == 0)
    {
        return 0;
    }
    else if (scores.size() == 1)
    {
        return scores[0];
    }
    else
    {
        return sum() - minimum();
    }
}
```

Step 4   Assemble and test the program.

Place your methods into a class. Review your code and check that you handle both normal and exceptional situations. What happens with an empty array? One that contains a single element? When no match is found? When there are multiple matches? Consider these boundary conditions and make sure that your program works correctly.

In our example, it is impossible to compute the minimum if the array is empty. In that case, we should terminate the program with an error message *before* attempting to call the minimum method.

What if the minimum value occurs more than once? That means that a student had more than one test with the same low score. We subtract only one of the occurrences of that low score, and that is the desired behavior.

The following table shows test cases and their expected output:

Test Case	Expected Output	Comment
8 7 8.5 9.5 7 5 10	50	See Step 1.
8 7 7 9	24	Only one instance of the low score should be removed.
8	0	After removing the low score, no score remains.
(no inputs)	**Error**	That is not a legal input.

The complete program is in the how_to_1 folder of your companion code.

WORKED EXAMPLE 7.1　　**Rolling the Dice**

Learn how to analyze a set of die tosses to see whether the die is "fair". Go to wiley.com/go/javaexamples and download the file for Worked Example 7.1.

7.5 Problem Solving: Discovering Algorithms by Manipulating Physical Objects

In Section 7.4, you saw how to solve a problem by combining and adapting known algorithms. But what do you do when none of the standard algorithms is sufficient for your task? In this section, you will learn a technique for discovering algorithms by manipulating physical objects.

Consider the following task: You are given an array whose size is an even number, and you are to switch the first and the second half. For example, if the array contains the eight numbers

Manipulating physical objects can give you ideas for discovering algorithms.

| 9 | 13 | 21 | 4 | 11 | 7 | 1 | 3 |

then you should change it to

| 11 | 7 | 1 | 3 | 9 | 13 | 21 | 4 |

Many students find it quite challenging to come up with an algorithm. They may know that a loop is required, and they may realize that elements should be inserted (Section 7.3.7) or swapped (Section 7.3.8), but they do not have sufficient intuition to draw diagrams, describe an algorithm, or write down pseudocode.

Use a sequence of coins, playing cards, or toys to visualize an array of values.

One useful technique for discovering an algorithm is to manipulate physical objects. Start by lining up some objects to denote an array. Coins, playing cards, or small toys are good choices.

Here we arrange eight coins:

Now let's step back and see what we can do to change the order of the coins. We can remove a coin (Section 7.3.6):

Visualizing the removal of an array element

We can insert a coin (Section 7.3.7):

Visualizing the insertion of an array element

Or we can swap two coins (Section 7.3.8).

Visualizing the swapping of two array elements

Go ahead—line up some coins and try out these three operations right now so that you get a feel for them.

Now how does that help us with our problem, switching the first and the second half of the array?

Let's put the first coin into place, by swapping it with the fifth coin. However, as Java programmers, we will say that we swap the coins in positions 0 and 4:

Next, we swap the coins in positions 1 and 5:

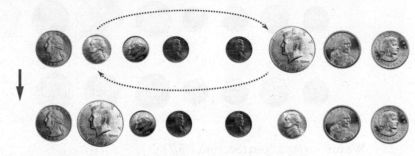

Two more swaps, and we are done:

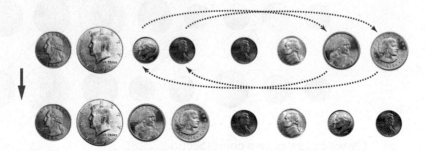

Now an algorithm is becoming apparent:

```
i = 0
j = ... (we'll think about that in a minute)
While (don't know yet)
    Swap elements at positions i and j
    i++
    j++
```

Where does the variable j start? When we have eight coins, the coin at position zero is moved to position 4. In general, it is moved to the middle of the array, or to position **size / 2**.

And how many iterations do we make? We need to swap all coins in the first half. That is, we need to swap **size / 2** coins.

The pseudocode is

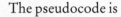
FULL CODE EXAMPLE
Go to wiley.com/go/
javacode to download
a program that
implements the
algorithm that
switches the first
and second halves
of an array.

```
i = 0
j = size / 2
While (i < size / 2)
    Swap elements at positions i and j
    i++
    j++
```

It is a good idea to make a walkthrough of the pseudocode (see Section 6.2). You can use paper clips to denote the positions of the variables i and j. If the walkthrough is successful, then we know that there was no "off-by-one" error in the pseudocode. Self Check 25 asks you to carry out the walkthrough, and Exercise E.7.9 asks you to translate the pseudocode to Java. Exercise R7.26 suggests a different algorithm for switching the two halves of an array, by repeatedly removing and inserting coins.

You can use paper clips as position markers or counters.

Many people find that the manipulation of physical objects is less intimidating than drawing diagrams or mentally envisioning algorithms. Give it a try when you need to design a new algorithm!

SELF CHECK

25. Walk through the algorithm that we developed in this section, using two paper clips to indicate the positions for I and J. Explain why there are no bounds errors in the pseudocode.

26. Take out some coins and simulate the following pseudocode, using two paper clips to indicate the positions for i and j.

```
i = 0
j = size - 1
While (i < j)
    Swap elements at positions i and j
    i++
    j--
```

What does the algorithm do?

27. Consider the task of rearranging all elements in an array so that the even numbers come first. Otherwise, the order doesn't matter. For example, the array

```
1 4 14 2 1 3 5 6 23
```

could be rearranged to

```
4 2 14 6 1 5 3 23 1
```

Using coins and paperclips, discover an algorithm that solves this task by swapping elements, then describe it in pseudocode.

28. Discover an algorithm for the task of Self Check 27 that uses removal and insertion of elements instead of swapping.

29. Consider the algorithm in Section 6.7.5 that finds the largest element in a sequence of inputs—*not* the largest element in an array. Why is this algorithm better visualized by picking playing cards from a deck rather than arranging toy soldiers in a sequence?

Practice It   Now you can try these exercises at the end of the chapter: R7.26, R7.27, E7.9.

7.6 Two-Dimensional Arrays

It often happens that you want to store collections of values that have a two-dimensional layout. Such data sets commonly occur in financial and scientific applications. An arrangement consisting of rows and columns of values is called a **two-dimensional array**, or a *matrix*.

Let's explore how to store the example data shown in Figure 13: the medal counts of the figure skating competitions at the 2010 Winter Olympics.

	Gold	Silver	Bronze
Canada	1	0	1
China	1	1	0
Germany	0	0	1
Korea	1	0	0
Japan	0	1	1
Russia	0	1	1
United States	1	1	0

Figure 13 Figure Skating Medal Counts

7.6.1 Declaring Two-Dimensional Arrays

> Use a two-dimensional array to store tabular data.

In Java, you obtain a two-dimensional array by supplying the number of rows and columns. For example, `new int[7][3]` is an array with seven rows and three columns. You store a reference to such an array in a variable of type `int[][]`. Here is a complete declaration of a two-dimensional array, suitable for holding our medal count data:

```
final int COUNTRIES = 7;
final int MEDALS = 3;
int[][] counts = new int[COUNTRIES][MEDALS];
```

Alternatively, you can declare and initialize the array by grouping each row:

```
int[][] counts =
   {
      { 1, 0, 1 },
      { 1, 1, 0 },
      { 0, 0, 1 },
      { 1, 0, 0 },
      { 0, 1, 1 },
      { 0, 1, 1 },
      { 1, 1, 0 }
   };
```

Syntax 7.3   Two-Dimensional Array Declaration

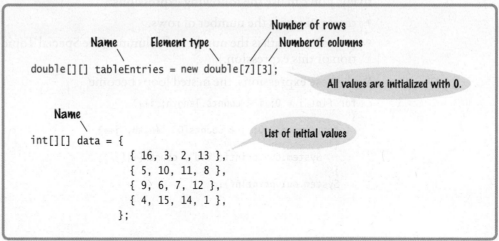

As with one-dimensional arrays, you cannot change the size of a two-dimensional array once it has been declared.

7.6.2 Accessing Elements

Individual elements in a two-dimensional array are accessed by using two index values, *array*[i][j].

To access a particular element in the two-dimensional array, you need to specify two index values in separate brackets to select the row and column, respectively (see Figure 14):

```
int medalCount = counts[3][1];
```

To access all elements in a two-dimensional array, you use nested loops. For example, the following loop prints all elements of counts:

```
for (int i = 0; i < COUNTRIES; i++)
{
    // Process the ith row
    for (int j = 0; j < MEDALS; j++)
    {
        // Process the jth column in the ith row
        System.out.printf("%8d", counts[i][j]);
    }
    System.out.println(); // Start a new line at the end of the row
}
```

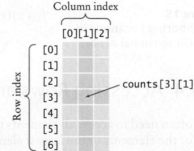

Figure 14
Accessing an Element in a
Two-Dimensional Array

In these loops, the number of rows and colums were given as constants. Alternatively, you can use the following expressions:

- `counts.length` is the number of rows.
- `counts[0].length` is the number of columns. (See Special Topic 7.3 for an explanation of this expression.)

With these expressions, the nested loops become

```
for (int i = 0; i < counts.length; i++)
{
   for (int j = 0; j < counts[0].length; j++)
   {
      System.out.printf("%8d", counts[i][j]);
   }
   System.out.println();
}
```

7.6.3 Locating Neighboring Elements

Some programs that work with two-dimensional arrays need to locate the elements that are adjacent to an element. This task is particularly common in games. Figure 15 shows how to compute the index values of the neighbors of an element.

For example, the neighbors of `counts[3][1]` to the left and right are `counts[3][0]` and `counts[3][2]`. The neighbors to the top and bottom are `counts[2][1]` and `counts[4][1]`.

You need to be careful about computing neighbors at the boundary of the array. For example, `counts[0][1]` has no neighbor to the top. Consider the task of computing the sum of the neighbors to the top and bottom of the element `count[i][j]`. You need to check whether the element is located at the top or bottom of the array:

```
int total = 0;
if (i > 0) { total = total + counts[i - 1][j]; }
if (i < ROWS - 1) { total = total + counts[i + 1][j]; }
```

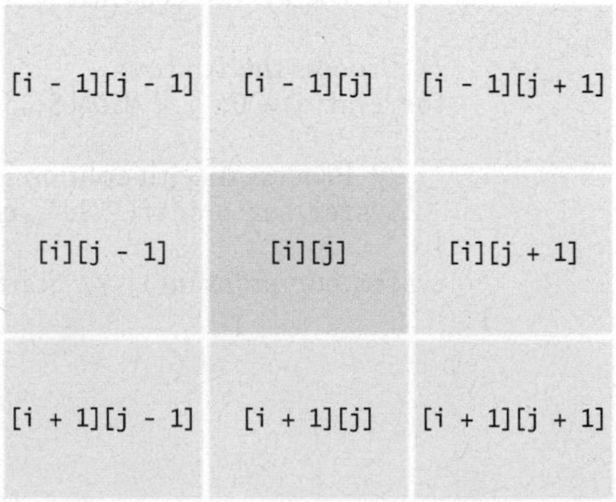

Figure 15
Neighboring Locations in a
Two-Dimensional Array

7.6.4 Accessing Rows and Columns

You often need to access all elements in a row or column, for example to compute the sum of the elements or the largest element in a row or column.

In our sample array, the row totals give us the total number of medals won by a particular country.

Finding the correct index values is a bit tricky, and it is a good idea to make a quick sketch. To compute the total of row i, we need to visit the following elements:

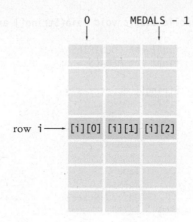

As you can see, we need to compute the sum of counts[i][j], where j ranges from 0 to MEDALS - 1. The following loop computes the total:

```
int total = 0;
for (int j = 0; j < MEDALS; j++)
{
    total = total + counts[i][j];
}
```

Computing column totals is similar. Form the sum of counts[i][j], where i ranges from 0 to COUNTRIES - 1.

```
int total = 0;
for (int i = 0; i < COUNTRIES; i++)
{
    total = total + counts[i][j];
}
```

ANIMATION
Tracing a Nested Loop in a 2D Array

Working with two-dimensional arrays is illustrated in the following program. The program prints out the medal counts and the row totals.

section_6/Medals.java

```java
1   /**
2      This program prints a table of medal winner counts with row totals.
3   */
4   public class Medals
5   {
6      public static void main(String[] args)
7      {
8         final int COUNTRIES = 7;
9         final int MEDALS = 3;
10
11        String[] countries =
12           {
13              "Canada",
14              "China",
15              "Germany",
16              "Korea",
17              "Japan",
18              "Russia",
19              "United States"
20           };
21
22        int[][] counts =
23           {
24              { 1, 0, 1 },
25              { 1, 1, 0 },
26              { 0, 0, 1 },
27              { 1, 0, 0 },
28              { 0, 1, 1 },
29              { 0, 1, 1 },
30              { 1, 1, 0 }
31           };
32
33        System.out.println("        Country    Gold  Silver  Bronze     Total");
34
35        // Print countries, counts, and row totals
36        for (int i = 0; i < COUNTRIES; i++)
37        {
38           // Process the ith row
39           System.out.printf("%15s", countries[i]);
40
41           int total = 0;
42
43           // Print each row element and update the row total
44           for (int j = 0; j < MEDALS; j++)
45           {
46              System.out.printf("%8d", counts[i][j]);
47              total = total + counts[i][j];
48           }
49
50           // Display the row total and print a new line
51           System.out.printf("%8d\n", total);
52        }
53     }
54  }
```

Program Run

Country	Gold	Silver	Bronze	Total
Canada	1	0	1	2
China	1	1	0	2
Germany	0	0	1	1
Korea	1	0	0	1
Japan	0	1	1	2
Russia	0	1	1	2
United States	1	1	0	2

SELF CHECK

30. What results do you get if you total the columns in our sample data?

31. Consider an 8 × 8 array for a board game:

```
int[][] board = new int[8][8];
```

Using two nested loops, initialize the board so that zeroes and ones alternate, as on a checkerboard:

```
0 1 0 1 0 1 0 1
1 0 1 0 1 0 1 0
0 1 0 1 0 1 0 1
. . .
1 0 1 0 1 0 1 0
```

Hint: Check whether i + j is even.

32. Declare a two-dimensional array for representing a tic-tac-toe board. The board has three rows and columns and contains strings "x", "o", and " ".

33. Write an assignment statement to place an "x" in the upper-right corner of the tic-tac-toe board in Self Check 32.

34. Which elements are on the diagonal joining the upper-left and the lower-right corners of the tic-tac-toe board in Self Check 32?

Practice It Now you can try these exercises at the end of the chapter: R7.28, E7.15, E7.16.

WORKED EXAMPLE 7.2 **A World Population Table**

Learn how to print world population data in a table with row and column headers, and with totals for each of the data columns. Go to wiley.com/go/javaexamples and download the file for Worked Example 7.2.

Special Topic 7.3

Two-Dimensional Arrays with Variable Row Lengths

When you declare a two-dimensional array with the command

```
int[][] a = new int[3][3];
```

you get a 3 × 3 matrix that can store 9 elements:

```
a[0][0] a[0][1] a[0][2]
a[1][0] a[1][1] a[1][2]
a[2][0] a[2][1] a[2][2]
```

In this matrix, all rows have the same length.

In Java it is possible to declare arrays in which the row length varies. For example, you can store an array that has a triangular shape, such as:

```
b[0][0]
b[1][0] b[1][1]
b[2][0] b[2][1] b[2][2]
```

To allocate such an array, you must work harder. First, you allocate space to hold three rows. Indicate that you will manually set each row by leaving the second array index empty:

```
double[][] b = new double[3][];
```

Then allocate each row separately (see Figure 16):

```
for (int i = 0; i < b.length; i++)
{
    b[i] = new double[i + 1];
}
```

You can access each array element as b[i][j]. The expression b[i] selects the ith row, and the [j] operator selects the jth element in that row.

Note that the number of rows is b.length, and the length of the ith row is b[i].length. For example, the following pair of loops prints a ragged array:

```
for (int i = 0; i < b.length; i++)
{
    for (int j = 0; j < b[i].length; j++)
    {
        System.out.print(b[i][j]);
    }
    System.out.println();
}
```

Alternatively, you can use two enhanced for loops:

```
for (double[] row : b)
{
    for (double element : row)
    {
        System.out.print(element);
    }
    System.out.println();
}
```

Naturally, such "ragged" arrays are not very common.

Java implements plain two-dimensional arrays in exactly the same way as ragged arrays: as arrays of one-dimensional arrays. The expression new int[3][3] automatically allocates an array of three rows, and three arrays for the rows' contents.

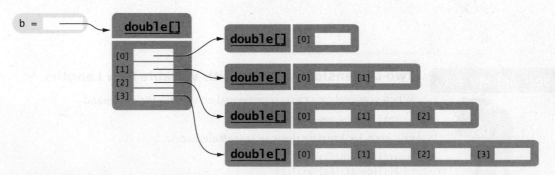

Figure 16 A Triangular Array

Multidimensional Arrays

You can declare arrays with more than two dimensions. For example, here is a three-dimensional array:

```
int[][][] rubiksCube = new int[3][3][3];
```

Each array element is specified by three index values:

```
rubiksCube[i][j][k]
```

7.7 Array Lists

An array list stores a sequence of values whose size can change.

When you write a program that collects inputs, you don't always know how many inputs you will have. In such a situation, an **array list** offers two significant advantages:

- Array lists can grow and shrink as needed.
- The ArrayList class supplies methods for common tasks, such as inserting and removing elements.

In the following sections, you will learn how to work with array lists.

An array list expands to hold as many elements as needed.

Syntax 7.4 Array Lists

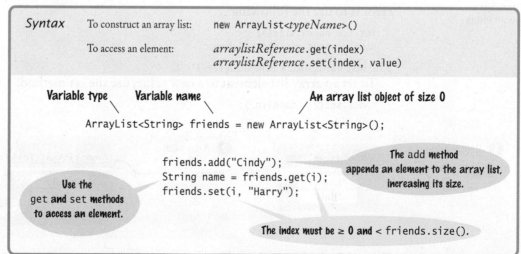

Syntax To construct an array list: `new ArrayList<typeName>()`

To access an element: `arraylistReference.get(index)`
`arraylistReference.set(index, value)`

Variable type   **Variable name**   **An array list object of size 0**

`ArrayList<String> friends = new ArrayList<String>();`

`friends.add("Cindy");`
`String name = friends.get(i);`
`friends.set(i, "Harry");`

The add method appends an element to the array list, increasing its size.

Use the get and set methods to access an element.

The index must be ≥ 0 and < friends.size().

7.7.1 Declaring and Using Array Lists

The following statement declares an array list of strings:

```
ArrayList<String> names = new ArrayList<String>();
```

The `ArrayList` class is contained in the `java.util` package. In order to use array lists in your program, you need to use the statement `import java.util.ArrayList`.

The type `ArrayList<String>` denotes an array list of `String` elements. The angle brackets around the `String` type tell you that `String` is a **type parameter**. You can replace `String` with any other class and get a different array list type. For that reason, `ArrayList` is called a **generic class**. However, you cannot use primitive types as type parameters—there is no `ArrayList<int>` or `ArrayList<double>`. Section 7.7.4 shows how you can collect numbers in an array list.

It is a common error to forget the initialization:

```
ArrayList<String> names;
names.add("Harry"); // Error—names not initialized
```

Here is the proper initialization:

```
ArrayList<String> names = new ArrayList<String>();
```

> The ArrayList class is a generic class: ArrayList<*Type*> collects elements of the specified type.

Note the `()` after `new ArrayList<String>` on the right-hand side of the initialization. It indicates that the **constructor** of the `ArrayList<String>` class is being called.

When the `ArrayList<String>` is first constructed, it has size 0. You use the `add` method to add an element to the end of the array list.

```
names.add("Emily"); // Now names has size 1 and element "Emily"
names.add("Bob"); // Now names has size 2 and elements "Emily", "Bob"
names.add("Cindy"); // names has size 3 and elements "Emily", "Bob", and "Cindy"
```

> Use the size method to obtain the current size of an array list.

The size increases after each call to `add` (see Figure 17). The `size` method yields the current size of the array list.

To obtain an array list element, use the `get` method, not the `[]` operator. As with arrays, index values start at 0. For example, `names.get(2)` retrieves the name with index 2, the third element in the array list:

```
String name = names.get(2);
```

> Use the get and set methods to access an array list element at a given index.

As with arrays, it is an error to access a nonexistent element. A very common bounds error is to use the following:

```
int i = names.size();
name = names.get(i);   // Error
```

The last valid index is `names.size() - 1`.

To set an array list element to a new value, use the `set` method:

```
names.set(2, "Carolyn");
```

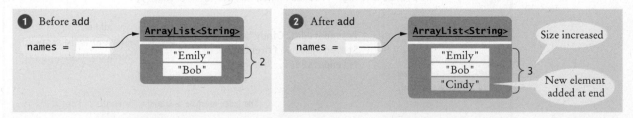

Figure 17 Adding an Array List Element with add

Figure 18
Adding and
Removing
Elements in the
Middle of an
Array List

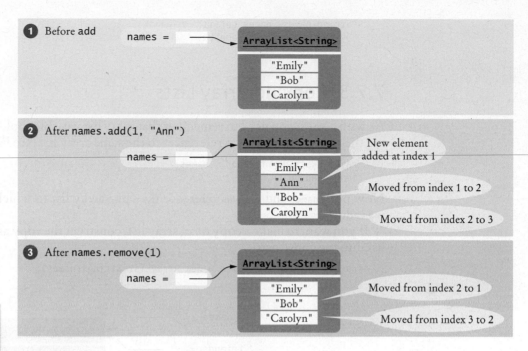

① Before add

```
names =
```
ArrayList<String>
"Emily"
"Bob"
"Carolyn"

② After names.add(1, "Ann")

```
names =
```
ArrayList<String>
"Emily"
"Ann"
"Bob"
"Carolyn"

New element
added at index 1

Moved from index 1 to 2

Moved from index 2 to 3

③ After names.remove(1)

```
names =
```
ArrayList<String>
"Emily"
"Bob"
"Carolyn"

Moved from index 2 to 1

Moved from index 3 to 2

*An array list has
methods for adding
and removing ele-
ments in the middle.*

Use the add and
remove methods to
add and remove
array list elements.

This call sets position 2 of the names array list to "Carolyn", overwriting whatever value
was there before.

The set method overwrites existing values. It is different from the add method,
which adds a new element to the array list.

You can insert an element in the middle of an array list. For example, the call
names.add(1, "Ann") adds a new element at position 1 and moves all elements with
index 1 or larger by one position. After each call to the add method, the size of the
array list increases by 1 (see Figure 18).

Conversely, the remove method removes the element at a given position, moves all
elements after the removed element down by one position, and reduces the size of the
array list by 1. Part 3 of Figure 18 illustrates the result of names.remove(1).

With an array list, it is very easy to get a quick printout. Simply pass the array list
to the println method:

```
System.out.println(names); // Prints [Emily, Bob, Carolyn]
```

7.7.2 Using the Enhanced for Loop with Array Lists

You can use the enhanced for loop to visit all elements of an array list. For example,
the following loop prints all names:

```
ArrayList<String> names = . . . ;
for (String name : names)
{
    System.out.println(name);
}
```

This loop is equivalent to the following basic for loop:

```
for (int i = 0; i < names.size(); i++)
{
```

```
        String name = names.get(i);
        System.out.println(name);
}
```

7.7.3 Copying Array Lists

As with arrays, you need to remember that array list variables hold references. Copying the reference yields two references to the same array list (see Figure 19).

```
ArrayList<String> friends = names;
friends.add("Harry");
```

Now both names and friends reference the same array list to which the string "Harry" was added.

If you want to make a copy of an array list, construct the copy and pass the original list into the constructor:

```
ArrayList<String> newNames = new ArrayList<String>(names);
```

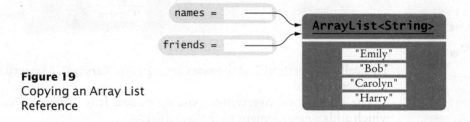

Figure 19
Copying an Array List
Reference

Table 2 Working with Array Lists

`ArrayList<String> names = new ArrayList<String>();`	Constructs an empty array list that can hold strings.
`names.add("Ann");` `names.add("Cindy");`	Adds elements to the end.
`System.out.println(names);`	Prints [Ann, Cindy].
`names.add(1, "Bob");`	Inserts an element at index 1. names is now [Ann, Bob, Cindy].
`names.remove(0);`	Removes the element at index 0. names is now [Bob, Cindy].
`names.set(0, "Bill");`	Replaces an element with a different value. names is now [Bill, Cindy].
`String name = names.get(i);`	Gets an element.
`String last = names.get(names.size() - 1);`	Gets the last element.

`ArrayList<Integer> squares = new ArrayList<Integer>();`
`for (int i = 0; i < 10; i++)`
`{`
`    squares.add(i * i);`
`}`
	Constructs an array list holding the first ten squares.

7.7.4 Wrappers and Auto-boxing

Like truffles that must be in a wrapper to be sold, a number must be placed in a wrapper to be stored in an array list.

To collect numbers in array lists, you must use wrapper classes.

In Java, you cannot directly insert primitive type values—numbers, characters, or boolean values—into array lists. For example, you cannot form an ArrayList<double>. Instead, you must use one of the **wrapper classes** shown in the following table.

Primitive Type	Wrapper Class
byte	Byte
boolean	Boolean
char	Character
double	Double
float	Float
int	Integer
long	Long
short	Short

For example, to collect double values in an array list, you use an ArrayList<Double>. Note that the wrapper class names start with uppercase letters, and that two of them differ from the names of the corresponding primitive type: Integer and Character.

Conversion between primitive types and the corresponding wrapper classes is automatic. This process is called **auto-boxing** (even though *auto-wrapping* would have been more consistent).

For example, if you assign a double value to a Double variable, the number is automatically "put into a box" (see Figure 20).

```
Double wrapper = 29.95;
```

Conversely, wrapper values are automatically "unboxed" to primitive types:

```
double x = wrapper;
```

Because boxing and unboxing is automatic, you don't need to think about it. Simply remember to use the wrapper type when you declare array lists of numbers. From then on, use the primitive type and rely on auto-boxing.

```
ArrayList<Double> values = new ArrayList<Double>();
values.add(29.95);
double x = values.get(0);
```

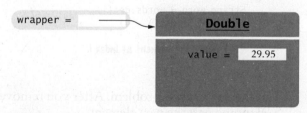

Figure 20 A Wrapper Class Variable

7.7.5   Using Array Algorithms with Array Lists

The array algorithms in Section 7.3 can be converted to array lists simply by using the array list methods instead of the array syntax (see Table 3 on page 354). For example, this code snippet finds the largest element in an array:

```java
double largest = values[0];
for (int i = 1; i < values.length; i++)
{
   if (values[i] > largest)
   {
      largest = values[i];
   }
}
```

Here is the same algorithm, now using an array list:

```java
double largest = values.get(0);
for (int i = 1; i < values.size(); i++)
{
   if (values.get(i) > largest)
   {
      largest = values.get(i);
   }
}
```

7.7.6   Storing Input Values in an Array List

When you collect an unknown number of inputs, array lists are *much* easier to use than arrays. Simply read inputs and add them to an array list:

```java
ArrayList<Double> inputs = new ArrayList<Double>();
while (in.hasNextDouble())
{
   inputs.add(in.nextDouble());
}
```

7.7.7 Removing Matches

It is easy to remove elements from an array list, by calling the remove method. A common processing task is to remove all elements that match a particular condition. Suppose, for example, that we want to remove all strings of length < 4 from an array list.
   Of course, you traverse the array list and look for matching elements:

```java
ArrayList<String> words = ...;
for (int i = 0; i < words.size(); i++)
{
   String word = words.get(i);
   if (word.length() < 4)
   {
      Remove the element at index i.
   }
}
```

But there is a subtle problem. After you remove the element, the for loop increments i, skipping past the *next* element.

Consider this concrete example, where words contains the strings "Welcome", "to", "the", "island!". When i is 1, we remove the word "to" at index 1. Then i is incremented to 2, and the word "the", which is now at position 1, is never examined.

i	words
~~0~~	~~"Welcome", "to", "the", "island"~~
~~1~~	"Welcome", "the", "island"
2	

We should not increment the index when removing a word. The appropriate pseudocode is

If the element at index i matches the condition
 Remove the element.
Else
 Increment i.

Because we don't always increment the index, a for loop is not appropriate for this algorithm. Instead, use a while loop:

```
int i = 0;
while (i < words.size())
{
    String word = words.get(i);
    if (word.length() < 4)
    {
        words.remove(i);
    }
    else
    {
        i++;
    }
}
```

7.7.8 Choosing Between Array Lists and Arrays

For most programming tasks, array lists are easier to use than arrays. Array lists can grow and shrink. On the other hand, arrays have a nicer syntax for element access and initialization.

Which of the two should you choose? Here are some recommendations.

- If the size of a collection never changes, use an array.

- If you collect a long sequence of primitive type values and you are concerned about efficiency, use an array.

- Otherwise, use an array list.

FULL CODE EXAMPLE

Go to wiley.com/go/ javacode to download a version of the Student class using an array list.

The following program shows how to mark the largest value in a sequence of values. This program uses an array list. Note how the program is an improvement over the array version on page 329. This program can process input sequences of arbitrary length.

Table 3 Comparing Array and Array List Operations

Operation	Arrays	Array Lists
Get an element.	`x = values[4];`	`x = values.get(4)`
Replace an element.	`values[4] = 35;`	`values.set(4, 35);`
Number of elements.	`values.length`	`values.size()`
Number of filled elements.	`currentSize` (companion variable, see Section 7.1.4)	`values.size()`
Remove an element.	See Section 7.3.6	`values.remove(4);`
Add an element, growing the collection.	See Section 7.3.7	`values.add(35);`
Initializing a collection.	`int[] values = { 1, 4, 9 };`	No initializer list syntax; call add three times.

section_7/LargestInArrayList.java

```java
1   import java.util.ArrayList;
2   import java.util.Scanner;
3
4   /**
5      This program reads a sequence of values and prints them, marking the largest value.
6   */
7   public class LargestInArrayList
8   {
9      public static void main(String[] args)
10     {
11        ArrayList<Double> values = new ArrayList<Double>();
12
13        // Read inputs
14
15        System.out.println("Please enter values, Q to quit:");
16        Scanner in = new Scanner(System.in);
17        while (in.hasNextDouble())
18        {
19           values.add(in.nextDouble());
20        }
21
22        // Find the largest value
23
24        double largest = values.get(0);
25        for (int i = 1; i < values.size(); i++)
26        {
27           if (values.get(i) > largest)
28           {
29              largest = values.get(i);
30           }
31        }
32
33        // Print all values, marking the largest
34
```

```
35        for (double element : values)
36        {
37            System.out.print(element);
38            if (element == largest)
39            {
40                System.out.print(" <== largest value");
41            }
42            System.out.println();
43        }
44    }
45 }
```

Program Run

```
Please enter values, Q to quit:
35 80 115 44.5 Q
35
80
115 <== largest value
44.5
```

SELF CHECK

35. Declare an array list primes of integers that contains the first five prime numbers (2, 3, 5, 7, and 11).

36. Given the array list primes declared in Self Check 35, write a loop to print its elements in reverse order, starting with the last element.

37. What does the array list names contain after the following statements?

```
ArrayList<String> names = new ArrayList<String>;
names.add("Bob");
names.add(0, "Ann");
names.remove(1);
names.add("Cal");
```

38. What is wrong with this code snippet?

```
ArrayList<String> names;
names.add(Bob);
```

39. Consider this method that appends the elements of one array list to another:

```
public void append(ArrayList<String> target, ArrayList<String> source)
{
    for (int i = 0; i < source.size(); i++)
    {
        target.add(source.get(i));
    }
}
```

What are the contents of names1 and names2 after these statements?

```
ArrayList<String> names1 = new ArrayList<String>();
names1.add("Emily");
names1.add("Bob");
names1.add("Cindy");
ArrayList<String> names2 = new ArrayList<String>();
names2.add("Dave");
append(names1, names2);
```

40. Suppose you want to store the names of the weekdays. Should you use an array list or an array of seven strings?

41. The ch07/section_7 directory of your source code contains an alternate implementation of the problem solution in How To 7.1 on page 334. Compare the array and array list implementations. What is the primary advantage of the latter?

Practice It   Now you can try these exercises at the end of the chapter: R7.10, R7.32, E7.17, E7.19.

Common Error 7.4

Length and Size

Unfortunately, the Java syntax for determining the number of elements in an array, an array list, and a string is not at all consistent. It is a common error to confuse these. You just have to remember the correct syntax for every data type.

Data Type	Number of Elements
Array	`a.length`
Array list	`a.size()`
String	`a.length()`

Special Topic 7.5

The Diamond Syntax in Java 7

Java 7 introduces a convenient syntax enhancement for declaring array lists and other generic classes. In a statement that declares and constructs an array list, you need not repeat the type parameter in the constructor. That is, you can write

```
ArrayList<String> names = new ArrayList<>();
```

instead of

```
ArrayList<String> names = new ArrayList<String>();
```

This shortcut is called the "diamond syntax" because the empty brackets <> look like a diamond shape.

7.8 Regression Testing

> A test suite is a set of tests for repeated testing.

It is a common and useful practice to make a new test whenever you find a program bug. You can use that test to verify that your bug fix really works. Don't throw the test away; feed it to the next version after that and all subsequent versions. Such a collection of test cases is called a **test suite**.

You will be surprised how often a bug that you fixed will reappear in a future version. This is a phenomenon known as *cycling*. Sometimes you don't quite understand the reason for a bug and apply a quick fix that appears to work. Later, you apply a different quick fix that solves a second problem but makes the first problem appear again. Of course, it is always best to think through what really causes a bug and fix the root cause instead of doing a sequence of "Band-Aid" solutions. If you don't succeed in doing that, however, you at least want to have an honest appraisal of how well the program works. By keeping all old test cases around and testing them against every

Regression testing
involves repeating
previously run
tests to ensure that
known failures of
prior versions do
not appear in
new versions of
the software.

new version, you get that feedback. The process of checking each version of a program against a test suite is called **regression testing**.

How do you organize a suite of tests? An easy technique is to produce multiple tester classes, such as ScoreTester1, ScoreTester2, and so on, where each program runs with a separate set of test data. For example, here is a tester for the Student class:

```java
public class ScoreTester1
{
    public static void main(String[] args)
    {
        Scanner in = new Scanner(System.in);
        Student fred = new Student(100);
        fred.addScore(10);
        fred.addScore(20);
        fred.addScore(5);
        System.out.println("Final score: " + fred.finalScore());
        System.out.println("Expected: 30");
    }
}
```

Another useful approach is to provide a generic tester, and feed it inputs from multiple files, as in the following.

section_8/ScoreTester.java

```java
1   import java.util.Scanner;
2
3   public class ScoreTester
4   {
5       public static void main(String[] args)
6       {
7           Scanner in = new Scanner(System.in);
8           double expected = in.nextDouble();
9           Student fred = new Student(100);
10          while (in.hasNextDouble())
11          {
12              if (!fred.addScore(in.nextDouble()))
13              {
14                  System.out.println("Too many scores.");
15                  return;
16              }
17          }
18          System.out.println("Final score: " + fred.finalScore());
19          System.out.println("Expected: " + expected);
20      }
21  }
```

The program reads the expected result and the scores. By running the program with different inputs, we can test different scenarios.

Of course, it would be tedious to type in the input values by hand every time the test is executed. It is much better to save the inputs in a file, such as the following:

section_8/input1.txt

```
30
10
20
5
```

When running the program from a shell window, one can link the input file to the input of a program, as if all the characters in the file had actually been typed by a user. Type the following command into a shell window:

```
java ScoreTester < input1.txt
```

The program is executed, but it no longer reads input from the keyboard. Instead, the System.in object (and the Scanner that reads from System.in) gets the input from the file input1.txt. We discussed this process, called input **redirection**, in Special Topic 6.2.

The output is still displayed in the console window:

Program Run

```
Final score: 30
Expected: 30
```

You can also redirect output. To capture the program's output in a file, use the command

```
java ScoreTester < input1.txt > output1.txt
```

This is useful for archiving test cases.

SELF CHECK

42. Suppose you modified the code for a method. Why do you want to repeat tests that already passed with the previous version of the code?

43. Suppose a customer of your program finds an error. What action should you take beyond fixing the error?

44. Why doesn't the ScoreTester program contain prompts for the inputs?

Practice It   Now you can try these exercises at the end of the chapter: R7.34, R7.35.

Programming Tip 7.3

Batch Files and Shell Scripts

If you need to perform the same tasks repeatedly on the command line, then it is worth learning about the automation features offered by your operating system.

Under Windows, you use batch files to execute a number of commands automatically. For example, suppose you need to test a program by running three testers:

```
java ScoreTester1
java ScoreTester < input1.txt
java ScoreTester < input2.txt
```

Then you find a bug, fix it, and run the tests again. Now you need to type the three commands once more. There has to be a better way. Under Windows, put the commands in a text file and call it test.bat:

File test.bat

```
1   java ScoreTester1
2   java ScoreTester < input1.txt
3   java ScoreTester < input2.txt
```

Then you just type

```
test.bat
```

and the three commands in the batch file execute automatically.

Batch files are a feature of the operating system, not of Java. On Linux, Mac OS, and UNIX, shell scripts are used for the same purpose. In this simple example, you can execute the commands by typing

```
sh test.bat
```

There are many uses for batch files and shell scripts, and it is well worth it to learn more about their advanced features, such as parameters and loops.

Computing & Society 7.2   The Therac-25 Incidents

The Therac-25 is a computerized device to deliver radiation treatment to cancer patients (see the figure). Between June 1985 and January 1987, several of these machines delivered serious overdoses to at least six patients, killing some of them and seriously maiming the others.

The machines were controlled by a computer program. Bugs in the program were directly responsible for the overdoses. According to Leveson and Turner ("An Investigation of the Therac-25 Accidents," *IEEE Computer*, July 1993, pp. 18–41), the program was written by a single programmer, who had since left the manufacturing company producing the device and could not be located. None of the company employees interviewed could say anything about the educational level or qualifications of the programmer.

The investigation by the federal Food and Drug Administration (FDA) found that the program was poorly documented and that there was neither a specification document nor a formal test plan. (This should make you think. Do you have a formal test plan for your programs?)

The overdoses were caused by an amateurish design of the software that had to control different devices concurrently, namely the keyboard, the display, the printer, and of course the radiation device itself. Synchronization and data sharing between the tasks were done in an ad hoc way, even though safe multitasking techniques were known at the time. Had the programmer enjoyed a formal education that involved these techniques, or

taken the effort to study the literature, a safer machine could have been built. Such a machine would have probably involved a commercial multitasking system, which might have required a more expensive computer.

The same flaws were present in the software controlling the predecessor model, the Therac-20, but that machine had hardware interlocks that mechanically prevented overdoses. The hardware safety devices were removed in the Therac-25 and replaced by checks in the software, presumably to save cost.

Frank Houston of the FDA wrote in 1985: "A significant amount of soft-

ware for life-critical systems comes from small firms, especially in the medical device industry; firms that fit the profile of those resistant to or uninformed of the principles of either system safety or software engineering."

Who is to blame? The programmer? The manager who not only failed to ensure that the programmer was up to the task but also didn't insist on comprehensive testing? The hospitals that installed the device, or the FDA, for not reviewing the design process? Unfortunately, even today there are no firm standards of what constitutes a safe software design process.

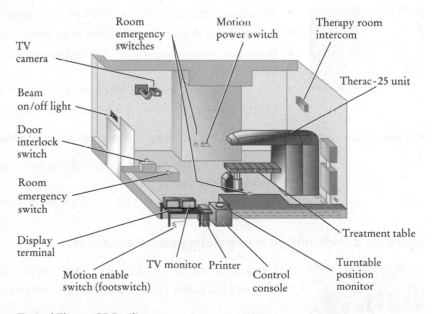

Typical Therac-25 Facility

CHAPTER SUMMARY

Use arrays for collecting values.

- An array collects a sequence of values of the same type.
- Individual elements in an array are accessed by an integer index i, using the notation *array*[i].
- An array element can be used like any variable.
- An array index must be at least zero and less than the size of the array.
- A bounds error, which occurs if you supply an invalid array index, can cause your program to terminate.
- Use the expression *array*.length to find the number of elements in an array.
- An array reference specifies the location of an array. Copying the reference yields a second reference to the same array.
- Arrays can occur as method arguments and return values.
- With a partially filled array, keep a companion variable for the current size.
- Avoid parallel arrays by changing them into arrays of objects.

Know when to use the enhanced for loop.

- You can use the enhanced for loop to visit all elements of an array.
- Use the enhanced for loop if you do not need the index values in the loop body.

Know and use common array algorithms.

- When separating elements, don't place a separator before the first element.
- A linear search inspects elements in sequence until a match is found.
- Before inserting an element, move elements to the end of the array *starting with the last one*.
- Use a temporary variable when swapping two elements.
- Use the Arrays.copyOf method to copy the elements of an array into a new array.

Combine and adapt algorithms for solving a programming problem.

- By combining fundamental algorithms, you can solve complex programming tasks.
- You should be familiar with the implementation of fundamental algorithms so that you can adapt them.

Discover algorithms by manipulating physical objects.

- Use a sequence of coins, playing cards, or toys to visualize an array of values.
- You can use paper clips as position markers or counters.

Use two-dimensional arrays for data that is arranged in rows and columns.

- Use a two-dimensional array to store tabular data.
- Individual elements in a two-dimensional array are accessed by using two index values, *array*[i][j].

Use array lists for managing collections whose size can change.

- An array list stores a sequence of values whose size can change.
- The ArrayList class is a generic class: ArrayList<*Type*> collects elements of the specified type.

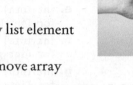

- Use the size method to obtain the current size of an array list.
- Use the get and set methods to access an array list element at a given index.
- Use the add and remove methods to add and remove array list elements.

- To collect numbers in array lists, you must use wrapper classes.

Describe the process of regression testing.

- A test suite is a set of tests for repeated testing.
- Regression testing involves repeating previously run tests to ensure that known failures of prior versions do not appear in new versions of the software.

STANDARD LIBRARY ITEMS INTRODUCED IN THIS CHAPTER

```
java.lang.Boolean                    java.util.ArrayList<E>
java.lang.Double                        add
java.lang.Integer                       get
java.util.Arrays                        remove
   copyOf                               set
   toString                             size
```

REVIEW QUESTIONS

•• R7.1 Write code that fills an array values with each set of numbers below.

a. 1	2	3	4	5	6	7	8	9	10	
b. 0	2	4	6	8	10	12	14	16	18	20
c. 1	4	9	16	25	36	49	64	81	100	
d. 0	0	0	0	0	0	0	0	0	0	
e. 1	4	9	16	9	7	4	9	11		
f. 0	1	0	1	0	1	0	1	0	1	
g. 0	1	2	3	4	0	1	2	3	4	

■■ **R7.2** Consider the following array:

```
int[] a = { 1, 2, 3, 4, 5, 4, 3, 2, 1, 0 };
```

What is the value of total after the following loops complete?

a. int total = 0;
for (int i = 0; i < 10; i++) { total = total + a[i]; }

b. int total = 0;
for (int i = 0; i < 10; i = i + 2) { total = total + a[i]; }

c. int total = 0;
for (int i = 1; i < 10; i = i + 2) { total = total + a[i]; }

d. int total = 0;
for (int i = 2; i <= 10; i++) { total = total + a[i]; }

e. int total = 0;
for (int i = 1; i < 10; i = 2 * i) { total = total + a[i]; }

f. int total = 0;
for (int i = 9; i >= 0; i--) { total = total + a[i]; }

g. int total = 0;
for (int i = 9; i >= 0; i = i - 2) { total = total + a[i]; }

h. int total = 0;
for (int i = 0; i < 10; i++) { total = a[i] - total; }

■■ **R7.3** Consider the following array:

```
int[] a = { 1, 2, 3, 4, 5, 4, 3, 2, 1, 0 };
```

What are the contents of the array a after the following loops complete?

a. for (int i = 1; i < 10; i++) { a[i] = a[i - 1]; }

b. for (int i = 9; i > 0; i--) { a[i] = a[i - 1]; }

c. for (int i = 0; i < 9; i++) { a[i] = a[i + 1]; }

d. for (int i = 8; i >= 0; i--) { a[i] = a[i + 1]; }

e. for (int i = 1; i < 10; i++) { a[i] = a[i] + a[i - 1]; }

f. for (int i = 1; i < 10; i = i + 2) { a[i] = 0; }

g. for (int i = 0; i < 5; i++) { a[i + 5] = a[i]; }

h. for (int i = 1; i < 5; i++) { a[i] = a[9 - i]; }

■■■ **R7.4** Write a loop that fills an array values with ten random numbers between 1 and 100.
Write code for two nested loops that fill values with ten *different* random numbers
between 1 and 100.

■■ **R7.5** Write Java code for a loop that simultaneously computes both the maximum and
minimum of an array.

■ **R7.6** What is wrong with each of the following code segments?

a. int[] values = new int[10];
for (int i = 1; i <= 10; i++)
{
    values[i] = i * i;
}

b. int[] values;
for (int i = 0; i < values.length; i++)
{
    values[i] = i * i;
}

•• R7.7 Write enhanced for loops for the following tasks.

    a. Printing all elements of an array in a single row, separated by spaces.

    b. Computing the maximum of all elements in an array.

    c. Counting how many elements in an array are negative.

•• R7.8 Rewrite the following loops without using the enhanced for loop construct. Here, values is an array of floating-point numbers.

    a. `for (double x : values) { total = total + x; }`

    b. `for (double x : values) { if (x == target) { return true; } }`

    c. `int i = 0;`
       `for (double x : values) { values[i] = 2 * x; i++; }`

•• R7.9 Rewrite the following loops, using the enhanced for loop construct. Here, values is an array of floating-point numbers.

    a. `for (int i = 0; i < values.length; i++) { total = total + values[i]; }`

    b. `for (int i = 1; i < values.length; i++) { total = total + values[i]; }`

    c. `for (int i = 0; i < values.length; i++)`
       `{`
          `if (values[i] == target) { return i; }`
       `}`

• R7.10 What is wrong with each of the following code segments?

    a. `ArrayList<int> values = new ArrayList<int>();`

    b. `ArrayList<Integer> values = new ArrayList();`

    c. `ArrayList<Integer> values = new ArrayList<Integer>;`

    d. `ArrayList<Integer> values = new ArrayList<Integer>();`
       `for (int i = 1; i <= 10; i++)`
       `{`
          `values.set(i - 1, i * i);`
       `}`

    e. `ArrayList<Integer> values;`
       `for (int i = 1; i <= 10; i++)`
       `{`
          `values.add(i * i);`
       `}`

• R7.11 What is an index of an array? What are the legal index values? What is a bounds error?

• R7.12 Write a program that contains a bounds error. Run the program. What happens on your computer?

• R7.13 Write a loop that reads ten numbers and a second loop that displays them in the opposite order from which they were entered.

•• R7.14 For the operations on partially filled arrays below, provide the header of a method. Do not implement the methods.

    a. Sort the elements in decreasing order.

    b. Print all elements, separated by a given string.

    c. Count how many elements are less than a given value.

    d. Remove all elements that are less than a given value.

    e. Place all elements that are less than a given value in another array.

■ **R7.15** Trace the flow of the loop in Section 7.3.4 with the given example. Show two columns, one with the value of i and one with the output.

■ **R7.16** Consider the following loop for collecting all elements that match a condition; in this case, that the element is larger than 100.

```
ArrayList<Double> matches = new ArrayList<Double>();
for (double element : values)
{
   if (element > 100)
   {
      matches.add(element);
   }
}
```

Trace the flow of the loop, where values contains the elements 110 90 100 120 80. Show two columns, for element and matches.

■ **R7.17** Trace the flow of the loop in Section 7.3.5, where values contains the elements 80 90 100 120 110. Show two columns, for pos and found. Repeat the trace when values contains the elements 80 90 120 70.

■■ **R7.18** Trace the algorithm for removing an element described in Section 7.3.6. Use an array values with elements 110 90 100 120 80, and remove the element at index 2.

■■ **R7.19** Give pseudocode for an algorithm that rotates the elements of an array by one position, moving the initial element to the end of the array, like this:

■■ **R7.20** Give pseudocode for an algorithm that removes all negative values from an array, preserving the order of the remaining elements.

■■ **R7.21** Suppose values is a *sorted* array of integers. Give pseudocode that describes how a new value can be inserted in its proper position so that the resulting array stays sorted.

■■■ **R7.22** A *run* is a sequence of adjacent repeated values. Give pseudocode for computing the length of the longest run in an array. For example, the longest run in the array with elements

1 2 5 5 3 1 2 4 3 2 2 2 2 3 6 5 5 6 3 1

has length 4.

■■■ **R7.23** What is wrong with the following method that aims to fill an array with random numbers?

```
public void makeCombination(int[] values, int n)
{
   Random generator = new Random();
   int[] numbers = new int[values.length];
   for (int i = 0; i < numbers.length; i++)
   {
      numbers[i] = generator.nextInt(n);
   }
   values = numbers;
}
```

■■ R7.24 You are given two arrays denoting x- and y-coordinates of a set of points in the plane. For plotting the point set, we need to know the x- and y-coordinates of the smallest rectangle containing the points.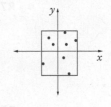

How can you obtain these values from the fundamental algorithms in Section 7.3?

■ R7.25 Solve the problem described in Section 7.4 by sorting the array first. How do you need to modify the algorithm for computing the total?

■■ R7.26 Solve the task described in Section 7.5 using an algorithm that removes and inserts elements instead of switching them. Write the pseudocode for the algorithm, assuming that methods for removal and insertion exist. Act out the algorithm with a sequence of coins and explain why it is less efficient than the swapping algorithm developed in Section 7.5.

■■ R7.27 Develop an algorithm for finding the most frequently occurring value in an array of numbers. Use a sequence of coins. Place paper clips below each coin that count how many other coins of the same value are in the sequence. Give the pseudocode for an algorithm that yields the correct answer, and describe how using the coins and paper clips helped you find the algorithm.

■■ R7.28 Write Java statements for performing the following tasks with an array declared as

```
int[][] values = new int[ROWS][COLUMNS];
```

- Fill all entries with 0.
- Fill elements alternately with 0s and 1s in a checkerboard pattern.
- Fill only the elements in the top and bottom rows with zeroes.
- Compute the sum of all elements.
- Print the array in tabular form.

■■ R7.29 Write pseudocode for an algorithm that fills the first and last columns as well as the first and last rows of a two-dimensional array of integers with −1.

■ R7.30 Section 7.7.7 shows that you must be careful about updating the index value when you remove elements from an array list. Show how you can avoid this problem by traversing the array list backwards.

■■ R7.31 True or false?
    a. All elements of an array are of the same type.
    b. Arrays cannot contain strings as elements.
    c. Two-dimensional arrays always have the same number of rows and columns.
    d. Elements of different columns in a two-dimensional array can have different types.
    e. A method cannot return a two-dimensional array.
    f. A method cannot change the length of an array argument.
    g. A method cannot change the number of columns of an argument that is a two-dimensional array.

■■ **R7.32** How do you perform the following tasks with array lists in Java?

a. Test that two array lists contain the same elements in the same order.

b. Copy one array list to another.

c. Fill an array list with zeroes, overwriting all elements in it.

d. Remove all elements from an array list.

■ **R7.33** True or false?

a. All elements of an array list are of the same type.

b. Array list index values must be integers.

c. Array lists cannot contain strings as elements.

d. Array lists can change their size, getting larger or smaller.

e. A method cannot return an array list.

f. A method cannot change the size of an array list argument.

■ **Testing R7.34** Define the terms regression testing and test suite.

■■ **Testing R7.35** What is the debugging phenomenon known as *cycling*? What can you do to avoid it?

PRACTICE EXERCISES

■■ **E7.1** Write a program that initializes an array with ten random integers and then prints four lines of output, containing

- Every element at an even index.
- Every even element.
- All elements in reverse order.
- Only the first and last element.

■■ **E7.2** Write array methods that carry out the following tasks for an array of integers by completing the ArrayMethods class below. For each method, provide a test program.

```java
public class ArrayMethods
{
    private int[] values;
    public ArrayMethods(int[] initialValues) { values = initialValues; }
    public void swapFirstAndLast() { ... }
    public void shiftRight() { ... }
    ...
}
```

a. Swap the first and last elements in the array.

b. Shift all elements by one to the right and move the last element into the first position. For example, 1 4 9 16 25 would be transformed into 25 1 4 9 16.

c. Replace all even elements with 0.

d. Replace each element except the first and last by the larger of its two neighbors.

e. Remove the middle element if the array length is odd, or the middle two elements if the length is even.

f. Move all even elements to the front, otherwise preserving the order of the elements.

g. Return the second-largest element in the array.

h. Return true if the array is currently sorted in increasing order.

i. Return true if the array contains two adjacent duplicate elements.

j. Return true if the array contains duplicate elements (which need not be adjacent).

■ **E7.3** Modify the `LargestInArray.java` program in Section 7.3 to mark both the smallest and the largest elements.

■■ **E7.4** Write a method `sumWithoutSmallest` that computes the sum of an array of values, except for the smallest one, in a single loop. In the loop, update the sum and the smallest value. After the loop, return the difference.

■ **E7.5** Add a method `removeMin` to the `Student` class of Section 7.4 that removes the minimum score without calling other methods.

■■ **E7.6** Compute the *alternating sum* of all elements in an array. For example, if your program reads the input

$$1 \quad 4 \quad 9 \quad 16 \quad 9 \quad 7 \quad 4 \quad 9 \quad 11$$

then it computes

$$1 - 4 + 9 - 16 + 9 - 7 + 4 - 9 + 11 = -2$$

■ **E7.7** Write a method that reverses the sequence of elements in an array. For example, if you call the method with the array

$$1 \quad 4 \quad 9 \quad 16 \quad 9 \quad 7 \quad 4 \quad 9 \quad 11$$

then the array is changed to

$$11 \quad 9 \quad 4 \quad 7 \quad 9 \quad 16 \quad 9 \quad 4 \quad 1$$

■■■ **E7.8** Write a program that produces ten random permutations of the numbers 1 to 10. To generate a random permutation, you need to fill an array with the numbers 1 to 10 so that no two entries of the array have the same contents. You could do it by brute force, by generating random values until you have a value that is not yet in the array. But that is inefficient. Instead, follow this algorithm.

> Make a second array and fill it with the numbers 1 to 10.
> Repeat 10 times
>   Pick a random element from the second array.
>   Remove it and append it to the permutation array.

■ **E7.9** Write a method that implements the algorithm developed in Section 7.5.

■■ **E7.10** Consider the following class:

```java
public class Sequence
{
    private int[] values;
    public Sequence(int size) { values = new int[size]; }
    public void set(int i, int n) { values[i] = n; }
}
```

Add a method

```java
public boolean equals(Sequence other)
```

that checks whether the two sequences have the same values in the same order.

E7.11 Add a method

```
public boolean sameValues(Sequence other)
```

to the Sequence class of Exercise E7.10 that checks whether two sequences have the same values in some order, ignoring duplicates. For example, the two sequences

$$1 \quad 4 \quad 9 \quad 16 \quad 9 \quad 7 \quad 4 \quad 9 \quad 11$$

and

$$11 \quad 11 \quad 7 \quad 9 \quad 16 \quad 4 \quad 1$$

would be considered identical. You will probably need one or more helper methods.

E7.12 Add a method

```
public boolean isPermutationOf(Sequence other)
```

to the Sequence class of Exercise E7.10 that checks whether two sequences have the same values in some order, with the same multiplicities. For example,

$$1 \quad 4 \quad 9 \quad 16 \quad 9 \quad 7 \quad 4 \quad 9 \quad 11$$

is a permutation of

$$11 \quad 1 \quad 4 \quad 9 \quad 16 \quad 9 \quad 7 \quad 4 \quad 9$$

but

$$1 \quad 4 \quad 9 \quad 16 \quad 9 \quad 7 \quad 4 \quad 9 \quad 11$$

is not a permutation of

$$11 \quad 11 \quad 7 \quad 9 \quad 16 \quad 4 \quad 1 \quad 4 \quad 9$$

You will probably need one or more helper methods.

E7.13 Write a program that generates a sequence of 20 random values between 0 and 99 in an array, prints the sequence, sorts it, and prints the sorted sequence. Use the sort method from the standard Java library.

E7.14 Consider the following class:

```
public class Table
{
    private int[][] values;
    public Table(int rows, int columns) { values = new int[rows][columns]; }
    public void set(int i, int j, int n) { values[i][j] = n; }
}
```

Add a method that computes the average of the neighbors of a table element in the eight directions shown in Figure 15.

```
public double neighborAverage(int row, int column)
```

However, if the element is located at the boundary of the array, only include the neighbors that are in the table. For example, if row and column are both 0, there are only three neighbors.

E7.15 *Magic squares.* An $n \times n$ matrix that is filled with the numbers $1, 2, 3, \ldots, n^2$ is a magic square if the sum of the elements in each row, in each column, and in the two diagonals is the same value.

Write a program that reads in 16 values from the keyboard and tests whether they form a magic square when put into a 4×4 array.

16	3	2	13
5	10	11	8
9	6	7	12
4	15	14	1

You need to test two features:

1. Does each of the numbers 1, 2, ..., 16 occur in the user input?

2. When the numbers are put into a square, are the sums of the rows, columns, and diagonals equal to each other?

••• E7.16 Implement the following algorithm to construct magic $n \times n$ squares; it works only if n is odd.

```
Set row = n - 1, column = n / 2.
For k = 1 ... n * n
    Place k at [row][column].
    Increment row and column.
    If the row or column is n, replace it with 0.
    If the element at [row][column] has already been filled
        Set row and column to their previous values.
        Decrement row.
```

Here is the 5 × 5 square that you get if you follow this method:

Write a program whose input is the number n and whose output is the magic square of order n if n is odd.

11	18	25	2	9
10	12	19	21	3
4	6	13	20	22
23	5	7	14	16
17	24	1	8	15

•• E7.17 Write a program that reads a sequence of input values and displays a bar chart of the values, using asterisks, like this:

```
**********************
******************************************
***************************
**************************
**************
```

You may assume that all values are positive. First figure out the maximum value. That value's bar should be drawn with 40 asterisks. Shorter bars should use proportionally fewer asterisks.

••• E7.18 Improve the program of Exercise E7.17 to work correctly when the data set contains negative values.

•• E7.19 Improve the program of Exercise E7.17 by adding captions for each bar. Prompt the user for the captions and data values. The output should look like this:

```
      Egypt ***********************
     France *******************************************
      Japan *****************************
    Uruguay **************************
Switzerland **************
```

• E7.20 Consider the following class:

```java
public class Sequence
{
    private ArrayList<Integer> values;
    public Sequence() { values = new ArrayList<Integer>(); }
    public void add(int n) { values.add(n); }
    public String toString() { return values.toString(); }
}
```

Add a method

```
public Sequence append(Sequence other)
```

that creates a new sequence, appending this and the other sequence, without modifying either sequence. For example, if a is

$$1 \quad 4 \quad 9 \quad 16$$

and b is the sequence

$$9 \quad 7 \quad 4 \quad 9 \quad 11$$

then the call a.append(b) returns the sequence

$$1 \quad 4 \quad 9 \quad 16 \quad 9 \quad 7 \quad 4 \quad 9 \quad 11$$

without modifying a or b.

■■ **E7.21** Add a method

```
public Sequence merge(Sequence other)
```

to the Sequence class of Exercise E7.20 that merges two sequences, alternating elements from both sequences. If one sequence is shorter than the other, then alternate as long as you can and then append the remaining elements from the longer sequence. For example, if a is

$$1 \quad 4 \quad 9 \quad 16$$

and b is

$$9 \quad 7 \quad 4 \quad 9 \quad 11$$

then a.merge(b) returns the sequence

$$1 \quad 9 \quad 4 \quad 7 \quad 9 \quad 4 \quad 16 \quad 9 \quad 11$$

without modifying a or b.

■■ **E7.22** Add a method

```
public Sequence mergeSorted(Sequence other)
```

to the Sequence class of Exercise E7.20 that merges two sorted sequences, producing a new sorted sequence. Keep an index into each sequence, indicating how much of it has been processed already. Each time, append the smallest unprocessed value from either sequence, then advance the index. For example, if a is

$$1 \quad 4 \quad 9 \quad 16$$

and b is

$$4 \quad 7 \quad 9 \quad 9 \quad 11$$

then a.mergeSorted(b) returns the sequence

$$1 \quad 4 \quad 4 \quad 7 \quad 9 \quad 9 \quad 9 \quad 11 \quad 16$$

If a or b is not sorted, merge the longest prefixes of a and b that are sorted.

PROGRAMMING PROJECTS

■■ **P7.1** A *run* is a sequence of adjacent repeated values. Write a program that generates a sequence of 20 random die tosses in an array and that prints the die values, marking the runs by including them in parentheses, like this:

1 2 (5 5) 3 1 2 4 3 (2 2 2 2) 3 6 (5 5) 6 3 1

Use the following pseudocode:

```
Set a boolean variable inRun to false.
For each valid index i in the array
    If inRun
        If values[i] is different from the preceding value
            Print ).
            inRun = false.
    If not inRun
        If values[i] is the same as the following value
            Print (.
            inRun = true.
    Print values[i].
If inRun, print ).
```

■■ P7.2 Write a program that generates a sequence of 20 random die tosses in an array and that prints the die values, marking only the longest run, like this:

```
1 2 5 5 3 1 2 4 3 (2 2 2 2) 3 6 5 5 6 3 1
```

If there is more than one run of maximum length, mark the first one.

■■ P7.3 It is a well-researched fact that men in a restroom generally prefer to maximize their distance from already occupied stalls, by occupying the middle of the longest sequence of unoccupied places.

For example, consider the situation where ten stalls are empty.

```
_ _ _ _ _ _ _ _ _ _
```

The first visitor will occupy a middle position:

```
_ _ _ _ _ X _ _ _ _
```

The next visitor will be in the middle of the empty area at the left.

```
_ _ X _ _ X _ _ _ _
```

Write a program that reads the number of stalls and then prints out diagrams in the format given above when the stalls become filled, one at a time. *Hint:* Use an array of boolean values to indicate whether a stall is occupied.

■■■ P7.4 In this assignment, you will model the game of *Bulgarian Solitaire*. The game starts with 45 cards. (They need not be playing cards. Unmarked index cards work just as well.) Randomly divide them into some number of piles of random size. For example, you might start with piles of size 20, 5, 1, 9, and 10. In each round, you take one card from each pile, forming a new pile with these cards. For example, the sample starting configuration would be transformed into piles of size 19, 4, 8, 9, and 5. The solitaire is over when the piles have size 1, 2, 3, 4, 5, 6, 7, 8, and 9, in some order. (It can be shown that you always end up with such a configuration.)

In your program, produce a random starting configuration and print it. Then keep applying the solitaire step and print the result. Stop when the solitaire final configuration is reached.

•• P7.5 A theater seating chart is implemented as a two-dimensional array of ticket prices, like this:

```
10 10 10 10 10 10 10 10 10 10
10 10 10 10 10 10 10 10 10 10
10 10 10 10 10 10 10 10 10 10
10 10 20 20 20 20 20 20 10 10
10 10 20 20 20 20 20 20 10 10
10 10 20 20 20 20 20 20 10 10
20 20 30 30 40 40 30 30 20 20
20 30 30 40 50 50 40 30 30 20
30 40 50 50 50 50 50 50 40 30
```

Write a program that prompts users to pick either a seat or a price. Mark sold seats by changing the price to 0. When a user specifies a seat, make sure it is available. When a user specifies a price, find any seat with that price.

••• P7.6 Write a program that plays tic-tac-toe. The tic-tac-toe game is played on a 3 × 3 grid as in the photo at right. The game is played by two players, who take turns. The first player marks moves with a circle, the second with a cross. The player who has formed a horizontal, vertical, or diagonal sequence of three marks wins. Your program should draw the game board, ask the user for the coordinates of the next mark, change the players after every successful move, and pronounce the winner.

••• P7.7 In this assignment, you will implement a simulation of a popular casino game usually called video poker. The card deck contains 52 cards, 13 of each suit. At the beginning of the game, the deck is shuffled. You need to devise a fair method for shuffling. (It does not have to be efficient.) The player pays a token for each game. Then the top five cards of the deck are presented to the player. The player can reject none, some, or all of the cards. The rejected cards are replaced from the top of the deck. Now the hand is scored. Your program should pronounce it to be one of the following:

- No pair—The lowest hand, containing five separate cards that do not match up to create any of the hands below.
- One pair—Two cards of the same value, for example two queens. Payout: 1
- Two pairs—Two pairs, for example two queens and two 5's. Payout: 2
- Three of a kind—Three cards of the same value, for example three queens. Payout: 3
- Straight—Five cards with consecutive values, not necessarily of the same suit, such as 4, 5, 6, 7, and 8. The ace can either precede a 2 or follow a king. Payout: 4
- Flush—Five cards, not necessarily in order, of the same suit. Payout: 5
- Full House—Three of a kind and a pair, for example three queens and two 5's. Payout: 6
- Four of a Kind—Four cards of the same value, such as four queens. Payout: 25
- Straight Flush—A straight and a flush: Five cards with consecutive values of the same suit. Payout: 50
- Royal Flush—The best possible hand in poker. A 10, jack, queen, king, and ace, all of the same suit. Payout: 250

••• P7.8 *The Game of Life* is a well-known mathematical game that gives rise to amazingly complex behavior, although it can be specified by a few simple rules. (It is not actually a game in the traditional sense, with players competing for a win.) Here are the rules. The game is played on a rectangular board. Each square can be either empty or occupied. At the beginning, you can specify empty and occupied cells in some way; then the game runs automatically. In each *generation*, the next generation is computed. A new cell is born on an empty square if it is surrounded by exactly three occupied neighbor cells. A cell dies of overcrowding if it is surrounded by four or more neighbors, and it dies of loneliness if it is surrounded by zero or one neighbor. A neighbor is an occupant of an adjacent square to the left, right, top, or bottom or in a diagonal direction. Figure 21 shows a cell and its neighbor cells.

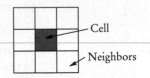

Figure 21
Neighborhood of a Cell

Many configurations show interesting behavior when subjected to these rules. Figure 22 shows a *glider*, observed over five generations. After four generations, it is transformed into the identical shape, but located one square to the right and below.

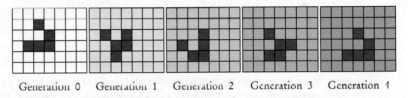

Generation 0   Generation 1   Generation 2   Generation 3   Generation 4

Figure 22   Glider

One of the more amazing configurations is the glider gun: a complex collection of cells that, after 30 moves, turns back into itself and a glider (see Figure 23).

Program the game to eliminate the drudgery of computing successive generations by hand. Use a two-dimensional array to store the rectangular configuration. Write a program that shows successive generations of the game. Ask the user to specify the original configuration, by typing in a configuration of spaces and o characters.

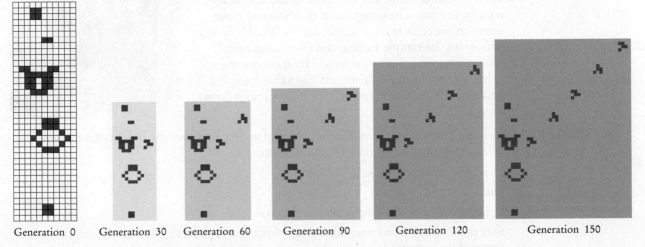

Generation 0   Generation 30   Generation 60   Generation 90   Generation 120   Generation 150

Figure 23   Glider Gun

■■ Business P7.9 A pet shop wants to give a discount to its clients if they buy one or more pets and at least five other items. The discount is equal to 20 percent of the cost of the other items, but not the pets.

Use a class `Item` to describe an item, with any needed methods and a constructor

```
public Item(double price, boolean isPet, int quantity)
```

An invoice holds a collection of `Item` objects; use an array or array list to store them. In the `Invoice` class, implement methods

```
public void add(Item anItem)
public double getDiscount()
```

Write a program that prompts a cashier to enter each price and quantity, and then a `Y` for a pet or `N` for another item. Use a price of –1 as a sentinel. In the loop, call the `add` method; after the loop, call the `getDiscount` method and display the returned value.

■■ Business P7.10 A supermarket wants to reward its best customer of each day, showing the customer's name on a screen in the supermarket. For that purpose, the store keeps an `ArrayList<Customer>`. In the `Store` class, implement methods

```
public void addSale(String customerName, double amount)
public String nameOfBestCustomer()
```

to record the sale and return the name of the customer with the largest sale.

Write a program that prompts the cashier to enter all prices and names, adds them to a `Store` object, and displays the best customer's name. Use a price of 0 as a sentinel.

■■■ Business P7.11 Improve the program of Exercise P7.10 so that it displays the top customers, that is, the `topN` customers with the largest sales, where `topN` is a value that the user of the program supplies. Implement a method

```
public ArrayList<String> nameOfBestCustomers(int topN)
```

If there were fewer than `topN` customers, include all of them.

■■ Science P7.12 Sounds can be represented by an array of "sample values" that describe the intensity of the sound at a point in time. The program in ch07/sound of your companion code reads a sound file (in WAV format), processes the sample values, and shows the result. Your task is to process the sound by introducing an echo. For each sound value, add the value from 0.2 seconds ago. Scale the result so that no value is larger than 32767.

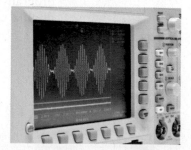

■■■ Science P7.13 You are given a two-dimensional array of values that give the height of a terrain at different points in a square. Write a constructor

```
public Terrain(double[][] heights)
```

and a method

```
public void printFloodMap(double waterLevel)
```

that prints out a flood map, showing which of the points in the terrain would be flooded if the water level was the given value.

In the flood map, print a * for each flooded point and a space for each point that is not flooded.

Here is a sample map:

Then write a program that reads one hundred terrain height values and shows how the terrain gets flooded when the water level increases in ten steps from the lowest point in the terrain to the highest.

■■ Science P7.14 Sample values from an experiment often need to be smoothed out. One simple approach is to replace each value in an array with the average of the value and its two neighboring values (or one neighboring value if it is at either end of the array). Given a class Data with instance fields

```
private double[] values;
private double valuesSize;
```

implement a method

```
public void smooth()
```

that carries out this operation. You should not create another array in your solution.

■■■ Science P7.15 Write a program that models the movement of an object with mass m that is attached to an oscillating spring. When a spring is displaced from its equilibrium position by an amount x, Hooke's law states that the restoring force is

$$F = -kx$$

where k is a constant that depends on the spring. (Use 10 N/m for this simulation.)

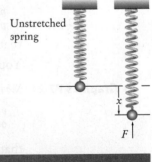

Unstretched spring

Start with a given displacement x (say, 0.5 meter). Set the initial velocity v to 0. Compute the acceleration a from Newton's law ($F = ma$) and Hooke's law, using a mass of 1 kg. Use a small time interval $\Delta t = 0.01$ second. Update the velocity—it changes by $a\Delta t$. Update the displacement—it changes by $v\Delta t$.

Every ten iterations, plot the spring displacement as a bar, where 1 pixel represents 1 cm, as shown here.

■■ Graphics P7.16 Generate the image of a checkerboard.

▪ Graphics P7.17 Generate the image of a sine wave. Draw a line of pixels for every five degrees.

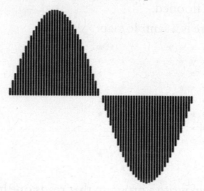

▪ Graphics P7.18 Implement a class `Cloud` that contains an array list of `Point2D.Double` objects. Support methods

```
public void add(Point2D.Double aPoint)
public void draw(Graphics2D g2)
```

Draw each point as a tiny circle. Write a graphical application that draws a cloud of 100 random points.

▪▪ Graphics P7.19 Implement a class `Polygon` that contains an array list of `Point2D.Double` objects. Support methods

```
public void add(Point2D.Double aPoint)
public void draw(Graphics2D g2)
```

Draw the polygon by joining adjacent points with a line, and then closing it up by joining the end and start points. Write a graphical application that draws a square and a pentagon using two `Polygon` objects.

▪ Graphics P7.20 Write a class `Chart` with methods

```
public void add(int value)
public void draw(Graphics2D g2)
```

that displays a stick chart of the added values, like this:

You may assume that the values are pixel positions.

▪▪ Graphics P7.21 Write a class `BarChart` with methods

```
public void add(double value)
public void draw(Graphics2D g2)
```

that displays a bar chart of the added values. You may assume that all added values are positive. Stretch the bars so that they fill the entire area of the screen. You must figure out the maximum of the values, then scale each bar.

▪▪▪ Graphics P7.22 Improve the `BarChart` class of Exercise P7.21 to work correctly when the data contains negative values.

▪▪ Graphics P7.23 Write a class `PieChart` with methods

```
public void add(double value)
public void draw(Graphics2D g2)
```

that displays a pie chart of the added values. Assume that all data values are positive.

ANSWERS TO SELF-CHECK QUESTIONS

1. `int[] primes = { 2, 3, 5, 7, 11 };`

2. 2, 3, 5, 3, 2

3. 3, 4, 6, 8, 12

4.
```
values[0] = 10;
values[9] = 10;   or better:
values[values.length - 1] = 10;
```

5. `String[] words = new String[10];`

6. `String[] words = { "Yes", "No" };`

7. No. Because you don't store the values, you need to print them when you read them. But you don't know where to add the <= until you have seen all values.

8.
```
public class Lottery
{
    public int[] getCombination(int n) { . . . }
    . . .
}
```

9. It counts how many elements of values are zero.

10.
```
for (double x : values)
{
    System.out.println(x);
}
```

11.
```
double product = 1;
for (double f : factors)
{
    product = product * f;
}
```

12. The loop writes a value into values[i]. The enhanced for loop does not have the index variable i.

13.
```
20 <== largest value
10
20 <== largest value
```

14.
```
int count = 0;
for (double x : values)
{
    if (x == 0) { count++; }
}
```

15. If all elements of values are negative, then the result is incorrectly computed as 0.

16.
```
for (int i = 0; i < values.length; i++)
{
    System.out.print(values[i]);
    if (i < values.length - 1)
    {
        System.out.print(" | ");
    }
}
```

}

Now you know why we set up the loop the other way.

17. If the array has no elements, then the program terminates with an exception.

18. If there is a match, then pos is incremented before the loop exits.

19. This loop sets all elements to values[pos].

20. Use the first algorithm. The order of elements does not matter when computing the sum.

21. Find the minimum value.
Calculate the sum.
Subtract the minimum value.

22. Use the algorithm for counting matches (Section 6.7.2) twice, once for counting the positive values and once for counting the negative values.

23. You need to modify the algorithm in Section 7.3.4.
```
boolean first = true;
for (int i = 0; i < values.length; i++)
{
    if (values[i] > 0))
    {
        if (first) { first = false; }
        else { System.out.print(", "); }
    }
    System.out.print(values[i]);
}
```

Note that you can no longer use i > 0 as the criterion for printing a separator.

24. Use the algorithm to collect all positive elements in an array, then use the algorithm in Section 7.3.4 to print the array of matches.

25. The paperclip for i assumes positions 0, 1, 2, 3. When i is incremented to 4, the condition i < size / 2 becomes false, and the loop ends. Similarly, the paperclip for j assumes positions 4, 5, 6, 7, which are the valid positions for the second half of the array.

26. It reverses the elements in the array.

27. Here is one solution. The basic idea is to move all odd elements to the end. Put one paper clip at the beginning of the array and one at the end. If the element at the first paper clip is odd, swap it with the one at the other paper clip and move that paper clip to the left. Otherwise, move the first paper clip to the right. Stop when the two paper clips meet. Here is the pseudocode:

i = 0
j = size - 1
While (i < j)
  If (a[i] is odd)
    Swap elements at positions i and j.
    j--
  Else
    i++

28. Here is one solution. The idea is to remove all odd elements and move them to the end. The trick is to know when to stop. Nothing is gained by moving odd elements into the area that already contains moved elements, so we want to mark that area with another paper clip.

i = 0
moved = size
While (i < moved)
  If (a[i] is odd)
    Remove the element at position i and add it
      at the end.
    moved--

29. When you read inputs, you get to see values one at a time, and you can't peek ahead. Picking cards one at a time from a deck of cards simulates this process better than looking at a sequence of items, all of which are revealed.

30. You get the total number of gold, silver, and bronze medals in the competition. In our example, there are four of each.

31.
```
for (int i = 0; i < 8; i++)
{
    for (int j = 0; j < 8; j++)
    {
        board[i][j] = (i + j) % 2;
    }
}
```

32. `String[][] board = new String[3][3];`

33. `board[0][2] = "x";`

34. `board[0][0], board[1][1], board[2][2]`

35.
```
ArrayList<Integer> primes =
    new ArrayList<Integer>();
primes.add(2);
primes.add(3);
primes.add(5);
primes.add(7);
primes.add(11);
```

36.
```
for (int i = primes.size() - 1; i >= 0; i--)
{
    System.out.println(primes.get(i));
}
```

37. `"Ann", "Cal"`

38. The names variable has not been initialized.

39. names1 contains `"Emily"`, `"Bob"`, `"Cindy"`, `"Dave"`; names2 contains `"Dave"`

40. Because the number of weekdays doesn't change, there is no disadvantage to using an array, and it is easier to initialize:

```
String[] weekdayNames = { "Monday", "Tuesday",
    "Wednesday", "Thursday", "Friday",
    "Saturday", "Sunday" };
```

41. Reading inputs into an array list is much easier.

42. It is possible to introduce errors when modifying code.

43. Add a test case to the test suite that verifies that the error is fixed.

44. There is no human user who would see the prompts because input is provided from a file.

CHAPTER 8

DESIGNING CLASSES

To learn how to choose appropriate
classes for a given problem

To understand the concept of cohesion

To minimize dependencies and
side effects

To learn how to find a data representation for a class

To understand static methods and variables

To learn about packages

To learn about unit testing frameworks

CHAPTER CONTENTS

Good design should be both functional and attractive. When designing classes, each class should be dedicated to a particular purpose, and classes should work well together. In this chapter, you will learn how to discover classes, design good methods, and choose appropriate data representations. You will also learn how to design features that belong to the class as a whole, not individual objects, by using static methods and variables. You will see how to use packages to organize your classes. Finally, we introduce the JUnit testing framework that lets you verify the functionality of your classes.

8.1 Discovering Classes

You have used a good number of classes in the preceding chapters and probably designed a few classes yourself as part of your programming assignments. Designing a class can be a challenge—it is not always easy to tell how to start or whether the result is of good quality.

What makes a good class? Most importantly, a class should *represent a single concept* from a problem domain. Some of the classes that you have seen represent concepts from mathematics:

> A class should represent a single concept from a problem domain, such as business, science, or mathematics.

- `Point`
- `Rectangle`
- `Ellipse`

Other classes are abstractions of real-life entities:

- `BankAccount`
- `CashRegister`

For these classes, the properties of a typical object are easy to understand. A `Rectangle` object has a width and height. Given a `BankAccount` object, you can deposit and withdraw money. Generally, concepts from a domain related to the program's purpose, such as science, business, or gaming, make good classes. The name for such a class should be a noun that describes the concept. In fact, a simple rule of thumb for getting started with class design is to look for nouns in the problem description.

One useful category of classes can be described as *actors*. Objects of an actor class carry out certain tasks for you. Examples of actors are the `Scanner` class of Chapter 4 and the `Random` class in Chapter 6. A `Scanner` object scans a stream for numbers and strings. A `Random` object generates random numbers. It is a good idea to choose class names for actors that end in "-er" or "-or". (A better name for the `Random` class might be `RandomNumberGenerator`.)

Very occasionally, a class has no objects, but it contains a collection of related static methods and constants. The `Math` class is an example. Such a class is called a *utility class*.

Finally, you have seen classes with only a `main` method. Their sole purpose is to start a program. From a design perspective, these are somewhat degenerate examples of classes.

What might not be a good class? If you can't tell from the class name what an object of the class is supposed to do, then you are probably not on the right track. For example, your homework assignment might ask you to write a program that prints paychecks. Suppose you start by trying to design a class PaycheckProgram. What would an object of this class do? An object of this class would have to do everything that the homework needs to do. That doesn't simplify anything. A better class would be Paycheck. Then your program can manipulate one or more Paycheck objects.

Another common mistake is to turn a single operation into a class. For example, if your homework assignment is to compute a paycheck, you may consider writing a class ComputePaycheck. But can you visualize a "ComputePaycheck" object? The fact that "ComputePaycheck" isn't a noun tips you off that you are on the wrong track. On the other hand, a Paycheck class makes intuitive sense. The word "paycheck" is a noun. You can visualize a paycheck object. You can then think about useful methods of the Paycheck class, such as computeTaxes, that help you solve the assignment.

SELF CHECK

1. What is a simple rule of thumb for finding classes?
2. Your job is to write a program that plays chess. Might ChessBoard be an appropriate class? How about MovePiece?

Practice It   Now you can try these exercises at the end of the chapter: R8.1, R8.2, R8.3.

8.2 Designing Good Methods

In the following sections, you will learn several useful criteria for analyzing and improving the public interface of a class.

8.2.1 Providing a Cohesive Public Interface

> The public interface of a class is cohesive if all of its features are related to the concept that the class represents.

A class should represent a single concept. All interface features should be closely related to the single concept that the class represents. Such a public interface is said to be **cohesive**.

The members of a cohesive team have a common goal.

If you find that the public interface of a class refers to multiple concepts, then that is a good sign that it may be time to use separate classes instead. Consider, for example, the public interface of the CashRegister class in Chapter 4:

```
public class CashRegister
{
    public static final double QUARTER_VALUE = 0.25;
    public static final double DIME_VALUE = 0.1;
    public static final double NICKEL_VALUE = 0.05;
    . . .
    public void receivePayment(int dollars, int quarters,
            int dimes, int nickels, int pennies)
    . . .
}
```

There are really two concepts here: a cash register that holds coins and computes their total, and the values of individual coins. (For simplicity, we assume that the cash register only holds coins, not bills. Exercise E8.3 discusses a more general solution.)

It makes sense to have a separate Coin class and have coins responsible for knowing their values.

```java
public class Coin
{
    . . .
    public Coin(double aValue, String aName) { . . . }
    public double getValue() { . . . }
    . . .
}
```

Then the CashRegister class can be simplified:

```java
public class CashRegister
{
    . . .
    public void receivePayment(int coinCount, Coin coinType) { . . . }
    {
        payment = payment + coinCount * coinType.getValue();
    }
    . . .
}
```

Now the CashRegister class no longer needs to know anything about coin values. The same class can equally well handle euros or zorkmids!

This is clearly a better solution, because it separates the responsibilities of the cash register and the coins. The only reason we didn't follow this approach in Chapter 4 was to keep the CashRegister example simple.

8.2.2 Minimizing Dependencies

A class depends on another class if its methods use that class in any way.

Many methods need other classes in order to do their jobs. For example, the receivePayment method of the restructured CashRegister class now uses the Coin class. We say that the CashRegister class *depends on* the Coin class.

To visualize relationships between classes, such as dependence, programmers draw class diagrams. In this book, we use the UML ("**Unified Modeling Language**") notation for objects and classes. UML is a notation for object-oriented analysis and design invented by Grady Booch, Ivar Jacobson, and James Rumbaugh, three leading researchers in object-oriented softare development. (Appendix H has a summary of the UML notation used in this book.) The UML notation distinguishes between *object diagrams* and class diagrams. In an object diagram the class names are underlined; in a class diagram the class names are not underlined. In a class diagram, you denote dependency by a dashed line with a ⤻-shaped open arrow tip that points to the dependent class. Figure 1 shows a class diagram indicating that the CashRegister class depends on the Coin class.

Note that the Coin class does *not* depend on the CashRegister class. All Coin methods can carry out their work without ever calling any method in the CashRegister class. Conceptually, coins have no idea that they are being collected in cash registers.

Here is an example of minimizing dependencies. Consider how we have always printed a bank balance:

```java
System.out.println("The balance is now $" + momsSavings.getBalance());
```

Figure 1
Dependency Relationship Between the CashRegister and Coin Classes

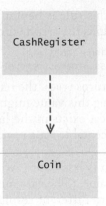

Why don't we simply have a printBalance method?

```
public void printBalance() // Not recommended
{
    System.out.println("The balance is now $" + balance);
}
```

The method depends on System.out. Not every computing environment has System.out. For example, an automatic teller machine doesn't display console messages. In other words, this design violates the rule of minimizing dependencies. The printBalance method couples the BankAccount class with the System and PrintStream classes.

It is best to place the code for producing output or consuming input in a separate class. That way, you decouple input/output from the actual work of your classes.

8.2.3 Separating Accessors and Mutators

A **mutator method** changes the state of an object. Conversely, an **accessor method** asks an object to compute a result, without changing the state.

Some classes have been designed to have only accessor methods and no mutator methods at all. Such classes are called **immutable**. An example is the String class. Once a string has been constructed, its content never changes. No method in the String class can modify the contents of a string. For example, the toUpperCase method does not change characters from the original string. Instead, it constructs a *new* string that contains the uppercase characters:

> An immutable class has no mutator methods.

```
String name = "John Q. Public";
String uppercased = name.toUpperCase(); // name is not changed
```

An immutable class has a major advantage: It is safe to give out references to its objects freely. If no method can change the object's value, then no code can modify the object at an unexpected time.

> References to objects of an immutable class can be safely shared.

Not every class should be immutable. Immutability makes most sense for classes that represent values, such as strings, dates, currency amounts, colors, and so on.

In mutable classes, it is still a good idea to cleanly separate accessors and mutators, in order to avoid accidental mutation. As a rule of thumb, a method that returns a value should not be a mutator. For example, one would not expect that calling getBalance on a BankAccount object would change the balance. (You would be pretty upset if your bank charged you a "balance inquiry fee".) If you follow this rule, then all mutators of your class have return type void.

Sometimes, this rule is bent a bit, and mutator methods return an informational value. For example, the `ArrayList` class has a `remove` method to remove an object.

```
ArrayList<String> names = ...;
boolean success = names.remove("Romeo");
```

That method returns `true` if the removal was successful; that is, if the list contained the object. Returning this value might be bad design if there was no other way to check whether an object exists in the list. However, there is such a method—the `contains` method. It is acceptable for a mutator to return a value if there is also an accessor that computes it.

The situation is less happy with the `Scanner` class. The `next` method is a mutator that returns a value. (The `next` method really is a mutator. If you call `next` twice in a row, it can return different results, so it must have mutated something inside the `Scanner` object.) Unfortunately, there is no accessor that returns the same value. This sometimes makes it awkward to use a `Scanner`. You must carefully hang on to the value that the `next` method returns because you have no second chance to ask for it. It would have been better if there was another method, say `peek`, that yields the next input without consuming it.

To check the temperature of the water in the bottle, you could take a sip, but that would be the equivalent of a mutator method.

8.2.4 Minimizing Side Effects

A **side effect** of a method is any kind of modification of data that is observable outside the method. Mutator methods have a side effect, namely the modification of the implicit parameter.

> A side effect of a method is any externally observable data modification.

There is another kind of side effect that you should avoid. A method should generally not modify its parameter variables. Consider this example:

```
/**
    Computes the total balance of the given accounts.
    @param accounts a list of bank accounts
*/
    public double getTotalBalance(ArrayList<String> accounts)
    {
        double sum = 0;
        while (studentNames.size() > 0)
        {
            BankAccount account = accounts.remove(0); // Not recommended
            sum = sum + account.getBalance();
        }
        return sum;
    }
}
```

This method *removes* all names from the accounts parameter variable. After a call

```
double total = getTotalBalance(allAccounts);
```

`allAccounts` is empty! Such a side effect would not be what most programmers expect. It is better if the method visits the elements from the list without removing them.

When designing methods, minimize side effects.

Another example of a side effect is output. Consider again the printBalance method that we discussed in Section 8.2.2:

```java
public void printBalance() // Not recommended
{
    System.out.println("The balance is now $" + balance);
}
```

This method mutates the System.out object, which is not a part of the BankAccount object. That is a side effect.

To avoid this side effect, keep most of your classes free from input and output operations, and concentrate input and output in one place, such as the main method of your program.

This taxi has an undesirable side effect, spraying bystanders with muddy water.

SELF CHECK

3. Why is the CashRegister class from Chapter 4 not cohesive?
4. Why does the Coin class not depend on the CashRegister class?
5. Why is it a good idea to minimize dependencies between classes?
6. Is the substring method of the String class an accessor or a mutator?
7. Is the Rectangle class immutable?
8. If a refers to a bank account, then the call a.deposit(100) modifies the bank account object. Is that a side effect?
9. Consider the Student class of Chapter 7. Suppose we add a method

```java
void read(Scanner in)
{
    while (in.hasNextDouble())
    {
        addScore(in.nextDouble());
    }
}
```

Does this method have a side effect other than mutating the scores?

Practice It   Now you can try these exercises at the end of the chapter: R8.4, R8.5, R8.9.

Programming Tip 8.1

Consistency

In this section you learned of two criteria for analyzing the quality of the public interface of a class. You should maximize cohesion and remove unnecessary dependencies. There is another criterion that we would like you to pay attention to—*consistency*. When you have a set of methods, follow a consistent scheme for their names and parameter variables. This is simply a sign of good craftsmanship.

Sadly, you can find any number of inconsistencies in the standard library. Here is an example: To show an input dialog box, you call

```java
JOptionPane.showInputDialog(promptString)
```

To show a message dialog box, you call

```
JOptionPane.showMessageDialog(null, messageString)
```

What's the `null` argument? It turns out that the `showMessage-Dialog` method needs an argument to specify the parent window, or `null` if no parent window is required. But the `showInputDialog` method requires no parent window. Why the inconsistency? There is no reason. It would have been an easy matter to supply a `showMessageDialog` method that exactly mirrors the `showInputDialog` method.

Inconsistencies such as these are not fatal flaws, but they are an annoyance, particularly because they can be so easily avoided.

While it is possible to eat with mismatched silverware, consistency is more pleasant.

Special Topic 8.1

Call by Value and Call by Reference

In Section 8.2.4, we recommended that you don't invoke a mutator method on a parameter variable. In this Special Topic, we discuss a related issue—what happens when you assign a new value to a parameter variable. Consider this method:

```java
public class BankAccount
{
   . . .
   /**
      Transfers money from this account and tries to add it to a balance.
      @param amount the amount of money to transfer
      @param otherBalance balance to add the amount to
   */
   public void transfer(double amount, double otherBalance) ❷
   {
      balance = balance - amount;
      otherBalance = otherBalance + amount;
         // Won't update the argument
   } ❸
}
```

Now let's see what happens when we call the method:

```java
double savingsBalance = 1000;
harrysChecking.transfer(500, savingsBalance); ❶
System.out.println(savingsBalance); ❹
```

You might expect that after the call, the `savingsBalance` variable has been incremented to 1500. However, that is not the case. As the method starts, the parameter variable `otherBalance` is set to the same value as `savingsBalance` (see Figure 2). Then the variable is set to a different value. That modification has no effect on `savingsBalance`, because `otherBalance` is a separate variable. When the method terminates, the `otherBalance` variable is removed, and `savingsBalance` isn't increased.

In Java, parameter variables are initialized with the values of the argument expressions. When the method exits, the parameter variables are removed. Computer scientists refer to this call mechanism as "call by value".

> In Java, a method can never change the contents of a variable that is passed to a method.

For that reason, a Java method can never change the contents of a variable that is passed as an argument—the method manipulates a different variable.

Other programming languages such as C++ support a mechanism, called "call by reference", that can change the arguments of a method call. You will sometimes read in Java books

ANIMATION
*A Method Cannot
Modify a Numeric
Parameter*

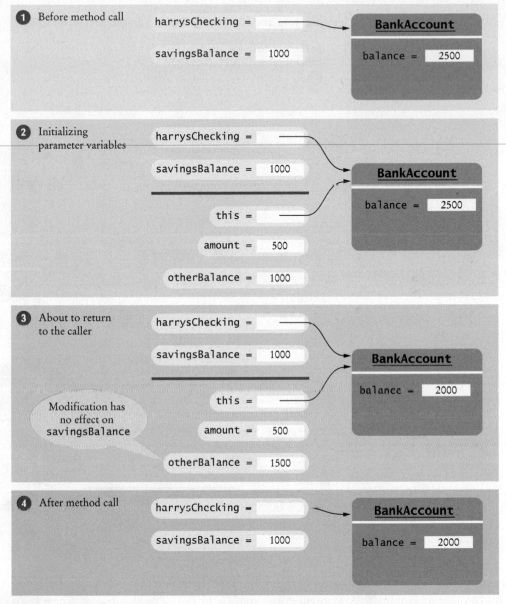

Figure 2   Modifying a Parameter Variable of a Primitive Type Has No Effect on Caller

that "numbers are passed by value, objects are passed by reference". That is technically not quite correct. In Java, objects themselves are never passed as arguments; instead, both numbers and *object references* are passed by value.

The confusion arises because a Java method can mutate an object when it receives an object reference as an argument (see Figure 3).

```
public class BankAccount
{
    . . .
    /**
        Transfers money from this account to another.
        @param amount the amount of money to transfer
        @param otherAccount account to add the amount to
```

```
        */
    public void transfer(double amount, BankAccount otherAccount)  ②
    {
        balance = balance - amount;
        otherAccount.deposit(amount);
    }  ③
}
```

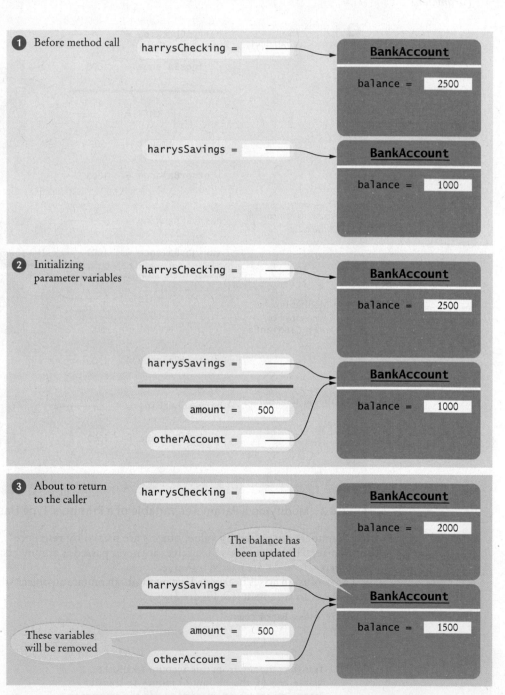

Figure 3 Methods Can Mutate Any Objects to Which They Hold References

Now we pass an object reference to the transfer method:

```
BankAccount harrysSavings = new BankAccount(1000);
harrysChecking.transfer(500, harrysSavings);  ❶
System.out.println(harrysSavings.getBalance());
```

This example works as expected. The parameter variable otherAccount contains a *copy* of the object reference harrysSavings. You saw in Section 2.8 what it means to make a copy of an object reference—you get another reference to the same object. Through that reference, the method is able to modify the object.

However, a method cannot *replace* an object reference that is passed as an argument. To appreciate this subtle difference, consider this method that tries to set the otherAccount parameter variable to a new object:

```
public class BankAccount
{
    . . .
    public void transfer(double amount, BankAccount otherAccount)
    {
        balance = balance - amount;
        double newBalance = otherAccount.balance + amount;
        otherAccount = new BankAccount(newBalance); // Won't work
    }
}
```

In this situation, we are not trying to change the state of the object to which the parameter variable otherAccount refers; instead, we are trying to replace the object with a different one (see Figure 4). Now the reference stored in parameter variable otherAccount is replaced with a reference to a new account. But if you call the method with

> In Java, a method can change the state of an object reference argument, but it cannot replace the object reference with another.

```
harrysChecking.transfer(500, savingsAccount);
```

then that change does not affect the savingsAccount variable that is supplied in the call. This example demonstrates that objects are not passed by reference.

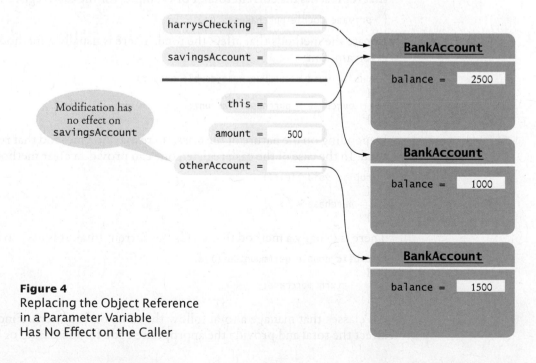

Figure 4
Replacing the Object Reference
in a Parameter Variable
Has No Effect on the Caller

To summarize:

- A Java method can't change the contents of any variable passed as an argument.
- A Java method can mutate an object when it receives a reference to it as an argument.

8.3 Problem Solving: Patterns for Object Data

When you design a class, you first consider the needs of the programmers who use the class. You provide the methods that the users of your class will call when they manipulate objects. When you implement the class, you need to come up with the instance variables for the class. It is not always obvious how to do this. Fortunately, there is a small set of recurring patterns that you can adapt when you design your own classes. We introduce these patterns in the following sections.

8.3.1 Keeping a Total

An instance variable for the total is updated in methods that increase or decrease the total amount.

Many classes need to keep track of a quantity that can go up or down as certain methods are called. Examples:

- A bank account has a balance that is increased by a deposit, decreased by a withdrawal.
- A cash register has a total that is increased when an item is added to the sale, cleared after the end of the sale.
- A car has gas in the tank, which is increased when fuel is added and decreased when the car drives.

In all of these cases, the implementation strategy is similar. Keep an instance variable that represents the current total. For example, for the cash register:

```java
private double purchase;
```

Locate the methods that affect the total. There is usually a method to increase it by a given amount:

```java
public void recordPurchase(double amount)
{
    purchase = purchase + amount;
}
```

Depending on the nature of the class, there may be a method that reduces or clears the total. In the case of the cash register, one can provide a clear method:

```java
public void clear()
{
    purchase = 0;
}
```

There is usually a method that yields the current total. It is easy to implement:

```java
public double getAmountDue()
{
    return purchase;
}
```

All classes that manage a total follow the same basic pattern. Find the methods that affect the total and provide the appropriate code for increasing or decreasing it. Find the methods that report or use the total, and have those methods read the current total.

8.3.2 Counting Events

A counter that counts events is incremented in methods that correspond to the events.

You often need to count how many times certain events occur in the life of an object. For example:

- In a cash register, you may want to know how many items have been added in a sale.
- A bank account charges a fee for each transaction; you need to count them.

Keep a counter, such as

```java
private int itemCount;
```

Increment the counter in those methods that correspond to the events that you want to count:

```java
public void recordPurchase(double amount)
{
    purchase = purchase + amount;
    itemCount++;
}
```

You may need to clear the counter, for example at the end of a sale or a statement period:

```java
public void clear()
{
    purchase = 0;
    itemCount = 0;
}
```

There may or may not be a method that reports the count to the class user. The count may only be used to compute a fee or an average. Find out which methods in your class make use of the count, and read the current value in those methods.

8.3.3 Collecting Values

Some objects collect numbers, strings, or other objects. For example, each multiple-choice question has a number of choices. A cash register may need to store all prices of the current sale.

An object can collect other objects in an array or array list.

Use an array list or an array to store the values. (An array list is usually simpler because you won't need to track the number of values.) For example,

```java
public class Question
{
    private ArrayList<String> choices;
    . . .
}
```

A shopping cart object needs to manage a collection of items.

In the constructor, initialize the instance variable to an empty collection:

```
public Question()
{
    choices = new ArrayList<String>();
}
```

You need to supply some mechanism for adding values. It is common to provide a method for appending a value to the collection:

```
public void add(String option)
{
    choices.add(option);
}
```

The user of a Question object can call this method multiple times to add the choices.

8.3.4 Managing Properties of an Object

An object property can be accessed with a getter method and changed with a setter method.

A property is a value of an object that an object user can set and retrieve. For example, a Student object may have a name and an ID. Provide an instance variable to store the property's value and methods to get and set it.

```
public class Student
{
    private String name;
    . . .
    public String getName() { return name; }
    public void setName(String newName) { name = newName; }
    . . .
}
```

It is common to add error checking to the setter method. For example, we may want to reject a blank name:

```
public void setName(String newName)
{
    if (newName.length() > 0) { name = newName; }
}
```

Some properties should not change after they have been set in the constructor. For example, a student's ID may be fixed (unlike the student's name, which may change). In that case, don't supply a setter method.

```
public class Student
{
    private int id;
    . . .
    public Student(int anId) { id = anId; }
    public String getId() { return id; }
    // No setId method
    . . .
}
```

8.3.5 Modeling Objects with Distinct States

Some objects have behavior that varies depending on what has happened in the past. For example, a Fish object may look for food when it is hungry and ignore food after it has eaten. Such an object would need to remember whether it has recently eaten.

If a fish is in a hungry state, its behavior changes.

If your object can have one of several states that affect the behavior, supply an instance variable for the current state.

Supply an instance variable that models the state, together with some constants for the state values:

```
public class Fish
{
    private int hungry;

    public static final int NOT_HUNGRY = 0;
    public static final int SOMEWHAT_HUNGRY = 1;
    public static final int VERY_HUNGRY = 2;
    . . .
}
```

(Alternatively, you can use an enumeration—see Special Topic 5.4.)

Determine which methods change the state. In this example, a fish that has just eaten won't be hungry. But as the fish moves, it will get hungrier:

```
public void eat()
{
    hungry = NOT_HUNGRY;
    . . .
}

public void move()
{
    . . .
    if (hungry < VERY_HUNGRY) { hungry++; }
}
```

Finally, determine where the state affects behavior. A fish that is very hungry will want to look for food first:

```
public void move()
{
    if (hungry == VERY_HUNGRY)
    {
        Look for food.
    }
    . . .
}
```

8.3.6 Describing the Position of an Object

To model a moving object, you need to store and update its position.

Some objects move around during their lifetime, and they remember their current position. For example,

- A train drives along a track and keeps track of the distance from the terminus.
- A simulated bug living on a grid crawls from one grid location to the next, or makes 90 degree turns to the left or right.
- A cannonball is shot into the air, then descends as it is pulled by the gravitational force.

Such objects need to store their position. Depending on the nature of their movement, they may also need to store their orientation or velocity.

A bug in a grid needs to store its row, column, and direction.

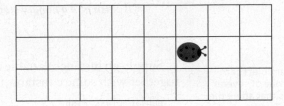

If the object moves along a line, you can represent the position as a distance from a fixed point:

```java
private double distanceFromTerminus;
```

If the object moves in a grid, remember its current location and direction in the grid:

```java
private int row;
private int column;
private int direction; // 0 = North, 1 = East, 2 = South, 3 = West
```

When you model a physical object such as a cannonball, you need to track both the position and the velocity, possibly in two or three dimensions. Here we model a cannonball that is shot upward into the air:

```java
private double zPosition;
private double zVelocity;
```

There will be methods that update the position. In the simplest case, you may be told by how much the object moves:

```java
public void move(double distanceMoved)
{
    distanceFromTerminus = distanceFromTerminus + distanceMoved;
}
```

If the movement happens in a grid, you need to update the row or column, depending on the current orientation.

```java
public void moveOneUnit()
{
    if (direction == NORTH) { row--; }
    else if (direction == EAST) { column++; }
    else if (direction == SOUTH) { row++; }
    else if (direction == WEST) { column--; }
}
```

FULL CODE EXAMPLE

Go to wiley.com/go/javacode to download classes that use these patterns for object data.

Exercise P8.6 shows you how to update the position of a physical object with known velocity.

Whenever you have a moving object, keep in mind that your program will simulate the actual movement in some way. Find out the rules of that simulation, such as movement along a line or in a grid with integer coordinates. Those rules determine how to represent the current position. Then locate the methods that move the object, and update the positions according to the rules of the simulation.

SELF CHECK

10. Suppose we want to count the number of transactions in a bank account in a statement period, and we add a counter to the BankAccount class:

```java
public class BankAccount
{
    private int transactionCount;
    . . .
```

}

In which methods does this counter need to be updated?

11. In How To 3.1, the CashRegister class does not have a getTotalPurchase method. Instead, you have to call receivePayment and then giveChange. Which recommendation of Section 8.2.4 does this design violate? What is a better alternative?

12. In the example in Section 8.3.3, why is the add method required? That is, why can't the user of a Question object just call the add method of the ArrayList<String> class?

13. Suppose we want to enhance the CashRegister class in How To 3.1 to track the prices of all purchased items for printing a receipt. Which instance variable should you provide? Which methods should you modify?

14. Consider an Employee class with properties for tax ID number and salary. Which of these properties should have only a getter method, and which should have getter and setter methods?

15. Suppose the setName method in Section 8.3.4 is changed so that it returns true if the new name is set, false if not. Is this a good idea?

16. Look at the direction instance variable in the bug example in Section 8.3.6. This is an example of which pattern?

Practice It   Now you can try these exercises at the end of the chapter: E8.21, E8.22, E8.23.

8.4 Static Variables and Methods

> A static variable belongs to the class, not to any object of the class.

Sometimes, a value properly belongs to a class, not to any object of the class. You use a **static variable** for this purpose. Here is a typical example: We want to assign bank account numbers sequentially. That is, we want the bank account constructor to construct the first account with number 1001, the next with number 1002, and so on. To solve this problem, we need to have a single value of lastAssignedNumber that is a property of the *class*, not any object of the class. Such a variable is called a static variable because you declare it using the static reserved word.

The reserved word static is a holdover from the C++ language. Its use in Java has no relationship to the normal use of the term.

```java
public class BankAccount
{
    private double balance;
    private int accountNumber;
    private static int lastAssignedNumber = 1000;

    public BankAccount()
    {
        lastAssignedNumber++;
        accountNumber = lastAssignedNumber;
    }
    . . .
}
```

Every BankAccount object has its own balance and accountNumber instance variables, but all objects share a single copy of the lastAssignedNumber variable (see Figure 5). That variable is stored in a separate location, outside any BankAccount objects.

Like instance variables, static variables should always be declared as private to ensure that methods of other classes do not change their values. However, static *constants* may be either private or public.

For example, the BankAccount class can define a public constant value, such as

```java
public class BankAccount
{
    public static final double OVERDRAFT_FEE = 29.95;
    . . .
}
```

Methods from any class can refer to such a constant as BankAccount.OVERDRAFT_FEE.

> A static method is not invoked on an object.

Sometimes a class defines methods that are not invoked on an object. Such a method is called a **static method**. A typical example of a static method is the sqrt method in the Math class. Because numbers aren't objects, you can't invoke methods on them. For example, if x is a number, then the call x.sqrt() is not legal in Java. Therefore, the Math class provides a static method that is invoked as Math.sqrt(x). No object of the Math class is constructed. The Math qualifier simply tells the compiler where to find the sqrt method.

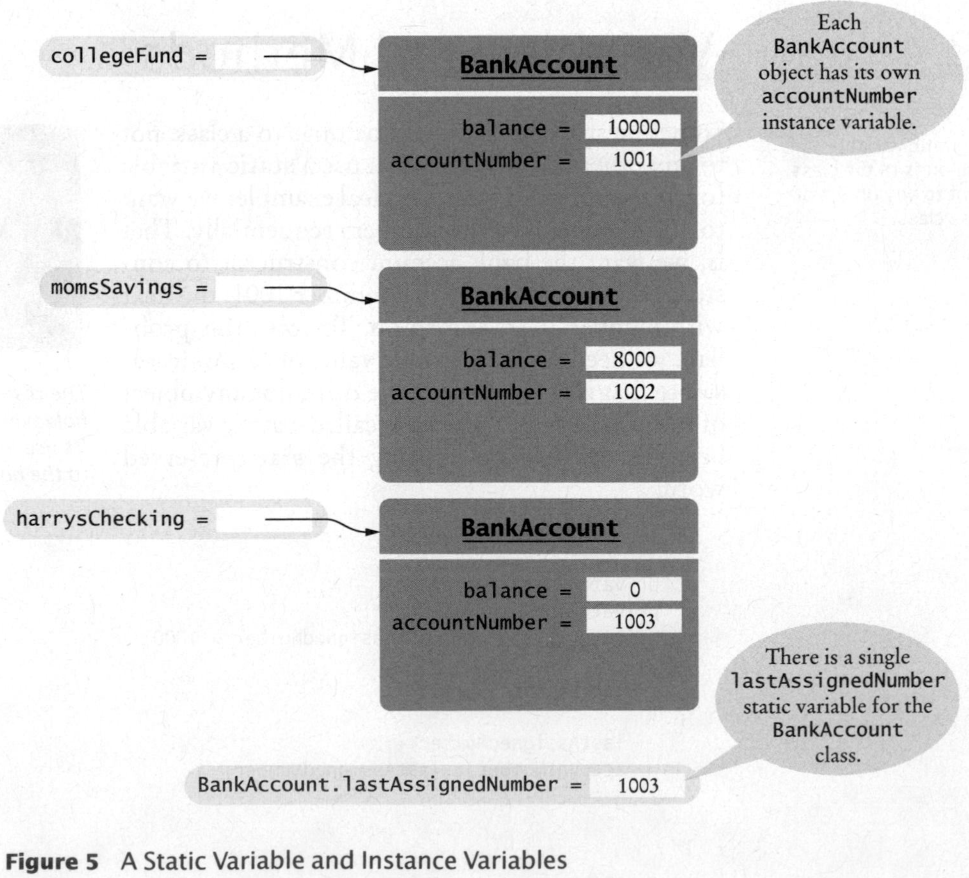

collegeFund =

BankAccount

balance = 10000
accountNumber = 1001

Each BankAccount object has its own accountNumber instance variable.

momsSavings =

BankAccount

balance = 8000
accountNumber = 1002

harrysChecking =

BankAccount

balance = 0
accountNumber = 1003

There is a single lastAssignedNumber static variable for the BankAccount class.

BankAccount.lastAssignedNumber = 1003

Figure 5 A Static Variable and Instance Variables

You can define your own static methods for use in other classes. Here is an example:

```
public class Financial
{
    /**
        Computes a percentage of an amount.
        @param percentage the percentage to apply
        @param amount the amount to which the percentage is applied
        @return the requested percentage of the amount
    */
    public static double percentOf(double percentage, double amount)
    {
        return (percentage / 100) * amount;
    }
}
```

FULL CODE EXAMPLE

Go to wiley.com/go/javacode to download a program with static methods and variables.

When calling this method, supply the name of the class containing it:

```
double tax = Financial.percentOf(taxRate, total);
```

In object-oriented programming, static methods are not very common. Nevertheless, the main method is always static. When the program starts, there aren't any objects. Therefore, the first method of a program must be a static method.

SELF CHECK

17. Name two static variables of the System class.

18. Name a static constant of the Math class.

19. The following method computes the average of an array of numbers:

```
public static double average(double[] values)
```

Why should it not be defined as an instance method?

20. Harry tells you that he has found a great way to avoid those pesky objects: Put all code into a single class and declare all methods and variables static. Then main can call the other static methods, and all of them can access the static variables. Will Harry's plan work? Is it a good idea?

Practice It Now you can try these exercises at the end of the chapter: R8.22, E8.5, E8.6.

Programming Tip 8.2

Minimize the Use of Static Methods

It is possible to solve programming problems by using classes with only static methods. In fact, before object-oriented programming was invented, that approach was quite common. However, it usually leads to a design that is not object-oriented and makes it hard to evolve a program.

Consider the task of How To 7.1. A program reads scores for a student and prints the final score, which is obtained by dropping the lowest one. We solved the problem by implementing a Student class that stores student scores. Of course, we could have simply written a program with a few static methods:

```
public class ScoreAnalyzer
{
    public static double[] readInputs() { . . . }
    public static double sum(double[] values) { . . . }
    public static double minimum(double[] values) { . . . }
```

```java
        public static double finalScore(double[] values)
        {
            if (values.length == 0) { return 0; }
            else if (values.length == 1) { return values[0]; }
            else { return sum(values) - minimum(values); }
        }

        public static void main(String[] args)
        {
            System.out.println(finalScore(readInputs()));
        }
    }
```

That solution is fine if one's sole objective is to solve a simple homework problem. But suppose you need to modify the program so that it deals with multiple students. An object-oriented program can evolve the Student class to store grades for many students. In contrast, adding more functionality to static methods gets messy quickly (see Exercise E8.7).

Common Error 8.1

Trying to Access Instance Variables in Static Methods

A static method does not operate on an object. In other words, it has no implicit parameter, and you cannot directly access any instance variables. For example, the following code is wrong:

```java
    public class SavingsAccount
    {
        private double balance;
        private double interestRate;

        public static double interest(double amount)
        {
            return (interestRate / 100) * amount;
            // ERROR: Static method accesses instance variable
        }
    }
```

Because different savings accounts can have different interest rates, the interest method should not be a static method.

Special Topic 8.2

Static Imports

Starting with Java version 5.0, there is a variant of the import directive that lets you use static methods and variables without class prefixes. For example,

```java
    import static java.lang.System.*;
    import static java.lang.Math.*;

    public class RootTester
    {
        public static void main(String[] args)
        {
            double r = sqrt(PI); // Instead of Math.sqrt(Math.PI)
            out.println(r);      // Instead of System.out
        }
```

}

Static imports can make programs easier to read, particularly if they use many mathematical functions.

Special Topic 8.3

Alternative Forms of Instance and Static Variable Initialization

As you have seen, instance variables are initialized with a default value (0, false, or null, depending on their type). You can then set them to any desired value in a constructor, and that is the style that we prefer in this book.

However, there are two other mechanisms to specify an initial value. Just as with local variables, you can specify initialization values for instance variables. For example,

```java
public class Coin
{
    private double value = 1;
    private String name = "Dollar";
    . . .
}
```

These default values are used for *every* object that is being constructed.

There is also another, much less common, syntax. You can place one or more *initialization blocks* inside the class declaration. All statements in that block are executed whenever an object is being constructed. Here is an example:

```java
public class Coin
{
    private double value;
    private String name;
    {
        value = 1;
        name = "Dollar";
    }
    . . .
}
```

For static variables, you use a static initialization block:

```java
public class BankAccount
{
    private static int lastAssignedNumber;
    static
    {
        lastAssignedNumber = 1000;
    }
    . . .
}
```

All statements in the static initialization block are executed once when the class is loaded. Initialization blocks are rarely used in practice.

When an object is constructed, the initializers and initialization blocks are executed in the order in which they appear. Then the code in the constructor is executed. Because the rules for the alternative initialization mechanisms are somewhat complex, we recommend that you simply use constructors to do the job of construction.

8.5 Packages

A package is a set of
related classes.

A Java program consists of a collection of classes. So far, most of your programs have consisted of a small number of classes. As programs get larger, however, simply distributing the classes over multiple files isn't enough. An additional structuring mechanism is needed.

In Java, packages provide this structuring mechanism. A Java **package** is a set of related classes. For example, the Java library consists of several hundred packages, some of which are listed in Table 1.

Table 1 Important Packages in the Java Library		
Package	Purpose	Sample Class
java.lang	Language support	Math
java.util	Utilities	Random
java.io	Input and output	PrintStream
java.awt	Abstract Windowing Toolkit	Color
java.applet	Applets	Applet
java.net	Networking	Socket
java.sql	Database access through Structured Query Language	ResultSet
javax.swing	Swing user interface	JButton
org.w3c.dom	Document Object Model for XML documents	Document

8.5.1 Organizing Related Classes into Packages

To put one of your classes in a package, you must place a line

    package packageName;

as the first instruction in the source file containing the class. A package name consists of one or more identifiers separated by periods. (See Section 8.5.3 for tips on constructing package names.)

For example, let's put the Financial class introduced in this chapter into a package named com.horstmann.bigjava. The Financial.java file must start as follows:

```
package com.horstmann.bigjava;
public class Financial
{
    . . .
}
```

In addition to the named packages (such as java.util or com.horstmann.bigjava), there is a special package, called the *default package*, which has no name. If you did not

In Java, related classes are grouped into packages.

include any package statement at the top of your source file, its classes are placed in the default package.

8.5.2 Importing Packages

If you want to use a class from a package, you can refer to it by its full name (package name plus class name). For example, java.util.Scanner refers to the Scanner class in the java.util package:

```
java.util.Scanner in = new java.util.Scanner(System.in);
```

Naturally, that is somewhat inconvenient. For that reason, you usually import a name with an import statement:

```
import java.util.Scanner;
```

Then you can refer to the class as Scanner without the package prefix.

> The import directive lets you refer to a class of a package by its class name, without the package prefix.

You can import *all classes* of a package with an import statement that ends in .*. For example, you can use the statement

```
import java.util.*;
```

to import all classes from the java.util package. That statement lets you refer to classes like Scanner or Random without a java.util prefix.

However, you never need to import the classes in the java.lang package explicitly. That is the package containing the most basic Java classes, such as Math and Object. These classes are always available to you. In effect, an automatic import java.lang.*; statement has been placed into every source file.

Finally, you don't need to import other classes in the same package. For example, when you implement the class homework1.Tester, you don't need to import the class homework1.Bank. The compiler will find the Bank class without an import statement because it is located in the same package, homework1.

8.5.3 Package Names

Placing related classes into a package is clearly a convenient mechanism to organize classes. However, there is a more important reason for packages: to avoid **name clashes**. In a large project, it is inevitable that two people will come up with the same name for the same concept. This even happens in the standard Java class library (which has now grown to thousands of classes). There is a class Timer in the java.util

Syntax 8.1 Package Specification

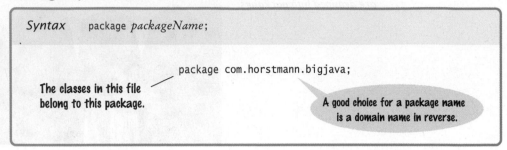

Syntax   package *packageName*;

package com.horstmann.bigjava;

The classes in this file belong to this package.

A good choice for a package name is a domain name in reverse.

package and another class called `Timer` in the `javax.swing` package. You can still tell the Java compiler exactly which `Timer` class you need, simply by referring to them as `java.util.Timer` and `javax.swing.Timer`.

Of course, for the package-naming convention to work, there must be some way to ensure that package names are unique. It wouldn't be good if the car maker BMW placed all its Java code into the package `bmw`, and some other programmer (perhaps Britney M. Walters) had the same bright idea. To avoid this problem, the inventors of Java recommend that you use a package-naming scheme that takes advantage of the uniqueness of Internet domain names.

> Use a domain name in reverse to construct an unambiguous package name.

For example, I have a domain name `horstmann.com`, and there is nobody else on the planet with the same domain name. (I was lucky that the domain name `horstmann.com` had not been taken by anyone else when I applied. If your name is Walters, you will sadly find that someone else beat you to `walters.com`.) To get a package name, turn the domain name around to produce a package name prefix, such as `com.horstmann`.

If you don't have your own domain name, you can still create a package name that has a high probability of being unique by writing your e-mail address backwards. For example, if Britney Walters has an e-mail address `walters@cs.sjsu.edu`, then she can use a package name `edu.sjsu.cs.walters` for her own classes.

Some instructors will want you to place each of your assignments into a separate package, such as `homework1`, `homework2`, and so on. The reason is again to avoid name collision. You can have two classes, `homework1.Bank` and `homework2.Bank`, with slightly different properties.

8.5.4 Packages and Source Files

> The path of a class file must match its package name.

A source file must be located in a subdirectory that matches the package name. The parts of the name between periods represent successively nested directories. For example, the source files for classes in the package `com.horstmann.bigjava` would be placed in a subdirectory `com/horstmann/bigjava`. You place the subdirectory inside the *base directory* holding your program's files. For example, if you do your homework assignment in a directory `/home/britney/hw8/problem1`, then you can place the class files for the `com.horstmann.bigjava` package into the directory `/home/britney/hw8/problem1/com/horstmann/bigjava`, as shown in Figure 6. (Here, we are using UNIX-style file names. Under Windows, you might use `c:\Users\Britney\hw8\problem1\com\horstmann\bigjava`.)

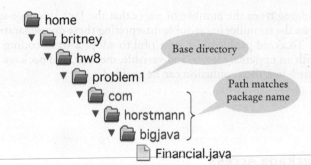

Figure 6 Base Directories and Subdirectories for Packages

SELF CHECK

21. Which of the following are packages?
    a. java
    b. java.lang
    c. java.util
    d. java.lang.Math

22. Is a Java program without import statements limited to using the default and java.lang packages?

23. Suppose your homework assignments are located in the directory /home/me/cs101 (c:\Users\Me\cs101 on Windows). Your instructor tells you to place your homework into packages. In which directory do you place the class hw1.problem1.TicTacToeTester?

Practice It   Now you can try these exercises at the end of the chapter: R8.25, E8.15, E8.16.

Common Error 8.2

Confusing Dots

In Java, the dot symbol (.) is used as a separator in the following situations:

- Between package names (java.util)
- Between package and class names (homework1.Bank)
- Between class and inner class names (Ellipse2D.Double)
- Between class and instance variable names (Math.PI)
- Between objects and methods (account.getBalance())

When you see a long chain of dot-separated names, it can be a challenge to find out which part is the package name, which part is the class name, which part is an instance variable name, and which part is a method name. Consider

```
java.lang.System.out.println(x);
```

Because println is followed by an opening parenthesis, it must be a method name. Therefore, out must be either an object or a class with a static println method. (Of course, we know that out is an object reference of type PrintStream.) Again, it is not at all clear, without context, whether System is another object, with a public variable out, or a class with a static variable.

Judging from the number of pages that the Java language specification devotes to this issue, even the compiler has trouble interpreting these dot-separated sequences of strings.

To avoid problems, it is helpful to adopt a strict coding style. If class names always start with an uppercase letter, and variable, method, and package names always start with a lowercase letter, then confusion can be avoided.

Special Topic 8.4

Package Access

If a class, instance variable, or method has no `public` or `private` modifier, then all methods of classes in the same package can access the feature. For example, if a class is declared as `public`, then all other classes in all packages can use it. But if a class is declared without an access modifier, then only the other classes in the *same* package can use it. Package access is a reasonable default for classes, but it is extremely unfortunate for instance variables.

> An instance variable or method that is not declared as `public` or `private` can be accessed by all classes in the same package, which is usually not desirable.

It is a common error to *forget* the reserved word `private`, thereby opening up a potential security hole. For example, at the time of this writing, the `Window` class in the `java.awt` package contained the following declaration:

```java
public class Window extends Container
{
    String warningString;
    . . .
}
```

There actually was no good reason to grant package access to the `warningString` instance variable—no other class accesses it.

Package access for instance variables is rarely useful and always a potential security risk. Most instance variables are given package access by accident because the programmer simply forgot the `private` reserved word. It is a good idea to get into the habit of scanning your instance variable declarations for missing `private` modifiers.

HOW TO 8.1

Programming with Packages

This How To explains in detail how to place your programs into packages.

Problem Statement Place each homework assignment into a separate package. That way, you can have classes with the same name but different implementations in separate packages (such as `homework1.problem1.Bank` and `homework1.problem2.Bank`).

Step 1   Come up with a package name.

Your instructor may give you a package name to use, such as `homework1.problem2`. Or, perhaps you want to use a package name that is unique to you. Start with your e-mail address, written backwards. For example, `walters@cs.sjsu.edu` becomes `edu.sjsu.cs.walters`. Then add a subpackage that describes your project, such as `edu.sjsu.cs.walters.cs1project`.

Step 2 Pick a *base directory*.

The base directory is the directory that contains the directories for your various packages, for example, /home/britney or c:\Users\Britney.

Step 3 Make a subdirectory from the base directory that matches your package name.

The subdirectory must be contained in your base directory. Each segment must match a segment of the package name. For example,

```
mkdir -p /home/britney/homework1/problem2 (in UNIX)
```

or

```
mkdir /s c:\Users\Britney\homework1\problem2 (in Windows)
```

Step 4 Place your source files into the package subdirectory.

For example, if your homework consists of the files Tester.java and Bank.java, then you place them into

```
/home/britney/homework1/problem2/Tester.java
/home/britney/homework1/problem2/Bank.java
```

or

```
c:\Users\Britney\homework1\problem2\Tester.java
c:\Users\Britney\homework1\problem2\Bank.java
```

Step 5 Use the package statement in each source file.

The first noncomment line of each file must be a package statement that lists the name of the package, such as

```
package homework1.problem2;
```

Step 6 Compile your source files from the *base directory*.

Change to the base directory (from Step 2) to compile your files. For example,

```
cd /home/britney
javac homework1/problem2/Tester.java
```

or

```
c:
cd \Users\Britney
javac homework1\problem2\Tester.java
```

Note that the Java compiler needs the *source file name and not the class name*. That is, you need to supply file separators (/ on UNIX, \ on Windows) and a file extension (.java).

Step 7 Run your program from the *base directory*.

Unlike the Java compiler, the Java interpreter needs the *class name (and not a file name) of the class containing the* main *method*. That is, use periods as package separators, and don't use a file extension. For example,

```
cd /home/britney
java homework1.problem2.Tester
```

or

```
c:
cd \Users\Britney
java homework1.problem2.Tester
```

Computing & Society 8.1 Personal Computing

In 1971, Marcian E. "Ted" Hoff, an engineer at Intel Corporation, was working on a chip for a manufacturer of electronic calculators. He realized that it would be a better idea to develop a *general-purpose* chip that could be *programmed* to interface with the keys and display of a calculator, rather than to do yet another custom design. Thus, the *microprocessor* was born. At the time, its primary application was as a controller for calculators, washing machines, and the like. It took years for the computer industry to notice that a genuine central processing unit was now available as a single chip.

Hobbyists were the first to catch on. In 1974 the first computer *kit,* the Altair 8800, was available from MITS Electronics for about $350. The kit consisted of the microprocessor, a circuit board, a very small amount of memory, toggle switches, and a row of display lights. Purchasers had to solder and assemble it, then program it in machine language through the toggle switches. It was not a big hit.

The first big hit was the Apple II. It was a real computer with a keyboard, a monitor, and a floppy disk drive. When it was first released, users had a $3,000 machine that could play Space Invaders, run a primitive bookkeeping program, or let users program it in BASIC. The original Apple II did not even support lowercase letters, making it worthless for word processing. The breakthrough came in 1979 with a new spreadsheet program, VisiCalc. In a spreadsheet, you enter financial data and their relationships into a grid of rows and columns (see the figure). Then you modify some of the data and watch in real time how the others change. For example, you can see how changing the mix of widgets in a manufacturing plant might affect estimated costs and profits. Corporate managers snapped up VisiCalc and the computer that was needed to run it. For them, the computer was a spreadsheet machine. More importantly, it was a personal device. The managers were free to do the calculations that they wanted to do, not just the ones that the "high priests" in the data center provided.

Personal computers have been with us ever since, and countless users have tinkered with their hardware and software, sometimes establishing highly successful companies or creating free software for millions of users. This "freedom to tinker" is an important part of personal computing. On a personal device, you should be able to install the software that you want to install to make you more productive or creative, even if that's not the same software that most people use. You should be able to add peripheral equipment of your choice. For the first thirty years of personal computing, this freedom was largely taken for granted.

We are now entering an era where smartphones, tablets, and smart TV sets are replacing functions that were traditionally fulfilled by personal computers. While it is amazing to carry more computing power in your cell phone than in the best personal computers of the 1990s, it is disturbing that we lose a degree of personal control. With some phone or tablet brands, you can only install those applications that the manufacturer publishes on the "app store". For example, Apple does not allow children to learn the Scratch language on the iPad. You'd think it would be in Apple's interest to encourage the next generation to be enthusiastic about programming, but they have a general policy of denying programmability on "their" devices, in order to thwart competitive environments such as Flash or Java.

When you select a device for making phone calls or watching movies, it is worth asking who is in control. Are you purchasing a personal device that you can use in any way you choose, or are you being tethered to a flow of data that is controlled by somebody else?

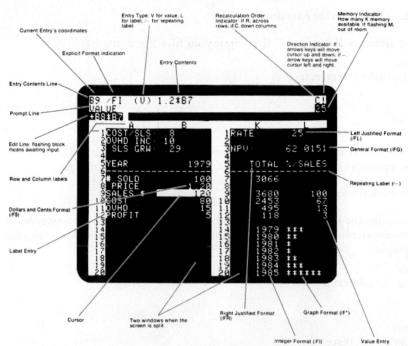

A **VISICALC**™ Screen:

The Visicalc Spreadsheet Running on an Apple II

8.6 Unit Test Frameworks

Up to now, we have used a very simple approach to testing. We provided tester classes whose main method computes values and prints actual and expected values. However, that approach has limitations. The main method gets messy if it contains many tests. And if an exception occurs during one of the tests, the remaining tests are not executed.

Unit testing frameworks were designed to quickly execute and evaluate test suites and to make it easy to incrementally add test cases. One of the most popular testing frameworks is JUnit. It is freely available at http://junit.org, and it is also built into a number of development environments, including BlueJ and Eclipse. Here we describe JUnit 4, the most current version of the library as this book is written.

> **Unit test frameworks simplify the task of writing classes that contain many test cases.**

When you use JUnit, you design a companion test class for each class that you develop. You provide a method for each test case that you want to have executed. You use "annotations" to mark the test methods. An annotation is an advanced Java feature that places a marker into the code that is interpreted by another tool. In the case of JUnit, the @Test annotation is used to mark test methods.

In each test case, you make some computations and then compute some condition that you believe to be true. You then pass the result to a method that communicates a test result to the framework, most commonly the assertEquals method. The assertEquals method takes as arguments the expected and actual values and, for floating-point numbers, a tolerance value.

It is also customary (but not required) that the name of the test class ends in Test, such as CashRegisterTest. Here is a typical example:

```
import org.junit.Test;
import org.junit.Assert;

public class CashRegisterTest
{
    @Test public void twoPurchases()
    {
        CashRegister register = new CashRegister();
        register.recordPurchase(0.75);
        register.recordPurchase(1.50);
        register.receivePayment(2, 0, 5, 0, 0);
        double expected = 0.25;
        Assert.assertEquals(expected, register.giveChange(), EPSILON);
    }
    // More test cases
    . . .
}
```

If all test cases pass, the JUnit tool shows a green bar (see Figure 7). If any of the test cases fail, the JUnit tool shows a red bar and an error message.

Your test class can also have other methods (whose names should not be annotated with @Test). These methods typically carry out steps that you want to share among test methods.

> **The JUnit philosophy is to run all tests whenever you change your code.**

The JUnit philosophy is simple. Whenever you implement a class, also make a companion test class. You design the tests as you design the program, one test method at a time. The test cases just keep accumulating in the test class. Whenever you have detected an actual failure, add a test case that flushes it out, so that you can be sure

Figure 7
Unit Testing with JUnit

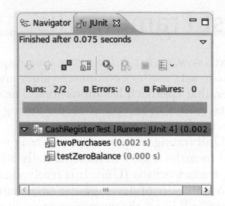

that you won't introduce that particular bug again. Whenever you modify your class, simply run the tests again.

If all tests pass, the user interface shows a green bar and you can relax. Otherwise, there is a red bar, but that's also good. It is much easier to fix a bug in isolation than inside a complex program.

SELF CHECK

24. Provide a JUnit test class with one test case for the Earthquake class in Chapter 5.

25. What is the significance of the EPSILON argument in the assertEquals method?

Practice It Now you can try these exercises at the end of the chapter: R8.27, E8.17, E8.18.

CHAPTER SUMMARY

Find classes that are appropriate for solving a programming problem.

- A class should represent a single concept from a problem domain, such as business, science, or mathematics.

Design methods that are cohesive, consistent, and minimize side effects.

- The public interface of a class is cohesive if all of its features are related to the concept that the class represents.
- A class depends on another class if its methods use that class in any way.
- An immutable class has no mutator methods.
- References to objects of an immutable class can be safely shared.
- A side effect of a method is any externally observable data modification.
- When designing methods, minimize side effects.
- In Java, a method can never change the contents of a variable that is passed to a method.
- In Java, a method can change the state of an object reference argument, but it cannot replace the object reference with another.

Use patterns to design the data representation of an object.

- An instance variable for the total is updated in methods that increase or decrease the total amount.
- A counter that counts events is incremented in methods that correspond to the events.
- An object can collect other objects in an array or array list.
- An object property can be accessed" with a getter method and changed with a setter method.
- If your object can have one of several states that affect the behavior, supply an instance variable for the current state.
- To model a moving object, you need to store and update its position.

Understand the behavior of static variables and static methods.

- A static variable belongs to the class, not to any object of the class.
- A static method is not invoked on an object.

Use packages to organize sets of related classes.

- A package is a set of related classes.
- The import directive lets you refer to a class of a package by its class name, without the package prefix.
- Use a domain name in reverse to construct an unambiguous package name.
- The path of a class file must match its package name.
- An instance variable or method that is not declared as public or private can be accessed by all classes in the same package, which is usually not desirable.

Use JUnit for writing unit tests.

- Unit test frameworks simplify the task of writing classes that contain many test cases.
- The JUnit philosophy is to run all tests whenever you change your code.

REVIEW QUESTIONS

- **R8.1** Your task is to write a program that simulates a vending machine. Users select a product and provide payment. If the payment is sufficient to cover the purchase price of the product, the product is dispensed and change is given. Otherwise, the payment is returned to the user. Name an appropriate class for implementing this program. Name two classes that would not be appropriate and explain why.

- **R8.2** Your task is to write a program that reads a customer's name and address, followed by a sequence of purchased items and their prices, and prints an invoice.

Discuss which of the following would be good classes for implementing this program:

    a. `Invoice`

    b. `InvoicePrinter`

    c. `PrintInvoice`

    d. `InvoiceProgram`

■■■ **R8.3** Your task is to write a program that computes paychecks. Employees are paid an hourly rate for each hour worked; however, if they worked more than 40 hours per week, they are paid at 150 percent of the regular rate for those overtime hours. Name an actor class that would be appropriate for implementing this program. Then name a class that isn't an actor class that would be an appropriate alternative. How does the choice between these alternatives affect the program structure?

■■ **R8.4** Look at the public interface of the `java.lang.System` class and discuss whether or not it is cohesive.

■■ **R8.5** Suppose an `Invoice` object contains descriptions of the products ordered, and the billing and shipping addresses of the customer. Draw a UML diagram showing the dependencies between the classes `Invoice`, `Address`, `Customer`, and `Product`.

■■ **R8.6** Suppose a vending machine contains products, and users insert coins into the vending machine to purchase products. Draw a UML diagram showing the dependencies between the classes `VendingMachine`, `Coin`, and `Product`.

■■ **R8.7** On which classes does the class `Integer` in the standard library depend?

■■ **R8.8** On which classes does the class `Rectangle` in the standard library depend?

■ **R8.9** Classify the methods of the class `Scanner` that are used in this book as accessors and mutators.

■ **R8.10** Classify the methods of the class `Rectangle` as accessors and mutators.

■ **R8.11** Is the `Resistor` class in Exercise P8.8 a mutable or immutable class? Why?

■ **R8.12** Which of the following classes are immutable?

    a. `Rectangle`

    b. `String`

    c. `Random`

■ **R8.13** Which of the following classes are immutable?

    a. `PrintStream`

    b. `Date`

    c. `Integer`

R8.14 Consider a method

```
public class DataSet
{
    /**
        Reads all numbers from a scanner and adds them to this data set.
        @param in a Scanner
    */
    public void read(Scanner in) { . . . }
    . . .
```

        }

Describe the side effects of the read method. Which of them are not recommended, according to Section 8.2.4? Which redesign eliminates the unwanted side effect? What is the effect of the redesign on coupling?

■■ **R8.15** What side effect, if any, do the following three methods have?

```java
public class Coin
{
    . . .
    public void print()
    {
        System.out.println(name + " " + value);
    }

    public void print(PrintStream stream)
    {
        stream.println(name + " " + value);
    }

    public String toString()
    {
        return name + " " + value;
    }
}
```

■■■ **R8.16** Ideally, a method should have no side effects. Can you write a program in which no method has a side effect? Would such a program be useful?

■■ **R8.17** Consider the following method that is intended to swap the values of two integers:

```java
public static void falseSwap(int a, int b)
{
    int temp = a;
    a = b;
    b = temp;
}

public static void main(String[] args)
{
    int x = 3;
    int y = 4;
    falseSwap(x, y);
    System.out.println(x + " " + y);
}
```

Why doesn't the method swap the contents of x and y?

■■■ **R8.18** How can you write a method that swaps two floating-point numbers?
Hint: java.awt.Point.

■■ **R8.19** Draw a memory diagram that shows why the following method can't swap two BankAccount objects:

```java
public static void falseSwap(BankAccount a, BankAccount b)
{
    BankAccount temp = a;
    a = b;
    b = temp;
}
```

■ R8.20 Consider an enhancement of the Die class of Chapter 6 with a static variable

```java
public class Die
{
    private int sides;
    private static Random generator = new Random();
    public Die(int s) { . . . }
    public int cast() { . . . }
}
```

Draw a memory diagram that shows three dice:

```java
Die d4 = new Die(4);
Die d6 = new Die(6);
Die d8 = new Die(8);
```

Be sure to indicate the values of the sides and generator variables.

■ R8.21 Try compiling the following program. Explain the error message that you get.

```java
public class Print13
{
    public void print(int x)
    {
        System.out.println(x);
    }

    public static void main(String[] args)
    {
        int n = 13;
        print(n);
    }
}
```

■ R8.22 Look at the methods in the Integer class. Which are static? Why?

■■ R8.23 Look at the methods in the String class (but ignore the ones that take an argument of type char[]). Which are static? Why?

■■ R8.24 The in and out variables of the System class are public static variables of the System class. Is that good design? If not, how could you improve on it?

■■ R8.25 Every Java program can be rewritten to avoid import statements. Explain how, and rewrite RectangleComponent.java from Section 2.9.3 to avoid import statements.

■ R8.26 What is the default package? Have you used it before this chapter in your programming?

■■ Testing R8.27 What does JUnit do when a test method throws an exception? Try it out and report your findings.

PRACTICE EXERCISES

■■ E8.1 Implement the Coin class described in Section 8.2. Modify the CashRegister class so that coins can be added to the cash register, by supplying a method

```java
void receivePayment(int coinCount, Coin coinType)
```

The caller needs to invoke this method multiple times, once for each type of coin that is present in the payment.

E8.2 Modify the giveChange method of the CashRegister class so that it returns the number of coins of a particular type to return:

```
int giveChange(Coin coinType)
```

The caller needs to invoke this method for each coin type, in decreasing value.

E8.3 Real cash registers can handle both bills and coins. Design a single class that expresses the commonality of these concepts. Redesign the CashRegister class and provide a method for entering payments that are described by your class. Your primary challenge is to come up with a good name for this class.

E8.4 Reimplement the BankAccount class so that it is immutable. The deposit and withdraw methods need to return new BankAccount objects with the appropriate balance.

E8.5 Write static methods

- `public static double cubeVolume(double h)`
- `public static double cubeSurface(double h)`
- `public static double sphereVolume(double r)`
- `public static double sphereSurface(double r)`
- `public static double cylinderVolume(double r, double h)`
- `public static double cylinderSurface(double r, double h)`
- `public static double coneVolume(double r, double h)`
- `public static double coneSurface(double r, double h)`

that compute the volume and surface area of a cube with height h, sphere with radius r, a cylinder with circular base with radius r and height h, and a cone with circular base with radius r and height h. Place them into a class Geometry. Then write a program that prompts the user for the values of r and h, calls the six methods, and prints the results.

E8.6 Solve Exercise E8.5 by implementing classes Cube, Sphere, Cylinder, and Cone. Which approach is more object-oriented?

E8.7 Modify the application of How To 7.1 so that it can deal with multiple students. First, ask the user for all student names. Then read in the scores for all quizzes, prompting for the score of each student. Finally, print the names of all students and their final scores. Use a single class and only static methods.

E8.8 Repeat Exercise E8.7, using multiple classes. Provide a GradeBook class that collects objects of type Student.

E8.9 Write methods

```
public static double perimeter(Ellipse2D.Double e);
public static double area(Ellipse2D.Double e);
```

that compute the area and the perimeter of the ellipse e. Add these methods to a class Geometry. The challenging part of this assignment is to find and implement an accurate formula for the perimeter. Why does it make sense to use a static method in this case?

E8.10 Write methods

```
public static double angle(Point2D.Double p, Point2D.Double q)
public static double slope(Point2D.Double p, Point2D.Double q)
```

that compute the angle between the *x*-axis and the line joining two points, measured in degrees, and the slope of that line. Add the methods to the class Geometry. Supply suitable preconditions. Why does it make sense to use a static method in this case?

■■■ **E8.11** Write methods

```
public static boolean isInside(Point2D.Double p, Ellipse2D.Double e)
public static boolean isOnBoundary(Point2D.Double p, Ellipse2D.Double e)
```

that test whether a point is inside or on the boundary of an ellipse. Add the methods to the class Geometry.

■ **E8.12** Write a method

```
public static int readInt(
        Scanner in, String prompt, String error, int min, int max)
```

that displays the prompt string, reads an integer, and tests whether it is between the minimum and maximum. If not, print an error message and repeat reading the input. Add the method to a class Input.

■■ **E8.13** Consider the following algorithm for computing x^n for an integer *n*. If n < 0, x^n is $1/x^{-n}$. If *n* is positive and even, then $x^n = (x^{n/2})^2$. If *n* is positive and odd, then $x^n = x^{n-1} \times x$. Implement a static method double intPower(double x, int n) that uses this algorithm. Add it to a class called Numeric.

■■ **E8.14** Improve the Die class of Chapter 6. Turn the generator variable into a static variable so that all needles share a single random number generator.

■■ **E8.15** Implement Coin and CashRegister classes as described in Exercise E8.1. Place the classes into a package called money. Keep the CashRegisterTester class in the default package.

■ **E8.16** Place a BankAccount class in a package whose name is derived from your e-mail address, as described in Section 8.5. Keep the BankAccountTester class in the default package.

■■ **Testing E8.17** Provide a JUnit test class StudentTest with three test methods, each of which tests a different method of the Student class in How To 7.1.

■■ **Testing E8.18** Provide JUnit test class TaxReturnTest with three test methods that test different tax situations for the TaxReturn class in Chapter 5.

■ **Graphics E8.19** Write methods

- public static void drawH(Graphics2D g2, Point2D.Double p);
- public static void drawE(Graphics2D g2, Point2D.Double p);
- public static void drawL(Graphics2D g2, Point2D.Double p);
- public static void drawO(Graphics2D g2, Point2D.Double p);

that show the letters H, E, L, O in the graphics window, where the point p is the top-left corner of the letter. Then call the methods to draw the words "HELLO" and "HOLE" on the graphics display. Draw lines and ellipses. Do not use the drawString method. Do not use System.out.

■■ **Graphics E8.20** Repeat Exercise E8.19 by designing classes LetterH, LetterE, LetterL, and LetterO, each with a constructor that takes a Point2D.Double parameter (the top-left corner) and a method draw(Graphics2D g2). Which solution is more object-oriented?

E8.21 Add a method ArrayList<Double> getStatement() to the BankAccount class that returns a list of all deposits and withdrawals as positive or negative values. Also add a method void clearStatement() that resets the statement.

E8.22 Implement a class LoginForm that simulates a login form that you find on many web pages. Supply methods

```
public void input(String text)
public void click(String button)
public boolean loggedIn()
```

The first input is the user name, the second input is the password. The click method can be called with arguments "Submit" and "Reset". Once a user has been successfully logged in, by supplying the user name, password, and clicking on the submit button, the loggedIn method returns true and further input has no effect. When a user tries to log in with an invalid user name and password, the form is reset.

Supply a constructor with the expected user name and password.

E8.23 Implement a class Robot that simulates a robot wandering on an infinite plane. The robot is located at a point with integer coordinates and faces north, east, south, or west. Supply methods

```
public void turnLeft()
public void turnRight()
public void move()
public Point getLocation()
public String getDirection()
```

The turnLeft and turnRight methods change the direction but not the location. The move method moves the robot by one unit in the direction it is facing. The getDirection method returns a string "N", "E", "S", or "W".

PROGRAMMING PROJECTS

••• P8.1 Declare a class ComboLock that works like the combination lock in a gym locker, as shown here. The lock is constructed with a combination—three numbers between 0 and 39. The reset method resets the dial so that it points to 0. The turnLeft and turnRight methods turn the dial by a given number of ticks to the left or right. The open method attempts to open the lock. The lock opens if the user first turned it right to the first number in the combination, then left to the second, and then right to the third.

```
public class ComboLock
{
    . . .
    public ComboLock(int secret1, int secret2, int secret3) { . . . }
    public void reset() { . . . }
    public void turnLeft(int ticks) { . . . }
    public void turnRight(int ticks) { . . . }
    public boolean open() { . . . }
}
```

••• Business P8.2 Implement a program that prints paychecks for a group of student assistants. Deduct federal and Social Security taxes. (You may want to use the tax computation used in Chapter 5. Find out about Social Security taxes on the Internet.) Your program should prompt for the names, hourly wages, and hours worked of each student.

■■■ **P8.3** For faster sorting of letters, the United States Postal Service encourages companies that send large volumes of mail to use a bar code denoting the ZIP code (see Figure 8).

The encoding scheme for a five-digit ZIP code is shown in Figure 8. There are full-height frame bars on each side. The five encoded digits are followed by a check digit, which is computed as follows: Add up all digits, and choose the check digit to make the sum a multiple of 10. For example, the sum of the digits in the ZIP code 95014 is 19, so the check digit is 1 to make the sum equal to 20.

Each digit of the ZIP code, and the check digit, is encoded according to the table at right, where 0 denotes a half bar and 1 a full bar. Note that they represent all combinations of two full and three half bars. The digit can be computed easily from the bar code using the column weights 7, 4, 2, 1, 0. For example, 01100 is

Digit	Weight				
	7	4	2	1	0
1	0	0	0	1	1
2	0	0	1	0	1
3	0	0	1	1	1
4	0	1	0	0	0
5	0	1	0	1	1
6	0	1	1	0	0
7	1	0	0	0	0
8	1	0	0	1	1
9	1	0	1	0	0
0	1	1	0	0	0

$$0 \times 7 + 1 \times 4 + 1 \times 2 + 0 \times 1 + 0 \times 0 = 6$$

The only exception is 0, which would yield 11 according to the weight formula.

Write a program that asks the user for a ZIP code and prints the bar code. Use : for half bars, | for full bars. For example, 95014 becomes

||:|:::|:|:|||:::::||:|::|:::|||

(Alternatively, write a graphical application that draws real bars.)

Your program should also be able to carry out the opposite conversion: Translate bars into their ZIP code, reporting any errors in the input format or a mismatch of the digits.

```
*************** ECRLOT ** CO57

CODE C671RTS2
JOHN DOE                              CO57
1009 FRANKLIN BLVD
SUNNYVALE      CA 95014 - 5143
```

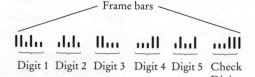

Digit 1   Digit 2   Digit 3   Digit 4   Digit 5   Check Digit

Frame bars

Figure 8 A Postal Bar Code

Figure 9 Encoding for Five-Digit Bar Codes

■■ **Business P8.4** Design a Customer class to handle a customer loyalty marketing campaign. After accumulating $100 in purchases, the customer receives a $10 discount on the next purchase.

Provide methods

- `void makePurchase(double amount)`
- `boolean discountReached()`

Provide a test program and test a scenario in which a customer has earned a discount and then made over $90, but less than $100 in purchases. This should not result in a second discount. Then add another purchase that results in the second discount.

■■■ Business P8.5   The Downtown Marketing Association wants to promote downtown shopping with a loyalty program similar to the one in Exercise P8.4. Shops are identified by a number between 1 and 20. Add a new parameter variable to the `makePurchase` method that indicates the shop. The discount is awarded if a customer makes purchases in at least three different shops, spending a total of $100 or more.

■■■ Science P8.6   Design a class `Cannonball` to model a cannonball that is fired into the air. A ball has

- An x- and a y-position.
- An x- and a y-velocity.

Supply the following methods:

- A constructor with an x-position (the y-position is initially 0)
- A method `move(double deltaSec)` that moves the ball to the next position First compute the distance traveled in `deltaSec` seconds, using the current velocities, then update the x- and y-positions; then update the y-velocity by taking into account the gravitational acceleration of -9.81 m/s^2; the x-velocity is unchanged.
- A method `Point getLocation()` that gets the current location of the cannonball, rounded to integer coordinates
- A method `ArrayList<Point> shoot(double alpha, double v, double deltaSec)` whose arguments are the angle α and initial velocity v (Compute the x-velocity as $v \cos \alpha$ and the y-velocity as $v \sin \alpha$; then keep calling `move` with the given time interval until the y-position is 0; return an array list of locations after each call to move.

Use this class in a program that prompts the user for the starting angle and the initial velocity. Then call `shoot` and print the locations.

■ Graphics P8.7   Continue Exercise P8.6, and draw the trajectory of the cannonball.

■■ Science P8.8   The colored bands on the top-most resistor shown in the photo at right indicate a resistance of 6.2 kΩ ±5 percent. The resistor tolerance of ±5 percent indicates the acceptable variation in the resistance. A 6.2 kΩ ±5 percent resistor could have a resistance as small as 5.89 kΩ or as large as 6.51 kΩ. We say that 6.2 kΩ is the *nominal value* of the

resistance and that the actual value of the resistance can be any value between 5.89 kΩ and 6.51 kΩ.

Write a program that represents a resistor as a class. Provide a single constructor that accepts values for the nominal resistance and tolerance and then determines the actual value randomly. The class should provide public methods to get the nominal resistance, tolerance, and the actual resistance.

Write a main method for the program that demonstrates that the class works properly by displaying actual resistances for ten 330 Ω ±10 percent resistors.

•• **Science P8.9** In the Resistor class from Exercise P8.8, supply a method that returns a description of the "color bands" for the resistance and tolerance. A resistor has four color bands:

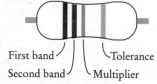

First band / Second band / Tolerance / Multiplier

- The first band is the first significant digit of the resistance value.
- The second band is the second significant digit of the resistance value.
- The third band is the decimal multiplier.
- The fourth band indicates the tolerance.

Color	Digit	Multiplier	Tolerance
Black	0	$\times 10^0$	—
Brown	1	$\times 10^1$	±1%
Red	2	$\times 10^2$	±2%
Orange	3	$\times 10^3$	—
Yellow	4	$\times 10^4$	—
Green	5	$\times 10^5$	±0.5%
Blue	6	$\times 10^6$	±0.25%
Violet	7	$\times 10^7$	±0.1%
Gray	8	$\times 10^8$	±0.05%
White	9	$\times 10^9$	—
Gold	—	$\times 10^{-1}$	±5%
Silver	—	$\times 10^{-2}$	±10%
None	—	—	±20%

For example (using the values from the table as a key), a resistor with red, violet, green, and gold bands (left to right) will have 2 as the first digit, 7 as the second digit, a multiplier of 10^5, and a tolerance of ±5 percent, for a resistance of 2,700 kΩ, plus or minus 5 percent.

•• **Science P8.10** The figure below shows a frequently used electric circuit called a "voltage divider". The input to the circuit is the voltage v_i. The output is the voltage v_o. The output of a voltage divider is proportional to the input, and the constant of proportionality is called the "gain" of the circuit. The voltage divider is represented by the equation

$$G = \frac{v_o}{v_i} = \frac{R_2}{R_1 + R_2}$$

where G is the gain and R_1 and R_2 are the resistances of the two resistors that comprise the voltage divider.

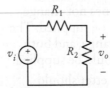

Manufacturing variations cause the actual resistance values to deviate from the nominal values, as described in Exercise P8.8. In turn, variations in the resistance values cause variations in the values of the gain of the voltage divider. We calculate the *nominal value of the gain* using the nominal resistance values and the *actual value of the gain* using actual resistance values.

Write a program that contains two classes, VoltageDivider and Resistor. The Resistor class is described in Exercise P8.8. The VoltageDivider class should have two instance variables that are objects of the Resistor class. Provide a single constructor that accepts two Resistor objects, nominal values for their resistances, and the resistor tolerance. The class should provide public methods to get the nominal and actual values of the voltage divider's gain.

Write a main method for the program that demonstrates that the class works properly by displaying nominal and actual gain for ten voltage dividers each consisting of 5 percent resistors having nominal values $R_1 = 250\ \Omega$ and $R_2 = 750\ \Omega$.

ANSWERS TO SELF-CHECK QUESTIONS

1. Look for nouns in the problem description.

2. Yes (ChessBoard) and no (MovePiece).

3. Some of its features deal with payments, others with coin values.

4. None of the coin operations require the CashRegister class.

5. If a class doesn't depend on another, it is not affected by interface changes in the other class.

6. It is an accessor—calling substring doesn't modify the string on which the method is invoked. In fact, all methods of the String class are accessors.

7. No—translate is a mutator method.

8. It is a side effect; this kind of side effect is common in object-oriented programming.

9. Yes—the method affects the state of the Scanner argument.

10. It needs to be incremented in the deposit and withdraw methods. There also needs to be some method to reset it after the end of a statement period.

11. The giveChange method is a mutator that returns a value that cannot be determined any other way. Here is a better design. The receivePayment method could decrease the purchase instance variable. Then the program user would call receivePayment, determine the change by calling getAmountDue, and call the clear method to reset the cash register for the next sale.

12. The ArrayList<String> instance variable is private, and the class users cannot acccess it.

13. You need to supply an instance variable that can hold the prices for all purchased items. This could be an ArrayList<Double> or ArrayList<String>, or it could simply be a String to which you append lines. The instance variable needs to be updated in the recordPurchase method. You also need a method that returns the receipt.

14. The tax ID of an employee does not change, and no setter method should be supplied. The salary of an employee can change, and both getter and setter methods should be supplied.

15. Section 8.2.3 suggests that a setter should return void, or perhaps a convenience value that the user can also determine in some other way. In this situation, the caller could check whether newName is blank, so the change is fine.

16. It is an example of the "state pattern" described in Section 8.3.5. The direction is a state that changes when the bug turns, and it affects how the bug moves.

17. System.in and System.out.

18. Math.PI

19. The method needs no data of any object. The only required input is the values argument.

20. Yes, it works. Static methods can access static variables of the same class. But it is a terrible idea. As your programming tasks get more complex, you will want to use objects and classes to organize your programs.

21. (a) No; (b) Yes; (c) Yes; (d) No

22. No—you can use fully qualified names for all other classes, such as java.util.Random and java.awt.Rectangle.

23. /home/me/cs101/hw1/problem1 or, on Windows, c:\Users\Me\cs101\hw1\problem1.

24. Here is one possible answer.

```
public class EarthquakeTest
{
    @Test public void testLevel4()
    {
        Earthquake quake = new Earthquake(4);
        Assert.assertEquals(
            "Felt by many people, no destruction",
            quake.getDescription());
    }
}
```

25. It is a tolerance threshold for comparing floating-point numbers. We want the equality test to pass if there is a small roundoff error.

Objects from related classes usually share common behavior. For example, cars, bicycles, and buses all provide transportation. In this chapter, you will learn how the notion of inheritance expresses the relationship between specialized and general classes. By using inheritance, you will be able to share code between classes and provide services that can be used by multiple classes.

9.1 Inheritance Hierarchies

> **A subclass inherits data and behavior from a superclass.**

In object-oriented design, **inheritance** is a relationship between a more general class (called the **superclass**) and a more specialized class (called the **subclass**). The subclass inherits data and behavior from the superclass. For example, consider the relationships between different kinds of vehicles depicted in Figure 1.

Every car *is a* vehicle. Cars share the common traits of all vehicles, such as the ability to transport people from one place to another. We say that the class Car inherits from the class Vehicle. In this relationship, the Vehicle class is the superclass and the Car class is the subclass. In Figure 2, the superclass and subclass are joined with an arrow that points to the superclass.

> **You can always use a subclass object in place of a superclass object.**

When you use inheritance in your programs, you can reuse code instead of duplicating it. This reuse comes in two forms. First, a subclass inherits the methods of the superclass. For example, if the Vehicle class has a drive method, then a subclass Car automatically inherits the method. It need not be duplicated.

The second form of reuse is more subtle. You can reuse algorithms that manipulate Vehicle objects. Because a car is a special kind of vehicle, we can use a Car object in such an algorithm, and it will work correctly. The **substitution principle** states that

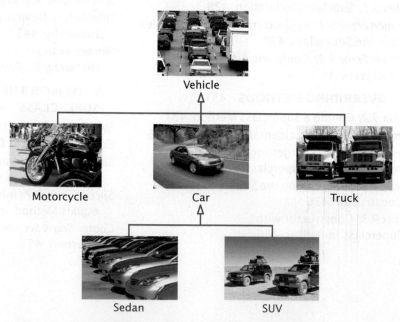

Vehicle

Motorcycle   Car   Truck

Sedan   SUV

Figure 1 An Inheritance Hierarchy of Vehicle Classes

Figure 2
An Inheritance Diagram

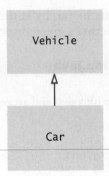

that you can always use a subclass object when a superclass object is expected. For example, consider a method that takes an argument of type Vehicle:

```
void processVehicle(Vehicle v)
```

Because Car is a subclass of Vehicle, you can call that method with a Car object:

```
Car myCar = new Car(. . .);
processVehicle(myCar);
```

Why provide a method that processes Vehicle objects instead of Car objects? That method is more useful because it can handle *any* kind of vehicle (including Truck and Motorcycle objects).

In this chapter, we will consider a simple hierarchy of classes. Most likely, you have taken computer-graded quizzes. A quiz consists of questions, and there are different kinds of questions:

- Fill-in-the-blank
- Choice (single or multiple)
- Numeric (where an approximate answer is ok; e.g., 1.33 when the actual answer is 4/3)
- Free response

We will develop a simple but flexible quiz-taking program to illustrate inheritance.

Figure 3 shows an inheritance hierarchy for these question types.

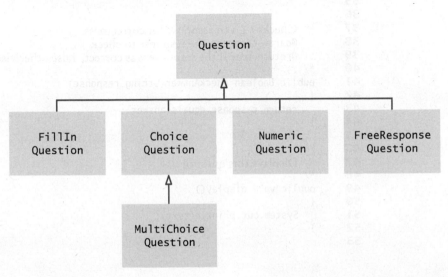

Figure 3
Inheritance Hierarchy
of Question Types

At the root of this hierarchy is the Question type. A question can display its text, and it can check whether a given response is a correct answer.

section_1/Question.java

```
1  /**
2      A question with a text and an answer.
3  */
4  public class Question
5  {
6     private String text;
7     private String answer;
8
9     /**
10        Constructs a question with empty question and answer.
11     */
12     public Question()
13     {
14        text = "";
15        answer = "";
16     }
17
18     /**
19        Sets the question text.
20        @param questionText the text of this question
21     */
22     public void setText(String questionText)
23     {
24        text = questionText;
25     }
26
27     /**
28        Sets the answer for this question.
29        @param correctResponse the answer
30     */
31     public void setAnswer(String correctResponse)
32     {
33        answer = correctResponse;
34     }
35
36     /**
37        Checks a given response for correctness.
38        @param response the response to check
39        @return true if the response was correct, false otherwise
40     */
41     public boolean checkAnswer(String response)
42     {
43        return response.equals(answer);
44     }
45
46     /**
47        Displays this question.
48     */
49     public void display()
50     {
51        System.out.println(text);
52     }
53  }
```

This Question class is very basic. It does not handle multiple-choice questions, numeric questions, and so on. In the following sections, you will see how to form subclasses of the Question class.

Here is a simple test program for the Question class:

section_1/QuestionDemo1.java

```java
1   import java.util.Scanner;
2
3   /**
4      This program shows a simple quiz with one question.
5   */
6   public class QuestionDemo1
7   {
8      public static void main(String[] args)
9      {
10        Scanner in = new Scanner(System.in);
11
12        Question q = new Question();
13        q.setText("Who was the inventor of Java?");
14        q.setAnswer("James Gosling");
15
16        q.display();
17        System.out.print("Your answer: ");
18        String response = in.nextLine();
19        System.out.println(q.checkAnswer(response));
20     }
21  }
```

Program Run

```
Who was the inventor of Java?
Your answer: James Gosling
true
```

SELF CHECK

1. Consider classes Manager and Employee. Which should be the superclass and which should be the subclass?

2. What are the inheritance relationships between classes BankAccount, Checking-Account, and SavingsAccount?

3. What are all the superclasses of the JFrame class? Consult the Java API documentation or Appendix D.

4. Consider the method doSomething(Car c). List all vehicle classes from Figure 1 whose objects *cannot* be passed to this method.

5. Should a class Quiz inherit from the class Question? Why or why not?

Practice It Now you can try these exercises at the end of the chapter: R9.1, R9.7, R9.9.

Use a Single Class for Variation in Values, Inheritance for Variation in Behavior

The purpose of inheritance is to model objects with different *behavior*. When students first learn about inheritance, they have a tendency to overuse it, by creating multiple classes even though the variation could be expressed with a simple instance variable.

Consider a program that tracks the fuel efficiency of a fleet of cars by logging the distance traveled and the refueling amounts. Some cars in the fleet are hybrids. Should you create a subclass HybridCar? Not in this application. Hybrids don't behave any differently than other cars when it comes to driving and refueling. They just have a better fuel efficiency. A single Car class with an instance variable

```
double milesPerGallon;
```

is entirely sufficient.

However, if you write a program that shows how to repair different kinds of vehicles, then it makes sense to have a separate class HybridCar. When it comes to repairs, hybrid cars behave differently from other cars.

9.2 Implementing Subclasses

In this section, you will see how to form a subclass and how a subclass automatically inherits functionality from its superclass.

Suppose you want to write a program that handles questions such as the following:

```
In which country was the inventor of Java born?
1. Australia
2. Canada
3. Denmark
4. United States
```

You could write a ChoiceQuestion class from scratch, with methods to set up the question, display it, and check the answer. But you don't have to. Instead, use inheritance and implement ChoiceQuestion as a subclass of the Question class (see Figure 4).

In Java, you form a subclass by specifying what makes the subclass *different from* its superclass.

> A subclass inherits all methods that it does not override.

Subclass objects automatically have the instance variables that are declared in the superclass. You only declare instance variables that are not part of the superclass objects.

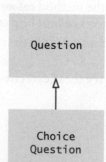

Figure 4
The ChoiceQuestion Class is a Subclass of the Question Class

Like the manufacturer of a stretch limo, who starts with a regular car and modifies it, a programmer makes a subclass by modifying another class.

A subclass can override a superclass method by providing a new implementation.

The subclass inherits all public methods from the superclass. You declare any methods that are *new* to the subclass, and *change* the implementation of inherited methods if the inherited behavior is not appropriate. When you supply a new implementation for an inherited method, you **override** the method.

A ChoiceQuestion object differs from a Question object in three ways:

- Its objects store the various choices for the answer.
- There is a method for adding answer choices.
- The display method of the ChoiceQuestion class shows these choices so that the respondent can choose one of them.

When the ChoiceQuestion class inherits from the Question class, it needs to spell out these three differences:

```
public class ChoiceQuestion extends Question
{
    // This instance variable is added to the subclass
    private ArrayList<String> choices;

    // This method is added to the subclass
    public void addChoice(String choice, boolean correct) { . . . }

    // This method overrides a method from the superclass
    public void display() { . . . }
}
```

The extends reserved word indicates that a class inherits from a superclass.

The reserved word extends denotes inheritance. Figure 5 shows how the methods and instance variables are captured in a UML diagram.

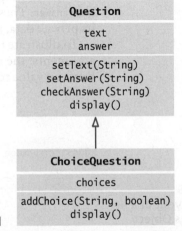

Question
text answer
setText(String) setAnswer(String) checkAnswer(String) display()

ChoiceQuestion
choices
addChoice(String, boolean) display()

Figure 5
The ChoiceQuestion Class Adds an Instance Variable and a Method, and Overrides a Method

Syntax 9.1   Subclass Declaration

```
Syntax    public class SubclassName extends SuperclassName
          {
              instance variables
              methods
          }
```

The reserved word extends denotes inheritance.

Declare instance variables that are added to the subclass.

Declare methods that are added to the subclass.

Declare methods that the subclass overrides.

Subclass   Superclass

```
public class ChoiceQuestion extends Question
{
    private ArrayList<String> choices;

    public void addChoice(String choice, boolean correct) { . . . }

    public void display() { . . . }
}
```

Figure 6 shows the layout of a ChoiceQuestion object. It has the text and answer instance variables that are declared in the Question superclass, and it adds an additional instance variable, choices.

The addChoice method is specific to the ChoiceQuestion class. You can only apply it to ChoiceQuestion objects, not general Question objects.

In contrast, the display method is a method that already exists in the superclass. The subclass overrides this method, so that the choices can be properly displayed.

All other methods of the Question class are automatically inherited by the Choice-Question class.

You can call the inherited methods on a subclass object:

```
choiceQuestion.setAnswer("2");
```

However, the private instance variables of the superclass are inaccessible. Because these variables are private data of the superclass, only the superclass has access to them. The subclass has no more access rights than any other class.

In particular, the ChoiceQuestion methods cannot directly access the instance variable answer. These methods must use the public interface of the Question class to access its private data, just like every other method.

To illustrate this point, let's implement the addChoice method. The method has two arguments: the choice to be added (which is appended to the list of choices), and a Boolean value to indicate whether this choice is correct.

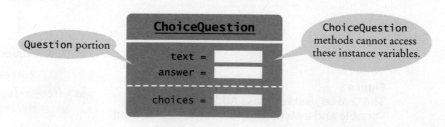

Figure 6
Data Layout of a
Subclass Object

For example,

```
question.addChoice("Canada", true);
```

The first argument is added to the `choices` variable. If the second argument is true, then the answer instance variable becomes the number of the current choice. For example, if `choices.size()` is 2, then answer is set to the string "2".

```
public void addChoice(String choice, boolean correct)
{
    choices.add(choice);
    if (correct)
    {
        // Convert choices.size() to string
        String choiceString = "" + choices.size();
        setAnswer(choiceString);
    }
}
```

You can't just access the answer variable in the superclass. Fortunately, the Question class has a setAnswer method. You can call that method. On which object? The question that you are currently modifying—that is, the implicit parameter of the ChoiceQuestion.addChoice method. Remember, if you invoke a method on the implicit parameter, you don't have to specify the implicit parameter and can write just the method name:

```
setAnswer(choiceString);
```

If you prefer, you can make it clear that the method is executed on the implicit parameter:

```
this.setAnswer(choiceString);
```

FULL CODE EXAMPLE

Go to wiley.com/go/javacode to download a program that shows a simple Car class extending a Vehicle class.

SELF CHECK

6. Suppose q is an object of the class Question and cq an object of the class Choice-Question. Which of the following calls are legal?

   a. `q.setAnswer(response)`

   b. `cq.setAnswer(response)`

   c. `q.addChoice(choice, true)`

   d. `cq.addChoice(choice, true)`

7. Suppose the class Employee is declared as follows:

```
public class Employee
{
    private String name;
    private double baseSalary;

    public void setName(String newName) { . . . }
    public void setBaseSalary(double newSalary) { . . . }
    public String getName() { . . . }
    public double getSalary() { . . . }
}
```

   Declare a class Manager that inherits from the class Employee and adds an instance variable bonus for storing a salary bonus. Omit constructors and methods.

8. Which instance variables does the Manager class from Self Check 7 have?

9. In the Manager class, provide the method header (but not the implementation) for a method that overrides the getSalary method from the class Employee.

10. Which methods does the Manager class from Self Check 9 inherit?

Practice It Now you can try these exercises at the end of the chapter: R9.3, E9.6, E9.10.

Common Error 9.1

Replicating Instance Variables from the Superclass

A subclass has no access to the private instance variables of the superclass.

```
public ChoiceQuestion(String questionText)
{
    text = questionText; // Error—tries to access private superclass variable
}
```

When faced with a compiler error, beginners commonly "solve" this issue by adding *another* instance variable with the same name to the subclass:

```
public class ChoiceQuestion extends Question
{
    private ArrayList<String> choices;
    private String text; // Don't!
    . . .
}
```

Sure, now the constructor compiles, but it doesn't set the correct text! Such a ChoiceQuestion object has two instance variables, both named text. The constructor sets one of them, and the display method displays the other. The correct solution is to access the instance variable of the superclass through the public interface of the superclass. In our example, the ChoiceQuestion constructor should call the setText method of the Question class.

ChoiceQuestion	
text =	
answer =	
choices =	
text =	

Question portion

Common Error 9.2

Confusing Super- and Subclasses

If you compare an object of type ChoiceQuestion with an object of type Question, you find that

- The reserved word extends suggests that the ChoiceQuestion object is an extended version of a Question.
- The ChoiceQuestion object is larger; it has an added instance variable, choices.
- The ChoiceQuestion object is more capable; it has an addChoice method.

It seems a superior object in every way. So why is ChoiceQuestion called the *subclass* and Question the *superclass*?

The *super/sub* terminology comes from set theory. Look at the set of all questions. Not all of them are ChoiceQuestion objects; some of them are other kinds of questions. Therefore, the set of ChoiceQuestion objects is a *subset* of the set of all Question objects, and the set of Question objects is a *superset* of the set of ChoiceQuestion objects. The more specialized objects in the subset have a richer state and more capabilities.

9.3 Overriding Methods

An overriding method can extend or replace the functionality of the superclass method.

The subclass inherits the methods from the superclass. If you are not satisfied with the behavior of an inherited method, you **override** it by specifying a new implementation in the subclass.

Consider the `display` method of the `ChoiceQuestion` class. It overrides the superclass `display` method in order to show the choices for the answer. This method *extends* the functionality of the superclass version. This means that the subclass method carries out the action of the superclass method (in our case, displaying the question text), and it also does some additional work (in our case, displaying the choices). In other cases, a subclass method *replaces* the functionality of a superclass method, implementing an entirely different behavior.

Let us turn to the implementation of the `display` method of the `ChoiceQuestion` class. The method needs to

- Display the question text.
- Display the answer choices.

The second part is easy because the answer choices are an instance variable of the subclass.

```
public class ChoiceQuestion
{
    . . .
    public void display()
    {
        // Display the question text
        . . .
        // Display the answer choices
        for (int i = 0; i < choices.size(); i++)
        {
            int choiceNumber = i + 1;
            System.out.println(choiceNumber + ": " + choices.get(i));
        }
    }
}
```

But how do you get the question text? You can't access the text variable of the superclass directly because it is private.

Syntax 9.2   Calling a Superclass Method

> *Syntax*   `super.methodName(parameters);`
>
> Calls the method of the superclass instead of the method of the current class.
>
> ```
> public void deposit(double amount)
> {
>     transactionCount++;
>     super.deposit(amount);
> }
> ```
>
> If you omit super, this method calls itself.
> See page 435.

Use the reserved
word super to call a
superclass method.

Instead, you can call the `display` method of the superclass, by using the reserved word super:

```
public void display()
{
    // Display the question text
    super.display(); // OK
    // Display the answer choices
    . . .
}
```

If you omit the reserved word super, then the method will not work as intended.

```
public void display()
{
    // Display the question text
    display(); // Error—invokes this.display()
    . . .
}
```

ANIMATION
Inheritance

Because the implicit parameter `this` is of type `ChoiceQuestion`, and there is a method named `display` in the `ChoiceQuestion` class, that method will be called—but that is just the method you are currently writing! The method would call itself over and over.

Note that super, unlike this, is *not* a reference to an object. There is no separate superclass object—the subclass object contains the instance variables of the superclass. Instead, super is simply a reserved word that forces execution of the superclass method.

Here is the complete program that lets you take a quiz consisting of two `Choice-Question` objects. We construct both objects and pass them to a method `presentQuestion`. That method displays the question to the user and checks whether the user response is correct.

section_3/QuestionDemo2.java

```
1  import java.util.Scanner;
2
3  /**
4     This program shows a simple quiz with two choice questions.
5  */
6  public class QuestionDemo2
7  {
8     public static void main(String[] args)
9     {
10        ChoiceQuestion first = new ChoiceQuestion();
11        first.setText("What was the original name of the Java language?");
12        first.addChoice("*7", false);
13        first.addChoice("Duke", false);
14        first.addChoice("Oak", true);
15        first.addChoice("Gosling", false);
16
17        ChoiceQuestion second = new ChoiceQuestion();
18        second.setText("In which country was the inventor of Java born?");
19        second.addChoice("Australia", false);
20        second.addChoice("Canada", true);
21        second.addChoice("Denmark", false);
22        second.addChoice("United States", false);
23
24        presentQuestion(first);
25        presentQuestion(second);
```

```
26      }
27
28      /**
29          Presents a question to the user and checks the response.
30          @param q the question
31      */
32      public static void presentQuestion(ChoiceQuestion q)
33      {
34          q.display();
35          System.out.print("Your answer: ");
36          Scanner in = new Scanner(System.in);
37          String response = in.nextLine();
38          System.out.println(q.checkAnswer(response));
39      }
40 }
```

section_3/ChoiceQuestion.java

```
1   import java.util.ArrayList;
2
3   /**
4       A question with multiple choices.
5   */
6   public class ChoiceQuestion extends Question
7   {
8       private ArrayList<String> choices;
9
10      /**
11          Constructs a choice question with no choices.
12      */
13      public ChoiceQuestion()
14      {
15          choices = new ArrayList<String>();
16      }
17
18      /**
19          Adds an answer choice to this question.
20          @param choice the choice to add
21          @param correct true if this is the correct choice, false otherwise
22      */
23      public void addChoice(String choice, boolean correct)
24      {
25          choices.add(choice);
26          if (correct)
27          {
28              // Convert choices.size() to string
29              String choiceString = "" + choices.size();
30              setAnswer(choiceString);
31          }
32      }
33
34      public void display()
35      {
36          // Display the question text
37          super.display();
38          // Display the answer choices
39          for (int i = 0; i < choices.size(); i++)
40          {
```

```
41          int choiceNumber = i + 1;
42          System.out.println(choiceNumber + ": " + choices.get(i));
43        }
44      }
45    }
```

Program Run

```
What was the original name of the Java language?
1: *7
2: Duke
3: Oak
4: Gosling
Your answer: *7
false
In which country was the inventor of Java born?
1: Australia
2: Canada
3: Denmark
4: United States
Your answer: 2
true
```

11. What is wrong with the following implementation of the `display` method?

```
public class ChoiceQuestion
{
   . . .
   public void display()
   {
      System.out.println(text);
      for (int i = 0; i < choices.size(); i++)
      {
         int choiceNumber = i + 1;
         System.out.println(choiceNumber + ": " + choices.get(i));
      }
   }
}
```

12. What is wrong with the following implementation of the `display` method?

```
public class ChoiceQuestion
{
   . . .
   public void display()
   {
      this.display();
      for (int i = 0; i < choices.size(); i++)
      {
         int choiceNumber = i + 1;
         System.out.println(choiceNumber + ": " + choices.get(i));
      }
   }
}
```

13. Look again at the implementation of the `addChoice` method that calls the `setAnswer` method of the superclass. Why don't you need to call `super.setAnswer`?

14. In the `Manager` class of Self Check 7, override the `getName` method so that managers have a * before their name (such as *Lin, Sally).

15. In the `Manager` class of Self Check 9, override the `getSalary` method so that it returns the sum of the salary and the bonus.

Practice It Now you can try these exercises at the end of the chapter: E9.1, E9.2, E9.11.

Common Error 9.3

Accidental Overloading

In Java, two methods can have the same name, provided they differ in their parameter types. For example, the `PrintStream` class has methods called `println` with headers

```
void println(int x)
```

and

```
void println(String x)
```

These are different methods, each with its own implementation. The Java compiler considers them to be completely unrelated. We say that the `println` name is **overloaded**. This is different from overriding, where a subclass method provides an implementation of a method whose parameter variables have the *same* types.

If you mean to override a method but use a parameter variable with a different type, then you accidentally introduce an overloaded method. For example,

```
public class ChoiceQuestion extends Question
{
   . . .
   public void display(PrintStream out)
   // Does not override void display()
   {
      . . .
   }
}
```

The compiler will not complain. It thinks that you want to provide a method just for `Print-Stream` arguments, while inheriting another method `void display()`.

When overriding a method, be sure to check that the types of the parameter variables match exactly.

Common Error 9.4

Forgetting to Use super When Invoking a Superclass Method

A common error in extending the functionality of a superclass method is to forget the reserved word `super`. For example, to compute the salary of a manager, get the salary of the underlying `Employee` object and add a bonus:

```
public class Manager
{
   . . .
   public double getSalary()
   {
      double baseSalary = getSalary();
         // Error: should be super.getSalary()
      return baseSalary + bonus;
   }
}
```

Here `getSalary()` refers to the `getSalary` method applied to the implicit parameter of the method. The implicit parameter is of type `Manager`, and there is a `getSalary` method in the

Manager class. Calling that method is a recursive call, which will never stop. Instead, you must tell the compiler to invoke the superclass method.

Whenever you call a superclass method from a subclass method with the same name, be sure to use the reserved word super.

Calling the Superclass Constructor

Consider the process of constructing a subclass object. A subclass constructor can only initialize the instance variables of the subclass. But the superclass instance variables also need to be initialized. Unless you specify otherwise, the superclass instance variables are initialized with the constructor of the superclass that has no arguments.

> Unless specified otherwise, the subclass constructor calls the superclass constructor with no arguments.

In order to specify another constructor, you use the super reserved word, together with the arguments of the superclass constructor, as the *first statement* of the subclass constructor.

For example, suppose the Question superclass had a constructor for setting the question text. Here is how a subclass constructor could call that superclass constructor:

> To call a superclass constructor, use the super reserved word in the first statement of the subclass constructor.

```
public ChoiceQuestion(String questionText)
{
    super(questionText);
    choices = new ArrayList<String>();
}
```

In our example program, we used the superclass constructor with no arguments. However, if all superclass constructors have arguments, you must use the super syntax and provide the arguments for a superclass constructor.

> The constructor of a subclass can pass arguments to a superclass constructor, using the reserved word super.

When the reserved word super is followed by a parenthesis, it indicates a call to the superclass constructor. When used in this way, the constructor call must be *the first statement of the subclass constructor*. If super is followed by a period and a method name, on the other hand, it indicates a call to a superclass method, as you saw in the preceding section. Such a call can be made anywhere in any subclass method.

Syntax 9.3   Constructor with Superclass Initializer

Syntax
```
public ClassName(parameterType parameterName, . . .)
{
    super(arguments);
    . . .
}
```

The superclass constructor is called first.

The constructor body can contain additional statements.

```
public ChoiceQuestion(String questionText)
{
    super(questionText);
    choices = new ArrayList<String>;
}
```

If you omit the superclass constructor call, the superclass constructor with no arguments is invoked.

9.4 Polymorphism

In this section, you will learn how to use inheritance for processing objects of different types in the same program.

Consider our first sample program. It presented two Question objects to the user. The second sample program presented two ChoiceQuestion objects. Can we write a program that shows a mixture of both question types?

With inheritance, this goal is very easy to realize. In order to present a question to the user, we need not know the exact type of the question. We just display the question and check whether the user supplied the correct answer. The Question superclass has methods for displaying and checking. Therefore, we can simply declare the parameter variable of the presentQuestion method to have the type Question:

```java
public static void presentQuestion(Question q)
{
    q.display();
    System.out.print("Your answer: ");
    Scanner in = new Scanner(System.in);
    String response = in.nextLine();
    System.out.println(q.checkAnswer(response));
}
```

A subclass reference can be used when a superclass reference is expected.

As discussed in Section 9.1, we can substitute a subclass object whenever a superclass object is expected:

```java
ChoiceQuestion second = new ChoiceQuestion();
. . .
presentQuestion(second); // OK to pass a ChoiceQuestion
```

When the presentQuestion method executes, the object references stored in second and q refer to the same object of type ChoiceQuestion (see Figure 7).

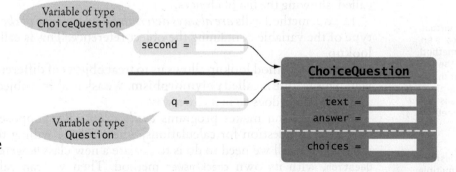

Figure 7
Variables of Different Types Referring to the Same Object

However, the *variable* q knows less than the full story about the object to which it refers (see Figure 8).

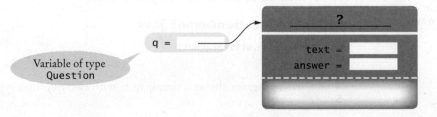

Figure 8
A Question Reference Can Refer to an Object of Any Subclass of Question

In the same way that vehicles can differ in their method of locomotion, polymorphic objects carry out tasks in different ways.

ANIMATION

Polymorphism

Because q is a variable of type Question, you can call the display and checkAnswer methods. You cannot call the addChoice method, though—it is not a method of the Question superclass.

This is as it should be. After all, it happens that in this method call, q refers to a ChoiceQuestion. In another method call, q might refer to a plain Question or an entirely different subclass of Question.

Now let's have a closer look inside the presentQuestion method. It starts with the call

```
q.display(); // Does it call Question.display or ChoiceQuestion.display?
```

Which display method is called? If you look at the program output on page 439, you will see that the method called depends on the contents of the parameter variable q. In the first case, q refers to a Question object, so the Question.display method is called. But in the second case, q refers to a ChoiceQuestion, so the ChoiceQuestion.display method is called, showing the list of choices.

> When the virtual machine calls an instance method, it locates the method of the implicit parameter's class. This is called dynamic method lookup.

In Java, method calls *are always determined by the type of the actual object*, not the type of the variable containing the object reference. This is called **dynamic method lookup**.

Dynamic method lookup allows us to treat objects of different classes in a uniform way. This feature is called **polymorphism**. We ask multiple objects to carry out a task, and each object does so in its own way.

> Polymorphism ("having multiple forms") allows us to manipulate objects that share a set of tasks, even though the tasks are executed in different ways.

Polymorphism makes programs *easily extensible*. Suppose we want to have a new kind of question for calculations, where we are willing to accept an approximate answer. All we need to do is to declare a new class NumericQuestion that extends Question, with its own checkAnswer method. Then we can call the presentQuestion method with a mixture of plain questions, choice questions, and numeric questions. The presentQuestion method need not be changed at all! Thanks to dynamic method lookup, method calls to the display and checkAnswer methods automatically select the correct method of the newly declared classes.

section_4/QuestionDemo3.java

```
1   import java.util.Scanner;
2
3   /**
4      This program shows a simple quiz with two question types.
5   */
```

```java
6   public class QuestionDemo3
7   {
8      public static void main(String[] args)
9      {
10        Question first = new Question();
11        first.setText("Who was the inventor of Java?");
12        first.setAnswer("James Gosling");
13
14        ChoiceQuestion second = new ChoiceQuestion();
15        second.setText("In which country was the inventor of Java born?");
16        second.addChoice("Australia", false);
17        second.addChoice("Canada", true);
18        second.addChoice("Denmark", false);
19        second.addChoice("United States", false);
20
21        presentQuestion(first);
22        presentQuestion(second);
23     }
24
25     /**
26        Presents a question to the user and checks the response.
27        @param q the question
28     */
29     public static void presentQuestion(Question q)
30     {
31        q.display();
32        System.out.print("Your answer: ");
33        Scanner in = new Scanner(System.in);
34        String response = in.nextLine();
35        System.out.println(q.checkAnswer(response));
36     }
37  }
```

Program Run

```
Who was the inventor of Java?
Your answer: Bjarne Stroustrup
false
In which country was the inventor of Java born?
1: Australia
2: Canada
3: Denmark
4: United States
Your answer: 2
true
```

SELF CHECK

16. Assuming SavingsAccount is a subclass of BankAccount, which of the following code fragments are valid in Java?

   a. BankAccount account = new SavingsAccount();

   b. SavingsAccount account2 = new BankAccount();

   c. BankAccount account = null;

   d. SavingsAccount account2 = account;

17. If account is a variable of type BankAccount that holds a non-null reference, what do you know about the object to which account refers?

18. Declare an array `quiz` that can hold a mixture of `Question` and `ChoiceQuestion` objects.

19. Consider the code fragment

```
ChoiceQuestion cq = . . .; // A non-null value
cq.display();
```

Which actual method is being called?

20. Is the method call `Math.sqrt(2)` resolved through dynamic method lookup?

Practice It Now you can try these exercises at the end of the chapter: R9.6, E9.4, E9.14.

Special Topic 9.2

Dynamic Method Lookup and the Implicit Parameter

Suppose we add the `presentQuestion` method to the `Question` class itself:

```
void presentQuestion()
{
    display();
    System.out.print("Your answer: ");
    Scanner in = new Scanner(System.in);
    String response = in.nextLine();
    System.out.println(checkAnswer(response));
}
```

Now consider the call

```
ChoiceQuestion cq = new ChoiceQuestion();
cq.setText("In which country was the inventor of Java born?");
. . .
cq.presentQuestion();
```

Which `display` and `checkAnswer` method will the `presentQuestion` method call? If you look inside the code of the `presentQuestion` method, you can see that these methods are executed on the implicit parameter:

```
public class Question
{
    public void presentQuestion()
    {
        this.display();
        System.out.print("Your answer: ");
        Scanner in = new Scanner(System.in);
        String response = in.nextLine();
        System.out.println(this.checkAnswer(response));
    }
}
```

The implicit parameter `this` in our call is a reference to an object of type `ChoiceQuestion`. Because of dynamic method lookup, the `ChoiceQuestion` versions of the `display` and `checkAnswer` methods are called automatically. This happens even though the `presentQuestion` method is declared in the `Question` class, which has *no knowledge* of the `ChoiceQuestion` class.

As you can see, polymorphism is a very powerful mechanism. The `Question` class supplies a `presentQuestion` method that specifies the common nature of presenting a question, namely to display it and check the response. How the displaying and checking are carried out is left to the subclasses.

Abstract Classes

When you extend an existing class, you have the choice whether or not to override the methods of the superclass. Sometimes, it is desirable to *force* programmers to override a method. That happens when there is no good default for the superclass, and only the subclass programmer can know how to implement the method properly.

Here is an example: Suppose the First National Bank of Java decides that every account type must have some monthly fees. Therefore, a deductFees method should be added to the Account class:

```
public class Account
{
    public void deductFees() { . . . }
    . . .
}
```

But what should this method do? Of course, we could have the method do nothing. But then a programmer implementing a new subclass might simply forget to implement the deductFees method, and the new account would inherit the do-nothing method of the superclass. There is a better way—declare the deductFees method as an **abstract method**:

```
public abstract void deductFees();
```

An abstract method has no implementation. This forces the implementors of subclasses to specify concrete implementations of this method. (Of course, some subclasses might decide to implement a do-nothing method, but then that is their choice—not a silently inherited default.)

You cannot construct objects of classes with abstract methods. For example, once the Account class has an abstract method, the compiler will flag an attempt to create a new Account() as an error.

A class for which you cannot create objects is called an **abstract class**. A class for which you can create objects is sometimes called a **concrete class**. In Java, you must declare all abstract classes with the reserved word abstract:

```
public abstract class Account
{
    public abstract void deductFees();
    . . .
}

public class SavingsAccount extends Account // Not abstract
{
    . . .
    public void deductFees() // Provides an implementation
    {
        . . .
    }
}
```

If a class extends an abstract class without providing an implementation of all abstract methods, it too is abstract.

```
public abstract class BusinessAccount
{
    // No implementation of deductFees
}
```

Note that you cannot construct an *object* of an abstract class, but you can still have an *object reference* whose type is an abstract class. Of course, the actual object to which it refers must be an instance of a concrete subclass:

```
Account anAccount; // OK
anAccount = new Account(); // Error—Account is abstract
anAccount = new SavingsAccount(); // OK
anAccount = null; // OK
```

When you declare a method as abstract, you force programmers to provide implementations in subclasses. This is better than coming up with a default that might be inherited accidentally.

Special Topic 9.4

Final Methods and Classes

In Special Topic 9.3 you saw how you can force other programmers to create subclasses of abstract classes and override abstract methods. Occasionally, you may want to do the opposite and *prevent* other programmers from creating subclasses or from overriding certain methods. In these situations, you use the final reserved word. For example, the String class in the standard Java library has been declared as

```
public final class String { . . . }
```

That means that nobody can extend the String class. When you have a reference of type String, it must contain a String object, never an object of a subclass.

You can also declare individual methods as final:

```
public class SecureAccount extends BankAccount
{
    . . .
    public final boolean checkPassword(String password)
    {
        . . .
    }
}
```

This way, nobody can override the checkPassword method with another method that simply returns true.

Special Topic 9.5

Protected Access

We ran into a hurdle when trying to implement the display method of the ChoiceQuestion class. That method wanted to access the instance variable text of the superclass. Our remedy was to use the appropriate method of the superclass to display the text.

Java offers another solution to this problem. The superclass can declare an instance variable as *protected*:

```
public class Question
{
    protected String text;
    . . .
}
```

Protected data in an object can be accessed by the methods of the object's class and all its subclasses. For example, ChoiceQuestion inherits from Question, so its methods can access the protected instance variables of the Question superclass.

Some programmers like the protected access feature because it seems to strike a balance between absolute protection (making instance variables private) and no protection at all (making instance variables public). However, experience has shown that protected instance variables are subject to the same kinds of problems as public instance variables. The designer of the superclass has no control over the authors of subclasses. Any of the subclass methods can corrupt the superclass data. Furthermore, classes with protected variables are hard to modify.

Even if the author of the superclass would like to change the data implementation, the protected variables cannot be changed, because someone somewhere out there might have written a subclass whose code depends on them.

In Java, protected variables have another drawback—they are accessible not just by subclasses, but also by other classes in the same package (see Special Topic 8.4).

It is best to leave all data private. If you want to grant access to the data to subclass methods only, consider making the *accessor* method protected.

HOW TO 9.1   Developing an Inheritance Hierarchy

When you work with a set of classes, some of which are more general and others more specialized, you want to organize them into an inheritance hierarchy. This enables you to process objects of different classes in a uniform way.

As an example, we will consider a bank that offers customers the following account types:

- A savings account that earns interest. The interest compounds monthly and is computed on the minimum monthly balance.

- A checking account that has no interest, gives you three free withdrawals per month, and charges a $1 transaction fee for each additional withdrawal.

Problem Statement   Design and implement a program that will manage a set of accounts of both types. It should be structured so that other account types can be added without affecting the main processing loop. Supply a menu

```
D)eposit W)ithdraw M)onth end Q)uit
```

For deposits and withdrawals, query the account number and amount. Print the balance of the account after each transaction.

In the "Month end" command, accumulate interest or clear the transaction counter, depending on the type of the bank account. Then print the balance of all accounts.

Step 1   List the classes that are part of the hierarchy.

In our case, the problem description yields two classes: SavingsAccount and CheckingAccount. Of course, you could implement each of them separately. But that would not be a good idea because the classes would have to repeat common functionality, such as updating an account balance. We need another class that can be responsible for that common functionality. The problem statement does not explicitly mention such a class. Therefore, we need to discover it. Of course, in this case, the solution is simple. Savings accounts and checking accounts are special cases of a bank account. Therefore, we will introduce a common superclass BankAccount.

Step 2   Organize the classes into an inheritance hierarchy.

Draw an inheritance diagram that shows super- and subclasses. Here is one for our example:

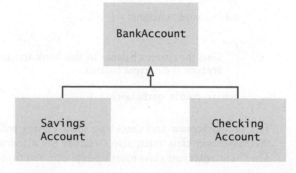

Step 3 Determine the common responsibilities.

In Step 2, you will have identified a class at the base of the hierarchy. That class needs to have sufficient responsibilities to carry out the tasks at hand. To find out what those tasks are, write pseudocode for processing the objects.

> For each user command
>   If it is a deposit or withdrawal
>   Deposit or withdraw the amount from the specified account.
>   Print the balance.
>   If it is month end processing
>   For each account
>   Call month end processing.
>   Print the balance.

From the pseudocode, we obtain the following list of common responsibilities that every bank account must carry out:

> Deposit money.
> Withdraw money.
> Get the balance.
> Carry out month end processing.

Step 4 Decide which methods are overridden in subclasses.

For each subclass and each of the common responsibilities, decide whether the behavior can be inherited or whether it needs to be overridden. Be sure to declare any methods that are inherited or overridden in the root of the hierarchy.

```java
public class BankAccount
{
   . . .
   /**
      Makes a deposit into this account.
      @param amount the amount of the deposit
   */
   public void deposit(double amount) { . . . }

   /**
      Makes a withdrawal from this account, or charges a penalty if
      sufficient funds are not available.
      @param amount the amount of the withdrawal
   */
   public void withdraw(double amount) { . . . }

   /**
      Carries out the end of month processing that is appropriate
      for this account.
   */
   public void monthEnd() { . . . }

   /**
      Gets the current balance of this bank account.
      @return the current balance
   */
   public double getBalance() { . . . }
}
```

The SavingsAccount and CheckingAccount classes will both override the monthEnd method. The SavingsAccount class must also override the withdraw method to track the minimum balance. The CheckingAccount class must update a transaction count in the withdraw method.

Step 5   Declare the public interface of each subclass.

Typically, subclasses have responsibilities other than those of the superclass. List those, as well as the methods that need to be overridden. You also need to specify how the objects of the subclasses should be constructed.

In this example, we need a way of setting the interest rate for the savings account. In addition, we need to specify constructors and overridden methods.

```java
public class SavingsAccount extends BankAccount
{
    . . .
    /**
        Constructs a savings account with a zero balance.
    */
    public SavingsAccount() { . . . }

    /**
        Sets the interest rate for this account.
        @param rate the monthly interest rate in percent
    */
    public void setInterestRate(double rate) { . . . }

    // These methods override superclass methods
    public void withdraw(double amount) { . . . }
    public void monthEnd() { . . . }
}

public class CheckingAccount extends BankAccount
{
    /**
        Constructs a checking account with a zero balance.
    */
    public CheckingAccount() { . . . }

    // These methods override superclass methods
    public void withdraw(double amount) { . . . }
    public void monthEnd() { . . . }
}
```

Step 6   Identify instance variables.

List the instance variables for each class. If you find an instance variable that is common to all classes, be sure to place it in the base of the hierarchy.

All accounts have a balance. We store that value in the BankAccount superclass:

```java
public class BankAccount
{
    private double balance;
    . . .
}
```

The SavingsAccount class needs to store the interest rate. It also needs to store the minimum monthly balance, which must be updated by all withdrawals.

```java
public class SavingsAccount extends BankAccount
{
    private double interestRate;
    private double minBalance;
    . . .
}
```

The CheckingAccount class needs to count the withdrawals, so that the charge can be applied after the free withdrawal limit is reached.

```java
public class CheckingAccount extends BankAccount
{
    private int withdrawals;
    . . .
}
```

Step 7 Implement constructors and methods.

The methods of the BankAccount class update or return the balance.

```java
public void deposit(double amount)
{
    balance = balance + amount;
}

public void withdraw(double amount)
{
    balance = balance - amount;
}

public double getBalance()
{
    return balance;
}
```

At the level of the BankAccount superclass, we can say nothing about end of month processing. We choose to make that method do nothing:

```java
public void monthEnd()
{
}
```

In the withdraw method of the SavingsAccount class, the minimum balance is updated. Note the call to the superclass method:

```java
public void withdraw(double amount)
{
    super.withdraw(amount);
    double balance = getBalance();
    if (balance < minBalance)
    {
        minBalance = balance;
    }
}
```

In the monthEnd method of the SavingsAccount class, the interest is deposited into the account. We must call the deposit method because we have no direct access to the balance instance variable. The minimum balance is reset for the next month.

```java
public void monthEnd()
{
    double interest = minBalance * interestRate / 100;
    deposit(interest);
    minBalance = getBalance();
}
```

The withdraw method of the CheckingAccount class needs to check the withdrawal count. If there have been too many withdrawals, a charge is applied. Again, note how the method invokes the superclass method:

```java
public void withdraw(double amount)
{
```

```
        final int FREE_WITHDRAWALS = 3;
        final int WITHDRAWAL_FEE = 1;

        super.withdraw(amount);
        withdrawals++;
        if (withdrawals > FREE_WITHDRAWALS)
        {
            super.withdraw(WITHDRAWAL_FEE);
        }
    }
}
```

End of month processing for a checking account simply resets the withdrawal count.

```
public void monthEnd()
{
    withdrawals = 0;
}
```

Step 8   Construct objects of different subclasses and process them.

In our sample program, we allocate five checking accounts and five savings accounts and store their addresses in an array of bank accounts. Then we accept user commands and execute deposits, withdrawals, and monthly processing.

```
BankAccount[] accounts = . . .;
. . .
Scanner in = new Scanner(System.in);
boolean done = false;
while (!done)
{
    System.out.print("D)eposit  W)ithdraw  M)onth end  Q)uit: ");
    String input = in.next();
    if (input.equals("D") || input.equals("W")) // Deposit or withdrawal
    {
        System.out.print("Enter account number and amount: ");
        int num = in.nextInt();
        double amount = in.nextDouble();

        if (input.equals("D")) { accounts[num].deposit(amount); }
        else { accounts[num].withdraw(amount); }

        System.out.println("Balance: " + accounts[num].getBalance());
    }
    else if (input.equals("M")) // Month end processing
    {
        for (int n = 0; n < accounts.length; n++)
        {
            accounts[n].monthEnd();
            System.out.println(n + " " + accounts[n].getBalance());
        }
    }
    else if (input == "Q")
    {
        done = true;
    }
}
```

FULL CODE EXAMPLE

Go to wiley.com/go/ javacode to download the program with BankAccount, SavingsAccount, and CheckingAccount classes.

WORKED EXAMPLE 9.1

**Implementing an Employee
Hierarchy for Payroll Processing**

Learn how to implement payroll processing that works
for different kinds of employees. Go to www.wiley.com/go/
javaexamples and download Worked Example 9.1.

9.5 Object: The Cosmic Superclass

In Java, every class that is declared without an explicit extends clause automatically
extends the class Object. That is, the class Object is the direct or indirect superclass of
every class in Java (see Figure 9). The Object class defines several very general methods, including

- toString, which yields a string describing the object (Section 9.5.1).
- equals, which compares objects with each other (Section 9.5.2).
- hashCode, which yields a numerical code for storing the object in a set (see Special
  Topic 15.1).

9.5.1 Overriding the toString Method

The toString method returns a string representation for each object. It is often used
for debugging.

For example, consider the Rectangle class in the standard Java library. Its toString
method shows the state of a rectangle:

```
Rectangle box = new Rectangle(5, 10, 20, 30);
String s = box.toString();
   // Sets s to "java.awt.Rectangle[x=5,y=10,width=20,height=30]"
```

The toString method is called automatically whenever you concatenate a string with
an object. Here is an example:

```
"box=" + box;
```

On one side of the + concatenation operator is a string, but on the other side is an
object reference. The Java compiler automatically invokes the toString method to
turn the object into a string. Then both strings are concatenated. In this case, the
result is the string

```
"box=java.awt.Rectangle[x=5,y=10,width=20,height=30]"
```

The compiler can invoke the toString method, because it knows that *every* object has
a toString method: Every class extends the Object class, and that class declares toString.

As you know, numbers are also converted to strings when they are concatenated
with other strings. For example,

```
int age = 18;
String s = "Harry's age is " + age;
   // Sets s to "Harry's age is 18"
```

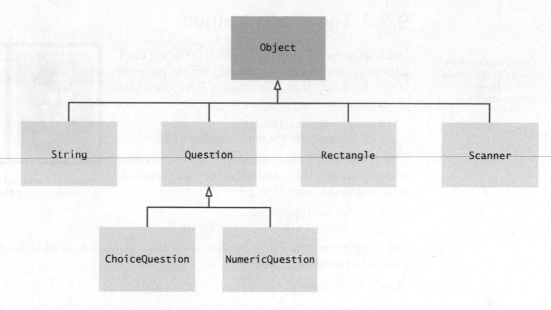

Figure 9   The `Object` Class Is the Superclass of Every Java Class

In this case, the `toString` method is *not* involved. Numbers are not objects, and there is no `toString` method for them. Fortunately, there is only a small set of primitive types, and the compiler knows how to convert them to strings.

Let's try the `toString` method for the `BankAccount` class:

```
BankAccount momsSavings = new BankAccount(5000);
String s = momsSavings.toString();
   // Sets s to something like "BankAccount@d24606bf"
```

That's disappointing—all that's printed is the name of the class, followed by the **hash code**, a seemingly random code. The hash code can be used to tell objects apart—different objects are likely to have different hash codes. (See Special Topic 15.1 for the details.)

We don't care about the hash code. We want to know what is *inside* the object. But, of course, the `toString` method of the `Object` class does not know what is inside the `BankAccount` class. Therefore, we have to override the method and supply our own version in the `BankAccount` class. We'll follow the same format that the `toString` method of the `Rectangle` class uses: first print the name of the class, and then the values of the instance variables inside brackets.

> Override the `toString` method to yield a string that describes the object's state.

```
public class BankAccount
{
   . . .
   public String toString()
   {
      return "BankAccount[balance=" + balance + "]";
   }
}
```

This works better:

```
BankAccount momsSavings = new BankAccount(5000);
String s = momsSavings.toString(); // Sets s to "BankAccount[balance=5000]"
```

9.5.2 The equals Method

> The equals method checks whether two objects have the same contents.

In addition to the toString method, the Object class also provides an equals method, whose purpose is to check whether two objects have the same contents:

```
if (stamp1.equals(stamp2)) . . .
    // Contents are the same—see Figure 10
```

This is different from the test with the == operator, which tests whether two references are identical, referring to the *same object:*

```
if (stamp1 == stamp2) . . .
    // Objects are the same—see Figure 11
```

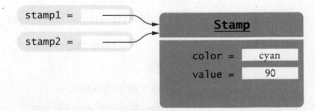

The equals *method checks whether two objects have the same contents.*

Let's implement the equals method for a Stamp class. You need to override the equals method of the Object class:

```
public class Stamp
{
    private String color;
    private int value;
    . . .
    public boolean equals(Object otherObject)
    {
        . . .
    }
    . . .
}
```

Now you have a slight problem. The Object class knows nothing about stamps, so it declares the otherObject parameter variable of the equals method to have the type Object. When overriding the method, you are not allowed to change the type of the parameter variable. Cast the parameter variable to the class Stamp:

```
Stamp other = (Stamp) otherObject;
```

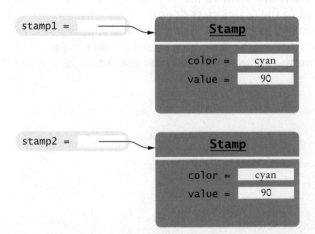

Figure 10 Two References to Equal Objects

Figure 11 Two References to the Same Object

Then you can compare the two stamps:

```java
public boolean equals(Object otherObject)
{
    Stamp other = (Stamp) otherObject;
    return color.equals(other.color)
            && value == other.value;
}
```

Note that this equals method can access the instance variables of *any* Stamp object: the access other.color is perfectly legal.

9.5.3 The instanceof Operator

As you have seen, it is legal to store a subclass reference in a superclass variable:

```java
ChoiceQuestion cq = new ChoiceQuestion();
Question q = cq; // OK
Object obj = cq; // OK
```

Very occasionally, you need to carry out the opposite conversion, from a superclass reference to a subclass reference.

For example, you may have a variable of type Object, and you happen to know that it actually holds a Question reference. In that case, you can use a cast to convert the type:

```java
Question q = (Question) obj;
```

However, this cast is somewhat dangerous. If you are wrong, and obj actually refers to an object of an unrelated type, then a "class cast" exception is thrown.

To protect against bad casts, you can use the instanceof operator. It tests whether an object belongs to a particular type. For example,

```java
obj instanceof Question
```

returns true if the type of obj is convertible to Question. This happens if obj refers to an actual Question or to a subclass such as ChoiceQuestion.

> If you know that an object belongs to a given class, use a cast to convert the type.

> The instanceof operator tests whether an object belongs to a particular type.

Syntax 9.4   The instanceof Operator

Syntax   *object* instanceof *TypeName*

If anObject is null, instanceof **returns** false.

Returns true if anObject **can be cast to a** Question.

The object may belong to a subclass of Question.

```java
if (anObject instanceof Question)
{
    Question q = (Question) anObject;
    . . .
}
```

You can invoke Question methods on this variable.

Two references to the same object.

Using the instanceof operator, a safe cast can be programmed as follows:

```
if (obj instanceof Question)
{
    Question q = (Question) obj;
}
```

Note that instanceof is *not* a method. It is an operator, just like + or <. However, it does not operate on numbers. To the left is an object, and to the right a type name.

FULL CODE EXAMPLE

Go to wiley.com/go/javacode to download a program that demonstrates the toString method and the instanceof operator.

Do *not* use the instanceof operator to bypass polymorphism:

```
if (q instanceof ChoiceQuestion) // Don't do this—see Common Error 9.5
{
    // Do the task the ChoiceQuestion way
}
else if (q instanceof Question)
{
    // Do the task the Question way
}
```

In this case, you should implement a method doTheTask in the Question class, override it in ChoiceQuestion, and call

```
q.doTheTask();
```

SELF CHECK

21. Why does the call

```
System.out.println(System.out);
```

produce a result such as java.io.PrintStream@7a84e4?

22. Will the following code fragment compile? Will it run? If not, what error is reported?

```
Object obj = "Hello";
System.out.println(obj.length());
```

23. Will the following code fragment compile? Will it run? If not, what error is reported?

```
Object obj = "Who was the inventor of Java?";
Question q = (Question) obj;
q.display();
```

24. Why don't we simply store all objects in variables of type Object?

25. Assuming that x is an object reference, what is the value of x instanceof Object?

Practice It Now you can try these exercises at the end of the chapter: E9.7, E9.8, E9.12.

Common Error 9.5

Don't Use Type Tests

Some programmers use specific type tests in order to implement behavior that varies with each class:

```
if (q instanceof ChoiceQuestion) // Don't do this
{
    // Do the task the ChoiceQuestion way
}
else if (q instanceof Question)
{
```

```
    // Do the task the Question way
}
```

This is a poor strategy. If a new class such as NumericQuestion is added, then you need to revise all parts of your program that make a type test, adding another case:

```
else if (q instanceof NumericQuestion)
{
    // Do the task the NumericQuestion way
}
```

In contrast, consider the addition of a class NumericQuestion to our quiz program. *Nothing* needs to change in that program because it uses polymorphism, not type tests.

Whenever you find yourself trying to use type tests in a hierarchy of classes, reconsider and use polymorphism instead. Declare a method doTheTask in the superclass, override it in the subclasses, and call

```
q.doTheTask();
```

Special Topic 9.6

Inheritance and the toString Method

You just saw how to write a toString method: Form a string consisting of the class name and the names and values of the instance variables. However, if you want your toString method to be usable by subclasses of your class, you need to work a bit harder.

Instead of hardcoding the class name, call the getClass method (which every class inherits from the Object class) to obtain an object that describes a class and its properties. Then invoke the getName method to get the name of the class:

```java
public String toString()
{
    return getClass().getName() + "[balance=" + balance + "]";
}
```

Then the toString method prints the correct class name when you apply it to a subclass, say a SavingsAccount.

```java
SavingsAccount momsSavings = . . . ;
System.out.println(momsSavings);
    // Prints "SavingsAccount[balance=10000]"
```

Of course, in the subclass, you should override toString and add the values of the subclass instance variables. Note that you must call super.toString to get the instance variables of the superclass—the subclass can't access them directly.

```java
public class SavingsAccount extends BankAccount
{
    . . .
    public String toString()
    {
        return super.toString() + "[interestRate=" + interestRate + "]";
    }
}
```

Now a savings account is converted to a string such as SavingsAccount[balance=10000][interestRate=5]. The brackets show which variables belong to the superclass.

Special Topic 9.7

Inheritance and the `equals` Method

You just saw how to write an `equals` method: Cast the `otherObject` parameter variable to the type of your class, and then compare the instance variables of the implicit parameter and the explicit parameter.

But what if someone called `stamp1.equals(x)` where x wasn't a `Stamp` object? Then the bad cast would generate an exception. It is a good idea to test whether `otherObject` really is an instance of the `Stamp` class. The easiest test would be with the `instanceof` operator. However, that test is not specific enough. It would be possible for `otherObject` to belong to some subclass of `Stamp`. To rule out that possibility, you should test whether the two objects belong to the same class. If not, return false.

```
if (getClass() != otherObject.getClass()) { return false; }
```

Moreover, the Java language specification demands that the `equals` method return false when `otherObject` is `null`.

Here is an improved version of the `equals` method that takes these two points into account:

```
public boolean equals(Object otherObject)
{
```

Computing & Society 9.1 Who Controls the Internet?

In 1962, J.C.R. Licklider was head of the first computer research program at DARPA, the Defense Advanced Research Projects Agency. He wrote a series of papers describing a "galactic network" through which computer users could access data and programs from other sites. This was well before computer networks were invented. By 1969, four computers—three in California and one in Utah—were connected to the ARPANET, the precursor of the Internet. The network grew quickly, linking computers at many universities and research organizations. It was originally thought that most network users wanted to run programs on remote computers. Using remote execution, a researcher at one institution would be able to access an underutilized computer at a different site. It quickly became apparent that remote execution was not what the network was actually used for. Instead, the "killer application" was electronic mail: the transfer of messages between computer users at different locations.

In 1972, Bob Kahn proposed to extend ARPANET into the *Internet:* a collection of interoperable networks. All networks on the Internet share common *protocols* for data transmission. Kahn and Vinton Cerf developed a protocol, now called TCP/IP (Transmission Control Protocol/Internet Protocol). On January 1, 1983, all hosts on the Internet simultaneously switched to the TCP/IP protocol (which is used to this day).

Over time, researchers, computer scientists, and hobbyists published increasing amounts of information on the Internet. For example, project Gutenberg makes available the text of important classical books, whose copyright has expired, in computer-readable form (www.gutenberg.org). In 1989, Tim Berners-Lee, a computer scientist at CERN (the European organization for nuclear research) started work on hyperlinked documents, allowing users to browse by following links to related documents. This infrastructure is now known as the World Wide Web.

The first interfaces to retrieve this information were, by today's standards, unbelievably clumsy and hard to use. In March 1993, WWW traffic was 0.1 percent of all Internet traffic. All that changed when Marc Andreesen, then a graduate student working for the National Center for Supercomputing Applications (NCSA), released Mosaic. Mosaic displayed web pages in graphical form, using images, fonts, and colors (see the figure). Andreesen went on to fame and fortune at Netscape, and Microsoft licensed the Mosaic code to create Internet Explorer. By 1996, WWW traffic accounted for more than half of the data transported on the Internet.

The Internet has a very democratic structure. Anyone can publish anything, and anyone can read whatever has been published. This does not always sit well with governments and corporations.

Many governments control the Internet infrastructure in their country. For example, an Internet user in China, searching for the Tiananmen Square

```
        if (otherObject == null) { return false; }
        if (getClass() != otherObject.getClass()) { return false; }
        Stamp other = (Stamp) otherObject;
        return color.equals(other.color) && value == other.value;
    }
```

When you implement equals in a subclass, you should first call equals in the superclass to check whether the superclass instance variables match. Here is an example:

```
public CollectibleStamp extends Stamp
{
    private int year;
    . . .
    public boolean equals(Object otherObject)
    {
        if (!super.equals(otherObject)) { return false; }
        CollectibleStamp other = (CollectibleStamp) otherObject;
        return year == other.year;
    }
}
```

massacre or air pollution in their hometown, may find nothing. Vietnam blocks access to Facebook, perhaps fearing that anti-government protesters might use it to organize themselves. The U.S. government has required publicly funded libraries and schools to install filters that block sexually explicit and hate speech.

When the Internet is delivered by phone or TV cable companies, those companies sometimes interfere with competing Internet offerings. Cell phone companies refused to carry Voice-over-IP services, and cable companies slowed down movie streaming.

The Internet has become a powerful force for delivering information—both good and bad. It is our responsibility as citizens to demand of our government that we can control which information to access.

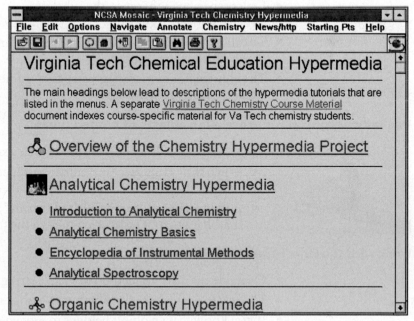

The NCSA Mosaic Browser

CHAPTER SUMMARY

Explain the notions of inheritance, superclass, and subclass.

- A subclass inherits data and behavior from a superclass.
- You can always use a subclass object in place of a superclass object.

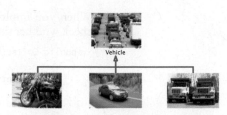

Implement subclasses in Java.

- A subclass inherits all methods that it does not override.
- A subclass can override a superclass method by providing a new implementation.
- The extends reserved word indicates that a class inherits from a superclass.

Implement methods that override methods from a superclass.

- An overriding method can extend or replace the functionality of the superclass method.
- Use the reserved word super to call a superclass method.
- Unless specified otherwise, the subclass constructor calls the superclass constructor with no arguments.
- To call a superclass constructor, use the super reserved word in the first statement of the subclass constructor.
- The constructor of a subclass can pass arguments to a superclass constructor, using the reserved word super.

Use polymorphism for processing objects of related types.

- A subclass reference can be used when a superclass reference is expected.
- When the virtual machine calls an instance method, it locates the method of the implicit parameter's class. This is called dynamic method lookup.
- Polymorphism ("having multiple forms") allows us to manipulate objects that share a set of tasks, even though the tasks are executed in different ways.

Work with the Object class and its methods.

- Override the toString method to yield a string that describes the object's state.
- The equals method checks whether two objects have the same contents.
- If you know that an object belongs to a given class, use a cast to convert the type.
- The instanceof operator tests whether an object belongs to a particular type.

REVIEW QUESTIONS

- **R9.1** Identify the superclass and subclass in each of the following pairs of classes.
    - **a.** Employee, Manager
    - **b.** GraduateStudent, Student
    - **c.** Person, Student
    - **d.** Employee, Professor
    - **e.** BankAccount, CheckingAccount
    - **f.** Vehicle, Car
    - **g.** Vehicle, Minivan
    - **h.** Car, Minivan
    - **i.** Truck, Vehicle

- **R9.2** Consider a program for managing inventory in a small appliance store. Why isn't it useful to have a superclass SmallAppliance and subclasses Toaster, CarVacuum, TravelIron, and so on?

- **R9.3** Which methods does the ChoiceQuestion class inherit from its superclass? Which methods does it override? Which methods does it add?

- **R9.4** Which methods does the SavingsAccount class in How To 9.1 inherit from its superclass? Which methods does it override? Which methods does it add?

- **R9.5** List the instance variables of a CheckingAccount object from How To 9.1.

- **R9.6** Suppose the class Sub extends the class Sandwich. Which of the following assignments are legal?

    ```
    Sandwich x = new Sandwich();
    Sub y = new Sub();
    ```
    - **a.** x = y;
    - **b.** y = x;
    - **c.** y = new Sandwich();
    - **d.** x = new Sub();

- **R9.7** Draw an inheritance diagram that shows the inheritance relationships between these classes.
    - Person
    - Employee
    - Student
    - Instructor
    - Classroom
    - Object

- **R9.8** In an object-oriented traffic simulation system, we have the classes listed below. Draw an inheritance diagram that shows the relationships between these classes.
    - Vehicle
    - Car
    - Truck
    - Sedan
    - Coupe
    - PickupTruck
    - SportUtilityVehicle
    - Minivan
    - Bicycle
    - Motorcycle

■ R9.9 What inheritance relationships would you establish among the following classes?

- Student
- Professor
- TeachingAssistant
- Employee
- Secretary

- DepartmentChair
- Janitor
- SeminarSpeaker
- Person
- Course

- Seminar
- Lecture
- ComputerLab

■■ R9.10 How does a cast such as (BankAccount) x differ from a cast of number values such as (int) x?

■■■ R9.11 Which of these conditions returns true? Check the Java documentation for the inheritance patterns. Recall that System.out is an object of the PrintStream class.

a. System.out instanceof PrintStream

b. System.out instanceof OutputStream

c. System.out instanceof LogStream

d. System.out instanceof Object

e. System.out instanceof String

f. System.out instanceof Writer

PRACTICE EXERCISES

■■ E9.1 Add a class NumericQuestion to the question hierarchy of Section 9.1. If the response and the expected answer differ by no more than 0.01, then accept the response as correct.

■■ E9.2 Add a class FillInQuestion to the question hierarchy of Section 9.1. Such a question is constructed with a string that contains the answer, surrounded by _ _, for example, "The inventor of Java was _James Gosling_". The question should be displayed as

```
The inventor of Java was _____
```

■ E9.3 Modify the checkAnswer method of the Question class so that it does not take into account different spaces or upper/lowercase characters. For example, the response "JAMES gosling" should match an answer of "James Gosling".

■■ E9.4 Add a class AnyCorrectChoiceQuestion to the question hierarchy of Section 9.1 that allows multiple correct choices. The respondent should provide any one of the correct choices. The answer string should contain all of the correct choices, separated by spaces. Provide instructions in the question text.

■■ E9.5 Add a class MultiChoiceQuestion to the question hierarchy of Section 9.1 that allows multiple correct choices. The respondent should provide all correct choices, separated by spaces. Provide instructions in the question text.

■■ E9.6 Add a method addText to the Question superclass and provide a different implementation of ChoiceQuestion that calls addText rather than storing an array list of choices.

■ E9.7 Provide toString methods for the Question and ChoiceQuestion classes.

■■ E9.8 Implement a superclass Person. Make two classes, Student and Instructor, that inherit from Person. A person has a name and a year of birth. A student has a major, and an instructor has a salary. Write the class declarations, the constructors, and the methods toString for all classes. Supply a test program that tests these classes and methods.

■■ E9.9 Make a class Employee with a name and salary. Make a class Manager inherit from Employee. Add an instance variable, named department, of type String. Supply a method toString that prints the manager's name, department, and salary. Make a class Executive inherit from Manager. Supply appropriate toString methods for all classes. Supply a test program that tests these classes and methods.

■■ E9.10 The java.awt.Rectangle class of the standard Java library does not supply a method to compute the area or perimeter of a rectangle. Provide a subclass BetterRectangle of the Rectangle class that has getPerimeter and getArea methods. *Do not add any instance variables*. In the constructor, call the setLocation and setSize methods of the Rectangle class. Provide a program that tests the methods that you supplied.

■■■ E9.11 Repeat Exercise E9.10, but in the BetterRectangle constructor, invoke the superclass constructor.

■■ E9.12 A labeled point has *x*- and *y*-coordinates and a string label. Provide a class Labeled-Point with a constructor LabeledPoint(int x, int y, String label) and a toString method that displays x, y, and the label.

■■ E9.13 Reimplement the LabeledPoint class of Exercise E9.12 by storing the location in a java.awt.Point object. Your toString method should invoke the toString method of the Point class.

■■ Business E9.14 Change the CheckingAccount class in How To 9.1 so that a $1 fee is levied for deposits or withdrawals in excess of three free monthly transactions. Place the code for computing the fee into a separate method that you call from the deposit and withdraw methods.

PROGRAMMING PROJECTS

■■ Business P9.1 Implement a superclass Appointment and subclasses Onetime, Daily, and Monthly. An appointment has a description (for example, "see the dentist") and a date. Write a method occursOn(int year, int month, int day) that checks whether the appointment occurs on that date. For example, for a monthly appointment, you must check whether the day of the month matches. Then fill an array of Appointment objects with a mixture of appointments. Have the user enter a date and print out all appointments that occur on that date.

■■ Business P9.2 Improve the appointment book program of Exercise P9.1. Give the user the option to add new appointments. The user must specify the type of the appointment, the description, and the date.

■■■ Business P9.3 Improve the appointment book program of Exercise P9.1 and P9.2 by letting the user save the appointment data to a file and reload the data from a file. The saving part is straightforward: Make a method save. Save the type, description, and date to a file. The loading part is not so easy. First determine the type of the appointment to be loaded, create an object of that type, and then call a load method to load the data.

■■ **Science P9.4**   Resonant circuits are used to select a signal (e.g., a radio station or TV channel) from among other competing signals. Resonant circuits are characterized by the frequency response shown in the figure below. The resonant frequency response is completely described by three parameters: the resonant frequency, ω_0, the bandwidth, B, and the gain at the resonant frequency, k.

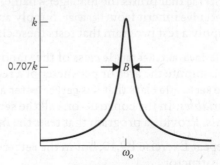

Frequency (rad/s, log scale)

Two simple resonant circuits are shown in the figure below. The circuit in (a) is called a *parallel resonant circuit*. The circuit in (b) is called a *series resonant circuit*. Both resonant circuits consist of a resistor having resistance R, a capacitor having capacitance C, and an inductor having inductance L.

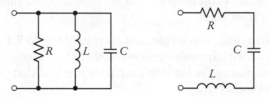

(a) Parallel resonant circuit   (b) Series resonant circuit

These circuits are designed by determining values of R, C, and L that cause the resonant frequency response to be described by specified values of ω_0, B, and k. The design equations for the parallel resonant circuit are:

$$R = k, \quad C = \frac{1}{BR}, \quad \text{and} \quad L = \frac{1}{\omega_0^2 C}$$

Similarly, the design equations for the series resonant circuit are:

$$R = \frac{1}{k}, \quad L = \frac{R}{B}, \quad \text{and} \quad C = \frac{1}{\omega_0^2 L}$$

Write a Java program that represents ResonantCircuit as a superclass and represents the SeriesResonantCircuit and ParallelResonantCircuit as subclasses. Give the superclass three private instance variables representing the parameters ω_0, B, and k of the resonant frequency response. The superclass should provide public instance methods to get and set each of these variables. The superclass should also provide a display method that prints a description of the resonant frequency response.

Each subclass should provide a method that designs the corresponding resonant circuit. The subclasses should also override the display method of the superclass to print descriptions of both the frequency response (the values of ω_o, B, and k) and the circuit (the values of R, C, and L).

All classes should provide appropriate constructors.

Supply a class that demonstrates that the subclasses all work properly.

■■■ Science P9.5 In this problem, you will model a circuit consisting of an arbitrary configuration of resistors. Provide a superclass `Circuit` with a instance method `getResistance`. Provide a subclass `Resistor` representing a single resistor. Provide subclasses `Serial` and `Parallel`, each of which contains an `ArrayList<Circuit>`. A `Serial` circuit models a series of circuits, each of which can be a single resistor or another circuit. Similarly, a `Parallel` circuit models a set of circuits in parallel. For example, the following circuit is a `Parallel` circuit containing a single resistor and one `Serial` circuit:

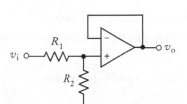

A `Serial` circuit

Use Ohm's law to compute the combined resistance.

■■ Science P9.6 Part (a) of the figure below shows a symbolic representation of an electric circuit called an *amplifier*. The input to the amplifier is the voltage v_i and the output is the voltage v_o. The output of an amplifier is proportional to the input. The constant of proportionality is called the "gain" of the amplifier.

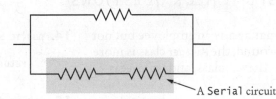

(a) Amplifier   (b) Inverting amplifier

(c) Noninverting amplifier   (d) Voltage divider amplifier

Parts (b), (c), and (d) show schematics of three specific types of amplifier: the *inverting amplifier*, *noninverting amplifier*, and *voltage divider amplifier*. Each of these three amplifiers consists of two resistors and an op amp. The value of the gain of each amplifier depends on the values of its resistances. In particular, the gain, g, of the inverting amplifier is given by $g = -\dfrac{R_2}{R_1}$. Similarly the gains of the noninverting amplifier and voltage divider amplifier are given by $g = 1 + \dfrac{R_2}{R_1}$ and $g = \dfrac{R_2}{R_1 + R_2}$, respectively.

Write a Java program that represents the amplifier as a superclass and represents the inverting, noninverting, and voltage divider amplifiers as subclasses. Give the subclass two methods, getGain and a `getDescription` method that returns a string identifying the amplifier. Each subclass should have a constructor with two arguments, the resistances of the amplifier.

The subclasses need to override the `getGain` and `getDescription` methods of the superclass.

Supply a class that demonstrates that the subclasses all work properly for sample values of the resistances.

ANSWERS TO SELF-CHECK QUESTIONS

1. Because every manager is an employee but not the other way around, the Manager class is more specialized. It is the subclass, and Employee is the superclass.

2. CheckingAccount and SavingsAccount both inherit from the more general class BankAccount.

3. The classes Frame, Window, and Component in the java.awt package, and the class Object in the java.lang package.

4. Vehicle, truck, motorcycle

5. It shouldn't. A quiz isn't a question; it *has* questions.

6. a, b, d

7.
```
public class Manager extends Employee
{
    private double bonus;
    // Constructors and methods omitted
}
```

8. name, baseSalary, and bonus

9.
```
public class Manager extends Employee
{
    . . .
    public double getSalary() { . . . }
}
```

10. getName, setName, setBaseSalary

11. The method is not allowed to access the instance variable text from the superclass.

12. The type of the this reference is ChoiceQuestion. Therefore, the display method of ChoiceQuestion is selected, and the method calls itself.

13. Because there is no ambiguity. The subclass doesn't have a setAnswer method.

14.
```
public String getName()
{
    return "*" + super.getName();
}
```

15.
```
public double getSalary()
{
    return super.getSalary() + bonus;
}
```

16. a only.

17. It belongs to the class BankAccount or one of its subclasses.

18. `Question[] quiz = new Question[SIZE];`

19. You cannot tell from the fragment—cq may be initialized with an object of a subclass of ChoiceQuestion. The display method of whatever object cq references is invoked.

20. No. This is a static method of the Math class. There is no implicit parameter object that could be used to dynamically look up a method.

21. Because the implementor of the PrintStream class did not supply a toString method.

22. The second line will not compile. The class Object does not have a method length.

23. The code will compile, but the second line will throw a class cast exception because Question is not a superclass of String.

24. There are only a few methods that can be invoked on variables of type Object.

25. The value is false if x is null and true otherwise.

CHAPTER **10**

INTERFACES

CHAPTER GOALS

To be able to declare and use interface types

To appreciate how interfaces can be used to decouple classes

To learn how to implement helper classes as inner classes

To implement event listeners in graphical applications

CHAPTER CONTENTS

A mixer rotates any tools that will attach to its motor's shaft. In other words, a single motor can be used with multiple tools. We want to be able to *reuse* software components in the same way. In this chapter, you will learn an important strategy for separating the reusable part of a computation from the parts that vary in each reuse scenario. The reusable part invokes methods of an *interface*, not caring how the methods are implemented—just as the mixer doesn't care about the shape of the attachment. In a program, the reusable code is combined with a class that implements the interface methods. To produce a different application, you plug in another class that implements the same interface.

10.1 Using Interfaces for Algorithm Reuse

It is often possible to make a service available to a wide set of inputs by focusing on the essential operations that the service requires. *Interface types* are used to express these common operations.

This restaurant is willing to serve anyone who conforms to the Customer *interface with* eat *and* pay *methods.*

10.1.1 Defining an Interface Type

Consider this average method that provides a service, namely to compute the average bank balance of an array of bank accounts:

```
public static double average(BankAccount[] objects)
{
    double sum = 0;
    for (BankAccount obj : objects)
    {
        sum = sum + obj.getBalance();
    }
    if (objects.length > 0) { return sum / objects.length; }
    else { return 0; }
}
```

Now suppose we want to compute an average of other objects. We have to write that method *again*. Here it is for Country objects:

```
public static double average(Country[] objects)
{
    double sum = 0;
    for (Country obj : objects)
    {
        sum = sum + obj.getArea();
```

```
        }
        if (objects.length > 0) { return sum / objects.length; }
        else { return 0; }
    }
```

Clearly, the algorithm for computing the average is the same in all cases, but the details of measurement differ. We would like to provide a *single* method that provides this service.

But there is a problem. Each class has a different name for the method that returns the value that is being averaged. In the BankAccount class, we call getBalance. In the Country class, we call getArea.

Suppose that the various classes agree on a method getMeasure that obtains the measure to be used in the data analysis. For bank accounts, getMeasure returns the balance. For countries, getMeasure returns the area, and so on.

Then we can implement a single method that computes

```
sum = sum + obj.getMeasure();
```

But agreeing on the name of the method is only half the solution. In Java, we also must declare the type of the variable obj. Of course, you can't write

```
BankAccount or Country or ... obj; // No
```

We need to invent a new type that describes any class whose objects can be measured.

In Java, an **interface type** is used to specify required operations. We will declare an interface type that we call Measurable:

A Java interface type declares methods but does not provide their implementations.

```
public interface Measurable
{
    double getMeasure();
}
```

The interface declaration lists all methods that the interface type requires. The Measurable interface type requires a single method, getMeasure. In general, an interface type can require multiple methods.

An interface type is similar to a class, but there are several important differences:

- An interface type does not have instance variables.
- All methods in an interface type are *abstract*; that is, they have a name, parameters, and a return type, but they don't have an implementation.
- All methods in an interface type are automatically public.
- An interface type has no constructor. Interfaces are not classes, and you cannot construct objects of an interface type.

Syntax 10.1   Declaring an Interface

Syntax
```
public interface InterfaceName
{
    method headers
}
```

```
public interface Measurable
{
    double getMeasure();
}
```

The methods of an interface are automatically public.

No implementation is provided.

Now that we have a type that denotes measurability, we can implement a reusable average method:

```java
public static double average(Measurable[] objects)
{
    double sum = 0;
    for (Measurable obj : objects)
    {
        sum = sum + obj.getMeasure();
    }
    if (objects.length > 0) { return sum / objects.length; }
    else { return 0; }
}
```

This method is useful for objects of any class that conforms to the Measurable type. In the next section, you will see what a class must do to make its objects measurable.

Note that the Measurable interface is not a type in the standard library—it was created specifically for this book, to provide a very simple example for studying the interface concept.

This standmixer provides the "rotation" service to any attachment that conforms to a common interface. Similarly, the average *method at the end of this section works with any class that implements a common interface.*

10.1.2 Implementing an Interface Type

Use the implements reserved word to indicate that a class implements an interface type.

The average method of the preceding section can process objects of any class that implements the Measurable interface. A class **implements an interface** type if it declares the interface in an implements clause, like this:

```java
public class BankAccount implements Measurable
```

The class should then implement the method or methods that the interface requires:

```java
public class BankAccount implements Measurable
{
    . . .
    public double getMeasure()
    {
        return balance;
    }
}
```

Note that the class must declare the method as public, whereas the interface need not—all methods in an interface are public.

Once the BankAccount class implements the Measurable interface type, BankAccount objects are instances of the Measurable type:

```java
Measurable obj = new BankAccount(); // OK
```

Syntax 10.2   Implementing an Interface

```
Syntax    public class ClassName implements InterfaceName, InterfaceName, . . .
          {
              instance variables
              methods
          }
```

```
                        public class BankAccount implements Measurable ——— List all interface types
                        {                                                     that this class implements.
          BankAccount       . . .
        instance variables  public double getMeasure()
                            {                              This method provides the implementation
                                return balance;            for the method declared in the interface.
            Other           }
       BankAccount methods  . . .

                        }
```

A variable of type Measurable holds a reference to an object of some class that implements the Measurable interface.

Similarly, it is an easy matter to modify the Country class to implement the Measurable interface:

```
public class Country implements Measurable
{
    public double getMeasure()
    {
        return area;
    }
    . . .
}
```

The program at the end of this section uses a single average method (placed in class Data) to compute the average of bank accounts and the average of countries.

This is a typical usage for interface types. By inventing the Measurable interface type, we have made the average method reusable.

Figure 1 shows the relationships between the Data class, the Measurable interface, and the classes that implement the interface. Note that the Data class depends only on the Measurable interface. It is decoupled from the BankAccount and Country classes.

Use interface types to make code more reusable.

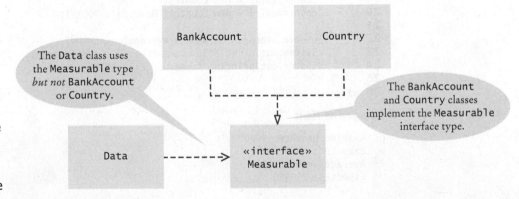

Figure 1
UML Diagram of the Data Class and the Classes that Implement the Measurable Interface

In the UML notation, interfaces are tagged with an indicator «interface». A dotted arrow with a triangular tip denotes the *implements* relationship between a class and an interface. You have to look carefully at the arrow tips—a dotted line with an open arrow tip (≫) denotes the *uses* relationship or dependency.

section_1/Data.java

```
1  public class Data
2  {
3     /**
4        Computes the average of the measures of the given objects.
5        @param objects an array of Measurable objects
6        @return the average of the measures
7     */
8     public static double average(Measurable[] objects)
9     {
10       double sum = 0;
11       for (Measurable obj : objects)
12       {
13          sum = sum + obj.getMeasure();
14       }
15       if (objects.length > 0) { return sum / objects.length;}
16       else { return 0; }
17    }
18 }
```

section_1/MeasurableTester.java

```
1  /**
2     This program demonstrates the measurable BankAccount and Country classes.
3  */
4  public class MeasurableTester
5  {
6     public static void main(String[] args)
7     {
8        Measurable[] accounts = new Measurable[3];
9        accounts[0] = new BankAccount(0);
10       accounts[1] = new BankAccount(10000);
11       accounts[2] = new BankAccount(2000);
12
13       double averageBalance = Data.average(accounts);
14       System.out.println("Average balance: " + averageBalance);
15       System.out.println("Expected: 4000");
16
17       Measurable[] countries = new Measurable[3];
18       countries[0] = new Country("Uruguay", 176220);
19       countries[1] = new Country("Thailand", 513120);
20       countries[2] = new Country("Belgium", 30510);
21
22       double averageArea = Data.average(countries);
23       System.out.println("Average area: " + averageArea);
24       System.out.println("Expected: 239950");
25    }
26 }
```

Program Run

```
Average balance: 4000
Expected: 4000
Average area: 239950
Expected: 239950
```

10.1.3 Comparing Interfaces and Inheritance

In Chapter 9, you saw how to use inheritance to model hierarchies of related classes, such as different kinds of quiz questions or bank accounts. Multiple-choice questions and fill-in questions are questions with specific characteristics.

Interfaces model a somewhat different relationship. Consider for example the BankAccount and Country classes in the preceding section. Both implement the Measurable interface type, but otherwise they have nothing in common. Being measurable is just one aspect of what it means to be a bank account or country. It is useful to model this common aspect, because it enables other programmers to write tools that exploit the commonality, such as the method for computing averages.

A class can implement more than one interface, for example

```
public class Country implements Measurable, Named
```

Here, Named is a different interface

```
public interface Named
{
    String getName();
}
```

In contrast, a class can only extend (inherit from) a single superclass.

An interface merely specifies the behavior that an implementing class should supply. It provides no implementation. In contrast, a superclass provides some implementation that a subclass inherits.

Special Topic 9.3 introduced abstract classes, which defer the implementation of some methods to subclasses. You can think of an interface as a class in which *every* method is abstract. However, interfaces have an advantage over such abstract classes —a class can implement more than one of them.

Generally, you will develop interfaces when you have code that processes objects of different classes in a common way. For example, a drawing program might have different objects that can be drawn, such as lines, images, text, and so on. In this situation, a Drawable interface with a draw method will be useful. Another example is a traffic simulation that models the movement of people, cars, dogs, balls, and so on. In this example, you might create a Moveable interface with methods move and getPosition.

SELF CHECK

1. Suppose you want to use the average method to find the average salary of an array of Employee objects. What condition must the Employee class fulfill?
2. Why can't the average method have a parameter variable of type Object[]?
3. Why can't you use the average method to find the average length of String objects?
4. What is wrong with this code?
   ```
   Measurable meas = new Measurable();
   System.out.println(meas.getMeasure());
   ```
5. What is wrong with this code?
   ```
   Measurable meas = new Country("Uruguay", 176220);
   System.out.println(meas.getName());
   ```

Practice It   Now you can try these exercises at the end of the chapter: E10.1, E10.2, E10.3.

Common Error 10.1

Forgetting to Declare Implementing Methods as Public

The methods in an interface are not declared as public, because they are public by default. However, the methods in a class are not public by default—their default access level is "package" access, which we discussed in Chapter 8. It is a common error to forget the public reserved word when declaring a method from an interface:

```
public class BankAccount implements Measurable
{
    . . .
    double getMeasure() // Oops—should be public
    {
        return balance;
    }
}
```

Then the compiler complains that the method has a weaker access level, namely package access instead of public access. The remedy is to declare the method as public.

Common Error 10.2

Trying to Instantiate an Interface

You can declare variables whose type is an interface, for example:

```
Measurable meas;
```

However, you can *never* construct an object of an interface type:

```
Measurable meas = new Measurable(); // Error
```

Interfaces aren't classes. There are no objects whose types are interfaces. If an interface variable refers to an object, then the object must belong to some class—a class that implements the interface:

```
Measurable meas = new BankAccount(); // OK
```

Special Topic 10.1

Constants in Interfaces

Interfaces cannot have instance variables, but it is legal to specify **constants**. For example, the SwingConstants interface declares various constants, such as SwingConstants.NORTH, Swing-Constants.EAST, and so on.

When declaring a constant in an interface, you can (and should) omit the reserved words public static final, because all variables in an interface are automatically public static final. For example,

```
public interface SwingConstants
{
    int NORTH = 1;
    int NORTHEAST = 2;
    int EAST = 3;
    . . .
}
```

10.2 Working with Interface Variables

In the following sections, you will learn how to work with variables whose types are interfaces.

10.2.1 Converting from Classes to Interfaces

Have a close look at the call

```
double averageBalance = Data.average(accounts);
```

from the program of the preceding section. Here, accounts is an array of BankAccount objects. However, the average method expects an array of Measurable objects:

```
public double average(Measurable[] objects)
```

It is legal to convert from the BankAccount type to the Measurable type. In general, you can convert from a class type to the type of any interface that the class implements. For example,

> You can convert from a class type to an interface type, provided the class implements the interface.

```
BankAccount account = new BankAccount(1000);
Measurable meas = account; // OK
```

Alternatively, a Measurable variable can refer to an object of the Country class of the preceding section because that class also implements the Measurable interface.

```
Country uruguay = new Country("Uruguay", 176220);
Measurable meas = uruguay; // Also OK
```

However, the Rectangle class from the standard library doesn't implement the Measurable interface. Therefore, the following assignment is an error:

```
Measurable meas = new Rectangle(5, 10, 20, 30); // Error
```

10.2.2 Invoking Methods on Interface Variables

Now suppose that the variable meas has been initialized with a reference to an object of some class that implements the Measurable interface. You don't know to which class that object belongs. But you do know that the class implements the methods of the interface type, and you can invoke them:

```
double result = meas.getMeasure();
```

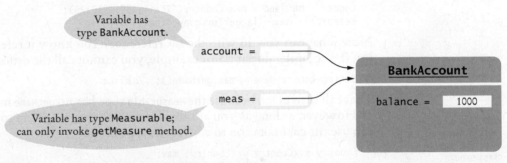

Figure 2 Variables of Class and Interface Types

Now let's think through the call to the getMeasure method more carefully. Which get-Measure method is called? The BankAccount and Country classes provide two different implementations of that method. How does the correct method get called if the caller doesn't even know the exact class to which meas belongs?

> Method calls on an interface reference are polymorphic. The appropriate method is determined at run time.

This is again polymorphism in action. (See Section 9.4 for a discussion of polymorphism.) The Java virtual machine locates the correct method by first looking at the class of the actual object, and then calling the method with the given name in that class. That is, if meas refers to a BankAccount object, then the BankAccount.getMeasure method is called. If meas refers to a Country object, then the Country.getMeasure method is called.

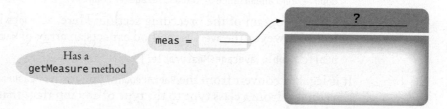

Figure 3
An Interface Reference Can Refer to an Object of Any Class that Implements the Interface

10.2.3 Casting from Interfaces to Classes

Occasionally, it happens that you store an object in an interface reference and you need to convert its type back. Consider this method that returns the object with the larger measure:

```java
public static Measurable larger(Measurable obj1, Measurable obj2)
{
    if (obj1.getMeasure() > obj2.getMeasure())
    {
        return obj1;
    }
    else
    {
        return obj2;
    }
}
```

The larger method returns the object with the larger measure, *as a* Measurable *reference*. It has no choice—it does not know the exact type of the object. Let's use the method:

```java
Country uruguay = new Country("Uruguay", 176220);
Country thailand = new Country("Thailand", 513120);
Measurable max = larger(uruguay, thailand);
```

Now what can you do with the max reference? *You* know it refers to a Country object, but the compiler doesn't. For example, you cannot call the getName method:

```java
String countryName = max.getName(); // Error
```

That call is an error, because the Measurable type has no getName method.

However, as long as you are absolutely sure that max refers to a Country object, you can use the **cast** notation to convert its type back:

> You need a cast to convert from an interface type to a class type.

```java
Country maxCountry = (Country) max;
String name = maxCountry.getName();
```

FULL CODE EXAMPLE

Go to wiley.com/go/ javacode to download a demonstration of conversions between class and interface types.

If you are wrong, and the object doesn't actually refer to a country, a run-time exception will occur.

If a Person object is actually a Superhero, you need a cast before you can apply any Superhero methods.

SELF CHECK

6. Can you use a cast (BankAccount) meas to convert a Measurable variable meas to a BankAccount reference?

7. If both BankAccount and Country implement the Measurable interface, can a Country reference be converted to a BankAccount reference?

8. Why is it impossible to construct a Measurable object?

9. Why can you nevertheless declare a variable whose type is Measurable?

10. What does this code fragment print? Why is this an example of polymorphism?

```
Measurable[] data = { new BankAccount(10000), new Country("Belgium", 30510) };
System.out.println(average(data));
```

Practice It Now you can try these exercises at the end of the chapter: R10.1, R10.2, R10.3.

WORKED EXAMPLE 10.1 **Investigating Number Sequences**

Learn how to use a Sequence interface to investigate properties of arbitrary number sequences. Go to wiley.com/go/javaexamples and download Worked Example 10.1.

10.3 The Comparable Interface

Implement the Comparable interface so that objects of your class can be compared, for example, in a sort method.

In the preceding sections, we defined the Measurable interface and provided an average method that works with any classes implementing that interface. In this section, you will learn about the Comparable interface of the standard Java library.

The Measurable interface is used for measuring a single object. The Comparable interface is more complex because comparisons involve two objects. The interface declares a compareTo method. The call

```
a.compareTo(b)
```

must return a negative number if a should come before b, zero if a and b are the same, and a positive number if b should come before a.

The Comparable interface has a single method:

```
public interface Comparable
{
    int compareTo(Object otherObject);
}
```

For example, the BankAccount class can implement Comparable like this:

```java
public class BankAccount implements Comparable
{
    . . .
    public int compareTo(Object otherObject)
    {
        BankAccount other = (BankAccount) otherObject;
        if (balance < other.balance) { return -1; }
        if (balance > other.balance) { return 1; }
        return 0;
    }
    . . .
}
```

This compareTo method compares bank accounts by their balance. Note that the compareTo method has a parameter variable of type Object. To turn it into a BankAccount reference, we use a cast:

```java
BankAccount other = (BankAccount) otherObject;
```

FULL CODE EXAMPLE

Go to wiley.com/go/ javacode to download a program that demonstrates the Comparable interface with bank accounts.

Once the BankAccount class implements the Comparable interface, you can sort an array of bank accounts with the Arrays.sort method:

```java
BankAccount[] accounts = new BankAccount[3];
accounts[0] = new BankAccount(10000);
accounts[1] = new BankAccount(0);
accounts[2] = new BankAccount(2000);
Arrays.sort(accounts);
```

The accounts array is now sorted by increasing balance.

The compareTo *method checks whether another object is larger or smaller.*

SELF CHECK

11. How can you sort an array of Country objects by increasing area?

12. Can you use the Arrays.sort method to sort an array of String objects? Check the API documentation for the String class.

13. Can you use the Arrays.sort method to sort an array of Rectangle objects? Check the API documentation for the Rectangle class.

14. Write a method max that finds the larger of any two Comparable objects.

15. Write a call to the method of Self Check 14 that computes the larger of two bank accounts, then prints its balance.

Practice It Now you can try these exercises at the end of the chapter: E10.6, E10.23.

The clone Method and the Cloneable Interface

You know that copying an object reference simply gives you two references to the same object:

```
BankAccount account = new BankAccount(1000);
BankAccount account2 = account;
account2.deposit(500);
    // Now both account and account2 refer to a bank account with a balance of 1500
```

What can you do if you actually want to make a copy of an object? That is the purpose of the clone method. The clone method must return a *new* object that has an identical state to the existing object (see Figure 4).

Here is how to call it:

```
BankAccount clonedAccount = (BankAccount) account.clone();
```

The return type of the clone method is the class Object. When you call the method, you must use a cast to inform the compiler that account.clone() really returns a BankAccount object.

The Object.clone method is the starting point for the clone methods in your own classes. It creates a new object of the same type as the original object. It also automatically copies the instance variables from the original object to the cloned object. Here is a first attempt to implement the clone method for the BankAccount class:

```
public class BankAccount
{
    . . .
    public Object clone()
    {
        // Not complete
        Object clonedAccount = super.clone();
        return clonedAccount;
    }
}
```

The clone *method makes an identical copy of an object.*

However, this Object.clone method must be used with care. It only shifts the problem of cloning by one level; it does not completely solve it. Specifically, if an object contains a reference to another object, then the Object.clone method makes a copy of that object reference, not a clone of that object. Figure 5 shows how the Object.clone method works with a Customer object that has references to a String object and a BankAccount object. As you can see, the Object.clone method copies the references to the cloned Customer object and does not clone the objects to which they refer. Such a copy is called a **shallow copy**.

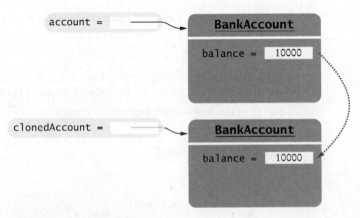

Figure 4   Cloning Objects

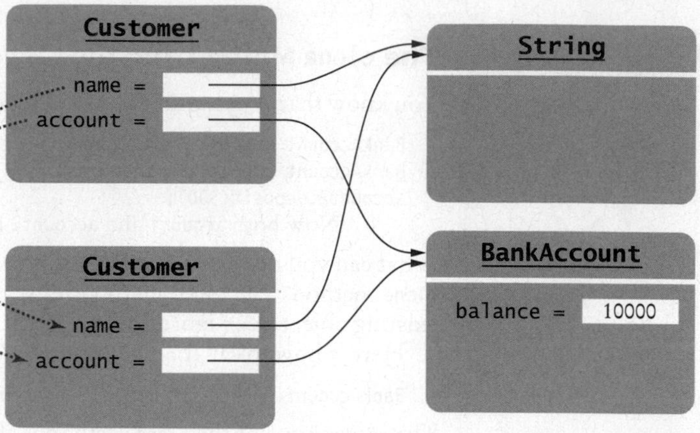

Figure 5
The `Object.clone`
Method Makes a
Shallow Copy

There is a reason why the `Object.clone` method does not systematically clone all sub-objects. In some situations, it is unnecessary. For example, if an object contains a reference to a string, there is no harm in copying the string reference, because Java string objects can never change their contents. The `Object.clone` method does the right thing if an object contains only numbers, Boolean values, and strings. But it must be used with caution when an object contains references to mutable objects.

For that reason, there are two safeguards built into the `Object.clone` method to ensure that it is not used accidentally. First, the method is declared `protected` (see Special Topic 9.5). This prevents you from accidentally calling `x.clone()` if the class to which x belongs hasn't declared `clone` to be public.

As a second precaution, `Object.clone` checks that the object being cloned implements the `Cloneable` interface. If not, it throws an exception. The `Object.clone` method looks like this:

```java
public class Object
{
    protected Object clone()
        throws CloneNotSupportedException
    {
        if (this instanceof Cloneable)
        {
            // Copy the instance variables
            . . .
        }
        else
        {
            throw new CloneNotSupportedException();
        }
    }
}
```

Unfortunately, all that safeguarding means that the legitimate callers of `Object.clone()` pay a price—they must catch that exception (see Chapter 11) *even if their class implements* `Cloneable`.

```java
public class BankAccount implements Cloneable
{
    . . .
    public Object clone()
    {
        try
        {
            return super.clone();
        }
```

```
        catch (CloneNotSupportedException e)
        {
            // Can't happen because we implement Cloneable but we still must catch it.
            return null;
        }
    }
}
```

If an object contains a reference to another mutable object, then you must call clone for that reference. For example, suppose the Customer class has an instance variable of class BankAccount. You can implement Customer.clone as follows:

```
public class Customer implements Cloneable
{
    private String name;
    private BankAccount account;
    . . .
    public Object clone()
    {
        try
        {
            Customer cloned = (Customer) super.clone();
            cloned.account = (BankAccount) account.clone();
            return cloned;
        }
        catch(CloneNotSupportedException e)
        { // Can't happen because we implement Cloneable
            return null;
        }
    }
}
```

In general, implementing the clone method requires these steps:
- Make the class implement the Cloneable interface type.
- In the clone method, call super.clone(). Catch the CloneNotSupportedException if the superclass is Object.
- Clone any mutable instance variables.

10.4 Using Interfaces for Callbacks

In this section, we introduce the notion of a **callback**, show how it leads to a more flexible average method, and study how a callback can be implemented in Java by using interface types.

To understand why a further improvement to the average method is desirable, consider these limitations of the Measurable interface:

- You can add the Measurable interface only to classes under your control. If you want to process a set of Rectangle objects, you cannot make the Rectangle class implement another interface—it is a library class, which you cannot change.
- You can measure an object in only one way. If you want to analyze a set of cars both by speed and price, you are stuck.

Therefore, let's rethink the average method. The method measures objects, requiring them to be of type Measurable. The responsibility of measuring lies with the added objects themselves. That is the cause for the limitations.

A callback object waits to be called. The algorithm that has the callback object only calls it when it needs to have the information that the callback can provide.

> A callback is a mechanism for specifying code that is executed at a later time.

It would be better if we could give the average method the data to be averaged, and separately a method for measuring the objects. When collecting rectangles, we might give it a method for computing the area of a rectangle. When collecting cars, we might give it a method for getting the car's price.

Such a method is called a **callback**. A callback is a mechanism for bundling up a block of code so that it can be invoked at a later time.

In some programming languages, it is possible to specify callbacks directly, as blocks of code or names of methods. But Java is an object-oriented programming language. Therefore, you turn callbacks into objects. This process starts by declaring an interface for the callback:

```java
public interface Measurer
{
    double measure(Object anObject);
}
```

The measure method measures an object and returns its measurement. Here we use the fact that all objects can be converted to the type Object.

The code that makes the call to the callback receives an object of a class that implements this interface. In our case, the improved average method receives a Measurer object.

```java
public static double average(Object[] objects, Measurer meas)
{
    double sum = 0;
    for (Object obj : objects)
    {
        sum = sum + meas.measure(obj);
    }
    if (objects.length > 0) { return sum / objects.length; }
    else { return 0; }
}
```

The average method simply makes a callback to the measure method whenever it needs to measure any object.

Finally, a specific callback is obtained by implementing the Measurer interface. For example, here is how you can measure rectangles by area. Provide a class

```java
public class AreaMeasurer implements Measurer
{
    public double measure(Object anObject)
    {
        Rectangle aRectangle = (Rectangle) anObject;
        double area = aRectangle.getWidth() * aRectangle.getHeight();
        return area;
    }
}
```

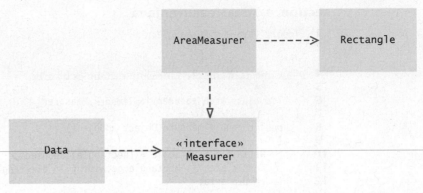

Figure 6   UML Diagram of the Data Class and the Measurer Interface

Note that the measure method has a parameter variable of type Object, even though this particular measurer just wants to measure rectangles. The method parameter types must match those of the measure method in the Measurer interface. Therefore, the anObject parameter variable is cast to the Rectangle type:

```
Rectangle aRectangle = (Rectangle) anObject;
```

What can you do with an AreaMeasurer? You need it to compute the average area of rectangles. Construct an object of the AreaMeasurer class and pass it to the average method:

```
Measurer areaMeas = new AreaMeasurer();
Rectangle[] rects
    = { new Rectangle(5, 10, 20, 30), new Rectangle(10, 20, 30, 40) };
double averageArea = average(rects, areaMeas);
```

The average method will ask the AreaMeasurer object to measure the rectangles.

Figure 6 shows the UML diagram of the classes and interfaces of this solution. As in Figure 1, the Data class (which holds the average method) is decoupled from the class whose objects it processes (Rectangle). However, unlike in Figure 1, the Rectangle class is no longer coupled with another class. Instead, to process rectangles, you provide a small "helper" class AreaMeasurer. This helper class has only one purpose: to tell the average method how to measure its objects.

Here is the complete program:

section_4/Measurer.java

```
1  /**
2       Describes any class whose objects can measure other objects.
3  */
4  public interface Measurer
5  {
6     /**
7         Computes the measure of an object.
8         @param anObject  the object to be measured
9         @return  the measure
10    */
11    double measure(Object anObject);
12 }
```

section_4/AreaMeasurer.java

```
1   import java.awt.Rectangle;
2
3   /**
4       Objects of this class measure rectangles by area.
5   */
6   public class AreaMeasurer implements Measurer
7   {
8       public double measure(Object anObject)
9       {
10          Rectangle aRectangle = (Rectangle) anObject;
11          double area = aRectangle.getWidth() * aRectangle.getHeight();
12          return area;
13      }
14  }
```

section_4/Data.java

```
1   public class Data
2   {
3       /**
4           Computes the average of the measures of the given objects.
5           @param objects an array of objects
6           @param meas the measurer for the objects
7           @return the average of the measures
8       */
9       public static double average(Object[] objects, Measurer meas)
10      {
11          double sum = 0;
12          for (Object obj : objects)
13          {
14              sum = sum + meas.measure(obj);
15          }
16          if (objects.length > 0) { return sum / objects.length; }
17          else { return 0; }
18      }
19  }
```

section_4/MeasurerTester.java

```
1   import java.awt.Rectangle;
2
3   /**
4       This program demonstrates the use of a Measurer.
5   */
6   public class MeasurerTester
7   {
8       public static void main(String[] args)
9       {
10          Measurer areaMeas = new AreaMeasurer();
11
12          Rectangle[] rects = new Rectangle[]
13              {
14                  new Rectangle(5, 10, 20, 30),
15                  new Rectangle(10, 20, 30, 40),
16                  new Rectangle(20, 30, 5, 15)
17              };
18
```

```
19        double averageArea = Data.average(rects, areaMeas);
20        System.out.println("Average area: " + averageArea);
21        System.out.println("Expected: 625");
22     }
23  }
```

Program Run

```
Average area: 625
Expected: 625
```

SELF CHECK

16. Suppose you want to use the average method of Section 10.1 to find the average length of String objects. Why can't this work?

17. How can you use the average class of this section to find the average length of String objects?

18. Why does the measure method of the Measurer interface have one more argument than the getMeasure method of the Measurable interface?

19. Write a method max with three arguments that finds the larger of any two objects, using a Measurer to compare them.

20. Write a call to the method of Self Check 19 that computes the larger of two rectangles, then prints its width and height.

Practice It   Now you can try these exercises at the end of the chapter: R10.7, E10.4, E10.5.

10.5 Inner Classes

An inner class is a class that is declared inside another class.

The AreaMeasurer class of the preceding section is a very trivial class. We need this class only because the average method needs an object of some class that implements the Measurer interface. When you have a class that serves a very limited purpose, such as this one, you can declare the class inside the method that needs it:

```
public class MeasurerTester
{
   public static void main(String[] args)
   {
      class AreaMeasurer implements Measurer
      {
         . . .
      }

      . . .
      Measurer areaMeas = new AreaMeasurer();
      double averageArea = Data.average(rects, areaMeas);
      . . .
   }
}
```

An inner class is declared inside another class.

A class that is declared inside another class, such as the AreaMeasurer class in this example, is called an **inner class**. This arrangement signals to the reader of your program that the AreaMeasurer class is not interesting beyond the scope of this method. Since an inner class inside a method is not a publicly accessible feature, you don't need to document it as thoroughly.

Inner classes are commonly used for utility classes that should not be visible elsewhere in a program.

You can also declare an inner class inside an enclosing class, but outside of its methods. Then the inner class is available to all methods of the enclosing class.

```java
public class MeasurerTester
{
    class AreaMeasurer implements Measurer
    {
        . . .
    }

    public static void main(String[] args)
    {

        Measurer areaMeas = new AreaMeasurer();
        double averageArea = Data.average(rects, areaMeas);
        . . .
    }
}
```

When you compile the source files for a program that uses inner classes, have a look at the class files in your program directory—you will find that the inner classes are stored in files with curious names, such as `MeasurerTester$1AreaMeasurer.class`. The exact names aren't important. The point is that the compiler turns an inner class into a regular class file.

SELF CHECK

21. Why would you use an inner class instead of a regular class?
22. When would you place an inner class inside a class but outside any methods?
23. How many class files are produced when you compile the `MeasurerTester` program from this section?

Practice It   Now you can try these exercises at the end of the chapter: E10.7, E10.9.

Special Topic 10.3

Anonymous Classes

An entity is *anonymous* if it does not have a name. In a program, something that is only used once doesn't usually need a name. For example, you can replace

```java
Country belgium = new Country("Belgium", 30510);
countries.add(belgium);
```

with

```java
countries.add(new Country("Belgium", 30510));
```

if the country is not used elsewhere in the same method. The object `new Country("Belgium", 30510)` is an **anonymous object**. Programmers like anonymous objects, because they don't have to go through the trouble of coming up with a name. If you have struggled with the decision whether to call a coin `c`, `dime`, or `aCoin`, you'll understand this sentiment.

Inner classes often give rise to a similar situation. After a single object of the `AreaMeasurer` has been constructed, the class is never used again. In Java, it is possible to declare **anonymous classes** if all you ever need is a single object of the class.

```java
public static void main(String[] args)
{
    // Construct an object of an anonymous class
    Measurer m = new Measurer()
        // Class declaration starts here
        {
```

```
            public double measure(Object anObject)
            {
                Rectangle aRectangle = (Rectangle) anObject;
                return aRectangle.getWidth() * aRectangle.getHeight();
            }
        };

        double result = Data.average(rectangles, m);
        . . .
    }
```

This means: Construct an object of a class that implements the Measurer interface by declaring the measure method as specified. Many programmers like this style, but we will not use it in this book.

10.6 Mock Objects

When you work on a program that consists of multiple classes, you often want to test some of the classes before the entire program has been completed. A very effective technique for this purpose is the use of **mock objects**. A mock object provides the same services as another object, but in a simplified manner.

Consider a grade book application that manages quiz scores for students. This calls for a class GradeBook with methods such as

> A mock object provides the same services as another object, but in a simplified manner.

```
public void addScore(int studentId, double score)
public double getAverageScore(int studentId)
public void save(String filename)
```

Now consider the class GradingProgram that manipulates a GradeBook object. That class calls the methods of the GradeBook class. We would like to test the GradingProgram class without having a fully functional GradeBook class.

To make this work, declare an interface type with the same methods that the Grade-Book class provides. A common convention is to use the letter I as the prefix for such an interface:

```
public interface IGradeBook
{
    void addScore(int studentId, double score);
    double getAverageScore(int studentId);
    void save(String filename);
    . . .
}
```

If you just want to practice arranging the Christmas decorations, you don't need a real tree. Similarly, when you develop a computer program, you can use mock objects to test parts of your program.

The GradingProgram class should *only* use this interface, never the GradeBook class. Of course, the GradeBook class will implement this interface, but as already mentioned, it may not be ready for some time.

In the meantime, provide a mock implementation that makes some simplifying assumptions. Saving is not actually necessary for testing the user interface. We can temporarily restrict to the case of a single student.

Both the mock class and the actual class implement the same interface.

```java
public class MockGradeBook implements IGradeBook
{
    private ArrayList<Double> scores;

    public MockGradeBook() { scores = new ArrayList<Double>(); }

    public void addScore(int studentId, double score)
    {
        // Ignore studentId
        scores.add(score);
    }
    public double getAverageScore(int studentId)
    {
        double total = 0;
        for (double x : scores) { total = total + x; }
        return total / scores.size();
    }
    public void save(String filename)
    {
        // Do nothing
    }
    . . .
}
```

FULL CODE EXAMPLE

Go to wiley.com/go/javacode to download a program that demonstrates the use of mock objects for testing.

Now construct an instance of MockGradeBook and use it in the GradingProgram class. You can immediately test the GradingProgram class. When you are ready to test the actual class, simply use a GradeBook instance instead. Don't erase the mock class—it will still come in handy for regression testing.

SELF CHECK

24. Why is it necessary that the real class and the mock class implement the same interface type?

25. Why is the technique of mock objects particularly effective when the GradeBook and GradingProgram class are developed by two programmers?

Practice It   Now you can try these exercises at the end of the chapter: P10.12, P10.13.

10.7 Event Handling

This and the following sections continue the book's graphics track. You will learn how interfaces are used when programming graphical user interfaces.

In the applications that you have written so far, user input was under control of the *program*. The program asked the user for input in a specific order. For example, a program might ask the user to supply first a name, then a dollar amount. But the programs that you use every day on your computer don't work like that. In a program with a graphical user interface, the *user* is in control. The user can use both the mouse and the keyboard and can manipulate many parts of the user interface in any desired order. For example, the user can enter information into text fields, pull down menus, click buttons, and drag scroll bars in any order. The program must react to the user commands in whatever order they arrive. Having to deal with many possible inputs in random order is quite a bit harder than simply forcing the user to supply input in a fixed order.

In the following sections, you will learn how to write Java programs that can react to user-interface events, such as menu selections and mouse clicks. The Java windowing toolkit has a very sophisticated mechanism that allows a program to specify the events in which it is interested and which objects to notify when one of these events occurs.

> User-interface events include key presses, mouse moves, button clicks, menu selections, and so on.

10.7.1 Listening to Events

Whenever the user of a graphical program types characters or uses the mouse anywhere inside one of the windows of the program, the Java windowing toolkit sends a notification to the program that an **event** has occurred. The windowing toolkit generates huge numbers of events. For example, whenever the mouse moves a tiny interval over a window, a "mouse move" event is generated. Whenever the mouse button is clicked, "mouse pressed" and "mouse released" events are generated. In addition, higher level events are generated when a user selects a menu item or button.

In an event-driven user interface, the program receives an event whenever the user manipulates an input component.

Most programs don't want to be flooded by irrelevant events. For example, consider what happens when selecting a menu item with the mouse. The mouse moves over the menu item, then the mouse button is pressed, and finally the mouse button is released. Rather than receiving all these mouse events, a program can indicate that it only cares about menu selections, not about the underlying mouse events. However, if the mouse input is used for drawing shapes on a virtual canvas, it is necessary to closely track mouse events.

Every program must indicate which events it needs to receive. It does that by installing **event listener** objects. An event listener object belongs to a class that you provide. The methods of your event listener classes contain the instructions that you want to have executed when the events occur.

To install a listener, you need to know the **event source**. The event source is the user-interface component that generates a particular event. You add an event listener object to the appropriate event sources. Whenever the event occurs, the event source calls the appropriate methods of all attached event listeners.

> An event listener belongs to a class that is provided by the application programmer. Its methods describe the actions to be taken when an event occurs.

> Event sources report on events. When an event occurs, the event source notifies all event listeners.

This sounds somewhat abstract, so let's run through an extremely simple program that prints a message whenever a button is clicked (see Figure 7). Button listeners must belong to a class that implements the ActionListener interface:

```
public interface ActionListener
{
    void actionPerformed(ActionEvent event);
}
```

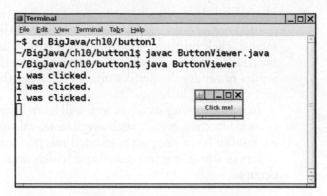

Figure 7 Implementing an Action Listener

This particular interface has a single method, `actionPerformed`. It is your job to supply a class whose `actionPerformed` method contains the instructions that you want executed whenever the button is clicked. Here is a very simple example of such a listener class:

section_7_1/ClickListener.java

```
1   import java.awt.event.ActionEvent;
2   import java.awt.event.ActionListener;
3
4   /**
5       An action listener that prints a message.
6   */
7   public class ClickListener implements ActionListener
8   {
9       public void actionPerformed(ActionEvent event)
10      {
11          System.out.println("I was clicked.");
12      }
13  }
```

We ignore the values of the event parameter variable of the `actionPerformed` method—it contains additional details about the event, such as the time at which it occurred.

Once the listener class has been declared, we need to construct an object of the class and add it to the button:

```
ActionListener listener = new ClickListener();
button.addActionListener(listener);
```

Whenever the button is clicked, it calls

```
listener.actionPerformed(event);
```

As a result, the message is printed.

You can think of the `actionPerformed` method as another example of a callback, similar to the `measure` method of the `Measurer` class. The windowing toolkit calls the `actionPerformed` method whenever the button is pressed, whereas the `Data` class calls the `measure` method whenever it needs to measure an object.

The `ButtonViewer` class, shown below, constructs a frame with a button and adds a `ClickListener` to the button. You can test this program out by opening a console window, starting the `ButtonViewer` program from that console window, clicking the button, and watching the messages in the console window.

> Use `JButton` components for buttons. Attach an `ActionListener` to each button.

section_7_1/ButtonViewer.java

```java
1   import java.awt.event.ActionListener;
2   import javax.swing.JButton;
3   import javax.swing.JFrame;
4
5   /**
6      This program demonstrates how to install an action listener.
7   */
8   public class ButtonViewer
9   {
10     private static final int FRAME_WIDTH = 100;
11     private static final int FRAME_HEIGHT = 60;
12
13     public static void main(String[] args)
14     {
15        JFrame frame = new JFrame();
16        JButton button = new JButton("Click me!");
17        frame.add(button);
18
19        ActionListener listener = new ClickListener();
20        button.addActionListener(listener);
21
22        frame.setSize(FRAME_WIDTH, FRAME_HEIGHT);
23        frame.setDefaultCloseOperation(JFrame.EXIT_ON_CLOSE);
24        frame.setVisible(true);
25     }
26  }
```

10.7.2 Using Inner Classes for Listeners

In the preceding section, you saw how the code that is executed when a button is clicked is placed into a listener class. It is common to implement listener classes as inner classes like this:

```java
JButton button = new JButton(". . .");

// This inner class is declared in the same method as the button variable
class MyListener implements ActionListener
{
   . . .
};

ActionListener listener = new MyListener();
button.addActionListener(listener);
```

There are two advantages to making a listener class into an inner class. First, listener classes tend to be very short. You can put the inner class close to where it is needed, without cluttering up the remainder of the project. Moreover, inner classes have a very attractive feature: Their methods can access instance variables and methods of the surrounding class.

> **Methods of an inner class can access variables from the surrounding class.**

This feature is particularly useful when implementing event handlers. It allows the inner class to access variables without having to receive them as constructor or method arguments.

Let's look at an example. Suppose we want to add interest to a bank account whenever a button is clicked.

```
JButton button = new JButton("Add Interest");
final BankAccount account = new BankAccount(INITIAL_BALANCE);

// This inner class is declared in the same method as the account and button variables.
class AddInterestListener implements ActionListener
{
    public void actionPerformed(ActionEvent event)
    {
        // The listener method accesses the account variable
        // from the surrounding block
        double interest = account.getBalance() * INTEREST_RATE / 100;
        account.deposit(interest);
    }
};

ActionListener listener = new AddInterestListener();
button.addActionListener(listener);
```

> Local variables that are accessed by an inner class method must be declared as final.

There is a technical wrinkle. An inner class can access surrounding *local* variables only if they are declared as final. That sounds like a restriction, but it is usually not an issue in practice. Keep in mind that an object variable is final when the variable always refers to the same object. The state of the object can change, but the variable can't refer to a different object. For example, in our program, we never intended to have the account variable refer to multiple bank accounts, so there was no harm in declaring it as final.

An inner class can also access *instance* variables of the surrounding class, again with a restriction. The instance variable must belong to the object that constructed the inner class object. If the inner class object was created inside a static method, it can only access static variables.

Here is the source code for the program:

section_7_2/InvestmentViewer1.java

```
1   import java.awt.event.ActionEvent;
2   import java.awt.event.ActionListener;
3   import javax.swing.JButton;
4   import javax.swing.JFrame;
5
6   /**
7      This program demonstrates how an action listener can access
8      a variable from a surrounding block.
9   */
10  public class InvestmentViewer1
11  {
12     private static final int FRAME_WIDTH = 120;
13     private static final int FRAME_HEIGHT = 60;
14
15     private static final double INTEREST_RATE = 10;
16     private static final double INITIAL_BALANCE = 1000;
17
18     public static void main(String[] args)
19     {
20        JFrame frame = new JFrame();
21
22        // The button to trigger the calculation
23        JButton button = new JButton("Add Interest");
24        frame.add(button);
25
```

```
26        // The application adds interest to this bank account
27        final BankAccount account = new BankAccount(INITIAL_BALANCE);
28
29        class AddInterestListener implements ActionListener
30        {
31           public void actionPerformed(ActionEvent event)
32           {
33              // The listener method accesses the account variable
34              // from the surrounding block
35              double interest = account.getBalance() * INTEREST_RATE / 100;
36              account.deposit(interest);
37              System.out.println("balance: " + account.getBalance());
38           }
39        }
40
41        ActionListener listener = new AddInterestListener();
42        button.addActionListener(listener);
43
44        frame.setSize(FRAME_WIDTH, FRAME_HEIGHT);
45        frame.setDefaultCloseOperation(JFrame.EXIT_ON_CLOSE);
46        frame.setVisible(true);
47     }
48 }
```

Program Run

```
balance: 1100.0
balance: 1210.0
balance: 1331.0
balance: 1464.1
```

SELF CHECK

26. Which objects are the event source and the event listener in the ButtonViewer program?
27. Why is it legal to assign a ClickListener object to a variable of type ActionListener?
28. When do you call the actionPerformed method?
29. Why would an inner class method want to access a variable from a surrounding scope?
30. If an inner class accesses a local variable from a surrounding scope, what special rule applies?

Practice It   Now you can try these exercises at the end of the chapter: R10.14, R10.20, E10.13.

Common Error 10.3

Modifying Parameter Types in the Implementing Method

When you implement an interface, you must declare each method *exactly* as it is specified in the interface. Accidentally making small changes to the parameter types is a common error. Here is the classic example:

```
class MyListener implements ActionListener
{
   public void actionPerformed()
   // Oops . . . forgot ActionEvent parameter variable
   {
```

```
        . . .
     }
   }
```

As far as the compiler is concerned, this class fails to provide the method

```
public void actionPerformed(ActionEvent event)
```

You have to read the error message carefully and pay attention to the parameter and return types to find your error.

Common Error 10.4

Trying to Call Listener Methods

Some students try to call the listener methods themselves:

```
ActionEvent event = new ActionEvent(. ..); // Don't do this
listener.actionPerformed(event);
```

You should not call the listener. The Java user interface calls it when the program user has clicked a button.

10.8 Building Applications with Buttons

In this section, you will learn how to structure a graphical application that contains buttons. We will put a button to work in our simple investment viewer program. Whenever the button is clicked, interest is added to a bank account, and the new balance is displayed (see Figure 8).

First, we construct an object of the JButton class, passing the button label to the constructor, like this:

```
JButton button = new JButton("Add Interest");
```

We also need a user-interface component that displays a message, namely the current bank balance. Such a component is called a *label*. You pass the initial message string to the JLabel constructor, like this:

```
JLabel label = new JLabel("balance: " + account.getBalance());
```

Use a JPanel container to group multiple user-interface components together.

The frame of our application contains both the button and the label. However, we cannot simply add both components directly to the frame—they would be placed on top of each other. The solution is to put them into a **panel**, a container for other user-interface components, and then add the panel to the frame:

```
JPanel panel = new JPanel();
panel.add(button);
panel.add(label);
frame.add(panel);
```

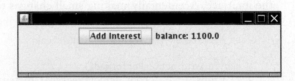

Figure 8 An Application with a Button

Whenever a button is pressed, the actionPerformed
method is called on all listeners.

Specify button
click actions
through classes
that implement
the ActionListener
interface.

Now we are ready for the hard part—the event listener that handles button clicks. As in the preceding section, it is necessary to provide a class that implements the Action-Listener interface, and to place the button action into the actionPerformed method. Our listener class adds interest to the account and displays the new balance:

```java
class AddInterestListener implements ActionListener
{
    public void actionPerformed(ActionEvent event)
    {
        double interest = account.getBalance() * INTEREST_RATE / 100;
        account.deposit(interest);
        label.setText("balance: " + account.getBalance());
    }
}
```

There is just a minor technicality. The actionPerformed method manipulates the account and label variables. These are local variables of the main method of the investment viewer program, not instance variables of the AddInterestListener class. We therefore need to declare the account and label variables as final so that the actionPerformed method can access them.

Let's put the pieces together:

```java
public static void main(String[] args)
{
    . . .
    JButton button = new JButton("Add Interest");
    final BankAccount account = new BankAccount(INITIAL_BALANCE);
    final JLabel label = new JLabel("balance: " + account.getBalance());

    class AddInterestListener implements ActionListener
    {
        public void actionPerformed(ActionEvent event)
        {
            double interest = account.getBalance() * INTEREST_RATE / 100;
            account.deposit(interest);
            label.setText("balance: " + account.getBalance());
        }
    }

    ActionListener listener = new AddInterestListener();
    button.addActionListener(listener);
    . . .
}
```

With a bit of practice, you will learn to glance at this code and translate it into plain English: "When the button is clicked, add interest and set the label text."

Here is the complete program. It demonstrates how to add multiple components to a frame, by using a panel, and how to implement listeners as inner classes.

section_8/InvestmentViewer2.java

```java
1   import java.awt.event.ActionEvent;
2   import java.awt.event.ActionListener;
3   import javax.swing.JButton;
4   import javax.swing.JFrame;
5   import javax.swing.JLabel;
6   import javax.swing.JPanel;
7
8   /**
9      This program displays the growth of an investment.
10  */
11  public class InvestmentViewer2
12  {
13     private static final int FRAME_WIDTH = 400;
14     private static final int FRAME_HEIGHT = 100;
15
16     private static final double INTEREST_RATE = 10;
17     private static final double INITIAL_BALANCE = 1000;
18
19     public static void main(String[] args)
20     {
21        JFrame frame = new JFrame();
22
23        // The button to trigger the calculation
24        JButton button = new JButton("Add Interest");
25
26        // The application adds interest to this bank account
27        final BankAccount account = new BankAccount(INITIAL_BALANCE);
28
29        // The label for displaying the results
30        final JLabel label = new JLabel("balance: " + account.getBalance());
31
32        // The panel that holds the user-interface components
33        JPanel panel = new JPanel();
34        panel.add(button);
35        panel.add(label);
36        frame.add(panel);
37
38        class AddInterestListener implements ActionListener
39        {
40           public void actionPerformed(ActionEvent event)
41           {
42              double interest = account.getBalance() * INTEREST_RATE / 100;
43              account.deposit(interest);
44              label.setText("balance: " + account.getBalance());
45           }
46        }
47
48        ActionListener listener = new AddInterestListener();
49        button.addActionListener(listener);
50
51        frame.setSize(FRAME_WIDTH, FRAME_HEIGHT);
52        frame.setDefaultCloseOperation(JFrame.EXIT_ON_CLOSE);
53        frame.setVisible(true);
54     }
55  }
```

31. How do you place the "balance: . . ." message to the left of the "Add Interest" button?

32. Why was it not necessary to declare the button variable as final?

Practice It   Now you can try these exercises at the end of the chapter: E10.14, E10.15, E10.16.

Common Error 10.5

Forgetting to Attach a Listener

If you run your program and find that your buttons seem to be dead, double-check that you attached the button listener. The same holds for other user-interface components. It is a surprisingly common error to program the listener class and the event handler action without actually attaching the listener to the event source.

Programming Tip 10.1

Don't Use a Container as a Listener

In this book, we use inner classes for event listeners. That approach works for many different event types. Once you master the technique, you don't have to think about it anymore. Many development environments automatically generate code with inner classes, so it is a good idea to be familiar with them.

However, some programmers bypass the event listener classes and instead turn a container (such as a panel or frame) into a listener. Here is a typical example. The actionPerformed method is added to the viewer class. That is, the viewer implements the ActionListener interface.

```java
public class InvestmentViewer
      implements ActionListener // This approach is not recommended
{
   public InvestmentViewer()
   {
      JButton button = new JButton("Add Interest");
      button.addActionListener(this);
      . . .
   }

   public void actionPerformed(ActionEvent event)
   {
      . . .
   }
   . . .
}
```

Now the actionPerformed method is a part of the InvestmentViewer class rather than part of a separate listener class. The listener is installed as this.

This technique has two major flaws. First, it separates the button declaration from the button action. Also, it doesn't *scale* well. If the viewer class contains two buttons that each generate action events, then the actionPerformed method must investigate the event source, which leads to code that is tedious and error-prone.

10.9 Processing Timer Events

In this section we will study timer events and show how you can use them to implement simple animations.

The Timer class in the javax.swing package generates a sequence of action events, spaced at even time intervals. (You can think of a timer as an invisible button that is automatically clicked.) This is useful whenever you want to have an object updated at regular intervals. For example, in an animation, you may want to update a scene ten times per second and redisplay the image to give the illusion of movement.

A Swing timer notifies a listener with each "tick".

> A timer generates timer events at fixed intervals.

When you use a timer, you specify the frequency of the events and an object of a class that implements the ActionListener interface. Place whatever action you want to occur inside the actionPerformed method. Finally, start the timer.

```java
class MyListener implements ActionListener
{
   public void actionPerformed(ActionEvent event)
   {
      Action that is executed at each timer event
   }
}

MyListener listener = new MyListener();
Timer t = new Timer(interval, listener);
t.start();
```

Then the timer calls the actionPerformed method of the listener object every interval milliseconds.

Our sample program will display a moving rectangle. We first supply a Rectangle-Component class with a moveRectangleBy method that moves the rectangle by a given amount.

section_9/RectangleComponent.java

```java
 1   import java.awt.Graphics;
 2   import java.awt.Graphics2D;
 3   import java.awt.Rectangle;
 4   import javx.swing.JComponent;
 5
 6   /**
 7      This component displays a rectangle that can be moved.
 8   */
 9   public class RectangleComponent extends JComponent
10   {
11      private static final int BOX_X = 100;
12      private static final int BOX_Y = 100;
13      private static final int BOX_WIDTH = 20;
14      private static final int BOX_HEIGHT = 30;
15
16      private Rectangle box;
17
18      public RectangleComponent()
19      {
```

```
20          // The rectangle that the paintComponent method draws
21          box = new Rectangle(BOX_X, BOX_Y, BOX_WIDTH, BOX_HEIGHT);
22       }
23
24       public void paintComponent(Graphics g)
25       {
26          Graphics2D g2 = (Graphics2D) g;
27          g2.draw(box);
28       }
29
30       /**
31          Moves the rectangle by a given amount.
32          @param dx the amount to move in the x-direction
33          @param dy the amount to move in the y-direction
34       */
35       public void moveRectangleBy(int dx, int dy)
36       {
37          box.translate(dx, dy);
38          repaint();
39       }
40    }
```

The repaint method causes a component to repaint itself. Call repaint whenever you modify the shapes that the paintComponent method draws.

Note the call to repaint in the moveRectangleBy method. This call is necessary to ensure that the component is repainted after the state of the rectangle object has been changed. Keep in mind that the component object does not contain the pixels that show the drawing. The component merely contains a Rectangle object, which itself contains four coordinate values. Calling translate updates the rectangle coordinate values. The call to repaint forces a call to the paintComponent method. The paintComponent method redraws the component, causing the rectangle to appear at the updated location.

The actionPerformed method of the timer listener simply calls component.moveBy(1, 1). This moves the rectangle one pixel down and to the right. Because the actionPerformed method is called many times per second, the rectangle appears to move smoothly across the frame.

section_9/RectangleFrame.java

```
1    import java.awt.event.ActionEvent;
2    import java.awt.event.ActionListener;
3    import javax.swing.JFrame;
4    import javax.swing.Timer;
5
6    /**
7       This frame contains a moving rectangle.
8    */
9    public class RectangleFrame extends JFrame
10   {
11      private static final int FRAME_WIDTH = 300;
12      private static final int FRAME_HEIGHT = 400;
13
14      private RectangleComponent scene;
15
16      class TimerListener implements ActionListener
17      {
18         public void actionPerformed(ActionEvent event)
19         {
20            scene.moveRectangleBy(1, 1);
```

```
21          }
22       }
23
24       public RectangleFrame()
25       {
26          scene = new RectangleComponent();
27          add(scene);
28
29          setSize(FRAME_WIDTH, FRAME_HEIGHT);
30
31          ActionListener listener = new TimerListener();
32
33          final int DELAY = 100; // Milliseconds between timer ticks
34          Timer t = new Timer(DELAY, listener);
35          t.start();
36       }
37    }
```

section_9/RectangleViewer.java

```
1    import javax.swing.JFrame;
2
3    /**
4       This program moves the rectangle.
5    */
6    public class RectangleViewer
7    {
8       public static void main(String[] args)
9       {
10          JFrame frame = new RectangleFrame();
11          frame.setTitle("An animated rectangle");
12          frame.setDefaultCloseOperation(JFrame.EXIT_ON_CLOSE);
13          frame.setVisible(true);
14       }
15    }
```

SELF CHECK

33. Why does a timer require a listener object?

34. What would happen if you omitted the call to repaint in the moveBy method?

Practice It   Now you can try these exercises at the end of the chapter: E10.20, E10.21.

Common Error 10.6

Forgetting to Repaint

You have to be careful when your event handlers change the data in a painted component. When you make a change to the data, the component is not automatically painted with the new data. You must call the repaint method of the component, either in the event handler or in the component's mutator methods. Your component's paintComponent method will then be invoked with an appropriate Graphics object. Note that you should not call the paintComponent method directly.

This is a concern only for your own painted components. When you make a change to a standard Swing component such as a JLabel, the component is automatically repainted.

10.10 Mouse Events

Use a mouse listener to capture mouse events.

If you write programs that show drawings, and you want users to manipulate the drawings with a mouse, then you need to process mouse events. Mouse events are more complex than button clicks or timer ticks.

A mouse listener must implement the `MouseListener` interface, which contains the following five methods:

```
public interface MouseListener
{
    void mousePressed(MouseEvent event);
        // Called when a mouse button has been pressed on a component
    void mouseReleased(MouseEvent event);
        // Called when a mouse button has been released on a component
    void mouseClicked(MouseEvent event);
        // Called when the mouse has been clicked on a component
    void mouseEntered(MouseEvent event);
        // Called when the mouse enters a component
    void mouseExited(MouseEvent event);
        // Called when the mouse exits a component
}
```

The `mousePressed` and `mouseReleased` methods are called whenever a mouse button is pressed or released. If a button is pressed and released in quick succession, and the mouse has not moved, then the `mouseClicked` method is called as well. The `mouseEntered` and `mouseExited` methods can be used to paint a user-interface component in a special way whenever the mouse is pointing inside it.

In Swing, a mouse event isn't a gathering of rodents; it's notification of a mouse click by the program user.

The most commonly used method is `mousePressed`. Users generally expect that their actions are processed as soon as the mouse button is pressed.

You add a mouse listener to a component by calling the `addMouseListener` method:

```
public class MyMouseListener implements MouseListener
{
    // Implements five methods
}

MouseListener listener = new MyMouseListener();
component.addMouseListener(listener);
```

In our sample program, a user clicks on a component containing a rectangle. Whenever the mouse button is pressed, the rectangle is moved to the mouse location. We first enhance the `RectangleComponent` class and add a `moveRectangleTo` method to move the rectangle to a new position.

section_10/RectangleComponent2.java

```
1   import java.awt.Graphics;
2   import java.awt.Graphics2D;
3   import java.awt.Rectangle;
4   import javax.swing.JComponent;
```

```
 5
 6   /**
 7       This component displays a rectangle that can be moved.
 8   */
 9   public class RectangleComponent2 extends JComponent
10   {
11      private static final int BOX_X = 100;
12      private static final int BOX_Y = 100;
13      private static final int BOX_WIDTH = 20;
14      private static final int BOX_HEIGHT = 30;
15
16      private Rectangle box;
17
18      public RectangleComponent2()
19      {
20         // The rectangle that the paintComponent method draws
21         box = new Rectangle(BOX_X, BOX_Y, BOX_WIDTH, BOX_HEIGHT);
22      }
23
24      public void paintComponent(Graphics g)
25      {
26         Graphics2D g2 = (Graphics2D) g;
27         g2.draw(box);
28      }
29
30      /**
31          Moves the rectangle to the given location.
32          @param x the x-position of the new location
33          @param y the y-position of the new location
34      */
35      public void moveRectangleTo(int x, int y)
36      {
37         box.setLocation(x, y);
38         repaint();
39      }
40   }
```

Note the call to repaint in the moveRectangleTo method. As explained in the preceding section, this call causes the component to repaint itself and show the rectangle in the new position.

Now, add a mouse listener to the component. Whenever the mouse is pressed, the listener moves the rectangle to the mouse location.

```
class MousePressListener implements MouseListener
{
    public void mousePressed(MouseEvent event)
    {
        int x = event.getX();
        int y = event.getY();
        component.moveRectangleTo(x, y);
    }

    // Do-nothing methods
    public void mouseReleased(MouseEvent event) {}
    public void mouseClicked(MouseEvent event) {}
    public void mouseEntered(MouseEvent event) {}
    public void mouseExited(MouseEvent event) {}
}
```

Figure 9
Clicking the Mouse Moves
the Rectangle

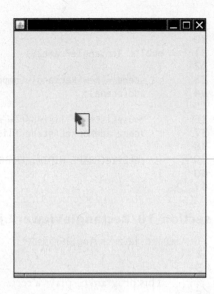

It often happens that a particular listener specifies actions only for one or two of the listener methods. Nevertheless, all five methods of the interface must be implemented. The unused methods are simply implemented as do-nothing methods.

Go ahead and run the RectangleViewer2 program. Whenever you click the mouse inside the frame, the top-left corner of the rectangle moves to the mouse pointer (see Figure 9).

section_10/RectangleFrame2.java

```java
1   import java.awt.event.MouseListener;
2   import java.awt.event.MouseEvent;
3   import javax.swing.JFrame;
4
5   /**
6      This frame contains a moving rectangle.
7   */
8   public class RectangleFrame2 extends JFrame
9   {
10     private static final int FRAME_WIDTH = 300;
11     private static final int FRAME_HEIGHT = 400;
12
13     private RectangleComponent2 scene;
14
15     class MousePressListener implements MouseListener
16     {
17        public void mousePressed(MouseEvent event)
18        {
19           int x = event.getX();
20           int y = event.getY();
21           scene.moveRectangleTo(x, y);
22        }
23
24        // Do-nothing methods
25        public void mouseReleased(MouseEvent event) {}
26        public void mouseClicked(MouseEvent event) {}
27        public void mouseEntered(MouseEvent event) {}
28        public void mouseExited(MouseEvent event) {}
```

```
29        }
30
31      public RectangleFrame2()
32      {
33          scene = new RectangleComponent2();
34          add(scene);
35
36          MouseListener listener = new MousePressListener();
37          scene.addMouseListener(listener);
38
39          setSize(FRAME_WIDTH, FRAME_HEIGHT);
40      }
41  }
```

section_10/RectangleViewer2.java

```
1   import javax.swing.JFrame;
2
3   /**
4       This program displays a rectangle that can be moved with the mouse.
5   */
6   public class RectangleViewer2
7   {
8       public static void main(String[] args)
9       {
10          JFrame frame = new RectangleFrame2();
11          frame.setDefaultCloseOperation(JFrame.EXIT_ON_CLOSE);
12          frame.setVisible(true);
13      }
14  }
```

SELF CHECK

35. Why was the moveRectangleBy method in the RectangleComponent replaced with a moveRectangleTo method?

36. Why must the MousePressListener class supply five methods?

Practice It   Now you can try these exercises at the end of the chapter: R10.17, E10.22.

Special Topic 10.4

Keyboard Events

If you program a game, you may want to process keystrokes, such as the arrow keys. Add a key listener to the component on which you draw the game scene. The KeyListener interface has three methods. As with a mouse listener, you are most interested in key press events, and you can leave the other two methods empty. Your key listener class should look like this:

```
class MyKeyListener implements KeyListener
{
    public void keyPressed(KeyEvent event)
    {
        String key = KeyStroke.getKeyStrokeForEvent(event).toString();
        key = key.replace("pressed ", "");
        Process key.
    }

    // Do-nothing methods
    public void keyReleased(KeyEvent event) {}
```

```
    public void keyTyped(KeyEvent event) {}
}
```

The call `KeyStroke.getKeyStrokeForEvent(event).toString()`
turns the event object into a text description of the key,
such as "pressed LEFT". In the next line, we eliminate the
"pressed " prefix. The remainder is a string such as "LEFT"
or "A" that describes the key that was pressed. You can
find a list of all key names in the API documentation of
the KeyStroke class.

As always, remember to attach the listener to the event
source:

*Whenever the program user presses
a key, a key event is generated.*

```
KeyListener listener = new MyKeyListener();
scene.addKeyListener(listener);
```

In order to receive key events, your component must call

```
scene.setFocusable(true);
```

FULL CODE EXAMPLE

Go to wiley.com/go/
javacode to download
a program that uses
the arrow keys to
move a rectangle.

Special Topic 10.5

Event Adapters

In the preceding section you saw how to install a mouse listener into a mouse event source and
how the listener methods are called when an event occurs. Usually, a program is not interested
in all listener notifications. For example, a program may only be interested in mouse clicks and
may not care that these mouse clicks are composed of "mouse pressed" and "mouse released"
events. Of course, the program could supply a listener that implements all those methods in
which it has no interest as "do-nothing" methods, for example:

```
class MouseClickListener implements MouseListener
{
    public void mouseClicked(MouseEvent event)
    {
        Mouse click action
    }

    // Four do-nothing methods
    public void mouseEntered(MouseEvent event) {}
    public void mouseExited(MouseEvent event) {}
    public void mousePressed(MouseEvent event) {}
    public void mouseReleased(MouseEvent event) {}
}
```

To avoid this labor, some friendly soul has created a MouseAdapter class that implements the
MouseListener interface such that all methods do nothing. You can *extend* that class, inheriting
the do-nothing methods and overriding the methods that you care about, like this:

```
class MouseClickListener extends MouseAdapter
{
    public void mouseClicked(MouseEvent event)
    {
        Mouse click action
    }
}
```

There is also a KeyAdapter class that implements the KeyListener interface with three do-nothing
methods.

Computing & Society 10.1 Open Source and Free Software

Most companies that produce software regard the source code as a trade secret. After all, if customers or competitors had access to the source code, they could study it and create similar programs without paying the original vendor. For the same reason, customers dislike secret source code. If a company goes out of business or decides to discontinue support for a computer program, its users are left stranded. They are unable to fix bugs or adapt the program to a new operating system. Nowadays, some software packages are distributed with "open source" or "free software" licenses. Here, the term "free" doesn't refer to price, but to the freedom to inspect and modify the source code. Richard Stallman, a famous computer scientist and winner of a MacArthur "genius" grant, pioneered the concept of free software. He is the inventor of the Emacs text editor and the originator of the GNU project that aims to create an entirely free version of a UNIX compatible operating system. All programs of the GNU project are licensed under the General Public License (GPL). The GPL allows you to make as many copies as you wish, make any modifications to the source, and redistribute the original and modified programs, charging nothing at all or whatever the market will bear. In return, you must agree that

your modifications also fall under the GPL. You must give out the source code to any changes that you distribute, and anyone else can distribute them under the same conditions. The GPL, and similar open source licenses, form a social contract. Users of the software enjoy the freedom to use and modify the software, and in return they are obligated to share any improvements that they make. Many programs, such as the Linux operating system and the GNU C++ compiler, are distributed under the GPL.

Some commercial software vendors have attacked the GPL as "viral" and "undermining the commercial software sector". Other companies have a more nuanced strategy, producing proprietary software while also contributing to open source projects.

Frankly, open source is not a panacea and there is plenty of room for the commercial software sector. Open source software often lacks the polish of commercial software because many of the programmers are volunteers who are interested in solving their own problems, not in making a product that is easy to use by others. Some product categories are not available at all as open source software because the development work is unattractive when there is little promise of commercial gain. Open source software has been most successful in areas that are

of interest to programmers, such as the Linux operating system, Web servers, and programming tools.

On the positive side, the open software community can be very competitive and creative. It is quite common to see several competing projects that take ideas from each other, all rapidly becoming more capable. Having many programmers involved, all reading the source code, often means that bugs tend to get squashed quickly. Eric Raymond describes open source development in his famous article "The Cathedral and the Bazaar" (http://catb.org/~esr/writings/cathedral-bazaar/cathedral-bazaar/index.html). He writes "Given enough eyeballs, all bugs are shallow".

Richard Stallman, a pioneer of the free source movement

CHAPTER SUMMARY

Use interfaces for making a service available to multiple classes.

- A Java interface type declares methods but does not provide their implementations.
- Use the implements reserved word to indicate that a class implements an interface type.
- Use interface types to make code more reusable.

Describe how to convert between class and interface types.

- You can convert from a class type to an interface type, provided the class implements the interface.
- Method calls on an interface reference are polymorphic. The appropriate method is determined at run time.
- You need a cast to convert from an interface type to a class type.

Use the Comparable interface from the Java library.

- Implement the Comparable interface so that objects of your class can be compared, for example, in a sort method.

Describe how to use interface types for providing callbacks.

- A callback is a mechanism for specifying code that is executed at a later time.

Use inner classes to limit the scope of a utility class.

- An inner class is declared inside another class.
- Inner classes are commonly used for utility classes that should not be visible elsewhere in a program.

Use mock objects for supplying test versions of classes.

- A mock object provides the same services as another object, but in a simplified manner.
- Both the mock class and the actual class implement the same interface.

Implement event listeners to react to events in user-interface programming.

- User-interface events include key presses, mouse moves, button clicks, menu selections, and so on.
- An event listener belongs to a class that is provided by the application programmer. Its methods describe the actions to be taken when an event occurs.
- Event sources report on events. When an event occurs, the event source notifies all event listeners.
- Use JButton components for buttons. Attach an ActionListener to each button.
- Methods of an inner class can access local and instance variables from the surrounding scope.
- Local variables that are accessed by an inner class method must be declared as final.

Build graphical applications that use buttons.

- Use a JPanel container to group multiple user-interface components together.
- Specify button click actions through classes that implement the ActionListener interface.

Use a timer for drawing animations.

- A timer generates timer events at fixed intervals.
- The repaint method causes a component to repaint itself. Call repaint whenever you modify the shapes that the paintComponent method draws.

Write programs that process mouse events.

- Use a mouse listener to capture mouse events.

STANDARD LIBRARY ITEMS INTRODUCED IN THIS CHAPTER

java.awt.Component
  addKeyListener
  addMouseListener
  repaint
  setFocusable
java.awt.Container
  add
java.awt.Dimension
java.awt.Rectangle
  setLocation
java.awt.event.ActionListener
  actionPerformed

java.awt.event.KeyEvent
java.awt.event.KeyListener
  keyPressed
  keyReleased
  keyTyped
java.awt.event.MouseEvent
  getX
  getY
java.awt.event.MouseListener
  mouseClicked
  mouseEntered
  mouseExited

mousePressed
mouseReleased
javax.swing.AbstractButton
  addActionListener
javax.swing.JButton
javax.swing.JLabel
javax.swing.JPanel
javax.swing.KeyStroke
  getKeyStrokeForEvent
javax.swing.Timer
  start
  stop

REVIEW QUESTIONS

- **R10.1** Suppose C is a class that implements the interfaces I and J. Which of the following assignments require a cast?

  ```
  C c = . . .;
  I i = . . .;
  J j = . . .;
  ```

  a. c = i;

  b. j = c;

  c. i = j;

- **R10.2** Suppose C is a class that implements the interfaces I and J, and suppose i is declared as: I i = new C();

  Which of the following statements will throw an exception?

  a. C c = (C) i;

  b. J j = (J) i;

  c. i = (I) null;

- **R10.3** Suppose the class Sandwich implements the Edible interface, and you are given the variable declarations

  ```
  Sandwich sub = new Sandwich();
  Rectangle cerealBox = new Rectangle(5, 10, 20, 30);
  Edible e = null;
  ```

Which of the following assignment statements are legal?

a. e = sub;   **e.** e = cerealBox;

b. sub = e;   **f.** e = (Edible) cerealBox;

c. sub = (Sandwich) e;   **g.** e = (Rectangle) cerealBox;

d. sub = (Sandwich) cerealBox;   **h.** e = (Rectangle) null;

■■ **R10.4** The classes `Rectangle2D.Double`, `Ellipse2D.Double`, and `Line2D.Double` implement the `Shape` interface. The `Graphics2D` class depends on the `Shape` interface but not on the rectangle, ellipse, and line classes. Draw a UML diagram denoting these facts.

■■ **R10.5** Suppose r contains a reference to a new `Rectangle(5, 10, 20, 30)`. Which of the following assignments is legal? (Look inside the API documentation to check which interfaces the `Rectangle` class implements.)

a. Rectangle a = r;   **e.** Measurable e = r;

b. Shape b = r;   **f.** Serializable f = r;

c. String c = r;   **g.** Object g = r;

d. ActionListener d = r;

■■ **R10.6** Classes such as `Rectangle2D.Double`, `Ellipse2D.Double`, and `Line2D.Double` implement the `Shape` interface. The `Shape` interface has a method

```
Rectangle getBounds()
```

that returns a rectangle completely enclosing the shape. Consider the method call:

```
Shape s = . . .;
Rectangle r = s.getBounds();
```

Explain why this is an example of polymorphism.

■■ **R10.7** Suppose you need to process an array of employees to find the average salary. Discuss what you need to do to use the `Data.average` method in Section 10.1 (which processes `Measurable` objects). What do you need to do to use the second implementation (in Section 10.4)? Which is easier?

■ **R10.8** What happens if you try to use an array of `String` objects with the `Data.average` method in Section 10.1?

■■ **R10.9** How can you use the `Data.average` method in Section 10.4 if you want to compute the average length of the strings?

■■ **R10.10** What happens if you pass an array of strings and an `AreaMeasurer` to the `Data.average` method of Section 10.4?

■■ **R10.11** Consider this top-level and inner class. Which variables can the f method access?

```
public class T
{
    private int t;

    public void m(final int x, int y)
    {
        int a;
        final int b;

        class C implements I
        {
```

```
                    public void f()
                    {
                        . . .
                    }
                }
            final int c;
            . . .
        }
    }
```

R10.12 What happens when an inner class tries to access a non-final local variable? Try it out and explain your findings.

Graphics R10.13 How would you reorganize the InvestmentViewer1 program if you needed to make AddInterestListener into a top-level class (that is, not an inner class)?

Graphics R10.14 What is an event object? An event source? An event listener?

Graphics R10.15 From a programmer's perspective, what is the most important difference between the user interfaces of a console application and a graphical application?

Graphics R10.16 What is the difference between an ActionEvent and a MouseEvent?

Graphics R10.17 Why does the ActionListener interface have only one method, whereas the MouseListener has five methods?

Graphics R10.18 Can a class be an event source for multiple event types? If so, give an example.

Graphics R10.19 What information does an action event object carry? What additional information does a mouse event object carry?

Graphics R10.20 Why are we using inner classes for event listeners? If Java did not have inner classes, could we still implement event listeners? How?

Graphics R10.21 What is the difference between the paintComponent and repaint methods?

Graphics R10.22 What is the difference between a frame and a panel?

PRACTICE EXERCISES

E10.1 Add a method

```
public static Measurable max(Measurable[] objects)
```

to the Data class that returns the object with the largest measure.

E10.2 Implement a class Quiz that implements the Measurable interface. A quiz has a score and a letter grade (such as B+). Use the Data class of Exercise E10.1 to process an array of quizzes. Display the average score and the quiz with the highest score (both letter grade and score).

E10.3 A person has a name and a height in centimeters. Use the Data class of Exercise E10.1 to process an array of Person objects. Display the average height and the name of the tallest person.

E10.4 Add a method to the Data class that returns the object with the largest measure, as measured by the supplied measurer:

```
public static Object max(Object[] objects, Measurer m)
```

- **E10.5** Using a different `Measurer` object, process a set of `Rectangle` objects to find the rectangle with the largest perimeter.

- **E10.6** Modify the `Coin` class from Chapter 8 to have it implement the `Comparable` interface.

- **E10.7** Repeat Exercise E10.5, making the `Measurer` into an inner class inside the `main` method.

- **E10.8** Repeat Exercise E10.5, making the `Measurer` into an inner class outside the `main` method.

- ■■ **E10.9** Implement a class `Bag` that stores items represented as strings. Items can be repeated. Supply methods for adding an item, and for counting how many times an item has been added:

```java
public void add(String itemName)
public int count(String itemName)
```

Your `Bag` class should store the data in an `ArrayList<Item>`, where `Item` is an inner class with two instance variables: the name of the item and the quantity.

- ■■ **E10.10** Implement a class `Grid` that stores measurements in a rectangular grid. The grid has a given number of rows and columns, and a description string can be added for any grid location. Supply the following constructor and methods:

```java
public Grid(int numRows, int numColumns)
public void add(int row, int column, String description)
public String getDescription(int row, int column)
public ArrayList<Location> getDescribedLocations()
```

Here, `Location` is an inner class that encapsulates the row and the column of a grid location.

- ■■■ **E10.11** Reimplement Exercise E10.10 where the grid is unbounded. The constructor has no arguments, and the row and column parameter variables of the `add` and `getDescription` methods can be arbitrary integers.

- ■■■ **Graphics E10.12** Write a method `randomShape` that randomly generates objects implementing the `Shape` interface in the Java library API: some mixture of rectangles, ellipses, and lines, with random positions. Call it ten times and draw all of them.

- ■ **Graphics E10.13** Enhance the `ButtonViewer` program so that it prints a message "I was clicked *n* times!" whenever the button is clicked. The value *n* should be incremented with each click.

- ■■ **Graphics E10.14** Enhance the `ButtonViewer` program so that it has two buttons, each of which prints a message "I was clicked *n* times!" whenever the button is clicked. Each button should have a separate click count.

- ■■ **Graphics E10.15** Enhance the `ButtonViewer` program so that it has two buttons labeled A and B, each of which prints a message "Button *x* was clicked!", where *x* is A or B.

- ■■ **Graphics E10.16** Implement a `ButtonViewer` program as in Exercise E10.15, using only a single listener class.

- ■ **Graphics E10.17** Enhance the `ButtonViewer` program so that it prints the time at which the button was clicked.

- ■■■ **Graphics E10.18** Implement the `AddInterestListener` in the `InvestmentViewer1` program as a regular class (that is, not an inner class). *Hint:* Store a reference to the bank account. Add a constructor to the listener class that sets the reference.

■■■ Graphics E10.19 Implement the AddInterestListener in the InvestmentViewer2 program as a regular class (that is, not an inner class). *Hint:* Store references to the bank account and the label in the listener. Add a constructor to the listener class that sets the references.

■■ Graphics E10.20 Write a program that uses a timer to print the current time once a second. *Hint:* The following code prints the current time:

```
Date now = new Date();
System.out.println(now);
```

The Date class is in the java.util package.

■■■ Graphics E10.21 Change the RectangleComponent for the animation program in Section 10.9 so that the rectangle bounces off the edges of the component rather than simply moving outside.

■ Graphics E10.22 Change the RectangleComponent for the mouse listener program in Section 10.10 so that a new rectangle is added to the component whenever the mouse is clicked. *Hint:* Keep an ArrayList<Rectangle> and draw all rectangles in the paintComponent method.

■ E10.23 Supply a class Person that implements the Comparable interface. Compare persons by their names. Ask the user to input ten names and generate ten Person objects. Using the compareTo method, determine the first and last person among them and print them.

PROGRAMMING PROJECTS

■■ P10.1 Modify the display method of the LastDigitDistribution class of Worked Example 10.1 so that it produces a histogram, like this:

```
0: *************
1: *******************
2: *************
```

Scale the bars so that widest one has length 40.

■■ P10.2 Write a class PrimeSequence that implements the Sequence interface of Worked Example 10.1, and produces the sequence of prime numbers.

■ P10.3 Add a method hasNext to the Sequence interface of Worked Example 10.1 that returns false if the sequence has no more values. Implement a class MySequence producing a sequence of real data of your choice, such as populations of cities or countries, temperatures, or stock prices. Obtain the data from the Internet and reformat the values so that they are placed into an array. Return one value at a time in the next method, until you reach the end of the data. Your SequenceDemo class should display the distribution of the last digits of all sequence values.

■ P10.4 Provide a class FirstDigitDistribution that works just like the LastDigitDistribution class of Worked Example 10.1, except that it counts the distribution of the first digit of each value. (It is a well-known fact that the first digits of random values are *not* uniformly distributed. This fact has been used to detect accounting fraud, when sequences of transaction amounts had an unnatural distribution of their first digits.)

P10.5 Declare an interface Filter as follows:

```
public interface Filter
{
    boolean accept(Object x);
}
```

Modify the implementation of the Data class in Section 10.4 to use both a Measurer and a Filter object. Only objects that the filter accepts should be processed. Demonstrate your modification by processing a collection of bank accounts, filtering out all accounts with balances less than $1,000.

P10.6 The System.out.printf method has predefined formats for printing integers, floating-point numbers, and other data types. But it is also extensible. If you use the S format, you can print any class that implements the Formattable interface. That interface has a single method:

```
void formatTo(Formatter formatter, int flags, int width, int precision)
```

In this exercise, you should make the BankAccount class implement the Formattable interface. Ignore the flags and precision and simply format the bank balance, using the given width. In order to achieve this task, you need to get an Appendable reference like this:

```
Appendable a = formatter.out();
```

Appendable is another interface with a method

```
void append(CharSequence sequence)
```

CharSequence is yet another interface that is implemented by (among others) the String class. Construct a string by first converting the bank balance into a string and then padding it with spaces so that it has the desired width. Pass that string to the append method.

P10.7 Enhance the formatTo method of Exercise P10.6 by taking into account the precision.

Graphics P10.8 Write a program that displays a scrolling message in a panel. Use a timer for the scrolling effect. In the timer's action listener, move the starting position of the message and repaint. When the message has left the window, reset the starting position to the other corner. Provide a user interface to customize the message text, font, foreground and background colors, and the scrolling speed and direction.

Graphics P10.9 Write a program that allows the user to specify a triangle with three mouse presses. After the first mouse press, draw a small dot. After the second mouse press, draw a line joining the first two points. After the third mouse press, draw the entire triangle. The fourth mouse press erases the old triangle and starts a new one.

Graphics P10.10 Implement a program that allows two players to play tic-tac-toe. Draw the game grid and an indication of whose turn it is (X or O). Upon the next click, check that the mouse click falls into an empty location, fill the location with the mark of the current player, and give the other player a turn. If the game is won, indicate the winner. Also supply a button for starting over.

Graphics P10.11 Write a program that lets users design bar charts with a mouse. When the user clicks inside a bar, the next mouse click extends the length of the bar to the x-coordinate of the mouse click. (If it is at or near 0, the bar is removed.) When the user clicks below the last bar, a new bar is added whose length is the x-coordinate of the mouse click.

■ **Testing P10.12** Consider the task of writing a program that plays tic-tac-toe against a human opponent. A user interface `TicTacToeUI` reads the user's moves and displays the computer's moves and the board. A class `TicTacToeStrategy` determines the next move that the computer makes. A class `TicTacToeBoard` represents the current state of the board. Complete all classes except for the strategy class. Instead, use a mock class that simply picks the first available empty square.

■■ **Testing P10.13** Consider the task of translating a plain text book from Project Gutenberg (`http://gutenberg.org`) to HTML. For example, here is the start of the first chapter of Tolstoy's Anna Karenina:

```
Chapter 1

Happy families are all alike; every unhappy family is unhappy in its own way.

Everything was in confusion in the Oblonskys' house. The wife had discovered
that the husband was carrying on an intrigue with a French girl, who had been a
governess in their family, and she had announced to her husband that she could
not go on living in the same house with him ...
```

The equivalent HTML is:

```
<h1>Chapter 1</h1>
<p>Happy families are all alike; every unhappy
family is unhappy in its own way.</p>
<p>Everything was in confusion in the
Oblonskys&rsquo; house. The wife had discovered
that the husband was carrying on an intrigue
with a French girl, who had been a governess in
their family, and she had announced to her
husband that she could not go on living in the
same house with him ...</p>
```

Plain Text	HTML
" "	“ (left) *or* ” (right)
' '	‘ (left) *or* ’ (right)
—	&emdash;
<	&lt;
>	&gt;
&	&amp;

The HTML conversion can be carried out in two steps. First, the plain text is assembled into *segments*, blocks of text of the same kind (heading, paragraph, and so on). Then each segment is converted, by surrounding it with the HTML tags and converting special characters.

Fetching the text from the Internet and breaking it into segments is a challenging task. Provide an interface and a mock implementation. Combine it with a class that uses the mock implementation to finish the formatting task.

■■ **Graphics P10.14** Write a program that demonstrates the growth of a roach population. Start with two roaches and double the number of roaches with each button click.

■■ **Graphics P10.15** Write a program that animates a car so that it moves across a frame.

■■■ **Graphics P10.16** Write a program that animates two cars moving across a frame in opposite directions (but at different heights so that they don't collide.)

■■ **Graphics P10.17** Write a program that prompts the user to enter the *x*- and *y*-positions of the center and a radius, using `JOptionPane` dialogs. When the user clicks a "Draw" button, prompt for the inputs and draw a circle with that center and radius in a component.

■■ **Graphics P10.18** Write a program that allows the user to specify a circle by clicking on the center and then typing the radius in a `JOptionPane`. Note that you don't need a "Draw" button.

■■■ **Graphics P10.19** Write a program that allows the user to specify a circle with two mouse presses, the first one on the center and the second on a point on the periphery. *Hint:* In the mouse press handler, you must keep track of whether you already received the center point in a previous mouse press.

■ **Graphics P10.20** Design an interface MoveableShape that can be used as a generic mechanism for animating a shape. A moveable shape must have two methods: move and draw. Write a generic AnimationPanel that paints and moves any MoveableShape (or array list of MoveableShape objects). Supply moveable rectangle and car shapes.

■ **P10.21** Your task is to design a general program for managing board games with two players. Your program should be flexible enough to handle games such as tic-tac-toe, chess, or the Game of Nim of Project 6.2.

Design an interface Game that describes a board game. Think about what your program needs to do. It asks the first player to input a move—a string in a game-specific format, such as Be3 in chess. Your program knows nothing about specific games, so the Game interface must have a method such as

```
boolean isValidMove(String move)
```

Once the move is found to be valid, it needs to be executed—the interface needs another method executeMove. Next, your program needs to check whether the game is over. If not, the other player's move is processed. You should also provide some mechanism for displaying the current state of the board.

Design the Game interface and provide two implementations of your choice—such as Nim and Chess (or TicTacToe if you are less ambitious). Your GamePlayer class should manage a Game reference without knowing which game is played, and process the moves from both players. Supply two programs that differ only in the initialization of the Game reference.

ANSWERS TO SELF-CHECK QUESTIONS

1. It must implement the Measurable interface, and its getMeasure method must return the salary.

2. The Object class doesn't have a getMeasure method.

3. You cannot modify the String class to implement Measurable—String is a library class. See Section 10.4 for a solution.

4. Measurable is not a class. You cannot construct objects of type Measurable.

5. The variable meas is of type Measurable, and that type has no getName method.

6. Only if meas actually refers to a BankAccount object.

7. No—a Country reference can be converted to a Measurable reference, but if you attempt to cast that reference to a BankAccount, an exception occurs.

8. Measurable is an interface. Interfaces have no instance variables and no method implementations.

9. That variable never refers to a Measurable object. It refers to an object of some class—a class that implements the Measurable interface.

10. The code fragment prints 20255. The average method calls getMeasure on each object in the array. In the first call, the object is a BankAccount. In the second call, the object is a Country. A different getMeasure method is called in each case. The first call returns the account balance, the second one the area, which are then averaged.

11. Have the Country class implement the Comparable interface, as shown below, and call Arrays.sort.

```
public class Country implements Comparable
{
    . . .
```

```
    public int compareTo(Object otherObject)
    {
        Country other = (Country) otherObject;
        if (area < other.area) { return -1; }
        if (area > other.area) { return 1; }
        return 0;
    }
}
```

12. Yes, you can, because `String` implements the `Comparable` interface type.

13. No. The `Rectangle` class does not implement the `Comparable` interface.

14.
```
public static Comparable max(
    Comparable a, Comparable b)
{
    if (a.compareTo(b) > 0) { return a; }
    else { return b; }
}
```

15.
```
BankAccount larger
    = (BankAccount) max(first, second);
System.out.println(larger.getBalance());
```

Note that the result must be cast from `Comparable` to `BankAccount` so that you can invoke the `getBalance` method.

16. The `String` class doesn't implement the `Measurable` interface.

17. Implement a class `StringMeasurer` that implements the `Measurer` interface.

18. A `Measurer` measures an object, whereas `getMeasure` measures "itself", that is, the implicit parameter.

19.
```
public static Object max(
    Object a, Object b, Measurer m)
{
    if (m.getMeasure(a) > m.getMeasure(b))
    {
        return a;
    }
    else { return b; }
}
```

20.
```
Rectangle larger = (Rectangle) max(
    first, second, areaMeas);
System.out.println(larger.getWidth() + " by "
    + larger.getHeight());
```

Note that the result of `max` must be cast from `Object` to `Rectangle` so that you can invoke the `getWidth` and `getHeight` methods.

21. Inner classes are convenient for insignificant classes. Also, their methods can access local and instance variables from the surrounding scope.

22. When the inner class is needed by more than one method of the classes.

23. Four: one for the outer class, one for the inner class, and two for the `Data` and `Measurer` classes.

24. You want to implement the `GradingProgram` class in terms of that interface so that it doesn't have to change when you switch between the mock class and the actual class.

25. Because the developer of `GradingProgram` doesn't have to wait for the `GradeBook` class to be complete.

26. The `button` object is the event source. The `listener` object is the event listener.

27. The `ClickListener` class implements the `ActionListener` interface.

28. You don't. It is called whenever the button is clicked.

29. Direct access is simpler than the alternative — passing the variable as an argument to a constructor or method.

30. The local variable must be declared as `final`.

31. First add `label` to the panel, then add `button`.

32. The `actionPerformed` method does not access that variable.

33. The timer needs to call some method whenever the time interval expires. It calls the `actionPerformed` method of the listener object.

34. The moved rectangles won't be painted, and the rectangle will appear to be stationary until the frame is repainted for an external reason.

35. Because you know the current mouse position, not the amount by which the mouse has moved.

36. It implements the `MouseListener` interface, which has five methods.

CHAPTER 11

INPUT/OUTPUT AND EXCEPTION HANDLING

CHAPTER GOALS

To read and write text files

To process command line arguments

To throw and catch exceptions

To implement programs that propagate checked exceptions

CHAPTER CONTENTS

In this chapter, you will learn how to read and write files—a very useful skill for processing real world data. As an application, you will learn how to encrypt data. (The Enigma machine shown at left is an encryption device used by Germany in World War II. Pioneering British computer scientists broke the code and were able to intercept encoded messages, which was a significant help in winning the war.) The remainder of this chapter tells you how your programs can report and recover from problems, such as missing files or malformed content, using the exception-handling mechanism of the Java language.

11.1 Reading and Writing Text Files

We begin this chapter by discussing the common task of reading and writing files that contain text. Examples of text files include not only files that are created with a simple text editor, such as Windows Notepad, but also Java source code and HTML files.

> Use the Scanner class for reading text files.

In Java, the most convenient mechanism for reading text is to use the Scanner class. You already know how to use a Scanner for reading console input. To read input from a disk file, the Scanner class relies on another class, File, which describes disk files and directories. (The File class has many methods that we do not discuss in this book; for example, methods that delete or rename a file.)

To begin, construct a File object with the name of the input file:

```
File inputFile = new File("input.txt");
```

Then use the File object to construct a Scanner object:

```
Scanner in = new Scanner(inputFile);
```

This Scanner object reads text from the file input.txt. You can use the Scanner methods (such as nextInt, nextDouble, and next) to read data from the input file.

For example, you can use the following loop to process numbers in the input file:

```
while (in.hasNextDouble())
{
    double value = in.nextDouble();
    Process value.
}
```

> When writing text files, use the PrintWriter class and the print/println/printf methods.

To write output to a file, you construct a PrintWriter object with the desired file name, for example

```
PrintWriter out = new PrintWriter("output.txt");
```

If the output file already exists, it is emptied before the new data are written into it. If the file doesn't exist, an empty file is created.

The PrintWriter class is an enhancement of the PrintStream class that you already know—System.out is a PrintStream object. You can use the familiar print, println, and printf methods with any PrintWriter object:

```
out.println("Hello, World!");
out.printf("Total: %8.2f\n", total);
```

Close all files
when you are done
processing them.

When you are done processing a file, be sure to *close* the Scanner or PrintWriter:

```
in.close();
out.close();
```

If your program exits without closing the PrintWriter, some of the output may not be written to the disk file.

The following program puts these concepts to work. It reads a file containing numbers and writes the numbers, lined up in a column and followed by their total, to another file.

For example, if the input file has the contents

```
32 54 67.5 29 35 80
115 44.5 100 65
```

then the output file is

```
        32.00
        54.00
        67.50
        29.00
        35.00
        80.00
       115.00
        44.50
       100.00
        65.00
Total:  622.00
```

There is one additional issue that we need to tackle. If the input or output file for a Scanner doesn't exist, a FileNotFoundException occurs when the Scanner object is constructed. The compiler insists that we specify what the program should do when that happens. Similarly, the PrintWriter constructor generates this exception if it cannot open the file for writing. (This can happen if the name is illegal or the user does not have the authority to create a file in the given location.) In our sample program, we want to terminate the main method if the exception occurs. To achieve this, we label the main method with a throws declaration:

```
public static void main(String[] args) throws FileNotFoundException
```

You will see in Section 11.4 how to deal with exceptions in a more professional way.

The File, PrintWriter, and FileNotFoundException classes are contained in the java.io package.

section_1/Total.java

```
 1  import java.io.File;
 2  import java.io.FileNotFoundException;
 3  import java.io.PrintWriter;
 4  import java.util.Scanner;
 5
 6  /**
 7     This program reads a file with numbers, and writes the numbers to another
 8     file, lined up in a column and followed by their total.
 9  */
10  public class Total
11  {
12     public static void main(String[] args) throws FileNotFoundException
13     {
```

```
14          // Prompt for the input and output file names
15
16          Scanner console = new Scanner(System.in);
17          System.out.print("Input file: ");
18          String inputFileName = console.next();
19          System.out.print("Output file: ");
20          String outputFileName = console.next();
21
22          // Construct the Scanner and PrintWriter objects for reading and writing
23
24          File inputFile = new File(inputFileName);
25          Scanner in = new Scanner(inputFile);
26          PrintWriter out = new PrintWriter(outputFileName);
27
28          // Read the input and write the output
29
30          double total = 0;
31
32          while (in.hasNextDouble())
33          {
34             double value = in.nextDouble();
35             out.printf("%15.2f\n", value);
36             total = total + value;
37          }
38
39          out.printf("Total: %8.2f\n", total);
40
41          in.close();
42          out.close();
43       }
44    }
```

SELF CHECK

1. What happens when you supply the same name for the input and output files to the Total program? Try it out if you are not sure.

2. What happens when you supply the name of a nonexistent input file to the Total program? Try it out if you are not sure.

3. Suppose you wanted to add the total to an existing file instead of writing a new file. Self Check 1 indicates that you cannot simply do this by specifying the same file for input and output. How can you achieve this task? Provide the pseudocode for the solution.

4. How do you modify the program so that it shows the average, not the total, of the inputs?

5. How can you modify the Total program so that it writes the values in two columns, like this:

```
    32.00    54.00
    67.50    29.00
    35.00    80.00
   115.00    44.50
   100.00    65.00
 Total:     622.00
```

Practice It   Now you can try these exercises at the end of the chapter: R11.1, R11.2, E11.1.

Common Error 11.1

Backslashes in File Names

When you specify a file name as a string literal, and the name contains backslash characters (as in a Windows file name), you must supply each backslash twice:

```
File inputFile = new File("c:\\homework\\input.dat");
```

A single backslash inside a quoted string is an **escape character** that is combined with the following character to form a special meaning, such as \n for a newline character. The \\ combination denotes a single backslash.

When a user supplies a file name to a program, however, the user should not type the backslash twice.

Common Error 11.2

Constructing a Scanner with a String

When you construct a PrintWriter with a string, it writes to a file:

```
PrintWriter out = new PrintWriter("output.txt");
```

However, this does *not* work for a Scanner. The statement

```
Scanner in = new Scanner("input.txt"); // Error?
```

does *not* open a file. Instead, it simply reads through the string: in.next() returns the string "input.txt". (This is occasionally useful—see Section 11.2.5.)

You must simply remember to use File objects in the Scanner constructor:

```
Scanner in = new Scanner(new File("input.txt")); // OK
```

Special Topic 11.1

Reading Web Pages

You can read the contents of a web page with this sequence of commands:

```
String address = "http://horstmann.com/index.html";
URL pageLocation = new URL(address);
Scanner in = new Scanner(pageLocation.openStream());
```

Now simply read the contents of the web page with the Scanner in the usual way. The URL constructor and the openStream method can throw an IOException, so you need to tag the main method with throws IOException. (See Section 11.4.3 for more information on the throws clause.)

The URL class is contained in the java.net package.

 FULL CODE EXAMPLE

Go to wiley.com/go/ javacode to download a program that reads data from a web page.

Special Topic 11.2

File Dialog Boxes

In a program with a graphical user interface, you will want to use a file dialog box (such as the one shown in the figure below) whenever the users of your program need to pick a file. The JFileChooser class implements a file dialog box for the Swing user-interface toolkit.

The JFileChooser class has many options to fine-tune the display of the dialog box, but in its most basic form it is quite simple: Construct a file chooser object; then call the showOpenDialog or showSaveDialog method. Both methods show the same dialog box, but the button for selecting a file is labeled "Open" or "Save", depending on which method you call.

For better placement of the dialog box on the screen, you can specify the user-interface component over which to pop up the dialog box. If you don't care where the dialog box pops up, you can simply pass null. The showOpenDialog and showSaveDialog methods return either JFileChooser.APPROVE_OPTION, if the user has chosen a file, or JFileChooser.CANCEL_OPTION, if the user canceled the selection. If a file was chosen, then you call the getSelectedFile method to obtain a File object that describes the file. Here is a complete example:

FULL CODE EXAMPLE

Go to wiley.com/go/javacode to download a program that demonstrates how to use a file chooser.

```
JFileChooser chooser = new JFileChooser();
Scanner in = null;
if (chooser.showOpenDialog(null) == JFileChooser.APPROVE_OPTION)
{
    File selectedFile = chooser.getSelectedFile();
    in = new Scanner(selectedFile);
    . . .
}
```

Call with showOpenDialog method

Button is "Save" when showSaveDialog method is called

A JFileChooser *Dialog Box*

Special Topic 11.3

Character Encodings

A **character** (such as the letter A, the digit 0, the accented character é, the Greek letter π, the symbol ∫, or the Chinese character 中) is encoded as a sequence of bytes. Each byte is a value between 0 and 255.

Unfortunately, the encoding is not uniform. In 1963, ASCII (the American Standard Code for Information Interchange) defined an encoding for 128 characters, which you can find in Appendix A. ASCII encodes all upper- and lowercase Latin letters and digits, as well as common symbols such as + * %, as values between 0 and 127. For example, the code for the letter A is 65.

As different populations felt the need to encode their own alphabets, they designed their own codes. Many of them built upon ASCII, using the values in the range from 128 to 255 for their own language. For example, in Spain, the letter é was encoded as 233. But in Greece, the code 233 denoted the letter ι (a lowercase iota). As you can imagine, if a Spanish tourist named José sent an e-mail to a Greek hotel, this created a problem.

To resolve this issue, the design of **Unicode** was begun in 1987. As described in Computing & Society 4.2, each character in the world is given a unique integer value. However, there are still multiple encodings of those integers in binary. The most popular encoding is called UTF-8. It encodes each character as a sequence of one to four bytes. For example, an A is still 65, as in ASCII, but an é is 195 169. The details of the encoding don't matter, as long as you specify that you want UTF-8 when you read and write a file.

As this book goes to print, the Windows and Macintosh operating systems have not yet made the switch to UTF-8. Java picks up the character encoding from the operating system. Unless you specifally request otherwise, the Scanner and PrintWriter classes will read and write files in that encoding. That's fine if your files contain only ASCII characters, or if the creator and the recipient use the same encoding. But if you need to process files with accented characters, Chinese characters, or special symbols, you should specifically request the UTF-8 encoding. Construct a scanner with

```
Scanner in = new Scanner(file, "UTF-8");
```

and a print writer with

```
PrintWriter out = new PrintWriter(file, "UTF-8");
```

You may wonder why Java can't just figure out the character encoding. However, consider the string José. In UTF-8, that's 74 111 115 195 169. The first three bytes, for Jos, are in the ASCII range and pose no problem. But the next two bytes, 195 169, could be é in UTF-8 or Ã¡ in the traditional Spanish encoding. The Scanner object doesn't understand Spanish, and it can't decide which encoding to choose.

Therefore, you should always specify the UTF-8 encoding when you exchange files with users from other parts of the world.

11.2 Text Input and Output

In the following sections, you will learn how to process text with complex contents, and you will learn how to cope with challenges that often occur with real data.

11.2.1 Reading Words

The next method of the Scanner class reads the next string. Consider the loop

The next method reads a string that is delimited by white space.

```
while (in.hasNext())
{
    String input = in.next();
    System.out.println(input);
}
```

If the user provides the input:

```
Mary had a little lamb
```

this loop prints each word on a separate line:

```
Mary
had
a
little
lamb
```

However, the words can contain punctuation marks and other symbols. The next method returns any sequence of characters that is not white space. **White space** includes spaces, tab characters, and the newline characters that separate lines. For example, the following strings are considered "words" by the next method:

```
snow.
1729
C++
```

(Note the period after snow—it is considered a part of the word because it is not white space.)

Here is precisely what happens when the next method is executed. Input characters that are white space are *consumed*—that is, removed from the input. However, they do not become part of the word. The first character that is not white space becomes the first character of the word. More characters are added until either another white space character occurs, or the end of the input file has been reached. However, if the end of the input file is reached before any character was added to the word, a "no such element exception" occurs.

Sometimes, you want to read just the words and discard anything that isn't a letter. You achieve this task by calling the useDelimiter method on your Scanner object:

```
Scanner in = new Scanner(. . .);
in.useDelimiter("[^A-Za-z]+");
```

Here, we set the character pattern that separates words to "any sequence of characters other than letters". (See Special Topic 11.4.) With this setting, punctuation and numbers are not included in the words returned by the next method.

11.2.2 Reading Characters

Sometimes, you want to read a file one character at a time. You will see an example in Section 11.3 where we encrypt the characters of a file. You achieve this task by calling the useDelimiter method on your Scanner object with an empty string:

```
Scanner in = new Scanner(. . .);
in.useDelimiter("");
```

Now each call to next returns a string consisting of a single character. Here is how you can process the characters:

```
while (in.hasNext())
{
    char ch = in.next().charAt(0);
    Process ch.
}
```

11.2.3 Classifying Characters

The Character class has methods for classifying characters.

When you read a character, or when you analyze the characters in a word or line, you often want to know what kind of character it is. The Character class declares several useful methods for this purpose. Each of them has an argument of type char and returns a boolean value (see Table 1).

For example, the call

```
Character.isDigit(ch)
```

returns true if ch is a digit ('0' . . . '9' or a digit in another writing system—see Computing & Society 4.2), false otherwise.

Table 1 Character Testing Methods

Method	Examples of Accepted Characters
isDigit	0, 1, 2
isLetter	A, B, C, a, b, c
isUpperCase	A, B, C
isLowerCase	a, b, c
isWhiteSpace	space, newline, tab

11.2.4 Reading Lines

> The nextLine method reads an entire line.

When each line of a file is a data record, it is often best to read entire lines with the nextLine method:

```
String line = in.nextLine();
```

The next input line (without the newline character) is placed into the string line. You can then take the line apart for further processing.

The hasNextLine method returns true if there is at least one more line in the input, false when all lines have been read. To ensure that there is another line to process, call the hasNextLine method before calling nextLine.

Here is a typical example of processing lines in a file. A file with population data from the CIA Fact Book site (https://www.cia.gov/library/publications/the-world-factbook/index.html) contains lines such as the following:

```
China   1330044605
India   1147995898
United States 303824646
. . .
```

Because some country names have more than one word, it would be tedious to read this file using the next method. For example, after reading United, how would your program know that it needs to read another word before reading the population count?

Instead, read each input line into a string:

```
while (in.hasNextLine())
{
    String line = nextLine();
    Process line.
}
```

Use the isDigit and isWhiteSpace methods in Table 1 to find out where the name ends and the number starts.

Locate the first digit:

```
int i = 0;
while (!Character.isDigit(line.charAt(i))) { i++; }
```

Then extract the country name and population:

```
String countryName = line.substring(0, i);
String population = line.substring(i);
```

However, the country name contains one or more spaces at the end. Use the trim method to remove them:

```
countryName = countryName.trim();
```

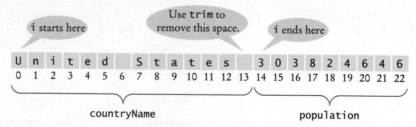

The trim method returns the string with all white space at the beginning and end removed.

There is one additional problem. The population is stored in a string, not a number. In Section 11.2.6, you will see how to convert the string to a number.

11.2.5 Scanning a String

In the preceding section, you saw how to break a string into parts by looking at individual characters. Another approach is occasionally easier. You can use a Scanner object to read the characters from a string:

```
Scanner lineScanner = new Scanner(line);
```

Then you can use lineScanner like any other Scanner object, reading words and numbers:

```
String countryName = lineScanner.next(); // Read first word
// Add more words to countryName until number encountered
while (!lineScanner.hasNextInt())
{
    countryName = countryName + " " + lineScanner.next();
}
int populationValue = lineScanner.nextInt();
```

11.2.6 Converting Strings to Numbers

Sometimes you have a string that contains a number, such as the population string in Section 11.2.4. For example, suppose that the string is the character sequence "303824646". To get the integer value 303824646, you use the Integer.parseInt method:

```
int populationValue = Integer.parseInt(population);
    // populationValue is the integer 303824646
```

To convert a string containing floating-point digits to its floating-point value, use the Double.parseDouble method. For example, suppose input is the string "3.95".

```
double price = Double.parseDouble(input);
    // price is the floating-point number 3.95
```

If a string contains the digits of a number, you use the Integer.parseInt or Double.parseDouble method to obtain the number value.

You need to be careful when calling the Integer.parseInt and Double.parseDouble methods. The argument must be a string containing the digits of an integer, without any additional characters. Not even spaces are allowed! In our situation, we happen to know that there won't be any spaces at the beginning of the string, but there might be some at the end. Therefore, we use the `trim` method:

```
int populationValue = Integer.parseInt(population.trim());
```

How To 11.1 on page 530 continues this example.

11.2.7 Avoiding Errors When Reading Numbers

You have used the `nextInt` and `nextDouble` methods of the `Scanner` class many times, but here we will have a look at what happens in "abnormal" situations. Suppose you call

```
int value = in.nextInt();
```

The `nextInt` method recognizes numbers such as 3 or -21. However, if the input is not a properly formatted number, an "input mismatch exception" occurs. For example, consider an input containing the characters

```
2 1 s t   c e n t u r y
```

White space is consumed and the word 21st is read. However, this word is not a properly formatted number, causing an input mismatch exception in the `nextInt` method.

If there is no input at all when you call `nextInt` or `nextDouble`, a "no such element exception" occurs. To avoid exceptions, use the `hasNextInt` method to screen the input when reading an integer. For example,

```
if (in.hasNextInt())
{
    int value = in.nextInt();
    . . .
}
```

Similarly, you should call the `hasNextDouble` method before calling `nextDouble`.

11.2.8 Mixing Number, Word, and Line Input

The `nextInt`, `nextDouble`, and `next` methods *do not* consume the white space that follows the number or word. This can be a problem if you alternate between calling `nextInt`/`nextDouble`/`next` and `nextLine`. Suppose a file contains country names and population values in this format:

```
China
1330044605
India
1147995898
United States
303824646
```

Now suppose you read the file with these instructions:

```
while (in.hasNextLine())
{
    String countryName = in.nextLine();
    int population = in.nextInt();
    Process the country name and population.
}
```

Initially, the input contains

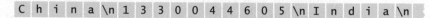

`C h i n a \n 1 3 3 0 0 4 4 6 0 5 \n I n d i a \n`

After the first call to the `nextLine` method, the input contains

`1 3 3 0 0 4 4 6 0 5 \n I n d i a \n`

After the call to `nextInt`, the input contains

`\n I n d i a \n`

Note that the `nextInt` call did *not* consume the newline character. Therefore, the second call to `nextLine` reads an empty string!

The remedy is to add a call to `nextLine` after reading the population value:

```
String countryName = in.nextLine();
int population = in.nextInt();
in.nextLine(); // Consume the newline
```

The call to `nextLine` consumes any remaining white space *and* the newline character.

11.2.9 Formatting Output

When you write numbers or strings, you often want to control how they appear. For example, dollar amounts are usually formatted with two significant digits, such as

```
Cookies:      3.20
```

You know from Section 4.3.2 how to achieve this output with the `printf` method. In this section, we discuss additional options of the `printf` method.

Suppose you need to print a table of items and prices, each stored in an array, such as

```
Cookies:      3.20
Linguine:     2.95
Clams:       17.29
```

Note that the item strings line up to the left, whereas the numbers line up to the right. By default, the `printf` method lines up values to the right.

Table 2 Format Flags		
Flag	Meaning	Example
-	Left alignment	1.23 followed by spaces
0	Show leading zeroes	001.23
+	Show a plus sign for positive numbers	+1.23
(	Enclose negative numbers in parentheses	(1.23)
,	Show decimal separators	12,300
^	Convert letters to uppercase	1.23E+1

To specify left alignment, you add a hyphen (-) before the field width:

```
System.out.printf("%-10s%10.2f", items[i] + ":", prices[i]);
```

Here, we have two format specifiers.

- %-10s formats a left-justified string. The string items[i] + ":" is padded with spaces so it becomes ten characters wide. The - indicates that the string is placed on the left, followed by sufficient spaces to reach a width of 10.

- %10.2f formats a floating-point number, also in a field that is ten characters wide. However, the spaces appear to the left and the value to the right.

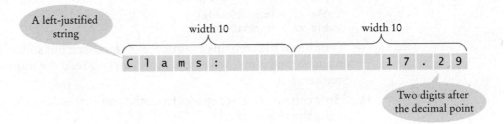

A construct such as %-10s or %10.2f is called a *format specifier:* it describes how a value should be formatted.

A format specifier has the following structure:

- The first character is a %.

- Next, there are optional "flags" that modify the format, such as - to indicate left alignment. See Table 2 for the most common format flags.

- Next is the field width, the total number of characters in the field (including the spaces used for padding), followed by an optional precision for floating-point numbers.

- The format specifier ends with the format type, such as f for floating-point values or s for strings. There are quite a few format types—Table 3 shows the most important ones.

FULL CODE EXAMPLE

Go to wiley.com/go/javacode to download a program that processes a file containing a mixture of text and numbers.

Table 3 Format Types		
Code	Type	Example
d	Decimal integer	123
f	Fixed floating-point	12.30
e	Exponential floating-point	1.23e+1
g	General floating-point (exponential notation is used for very large or very small values)	12.3
s	String	Tax:

SELF CHECK

6. Suppose the input contains the characters `Hello, World!`. What are the values of `word` and `input` after this code fragment?

    ```
    String word = in.next();
    String input = in.nextLine();
    ```

7. Suppose the input contains the characters `995.0 Fred`. What are the values of `number` and `input` after this code fragment?

    ```
    int number = 0;
    if (in.hasNextInt()) { number = in.nextInt(); }
    String input = in.next();
    ```

8. Suppose the input contains the characters `6E6 6,995.00`. What are the values of `x1` and `x2` after this code fragment?

    ```
    double x1 = in.nextDouble();
    double x2 = in.nextDouble();
    ```

9. Your input file contains a sequence of numbers, but sometimes a value is not available and is marked as `N/A`. How can you read the numbers and skip over the markers?

10. How can you remove spaces from the country name in Section 11.2.4 without using the `trim` method?

Practice It   Now you can try these exercises at the end of the chapter: E11.2, E11.4, E11.5.

Special Topic 11.4

Regular Expressions

Regular expressions describe character patterns. For example, numbers have a simple form. They contain one or more digits. The regular expression describing numbers is `[0-9]+`. The set `[0-9]` denotes any digit between 0 and 9, and the + means "one or more".

The search commands of professional programming editors understand regular expressions. Moreover, several utility programs use regular expressions to locate matching text. A commonly used program that uses regular expressions is **grep** (which stands for "global regular expression print"). You can run grep from a command line or from inside some compilation environments. Grep is part of the UNIX operating system, and versions are available for Windows. It needs a regular expression and one or more files to search. When grep runs, it displays a set of lines that match the regular expression.

Suppose you want to find all magic numbers (see Programming Tip 4.1) in a file.

    grep [0-9]+ Homework.java

lists all lines in the file `Homework.java` that contain sequences of digits. That isn't terribly useful; lines with variable names x1 will be listed. OK, you want sequences of digits that do *not* immediately follow letters:

    grep [^A-Za-z][0-9]+ Homework.java

The set `[^A-Za-z]` denotes any characters that are *not* in the ranges A to Z and a to z. This works much better, and it shows only lines that contain actual numbers.

The `useDelimiter` method of the `Scanner` class accepts a regular expression to describe delimiters—the blocks of text that separate words. As already mentioned, if you set the delimiter pattern to `[^A-Za-z]+`, a delimiter is a sequence of one or more characters that are not letters.

For more information on regular expressions, consult one of the many tutorials on the Internet by pointing your search engine to "regular expression tutorial".

11.3 Command Line Arguments

Depending on the operating system and Java development environment used, there are different methods of starting a program—for example, by selecting "Run" in the compilation environment, by clicking on an icon, or by typing the name of the program at the prompt in a command shell window. The latter method is called "invoking the program from the command line". When you use this method, you must of course type the name of the program, but you can also type in additional information that the program can use. These additional strings are called **command line arguments**. For example, if you start a program with the command line

```
java ProgramClass -v input.dat
```

then the program receives two command line arguments: the strings "-v" and "input. dat". It is entirely up to the program what to do with these strings. It is customary to interpret strings starting with a hyphen (-) as program options.

Should you support command line arguments for your programs, or should you prompt users, perhaps with a graphical user interface? For a casual and infrequent user, an interactive user interface is much better. The user interface guides the user along and makes it possible to navigate the application without much knowledge. But for a frequent user, a command line interface has a major advantage: it is easy to automate. If you need to process hundreds of files every day, you could spend all your time typing file names into file chooser dialog boxes. However, by using batch files or shell scripts (a feature of your computer's operating system), you can automatically call a program many times with different command line arguments.

Your program receives its command line arguments in the args parameter of the main method:

```
public static void main(String[] args)
```

In our example, args is an array of length 2, containing the strings

```
args[0]:    "-v"
args[1]:    "input.dat"
```

> Programs that start from the command line receive the command line arguments in the main method.

Let us write a program that *encrypts* a file—that is, scrambles it so that it is unreadable except to those who know the decryption method. Ignoring 2,000 years of progress in the field of encryption, we will use a method familiar to Julius Caesar, replacing A with a D, B with an E, and so on (see Figure 1).

The emperor Julius Caesar used a simple scheme to encrypt messages.

Plain text   M e e t   m e   a t   t h e

Encrypted text   P h h w   p h   d w   w k h

Figure 1
Caesar Cipher

The program takes the following command line arguments:

- An optional -d flag to indicate decryption instead of encryption
- The input file name
- The output file name

For example,

```
java CaesarCipher input.txt encrypt.txt
```

encrypts the file input.txt and places the result into encrypt.txt.

```
java CaesarCipher -d encrypt.txt output.txt
```

decrypts the file encrypt.txt and places the result into output.txt.

section_3/CaesarCipher.java

```java
1   import java.io.File;
2   import java.io.FileNotFoundException;
3   import java.io.PrintWriter;
4   import java.util.Scanner;
5
6   /**
7      This program encrypts a file using the Caesar cipher.
8   */
9   public class CaesarCipher
10  {
11     public static void main(String[] args) throws FileNotFoundException
12     {
13        final int DEFAULT_KEY = 3;
14        int key = DEFAULT_KEY;
15        String inFile = "";
16        String outFile = "";
17        int files = 0; // Number of command line arguments that are files
18
19        for (int i = 0; i < args.length; i++)
20        {
21           String arg = args[i];
22           if (arg.charAt(0) == '-')
23           {
24              // It is a command line option
25
26              char option = arg.charAt(1);
27              if (option == 'd') { key = -key; }
28              else { usage(); return; }
29           }
30           else
31           {
32              // It is a file name
33
34              files++;
35              if (files == 1) { inFile = arg; }
36              else if (files == 2) { outFile = arg; }
37           }
38        }
39        if (files != 2) { usage(); return; }
40
```

```
41        Scanner in = new Scanner(new File(inFile));
42        in.useDelimiter(""); // Process individual characters
43        PrintWriter out = new PrintWriter(outFile);
44
45        while (in.hasNext())
46        {
47           char from = in.next().charAt(0);
48           char to = encrypt(from, key);
49           out.print(to);
50        }
51        in.close();
52        out.close();
53     }
54
55     /**
56        Encrypts upper- and lowercase characters by shifting them
57        according to a key.
58        @param ch the letter to be encrypted
59        @param key the encryption key
60        @return the encrypted letter
61     */
62     public static char encrypt(char ch, int key)
63     {
64        int base = 0;
65        if ('A' <= ch && ch <= 'Z') { base = 'A'; }
66        else if ('a' <= ch && ch <= 'z') { base = 'a'; }
67        else { return ch; } // Not a letter
68        int offset = ch - base + key;
69        final int LETTERS = 26; // Number of letters in the Roman alphabet
70        if (offset > LETTERS) { offset = offset - LETTERS; }
71        else if (offset < 0) { offset = offset + LETTERS; }
72        return (char) (base + offset);
73     }
74
75     /**
76        Prints a message describing proper usage.
77     */
78     public static void usage()
79     {
80        System.out.println("Usage: java CaesarCipher [-d] infile outfile");
81     }
82  }
```

SELF CHECK

11. If the program is invoked with java CaesarCipher -d file1.txt, what are the elements of args?

12. Trace the program when it is invoked as in Self Check 11.

13. Will the program run correctly if the program is invoked with java CaesarCipher file1.txt file2.txt -d? If so, why? If not, why not?

14. Encrypt CAESAR using the Caesar cipher.

15. How can you modify the program so that the user can specify an encryption key other than 3 with a -k option, for example

    java CaesarCipher -k15 input.txt output.txt

Practice It Now you can try these exercises at the end of the chapter: R11.4, E11.8, E11.9.

HOW TO 11.1

Processing Text Files

Processing text files that contain real data can be surprisingly challenging. This How To gives you step-by-step guidance using world population data.

Problem Statement Read two country data files, `worldpop.txt` and `worldarea.txt` (supplied with your source code). Both files contain the same countries in the same order. Write a file `world_pop_density.txt` that contains country names and population densities (people per square km), with the country names aligned left and the numbers aligned right:

```
Afghanistan                 50.56
Akrotiri                   127.64
Albania                    125.91
Algeria                     14.18
American Samoa             288.92
 . . .
```

Singapore is one of the most densely populated countries in the world.

Step 1 Understand the processing task.

As always, you need to have a clear understanding of the task before designing a solution. Can you carry out the task by hand (perhaps with smaller input files)? If not, get more information about the problem.

One important consideration is whether you can process the data as it becomes available, or whether you need to store it first. For example, if you are asked to write out sorted data, you first need to collect all input, perhaps by placing it in an array list. However, it is often possible to process the data "on the go", without storing it.

In our example, we can read each file one line at a time and compute the density for each line because our input files store the population and area data in the same order.

The following pseudocode describes our processing task.

> **While there are more lines to be read**
> **Read a line from each file.**
> **Extract the country name.**
> **population = number following the country name in the line from the first file**
> **area = number following the country name in the line from the second file**
> **If area != 0**
> **density = population / area**
> **Print country name and density.**

Step 2 Determine which files you need to read and write.

This should be clear from the problem. In our example, there are two input files, the population data and the area data, and one output file.

Step 3 Choose a mechanism for obtaining the file names.

There are three options:

- Hard-coding the file names (such as "worldpop.txt").
- Asking the user:
  ```
  Scanner in = new Scanner(System.in);
  System.out.print("Enter filename: ");
  String inFile = in.nextLine();
  ```
- Using command-line arguments for the file names.

In our example, we use hard-coded file names for simplicity.

Step 4 Choose between line, word, and character-based input.

As a rule of thumb, read lines if the input data is grouped by lines. That is the case with tabular data, such as in our example, or when you need to report line numbers.

When gathering data that can be distributed over several lines, then it makes more sense to read words. Keep in mind that you lose all white space when you read words.

Reading characters is mostly useful for tasks that require access to individual characters. Examples include analyzing character frequencies, changing tabs to spaces, or encryption.

Step 5 With line-oriented input, extract the required data.

It is simple to read a line of input with the `nextLine` method. Then you need to get the data out of that line. You can extract substrings, as described in Section 11.2.4.

Typically, you will use methods such as `Character.isWhitespace` and `Character.isDigit` to find the boundaries of substrings.

If you need any of the substrings as numbers, you must convert them, using `Integer.parseInt` or `Double.parseDouble`.

Step 6 Use classes and methods to factor out common tasks.

Processing input files usually has repetitive tasks, such as skipping over white space or extracting numbers from strings. It really pays off to isolate these tedious operations from the remainder of the code.

In our example, we have a task that occurs twice: splitting an input line into the country name and the value that follows. We implement a simple `CountryValue` class for this purpose, using the technique described in Section 11.2.4.

Here is the complete source code:

how_to_1/CountryValue.java

```
1   /**
2        Describes a value that is associated with a country.
3   */
4   public class CountryValue
5   {
6      private String country;
7      private double value;
8
9      /**
10         Constructs a CountryValue from an input line.
11         @param line a line containing a country name, followed by a value
12      */
13      public CountryValue(String line)
14      {
15         int i = 0; // Locate the start of the first digit
16         while (!Character.isDigit(line.charAt(i))) { i++; }
17         int j = i - 1; // Locate the end of the preceding word
18         while (Character.isWhitespace(line.charAt(j))) { j--; }
19         country = line.substring(0, j + 1); // Extract the country name
20         value = Double.parseDouble(line.substring(i).trim()); // Extract the value
21      }
22
23      /**
24         Gets the country name.
25         @return the country name
26      */
27      public String getCountry() { return country; }
28
```

```
29    /**
30        Gets the associated value.
31        @return the value associated with the country
32    */
33    public double getValue() { return value; }
34 }
```

how_to_1/PopulationDensity.java

```java
1  import java.io.File;
2  import java.io.FileNotFoundException;
3  import java.io.PrintWriter;
4  import java.util.Scanner;
5
6  public class PopulationDensity
7  {
8     public static void main(String[] args) throws FileNotFoundException
9     {
10       // Open input files
11       Scanner in1 = new Scanner(new File("worldpop.txt"));
12       Scanner in2 = new Scanner(new File("worldarea.txt"));
13
14       // Open output file
15       PrintWriter out = new PrintWriter("world_pop_density.txt");
16
17       // Read lines from each file
18       while (in1.hasNextLine() && in2.hasNextLine())
19       {
20          CountryValue population = new CountryValue(in1.nextLine());
21          CountryValue area = new CountryValue(in2.nextLine());
22
23          // Compute and print the population density
24          double density = 0;
25          if (area.getValue() != 0) // Protect against division by zero
26          {
27             density = population.getValue() / area.getValue();
28          }
29          out.printf("%-40s%15.2f\n", population.getCountry(), density);
30       }
31
32       in1.close();
33       in2.close();
34       out.close();
35    }
36 }
```

WORKED EXAMPLE 11.1   Analyzing Baby Names

Learn how to use data from the Social Security
Administration to analyze the most popular baby
names. Go to wiley.com/go/javaexamples and download Worked Example 11.1.

Computing & Society 11.1 Encryption Algorithms

This chapter's exercise section gives a few algorithms for encrypting text. Don't actually use any of those methods to send secret messages to your lover. Any skilled cryptographer can *break* these schemes in a very short time—that is, reconstruct the original text without knowing the secret keyword.

In 1978 Ron Rivest, Adi Shamir, and Leonard Adleman introduced an encryption method that is much more powerful. The method is called *RSA encryption*, after the last names of its inventors. The exact scheme is too complicated to present here, but it is not actually difficult to follow. You can find the details in http://theory.lcs.mit.edu/~rivest/rsapaper.pdf.

RSA is a remarkable encryption method. There are two keys: a public key and a private key (see the figure). You can print the public key on your business card (or in your e-mail signature block) and give it to anyone. Then anyone can send you messages that only you can decrypt. Even though everyone else knows the public key, and even if they intercept all the messages coming to you, they cannot break the scheme and actually read the messages. In 1994, hundreds of researchers, collaborating over the Internet, cracked an RSA message encrypted with a 129-digit key. Messages encrypted with a key of 230 digits or more are expected to be secure.

The inventors of the algorithm obtained a *patent* for it. A patent is a deal that society makes with an inventor. For a period of 20 years, the inventor has an exclusive right to its commercialization, may collect royalties from others wishing to manufacture the invention, and may even stop competitors from using it altogether. In return, the inventor must publish the invention, so that others may learn from it, and must relinquish all claim to it after the monopoly period ends. The presumption is that in the absence of patent law, inventors would be reluctant to go through the trouble of inventing, or they would try to cloak their techniques to prevent others from copying their devices.

There has been some controversy about the RSA patent. Had there not been patent protection, would the inventors have published the method anyway, thereby giving the benefit to society without the cost of the 20-year monopoly? In this case, the answer is probably yes. The inventors were academic researchers who live on salaries rather than sales receipts and are usually rewarded for their discoveries by a boost in their reputation and careers. Would their followers have been as active in discovering (and patenting) improvements? There is no way of knowing, of course. Is an algorithm even patentable, or is it a mathematical fact that belongs to nobody? The patent office did take the latter attitude for a long time. The RSA inventors and many others described their inventions in terms of imaginary electronic devices, rather than algorithms, to circumvent that restriction. Nowadays, the patent office will award software patents.

There is another interesting aspect to the RSA story. A programmer, Phil Zimmermann, developed a program called PGP (for *Pretty Good Privacy*) that is based on RSA. Anyone can use the program to encrypt messages, and decryption is not feasible even with the most powerful computers. You can get a copy of a free PGP implementation from the GNU project (http://www.gnupg.org). The existence of strong encryption methods bothers the United States government to no end. Criminals and foreign agents can send communications that the police and intelligence agencies cannot decipher. The government considered charging Zimmermann with breaching a law that forbids the unauthorized export of munitions, arguing that he should have known that his program would appear on the Internet. There have been serious proposals to make it illegal for private citizens to use these encryption methods, or to keep the keys secret from law enforcement.

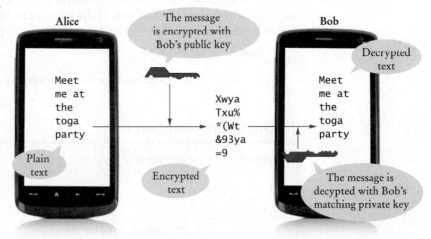

Public-Key Encryption

11.4 Exception Handling

There are two aspects to dealing with program errors: *detection* and *handling*. For example, the Scanner constructor can detect an attempt to read from a non-existent file. However, it cannot handle that error. A satisfactory way of handling the error might be to terminate the program, or to ask the user for another file name. The Scanner class cannot choose between these alternatives. It needs to report the error to another part of the program.

In Java, *exception handling* provides a flexible mechanism for passing control from the point of error detection to a handler that can deal with the error. In the following sections, we will look into the details of this mechanism.

11.4.1 Throwing Exceptions

> To signal an exceptional condition, use the throw statement to throw an exception object.

When you detect an error condition, your job is really easy. You just *throw* an appropriate exception object, and you are done. For example, suppose someone tries to withdraw too much money from a bank account.

```
if (amount > balance)
{
    // Now what?
}
```

First look for an appropriate exception class. The Java library provides many classes to signal all sorts of exceptional conditions. Figure 2 shows the most useful ones. (The classes are arranged as a tree-shaped inheritance hierarchy, with more specialized classes at the bottom of the tree.)

Look around for an exception type that might describe your situation. How about the ArithmeticException? Is it an arithmetic error to have a negative balance? No—Java can deal with negative numbers. Is the amount to be withdrawn illegal? Indeed it is. It is just too large. Therefore, let's throw an IllegalArgumentException.

```
if (amount > balance)
{
    throw new IllegalArgumentException("Amount exceeds balance");
}
```

Syntax 11.1 Throwing an Exception

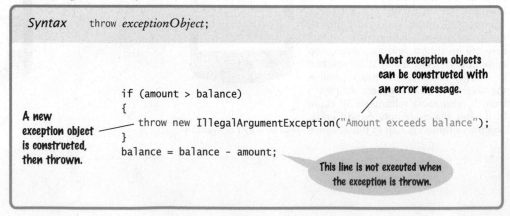

Syntax   throw *exceptionObject*;

Most exception objects can be constructed with an error message.

```
if (amount > balance)
{
    throw new IllegalArgumentException("Amount exceeds balance");
}
balance = balance - amount;
```

A new exception object is constructed, then thrown.

This line is not executed when the exception is thrown.

When you throw
an exception,
processing
continues in an
exception handler.

When you **throw an exception,** execution does not continue with the next statement but with an **exception handler.** That is the topic of the next section.

When you throw an exception, the normal control flow is terminated. This is similar to a circuit breaker that cuts off the flow of electricity in a dangerous situation.

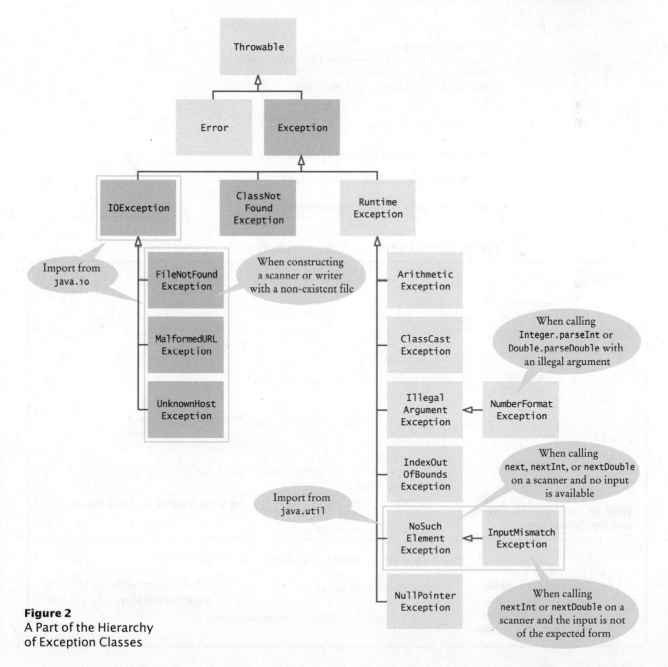

Figure 2
A Part of the Hierarchy
of Exception Classes

11.4.2 Catching Exceptions

Place the statements that can cause an exception inside a try block, and the handler inside a catch clause.

Every exception should be handled somewhere in your program. If an exception has no handler, an error message is printed, and your program terminates. Of course, such an unhandled exception is confusing to program users.

You handle exceptions with the try/catch statement. Place the statement into a location of your program that knows how to handle a particular exception. The **try block** contains one or more statements that may cause an exception of the kind that you are willing to handle. Each catch clause contains the handler for an exception type. Here is an example:

```
try
{
   String filename = . . .;
   Scanner in = new Scanner(new File(filename));
   String input = in.next();
   int value = Integer.parseInt(input);
   . . .
}
catch (IOException exception)
{
   exception.printStackTrace();
}
catch (NumberFormatException exception)
{
   System.out.println(exception.getMessage());
}
```

Syntax 11.2   Catching Exceptions

Syntax
```
try
{
    statement
    statement
    . . .
}
catch (ExceptionClass exceptionObject)
{
    statement
    statement
    . . .
}
```

This constructor can throw a FileNotFoundException.

```
try
{
   Scanner in = new Scanner(new File("input.txt"));
   String input = in.next();
   process(input);
}
catch (IOException exception)
{
   System.out.println("Could not open input file");
}
catch (Exception except)
{
   System.out.println(except.getMessage());
}
```

When an IOException is thrown, execution resumes here.

This is the exception that was thrown.

Additional catch clauses can appear here. Place more specific exceptions before more general ones.

A FileNotFoundException is a special case of an IOException.

Three exceptions may be thrown in this try block:

- The Scanner constructor can throw a FileNotFoundException.
- Scanner.next can throw a NoSuchElementException.
- Integer.parseInt can throw a NumberFormatException.

If any of these exceptions is actually thrown, then the rest of the instructions in the try block are skipped. Here is what happens for the various exception types:

You should only catch those exceptions that you can handle.

ANIMATION
Exception Handling

- If a FileNotFoundException is thrown, then the catch clause for the IOException is executed. (If you look at Figure 2, you will note that FileNotFoundException is a descendant of IOException.) If you want to show the user a different message for a FileNotFoundException, you must place the catch clause *before* the clause for an IOException.
- If a NumberFormatException occurs, then the second catch clause is executed.
- A NoSuchElementException is *not caught* by any of the catch clauses. The exception remains thrown until it is caught by another try block.

Each catch clause contains a handler. When the catch (IOException exception) block is executed, then some method in the try block has failed with an IOException (or one of its descendants).

In this handler, we produce a printout of the chain of method calls that led to the exception, by calling

```
exception.printStackTrace()
```

In the second exception handler, we call exception.getMessage() to retrieve the message associated with the exception. When the parseInt method throws a NumberFormat-Exception, the message contains the string that it was unable to format. When you throw an exception, you can provide your own message string. For example, when you call

```
throw new IllegalArgumentException("Amount exceeds balance");
```

the message of the exception is the string provided in the constructor.

In these sample catch clauses, we merely inform the user of the source of the problem. Often, it is better to give the user another chance to provide a correct input—see Section 11.5 for a solution.

11.4.3 Checked Exceptions

In Java, the exceptions that you can throw and catch fall into three categories.

- Internal errors are reported by descendants of the type Error. One example is the OutOfMemoryError, which is thrown when all available computer memory has been used up. These are fatal errors that happen rarely, and we will not consider them in this book.
- Descendants of RuntimeException, such as as IndexOutOfBoundsException or Illegal-ArgumentException indicate errors in your code. They are called **unchecked exceptions**.

Checked exceptions are due to external circumstances that the programmer cannot prevent. The compiler checks that your program handles these exceptions.

- All other exceptions are **checked exceptions**. These exceptions indicate that something has gone wrong for some external reason beyond your control. In Figure 2, the checked exceptions are shaded in a darker color.

Why have two kinds of exceptions? A checked exception describes a problem that can occur, no matter how careful you are. For example, an IOException can be caused by forces beyond your control, such as a disk error or a broken network connection. The compiler takes checked exceptions very seriously and ensures that they are handled. Your program will not compile if you don't indicate how to deal with a checked exception.

The unchecked exceptions, on the other hand, are your fault. The compiler does not check whether you handle an unchecked exception, such as an IndexOutOfBoundsException. After all, you should check your index values rather than install a handler for that exception.

If you have a handler for a checked exception in the same method that may throw it, then the compiler is satisfied. For example,

```
try
{
    File inFile = new File(filename);
    Scanner in = new Scanner(inFile); // Throws FileNotFoundException
    . . .
}
catch (FileNotFoundException exception) // Exception caught here
{
    . . .
}
```

Add a throws clause to a method that can throw a checked exception.

However, it commonly happens that the current method *cannot handle* the exception. In that case, you need to tell the compiler that you are aware of this exception and that you want your method to be terminated when it occurs. You supply the method with a throws clause:

```
public void readData(String filename) throws FileNotFoundException
{
    File inFile = new File(filename);
    Scanner in = new Scanner(inFile);
    . . .
}
```

The **throws clause** signals to the caller of your method that it may encounter a FileNotFoundException. Then the caller needs to make the same decision— handle the exception, or declare that the exception may be thrown.

It sounds somehow irresponsible not to handle an exception when you know that it happened. Actually, the opposite is true. Java provides an exception handling facility so that an exception can be sent to the *appropriate* handler. Some methods detect errors, some methods handle them, and some methods just pass them along. The throws clause simply ensures that no exceptions get lost along the way.

Just as trucks with large or hazardous loads carry warning signs, the throws *clause warns the caller that an exception may occur.*

Syntax 11.3 The throws Clause

> *Syntax*   *modifiers returnType methodName(parameterType parameterName, . . .)*
>   throws *ExceptionClass, ExceptionClass, . . .*
>
>   public void readData(String filename)
>   throws FileNotFoundException, NumberFormatException
>
> **You must specify all checked exceptions that this method may throw.**   **You may also list unchecked exceptions.**

11.4.4 The finally Clause

> Once a try block is entered, the statements in a finally clause are guaranteed to be executed, whether or not an exception is thrown.

Occasionally, you need to take some action whether or not an exception is thrown. The **finally clause** is used to handle this situation.

Here is a typical example: It is important to close a PrintWriter to ensure that all output is written to the file. In the following code segment, we open a stream, call one or more methods, and then close the stream:

```java
PrintWriter out = new PrintWriter(filename);
writeData(out);
out.close(); // May never get here
```

Now suppose that one of the methods before the last line throws an exception. Then the call to close is never executed! You solve this problem by placing the call to close inside a finally clause:

```java
PrintWriter out = new PrintWriter(filename);
try
{
    writeData(out);
}
finally
{
    out.close();
}
```

FULL CODE EXAMPLE

Go to wiley.com/go/
javacode to download
a program that
demonstrates
throwing and
catching exceptions.

In a normal case, there will be no problem. When the try block is completed, the finally clause is executed, and the writer is closed. However, if an exception occurs, the finally clause is also executed before the exception is passed to its handler.

Use the finally clause whenever you need to do some clean up, such as closing a file, to ensure that the clean up happens no matter how the method exits.

All visitors to a foreign country have to go through passport control, no matter what happened on their trip. Similarly, the code in a finally clause is always executed, even when an exception has occurred.

Syntax 11.4   The `finally` Clause

```
Syntax      try
            {
                statement
                statement
                . . .
            }
            finally
            {
                statement
                statement
                . . .
            }
```

This variable must be declared outside the `try` block so that the `finally` clause can access it.

```
PrintWriter out = new PrintWriter(filename);
try
```

This code may throw exceptions.

```
{
    writeData(out);
}
finally
```

This code is always executed, even if an exception occurs.

```
{
    out.close();
}
```

11.4.5 Designing Your Own Exception Types

Sometimes none of the standard exception types describe your particular error condition well enough. In that case, you can design your own exception class. Consider a bank account. Let's report an `InsufficientFundsException` when an attempt is made to withdraw an amount from a bank account that exceeds the current balance.

```
if (amount > balance)
{
    throw new InsufficientFundsException(
        "withdrawal of " + amount + " exceeds balance of " + balance);
}
```

To describe an error condition, provide a subclass of an existing exception class.

Now you need to provide the `InsufficientFundsException` class. Should it be a checked or an unchecked exception? Is it the fault of some external event, or is it the fault of the programmer? We take the position that the programmer could have prevented the exceptional condition—after all, it would have been an easy matter to check whether `amount <= account.getBalance()` before calling the `withdraw` method. Therefore, the exception should be an unchecked exception and extend the `RuntimeException` class or one of its subclasses.

It is a good idea to extend an appropriate class in the exception hierarchy. For example, we can consider an `InsufficientFundsException` a special case of an `Illegal-ArgumentException`. This enables other programmers to catch the exception as an `IllegalArgumentException` if they are not interested in the exact nature of the problem.

It is customary to provide two constructors for an exception class: a constructor with no arguments and a constructor that accepts a message string describing the reason for the exception. Here is the declaration of the exception class:

```java
public class InsufficientFundsException extends IllegalArgumentException
{
    public InsufficientFundsException() {}

    public InsufficientFundsException(String message)
    {
        super(message);
    }
}
```

When the exception is caught, its message string can be retrieved using the getMessage method of the Throwable class.

SELF CHECK

16. Suppose balance is 100 and amount is 200. What is the value of balance after these statements?

```java
if (amount > balance)
{
    throw new IllegalArgumentException("Amount exceeds balance");
}
balance = balance - amount;
```

17. When depositing an amount into a bank account, we don't have to worry about overdrafts—except when the amount is negative. Write a statement that throws an appropriate exception in that case.

18. Consider the method

```java
public static void main(String[] args)
{
    try
    {
        Scanner in = new Scanner(new File("input.txt"));
        int value = in.nextInt();
        System.out.println(value);
    }
    catch (IOException exception)
    {
        System.out.println("Error opening file.");
    }
}
```

Suppose the file with the given file name exists and has no contents. Trace the flow of execution.

19. Why is an ArrayIndexOutOfBoundsException not a checked exception?

20. Is there a difference between catching checked and unchecked exceptions?

21. What is wrong with the following code, and how can you fix it?

```java
public static void writeAll(String[] lines, String filename)
{
    PrintWriter out = new PrintWriter(filename);
    for (String line : lines)
    {
        out.println(line.toUpperCase());
    }
    out.close();
```

}

22. What is the purpose of the call super(message) in the second InsufficientFunds-Exception constructor?

23. Suppose you read bank account data from a file. Contrary to your expectation, the next input value is not of type double. You decide to implement a BadData-Exception. Which exception class should you extend?

Practice It   Now you can try these exercises at the end of the chapter: R11.7, R11.8, R11.9.

Programming Tip 11.1

Throw Early, Catch Late

When a method detects a problem that it cannot solve, it is better to throw an exception rather than try to come up with an imperfect fix. For example, suppose a method expects to read a number from a file, and the file doesn't contain a number. Simply using a zero value would be a poor choice because it hides the actual problem and perhaps causes a different problem elsewhere.

> Throw an exception as soon as a problem is detected. Catch it only when the problem can be handled.

Conversely, a method should only catch an exception if it can really remedy the situation. Otherwise, the best remedy is simply to have the exception propagate to its caller, allowing it to be caught by a competent handler.

These principles can be summarized with the slogan "throw early, catch late".

Programming Tip 11.2

Do Not Squelch Exceptions

When you call a method that throws a checked exception and you haven't specified a handler, the compiler complains. In your eagerness to continue your work, it is an understandable impulse to shut the compiler up by squelching the exception:

```
try
{
    Scanner in = new Scanner(new File(filename));
    // Compiler complained about FileNotFoundException
    . . .
}
catch (FileNotFoundException e) {} // So there!
```

The do-nothing exception handler fools the compiler into thinking that the exception has been handled. In the long run, this is clearly a bad idea. Exceptions were designed to transmit problem reports to a competent handler. Installing an incompetent handler simply hides an error condition that could be serious.

Programming Tip 11.3

Do Not Use catch and finally in the Same try Statement

It is possible to have a finally clause following one or more catch clauses. Then the code in the finally clause is executed whenever the try block is exited in any of three ways:

1. After completing the last statement of the try block

2. After completing the last statement of a catch clause, if this try block caught an exception

3. When an exception was thrown in the try block and not caught

It is tempting to combine catch and finally clauses, but the resulting code can be hard to understand, and it is often incorrect. Instead, use two statements:

- a try/finally statement to close resources
- a separate try/catch statement to handle errors

For example,

```java
try
{
    PrintWriter out = new PrintWriter(filename);
    try
    {
        Write output.
    }
    finally
    {
        out.close();
    }
}
catch (IOException exception)
{
    Handle exception.
}
```

Note that the nested statements work correctly even if the PrintWriter constructor throws an exception.

Programming Tip 11.4

Do Throw Specific Exceptions

When throwing an exception, you should choose an exception class that describes the situation as closely as possible. For example, it would be a bad idea to simply throw a RuntimeException object when a bank account has insufficient funds. This would make it far too difficult to catch the exception. After all, if you caught all exceptions of type RuntimeException, your catch clause would also be activated by exceptions of the type NullPointerException, ArrayIndexOutOfBoundsException, and so on. You would then need to carefully examine the exception object and attempt to deduce whether the exception was caused by insufficient funds.

If the standard library does not have an exception class that describes your particular error situation, simply provide a new exception class.

Special Topic 11.5

Assertions

An **assertion** is a condition that you believe to be true at all times in a particular program location. An assertion check tests whether an assertion is true. Here is a typical assertion check:

```java
public double deposit (double amount)
{
    assert amount >= 0;
    balance = balance + amount;
}
```

In this method, the programmer expects that the quantity amount can never be negative. When the assertion is correct, no harm is done, and the program works in the normal way. If, for some reason, the assertion fails, and assertion checking is enabled, then the assert statement throws an exception of type AssertionError, causing the program to terminate.

However, if assertion checking is disabled, then the assertion is never checked, and the program runs at full speed. By default, assertion checking is disabled when you execute a program.

To execute a program with assertion checking turned on, use this command:

```
java -enableassertions MainClass
```

You can also use the shortcut -ea instead of -enableassertions. You should turn assertion checking on during program development and testing.

Special Topic 11.6

Automatic Resource Management in Java 7

In Java 7, you can use a new form of the try block that automatically closes a PrintWriter or Scanner object. Here is the syntax:

```
try (PrintWriter out = new PrintWriter(filename))
{
    Write output to out.
}
```

The close method is automatically invoked on the out object when the try block ends, whether or not an exception has occurred. A finally statement is not required.

Computing & Society 11.2 The Ariane Rocket Incident

The European Space Agency (ESA), Europe's counterpart to NASA, had developed a rocket model called Ariane that it had successfully used several times to launch satellites and scientific experiments into space. However, when a new version, the Ariane 5, was launched on June 4, 1996, from ESA's launch site in Kourou, French Guiana, the rocket veered off course about 40 seconds after liftoff. Flying at an angle of more than 20 degrees, rather than straight up, exerted such an aerodynamic force that the boosters separated, which triggered the automatic self-destruction mechanism. The rocket blew itself up.

The ultimate cause of this accident was an unhandled exception! The rocket contained two identical devices (called inertial reference systems) that processed flight data from measuring devices and turned the data into information about the rocket position.

The onboard computer used the position information for controlling the boosters. The same inertial reference systems and computer software had worked fine on the Ariane 4.

However, due to design changes to the rocket, one of the sensors measured a larger acceleration force than had been encountered in the Ariane 4. That value, expressed as a floating-point value, was stored in a 16-bit integer (like a short variable in Java). Unlike Java, the Ada language, used for the device software, generates an exception if a floating-point number is too large to be converted to an integer. Unfortunately, the programmers of the device had decided that this situation would never happen and didn't provide an exception handler.

When the overflow did happen, the exception was triggered and, because there was no handler, the device shut itself off. The onboard computer sensed the failure and switched over to the backup device. However, that device had shut itself off for exactly the same reason, something that the designers of the rocket had not expected. They figured that the devices might fail for mechanical reasons, but the chance of them having the same mechanical failure was remote. At that point, the rocket was without reliable position information and went off course.

Perhaps it would have been better if the software hadn't been so thorough? If it had ignored the overflow, the device wouldn't have been shut off. It would have computed bad data. But then the device would have reported wrong position data, which could have been just as fatal. Instead, a correct implementation should have caught overflow exceptions and come up with some strategy to recompute the flight data. Clearly, giving up was not a reasonable option in this context.

The advantage of the exception-handling mechanism is that it makes these issues explicit to programmers—something to think about when you curse the Java compiler for complaining about uncaught exceptions.

The Explosion of the Ariane Rocket

11.5 Application: Handling Input Errors

This section walks through a complete example of a program with exception handling. The program asks a user for the name of a file. The file is expected to contain data values. The first line of the file contains the total number of values, and the remaining lines contain the data. A typical input file looks like this:

```
3
1.45
-2.1
0.05
```

What can go wrong? There are two principal risks.

- The file might not exist.
- The file might have data in the wrong format.

Who can detect these faults? The Scanner constructor will throw an exception when the file does not exist. The methods that process the input values need to throw an exception when they find an error in the data format.

What exceptions can be thrown? The Scanner constructor throws a FileNotFoundException when the file does not exist, which is appropriate in our situation. When the file data is in the wrong format, we will throw a BadDataException, a custom checked exception class. We use a checked exception because corruption of a data file is beyond the control of the programmer.

Who can remedy the faults that the exceptions report? Only the main method of the DataAnalyzer program interacts with the user. It catches the exceptions, prints appropriate error messages, and gives the user another chance to enter a correct file.

> When designing a program, ask yourself what kinds of exceptions can occur.

> For each exception, you need to decide which part of your program can competently handle it.

section_5/DataAnalyzer.java

```java
1   import java.io.FileNotFoundException;
2   import java.io.IOException;
3   import java.util.Scanner;
4
5   /**
6      This program reads a file containing numbers and analyzes its contents.
7      If the file doesn't exist or contains strings that are not numbers, an
8      error message is displayed.
9   */
10  public class DataAnalyzer
11  {
12     public static void main(String[] args)
13     {
14        Scanner in = new Scanner(System.in);
15        DataSetReader reader = new DataSetReader();
16
17        boolean done = false;
18        while (!done)
19        {
20           try
21           {
22              System.out.println("Please enter the file name: ");
23              String filename = in.next();
24
25              double[] data = reader.readFile(filename);
26              double sum = 0;
```

```
27            for (double d : data) { sum = sum + d; }
28            System.out.println("The sum is " + sum);
29            done = true;
30         }
31         catch (FileNotFoundException exception)
32         {
33            System.out.println("File not found.");
34         }
35         catch (BadDataException exception)
36         {
37            System.out.println("Bad data: " + exception.getMessage());
38         }
39         catch (IOException exception)
40         {
41            exception.printStackTrace();
42         }
43      }
44   }
45 }
```

The catch clauses in the main method give a human-readable error report if the file was not found or bad data was encountered.

The following readFile method of the DataSetReader class constructs the Scanner object and calls the readData method. It is completely unconcerned with any exceptions. If there is a problem with the input file, it simply passes the exception to its caller.

```
public double[] readFile(String filename) throws IOException
{
   File inFile = new File(filename);
   Scanner in = new Scanner(inFile);
   try
   {
      readData(in);
      return data;
   }
   finally
   {
      in.close();
   }
}
```

The method throws an IOException, the common superclass of FileNotFoundException (thrown by the Scanner constructor) and BadDataException (thrown by the readData method).

Next, here is the readData method of the DataSetReader class. It reads the number of values, constructs an array, and calls readValue for each data value.

```
private void readData(Scanner in) throws BadDataException
{
   if (!in.hasNextInt())
   {
      throw new BadDataException("Length expected");
   }
   int numberOfValues = in.nextInt();
   data = new double[numberOfValues];

   for (int i = 0; i < numberOfValues; i++)
   {
```

```
            readValue(in, i);
        }

        if (in.hasNext())
        {
            throw new BadDataException("End of file expected");
        }
    }
}
```

This method checks for two potential errors. The file might not start with an integer, or it might have additional data after reading all values.

However, this method makes no attempt to catch any exceptions. Plus, if the read-Value method throws an exception—which it will if there aren't enough values in the file—the exception is simply passed on to the caller.

Here is the readValue method:

```
private void readValue(Scanner in, int i) throws BadDataException
{
    if (!in.hasNextDouble())
    {
        throw new BadDataException("Data value expected");
    }
    data[i] = in.nextDouble();
}
```

To see the exception handling at work, look at a specific error scenario:

1. DataAnalyzer.main calls DataSetReader.readFile.

2. readFile calls readData.

3. readData calls readValue.

4. readValue doesn't find the expected value and throws a BadDataException.

5. readValue has no handler for the exception and terminates immediately.

6. readData has no handler for the exception and terminates immediately.

7. readFile has no handler for the exception and terminates immediately after executing the finally clause and closing the Scanner object.

8. DataAnalyzer.main has a handler for a BadDataException. That handler prints a message to the user. Afterward, the user is given another chance to enter a file name. Note that the statements computing the sum of the values have been skipped.

This example shows the separation between error detection (in the DataSetReader.readValue method) and error handling (in the DataAnalyzer.main method). In between the two are the readData and readFile methods, which just pass exceptions along.

section_5/DataSetReader.java

```
1   import java.io.File;
2   import java.io.IOException;
3   import java.util.Scanner;
4
5   /**
6       Reads a data set from a file. The file must have the format
7       numberOfValues
8       value1
9       value2
10      . . .
```

```
11  */
12  public class DataSetReader
13  {
14     private double[] data;
15
16     /**
17        Reads a data set.
18        @param filename the name of the file holding the data
19        @return the data in the file
20     */
21     public double[] readFile(String filename) throws IOException
22     {
23        File inFile = new File(filename);
24        Scanner in = new Scanner(inFile);
25        try
26        {
27           readData(in);
28           return data;
29        }
30        finally
31        {
32           in.close();
33        }
34     }
35
36     /**
37        Reads all data.
38        @param in the scanner that scans the data
39     */
40     private void readData(Scanner in) throws BadDataException
41     {
42        if (!in.hasNextInt())
43        {
44           throw new BadDataException("Length expected");
45        }
46        int numberOfValues = in.nextInt();
47        data = new double[numberOfValues];
48
49        for (int i = 0; i < numberOfValues; i++)
50        {
51           readValue(in, i);
52        }
53
54        if (in.hasNext())
55        {
56           throw new BadDataException("End of file expected");
57        }
58     }
59
60     /**
61        Reads one data value.
62        @param in the scanner that scans the data
63        @param i the position of the value to read
64     */
65     private void readValue(Scanner in, int i) throws BadDataException
66     {
67        if (!in.hasNextDouble())
68        {
69           throw new BadDataException("Data value expected");
70        }
```

```
71          data[i] = in.nextDouble();
72      }
73  }
```

section_5/BadDataException.java

```
1   import java.io.IOException;
2
3   /**
4       This class reports bad input data.
5   */
6   public class BadDataException extends IOException
7   {
8       public BadDataException() {}
9       public BadDataException(String message)
10      {
11          super(message);
12      }
13  }
```

SELF CHECK

24. Why doesn't the DataSetReader.readFile method catch any exceptions?

25. Suppose the user specifies a file that exists and is empty. Trace the flow of execution.

26. If the readValue method had to throw a NoSuchElementException instead of a Bad-DataException when the next input isn't a floating-point number, how would the implementation change?

27. Consider the try/finally statement in the readFile method. Why was the in variable declared outside the try block?

28. How can the program be simplified when you use the "automatic resource management" feature described in Special Topic 11.6?

Practice It   Now you can try these exercises at the end of the chapter: R11.15, R11.16, E11.11.

CHAPTER SUMMARY

Develop programs that read and write files.

- Use the Scanner class for reading text files.
- When writing text files, use the PrintWriter class and the print/println/printf methods.
- Close all files when you are done processing them.

Be able to process text in files.

- The next method reads a string that is delimited by white space.
- The Character class has methods for classifying characters.
- The nextLine method reads an entire line.
- If a string contains the digits of a number, you use the Integer.parseInt or Double.parseDouble method to obtain the number value.

Process the command line arguments of a program.

- Programs that start from the command line receive the command line arguments in the main method.

Use exception handling to transfer control from an error location to an error handler.

- To signal an exceptional condition, use the throw statement to throw an exception object.
- When you throw an exception, processing continues in an exception handler.
- Place the statements that can cause an exception inside a try block, and the handler inside a catch clause.

- Checked exceptions are due to external circumstances that the programmer cannot prevent. The compiler checks that your program handles these exceptions.
- Add a throws clause to a method that can throw a checked exception.

- Once a try block is entered, the statements in a finally clause are guaranteed to be executed, whether or not an exception is thrown.
- To describe an error condition, provide a subclass of an existing exception class.
- Throw an exception as soon as a problem is detected. Catch it only when the problem can be handled.

Use exception handling in a program that processes input.

- When designing a program, ask yourself what kinds of exceptions can occur.
- For each exception, you need to decide which part of your program can competently handle it.

STANDARD LIBRARY ITEMS INTRODUCED IN THIS CHAPTER

java.io.File	java.lang.NumberFormatException
java.io.FileNotFoundException	java.lang.RuntimeException
java.io.IOException	java.lang.Throwable
java.io.PrintWriter	getMessage
close	printStackTrace
java.lang.Character	java.net.URL
isDigit	openStream
isLetter	java.util.InputMismatchException
isLowerCase	java.util.NoSuchElementException
isUpperCase	java.util.Scanner
isWhiteSpace	close
java.lang.Double	hasNextLine
parseDouble	nextLine
java.lang.Error	useDelimiter
java.lang.Integer	javax.swing.JFileChooser
parseInt	getSelectedFile
java.lang.IllegalArgumentException	showOpenDialog
java.lang.NullPointerException	showSaveDialog

REVIEW QUESTIONS

■■ R11.1 What happens if you try to open a file for reading that doesn't exist? What happens if you try to open a file for writing that doesn't exist?

■■ R11.2 What happens if you try to open a file for writing, but the file or device is write-protected (sometimes called read-only)? Try it out with a short test program.

■ R11.3 How do you open a file whose name contains a backslash, like `c:temp\output.dat`?

■ R11.4 If a program Woozle is started with the command

```
java Woozle -Dname=piglet -I\eeyore -v heff.txt a.txt lump.txt
```

what are the values of `args[0]`, `args[1]`, and so on?

■ R11.5 What is the difference between throwing an exception and catching an exception?

■ R11.6 What is a checked exception? What is an unchecked exception? Give an example for each. Which exceptions do you need to declare with the `throws` reserved word?

■■ R11.7 Why don't you need to declare that your method might throw an `IndexOutOfBounds-Exception`?

■■ R11.8 When your program executes a `throw` statement, which statement is executed next?

■■ R11.9 What happens if an exception does not have a matching `catch` clause?

■■ R11.10 What can your program do with the exception object that a `catch` clause receives?

■■ R11.11 Is the type of the exception object always the same as the type declared in the `catch` clause that catches it? If not, why not?

■ R11.12 What is the purpose of the `finally` clause? Give an example of how it can be used.

■■ R11.13 What happens when an exception is thrown, the code of a `finally` clause executes, and that code throws an exception of a different kind than the original one? Which one is caught by a surrounding `catch` clause? Write a sample program to try it out.

■■ R11.14 Which exceptions can the `next` and `nextInt` methods of the `Scanner` class throw? Are they checked exceptions or unchecked exceptions?

■■ R11.15 Suppose the program in Section 11.5 reads a file containing the following values:

```
1
2
3
4
```

What is the outcome? How could the program be improved to give a more accurate error report?

■■ R11.16 Can the `readFile` method in Section 11.5 throw a `NullPointerException`? If so, how?

■■■ R11.17 Suppose the code in Programming Tip 11.3 had been condensed to a single try/catch/finally statement:

```
PrintWriter out = new PrintWriter(filename);
try
{
    Write output.
```

```
    }
    catch (IOException exception)
    {
        Handle exception.
    }
    finally
    {
        out.close();
    }
```

What is the disadvantage of this version? (*Hint:* What happens when the `PrintWriter` constructor throws an exception?) Why can't you solve the problem by moving the declaration of the out variable inside the try block?

PRACTICE EXERCISES

- **E11.1** Write a program that carries out the following tasks:

    Open a file with the name hello.txt.
    Store the message "Hello, World!" in the file.
    Close the file.
    Open the same file again.
    Read the message into a string variable and print it.

- **E11.2** Write a program that reads a file containing text. Read each line and send it to the output file, preceded by *line numbers*. If the input file is

    ```
    Mary had a little lamb
    Whose fleece was white as snow.
    And everywhere that Mary went,
    The lamb was sure to go!
    ```

    then the program produces the output file

    ```
    /* 1 */ Mary had a little lamb
    /* 2 */ Whose fleece was white as snow.
    /* 3 */ And everywhere that Mary went,
    /* 4 */ The lamb was sure to go!
    ```

    The line numbers are enclosed in /* */ delimiters so that the program can be used for numbering Java source files.
    Prompt the user for the input and output file names.

- **E11.3** Repeat Exercise E11.2, but allow the user to specify the file name on the command-line. If the user doesn't specify any file name, then prompt the user for the name.

- **E11.4** Write a program that reads a file containing two columns of floating-point numbers. Prompt the user for the file name. Print the average of each column.

- **E11.5** Write a program that asks the user for a file name and prints the number of characters, words, and lines in that file.

- **E11.6** Write a program `Find` that searches all files specified on the command line and prints out all lines containing a specified word. For example, if you call

    ```
    java Find ring report.txt address.txt Homework.java
    ```

then the program might print

```
report.txt: has broken up an international ring of DVD bootleggers that
address.txt: Kris Kringle, North Pole
address.txt: Homer Simpson, Springfield
Homework.java: String filename;
```

The specified word is always the first command line argument.

•• **E11.7** Write a program that checks the spelling of all words in a file. It should read each word of a file and check whether it is contained in a word list. A word list is available on most Linux systems in the file /usr/share/dict/words. (If you don't have access to a Linux system, your instructor should be able to get you a copy.) The program should print out all words that it cannot find in the word list.

•• **E11.8** Write a program that replaces each line of a file with its reverse. For example, if you run

```
java Reverse HelloPrinter.java
```

then the contents of HelloPrinter.java are changed to

```
retnirPolleH ssalc cilbup
{
)sgra ][gnirtS(niam diov citats cilbup
{
wodniw elosnoc eht ni gniteerg a yalpsiD //

;)"!dlroW ,olleH"(nltnirp.tuo.metsyS
}
]
```

Of course, if you run Reverse twice on the same file, you get back the original file.

•• **E11.9** Write a program that reads each line in a file, reverses its lines, and writes them to another file. For example, if the file input.txt contains the lines

```
Mary had a little lamb
Its fleece was white as snow
And everywhere that Mary went
The lamb was sure to go.
```

and you run

```
reverse input.txt output.txt
```

then output.txt contains

```
The lamb was sure to go.
And everywhere that Mary went
Its fleece was white as snow
Mary had a little lamb
```

•• **E11.10** Get the data for names in prior decades from the Social Security Administration. Paste the table data in files named babynames80s.txt, etc. Modify the worked_example_1/ BabyNames.java program so that it prompts the user for a file name. The numbers in the files have comma separators, so modify the program to handle them. Can you spot a trend in the frequencies?

•• **E11.11** Write a program that asks the user to input a set of floating-point values. When the user enters a value that is not a number, give the user a second chance to enter the value. After two chances, quit reading input. Add all correctly specified values and print the sum when the user is done entering data. Use exception handling to detect improper inputs.

- **E11.12** Modify the `BankAccount` class to throw an `IllegalArgumentException` when the account is constructed with a negative balance, when a negative amount is deposited, or when an amount that is not between 0 and the current balance is withdrawn. Write a test program that causes all three exceptions to occur and that catches them all.

- **E11.13** Repeat Exercise E11.12, but throw exceptions of three exception types that you provide.

- **E11.14** Modify the `DataSetReader` class so that you do not call `hasNextInt` or `hasNextDouble`. Simply have `nextInt` and `nextDouble` throw a `NoSuchElementException` and catch it in the `main` method.

PROGRAMMING PROJECTS

- **P11.1** Write a program that reads in `worked_example_1/babynames.txt` and produces two files, `boynames.txt` and `girlnames.txt`, separating the data for the boys and girls.

- **P11.2** Write a program that reads a file in the same format as `worked_example_1/babynames.txt` and prints all names that are both boy and girl names (such as Alexis or Morgan).

- **P11.3** Using the mechanism described in Special Topic 11.1, write a program that reads all data from a web page and writes them to a file. Prompt the user for the web page URL and the file.

- **P11.4** Using the mechanism described in Special Topic 11.1, write a program that reads all data from a web page and prints all hyperlinks of the form

    ```
    <a href="link">link text</a>
    ```

    Extra credit if your program can follow the links that it finds and find links in those web pages as well. (This is the method that search engines such as Google use to find web sites.)

- **P11.5** Write a program that reads in a set of coin descriptions from a file. The input file has the format

    ```
    coinName1 coinValue1
    coinName2 coinValue2
    . . .
    ```

    Add a method

    ```
    void read(Scanner in) throws FileNotFoundException
    ```

    to the `Coin` class of Section 8.2. Throw an exception if the current line is not properly formatted. Then implement a method

    ```
    static ArrayList<Coin> readFile(String filename) throws FileNotFoundException
    ```

    In the `main` method, call `readFile`. If an exception is thrown, give the user a chance to select another file. If you read all coins successfully, print the total value.

- **P11.6** Design a class `Bank` that contains a number of bank accounts. Each account has an account number and a current balance. Add an `accountNumber` field to the `BankAccount` class. Store the bank accounts in an array list. Write a `readFile` method of the `Bank` class for reading a file with the format

    ```
    accountNumber1  balance1
    accountNumber2  balance2
    . . .
    ```

Implement read methods for the Bank and BankAccount classes. Write a sample program to read in a file with bank accounts, then print the account with the highest balance. If the file is not properly formatted, give the user a chance to select another file.

■■ Business P11.7 A hotel salesperson enters sales in a text file. Each line contains the following, separated by semicolons: The name of the client, the service sold (such as Dinner, Conference, Lodging, and so on), the amount of the sale, and the date of that event. Write a program that reads such a file and displays the total amount for each service category. Display an error if the file does not exist or the format is incorrect.

■■ Business P11.8 Write a program that reads a text file as described in Exercise P11.7, and that writes a separate file for each service category, containing the entries for that category. Name the output files Dinner.txt, Conference.txt, and so on.

■■ Business P11.9 A store owner keeps a record of daily cash transactions in a text file. Each line contains three items: The invoice number, the cash amount, and the letter P if the amount was paid or R if it was received. Items are separated by spaces. Write a program that prompts the store owner for the amount of cash at the beginning and end of the day, and the name of the file. Your program should check whether the actual amount of cash at the end of the day equals the expected value.

■■■ Science P11.10 After the switch in the figure below closes, the voltage (in volts) across the capacitor is represented by the equation

$$v(t) = B\left(1 - e^{-t/(RC)}\right)$$

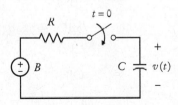

Suppose the parameters of the electric circuit are $B = 12$ volts, $R = 500\ \Omega$, and $C = 0.25\ \mu F$. Consequently

$$v(t) = 12\left(1 - e^{-0.008t}\right)$$

where t has units of μs. Read a file params.txt containing the values for B, R, C, and the starting and ending values for t. Write a file rc.txt of values for the time t and the corresponding capacitor voltage $v(t)$, where t goes from the given starting value to the given ending value in 100 steps. In our example, if t goes from 0 to 1,000 μs, the twelfth entry in the output file would be:

110   7.02261

■■■ Science P11.11 The figure at right shows a plot of the capacitor voltage from the circuit shown in Exercise P11.10. The capacitor voltage increases from 0 volts to B volts. The "rise time" is defined as the time required for the capacitor voltage to change from $v_1 = 0.05 \times B$ to $v_2 = 0.95 \times B$.

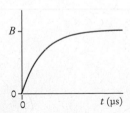

The file rc.txt contains a list of values of time t and the corresponding capacitor voltage $v(t)$. A time in µs and the corresponding voltage in volts are printed on the same line. For example, the line

    110   7.02261

indicates that the capacitor voltage is 7.02261 volts when the time is 110 µs. The time is increasing in the data file.

Write a program that reads the file rc.txt and uses the data to calculate the rise time. Approximate B by the voltage in the last line of the file, and find the data points that are closest to $0.05 \times B$ and $0.95 \times B$.

·· Science P11.12 Suppose a file contains bond energies and bond lengths for covalent bonds in the following format:

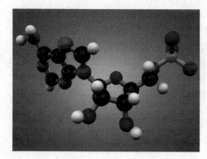

Single, double, or triple bond	Bond energy (kJ/mol)	Bond length (nm)
C|C	370	0.154
C||C	680	0.13
C|||C	890	0.12
C|H	435	0.11
C|N	305	0.15
C|O	360	0.14
C|F	450	0.14
C|Cl	340	0.18
O|H	500	0.10
O|O	220	0.15
O|Si	375	0.16
N|H	430	0.10
N|O	250	0.12
F|F	160	0.14
H|H	435	0.074

Write a program that accepts data from one column and returns the corresponding data from the other columns in the stored file. If input data matches different rows, then return all matching row data. For example, a bond length input of 0.12 should return triple bond C|||C and bond energy 890 kJ/mol *and* single bond N|O and bond energy 250 kJ/mol.

ANSWERS TO SELF-CHECK QUESTIONS

1. When the `PrintWriter` object is created, the output file is emptied. Sadly, that is the same file as the input file. The input file is now empty and the `while` loop exits immediately.

2. The program throws a `FileNotFoundException` and terminates.

3. Open a scanner for the file.
   For each number in the scanner
       Add the number to an array.
   Close the scanner.
   Set total to 0.
   Open a print writer for the file.
   For each number in the array
       Write the number to the print writer.
       Add the number to total.
   Write total to the print writer.
   Close the print writer.

4. Add a variable count that is incremented whenever a number is read. At the end, print the average, not the total, as

   ```
   out.printf("Average: %8.2f\n", total / count);
   ```

   Because the string "Average" is three characters longer than "Total", change the other output to `out.printf("%18.2f\n", value)`.

5. Add a variable count that is incremented whenever a number is read. Only write a new line when it is even.

   ```
   count++;
   out.printf("%8.2f", value);
   if (count % 2 == 0) { out.println(); }
   ```

   At the end of the loop, write a new line if count is odd, then write the total:

   ```
   if (count % 2 == 1) { out.println(); }
   out.printf("Total: %10.2f\n", total);
   ```

6. word is "Hello," and input is "World!"

7. Because 995.0 is not an integer, the call `in.hasNextInt()` returns false, and the call `in.nextInt()` is skipped. The value of number stays 0, and input is set to the string "995.0".

8. x1 is set to 6000000. Because a comma is not considered a part of a floating-point number in Java, the second call to `nextDouble` causes an input mismatch exception and x2 is not set.

9. Read them as strings, and convert those strings to numbers that are not equal to N/A:

   ```
   String input = in.next();
   if (!input.equals("N/A"))
   {
       double value = Double.parseDouble(input);
       Process value.
   }
   ```

10. Locate the last character of the country name:

    ```
    int j = i - 1;
    while (!Character.isWhiteSpace(line.charAt(j)))
    {
        j--;
    }
    ```

    Then extract the country name:

    ```
    String countryName = line.substring(0, j + 1);
    ```

11. args[0] is "-d" and args[1] is "file1.txt"

12.

key	inFile	outFile	i	arg
~~3~~	~~null~~	null	~~0~~	~~-d~~
-3	file1.txt		~~1~~	file1.txt
			2	

    Then the program prints a message

    ```
    Usage: java CaesarCipher [-d] infile outfile
    ```

13. The program will run correctly. The loop that parses the options does not depend on the positions in which the options appear.

14. FDHVDU

15. Add the lines

    ```
    else if (option == 'k')
    {
        key = Integer.parseInt(
            args[i].substring(2));
    }
    ```

    after line 27 and update the usage information.

16. It is still 100. The last statement was not executed because the exception was thrown.

17. ```
    if (amount < 0)
    {
        throw new IllegalArgumentException(
            "Negative amount");
    }
    ```

18. The Scanner constructor succeeds because the file exists. The nextInt method throws a NoSuchElementException. This is *not* an
    ```

IOException. Therefore, the error is not caught. Because there is no other handler, an error message is printed and the program terminates.

19. Because programmers should simply check that their array index values are valid instead of trying to handle an ArrayIndexOutOfBounds-Exception.

20. No. You can catch both exception types in the same way, as you can see in the code example on page 536.

21. There are two mistakes. The PrintWriter constructor can throw a FileNotFoundException. You should supply a throws clause. And if one of the array elements is null, a NullPointerException is thrown. In that case, the out.close() statement is never executed. You should use a try/finally statement.

22. To pass the exception message string to the IllegalArgumentException superclass.

23. Because file corruption is beyond the control of the programmer, this should be a checked exception, so it would be wrong to extend RuntimeException or IllegalArgumentException. Because the error is related to input, IOException would be a good choice.

24. It would not be able to do much with them. The DataSetReader class is a reusable class that may be used for systems with different languages and different user interfaces. Thus, it cannot engage in a dialog with the program user.

25. DataAnalyzer.main calls DataSetReader.readFile, which calls readData. The call in.hasNextInt() returns false, and readData throws a BadData-Exception. The readFile method doesn't catch it, so it propagates back to main, where it is caught.

26. It could simply be

```
private void readValue(Scanner in, int i)
{
    data[i] = in.nextDouble();
}
```

The nextDouble method throws a NoSuchElement-Exception or a InputMismatchException (which is a subclass of NoSuchElementException) when the next input isn't a floating-point number. That exception isn't a checked exception, so it need not be declared.

27. If it had been declared inside the try block, its scope would only have extended until the end of the try block, and it would not have been accessible in the finally clause.

28. The try/finally statement in the readFile method can be rewritten as

```
try (Scanner in = new Scanner(inFile))
{
    readData(in);
    return data;
}
```

OBJECT-ORIENTED DESIGN

CHAPTER GOALS

To learn how to discover new classes and methods

To use CRC cards for class discovery

To identify inheritance, aggregation, and dependency relationships between classes

To describe class relationships using UML class diagrams

To apply object-oriented design techniques to building complex programs

CHAPTER CONTENTS

Successfully implementing a software system—as simple as your next homework project or as complex as the next air traffic monitoring system—requires a great deal of planning and design. In fact, for larger projects, the amount of time spent on planning and design is much greater than the amount of time spent on programming and testing.

Do you find that most of your homework time is spent in front of the computer, keying in code and fixing bugs? If so, you can probably save time by focusing on a better design before you start coding. This chapter tells you how to approach the design of an object-oriented program in a systematic manner.

12.1 Classes and Their Responsibilities

When you design a program, you work from a *requirements specification*, a description of what your program should do. The designer's task is to discover structures that make it possible to implement the requirements in a computer program. In the following sections, we will examine the steps of the design process.

12.1.1 Discovering Classes

> To discover classes, look for nouns in the problem description.

When you solve a problem using objects and classes, you need to determine the classes required for the implementation. You may be able to reuse existing classes, or you may need to implement new ones.

One simple approach for discovering classes and methods is to look for the nouns and verbs in the requirements specification. Often, *nouns* correspond to classes, and *verbs* correspond to methods.

For example, suppose your job is to print an invoice such as the one in Figure 1.

INVOICE

Sam's Small Appliances
100 Main Street
Anytown, CA 98765

Item	Qty	Price	Total
Toaster	3	$29.95	$89.85
Hair Dryer	1	$24.95	$24.95
Car Vacuum	2	$19.99	$39.98

AMOUNT DUE: $154.78

Figure 1
An Invoice

Obvious classes that come to mind are `Invoice`, `LineItem`, and `Customer`. It is a good idea to keep a list of *candidate classes* on a whiteboard or a sheet of paper. As you brainstorm, simply put all ideas for classes onto the list. You can always cross out the ones that weren't useful after all.

In general, concepts from the problem domain, be it science, business, or a game, often make good classes. Examples are

Concepts from the problem domain are good candidates for classes.

- `Cannonball`
- `CashRegister`
- `Monster`

The name for such a class should be a noun that describes the concept.

Not all classes can be discovered from the program requirements. Most complex programs need classes for tactical purposes, such as file or database access, user interfaces, control mechanisms, and so on.

Some of the classes that you need may already exist, either in the standard library or in a program that you developed previously. You also may be able to use inheritance to extend existing classes into classes that match your needs.

A common error is to overdo the class discovery process. For example, should an address be an object of an `Address` class, or should it simply be a string? There is no perfect answer—it depends on the task that you want to solve. If your software needs to analyze addresses (for example, to determine shipping costs), then an `Address` class is an appropriate design. However, if your software will never need such a capability, you should not waste time on an overly complex design. It is your job to find a balanced design; one that is neither too limiting nor excessively general.

12.1.2 The CRC Card Method

Once you have identified a set of classes, you define the behavior for each class. Find out what methods you need to provide for each class in order to solve the programming problem. A simple rule for finding these methods is to look for *verbs* in the task description, then match the verbs to the appropriate objects. For example, in the invoice program, a class needs to compute the amount due. Now you need to figure out *which class* is responsible for this method. Do customers compute what they owe? Do invoices total up the amount due? Do the items total themselves up? The best choice is to make "compute amount due" the responsibility of the `Invoice` class.

In a class scheduling system, potential classes from the problem domain include Class, LectureHall, Instructor, and Student.

A CRC card
describes a class,
its responsibilities,
and its collaborating
classes.

An excellent way to carry out this task is the "**CRC card** method." *CRC* stands for "*classes*", "*responsibilities*", "*collaborators*", and in its simplest form, the method works as follows: Use an index card for each *class* (see Figure 2). As you think about verbs in the task description that indicate methods, you pick the card of the class that you think should be responsible, and write that *responsibility* on the card.

For each responsibility, you record which other classes are needed to fulfill it. Those classes are the **collaborators**.

For example, suppose you decide that an invoice should compute the amount due. Then you write "compute amount due" on the left-hand side of an index card with the title Invoice.

If a class can carry out that responsibility by itself, do nothing further. But if the class needs the help of other classes, write the names of these collaborators on the right-hand side of the card.

To compute the total, the invoice needs to ask each line item about its total price. Therefore, the LineItem class is a collaborator.

This is a good time to look up the index card for the LineItem class. Does it have a "get total price" method? If not, add one.

How do you know that you are on the right track? For each responsibility, ask yourself how it can actually be done, using the responsibilities written on the various cards. Many people find it helpful to group the cards on a table so that the collaborators are close to each other, and to simulate tasks by moving a token (such as a coin) from one card to the next to indicate which object is currently active.

Keep in mind that the responsibilities that you list on the CRC card are on a *high level*. Sometimes a single responsibility may need two or more Java methods for carrying it out. Some researchers say that a CRC card should have no more than three distinct responsibilities.

The CRC card method is informal on purpose, so that you can be creative and discover classes and their properties. Once you find that you have settled on a good set of classes, you will want to know how they are related to each other. Can you find classes with common properties, so that some responsibilities can be taken care of by a common superclass? Can you organize classes into clusters that are independent of each other? Finding class relationships and documenting them with diagrams is the topic of Section 12.2.

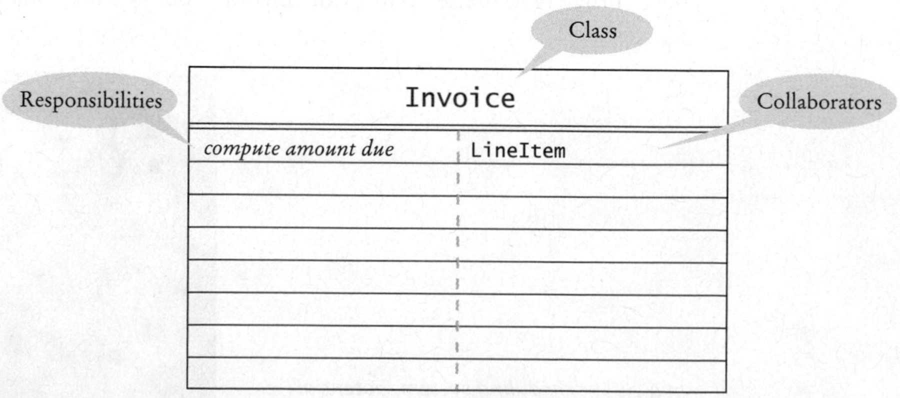

Figure 2 A CRC Card

1. What is the rule of thumb for finding classes?
2. Your job is to write a program that plays chess. Might ChessBoard be an appropriate class? How about MovePiece?
3. Suppose the invoice is to be saved to a file. Name a likely collaborator.
4. Looking at the invoice in Figure 1, what is a likely responsibility of the Customer class?
5. What do you do if a CRC card has ten responsibilities?

Practice It Now you can try these exercises at the end of the chapter: R12.4, R12.8.

12.2 Relationships Between Classes

When designing a program, it is useful to document the relationships between classes. This helps you in a number of ways. For example, if you find classes with common behavior, you can save effort by placing the common behavior into a superclass. If you know that some classes are *not* related to each other, you can assign different programmers to implement each of them, without worrying that one of them has to wait for the other.

In the following sections, we will describe the most common types of relationships.

12.2.1 Dependency

> A class depends on another class if it uses objects of that class.

Many classes need other classes in order to do their jobs. For example, in Section 8.2.2, we described a design of a CashRegister class that depends on the Coin class to determine the value of the payment.

The dependency relationship is sometimes nicknamed the "knows about" relationship. The cash register in Section 8.2.2 knows that there are coin objects. In contrast, the Coin class does *not* depend on the CashRegister class. Coins have no idea that they are being collected in cash registers, and they can carry out their work without ever calling any method in the CashRegister class.

As you saw in Section 8.2, dependency is denoted by a dashed line with a ≻-shaped open arrow tip. The arrow tip points to the class on which the other class depends. Figure 3 shows a class diagram indicating that the CashRegister class depends on the Coin class.

Too many dependencies make a system difficult to manage.

If many classes of a program depend on each other, then we say that the **coupling** between classes is high. Conversely, if there are few dependencies between classes, then we say that the coupling is low (see Figure 4).

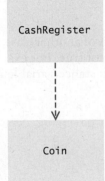

Figure 3
Dependency Relationship Between the CashRegister and Coin Classes

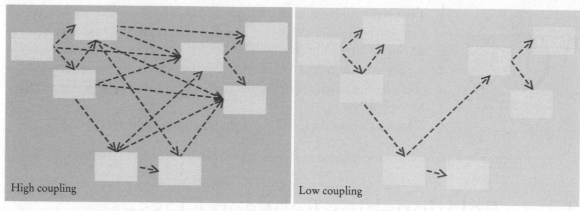

High coupling   Low coupling

Figure 4   High and Low Coupling Between Classes

It is a good practice to minimize the coupling (i.e., dependency) between classes.

Why does coupling matter? If the Coin class changes in the next release of the program, all the classes that depend on it may be affected. If the change is drastic, the coupled classes must all be updated. Furthermore, if we would like to use a class in another program, we have to take with it all the classes on which it depends. Thus, we want to remove unnecessary coupling between classes.

12.2.2 Aggregation

Another fundamental relationship between classes is the "aggregation" relationship (which is informally known as the "has-a" relationship).

A class aggregates another if its objects contain objects of the other class.

The **aggregation** relationship states that objects of one class contain objects of another class. Consider a quiz that is made up of questions. Because each quiz has one or more questions, we say that the class Quiz *aggregates* the class Question. In the UML notation, aggregation is denoted by a line with a diamond-shaped symbol attached to the aggregating class (see Figure 5).

Finding out about aggregation is very helpful for deciding how to implement classes. For example, when you implement the Quiz class, you will want to store the questions of a quiz as an instance variable.

FULL CODE EXAMPLE
Go to wiley.com/go/javacode to download the complete Quiz and Question classes.

Because a quiz can have any number of questions, an array or array list is a good choice for collecting them:

```
public class Quiz
{
    private ArrayList<Question> questions;
    . . .
}
```

Aggregation is a stronger form of dependency. If a class has objects of another class, it certainly knows about the other class. However, the converse is not true. For example, a class may use the Scanner class without ever declaring an instance variable of

Figure 5
Class Diagram
Showing Aggregation

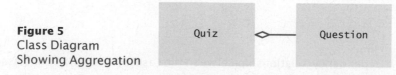

A car has a motor and tires. In object-oriented design, this "has-a" relationship is called aggregation.

class `Scanner`. The class may simply construct a local variable of type `Scanner`, or its methods may receive `Scanner` objects as arguments. This use is not aggregation because the objects of the class don't contain `Scanner` objects — they just create or receive them for the duration of a single method.

Generally, you need aggregation when an object needs to remember another object *between method calls*.

12.2.3 Inheritance

Inheritance is a relationship between a more general class (the superclass) and a more specialized class (the subclass). This relationship is often described as the "is-a" relationship. Every truck *is a* vehicle. Every savings account *is a* bank account.

Inheritance is sometimes abused. For example, consider a `Tire` class that describes a car tire. Should the class `Tire` be a subclass of a class `Circle`? It sounds convenient. There are quite a few useful methods in the `Circle` class — for example, the `Tire` class may inherit methods that compute the radius, perimeter, and center point, which should come in handy when drawing tire shapes. Though it may be convenient for the programmer, this arrangement makes no sense conceptually. It isn't true that every tire is a circle. Tires are car parts, whereas circles are geometric objects. There is a relationship between tires and circles, though. A tire *has a* circle as its boundary. Use aggregation:

> Inheritance (the *is-a* relationship) is sometimes inappropriately used when the *has-a* relationship would be more appropriate.

```
public class Tire
{
    private String rating;
    private Circle boundary;
    . . .
}
```

Here is another example: Every car *is a* vehicle. Every car *has a* tire (in fact, it typically has four or, if you count the spare, five). Thus, you would use inheritance from `Vehicle` and use aggregation of `Tire` objects (see Figure 6 for the UML diagram):

> Aggregation (the *has-a* relationship) denotes that objects of one class contain references to objects of another class.

```
public class Car extends Vehicle
{
    private Tire[] tires;
    . . .
}
```

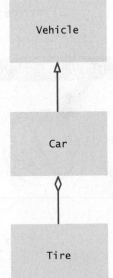

Figure 6
UML Notation for Inheritance and Aggregation

You need to be able to distinguish the UML notation for inheritance, interface implementation, aggregation, and dependency.

The arrows in the UML notation can get confusing. Table 1 shows a summary of the four UML relationship symbols that we use in this book.

Table 1 UML Relationship Symbols			
Relationship	Symbol	Line Style	Arrow Tip
Inheritance	———▷	Solid	Triangle
Interface Implementation	------▷	Dotted	Triangle
Aggregation	◇———	Solid	Diamond
Dependency	------>	Dotted	Open

SELF CHECK

6. Consider the CashRegisterTester class of Section 8.2. On which classes does it depend?

7. Consider the Question and ChoiceQuestion objects of Chapter 9. How are they related?

8. Consider the Quiz class described in Section 12.2.2. Suppose a quiz contains a mixture of Question and ChoiceQuestion objects. Which classes does the Quiz class depend on?

9. Why should coupling be minimized between classes?

10. In an e-mail system, messages are stored in a mailbox. Draw a UML diagram that shows the appropriate aggregation relationship.

11. You are implementing a system to manage a library, keeping track of which books are checked out by whom. Should the Book class aggregate Patron or the other way around?

12. In a library management system, what would be the relationship between classes Patron and Author?

Practice It Now you can try these exercises at the end of the chapter: R12.5, R12.6, R12.10.

HOW TO 12.1

Using CRC Cards and UML Diagrams in Program Design

Before writing code for a complex problem, you need to design a solution. The methodology introduced in this chapter suggests that you follow a design process that is composed of the following tasks:

- Discover classes.
- Determine the responsibilities of each class.
- Describe the relationships between the classes.

CRC cards and UML diagrams help you discover and record this information.

Step 1 Discover classes.

Highlight the nouns in the problem description. Make a list of the nouns. Cross out those that don't seem to be reasonable candidates for classes.

Step 2   Discover responsibilities.

Make a list of the major tasks that your system needs to fulfill. From those tasks, pick one that is not trivial and that is intuitive to you. Find a class that is responsible for carrying out that task. Make an index card and write the name and the task on it. Now ask yourself how an object of the class can carry out the task. It probably needs help from other objects. Then make CRC cards for the classes to which those objects belong and write the responsibilities on them.

Don't be afraid to cross out, move, split, or merge responsibilities. Rip up cards if they become too messy. This is an informal process.

You are done when you have walked through all major tasks and are satisfied that they can all be solved with the classes and responsibilities that you discovered.

Step 3   Describe relationships.

Make a class diagram that shows the relationships between all the classes that you discovered.

Start with inheritance—the *is-a* relationship between classes. Is any class a specialization of another? If so, draw inheritance arrows. Keep in mind that many designs, especially for simple programs, don't use inheritance extensively.

The "collaborators" column of the CRC card tells you which classes are used by that class. Draw dependency arrows for the collaborators on the CRC cards.

Some dependency relationships give rise to aggregations. For each of the dependency relationships, ask yourself: How does the object locate its collaborator? Does it navigate to it directly because it stores a reference? In that case, draw an aggregation arrow. Or is the collaborator a method parameter variable or return value? Then simply draw a dependency arrow.

Special Topic 12.1

Attributes and Methods in UML Diagrams

Sometimes it is useful to indicate class *attributes* and *methods* in a class diagram. An **attribute** is an externally observable property that objects of a class have. For example, name and price would be attributes of the Product class. Usually, attributes correspond to instance variables. But they don't have to—a class may have a different way of organizing its data. For example, a GregorianCalendar object from the Java library has attributes day, month, and year, and it would be appropriate to draw a UML diagram that shows these attributes. However, the class doesn't actually have instance variables that store these quantities. Instead, it internally represents all dates by counting the milliseconds from January 1, 1970—an implementation detail that a class user certainly doesn't need to know about.

You can indicate attributes and methods in a class diagram by dividing a class rectangle into three compartments, with the class name in the top, attributes in the middle, and methods in the bottom (see the figure below). You need not list *all* attributes and methods in a particular diagram. Just list the ones that are helpful for understanding whatever point you are making with a particular diagram.

Also, don't list as an attribute what you also draw as an aggregation. If you denote by aggregation the fact that a Car has Tire objects, don't add an attribute tires.

Attributes and Methods in a Class Diagram

BankAccount	Attributes
balance	
deposit() withdraw()	Methods

Special Topic 12.2

Multiplicities

Some designers like to write *multiplicities* at the end(s) of an aggregation relationship to denote how many objects are aggregated. The notations for the most common multiplicities are:

- any number (zero or more): *
- one or more: 1..*
- zero or one: 0..1
- exactly one: 1

The figure below shows that a customer has one or more bank accounts.

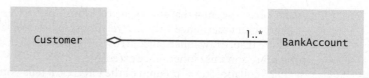

An Aggregation Relationship with Multiplicities

Special Topic 12.3

Aggregation, Association, and Composition

Some designers find the aggregation or *has-a* terminology unsatisfactory. For example, consider customers of a bank. Does the bank "have" customers? Do the customers "have" bank accounts, or does the bank "have" them? Which of these "has" relationships should be modeled by aggregation? This line of thinking can lead us to premature implementation decisions.

Early in the design phase, it makes sense to use a more general relationship between classes called **association**. A class is associated with another if you can *navigate* from objects of one class to objects of the other class. For example, given a Bank object, you can navigate to Customer objects, perhaps by accessing an instance variable, or by making a database lookup.

The UML notation for an association relationship is a solid line, with optional arrows that show in which directions you can navigate the relationship. You can also add words to the line ends to further explain the nature of the relationship. The figure below shows that you can navigate from Bank objects to Customer objects, but you cannot navigate the other way around. That is, in this particular design, the Customer class has no mechanism to determine in which banks it keeps its money.

An Association Relationship

The UML standard also recognizes a stronger form of the aggregation relationship called **composition**, where the aggregated objects do not have an existence independent of the containing object. For example, composition models the relationship between a bank and its accounts. If a bank closes, the account objects cease to exist as well. In the UML notation, composition looks like aggregation with a filled-in diamond.

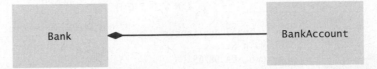

A Composition Relationship

Frankly, the differences between aggregation, association, and composition can be confusing, even to experienced designers. If you find the distinction helpful, by all means use the relationship that you find most appropriate. But don't spend time pondering subtle differences between these concepts. From the practical point of view of a Java programmer, it is useful to know when objects of one class have references to objects of another class. The aggregation or *has-a* relationship accurately describes this phenomenon.

12.3 Application: Printing an Invoice

In this book, we discuss a five-part program development process that is particularly well suited for beginning programmers:

1. Gather requirements.
2. Use CRC cards to find classes, responsibilities, and collaborators.
3. Use UML diagrams to record class relationships.
4. Use javadoc to document method behavior.
5. Implement your program.

There isn't a lot of notation to learn. The class diagrams are simple to draw. The deliverables of the design phase are obviously useful for the implementation phase—you simply take the source files and start adding the method code. Of course, as your projects get more complex, you will want to learn more about formal design methods. There are many techniques to describe object scenarios, call sequencing, the large-scale structure of programs, and so on, that are very beneficial even for relatively simple projects. *The Unified Modeling Language User Guide* gives a good overview of these techniques.

In this section, we will walk through the object-oriented design technique with a very simple example. In this case, the methodology may feel overblown, but it is a good introduction to the mechanics of each step. You will then be better prepared for the more complex programs that you will encounter in the future.

12.3.1 Requirements

Start the development process by gathering and documenting program requirements.

Before you begin designing a solution, you should gather all requirements for your program in plain English. Write down what your program should do. It is helpful to include typical scenarios in addition to a general description.

The task of our sample program is to print out an invoice. An invoice describes the charges for a set of products in certain quantities. (We omit complexities such as dates, taxes, and invoice and customer numbers.) The program simply prints the billing address, all line items, and the amount due. Each line item contains the description and unit price of a product, the quantity ordered, and the total price.

An invoice lists the charges for each item and the amount due.

```
             I N V O I C E

Sam's Small Appliances
100 Main Street
Anytown, CA 98765

Description                  Price  Qty  Total
Toaster                      29.95   3   89.85
Hair dryer                   24.95   1   24.95
Car vacuum                   19.99   2   39.98

AMOUNT DUE: $154.78
```

Also, in the interest of simplicity, we do not provide a user interface. We just supply a test program that adds line items to the invoice and then prints it.

12.3.2 CRC Cards

Use CRC cards to find classes, responsibilities, and collaborators.

When designing an object-oriented program, you need to discover classes. Classes correspond to nouns in the requirements specification. In this problem, it is pretty obvious what the nouns are:

```
Invoice        Address      LineItem      Product
Description    Price        Quantity      Total
                                                     Amount due
```

(Of course, Toaster doesn't count—it is the description of a LineItem object and therefore a data value, not the name of a class.)

Description and price are attributes of the Product class. What about the quantity? The quantity is not an attribute of a Product. Just as in the printed invoice, let's have a class LineItem that records the product and the quantity (such as "3 toasters").

The total and amount due are computed—not stored anywhere. Thus, they don't lead to classes.

After this process of elimination, we are left with four candidates for classes:

```
Invoice    Address    LineItem    Product
```

Each of them represents a useful concept, so let's make them all into classes.

The purpose of the program is to print an invoice. However, the Invoice class won't necessarily know whether to display the output in System.out, in a text area, or in a file. Therefore, let's relax the task slightly and make the invoice responsible for *formatting* the invoice. The result is a string (containing multiple lines) that can be printed out or displayed. Record that responsibility on a CRC card:

Invoice
format the invoice

How does an invoice format itself? It must format the billing address, format all line items, and then add the amount due. How can the invoice format an address? It can't—that really is the responsibility of the Address class. This leads to a second CRC card:

Address	
format the address	

Similarly, formatting of a line item is the responsibility of the LineItem class.

The format method of the Invoice class calls the format methods of the Address and LineItem classes. Whenever a method uses another class, you list that other class as a collaborator. In other words, Address and LineItem are collaborators of Invoice:

Invoice	
format the invoice	Address
	LineItem

When formatting the invoice, the invoice also needs to compute the total amount due. To obtain that amount, it must ask each line item about the total price of the item.

How does a line item obtain that total? It must ask the product for the unit price, and then multiply it by the quantity. That is, the Product class must reveal the unit price, and it is a collaborator of the LineItem class.

Product	
get description	
get unit price	

LineItem	
format the item	Product
get total price	

Finally, the invoice must be populated with products and quantities, so that it makes sense to format the result. That too is a responsibility of the Invoice class.

Invoice	
format the invoice	Address
add a product and quantity	LineItem
	Product

We now have a set of CRC cards that completes the CRC card process.

12.3.3 UML Diagrams

Use UML diagrams to record class relationships.

After you have discovered classes and their relationships with CRC cards, you should record your findings in a UML diagram. The dependency relationships come from the collaboration column on the CRC cards. Each class depends on the classes with which it collaborates. In our example, the Invoice class collaborates with the Address, LineItem, and Product classes. The LineItem class collaborates with the Product class.

Now ask yourself which of these dependencies are actually aggregations. How does an invoice know about the address, line item, and product objects with which it collaborates? An invoice object must hold references to the address and the line items when it formats the invoice. But an invoice object need not hold a reference to a product object when adding a product. The product is turned into a line item, and then it is the item's responsibility to hold a reference to it.

Therefore, the Invoice class aggregates the Address and LineItem classes. The LineItem class aggregates the Product class. However, there is no *has-a* relationship between an invoice and a product. An invoice doesn't store products directly—they are stored in the LineItem objects.

There is no inheritance in this example.

Figure 7 shows the class relationships that we discovered.

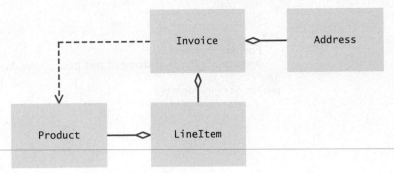

Figure 7 The Relationships Between the Invoice Classes

12.3.4 Method Documentation

Use javadoc comments (with the method bodies left blank) to record the behavior of classes.

The final step of the design phase is to write the documentation of the discovered classes and methods. Simply write a Java source file for each class, write the method comments for those methods that you have discovered, and leave the bodies of the methods blank.

```java
/**
    Describes an invoice for a set of purchased products.
*/
public class Invoice
{
    /**
        Adds a charge for a product to this invoice.
        @param aProduct the product that the customer ordered
        @param quantity the quantity of the product
    */
    public void add(Product aProduct, int quantity)
    {
    }

    /**
        Formats the invoice.
        @return the formatted invoice
    */
    public String format()
    {
    }
}


/**
    Describes a quantity of an article to purchase.
*/
public class LineItem
{
    /**
        Computes the total cost of this line item.
        @return the total price
    */
    public double getTotalPrice()
    {
```

```
      }

      /**
         Formats this item.
         @return a formatted string of this item
      */
      public String format()
      {
      }
}


/**
   Describes a product with a description and a price.
*/
public class Product
{
   /**
      Gets the product description.
      @return the description
   */
   public String getDescription()
   {
   }

   /**
      Gets the product price.
      @return the unit price
   */
   public double getPrice()
   {
   }
}


/**
   Describes a mailing address.
*/
public class Address
{
   /**
      Formats the address.
      @return the address as a string with three lines
   */
   public String format()
   {
   }
}
```

Then run the javadoc program to obtain a neatly formatted version of your documentation in HTML format (see Figure 8).

This approach for documenting your classes has a number of advantages. You can share the HTML documentation with others if you work in a team. You use a format that is immediately useful—Java source files that you can carry into the implementation phase. And, most importantly, you supply the comments for the key methods—a task that less prepared programmers leave for later, and often neglect for lack of time.

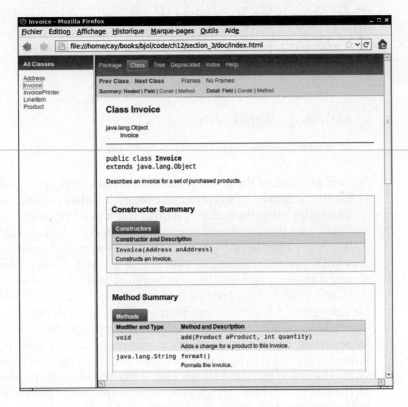

Figure 8
Class Documentation
in HTML Format

12.3.5 Implementation

After completing the
design, implement
your classes.

After you have completed the object-oriented design, you are ready to implement the classes.

You already have the method parameter variables and comments from the previous step. Now look at the UML diagram to add instance variables. Aggregated classes yield instance variables. Start with the Invoice class. An invoice aggregates Address and LineItem. Every invoice has one billing address, but it can have many line items. To store multiple LineItem objects, you can use an array list. Now you have the instance variables of the Invoice class:

```
public class Invoice
{
    private Address billingAddress;
    private ArrayList<LineItem> items;
    . . .
}
```

A line item needs to store a Product object and the product quantity. That leads to the following instance variables:

```
public class LineItem
{
    private int quantity;
    private Product theProduct;
    . . .
}
```

The methods themselves are now easy to implement. Here is a typical example. You already know what the getTotalPrice method of the LineItem class needs to do—get the unit price of the product and multiply it with the quantity.

```
/**
    Computes the total cost of this line item.
    @return the total price
*/
public double getTotalPrice()
{
    return theProduct.getPrice() * quantity;
}
```

We will not discuss the other methods in detail—they are equally straightforward.

Finally, you need to supply constructors, another routine task.

The entire program is shown below. It is a good practice to go through it in detail and match up the classes and methods to the CRC cards and UML diagram.

Worked Example 12.1 (at wiley.com/go/javaexamples) demonstrates the design process with a more challenging problem, a simulated automatic teller machine. You should download and study that example as well.

In this chapter, you learned a systematic approach for building a relatively complex program. However, object-oriented design is definitely not a spectator sport. To really learn how to design and implement programs, you have to gain experience by repeating this process with your own projects. It is quite possible that you don't immediately home in on a good solution and that you need to go back and reorganize your classes and responsibilities. That is normal and only to be expected. The purpose of the object-oriented design process is to spot these problems in the design phase, when they are still easy to rectify, instead of in the implementation phase, when massive reorganization is more difficult and time consuming.

section_3/InvoicePrinter.java

```
1   /**
2       This program demonstrates the invoice classes by
3       printing a sample invoice.
4   */
5   public class InvoicePrinter
6   {
7       public static void main(String[] args)
8       {
9           Address samsAddress
10              = new Address("Sam's Small Appliances",
11              "100 Main Street", "Anytown", "CA", "98765");
12
13          Invoice samsInvoice = new Invoice(samsAddress);
14          samsInvoice.add(new Product("Toaster", 29.95), 3);
15          samsInvoice.add(new Product("Hair dryer", 24.95), 1);
16          samsInvoice.add(new Product("Car vacuum", 19.99), 2);
17
18          System.out.println(samsInvoice.format());
19      }
20  }
```

section_3/Invoice.java

```
1   import java.util.ArrayList;
2
```

```java
 3   /**
 4       Describes an invoice for a set of purchased products.
 5   */
 6   public class Invoice
 7   {
 8      private Address billingAddress;
 9      private ArrayList<LineItem> items;
10
11      /**
12          Constructs an invoice.
13          @param anAddress the billing address
14      */
15      public Invoice(Address anAddress)
16      {
17         items = new ArrayList<LineItem>();
18         billingAddress = anAddress;
19      }
20
21      /**
22          Adds a charge for a product to this invoice.
23          @param aProduct the product that the customer ordered
24          @param quantity the quantity of the product
25      */
26      public void add(Product aProduct, int quantity)
27      {
28         LineItem anItem = new LineItem(aProduct, quantity);
29         items.add(anItem);
30      }
31
32      /**
33          Formats the invoice.
34          @return the formatted invoice
35      */
36      public String format()
37      {
38         String r = "                       I N V O I C E\n\n"
39             + billingAddress.format()
40             + String.format("\n\n%-30s%8s%5s%8s\n",
41             "Description", "Price", "Qty", "Total");
42
43         for (LineItem item : items)
44         {
45            r = r + item.format() + "\n";
46         }
47
48         r = r + String.format("\nAMOUNT DUE: $%8.2f", getAmountDue());
49
50         return r;
51      }
52
53      /**
54          Computes the total amount due.
55          @return the amount due
56      */
57      private double getAmountDue()
58      {
59         double amountDue = 0;
60         for (LineItem item : items)
61         {
62            amountDue = amountDue + item.getTotalPrice();
```

```
63         }
64         return amountDue;
65      }
66   }
```

section_3/LineItem.java

```
1    /**
2        Describes a quantity of an article to purchase.
3    */
4    public class LineItem
5    {
6       private int quantity;
7       private Product theProduct;
8
9       /**
10          Constructs an item from the product and quantity.
11          @param aProduct the product
12          @param aQuantity the item quantity
13       */
14       public LineItem(Product aProduct, int aQuantity)
15       {
16          theProduct = aProduct;
17          quantity = aQuantity;
18       }
19
20       /**
21          Computes the total cost of this line item.
22          @return the total price
23       */
24       public double getTotalPrice()
25       {
26          return theProduct.getPrice() * quantity;
27       }
28
29       /**
30          Formats this item.
31          @return a formatted string of this line item
32       */
33       public String format()
34       {
35          return String.format("%-30s%8.2f%5d%8.2f",
36             theProduct.getDescription(), theProduct.getPrice(),
37             quantity, getTotalPrice());
38       }
39   }
```

section_3/Product.java

```
1    /**
2        Describes a product with a description and a price.
3    */
4    public class Product
5    {
6       private String description;
7       private double price;
8
9       /**
10          Constructs a product from a description and a price.
11          @param aDescription the product description
```

```
12          @param aPrice  the product price
13       */
14       public Product(String aDescription, double aPrice)
15       {
16          description = aDescription;
17          price = aPrice;
18       }
19
20       /**
21          Gets the product description.
22          @return  the description
23       */
24       public String getDescription()
25       {
26          return description;
27       }
28
29       /**
30          Gets the product price.
31          @return  the unit price
32       */
33       public double getPrice()
34       {
35          return price;
36       }
37    }
```

section_3/Address.java

```
 1    /**
 2       Describes a mailing address.
 3    */
 4    public class Address
 5    {
 6       private String name;
 7       private String street;
 8       private String city;
 9       private String state;
10       private String zip;
11
12       /**
13          Constructs a mailing address.
14          @param aName  the recipient name
15          @param aStreet  the street
16          @param aCity  the city
17          @param aState  the two-letter state code
18          @param aZip  the ZIP postal code
19       */
20       public Address(String aName, String aStreet,
21             String aCity, String aState, String aZip)
22       {
23          name = aName;
24          street = aStreet;
25          city = aCity;
26          state = aState;
27          zip = aZip;
28       }
29
30       /**
31          Formats the address.
```

```
32          @return the address as a string with three lines
33      */
34      public String format()
35      {
36          return name + "\n" + street + "\n"
37              + city + ", " + state + " " + zip;
38      }
39  }
```

13. Which class is responsible for computing the amount due? What are its collaborators for this task?

14. Why do the `format` methods return `String` objects instead of directly printing to `System.out`?

Practice It   Now you can try these exercises at the end of the chapter: R12.15, E12.4, E12.5.

Computing & Society 12.1 Databases and Privacy

Most companies use computers to keep huge databases of customer records and other business information. Databases not only lower the cost of doing business, they improve the quality of service that companies can offer. Nowadays it is almost unimaginable how time-consuming it used to be to withdraw money from a bank branch or to make travel reservations.

As these databases became ubiquitous, they started creating problems for citizens. Consider the "no fly list" maintained by the U.S. government, which lists names used by suspected terrorists. On March 1, 2007, Professor Walter Murphy, a constitutional scholar of Princeton University and a decorated former Marine, was denied a boarding pass. The airline employee asked him, "Have you been in any peace marches? We ban a lot of people from flying because of that." As Murphy tells it, "I explained that I had not so marched but had, in September 2006, given a lecture at Princeton, televised and put on the Web, highly critical of George Bush for his many violations of the constitution. 'That'll do it,' the man said."

We do not actually know if Professor Murphy's name was on the list because he was critical of the Bush administration or because some other potentially dangerous person had traveled under the same name. Travelers with similar misfortunes had serious difficulties trying to get themselves off the list.

Problems such as these have become commonplace. Companies and the government routinely merge multiple databases, derive information about us that may be quite inaccurate, and then use that information to make decisions. An insurance company may deny coverage, or charge a higher premium, if it finds that you have too many relatives with a certain disease. You may be denied a job because of a credit or medical report. You do not usually know what information about you is stored or how it is used. In cases where the information can be checked—such as credit reports—it is often difficult to correct errors.

Another issue of concern is privacy. Most people do something, at one time or another in their lives, that they do not want everyone to know about. As judge Louis Brandeis wrote in 1928, "Privacy is the right to be alone—the most comprehensive of rights, and the right most valued by civilized man." When employers can see your old Facebook posts, divorce lawyers have access to tollroad records, and Google mines your e-mails and searches to present you "targeted" advertising, you have little privacy left.

The 1948 "universal declaration of human rights" by the United Nations states, "No one shall be subjected to arbitrary interference with his privacy, family, home or correspondence, nor to attacks upon his honour and reputation. Everyone has the right to the protection of the law against such interference or attacks." The United States has surprisingly few legal protections against privacy invasion, apart from federal laws protecting student records and video rentals (the latter was passed after a Supreme Court nominee's video rental records were published). Other industrialized countries have gone much further and recognize every citizen's right to control what information about them should be communicated to others and under what circumstances.

If you pay road or bridge tolls with an electronic pass, your records may not be private.

 WORKED EXAMPLE 12.1   **Simulating an Automatic Teller Machine**

Learn to apply the object-oriented design methodology to the simulation of an automatic teller machine that works with both a console-based and graphical user interface. Go to wiley.com/go/javaexamples and download Worked Example 12.1.

CHAPTER SUMMARY

Recognize how to discover classes and their responsibilities.

- To discover classes, look for nouns in the problem description.
- Concepts from the problem domain are good candidates for classes.
- A CRC card describes a class, its responsibilities, and its collaborating classes.

Categorize class relationships and produce UML diagrams that describe them.

- A class depends on another class if it uses objects of that class.
- It is a good practice to minimize the coupling (i.e., dependency) between classes.
- A class aggregates another if its objects contain objects of the other class.
- Inheritance (the *is-a* relationship) is sometimes inappropriately used when the *has-a* relationship would be more appropriate.

- Aggregation (the *has-a* relationship) denotes that objects of one class contain references to objects of another class.
- You need to be able to distinguish the UML notation for inheritance, interface implementation, aggregation, and dependency.

Apply an object-oriented development process to designing a program.

- Start the development process by gathering and documenting program requirements.
- Use CRC cards to find classes, responsibilities, and collaborators.
- Use UML diagrams to record class relationships.
- Use javadoc comments (with the method bodies left blank) to record the behavior of classes.
- After completing the design, implement your classes.

REVIEW QUESTIONS

■■ **R12.1** List the steps in the process of object-oriented design that this chapter recommends for student use.

■ **R12.2** Give a rule of thumb for how to find classes when designing a program.

■ **R12.3** Give a rule of thumb for how to find methods when designing a program.

■■ **R12.4** After discovering a method, why is it important to identify the object that is *responsible* for carrying out the action?

■■ **R12.5** What relationship is appropriate between the following classes: aggregation, inheritance, or neither?

    a. University–Student   **e.** Car–Door

    b. Student–TeachingAssistant   **f.** Truck–Vehicle

    c. Student–Freshman   **g.** Traffic–TrafficSign

    d. Student–Professor   **h.** TrafficSign–Color

■■ **R12.6** Every BMW is a vehicle. Should a class BMW inherit from the class Vehicle? BMW is a vehicle manufacturer. Does that mean that the class BMW should inherit from the class VehicleManufacturer?

■■ **R12.7** Some books on object-oriented programming recommend using inheritance so that the class Circle extends the class java.awt.Point. Then the Circle class inherits the setLocation method from the Point superclass. Explain why the setLocation method need not be overridden in the subclass. Why is it nevertheless not a good idea to have Circle inherit from Point? Conversely, would inheriting Point from Circle fulfill the *is-a* rule? Would it be a good idea?

■ **R12.8** Write CRC cards for the Coin and CashRegister classes described in Section 8.2.

■ **R12.9** Write CRC cards for the Quiz and Question classes in Section 12.2.2.

■■ **R12.10** Draw a UML diagram for the Quiz, Question, and ChoiceQuestion classes. The Quiz class is described in Section 12.2.2.

■■■ **R12.11** A file contains a set of records describing countries. Each record consists of the name of the country, its population, and its area. Suppose your task is to write a program that reads in such a file and prints

- The country with the largest area
- The country with the largest population
- The country with the largest population density (people per square kilometer)

Think through the problems that you need to solve. What classes and methods will you need? Produce a set of CRC cards, a UML diagram, and a set of javadoc comments.

■■■ **R12.12** Discover classes and methods for generating a student report card that lists all classes, grades, and the grade point average for a semester. Produce a set of CRC cards, a UML diagram, and a set of javadoc comments.

■■ **R12.13** Consider the following problem description:

> Users place coins in a vending machine and select a product by pushing a button. If the inserted coins are sufficient to cover the purchase price of the product, the product is dispensed and change is given. Otherwise, the inserted coins are returned to the user.

What classes should you use to implement a solution?

■■ **R12.14** Consider the following problem description:

> Employees receive their biweekly paychecks. They are paid their hourly rates for each hour worked; however, if they worked more than 40 hours per week, they are paid overtime at 150 percent of their regular wage.

What classes should you use to implement a solution?

■■ **R12.15** Consider the following problem description:

Customers order products from a store. Invoices are generated to list the items and quantities ordered, payments received, and amounts still due. Products are shipped to the shipping address of the customer, and invoices are sent to the billing address.

Draw a UML diagram showing the aggregation relationships between the classes Invoice, Address, Customer, and Product.

PRACTICE EXERCISES

■ **E12.1** Enhance the invoice-printing program by providing for two kinds of line items: One kind describes products that are purchased in certain numerical quantities (such as "3 toasters"), another describes a fixed charge (such as "shipping: $5.00"). *Hint:* Use inheritance. Produce a UML diagram of your modified implementation.

■■ **E12.2** The invoice-printing program is somewhat unrealistic because the formatting of the LineItem objects won't lead to good visual results when the prices and quantities have varying numbers of digits. Enhance the format method in two ways: Accept an int[] array of column widths as an argument. Use the NumberFormat class to format the currency values.

■■ **E12.3** The invoice-printing program has an unfortunate flaw—it mixes "application logic" (the computation of total charges) and "presentation" (the visual appearance of the invoice). To appreciate this flaw, imagine the changes that would be necessary to draw the invoice in HTML for presentation on the Web. Reimplement the program, using a separate InvoiceFormatter class to format the invoice. That is, the Invoice and LineItem methods are no longer responsible for formatting. However, they will acquire other responsibilities, because the InvoiceFormatter class needs to query them for the values that it requires.

■■■ **E12.4** Write a program that teaches arithmetic to a young child. The program tests addition and subtraction. In level 1, it tests only addition of numbers less than 10 whose sum is less than 10. In level 2, it tests addition of arbitrary one-digit numbers. In level 3, it tests subtraction of one-digit numbers with a nonnegative difference.

Generate random problems and get the player's input. The player gets up to two tries per problem. Advance from one level to the next when the player has achieved a score of five points.

■■■ **E12.5** Implement a simple e-mail messaging system. A message has a recipient, a sender, and a message text. A mailbox can store messages. Supply a number of mailboxes for different users and a user interface for users to log in, send messages to other users, read their own messages, and log out. Follow the design process that was described in this chapter.

■■ **E12.6** Modify the implementation of the classes in the ATM simulation in Worked Example 12.1 so that the bank manages a collection of bank accounts and a separate collection of customers. Allow joint accounts in which some accounts can have more than one customer.

PROGRAMMING PROJECTS

■■ P12.1   Write a program that simulates a vending machine. Products can be purchased by inserting coins with a value at least equal to the cost of the product. A user selects a product from a list of available products, adds coins, and either gets the product or gets the coins returned. The coins are returned if insufficient money was supplied or if the product is sold out. The machine does not give change if too much money was added. Products can be restocked and money removed by an operator. Follow the design process that was described in this chapter. Your solution should include a class VendingMachine that is not coupled with the Scanner or PrintStream classes.

■■■ P12.2   Write a program to design an appointment calendar. An appointment includes the date, starting time, ending time, and a description; for example,

```
Dentist 2012/10/1 17:30 18:30
CS1 class 2012/10/2 08:30 10:00
```

Supply a user interface to add appointments, remove canceled appointments, and print out a list of appointments for a particular day. Follow the design process that was described in this chapter. Your solution should include a class Appointment-Calendar that is not coupled with the Scanner or PrintStream classes.

■■■ P12.3   Write a program that administers and grades quizzes. A quiz consists of questions. There are four types of questions: text questions, number questions, choice questions with a single answer, and choice questions with multiple answers. When grading a text question, ignore leading or trailing spaces and letter case. When grading a numeric question, accept a response that is approximately the same as the answer.

A quiz is specified in a text file. Each question starts with a letter indicating the question type (T, N, S, M), followed by a line containing the question text. The next line of a non-choice question contains the answer. Choice questions have a list of choices that is terminated by a blank line. Each choice starts with + (correct) or - (incorrect). Here is a sample file:

```
T
Which Java reserved word is used to declare a subclass?
extends
S
What is the original name of the Java language?
- *7
- C--
+ Oak
- Gosling

M
Which of the following types are supertypes of Rectangle?
- PrintStream
+ Shape
+ RectangularShape
+ Object
- String

N
What is the square root of 2?
1.41421356
```

Your program should read in a quiz file, prompt the user for responses to all questions, and grade the responses. Follow the design process described in this chapter.

•• P12.4 Produce a requirements document for a program that allows a company to send out personalized mailings, either by e-mail or through the postal service. Template files contain the message text, together with variable fields (such as Dear [Title] [Last Name]...). A database (stored as a text file) contains the field values for each recipient. Use HTML as the output file format. Then design and implement the program.

••• P12.5 Write a tic-tac-toe game that allows a human player to play against the computer. Your program will play many turns against a human opponent, and it will learn. When it is the computer's turn, the computer randomly selects an empty field, except that it won't ever choose a losing combination. For that purpose, your program must keep an array of losing combinations. Whenever the human wins, the immediately preceding combination is stored as losing. For example, suppose that X = computer and O = human.

Suppose the current combination is

```
 O | X | X
---+---+---
   | O |
---+---+---
   |   |
```

Now it is the human's turn, who will of course choose

```
 O | X | X
---+---+---
   | O |
---+---+---
   |   | O
```

The computer should then remember the preceding combination

```
 O | X | X
---+---+---
   | O |
---+---+---
   |   |
```

as a losing combination. As a result, the computer will never again choose that combination from

```
 O | X              or          O |   | X
---+---+---                     ---+---+---
   | O |                           | O |
---+---+---                     ---+---+---
   |   |                           |   |
```

Discover classes and supply a UML diagram before you begin to program.

••• Business P12.6 *Airline seating.* Write a program that assigns seats on an airplane. Assume the airplane has 20 seats in first class (5 rows of 4 seats each, separated by an aisle) and 90 seats in economy class (15 rows of 6 seats each, separated by an aisle). Your program should take three commands: add passengers, show seating, and quit. When passengers are added, ask for the class (first or economy), the number of passengers traveling together (1 or 2 in first class; 1 to 3 in economy), and the seating preference (aisle or window in first class; aisle, center, or window in economy). Then try to find a match and assign the seats. If no match exists, print a message. Your solution should include a class `Airplane` that is not coupled with the `Scanner` or `PrintStream` classes. Follow the design process that was described in this chapter.

••• Business P12.7 In an airplane, each passenger has a touch screen for ordering a drink and a snack. Some items are free and some are not. The system prepares two reports for speeding up service:

1. A list of all seats, ordered by row, showing the charges that must be collected.

2. A list of how many drinks and snacks of each type must be prepared for the front and the rear of the plane.

Follow the design process that was described in this chapter to identify classes, and implement a program that simulates the system.

■■■ Graphics P12.8 Implement a program to teach a young child to read the clock. In the game, present an analog clock, such as the one shown at left. Generate random times and display the clock. Accept guesses from the player. Reward the player for correct guesses. After two incorrect guesses, display the correct answer and make a new random time. Implement several levels of play. In level 1, only show full hours. In level 2, show quarter hours. In level 3, show five-minute multiples, and in level 4, show any number of minutes. After a player has achieved five correct guesses at one level, advance to the next level.

An Analog Clock

■■■ Graphics P12.9 Write a program that can be used to design a suburban scene, with houses, streets, and cars. Users can add houses and cars of various colors to a street. Write more specific requirements that include a detailed description of the user interface. Then, discover classes and methods, provide UML diagrams, and implement your program.

■■■ Graphics P12.10 Write a simple graphics editor that allows users to add a mixture of shapes (ellipses, rectangles, and lines in different colors) to a panel. Supply commands to load and save the picture. Discover classes, supply a UML diagram, and implement your program.

ANSWERS TO SELF-CHECK QUESTIONS

1. Look for nouns in the problem description.
2. Yes (ChessBoard) and no (MovePiece).
3. PrintStream.
4. To produce the shipping address of the customer.
5. Reword the responsibilities so that they are at a higher level, or come up with more classes to handle the responsibilities.
6. The CashRegisterTester class depends on the CashRegister, Coin, and System classes.
7. The ChoiceQuestion class inherits from the Question class.
8. The Quiz class depends on the Question class but probably not ChoiceQuestion, if we assume that the methods of the Quiz class manipulate generic Question objects, as they did in Chapter 9.
9. If a class doesn't depend on another, it is not affected by interface changes in the other class.
10.

11. Typically, a library system wants to track which books a patron has checked out, so it makes more sense to have Patron aggregate Book. However, there is not always one true answer in design. If you feel strongly that it is important to identify the patron who checked out a particular book (perhaps to notify the patron to return it because it was requested by someone else), then you can argue that the aggregation should go the other way around.
12. There would be no relationship.
13. The Invoice class is responsible for computing the amount due. It collaborates with the LineItem class.
14. This design decision reduces coupling. It enables us to reuse the classes when we want to show the invoice in a dialog box or on a web page.

THE BASIC LATIN AND LATIN-1 SUBSETS OF UNICODE

This appendix lists the Unicode characters that are most commonly used for processing Western European languages. A complete listing of Unicode characters can be found at http://unicode.org.

Table 1 Selected Control Characters			
Character	Code	Decimal	Escape Sequence
Tab	'\u0009'	9	'\t'
Newline	'\u000A'	10	'\n'
Return	'\u000D'	13	'\r'
Space	'\u0020'	32	

Table 2 The Basic Latin (ASCII) Subset of Unicode

Char.	Code	Dec.	Char.	Code	Dec.	Char.	Code	Dec.
			@	'\u0040'	64	`	'\u0060'	96
!	'\u0021'	33	A	'\u0041'	65	a	'\u0061'	97
"	'\u0022'	34	B	'\u0042'	66	b	'\u0062'	98
#	'\u0023'	35	C	'\u0043'	67	c	'\u0063'	99
$	'\u0024'	36	D	'\u0044'	68	d	'\u0064'	100
%	'\u0025'	37	E	'\u0045'	69	e	'\u0065'	101
&	'\u0026'	38	F	'\u0046'	70	f	'\u0066'	102
'	'\u0027'	39	G	'\u0047'	71	g	'\u0067'	103
(	'\u0028'	40	H	'\u0048'	72	h	'\u0068'	104
)	'\u0029'	41	I	'\u0049'	73	i	'\u0069'	105
*	'\u002A'	42	J	'\u004A'	74	j	'\u006A'	106
+	'\u002B'	43	K	'\u004B'	75	k	'\u006B'	107
,	'\u002C'	44	L	'\u004C'	76	l	'\u006C'	108
-	'\u002D'	45	M	'\u004D'	77	m	'\u006D'	109
.	'\u002E'	46	N	'\u004E'	78	n	'\u006E'	110
/	'\u002F'	47	O	'\u004F'	79	o	'\u006F'	111
0	'\u0030'	48	P	'\u0050'	80	p	'\u0070'	112
1	'\u0031'	49	Q	'\u0051'	81	q	'\u0071'	113
2	'\u0032'	50	R	'\u0052'	82	r	'\u0072'	114
3	'\u0033'	51	S	'\u0053'	83	s	'\u0073'	115
4	'\u0034'	52	T	'\u0054'	84	t	'\u0074'	116
5	'\u0035'	53	U	'\u0055'	85	u	'\u0075'	117
6	'\u0036'	54	V	'\u0056'	86	v	'\u0076'	118
7	'\u0037'	55	W	'\u0057'	87	w	'\u0077'	119
8	'\u0038'	56	X	'\u0058'	88	x	'\u0078'	120
9	'\u0039'	57	Y	'\u0059'	89	y	'\u0079'	121
:	'\u003A'	58	Z	'\u005A'	90	z	'\u007A'	122
;	'\u003B'	59	[	'\u005B'	91	{	'\u007B'	123
<	'\u003C'	60	\'	'\u005C'	92	|	'\u007C'	124
=	'\u003D'	61	]	'\u005D'	93	}	'\u007D'	125
>	'\u003E'	62	^	'\u005E'	94	~	'\u007E'	126
?	'\u003F'	63	_	'\u005F'	95			

Table 3 The Latin-1 Subset of Unicode

Char.	Code	Dec.	Char.	Code	Dec.	Char.	Code	Dec.
			À	'\u00C0'	192	à	'\u00E0'	224
¡	'\u00A1'	161	Á	'\u00C1'	193	á	'\u00E1'	225
¢	'\u00A2'	162	Â	'\u00C2'	194	â	'\u00E2'	226
£	'\u00A3'	163	Ã	'\u00C3'	195	ã	'\u00E3'	227
¤	'\u00A4'	164	Ä	'\u00C4'	196	ä	'\u00E4'	228
¥	'\u00A5'	165	Å	'\u00C5'	197	å	'\u00E5'	229
¦	'\u00A6'	166	Æ	'\u00C6'	198	æ	'\u00E6'	230
§	'\u00A7'	167	Ç	'\u00C7'	199	ç	'\u00E7'	231
¨	'\u00A8'	168	È	'\u00C8'	200	è	'\u00E8'	232
©	'\u00A9'	169	É	'\u00C9'	201	é	'\u00E9'	233
ª	'\u00AA'	170	Ê	'\u00CA'	202	ê	'\u00EA'	234
«	'\u00AB'	171	Ë	'\u00CB'	203	ë	'\u00EB'	235
¬	'\u00AC'	172	Ì	'\u00CC'	204	ì	'\u00EC'	236
	'\u00AD'	173	Í	'\u00CD'	205	í	'\u00ED'	237
®	'\u00AE'	174	Î	'\u00CE'	206	î	'\u00EE'	238
¯	'\u00AF'	175	Ï	'\u00CF'	207	ï	'\u00EF'	239
°	'\u00B0'	176	Ð	'\u00D0'	208	ð	'\u00F0'	240
±	'\u00B1'	177	Ñ	'\u00D1'	209	ñ	'\u00F1'	241
²	'\u00B2'	178	Ò	'\u00D2'	210	ò	'\u00F2'	242
³	'\u00B3'	179	Ó	'\u00D3'	211	ó	'\u00F3'	243
´	'\u00B4'	180	Ô	'\u00D4'	212	ô	'\u00F4'	244
µ	'\u00B5'	181	Õ	'\u00D5'	213	õ	'\u00F5'	245
¶	'\u00B6'	182	Ö	'\u00D6'	214	ö	'\u00F6'	246
·	'\u00B7'	183	×	'\u00D7'	215	÷	'\u00F7'	247
¸	'\u00B8'	184	Ø	'\u00D8'	216	ø	'\u00F8'	248
¹	'\u00B9'	185	Ù	'\u00D9'	217	ù	'\u00F9'	249
º	'\u00BA'	186	Ú	'\u00DA'	218	ú	'\u00FA'	250
»	'\u00BB'	187	Û	'\u00DB'	219	û	'\u00FB'	251
¼	'\u00BC'	188	Ü	'\u00DC'	220	ü	'\u00FC'	252
½	'\u00BD'	189	Ý	'\u00DD'	221	ý	'\u00FD'	253
¾	'\u00BE'	190	Þ	'\u00DE'	222	þ	'\u00FE'	254
¿	'\u00BF'	191	ß	'\u00DF'	223	ÿ	'\u00FF'	255

JAVA OPERATOR SUMMARY

The Java operators are listed in groups of decreasing *precedence* in the table below. The horizontal lines in the table indicate a change in operator precedence. Operators with higher precedence bind more strongly than those with lower precedence. For example, x + y * z means x + (y * z) because the * operator has higher precedence than the + operator. Looking at the table below, you can tell that x && y || z means (x && y) || z because the || operator has lower precedence.

The *associativity* of an operator indicates whether it groups left to right, or right to left. For example, the - operator binds left to right. Therefore, x - y - z means (x - y) - z. But the = operator binds right to left, and x = y = z means x = (y = z).

Operator	Description	Associativity
.	Access class feature	
[]	Array subscript	Left to right
()	Function call	
++	Increment	
--	Decrement	
!	Boolean *not*	
~	Bitwise *not*	
+ *(unary)*	(Has no effect)	Right to left
- *(unary)*	Negative	
(*TypeName*)	Cast	
new	Object allocation	
*	Multiplication	
/	Division or integer division	Left to right
%	Integer remainder	
+	Addition, string concatenation	Left to right
-	Subtraction	
<<	Shift left	
>>	Right shift with sign extension	Left to right
>>>	Right shift with zero extension	

Operator	Description	Associativity
<	Less than	
<=	Less than or equal	
>	Greater than	Left to right
>=	Greater than or equal	
instanceof	Tests whether an object's type is a given type or a subtype thereof	
==	Equal	Left to right
!=	Not equal	
&	Bitwise *and*	Left to right
^	Bitwise exclusive *or*	Left to right
|	Bitwise *or*	Left to right
&&	Boolean "short circuit" *and*	Left to right
||	Boolean "short circuit" *or*	Left to right
? :	Conditional	Right to left
=	Assignment	
op=	Assignment with binary operator (*op* is one of +, -, *, /, &, |, ^, <<, >>, >>>)	Right to left

JAVA RESERVED
WORD SUMMARY

Reserved Word	Description
abstract	An abstract class or method
assert	An assertion that a condition is fulfilled
boolean	The Boolean type
break	Breaks out of the current loop or labeled statement
byte	The 8-bit signed integer type
case	A label in a switch statement
catch	The handler for an exception in a try block
char	The 16-bit Unicode character type
class	Defines a class
const	Not used
continue	Skips the remainder of a loop body
default	The default label in a switch statement
do	A loop whose body is executed at least once
double	The 64-bit double-precision floating-point type
else	The alternative clause in an if statement
enum	An enumeration type
extends	Indicates that a class is a subclass of another class
final	A value that cannot be changed after it has been initialized, a method that cannot be overridden, or a class that cannot be extended
finally	A clause of a try block that is always executed
float	The 32-bit single-precision floating-point type
for	A loop with initialization, condition, and update expressions
goto	Not used
if	A conditional branch statement
implements	Indicates that a class realizes an interface

Reserved Word	Description
import	Allows the use of class names without the package name
instanceof	Tests whether an object's type is a given type or a subtype thereof
int	The 32-bit integer type
interface	An abstract type with only abstract methods and constants
long	The 64-bit integer type
native	A method implemented in non-Java code
new	Allocates an object
package	A collection of related classes
private	A feature that is accessible only by methods of the same class
protected	A feature that is accessible only by methods of the same class, a subclass, or another class in the same package
public	A feature that is accessible by all methods
return	Returns from a method
short	The 16-bit integer type
static	A feature that is defined for a class, not for individual instances
strictfp	Uses strict rules for floating-point computations
super	Invokes the superclass constructor or a superclass method
switch	A selection statement
synchronized	A block of code that is accessible to only one thread at a time
this	The implicit parameter of a method; or invocation of another constructor of the same class
throw	Throws an exception
throws	Indicates the exceptions that a method may throw
transient	Instance variables that should not be serialized
try	A block of code with exception handlers or a finally handler
void	Tags a method that doesn't return a value
volatile	A variable that may be accessed by multiple threads without synchronization
while	A loop statement

THE JAVA LIBRARY

This appendix lists all classes and methods from the standard Java library that are used in this book.

In the following inheritance hierarchy, superclasses that are not used in this book are shown in gray type. Some classes implement interfaces not covered in this book; they are omitted. Classes are sorted first by package, then alphabetically within a package.

```
java.awt.Shape
java.lang.Cloneable
java.lang.Object
    java.awt.BorderLayout
    java.awt.Color
    java.awt.Component
        java.awt.Container
            javax.swing.JComponent
                javax.swing.AbstractButton
                    javax.swing.JButton
                    javax.swing.JMenuItem
                        javax.swing.JMenu
                    javax.swing.JToggleButton
                        javax.swing.JCheckBox
                        javax.swing.JRadioButton
                javax.swing.JComboBox
                javax.swing.JFileChooser
                javax.swing.JLabel
                javax.swing.JMenuBar
                javax.swing.JPanel
                javax.swing.JOptionPane
                javax.swing.JScrollPane
                javax.swing.JSlider
                javax.swing.text.JTextComponent
                    javax.swing.JTextArea
                    javax.swing.JTextField
        java.awt.Window
            java.awt.Frame
                javax.swing.JFrame
    java.awt.Dimension2D
        java.awt.Dimension implements Cloneable
    java.awt.FlowLayout
    java.awt.Font
    java.awt.Graphics
        java.awt.Graphics2D;
    java.awt.GridLayout
    java.awt.event.MouseAdapter implements MouseListener
    java.awt.geom.Line2D implements Cloneable, Shape
        java.awt.geom.Line2D.Double
    java.awt.geom.Point2D implements Cloneable
        java.awt.geom.Point2D.Double
    java.awt.geom.RectangularShape implements Cloneable, Shape
```

```
                    java.awt.geom.Rectangle2D
                       java.awt.Rectangle
                    java.awt.geom.Ellipse2D
                       java.awt.geom.Ellipse2D.Double
              java.io.File implements Comparable<File>
              java.io.InputStream
                 java.io.FileInputStream
              java.io.OutputStream
                 java.io.FileOutputStream
                 java.io.FilterOutputStream
                    java.io.PrintStream
              java.io.Writer
                 java.io.PrintWriter
              java.lang.Boolean implements Comparable<Boolean>
              java.lang.Character implements Comparable<Character>
              java.lang.Class
              java.lang.Math
              java.lang.Number
                 java.math.BigDecimal implements Comparable<BigDecimal>
                 java.math.BigInteger implements Comparable<BigInteger>
                 java.lang.Double implements Comparable<Double>
                 java.lang.Integer implements Comparable<Integer>
              java.lang.String implements Comparable<String>
              java.lang.System
              java.lang.Throwable
                 java.lang.Error
                 java.lang.Exception
                    java.lang.CloneNotSupportedException
                    java.lang.InterruptedException
                    java.io.IOException
                       java.io.EOFException
                       java.io.FileNotFoundException
                    java.lang.RuntimeException
                       java.lang.IllegalArgumentException
                          java.lang.NumberFormatException
                       java.lang.IllegalStateException
                       java.util.NoSuchElementException
                          java.util.InputMismatchException
                       java.lang.NullPointerException
              java.net.URL
              java.net.URLConnection
              java.text.Format
                 java.text.DateFormat
              java.util.AbstractCollection<E>
                 java.util.AbstractList<E>
                    java.util.AbstractSequentialList<E>
                       java.util.LinkedList<E> implements List<E>, Queue<E>
                    java.util.ArrayList<E> implements List<E>
                 java.util.AbstractQueue<E>
                    java.util.PriorityQueue<E>
                 java.util.AbstractSet<E>
                    java.util.HashSet<E> implements Set<E>
                    java.util.TreeSet<E> implements SortedSet<E>
              java.util.AbstractMap<K, V>
                 java.util.HashMap<K, V> implements Map<K, V>
                    java.util.LinkedHashMap<K, V>
                 java.util.TreeMap<K, V> implements Map<K, V>
              java.util.Arrays
              java.util.Collections
```

```
        java.util.Calendar
            java.util.GregorianCalendar
        java.util.Date
        java.util.EventObject
            java.awt.AWTEvent
                java.awt.event.ActionEvent
                java.awt.event.ComponentEvent
                    java.awt.event.InputEvent
                        java.awt.event.KeyEvent
                        java.awt.event.MouseEvent
            javax.swing.event.ChangeEvent
        java.util.Random
        java.util.Scanner
        java.util.logging.Level
        java.util.logging.Logger
        javax.swing.ButtonGroup
        javax.swing.ImageIcon
        javax.swing.Keystroke
        javax.swing.Timer
        javax.swing.border.AbstractBorder
            javax.swing.border.EtchedBorder
            javax.swing.border.TitledBorder
java.lang.Comparable<T>
java.util.Collection<E>
    java.util.List<E>
    java.util.Set<E>
        java.util.SortedSet<E>
java.util.Comparator<T>
java.util.EventListener
    java.awt.event.ActionListener
    java.awt.event.KeyListener
    java.awt.event.MouseListener
    javax.swing.event.ChangeListener
java.util.Iterator<E>
    java.util.ListIterator<E>
java.util.Map<K, V>
java.util.Queue<E> extends Collection<E>
```

In the following descriptions, the phrase "this object" ("this component", "this container", and so forth) means the object (component, container, and so forth) on which the method is invoked (the implicit parameter, this).

Package java.awt

Class java.awt.BorderLayout

- `BorderLayout()`
  This constructs a border layout. A border layout has five regions for adding components, called "NORTH", "EAST", "SOUTH", "WEST", and "CENTER".

- `static final int CENTER`
  This value identifies the center position of a border layout.

- `static final int EAST`
  This value identifies the east position of a border layout.

- `static final int NORTH`
  This value identifies the north position of a border layout.
- `static final int SOUTH`
  This value identifies the south position of a border layout.
- `static final int WEST`
  This value identifies the west position of a border layout.

Class java.awt.Color

- `Color(int red, int green, int blue)`
  This creates a color with the specified red, green, and blue values between 0 and 255.
  Parameters: red   The red component
    green   The green component
    blue   The blue component

Class java.awt.Component

- `void addKeyListener(KeyListener listener)`
  This method adds a key listener to the component.
  Parameters: listener   The key listener to be added
- `void addMouseListener(MouseListener listener)`
  This method adds a mouse listener to the component.
  Parameters: listener   The mouse listener to be added
- `int getHeight()`
  This method gets the height of this component.
  Returns: The height in pixels
- `int getWidth()`
  This method gets the width of this component.
  Returns: The width in pixels
- `void repaint()`
  This method repaints this component by scheduling a call to the paint method.
- `void setFocusable(boolean focusable)`
  This method controls whether or not the component can receive input focus.
  Parameters: focusable   true to have focus, or false to lose focus
- `void setPreferredSize(Dimension preferredSize)`
  This method sets the preferred size of this component.
- `void setSize(int width, int height)`
  This method sets the size of this component.
  Parameters: width   the component width
    height   the component height
- `void setVisible(boolean visible)`
  This method shows or hides the component.
  Parameters: visible   true to show the component, or false to hide it

Class `java.awt.Container`

- void **add**(Component c)
- void **add**(Component c, Object position)

These methods add a component to the end of this container. If a position is given, the layout manager is called to position the component.

Parameters: c   The component to be added

position   An object expressing position information for the layout manager

- void **setLayout**(LayoutManager manager)

This method sets the layout manager for this container.

Parameters: manager   A layout manager

Class `java.awt.Dimension`

- **Dimension**(int width, int height)

This constructs a Dimension object with the given width and height.

Parameters: width   The width

height   The height

Class `java.awt.FlowLayout`

- **FlowLayout**()

This constructs a new flow layout. A flow layout places as many components as possible in a row, without changing their size, and starts new rows as needed.

Class `java.awt.Font`

- **Font**(String name, int style, int size)

This constructs a font object from the specified name, style, and point size.

Parameters: name   The font name, either a font face name or a logical font name, which must be one of "Dialog", "DialogInput", "Monospaced", "Serif", or "SansSerif"

style   One of Font.PLAIN, Font.ITALIC, Font.BOLD, or Font.ITALIC+Font.BOLD

size   The point size of the font

Class `java.awt.Frame`

- void **setTitle**(String title)

This method sets the frame title.

Parameters: title   The title to be displayed in the border of the frame

Class `java.awt.Graphics`

- void **drawLine**(int x1, int y1, int x2, int y2)

Draws a line between two points.

Parameters: x1, y1   The starting point

x2, y2   The endpoint

- void **setColor**(Color c)

  This method sets the current color. After the method call, all graphics operations use this color.

  Parameters: c The new drawing color

Class java.awt.Graphics2D

- void **draw**(Shape s)

  This method draws the outline of the given shape. Many classes—among them Rectangle and Line2D.Double—implement the Shape interface.

  Parameters: s The shape to be drawn

- void **drawString**(String s, int x, int y)
- void **drawString**(String s, float x, float y)

  These methods draw a string in the current font.

  Parameters: s The string to draw

  x,y The basepoint of the first character in the string

- void **fill**(Shape s)

  This method draws the given shape and fills it with the current color.

  Parameters: s The shape to be filled

Class java.awt.GridLayout

- **GridLayout**(int rows, int cols)

  This constructor creates a grid layout with the specified number of rows and columns. The components in a grid layout are arranged in a grid with equal widths and heights. One, but not both, of rows and cols can be zero, in which case any number of objects can be placed in a row or in a column, respectively.

  Parameters: rows The number of rows in the grid

  cols The number of columns in the grid

Class java.awt.Rectangle

- **Rectangle**()

  This constructs a rectangle with a top-left corner at (0, 0) and width and height set to 0.

- **Rectangle**(int x, int y, int width, int height)

  This constructs a rectangle with given top-left corner and size.

  Parameters: x, y The top-left corner

  width The width

  height The height

- double **getHeight**()
- double **getWidth**()

  These methods get the height and width of the rectangle.

- double **getX**()
- double **getY**()

  These methods get the x- and y-coordinates of the top-left corner of the rectangle.

- void **grow**(int dw, int dh)

  This method adjusts the width and height of this rectangle.

  Parameters: dw The amount to add to the width (can be negative)

  dh The amount to add to the height (can be negative)

- Rectangle **intersection**(Rectangle other)

  This method computes the intersection of this rectangle with the specified rectangle.

  Parameters: other A rectangle

  Returns: The largest rectangle contained in both this and other

- void **setLocation**(int x, int y)

  This method moves this rectangle to a new location.

  Parameters: x, y The new top-left corner

- void **setSize**(int width, int height)

  This method sets the width and height of this rectangle to new values.

  Parameters: width The new width

  height The new height

- void **translate**(int dx, int dy)

  This method moves this rectangle.

  Parameters: dx The distance to move along the x-axis

  dy The distance to move along the y-axis

- Rectangle **union**(Rectangle other)

  This method computes the union of this rectangle with the specified rectangle. This is not the set-theoretic union but the smallest rectangle that contains both this and other.

  Parameters: other A rectangle

  Returns: The smallest rectangle containing both this and other

Interface java.awt.Shape

This interface describes shapes that can be drawn and filled by a Graphics2D object.

Package java.awt.event

Interface java.awt.event.ActionListener

- void **actionPerformed**(ActionEvent e)

  The event source calls this method when an action occurs.

Class java.awt.event.KeyEvent

This event is passed to the KeyListener methods. Use the KeyStroke class to obtain the key information from the key event.

Interface java.awt.event.KeyListener

- void **keyPressed**(KeyEvent e)
- void **keyReleased**(KeyEvent e)

  These methods are called when a key has been pressed or released.

- void **keyTyped**(KeyEvent e)

  This method is called when a keystroke has been composed by pressing and releasing one or more keys.

Class java.awt.event.MouseEvent

- int **getX**()

  This method returns the horizontal position of the mouse when the event occurred.

  Returns: The x-position of the mouse

- int **getY**()

  This method returns the vertical position of the mouse when the event occurred.

  Returns: The y-position of the mouse

Interface java.awt.event.MouseListener

- void **mouseClicked**(MouseEvent e)

  This method is called when the mouse has been clicked (that is, pressed and released in quick succession).

- void **mouseEntered**(MouseEvent e)

  This method is called when the mouse has entered the component to which this listener was added.

- void **mouseExited**(MouseEvent e)

  This method is called when the mouse has exited the component to which this listener was added.

- void **mousePressed**(MouseEvent e)

  This method is called when a mouse button has been pressed.

- void **mouseReleased**(MouseEvent e)

  This method is called when a mouse button has been released.

Package java.awt.geom

Class java.awt.geom.Ellipse2D.Double

- **Ellipse2D.Double**(double x, double y, double w, double h)

  This constructs an ellipse from the specified coordinates.

  Parameters: x, y The top-left corner of the bounding rectangle
  w The width of the bounding rectangle
  h The height of the bounding rectangle

Class java.awt.geom.Line2D

- double **getX1**()
- double **getX2**()
- double **getY1**()
- double **getY2**()

  These methods get the requested coordinate of an endpoint of this line.

  Returns: The x- or y-coordinate of the first or second endpoint

- void **setLine**(double x1, double y1, double x2, double y2)
  This methods sets the endpoints of this line.
  Parameters: x1, y1 A new endpoint of this line
                 x2, y2 The other new endpoint

Class java.awt.geom.Line2D.Double

- **Line2D.Double**(double x1, double y1, double x2, double y2)
  This constructs a line from the specified coordinates.
  Parameters: x1, y1 One endpoint of the line
                 x2, y2 The other endpoint
- **Line2D.Double**(Point2D p1, Point2D p2)
  This constructs a line from the two endpoints.
  Parameters: p1, p2 The endpoints of the line

Class java.awt.geom.Point2D

- double **getX**()
- double **getY**()
  These methods get the requested coordinates of this point.
  Returns: The x- or y-coordinate of this point
- void **setLocation**(double x, double y)
  This method sets the x- and y-coordinates of this point.
  Parameters: x, y The new location of this point

Class java.awt.geom.Point2D.Double

- **Point2D.Double**(double x, double y)
  This constructs a point with the specified coordinates.
  Parameters: x, y The coordinates of the point

Class java.awt.geom.RectangularShape

- int **getHeight**()
- int **getWidth**()
  These methods get the height or width of the bounding rectangle of this
  rectangular shape.
  Returns: The height or width, respectively
- double **getCenterX**()
- double **getCenterY**()
- double **getMaxX**()
- double **getMaxY**()
- double **getMinX**()
- double **getMinY**()
  These methods get the requested coordinate value of the corners or center of the
  bounding rectangle of this shape.
  Returns: The center, maximum, or minimum x- and y-coordinates

Package `java.io`

Class `java.io.EOFException`

- `EOFException`(String message)
  This constructs an "end of file" exception object.
  Parameters: message   The detail message

Class `java.io.File`

- `File`(String name)
  This constructs a `File` object that describes a file (which may or may not exist) with the given name.
  Parameters: name   The name of the file
- boolean `exists`()
  This method checks whether there is a file in the local file system that matches this `File` object.
  Returns: true if there is a matching file, false otherwise
- static final String pathSeparator
  The sytem-dependent separator between path names. A colon (:) in Linux or Mac OS X; a semicolon (;) in Windows.

Class `java.io.FileInputStream`

- `FileInputStream`(File f)
  This constructs a file input stream and opens the chosen file. If the file cannot be opened for reading, a `FileNotFoundException` is thrown.
  Parameters: f   The file to be opened for reading
- `FileInputStream`(String name)
  This constructs a file input stream and opens the named file. If the file cannot be opened for reading, a `FileNotFoundException` is thrown.
  Parameters: name   The name of the file to be opened for reading

Class `java.io.FileNotFoundException`

This exception is thrown when a file could not be opened.

Class `java.io.FileOutputStream`

- `FileOutputStream`(File f)
  This constructs a file output stream and opens the chosen file. If the file cannot be opened for writing, a `FileNotFoundException` is thrown.
  Parameters: f   The file to be opened for writing
- `FileOutputStream`(String name)
  This constructs a file output stream and opens the named file. If the file cannot be opened for writing, a `FileNotFoundException` is thrown.
  Parameters: name   The name of the file to be opened for writing

Class java.io.InputStream

- void **close**()
  This method closes this input stream (such as a `FileInputStream`) and releases any system resources associated with the stream.
- int **read**()
  This method reads the next byte of data from this input stream.
  Returns: The next byte of data, or –1 if the end of the stream is reached

Class java.io.InputStreamReader

- **InputStreamReader**(InputStream in)
  This constructs a reader from a specified input stream.
  Parameters: in The stream to read from

Class java.io.IOException

This type of exception is thrown when an input/output error is encountered.

Class java.io.OutputStream

- void **close**()
  This method closes this output stream (such as a `FileOutputStream`) and releases any system resources associated with this stream. A closed stream cannot perform output operations and cannot be reopened.
- void **write**(int b)
  This method writes the lowest byte of b to this output stream.
  Parameters: b The integer whose lowest byte is written

Class java.io.PrintStream / Class java.io.PrintWriter

- **PrintStream**(String name)
- **PrintWriter**(String name)
  This constructs a `PrintStream` or `PrintWriter` and opens the named file. If the file cannot be opened for writing, a `FileNotFoundException` is thrown.
  Parameters: name The name of the file to be opened for writing
- void **close**()
  This method closes this stream or writer and releases any associated system resources.
- void **print**(int x)
- void **print**(double x)
- void **print**(Object x)
- void **print**(String x)
- void **println**()
- void **println**(int x)
- void **println**(double x)

- void **println**(Object x)
- void **println**(String x)

These methods print a value to this PrintStream or PrintWriter. The println methods print a newline after the value. Objects are printed by converting them to strings with their toString methods.

Parameters: x   The value to be printed

- PrintStream **printf**(String format, Object... values)
- Printwriter **printf**(String format, Object... values)

These methods print the format string to this PrintStream or PrintWriter, substituting the given values for placeholders that start with %.

Parameters: format   The format string
                 values   The values to be printed. You can supply any number
                          of values

Returns: The implicit parameter

Package java.lang

Class java.lang.Boolean

- **Boolean**(boolean value)

This constructs a wrapper object for a boolean value.

Parameters: value   The value to store in this object

- boolean **booleanValue**()

This method returns the value stored in this boolean object.

Returns: The Boolean value of this object

Class java.lang.Character

- static boolean **isDigit**(ch)

This method tests whether a given character is a Unicode digit.

Parameters: ch   The character to test
Returns: true if the character is a digit

- static boolean **isLetter**(ch)

This method tests whether a given character is a Unicode letter.

Parameters: ch   The character to test
Returns: true if the character is a letter

- static boolean **isLowerCase**(ch)

This method tests whether a given character is a lowercase Unicode letter.

Parameters: ch   The character to test
Returns: true if the character is a lowercase letter

- static boolean **isUpperCase**(ch)

This method tests whether a given character is an uppercase Unicode letter.

Parameters: ch   The character to test
Returns: true if the character is an uppercase letter

Class java.lang.Class

- static Class **forName**(String className)

  This method loads a class with a given name. Loading a class initializes its static variables.

  Parameters: className The name of the class to load

  Returns: The type descriptor of the class

Interface java.lang.Cloneable

A class implements this interface to indicate that the Object.clone method is allowed to make a shallow copy of its instance variables.

Class java.lang.CloneNotSupportedException

This exception is thrown when a program tries to use Object.clone to make a shallow copy of an object of a class that does not implement the Cloneable interface.

Interface java.lang.Comparable<T>

- int **compareTo**(T other)

  This method compares this object with the other object.

  Parameters: other The object to be compared

  Returns: A negative integer if this object is less than the other, zero if they are equal, or a positive integer otherwise

Class java.lang.Double

- **Double**(double value)

  This constructs a wrapper object for a double-precision floating-point number.

  Parameters: value The value to store in this object

- double **doubleValue**()

  This method returns the floating-point value stored in this Double wrapper object.

  Returns: The value stored in the object

- static double **parseDouble**(String s)

  This method returns the floating-point number that the string represents. If the string cannot be interpreted as a number, a NumberFormatException is thrown.

  Parameters: s The string to be parsed

  Returns: The value represented by the string argument

Class java.lang.Error

This is the superclass for all unchecked system errors.

Class java.lang.IllegalArgumentException

- **IllegalArgumentException**()

  This constructs an IllegalArgumentException with no detail message.

Class java.lang.`IllegalStateException`

This exception is thrown if the state of an object indicates that a method cannot currently be applied.

Class java.lang.`Integer`

- `Integer(int value)`
  This constructs a wrapper object for an integer.
  Parameters: value   The value to store in this object

- int `intValue()`
  This method returns the integer value stored in this wrapper object.
  Returns: The value stored in the object

- static int `parseInt(String s)`
  This method returns the integer that the string represents. If the string cannot be interpreted as an integer, a `NumberFormatException` is thrown.
  Parameters: s   The string to be parsed
  Returns: The value represented by the string argument

- static Integer `parseInt(String s, int base)`
  This method returns the integer value that the string represents in a given number system. If the string cannot be interpreted as an integer, a `NumberFormatException` is thrown.
  Parameters: s   The string to be parsed
                        base   The base of the number system (such as 2 or 16)
  Returns: The value represented by the string argument

- static String `toString(int i)`
- static String `toString(int i, int base)`
  This method creates a string representation of an integer in a given number system. If no base is given, a decimal representation is created.
  Parameters: i   An integer number
                        base   The base of the number system (such as 2 or 16)
  Returns: A string representation of the argument in the number system

- static final int MAX_VALUE
  This constant is the largest value of type int.

- static final int MIN_VALUE
  This constant is the smallest (negative) value of type int.

Class java.lang.`InterruptedException`

This exception is thrown to interrupt a thread, usually with the intention of terminating it.

Class java.lang.`Math`

- static double `abs(double x)`
  This method returns the absolute value $|x|$.
  Parameters: x   A floating-point value
  Returns: The absolute value of the argument

- `static double` **acos**`(double x)`
  This method returns the angle with the given cosine, $\cos^{-1} x \in [0, \pi]$.
  Parameters: x A floating-point value between −1 and 1
  Returns: The arc cosine of the argument, in radians

- `static double` **asin**`(double x)`
  This method returns the angle with the given sine, $\sin^{-1} x \in [-\pi/2, \pi/2]$.
  Parameters: x A floating-point value between −1 and 1
  Returns: The arc sine of the argument, in radians

- `static double` **atan**`(double x)`
  This method returns the angle with the given tangent, $\tan^{-1} x \, (-\pi/2, \pi/2)$.
  Parameters: x A floating-point value
  Returns: The arc tangent of the argument, in radians

- `static double` **atan2**`(double y, double x)`
  This method returns the arc tangent, $\tan^{-1} (y/x) \in (-\pi, \pi)$. If x can equal zero, or if it is necessary to distinguish "northwest" from "southeast" and "northeast" from "southwest", use this method instead of atan(y/x).
  Parameters: y, x Two floating-point values
  Returns: The angle, in radians, between the points (0,0) and (x,y)

- `static double` **ceil**`(double x)`
  This method returns the smallest integer $\geq x$ (as a `double`).
  Parameters: x A floating-point value
  Returns: The smallest integer greater than or equal to the argument

- `static double` **cos**`(double radians)`
  This method returns the cosine of an angle given in radians.
  Parameters: radians An angle, in radians
  Returns: The cosine of the argument

- `static double` **exp**`(double x)`
  This method returns the value e^x, where e is the base of the natural logarithms.
  Parameters: x A floating-point value
  Returns: e^x

- `static double` **floor**`(double x)`
  This method returns the largest integer $\leq x$ (as a `double`).
  Parameters: x A floating-point value
  Returns: The largest integer less than or equal to the argument

- `static double` **log**`(double x)`
- `static double` **log10**`(double x)`
  This method returns the natural (base e) or decimal (base 10) logarithm of x, $\ln x$.
  Parameters: x A number greater than 0.0
  Returns: The natural logarithm of the argument

- `static int` **max**`(int x, int y)`
- `static double` **max**`(double x, double y)`
  These methods return the larger of the given arguments.
  Parameters: x, y Two integers or floating-point values
  Returns: The maximum of the arguments

- `static int min(int x, int y)`
- `static double min(double x, double y)`

  These methods return the smaller of the given arguments.

  Parameters: x, y   Two integers or floating-point values

  Returns: The minimum of the arguments

- `static double pow(double x, double y)`

  This method returns the value x^y ($x > 0$, or $x = 0$ and $y > 0$, or $x < 0$ and y is an integer).

  Parameters: x, y   Two floating-point values

  Returns: The value of the first argument raised to the power of the second argument

- `static long round(double x)`

  This method returns the closest `long` integer to the argument.

  Parameters: x   A floating-point value

  Returns: The argument rounded to the nearest `long` value

- `static double sin(double radians)`

  This method returns the sine of an angle given in radians.

  Parameters: radians   An angle, in radians

  Returns: The sine of the argument

- `static double sqrt(double x)`

  This method returns the square root of x, $\sqrt{x}$.

  Parameters: x   A nonnegative floating-point value

  Returns: The square root of the argument

- `static double tan(double radians)`

  This method returns the tangent of an angle given in radians.

  Parameters: radians   An angle, in radians

  Returns: The tangent of the argument

- `static double toDegrees(double radians)`

  This method converts radians to degrees.

  Parameters: radians   An angle, in radians

  Returns: The angle in degrees

- `static double toRadians(double degrees)`

  This methods converts degrees to radians.

  Parameters: degrees   An angle, in degrees

  Returns: The angle in radians

- `static final double E`

  This constant is the value of e, the base of the natural logarithms.

- `static final double PI`

  This constant is the value of π.

Class java.lang.NullPointerException

This exception is thrown when a program tries to use an object through a `null` reference.

Class java.lang.NumberFormatException

This exception is thrown when a program tries to parse the numerical value of a string that is not a number.

Class java.lang.Object

- `protected Object clone()`

This constructs and returns a shallow copy of this object whose instance variables are copies of the instance variables of this object. If an instance variable of the object is an object reference itself, only the reference is copied, not the object itself. However, if the class does not implement the `Cloneable` interface, a `CloneNotSupportedException` is thrown. Subclasses should redefine this method to make a deep copy.

Returns: A copy of this object

- `boolean equals(Object other)`

This method tests whether this and the other object are equal. This method tests only whether the object references are to the same object. Subclasses should redefine this method to compare the instance variables.

Parameters: other   The object with which to compare

Returns: true if the objects are equal, false otherwise

- `String toString()`

This method returns a string representation of this object. This method produces only the class name and locations of the objects. Subclasses should redefine this method to print the instance variables.

Returns: A string describing this object

Class java.lang.RuntimeException

This is the superclass for all unchecked exceptions.

Class java.lang.String

- `int compareTo(String other)`

This method compares this string and the other string lexicographically.

Parameters: other   The other string to be compared

Returns: A value less than 0 if this string is lexicographically less than the other, 0 if the strings are equal, and a value greater than 0 otherwise

- `boolean equals(String other)`
- `boolean equalsIgnoreCase(String other)`

These methods test whether two strings are equal, or whether they are equal when letter case is ignored.

Parameters: other   The other string to be compared

Returns: true if the strings are equal

- `static String` **`format`**`(String format, Object... values)`
This method formats the given string by substituting placeholders beginning with % with the given values.
  Parameters: `format` The string with the placeholders
                  `values` The values to be substituted for the placeholders
  Returns: The formatted string, with the placeholders replaced by the given values

- `int` **`length`**`()`
This method returns the length of this string.
  Returns: The count of characters in this string

- `String` **`replace`**`(String match, String replacement)`
This method replaces matching substrings with a given replacement.
  Parameters: `match` The string whose matches are to be replaced
                  `replacement` The string with which matching substrings are replaced
  Returns: A string that is identical to this string, with all matching substrings replaced by the given replacement

- `String` **`substring`**`(int begin)`
- `String` **`substring`**`(int begin, int pastEnd)`
These methods return a new string that is a substring of this string, made up of all characters starting at position `begin` and up to either position `pastEnd - 1`, if it is given, or the end of the string.
  Parameters: `begin` The beginning index, inclusive
                  `pastEnd` The ending index, exclusive
  Returns: The specified substring

- `String` **`toLowerCase`**`()`
This method returns a new string that consists of all characters in this string converted to lowercase.
  Returns: A string with all characters in this string converted to lowercase

- `String` **`toUpperCase`**`()`
This method returns a new string that consists of all characters in this string converted to uppercase.
  Returns: A string with all characters in this string converted to uppercase

Class java.lang.System

- `static long` **`currentTimeMillis`**`()`
This method returns the difference, measured in milliseconds, between the current time and midnight, Universal Time, January 1, 1970.
  Returns: The current time in milliseconds since January 1, 1970.

- `static void` **`exit`**`(int status)`
This method terminates the program.
  Parameters: `status` Exit status. A nonzero status code indicates abnormal termination

- `static final InputStream` **`in`**
This object is the "standard input" stream. Reading from this stream typically reads keyboard input.

- `static final PrintStream out`
This object is the "standard output" stream. Printing to this stream typically sends output to the console window.

Class java.lang.Throwable

This is the superclass of exceptions and errors.

- `Throwable()`
This constructs a `Throwable` with no detail message.

- `String getMessage()`
This method gets the message that describes the exception or error.
Returns: The message

- `void printStackTrace()`
This method prints a stack trace to the "standard error" stream. The stack trace contains lists this object and all calls that were pending when it was created.

Package java.math

Class java.math.BigDecimal

- `BigDecimal(String value)`
This constructs an arbitrary-precision floating-point number from the digits in the given string.
Parameters: value A string representing the floating-point number

- `BigDecimal add(BigDecimal other)`
- `BigDecimal multiply(BigDecimal other)`
- `BigDecimal subtract(BigDecimal other)`
These methods return a `BigDecimal` whose value is the sum, difference, product, or quotient of this number and the other.
Parameters: other The other number
Returns: The result of the arithmetic operation

Class java.math.BigInteger

- `BigInteger(String value)`
This constructs an arbitrary-precision integer from the digits in the given string.
Parameters: value A string representing an arbitrary-precision integer

- `BigInteger add(BigInteger other)`
- `BigInteger divide(BigInteger other)`
- `BigInteger mod(BigInteger other)`
- `BigInteger multiply(BigInteger other)`
- `BigInteger subtract(BigInteger other)`
These methods return a `BigInteger` whose value is the sum, quotient, remainder, product, or difference of this number and the other.
Parameters: other The other number
Returns: The result of the arithmetic operation

Package java.net

Class java.net.URL

- `URL(String s)`
  This constructs a URL object from a string containing the URL.
  Parameters: s   The URL string, such as `"http://horstmann.com/index.html"`

- `InputStream openStream()`
  This method gets the input stream through which the client can read the information that the server sends.
  Returns: The input stream associated with this URL

Package java.util

Class java.util.ArrayList<E>

- `ArrayList()`
  This constructs an empty array list.

- `boolean add(E element)`
  This method appends an element to the end of this array list.
  Parameters: element   The element to add
  Returns: true (This method returns a value because it overrides a method in the List interface.)

- `void add(int index, E element)`
  This method inserts an element into this array list at the given position.
  Parameters: index   Insert position
                      element   The element to insert

- `E get(int index)`
  This method gets the element at the specified position in this array list.
  Parameters: index   Position of the element to return
  Returns: The requested element

- `E remove(int index)`
  This method removes the element at the specified position in this array list and returns it.
  Parameters: index   Position of the element to remove
  Returns: The removed element

- `E set(int index, E element)`
  This method replaces the element at a specified position in this array list.
  Parameters: index   Position of element to replace
                      element   Element to be stored at the specified position
  Returns: The element previously at the specified position

- `int size()`
  This method returns the number of elements in this array list.
  Returns: The number of elements in this array list

Class java.util.Arrays

- static int **binarySearch**(Object[] a, Object key)

  This method searches the specified array for the specified object using the binary search algorithm. The array elements must implement the Comparable interface. The array must be sorted in ascending order.

  Parameters: a The array to be searched

                  key The value to be searched for

  Returns: The position of the search key, if it is contained in the array; otherwise, *-index* – 1, where *index* is the position where the element may be inserted

- static *T*[] **copyOf**(*T*[] a, int newLength)

  This method copies the elements of the array a, or the first newLength elements if a.length > newLength, into an array of length newLength and returns that array. *T* can be a primitive type, class, or interface type.

  Parameters: a The array to be copied

                  key The value to be searched for

  Returns: The position of the search key, if it is contained in the array; otherwise, *-index* – 1, where *index* is the position where the element may be inserted

- static void **sort**(Object[] a)

  This method sorts the specified array of objects into ascending order. Its elements must implement the Comparable interface.

  Parameters: a The array to be sorted

- static String **toString**(*T*[] a)

  This method creates and returns a string containing the array elements. *T* can be a primitive type, class, or interface type.

  Parameters: a An array

  Returns: A string containing a comma-separated list of string representations of the array elements, surrounded by brackets.

Class java.util.Calendar

- int **get**(int field)

  This method returns the value of the given field.

  Parameters: field   One of Calendar.YEAR, Calendar.MONTH, Calendar.DAY_OF_MONTH, Calendar.HOUR, Calendar.MINUTE, Calendar.SECOND, or Calendar.MILLISECOND

Interface java.util.Collection<E>

- boolean **add**(E element)

  This method adds an element to this collection.

  Parameters: element The element to add

  Returns: true if adding the element changes the collection

- boolean **contains**(E element)

  This method tests whether an element is present in this collection.

  Parameters: element The element to find

  Returns: true if the element is contained in the collection

- Iterator **iterator**()
  This method returns an iterator that can be used to traverse the elements of this collection.
  Returns: An object of a class implementing the Iterator interface
- boolean **remove**(E element)
  This method removes an element from this collection.
  Parameters: element   The element to remove
  Returns: true if removing the element changes the collection
- int **size**()
  This method returns the number of elements in this collection.
  Returns: The number of elements in this collection

Class java.util.Collections

- static <T> int **binarySearch**(List<T> a, T key)
  This method searches the specified list for the specified object using the binary search algorithm. The list elements must implement the Comparable interface. The list must be sorted in ascending order.
  Parameters: a   The list to be searched
                      key   The value to be searched for
  Returns: The position of the search key, if it is contained in the list; otherwise, *–index* – 1, where *index* is the position where the element may be inserted
- static <T> void **sort**(List<T> a)
  This method sorts the specified list of objects into ascending order. Its elements must implement the Comparable interface.
  Parameters: a   The list to be sorted

Interface java.util.Comparator<T>

- int **compare**(T first, T second)
  This method compares the given objects.
  Parameters: first, second   The objects to be compared
  Returns: A negative integer if the first object is less than the second, zero if they are equal, or a positive integer otherwise

Class java.util.Date

- **Date**()
  This constructs an object that represents the current date and time.

Class java.util.EventObject

- Object **getSource**()
  This method returns a reference to the object on which this event initially occurred.
  Returns: The source of this event

Class java.util.GregorianCalendar

- **GregorianCalendar**()
  This constructs a calendar object that represents the current date and time.

- **GregorianCalendar**(int year, int month, int day)
  This constructs a calendar object that represents the start of the given date.
  Parameters: year, month, day   The given date

Class java.util.HashMap<K, V>

- **HashMap**<K, V>()
  This constructs an empty hash map.

Class java.util.HashSet<E>

- **HashSet**<E>()
  This constructs an empty hash set.

Class java.util.InputMismatchException

This exception is thrown if the next available input item does not match the type of the requested item.

Interface java.util.Iterator<E>

- boolean **hasNext**()
  This method checks whether the iterator is past the end of the list.
  Returns: true if the iterator is not yet past the end of the list

- F **next**()
  This method moves the iterator over the next element in the linked list. This method throws an exception if the iterator is past the end of the list.
  Returns: The object that was just skipped over

- void **remove**()
  This method removes the element that was returned by the last call to next or previous. This method throws an exception if there was an add or remove operation after the last call to next or previous.

Class java.util.LinkedList<E>

- void **addFirst**(E element)
- void **addLast**(E element)
  These methods add an element before the first or after the last element in this list.
  Parameters: element   The element to be added

- E **getFirst**()
- E **getLast**()
  These methods return a reference to the specified element from this list.
  Returns: The first or last element

- E **removeFirst**()
- E **removeLast**()

These methods remove the specified element from this list.

Returns: A reference to the removed element

Interface java.util.List<E>

- ListIterator<E> **listIterator**()

This method gets an iterator to visit the elements in this list.

Returns: An iterator that points before the first element in this list

Interface java.util.ListIterator<E>

Objects implementing this interface are created by the listIterator methods of list classes.

- void **add**(E element)

This method adds an element after the iterator position and moves the iterator after the new element.

Parameters: element The element to be added

- boolean **hasPrevious**()

This method checks whether the iterator is before the first element of the list.

Returns: true if the iterator is not before the first element of the list

- E **previous**()

This method moves the iterator over the previous element in the linked list. This method throws an exception if the iterator is before the first element of the list.

Returns: The object that was just skipped over

- void **set**(E element)

This method replaces the element that was returned by the last call to next or previous. This method throws an exception if there was an add or remove operation after the last call to next or previous.

Parameters: element The element that replaces the old list element

Interface java.util.Map<K, V>

- V **get**(K key)

Gets the value associated with a key in this map.

Parameters: key The key for which to find the associated value

Returns: The value associated with the key, or null if the key is not present in the map

- Set<K> **keySet**()

This method returns all keys this map.

Returns: A set of all keys in this map

- V **put**(K key, V value)

This method associates a value with a key in this map.

Parameters: key The lookup key
value The value to associate with the key

Returns: The value previously associated with the key, or null if the key was not present in the map

- V **remove**(K key)

  This method removes a key and its associated value from this map.

  Parameters: key   The lookup key

  Returns: The value previously associated with the key, or null if the key was not present in the map

Class java.util.NoSuchElementException

This exception is thrown if an attempt is made to retrieve a value that does not exist.

Class java.util.PriorityQueue<E>

- **PriorityQueue**<E>()

  This constructs an empty priority queue. The element type E must implement the Comparable interface.

- E **remove**()

  This method removes the smallest element in the priority queue.

  Returns: The removed value

Interface java.util.Queue<E>

- E **peek**()

  Gets the element at the head of the queue without removing it.

  Returns: The head element or null if the queue is empty

Class java.util.Random

- **Random**()

  This constructs a new random number generator.

- double **nextDouble**()

  This method returns the next pseudorandom, uniformly distributed floating-point number between 0.0 (inclusive) and 1.0 (exclusive) from this random number generator's sequence.

  Returns: The next pseudorandom floating-point number

- int **nextInt**(int n)

  This method returns the next pseudorandom, uniformly distributed integer between 0 (inclusive) and the specified value (exclusive) drawn from this random number generator's sequence.

  Parameters: n   Number of values to draw from

  Returns: The next pseudorandom integer

Class java.util.Scanner

- **Scanner**(File in)
- **Scanner**(InputStream in)
- **Scanner**(Reader in)

  These construct a scanner that reads from the given file, input stream, or reader.

  Parameters: in   The file, input stream, or reader from which to read

- void **close**()
  This method closes this scanner and releases any associated system resources.
- boolean **hasNext**()
- boolean **hasNextDouble**()
- boolean **hasNextInt**()
- boolean **hasNextLine**()
  These methods test whether it is possible to read any non-empty string, a floating-point value, an integer, or a line, as the next item.
  Returns: true if it is possible to read an item of the requested type, false otherwise (either because the end of the file has been reached, or because a number type was tested and the next item is not a number)
- String **next**()
- double **nextDouble**()
- int **nextInt**()
- String **nextLine**()
  These methods read the next whitespace-delimited string, floating-point value, integer, or line.
  Returns: The value that was read
- Scanner **useDelimiter**(String pattern)
  Sets the pattern for the delimiters between input tokens.
  Parameters: pattern   A regular expression for the delimiter pattern
  Returns: This scanner

Interface java.util.Set<E>

This interface describes a collection that contains no duplicate elements.

Class java.util.TreeMap<K, V>

- **TreeMap**<K, V>()
  This constructs an empty tree map. The iterator of a TreeMap visits the entries in sorted order.

Class java.util.TreeSet<E>

- **TreeSet**<E>()
  This constructs an empty tree set.

Package java.util.logging

Class java.util.logging.Level

- static final int INFO
  This value indicates informational logging.
- static final int OFF
  This value indicates logging of no messages.

Class java.util.logging.Logger

- static Logger **getGlobal**()
  This method gets the global logger. For Java 5 and 6, use getLogger("global") instead.
  Returns: The global logger that, by default, displays messages with level INFO or a higher severity on the console.
- void **info**(String message)
  This method logs an informational message.
  Parameters: message   The message to log
- void **setLevel**(Level aLevel)
  This method sets the logging level. Logging messages with a lesser severity than the current level are ignored.
  Parameters: aLevel   The minimum level for logging messages

Package javax.swing

Class javax.swing.AbstractButton

- void **addActionListener**(ActionListener listener)
  This method adds an action listener to the button.
  Parameters: listener   The action listener to be added
- boolean **isSelected**()
  This method returns the selection state of the button.
  Returns: true if the button is selected
- void **setSelected**(boolean state)
  This method sets the selection state of the button. This method updates the button but does not trigger an action event.
  Parameters: state   true to select, false to deselect

Class javax.swing.ButtonGroup

- void **add**(AbstractButton button)
  This method adds the button to the group.
  Parameters: button   The button to add

Class javax.swing.ImageIcon

- **ImageIcon**(String filename)
  This constructs an image icon from the specified graphics file.
  Parameters: filename   A string specifying a file name

Class javax.swing.JButton

- **JButton**(String label)
  This constructs a button with the given label.
  Parameters: label   The button label

Class javax.swing.JCheckBox

- **JCheckBox**(String text)
  This constructs a check box with the given text, which is initially deselected.
  (Use the setSelected method to make the box selected; see the javax.swing.
  AbstractButton class.)
  Parameters: text   The text displayed next to the check box

Class javax.swing.JComboBox

- **JComboBox**()
  This constructs a combo box with no items.
- void **addItem**(Object item)
  This method adds an item to the item list of this combo box.
  Parameters: item   The item to add
- Object **getSelectedItem**()
  This method gets the currently selected item of this combo box.
  Returns: The currently selected item
- boolean **isEditable**()
  This method checks whether the combo box is editable. An editable combo box
  allows the user to type into the text field of the combo box.
  Returns: true if the combo box is editable
- void **setEditable**(boolean state)
  This method is used to make the combo box editable or not.
  Parameters: state   true to make editable, false to disable editing
- void **setSelectedItem**(Object item)
  This method sets the item that is shown in the display area of the combo box as
  selected.
  Parameters: item   The item to be displayed as selected

Class javax.swing.JComponent

- protected void **paintComponent**(Graphics g)
  Override this method to paint the surface of a component. Your method needs to
  call super.paintComponent(g).
  Parameters: g   The graphics context used for drawing
- void **setBorder**(Border b)
  This method sets the border of this component.
  Parameters: b   The border to surround this component
- void **setFont**(Font f)
  Sets the font used for the text in this component.
  Parameters: f   A font

Class javax.swing.JFileChooser

- **JFileChooser**()
  This constructs a file chooser.

- File **getSelectedFile**()
  This method gets the selected file from this file chooser.
  Returns: The selected file
- int **showOpenDialog**(Component parent)
  This method displays an "Open File" file chooser dialog box.
  Parameters: parent The parent component or null
  Returns: The return state of this file chooser after it has been closed by
                        the user: either APPROVE_OPTION or CANCEL_OPTION. If APPROVE_OPTION is
                        returned, call getSelectedFile() on this file chooser to get the file
- int **showSaveDialog**(Component parent)
  This method displays a "Save File" file chooser dialog box.
  Parameters: parent The parent component or null
  Returns: The return state of the file chooser after it has been closed by the
                        user: either APPROVE_OPTION or CANCEL_OPTION

Class javax.swing.JFrame

- void **setDefaultCloseOperation**(int operation)
  This method sets the default action for closing the frame.
  Parameters: operation The desired close operation. Choose among
                        DO_NOTHING_ON_CLOSE, HIDE_ON_CLOSE (the default), DISPOSE_ON_CLOSE,
                        or EXIT_ON_CLOSE
- void **setJMenuBar**(JMenuBar mb)
  This method sets the menu bar for this frame.
  Parameters: mb The menu bar. If mb is null, then the current menu bar is
                        removed
- static final int EXIT_ON_CLOSE
  This value indicates that when the user closes this frame, the application is to exit.

Class javax.swing.JLabel

- **JLabel**(String text)
- **JLabel**(String text, int alignment)
  These containers create a JLabel instance with the specified text and horizontal
  alignment.
  Parameters: text The label text to be displayed by the label
                        alignment One of SwingConstants.LEFT, SwingConstants.CENTER, or
                        SwingConstants.RIGHT

Class javax.swing.JMenu

- **JMenu**()
  This constructs a menu with no items.
- JMenuItem **add**(JMenuItem menuItem)
  This method appends a menu item to the end of this menu.
  Parameters: menuItem The menu item to be added
  Returns: The menu item that was added

Class javax.swing.JMenuBar

- **JMenuBar()**
  This constructs a menu bar with no menus.

- JMenu **add**(JMenu menu)
  This method appends a menu to the end of this menu bar.
  Parameters: menu   The menu to be added
  Returns: The menu that was added

Class javax.swing.JMenuItem

- **JMenuItem**(String text)
  This constructs a menu item.
  Parameters: text   The text to appear in the menu item

Class javax.swing.JOptionPane

- static String **showInputDialog**(Object prompt)
  This method brings up a modal input dialog box, which displays a prompt and waits for the user to enter an input in a text field, preventing the user from doing anything else in this program.
  Parameters: prompt   The prompt to display
  Returns: The string that the user typed

- static void **showMessageDialog**(Component parent, Object message)
  This method brings up a confirmation dialog box that displays a message and waits for the user to confirm it.
  Parameters: parent   The parent component or null
  message   The message to display

Class javax.swing.JPanel

This class is a component without decorations. It can be used as an invisible container for other components.

Class javax.swing.JRadioButton

- **JRadioButton**(String text)
  This constructs a radio button having the given text that is initially deselected. (Use the setSelected method to select it; see the javax.swing.AbstractButton class.)
  Parameters: text   The string displayed next to the radio button

Class javax.swing.JScrollPane

- **JScrollPane**(Component c)
  This constructs a scroll pane around the given component.
  Parameters: c   The component that is decorated with scroll bars

Class javax.swing.JSlider

- **JSlider**(int min, int max, int value)
This constructor creates a horizontal slider using the specified minimum, maximum, and value.
Parameters: min   The smallest possible slider value
   max   The largest possible slider value
   value   The initial value of the slider

- void **addChangeListener**(ChangeListener listener)
This method adds a change listener to the slider.
Parameters: listener   The change listener to add

- int **getValue**()
This method returns the slider's value.
Returns: The current value of the slider

Class javax.swing.JTextArea

- **JTextArea**()
This constructs an empty text area.

- **JTextArea**(int rows, int columns)
This constructs an empty text area with the specified number of rows and columns.
Parameters: rows   The number of rows
   columns   The number of columns

- void **append**(String text)
This method appends text to this text area.
Parameters: text   The text to append

Class javax.swing.JTextField

- **JTextField**()
This constructs an empty text field.

- **JTextField**(int columns)
This constructs an empty text field with the specified number of columns.
Parameters: columns   The number of columns

Class javax.swing.KeyStroke

- static KeyStroke **getKeyStrokeForEvent**(KeyEvent event)
Gets a KeyStroke object describing the key stroke that caused the event.
Parameters: event   The key event to be analyzed
Returns: A KeyStroke object. Call toString on this object to get a string representation such as "pressed LEFT"

Class javax.swing.Timer

- **Timer**(int millis, ActionListener listener)
  This constructs a timer that notifies an action listener whenever a time interval has elapsed.
  Parameters: millis   The number of milliseconds between timer notifications
  listener   The object to be notified when the time interval has elapsed

- void **start**()
  This method starts the timer. Once the timer has started, it begins notifying its listener.

- void **stop**()
  This method stops the timer. Once the timer has stopped, it no longer notifies its listener.

Package javax.swing.event

Class javax.swing.event.ChangeEvent

Components such as sliders emit change events when they are manipulated by the user.

Interface javax.swing.event.ChangeListener

- void **stateChanged**(ChangeEvent e)
  This event is called when the event source has changed its state.
  Parameters: e   A change event

Package javax.swing.text

Class javax.swing.text.JTextComponent

- String **getText**()
  This method returns the text contained in this text component.
  Returns: The text

- boolean **isEditable**()
  This method checks whether this text component is editable.
  Returns: true if the component is editable

- void **setEditable**(boolean state)
  This method is used to make this text component editable or not.
  Parameters: state   true to make editable, false to disable editing

- void **setText**(String text)
  This method sets the text of this text component to the specified text. If the argument is the empty string, the old text is deleted.
  Parameters: text   The new text to be set

GLOSSARY

Abstract class A class that cannot be instantiated.

Abstract method A method with a name, parameter variable types, and return type but without an implementation.

Access specifier A reserved word that indicates the accessibility of a feature, such as private or public.

Accessor method A method that accesses an object but does not change it.

Aggregation The *has-a* relationship between classes.

Algorithm An unambiguous, executable, and terminating specification of a way to solve a problem.

Anonymous class A class that does not have a name.

Anonymous object An object that is not stored in a named variable.

API (Application Programming Interface) A code library for building programs.

API Documentation Information about each class in the Java library.

Applet A graphical Java program that executes inside a web browser or applet viewer.

Argument A value supplied in a method call, or one of the values combined by an operator.

Array A collection of values of the same type stored in contiguous memory locations, each of which can be accessed by an integer index.

Array list A Java class that implements a dynamically growable array of objects.

Assert A claim that a certain condition holds in a particular program location.

Assignment Placing a new value into a variable.

Association A relationship between classes in which one can navigate from objects of one class to objects of the other class, usually by following object references.

Asymmetric bounds Bounds that include the starting index but not the ending index.

Attribute A named property that an object is responsible for maintaining.

Auto-boxing Automatically converting a primitive type value into a wrapper type object.

Big-Oh notation The notation $g(n) = O(f(n))$, which denotes that the function g grows at a rate that is bounded by the growth rate of the function f with respect to n. For example, $10n^2 + 100n - 1000 = O(n^2)$.

Binary operator An operator that takes two arguments, for example + in $x + y$.

Binary search A fast algorithm for finding a value in a sorted array. It narrows the search down to half of the array in every step.

Bit Binary digit; the smallest unit of information, having two possible values: 0 and 1. A data element consisting of n bits has 2^n possible values.

Black-box testing Testing a method without knowing its implementation.

Block A group of statements bracketed by {}.

Body All statements of a method or block.

Boolean operator An operator that can be applied to Boolean values. Java has three Boolean operators: &&, ||, and !.

Boolean type   A type with two possible values: true and false.

Boundary test case   A test case involving values that are at the outer boundary of the set of legal values. For example, if a method is expected to work for all nonnegative integers, then 0 is a boundary test case.

Bounds error   Trying to access an array element that is outside the legal range.

break statement   A statement that terminates a loop or switch statement.

Breakpoint   A point in a program, specified in a debugger, at which the debugger stops executing the program and lets the user inspect the program state.

Buffer   A temporary storage location for holding values that have been produced (for example, characters typed by the user) and are waiting to be consumed (for example, read a line at a time).

Bug   A programming error.

Byte   A number made up of eight bits. Essentially all currently manufactured computers use a byte as the smallest unit of storage in memory.

Bytecode   Instructions for the Java virtual machine.

Call stack   The ordered set of all methods that currently have been called but not yet terminated, starting with the current method and ending with main.

Callback   A mechanism for specifying a block of code so it can be executed at a later time.

Case sensitive   Distinguishing upper- and lowercase characters.

Cast   Explicitly converting a value from one type to a different type. For example, the cast from a floating-point number x to an integer is expressed in Java by the cast notation (int) x.

catch clause   A part of a try block that is executed when a matching exception is thrown by any statement in the try block.

Central processing unit (CPU)   The part of a computer that executes the machine instructions.

Character   A single letter, digit, or symbol.

Checked exception   An exception that the compiler checks. All checked exceptions must be declared or caught.

Class   A programmer-defined data type.

Code coverage   A measure of the amount of source code that has been executed during testing.

Cohesive   A class is cohesive if its features support a single abstraction.

Collection   A data structure that provides a mechanism for adding, removing, and locating elements.

Collaborator   A class on which another class depends.

Command line   The line the user types to start a program in DOS or UNIX or a command window in Windows. It consists of the program name followed by any necessary arguments.

Comment   An explanation to help the human reader understand a section of a program; ignored by the compiler.

Compiler   A program that translates code in a high-level language (such as Java) to machine instructions (such as bytecode for the Java virtual machine).

Compile-time error   An error that is detected when a program is compiled.

Component   See **User-interface component**

Composition   An aggregation relationship where the aggregated objects do not have an existence independent of the containing object.

Computer program   A sequence of instructions that is executed by a computer.

Concatenation   Placing one string after another to form a new string.

Concrete class   A class that can be instantiated.

Console program   A Java program that does not have a graphical window. A console program reads input from the keyboard and writes output to the terminal screen.

Constant   A value that cannot be changed by a program. In Java, constants are defined with the reserved word final.

Constructor   A sequence of statements for initializing a newly instantiated object.

Construction   Setting a newly allocated object to an initial state.

Container   A user-interface component that can hold other components and present them together to the user. Also, a data structure, such as a list, that can hold a collection of objects and present them individually to a program.

Content pane   The part of a Swing frame that holds the user-interface components of the frame.

Coupling   The degree to which classes are related to each other by dependency.

CRC card   An index card representing a class that lists its responsibilities and collaborating classes.

De Morgan's Law   A law about logical operations that describes how to negate expressions formed with *and* and *or* operations.

Debugger   A program that lets a user run another program one or a few steps at a time, stop execution, and inspect the variables in order to analyze it for bugs.

Dependency   The *uses* relationship between classes, in which one class needs services provided by another class.

Directory   A structure on a disk that can hold files or other directories; also called a folder.

Documentation comment   A comment in a source file that can be automatically extracted into the program documentation by a program such as javadoc.

Dot notation   The notation *object.method(arguments)* or *object.variable* used to invoke a method or access a variable.

Doubly-linked list   A linked list in which each link has a reference to both its predecessor and successor links.

Dynamic method lookup   Selecting a method to be invoked at run time. In Java, dynamic method lookup considers the class of the implicit parameter object to select the appropriate method.

Editor   A program for writing and modifying text files.

Encapsulation   The hiding of implementation details.

Enumeration type   A type with a finite number of values, each of which has its own symbolic name.

Escape character   A character in text that is not taken literally but has a special meaning when combined with the character or characters that follow it. The \ character is an escape character in Java strings.

Escape sequence   A sequence of characters that starts with an escape character, such as \n or \".

Event   See **User-interface event**

Event class   A class that contains information about an event, such as its source.

Event adapter   A class that implements an event listener interface by defining all methods to do nothing.

Event handler   A method that is executed when an event occurs.

Event listener   An object that is notified by an event source when an event occurs.

Event source   An object that can notify other classes of events.

Exception   A class that signals a condition that prevents the program from continuing normally. When such a condition occurs, an object of the exception class is thrown.

Exception handler   A sequence of statements that is given control when an exception of a particular type has been thrown and caught.

Explicit parameter   A parameter of a method other than the object on which the method is invoked.

Expression   A syntactical construct that is made up of constants, variables, method calls, and the operators combining them.

Extension   The last part of a file name, which specifies the file type. For example, the extension .java denotes a Java file.

Fibonacci numbers   The sequence of numbers 1, 1, 2, 3, 5, 8, 13, . . . , in which every term is the sum of its two predecessors.

File   A sequence of bytes that is stored on disk.

finally clause   A part of a try block that is executed no matter how the try block is exited.

Flag   See **Boolean type**

Floating-point number   A number that can have a fractional part.

Folder   See **Directory**

Font   A set of character shapes in a particular style and size.

Frame   A window with a border and a title bar.

Garbage collection   Automatic reclamation of memory occupied by objects that are no longer referenced.

Generic class   A class with one or more type parameters.

Graphics context   A class through which a programmer can cause shapes to appear on a window or off-screen bitmap.

grep   The "global regular expression print" search program, useful for finding all strings matching a pattern in a set of files.

GUI (Graphical User Interface)   A user interface in which the user supplies inputs through graphical components such as buttons, menus, and text fields.

Hard disk   A device that stores information on rotating platters with magnetic coating.

Hardware   The physical equipment for a computer or another device.

Hash code   A value that is computed by a hash function.

Hash collision   Two different objects for which a hash function computes identical values.

Hash function   A function that computes an integer value from an object in such a way that different objects are likely to yield different values.

Hash table   A data structure in which elements are mapped to array positions according to their hash function values.

Heapsort algorithm   A sorting algorithm that inserts the values to be sorted into a heap.

High-level programming language   A programming language that provides an abstract view of a computer and allows programmers to focus on their problem domain.

IDE (Integrated Development Environment)   A programming environment that includes an editor, compiler, and debugger.

Immutable class   A class without a mutator method.

Implementing an interface   Implementing a class that defines all methods specified in the interface.

Implicit parameter   The object on which a method is invoked. For example, in the call x.f(y), the object x is the implicit parameter of the method f.

Importing a class or package   Indicating the intention of referring to a class, or all classes in a package, by the simple name rather than the qualified name.

Inheritance   The *is-a* relationship between a more general superclass and a more specialized subclass.

Initialize   Set a variable to a well-defined value when it is created.

Inner class   A class that is defined inside another class.

Instance method   A method with an implicit parameter; that is, a method that is invoked on an instance of a class.

Instance of a class   An object whose type is that class.

Instance variable   A variable defined in a class for which every object of the class has its own value.

Instantiation of a class   Construction of an object of that class.

Integer   A number that cannot have a fractional part.

Integer division   Taking the quotient of two integers and discarding the remainder. In Java the / symbol denotes integer division if both arguments are integers. For example, 11/4 is 2, not 2.75.

Interface type   A type with no instance variables, only abstract methods and constants.

Iterator   An object that can inspect all elements in a container such as a linked list.

javadoc   The documentation generator in the Java SDK. It extracts documentation comments from Java source files and produces a set of linked HTML files.

Lexicographic ordering   Ordering strings in the same order as in a dictionary, by skipping all matching characters and comparing the first non-matching characters of both strings. For example, "orbit" comes before "orchid" in lexicographic ordering. Note that in Java, unlike a dictionary, the ordering is case sensitive: Z comes before a.

Library   A set of precompiled classes that can be included in programs.

Linear search   Searching a container (such as an array or list) for an object by inspecting each element in turn.

Linked list   A data structure that can hold an arbitrary number of objects, each of which is stored in a link object, which contains a pointer to the next link.

Literal   A notation for a fixed value in a program, such as −2, 3.14, 6.02214115E23, "Harry", or 'H'.

Local variable   A variable whose scope is a block.

Logging   Sending messages that trace the progress of a program to a file or window.

Logical operator   See **Boolean operator**.

Logic error   An error in a syntactically correct program that causes it to act differently from its specification. (A form of run-time error.)

Loop   A sequence of instructions that is executed repeatedly.

Loop and a half   A loop whose termination decision is neither at the beginning nor at the end.

Machine code   Instructions that can be executed directly by the CPU.

Magic number   A number that appears in a program without explanation.

main method   The method that is first called when a Java application executes.

Map   A data structure that keeps associations between key and value objects.

Memory location   A value that specifies the location of data in computer memory.

Merge sort   A sorting algorithm that first sorts two halves of a data structure and then merges the sorted subarrays together.

Method   A sequence of statements that has a name, may have parameter variables, and may return a value. A method can be invoked any number of times, with different values for its parameter variables.

Modifier   A reserved word that indicates the accessibility of a feature, such as private or public.

Modulus   The % operator that computes the remainder of an integer division.

Mock object   An object that is used during program testing, replacing another object and providing similar behavior. Usually, the mock object is simpler to implement or provides better support for testing.

Mutator method   A method that changes the state of an object.

Mutual recursion   Cooperating methods that call each other.

Name clash   Accidentally using the same name to denote two program features in a way that cannot be resolved by the compiler.

Nested loop   A loop that is contained in another loop.

Networks   An interconnected system of computers and other devices.

new operator   An operator that allocates new objects.

Newline   The '\n' character, which indicates the end of a line.

No-argument constructor   A constructor that takes no arguments.

Null reference   A reference that does not refer to any object.

Number literal   A fixed value in a program this is explicitly written as a number, such as –2 or 6.02214115E23.

Object   A value of a class type.

Object-oriented programming   Designing a program by discovering objects, their properties, and their relationships.

Object reference   A value that denotes the location of an object in memory. In Java, a variable whose type is a class contains a reference to an object of that class.

Off-by-one error   A common programming error in which a value is one larger or smaller than it should be.

Opening a file   Preparing a file for reading or writing.

Operating system   The software that launches application programs and provides services (such as a file system) for those programs.

Operator   A symbol denoting a mathematical or logical operation, such as + or &&.

Operator associativity   The rule that governs in which order operators of the same precedence are executed. For example, in Java the - operator is left-associative because a - b - c is interpreted as (a - b) - c, and = is right-associative because a = b = c is interpreted as a = (b = c).

Operator precedence   The rule that governs which operator is evaluated first. For example, in Java the && operator has a higher precedence than the || operator. Hence a || b && c is interpreted as a || (b && c). (See Appendix B.)

Overloading   Giving more than one meaning to a method name.

Overriding   Redefining a method in a subclass.

Package   A collection of related classes. The import statement is used to access one or more classes in a package.

Panel   A user-interface component with no visual appearance. It can be used to group other components.

Parallel arrays   Arrays of the same length, in which corresponding elements are logically related.

Parameter passing   Specifying expressions to be arguments for a method when it is called.

Parameter variable   A variable of a method that is initialized with a value when the method is called.

Partially filled array   An array that is not filled to capacity, together with a companion variable that indicates the number of elements actually stored.

Permutation   A rearrangement of a set of values.

Polymorphism   Selecting a method among several methods that have the same name on the basis of the actual types of the implicit parameters.

Primitive type   In Java, a number type or boolean.

Priority queue   An abstract data type that enables efficient insertion of elements and efficient removal of the smallest element.

Programming   The act of designing and implementing computer programs.

Project   A collection of source files and their dependencies.

Prompt   A string that tells the user to provide input.

Pseudocode   A high-level description of the actions of a program or algorithm, using a mixture of English and informal programming language syntax.

Pseudorandom number   A number that appears to be random but is generated by a mathematical formula.

Public interface   The features (methods, variables, and nested types) of a class that are accessible to all clients.

Queue   A collection of items with "first in, first out" retrieval.

Quicksort   A generally fast sorting algorithm that picks an element, called the pivot, partitions the sequence into the elements smaller than the pivot and those larger than the pivot, and then recursively sorts the subsequences.

Reader   In the Java input/output library, a class from which to read characters.

Recursion   A method for computing a result by decomposing the inputs into simpler values and applying the same method to them.

Recursive method   A method that can call itself with simpler values. It must handle the simplest values without calling itself.

Redirection   Linking the input or output of a program to a file instead of the keyboard or display.

Reference   See **Object reference**

Regression testing   Keeping old test cases and testing every revision of a program against them.

Regular expression   A string that defines a set of matching strings according to their content. Each part of a regular expression can be a specific required character; one of a set of permitted characters such as [abc], which can be a range such as [a-z]; any character not in a set of forbidden characters, such as [^0-9]; a repetition of one or more matches, such as [0-9]+, or zero or more, such as [ACGT]; one of a set of alternatives, such as and|et|und; or various other possibilities. For example, "[A-Za-z][0-9]+" matches "Cloud9" or "007" but not "Jack".

Relational operator   An operator that compares two values, yielding a Boolean result.

Reserved word   A word that has a special meaning in a programming language and therefore cannot be used as a name by the programmer.

Return value   The value returned by a method through a return statement.

Reverse Polish notation   A style of writing expressions in which the operators are written following the operands, such as 2 3 4 * + for 2 + 3 * 4.

Roundoff error   An error introduced by the fact that the computer can store only a finite number of digits of a floating-point number.

Run-time error   An error in a syntactically correct program that causes it to act differently from its specification.

Run-time stack   The data structure that stores the local variables of all called methods as a program runs.

Scope   The part of a program in which a variable is defined.

Secondary storage   Storage that persists without electricity, e.g., a hard disk.

Selection sort   A sorting algorithm in which the smallest element is repeatedly found and removed until no elements remain.

Sentinel   A value in input that is not to be used as an actual input value but to signal the end of input.

Sequential search   See **Linear search**

Set   An unordered collection that allows efficient addition, location, and removal of elements.

Shadowing   Hiding a variable by defining another one with the same name.

Shallow copy   Copying only the reference to an object.

Shell script   A file that contains commands for running programs and manipulating files. Typing the name of the shell script file on the command line causes those commands to be executed.

Shell window   A window for interacting with an operating system through textual commands.

Short-circuit evaluation   Evaluating only a part of an expression if the remainder cannot change the result.

Side effect   An effect of a method other than returning a value.

Software   The intangible instructions and data that are necessary for operating a computer or another device.

Source code   Instructions in a programming language that need to be translated before execution on a computer.

Source file   A file containing instructions in a programming language such as Java.

Stack   A data structure with "last-in, first-out" retrieval. Elements can be added and removed only at one position, called the top of the stack.

Stack trace   A printout of the call stack, listing all currently pending method calls.

State   The current value of an object, which is determined by the cumulative action of all methods that were invoked on it.

State diagram   A diagram that depicts state transitions and their causes.

Statement   A syntactical unit in a program. In Java a statement is either a simple statement, a compound statement, or a block.

Static method   A method with no implicit parameter.

Static variable   A variable defined in a class that has only one value for the whole class, and which can be accessed and changed by any method of that class.

String   A sequence of characters.

Subclass   A class that inherits variables and methods from a superclass but may also add instance variables, add methods, or redefine methods.

Substitution principle   The principle that a subclass object can be used in place of any superclass object.

Superclass   A general class from which a more specialized class (a subclass) inherits.

Swing   A Java toolkit for implementing graphical user interfaces.

Symmetric bounds   Bounds that include the starting index and the ending index.

Syntax   Rules that define how to form instructions in a particular programming language.

Syntax diagram   A graphical representation of grammar rules.

Syntax error   An instruction that does not follow the programming language rules and is rejected by the compiler. (A form of compile-time error.)

Tab character   The '\t' character, which advances the next character on the line to the next one of a set of fixed positions known as tab stops.

Ternary operator   An operator with three arguments. Java has one ternary operator, a ? b : c.

Test suite   A set of test cases for a program.

Text file   A file in which values are stored in their text representation.

Throw an exception   Indicate an abnormal condition by terminating the normal control flow of a program and transferring control to a matching catch clause.

throws clause   Indicates the types of the checked exceptions that a method may throw.

Token   A sequence of consecutive characters from an input source that belongs together for the purpose of analyzing the input. For example, a token can be a sequence of characters other than white space.

Trace message   A message that is printed during a program run for debugging purposes.

try block   A block of statements that contains exception processing clauses. A try block contains at least one catch or finally clause.

Turing machine   A very simple model of computation that is used in theoretical computer science to explore computability of problems.

Two-dimensional array   A tabular arrangement of elements in which an element is specified by a row and a column index.

Type   A named set of values and the operations that can be carried out with them.

Type parameter   A parameter in a generic class or method that can be replaced with an actual type.

Unary operator   An operator with one argument.

Unchecked exception   An exception that the compiler doesn't check.

Unicode   A standard code that assigns code values consisting of two bytes to characters used in scripts around the world. Java stores all characters as their Unicode values.

Unified Modeling Language (UML)   A notation for specifying, visualizing, constructing, and documenting the artifacts of software systems.

Uninitialized variable   A variable that has not been set to a particular value. In Java, using an uninitialized local variable is a syntax error.

Unit testing   Testing a method by itself, isolated from the remainder of the program.

URL (Uniform Resource Locator)   A pointer to an information resource (such as a web page or an image) on the World Wide Web.

User-interface component   A building block for a graphical user interface, such as a button or a text field. User-interface components are used to present information to the user and allow the user to enter information to the program.

User-interface event   A notification to a program that a user action such as a key press, mouse move, or menu selection has occurred.

Variable   A symbol in a program that identifies a storage location that can hold different values.

Virtual machine   A program that simulates a CPU that can be implemented efficiently on a variety of actual machines. A given program in Java bytecode can be executed by any Java virtual machine, regardless of which CPU is used to run the virtual machine itself.

void   A reserved word indicating no type or an unknown type.

Walkthrough   A step-by-step manual simulation of a computer program.

White-box testing   Testing methods by taking their implementations into account, in contrast to black-box testing; for example, by selecting boundary test cases and ensuring that all branches of the code are covered by some test case.

White space   Any sequence of only space, tab, and newline characters.

Wrapper class   A class that contains a primitive type value, such as Integer.

Writer   In the Java input/output library, a class to which characters are to be sent.

INDEX

ILLUSTRATION CREDITS

Preface
Page v: © Terraxplorer/iStockphoto.

Icons
Animation icon: (camera) © james Steidl/iStockphoto; (globe) Alex Slobodkin/iStockphoto.
Common Error icon: (spider) © John Bell/iStockphoto.
Computing & Society icon: (rhinoceros) Media Bakery.
How To icon: (compass) © Steve Simzer/iStockphoto.
Paperclips: © Yvan Dube/iStockphoto.
Programming Tip icon: (toucan) Eric Isselé/iStockphoto.
Self Check icon: (stopwatch) © Nicholas Homrich/iStockphoto.
Special Topic icon: (tiger) © Eric Isselé/iStockphoto.
Worked Example icon: (globe) Alex Slobodkin/iStockphoto.
Web only icon: (globe) Alex Slobodkin/iStockphoto.

Chapter 1
Page 1, 2: © JanPietruszka/iStockphoto.
Page 3 (top), 24: © Amorphis/iStockphoto.
Page 3 (bottom): PhotoDisc, Inc./Getty Images.
Page 5 (top): © Maurice Savage/Alamy Limited.
Page 5 (bottom): © UPPA/Photoshot.
Page 6, 24: James Sullivan/Getty Images.
Page 11, 24: © Tatiana Popova/iStockphoto.
Page 12, 24: © Amanda Rohde/iStockphoto
Page 15, 25: © Martin Carlsson/iStockphoto.
Page 17 (top): © mammamaart/iStockphoto.
Page 17 (bottom), 25: © Claudiad/iStockphoto.
Page 20: © dlewis33/iStockphoto.
Page 22: © rban/iStockphoto.
Page 30: © Skip ODonnell/iStockphoto.
Page 31: © Don Bayley/iStockphoto.

Chapter 2
Page 33, 34: © Lisa F. Young/iStockphoto.
Page 34 (middle), 70: © Luc Meaille/iStockphoto.
Page 35: © Steven Frame/iStockphoto.
Page 36 (top): © Peter Mukherjee/iStockphoto.
Page 36 (bottom): Javier Larrea/Age Fotostock.
Page 37, 70: © Ingenui/iStockphoto.
Page 39, 70: © GlobalP/iStockphoto.
Page 44: © Damir Cudic/iStockphoto.
Page 45, 71: © Leontura/iStockphoto.
Page 48, 71: © sinankocasian/iStockphoto.
Page 57 (top): © Constance Bannister Corp/Hulton Archive/Getty Images, Inc.
Page 57 (bottom): Cay Horstmann.

Page 58, 71: © Jacob Wackerhausen/iStockphoto.
Page 60: Corbis Digital Stock.
Page 61, 72: © Eduardo Jose Bernardino/iStockphoto.
Page 66, 72: © Alexey Avdeev/iStockphoto.
Page 74: © PeskyMonkey/iStockphoto.
Page 77: © Feng Yu/iStockphoto.
Worked Example 2.1, WE1: © Constance Bannister Corp/Hulton Archive/ Getty Images, Inc.
Worked Example 2.2, WE3, WE6: Cay Horstmann.

Chapter 3

Page 81, 82: © Kris Hanke/iStockphoto.
Page 82 (bottom): © Jasmin Awad/iStockphoto.
Page 83, 119: © Mark Evans/iStockphoto.
Page 85, 119: © yenwen/iStockphoto.
Page 93, 120: © migin/iStockphoto.
Page 94: © Ann Marie Kurtz/iStockphoto.
Page 98: © Z5006 Karlheinz Schindler Deutsche Presse Agentur/NewsCom.
Page 101: © Mark Evans/iStockphoto.
Page 102, 120: © Chris Fertnig/iStockphoto.
Page 104 (left): © Peter Nguyen/iStockphoto.
Page 104 (middle): © Lisa F. Young/iStockphoto.
Page 107: © plusphoto/iStockphoto.
Page 116, 120: © Punchstock.
Worked Example 3.1, WE1: © Mark Evans/iStockphoto.

Chapter 4

Page 131, 132: Eyeidea/iStockphoto.
Page 133, 163: © Douglas Allen/iStockphoto
Page 134: © caracterdesign/iStockphoto.
Page 139 (top): © FinnBrandt/iStockphoto.
Page 139 (bottom): © hocus-focus/iStockphoto.
Page 140, 164: © Michael Flippo/iStockphoto.
Page 144: © Croko/iStockphoto.
Page 146: (graph) © Courtesy of Larry Hoyle, Institute for Policy & Social Research, University of Kansas.
Page 147, 164: © Media Bakery.
Page 148, 164: © Koele/iStockphoto.
Page 149: (cans) © blackred/iStockphoto; (bottle) © travismanley/iStockphoto.
Page 153: Photos.com/Jupiter Images.
Page 154: © Holger Mette/iStockphoto.
Page 156 (top): Courtesy NASA/JPL-Caltech.
Page 156 (bottom), 164: © essxboy/iStockphoto.
Page 158, 164: © slpix/iStockphoto.
Page 160, 164: © Rich Legg/iStockphoto.
Page 163 (left): © pvachier/iStockphoto.
Page 163 (middle): © Joel Carillet/iStockphoto.
Page 163 (right): © Saipg/iStockphoto.
Page 167: © Media Bakery.
Page 170: © José Luis Gutiérrez/iStockphoto.

Page 171: © asiseeit/iStockphoto.
Page 173: © Captainflash/iStockphoto.
Page 175: © TebNad/iStockphoto.
🌐 Worked Example 4.1, WE1: © Holger Mette/iStockphoto.
🌐 Worked Example 4.2, WE5: Courtesy NASA/JPL-Caltech.

Chapter 5

Page 179, 180 (top): © zennie/iStockphoto.
Page 180: © DrGrounds/iStockphoto.
Page 181, 222: © Media Bakery.
Page 184: © Timothy Large/iStockphoto.
Page 185: Photo by Vincent LaRussa/John Wiley & Sons, Inc.
Page 186, 222: © arturbo/iStockphoto.
Page 189, 222: Corbis Digital Stock.
Page 193: © MikePanic/iStockphoto.
Page 195: Bob Daemmrich/Getty Images.
Page 196, 222: © kevinruss/iStockphoto.
Page 199: © travelpixpro/iStockphoto.
Page 200, 222: © ericsphotography/iStockphoto.
Page 203: © thomasd007/iStockphoto.
Page 205: (left) © jchamp/iStockphoto; (middle) © StevenCarrieJohnson/iStockphoto;
    (right) © jsmith/iStockphoto.
Page 209: © Ekspansio/iStockphoto.
Page 212: Bananastock/Media Bakery.
Page 213, 223: Cusp/SuperStock.
Page 214: © toos/iStockphoto.
Page 217: © YouraPechkin/iStockphoto.
Page 218, 223: Tetra Images/Media Bakery.
Page 220: © jeanma85/iStockphoto.
Page 221: Vaughn Youtz/Zuma Press.
Page 229: © rotofrank/iStockphoto.
Page 231: © lillisphotography/iStockphoto.
Page 233 (top): © Straitshooter/iStockphoto.
Page 233 (bottom): © Mark Evans/iStockphoto.
Page 234 (top): © drxy/iStockphoto.
Page 234 (bottom): © nano/iStockphoto
Page 235: © Photobuff/iStockphoto.
Page 236: © rotofrank/iStockphoto.
Page 237: Courtesy NASA/JPL-Caltech.

Chapter 6

Page 241, 242 (top): © photo75/iStockphoto.
Page 242 (middle): © AlterYourReality/iStockphoto.
Page 242 (bottom), 291: © mmac72/iStockphoto.
Page 247: © MsSponge/iStockphoto.
Page 248: © ohiophoto/iStockphoto.
Pages 250–251 (paperclip): © Yvan Dube/iStockphoto.
Page 253: © RapidEye/iStockphoto.
Page 254, 292: © Enrico Fianchini/iStockphoto.
Page 260: © akaplummer/iStockphoto.

Page 263, 292: © Rhoberazzi/iStockphoto.

Page 269: Courtesy of Martin Hardee.

Page 273 (top), 292: © Hiob/iStockphoto.

Page 273 (bottom): © drflet/iStockphoto.

Page 274: © CEFutcher/iStockphoto.

Page 275: © tingberg/iStockphoto.

Page 276: © Stevegeer/iStockphoto.

Page 279 (top): © MorePixels/iStockphoto.

Page 279 (bottom), 292: © davejkahn/iStockphoto.

Page 282: Cay Horstmann.

Page 283, 292: © ktsimage/iStockphoto.

Page 285: © timstarkey/iStockphoto.

Page 291 (top): © Mark Poprocki/iStockphoto.

Page 291 (middle): Courtesy of the Naval Surface Warfare Center, Dahlgren, VA., 1988. NHHC Collection.

Page 291 (boy, bottom): © thomasd007/iStockphoto.

Page 299: © Anthony Rosenberg/iStockphoto.

Page 300: © hatman12/iStockphoto.

Page 301: © GlobalP/iStockphoto.

Page 304 (top): © Charles Gibson/iStockphoto.

Page 304 (bottom): © MOF/iStockphoto.

Page 305: *Introduction to Engineering Programming: Solving Problems with Algorithms*, James P. Holloway (John Wiley & Sons, Inc., 2004). Reprinted with permission of John Wiley & Sons, Inc.

Page 306 (right): © Snowleopard1/iStockphoto.

Page 306 (left): © zig4photo/iStockphoto.

Worked Example 6.2, WE5: Cay Horstmann.

Chapter 7

Page 311, 312: © traveler1116/iStockphoto.

Page 314, 360: © Luckie8/iStockphoto.

Page 316, 360: © AlterYourReality/iStockphoto.

Page 321: © nullplus/iStockphoto.

Page 323 (top): © CEFutcher/iStockphoto.

Page 323 (bottom): © trutenka/iStockphoto.

Page 324, 360: © yekorzh/iStockphoto.

Page 331: © ProstoVova/iStockphoto.

Page 334 : Thierry Dosogne/The Image Bank/Getty Images, Inc.

Page 336 (middle): © ktsimage/iStockphoto.

Page 336 (bottom), 360: © JenCon/iStockphoto.

Page 337–338: (coins) © jamesbenet/iStockphoto; (dollar coins) Jorge Delgado/iStockphoto.

Page 339: © claudio.arnese/iStockphoto.

Page 340 (top), 361: © Trub/iStockphoto.

Page 340 (middle): © technotr/iStockphoto.

Page 347, 361: © digital94086/iStockphoto.

Page 349, 361: © Danijelm/iStockphoto.

Page 351, 361: © sandoclr/iStockphoto.

Page 372 (top): © lepas2004/iStockphoto.

Page 372 (bottom): © KathyMuller/iStockphoto.

Page 374 (top): © joshblake/iStockphoto.

Page 374 (bottom): © GordonHeeley/iStockphoto.

Page 375: © nicolamargaret/iStockphoto.

Page 377: (coins) © jamesbenet/iStockphoto; (dollar coins) Jorge Delgado/iStockphoto; (paperclip) © Yvan Dube/iStockphoto.

Worked Example 7.1, WE1 (top): © ktsimage/iStockphoto.

Worked Example 7.1, WE1 (bottom): © Ryan Ruffatti/iStockphoto.

Chapter 8

Page 379, 380: © Ivan Stevanovic/iStockphoto.

Page 381, 408: © Sergey Ivanov/iStockphoto.

Page 384, 408: © manley099/iStockphoto.

Page 385, 408: AP Photo/Frank Franklin II.

Page 386: Frank Rosenstein/Digital Vision/Getty Images, Inc.

Page 391, 409: © paul prescott/iStockphoto.

Page 393, 409: © John Alexander/iStockphoto.

Page 395, 409: © Diane Diederich/iStockphoto.

Page 401, 404, 409: © Don Wilkie/iStockphoto

Page 406: Reprint Courtesy of International Business Machines Corporation, © International Business Machines Corporation.

Page 413: © DNY59/iStockphoto.

Page 415: © pixhook/iStockphoto.

Page 417 (top): © ThreeJays/iStockphoto.

Page 417 (bottom): © Maria Toutoudaki/iStockphoto.

Chapter 9

Page 421, 422: © Jason Hosking/Photodisc/Getty Images, Inc.

Page 422, 456: © Richard Stouffer/iStockphoto (vehicles); © Ed Hidden/iStockphoto (motorcycle); © Yin Yang/iStockphoto (car); © Robert Pernell/iStockphoto (truck); Media Bakery (sedan); Cezary Wojtkowski/Age Fotostock America (SUV).

Page 423: © paul kline/iStockphoto.

Page 427, 456: Media Bakery.

Page 438, 456: © Alpophoto/iStockphoto.

Page 448: © Sean Locke/iStockphoto.

Page 450: © Ken Brown/iStockphoto.

Page 459: © Pali Rao/iStockphoto.

Worked Example 9.1, WE1: © Sean Locke/iStockphoto.

Chapter 10

Page 463, 464 (top): © supermimicry/iStockphoto.

Page 464, 502: © Oxana Oleynichenko/iStockphoto.

Page 466: © gregory horler/iStockphoto.

Page 473 (top), 503: © Andrew Rich/iStockphoto.

Page 473 (middle): © Norebbo/iStockphoto.

Page 474: © Janis Dreosti/iStockphoto.

Page 475: © Alex Gumerov/iStockphoto.

Page 478: © Dan Herrick/iStockphoto.

Page 481, 503: © maureenpr/iStockphoto.

Page 483: © Don Nichols/iStockphoto.

Page 485: © Seriy Tryapitsyn/iStockphoto.

Page 491, 503: © Eduard Andras/iStockphoto.
Page 494, 504: © jeff giniewicz/iStockphoto.
Page 497, 504: © james Brey/iStockphoto.
Page 501: © Dmitry Shironosov/iStockphoto.
Page 502: Courtesy of Richard Stallman.
Page 509: © KathyMuller/iStockphoto.
Worked Example 10.1, WE1: © Norebbo/iStockphoto.

Chapter 11

Page 513, 514 (top): James King-Holmes/Bletchley Park Trust/Photo Researchers, Inc.
Page 527, 550: © xyno/iStockphoto.
Page 530: © Oksana Perkins/iStockphoto.
Page 532: © Nancy Ross/iStockphoto.
Page 533: (mobile phone) © Anna Khomulo/iStockphoto.
Page 535, 550: © Lisa F. Young/iStockphoto.
Page 537, 550: © Andraz Cerar/iStockphoto.
Page 538, 550: © tillsonburg/iStockphoto.
Page 539, 550: © archives/iStockphoto.
Page 544: © AP/Wide World Photos.
Page 552: © Chris Price/iStockphoto.
Page 556: © Chris Dascher/iStockphoto.
Worked Example 11.1, WE1: © Nancy Ross/iStockphoto.

Chapter 12

Page 559, 560: © Petrea Alexandru/iStockphoto.
Page 561, 581: © Oleg Prikhodko/iStockphoto.
Page 563: © visual7/iStockphoto.
Page 565, 581: © bojan fatur/iStockphoto.
Page 570: © Scott Cramer/iStockphoto.
Page 580: © Greg Nicholas/iStockphoto
Page 581 (top): © Mark Evans/iStockphoto.
Worked Example 12.1, WE1: © Mark Evans/iStockphoto.

Chapters Available on the Web

Chapter 13

Page 587, 588 (top): © Nicolae Popovici/iStockphoto.
Page 588, 620: © Davis Mantel/iStockphoto.
Page 593, 620: © Nikada/iStockphoto.
Page 596, 620: © gerenme/iStockphoto.
Page 598, 621: © pagadesign/iStockphoto.
Page 603, 621: © Jeanine Groenwald/iStockphoto.
Page 606: Science Photo Library/Photo Researchers, Inc.
Page 614, 621: © Lanica Klein/iStockphoto.

Chapter 14

Page 629, 630 (top): © Volkan Ersoy/iStockphoto.
Page 630, 662: © Zone Creative/iStockphoto.
Page 640, 662: © Kirby Hamilton/iStockphoto.

Page 641, 662: © Rich Legg/iStockphoto.
Page 647: © Christopher Futcher/iStockphoto.
Page 652: Topham/The Image Works.
Page 653–657, 662, 669 (lightbulbs): © Kraska/iStockphoto.

Chapter 15

Page 671, 672: © nicholas belton/iStockphoto.
Page 673 (top left): © Filip Fuxa/iStockphoto.
Page 673 (top center), 704: © parema/iStockphoto.
Page 673 (top right): © Vladimir Trenin/iStockphoto.
Page 673 (books, bottom), 704: © david franklin/iStockphoto.
Page 675, 704: © andrea laurita/iStockphoto.
Page 680: © Denis Vorob'yev/iStockphoto.
Page 681, 704: © Alfredo Ragazzoni/iStockphoto.
Page 682, 704: © Volkan Ersoy/iStockphoto.
Page 688, 704: © Tom Hahn/iStockphoto.
Page 689: © Ermin Gutenberger/iStockphoto.
Page 690, 704: © one clear vision/iStockphoto.
Page 692 (top), 705: © John Madden/iStockphoto.
Page 692 (left): © budgetstockphoto/iStockphoto.
Page 693, 702, 705: Photodisc/Punchstock.
Page 695: © paul kline/iStockphoto.
Page 697, 705: © Jorge Delgado/iStockphoto.
Page 700: © Skip ODonnell/iStockphoto.
Page 703 (top): Courtesy of Nigel Tout.
Page 708: © martin mcelligott/iStockphoto.
Page 710: © Luis Carlos Torres/iStockphoto.

Input

```java
Scanner in = new Scanner(System.in);
  // Can also use new Scanner(new File("input.txt"));

int n = in.nextInt();
double x = in.nextDouble();
String word = in.next();
String line = in.nextLine();

while (in.hasNextDouble())
{
    double x = in.nextDouble();
    Process x
}
```

Output

Does not advance to new line.

```java
System.out.print("Enter a value: ");
```

Use + to concatenate values.

```java
System.out.println("Volume: " + volume);
```

Field width *Precision*

```java
System.out.printf("%-10s %10d %10.2f", name, qty, price);
```

Left-justified string *Integer* *Floating-point number*

```java
PrintWriter out = new PrintWriter("output.txt");

out.close();
```

Use print/println/printf to write output to file.

Remember to close output file.

Arrays

Element type *Element type* *Length* *All elements are zero.*

```java
int[] numbers = new int[5];
int[] squares = { 0, 1, 4, 9, 16 };
int[][] magicSquare =
    {
        { 16,  3,  2, 13},
        {  5, 10, 11,  8},
        {  9,  6,  7, 12},
        {  4, 15, 14,  1}
    };

for (int i = 0; i < numbers.length; i++)
{
    numbers[i] = i * i;
}

for (int element : numbers)
{
    Process element
}

System.out.println(Arrays.toString(numbers));
    // Prints [0, 1, 4, 9, 16]
```

Array Lists

Initially empty *Use wrapper type, Integer, Double, etc., for primitive types.*

Element type

```java
ArrayList<String> names = new ArrayList<String>();
```

Add elements to the end

```java
names.add("Ann");
names.add("Cindy"); // [Ann, Cindy], names.size() is now 2

names.add(1, "Bob"); // [Ann, Bob, Cindy]
names.remove(2); // [Ann, Bob]
names.set(1, "Bill"); // [Ann, Bill]

String name = names.get(0); // Gets "Ann"
System.out.println(names); // Prints [Ann, Bill]
```

Linked Lists, Sets, and Iterators

```java
LinkedList<String> names = new LinkedList<String>();
names.add("Bob"); // Adds at end

ListIterator<String> iter = names.listIterator();
iter.add("Ann"); // Adds before current position

String name = iter.next(); // Returns "Ann"
iter.remove(); // Removes "Ann"

Set<String> names = new HashSet<String>();
names.add("Ann"); // Adds to set if not present
names.remove("Bob"); // Removes if present

Iterator<String> iter = names.iterator();
while (iter.hasNext())
{
    Process iter.next()
}
```

Maps

Key type *Value type*

```java
Map<String, Integer> scores = new HashMap<String, Integer>();

scores.put("Bob", 10);
Integer score = scores.get("Bob");

for (String key : scores.keySet())
{
    Process key and scores.get(key)
}
```

Returns null if key not present

150018